Oracle Certified Professional Java SE 7 Programmer Exams 1Z0-804 and 1Z0-805

A Comprehensive OCPJP 7 Certification Guide

S G Ganesh
Tushar Sharma

Apress·

Oracle Certified Professional Java SE 7 Programmer Exams 1Z0-804 and 1Z0-805

ISBN-13 (pbk): 978-1-4302-4764-7

ISBN-13 (electronic): 978-1-4302-4765-4

President and Publisher: Paul Manning
Lead Editor: Saswata Mishra
Technical Reviewer: B V Kumar
Editorial Board: Steve Anglin, Ewan Buckingham, Gary Cornell, Louise Corrigan, Morgan Ertel,
    Jonathan Gennick, Jonathan Hassell, Robert Hutchinson, Michelle Lowman, James Markham,
    Saswata Mishra, Matthew Moodie, Morgan Ertel, Jeff Olson, Jeffrey Pepper, Douglas Pundick,
    Ben Renow-Clarke, Dominic Shakeshaft, Gwenan Spearing, Matt Wade, Tom Welsh
Coordinating Editor: Jill Balzano
Copy Editor: Mary Behr
Compositor: SPi Global
Indexer: SPi Global
Artist: SPi Global
Cover Designer: Anna Ishchenko

Distributed to the book trade worldwide by Springer Science+Business Media New York, 233 Spring Street, 6th Floor, New York, NY 10013. Phone 1-800-SPRINGER, fax (201) 348-4505, e-mail orders-ny@springer-sbm.com, or visit www.springeronline.com.

For information on translations, please e-mail rights@apress.com, or visit www.apress.com.

Apress and friends of ED books may be purchased in bulk for academic, corporate, or promotional use. eBook versions and licenses are also available for most titles. For more information, reference our Special Bulk Sales–eBook Licensing web page at www.apress.com/bulk-sales.

Any source code or other supplementary materials referenced by the author in this text is available to readers at www.apress.com. For detailed information about how to locate your book's source code, go to www.apress.com/source-code.

To my wonderful mom
—Ganesh

To my caring parents, loving wife, and cute son
—Tushar

Contents at a Glance

Contents

About the Authors

S G Ganesh is a practitioner working in the area of code quality management at Siemens Corporate Research and Technologies in Bangalore. He previously worked in HP's C++ compiler team and was also a member of the C++ standardization committee. His areas of interests include OO design, design patterns, and programming languages. He is a Software Engineering Certified Instructor (IEEE certification) and has an OCPJP 7 certification.

Tushar Sharma is a researcher and practitioner at Siemens Corporate Research and Technologies–India. He earned an MS from the Indian Institute of Technology–Madras (IIT-Madras). His interests include OO software design, OO programming, refactoring, and design patterns. He has an OCPJP 7 certification.

About the Technical Reviewer

Dr. B V Kumar is currently the Director at Altius Inc and is responsible for delivering technology-based services for corporate clients. Dr. Kumar has a master's degree in technology from the Indian Institute of Technology Kanpur and a PhD from the Indian Institute of Technology-Kharagpur. He has over 22 years of experience in the field of information technology at various levels and in organizations such as Computer Vision Corporation (Singapore), Parametric Technologies (Seoul, South Korea), Sun Microsystems (India), and Infosys Technologies Ltd.

Prior to initiating Altius Inc, Dr. Kumar was the Director and Chief Architect at the Global Technology Office of Cognizant Technology Solutions (India). He has been working on enterprise technology solutions for more than 12 years, focusing on Java, JEE, web services, service-oriented architecture, and open source technologies. He has also been working on content management systems through applications such as Joomla and Drupal and mobile platforms such as Android and iPhone.

As a Director of Altius Inc, Dr. Kumar is currently focusing on technology consultancy, technology training and evangelization, community development, and project support for corporate clients. Dr. Kumar has two patents in the IT space and has published many technological papers in national and international journals and conferences. He has also co-authored the following books on information technologies: *J2EE Architecture* (2007), *Web Services 2e: An Introduction* (2011), *Implementing SOA Using Java EE* (2009), and *Secure Java: For Web Application Development* (2010). Dr. Kumar is currently working on the second edition of *Java EE 7 Architecture*.

Acknowledgments

Our first and foremost thanks go to our acquisitions editor Saswata Mishra, who played a key role from the conceptualization to the production stage of the book. Saswata, thank you for your excellent support—you made writing this book an enjoyable experience!

Our special thanks to book editor Robert Hutchinson. Robert played a major role in improving the quality of the presentation in this book. His attention to detail is amazing. Robert, thank you for turning our raw initial writes into a publishable manuscript.

Another special thanks to our technical reviewer, Dr. B V Kumar. His careful and critical review played a key role in improving the technical quality of the book.

We would like to convey our sincere thanks to the entire Apress team, especially Jeffrey Pepper, Ms. Jill Balzano, Ms. Mary Behr, and Ms. Anna Ishchenko for their excellent contributions in producing this book.

Both of us have spent countless hours writing chapters quite late into the night and during the weekends and holidays. With kids in our respective homes screaming for attention, it was only the support of our spouses that made writing this book possible.

—S G Ganesh and Tushar Sharma

Introduction

This book is a comprehensive guide to preparing for the OCPJP 7 exam. This book covers the exam objectives of both OCPJP exams, *Java SE 7 Programmer II* (1Z0-804 exam) and *Upgrade to Java SE 7 Programmer* (1Z0-805 exam). The main objective of this book is to prepare the reader to take the OCPJP 7 exam and pass it with ease.

The book covers all of the exam topics for *Java SE 7 Programmer II* (1Z0-804 exam). The chapters and sections in this book map one-to-one to the exam objectives and subtopics. This one-to-one mapping between chapters and the exam objectives ensures that we cover only the topics to the required breadth and depth—no more, no less. If you're taking *Upgrade to Java SE 7 Programmer* (1Z0-805 exam), see Appendix A for the key to how the exam topics map to the chapters of this book.

A reader will find lots and lots of sample questions in the form of a pretest, numerous sample questions within each chapter, and two full-length mock tests. These sample questions not only help the reader prepare for taking the exam but also set realistic expectations for what the reader will find on the exam.

There are many features in this book designed to present the content in a smooth, example-driven flow to improve your reading and study experience. For instance, the chapters provide numerous programming and real-world examples to help you internalize each of the presented concepts. Additionally, in each chapter we use visual cues (such as caution signs and exam tips) to direct your attention to important and interesting aspects of the concepts that are of particular relevance to the OCPJP 7 exam.

Prerequisites

Since the OCAJP 7 (a.k.a. *Java SE 7 Programmer* I/1Z0-803) exam is a prerequisite for the more comprehensive OCPJP 7 exam (1Z0-804), we assume that the reader is already familiar with the fundamentals of the language. We focus only on the OCPJP 7 exam objectives, on the presumption that the reader has a working knowledge in Java.

Target Audience

This book is for you if any of the following is true:

- If you are a student or a Java programmer aspiring to crack the OCPJP 7 exam.

- If you have already passed any of the older versions of the OCPJP 7 exam (such as the SCJP 5 exam). This book will prepare you for the *Upgrade to OCPJP 7* exam (1Z0-805).

- If you're a trainer for OCPJP 7 exam. You can use this book as training material for OCPJP 7 exam preparation.

- If you just want to refresh your knowledge of Java programming or gain a better understanding of various Java APIs.

Please note, however, that this book is neither a tutorial for learning Java nor a comprehensive reference book for Java.

Roadmap for Reading This Book

To get the most out of reading this book, we recommend you follow these steps:

Step 0: Make sure you have JDK 7 installed on your machine and you're able to compile and run Java programs.

Step 1: First read the FAQ in Chapter 1 and get familiar with the exam (you may want to skip irrelevant questions or questions for which you already know the answers).

Step 2: Check the exam topics (Appendix A) and mark the topics you're not familiar with or comfortable with. Read the chapters or sections corresponding to the topics you've marked for preparation.

Step 3: Take the pretest in Chapter 2. If you've answered all the questions correctly for an exam chapter, you may want to skip reading the corresponding chapter. For those exam topics in which you did not scored well, mark those chapters and read them first. Try out as many sample programs as possible while you read the chapters.

Step 4: Once you feel you are ready to take the exam, take the first mock test (Appendix B). If you don't pass it, go back to the chapters in which you are weak, read them, and try out more code relating to those topics. Once you're confident, attempt the second mock test (Appendix C). If you've prepared well, you should be able to pass it.

Step 5: Register for the exam and take the exam based on your performance in the mock tests. The day before taking the exam, read Chapter 15, "OCPJP 7 Quick Refresher."

On Coding Examples in This Book

All the programs in this book are self-contained programs (with necessary `import` statements). You can download the source code of the programs from `www.apress.com/9781430247647`.

We've tested the coding examples in this book in two compilers, Oracle's Java compiler JDK 7 (javac) and the Eclipse Compiler for Java (ecj). For the error messages, we've provided javac's error messages. It is important that you use a Java compiler and a JVM that supports Java 7.

Java is a platform-independent language, but there are certain features that are better explained with a specific platform. Since Windows is the most widely used OS today, some of the programming examples (specifically some of the programs in the NIO.2 chapter) are written with the Windows OS in mind. You may require minor modifications to the programs to get them working under other OSs (Linux, MAC OS, etc).

Contact Us

In case of any queries, suggestions or corrections, please feel free to contact us at `sgganesh@gmail.com` or `tusharsharma@ieee.org`.

CHAPTER 1

▪ ▪ ▪

The OCPJP 7 Exam: FAQ

The singular acronym of the OCPJP 7 exam is shorthand for two separate but congruent exams:

- The Java SE 7 Programmer II exam (exam number 1Z0-804)

- The Upgrade to Java SE 7 Programmer exam (exam number 1Z0-805)

These two exams are alternative paths to the same certification. The 1Z0-804 and 1Z0-805 exams both qualify the candidates who pass them for the same credential: Oracle Certified Professional, Java SE 7 Programmer (OCPJP 7). This book prepares you to take the OCPJP 7 exams.

The 1Z0-804 exam syllabus (given in full in Appendix A) consists of twelve topics, mapping to the titles and subjects of Chapters 3-14 of this book. This book serves equally as preparation for the 1Z0-805 exam, whose six topics map to Chapters 5-6 and 9-14 of this book (see Appendix A).

In this preliminary chapter, we address the frequently asked questions (FAQs) that are apt to come to mind when you are preparing for the OCPJP 7 exam. Again, the term "OCPJP 7 exam" should be taken in the sense of encompassing both variants of the exam, the 1Z0-804 and 1Z0-805. The course of study, model questions, and practice tests presented in this book will prepare you equally well to take either one. Which variant of the OCPJP 7 exam you take will depend on your existing credentials, as explained below.

The FAQs we present in this chapter answer concerns such as the placement of OCPJP 7 certification in the suite of Oracle Java certifications, the difficulty level and prerequisites of the OCPJP 7 exam, the scope of the topics on the OCPJP 7 exam syllabus, the depth of the preparation for it, and the details of registering for and taking the exam. Broadly, this chapter consists of three sections:

- *Oracle Java Certifications*: *Overview*: FAQs 1-6 survey Oracle's various Java exams as they map onto Java certifications. It focuses in particular on the OCAJP 7 exam, because the Oracle Certified Associate, Java SE 7 Programmer (OCAJP 7) credential is a prerequisite for OCPJP 7 certification via the 1Z0-804 exam.

- *The OCPJP 7 Exam*: FAQs 7-15 concern the objectives of the OCPJP 7 exam, the kinds of questions on it, and the details about the preparation for it.

- *Taking the OCPJP 7 Exam*: FAQs 16, 17, and 18 cover the nuts and bolts of registering for exam, the various things you need to do on the day of the exam, and actually taking the exam.

Oracle Java Certifications: Overview
FAQ 1. What are the different levels of Oracle Java certification exams?

Table 1-1 shows four ascending expertise levels of Oracle exams (Associate, Professional, Expert, and Master) matched with examples of Java certifications at those levels, together with the qualifying exams by name and number.

Table 1-1. *Oracle Certification Levels with Examples of Corresponding Java Exams (OPCJP 7 exam, in bold)*

Certification Level	Java Certification (Example)	Exam Name	Exam Number
Oracle Certified Associate (OCA)	Oracle Certified Associate, Java SE 7 Programmer	Java SE 7 Programmer I	1Z0-803
Oracle Certified Professional (OCP)	**Oracle Certified Professional, Java SE 7 Programmer**	**Java SE 7 Programmer II**	**1Z0-804**
	Oracle Certified Professional, Java SE 7 Programmer	**Upgrade to Java SE 7 Programmer**	**1Z0-805**
Oracle Certified Expert (OCE)	Oracle Certified Expert, NetBeans Integrated Development Environment 6.1 Programmer	NetBeans Integrated Development Environment 6.1 Programmer Certified Expert Exam	1Z0-889
Oracle Certified Master (OCM)	Oracle Certified Master, Java SE6 Developer	Java Standard Edition 6 Developer Certified Master Essay Exam	1Z0-856

Pictorially, Java exams offered by Oracle and their path can be observed in Figure 1-1.

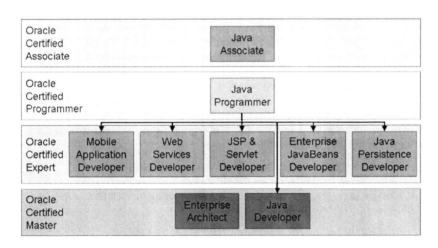

Figure 1-1. *Java certification path offered by Oracle*

FAQ 2. Can you compare the specifications of the 1Z0-803, 1Z0-804, and 1Z0-805 exams in relation to OCAJP 7 and OCPJP 7 certification?

Yes, see Table 1-2.

Table 1-2. *Comparison of the Oracle Exams Leading to OCAJP 7 and OCPJP 7 Certification*

Exam Number	1Z0-803	1Z0-804	1Z0-805
Expertise Level	Beginner	Intermediate	Intermediate
Exam Name	Java SE 7 Programmer I	Java SE 7 Programmer II	Upgrade to Java SE 7 Programmer
Associated Certification (abbreviation)	Oracle Certified Associate, Java SE 7 Programmer (OCAJP 7)	Oracle Certified Professional, Java SE 7 Programmer (OCPJP 7)	Oracle Certified Professional, Java SE 7 Programmer (OCPJP 7)
Prerequisite Certification	None	OCAJP 7	Any older OCPJP version or any version of SCJP
Exam Duration	2 hrs 30 minutes (150 mins)	2 hrs 30 minutes (150 mins)	3 hrs (180 mins)
Number of Questions	90 Questions	90 Questions	90 Questions
Pass Percentage	75%	65%	60%
Cost	~ USD 300	~ USD 300	~ USD 300
Exam Topics	Java Basics	Java Class Design	Language Enhancements
	Working With Java Data Types	Advanced Class Design	Design Patterns
	Creating and Manipulate Strings	Object-Oriented Design Principles	Java File I/O (NIO.2)
	Creating and Using Arrays	Generics and Collections	Describe the JDBC API
	Using Loop Constructs	String Processing	Concurrency
	Working with Methods and Encapsulation	Exceptions and Assertions	Localization
	Working with Inheritance	Java I/O Fundamentals	
	Handling Exceptions	Java File I/O (NIO.2)	
		Building Database Applications with JDBC	
		Threads	
		Concurrency	
		Localization	

Note 1: In the Cost row, the given USD cost of the exams is approximate as actual cost varies with currency of the country in which you take the exam: $300 in US, £202 in UK, Rs. 8,500 in India, etc.

Note 2: The Exam Topics row lists only the top-level topics. Note that the 1Z0-804 and 1Z0-805 exams share certain high-level topic names—such as "Java File I/O (NIO.2)," "Concurrency," and "Localization"—but that the subtopics are not identical between the two exams. The subtopics of the 1Z0-804 and 1Z0-805 exams are listed in Appendix A.

FAQ 3. OCAJP 7 certification is a prerequisite for OCPJP 7 certification via the 1Z0-804 exam. Does that mean that I have to take the OCAJP 7 exam before I can take the OCPJP 7 exam?

No, requirements for certification may be met in any order. You may take the OCPJP 7 exam before you take the OCAJP 7 exam, but you will not be granted OCPJP 7 certification until you have passed both the 1Z0-803 exam and the 1Z0-804 exam—unless you are eligible to take and pass the 1Z0-805 exam, for which OCAJP 7 certification is not a prerequisite.

FAQ 4. Is OCPJP 7 prerequisite for other Oracle certification exams?

Yes, OCPJP 7 is prerequisite for many other exams, such as

- Java Enterprise Edition 5 Web Component Developer Certified Professional Exam (1Z0-858)
- Oracle Certified Master, Java SE 6 Developer exam (1Z0-855 and 1Z0-856)

FAQ 5. Should I take the OCPJP 7 or OCPJP 6 exam?

Although you can still take exams for older certifications such as OCPJP 6, OCPJP 7 is the best professional credential to have.

FAQ 6. How does the Oracle OCPJP 7 exam differ from the OCPJP 6 and OCPJP 5 exams (and the previous Sun versions SCJP 6 and SCJP 5)?

Short answer: The OCPJP 7 exam is tougher and covers more topics.

Long answer: Here is a short list of differences between the OCPJP 7 exam (1Z0-804) versus the OCPJP 6 and OCPJP 5 exams (1Z0-851 and 1Z0-853, respectively) and the SCJP 5 and SCJP 6 exams (the former Sun Microsystems versions of the OCPJP 6 and OCPJP 5 exams, leading to Sun Certified Java Programmer 6 and 5 certifications):

- Like the former SCJP 6/SCJP 5 exams, the OCPJP 6 and 5 exams cover language fundamentals and some of the common APIs involving strings, arrays, and so on. At the Java SE 7 level, most of these topics have been moved to the OCAJP 7 exam, which is the prerequisite for OCPJP 7 certification through the 1Z0-804 exam path. Note that some questions in OCAJP 7 have the same difficulty level as OCPJP 7 questions.

- The OCPJP 7 exam covers more topics than the OCPJP 6 and 5 exams and their Sun predecessors, including JDBC, localization, NIO.2, and concurrency APIs.

- OCPJP 7 also covers new features of Java SE 7, including try-with-resources statements, new APIs in JDBC, string-based switches, and binary literals.

- The questions in the OCPJP 7 exam are tougher than those asked in the OCPJP 6 and 5 exams and their Sun predecessors.

- The OCPJP 7 exam has only multiple-choice questions, whereas the retired SCJP exams also had interactive questions (drag-and-drop, match-the-options, etc.).

The differences between the OCPJP 6 and OCPJP 7 exams are summarized in Table 1-3.

Table 1-3. *Comparison of the Oracle Exams Leading to OCPJP 6 and OCPJP 7 Certification*

Exam Number	1Z0-851	1Z0-804
Expertise Level	Beginner to intermediate	Intermediate
Pre-requisite Certification	None	OCAJP7
Exam Name	Java SE 6 Programmer	Java SE 7 Programmer II
Associated Certification	Oracle Certified Professional, Java SE 6 Programmer (OCPJP 6)	Oracle Certified Professional, Java SE 7 Programmer (OCPJP 7)
Exam Duration	2 hrs 30 minutes (150 mins)	2 hrs 30 minutes (150 mins)
Number of Questions	60 Questions	90 Questions
Pass Percentage	61%	65%
Cost	~ USD 300	~ USD 300
Exam Release Status	Released	Released
Exam Topics	Declarations, Initialization, and Scoping	Java Class Design
	Flow Control	Advanced Class Design
	API Contents	Object-Oriented Design Principles
	Concurrency	Generics and Collections
	OO Concepts	String Processing
	Collections/Generics	Exceptions and Assertions
	Fundamentals	Java I/O Fundamentals
		Java File I/O (NIO.2)
		Building Database Applications with JDBC
		Threads
		Concurrency
		Localization

The OCPJP 7 Exam

FAQ 7. How many questions are there in the OCPJP 7 exam?

In both the 1Z0-804 and 1Z0-805 versions of the OCPJP 7 exam, there are 90 questions.

FAQ 8. What is the duration of the OCPJP 7 exam?

The 1Z0-804 and 1Z0-805 versions of the OCPJP 7 exam last 150 and 180 minutes respectively (2 hours 30 minutes, and 3 hours).

FAQ 9. What is the cost of the OCPJP 7 exam?

The cost of the 1Z0-804 and 1Z0-805 versions of the OCPJP 7 exam is the same, but that cost varies according to the currency of the country in which you take the exam: currently $300 in US, £202 in UK, Rs. 8,500 in India, €238 in Eurozone countries, and so on. (The cost of the exam is shown on the Oracle web site in the viewer's local currency.)

FAQ 10. What are the passing scores for the OCPJP 7 exam?

The passing scores for the 1Z0-804 and 1Z0-805 versions of the OCPJP 7 exam are 65% and 60%, respectively. (There are no negative marks for wrong answers.)

FAQ 11. What kinds of questions are asked in the OCPJP 7 exam?

Some questions on the OCPJP 7 exam test your conceptual knowledge without reference to a specific program or code segment. But most of the questions are programming questions of the following types:

- Given a program or code segment, what is the output or expected behavior?

- Which option(s) would compile without errors or give the desired output?

- Which option(s) constitute the correct usage of a given API (in particular, newly introduced APIs such as those associated with new classes of JDBC)?

All questions are multiple-choice. Most of them present four or five options, but some have six or seven options. Many questions are designed to have a set of multiple correct answers. Such questions are clearly flagged (usually at the left top corner in the exam test screen) with the number of options you need to select.

Exam questions are not constrained to be exclusively from the topics on the exam syllabus. You might, for example, get questions on Java fundamentals (a topic in OCAJP syllabus) concerning the basics of exception handling and using wrapper types. You might also get questions on topics related to those on the exam syllabus but not specified in it. For example, serialization and use of the `transient` keyword are not explicitly mentioned in the OCPJP exam syllabus, but they can come up in the actual exam because they are related to reading and writing streams—and one of these is `ObjectStreams`, which relates to serialization!

A given question is not constrained to test only one topic. Some questions are designed to test multiple topics with a single question. For instance, you may find a question testing the concepts of threads and inner classes as they relate to each other.

FAQ 12. What does the OCPJP 7 exam test for?

The OCPJP 7 exam tests your understanding of the Java language features and APIs that are essential for developing real-world programs. The exam focuses on the following areas:

- *Language concepts that are useful for problem solving*: The exam tests not only your knowledge of how language features work, but also covers your grasp of the nitty-gritty and corner cases of language features. For example, you need to understand not only the generics feature in Java but also problems associated with type-erasure, mixing legacy containers with generic containers, and so on.

- *Java APIs*: The exam tests your familiarity with using the Java class library, as well as such unusual aspects or corner cases, such as the following:

    - What does the `remove()` method of Deque do? (Answer: It removes the first element from the underlying deque instance).

- What will happen if `sleep()` method is interrupted? (Answer: You'll get an `InterrputedException`).

- *Underlying concepts*: For example, the exam might test your understanding of how serialization works, the differences between overloading and overriding, how autoboxing and unboxing work in relation to generics, the different kinds of drivers in JDBC, how multithreaded programming is platform-dependent, the different kinds of liveness problems with threads, etc.

Although the exam does not test memory skills, some questions presume rote knowledge of key elements, such as the following:

- Letters used for creating custom date and time formats ("string patterns") for use with `SimpleDateFormat` class.

- Characters used for forming pattern strings in regular expressions.

- Format specifiers and their meaning for use in `format()` method in `String` and in `printf()`.

FAQ 13. I've been a Java programmer for last five years. Do I have to prepare for the OCPJP 7 exam?

Short answer: It's good that you have work experience, but you still need to prepare for the OCPJP 7 exam.

Long answer: No matter how much real-world programming experience you might have, there are two reasons why you should prepare for this exam to improve your chances of passing it:

- *You may not have been exposed to certain topics on the exam.* Java is vast, and you might not have had occasion to work on every topic covered in the exam. For example, you may not be familiar with localization if you have never dealt the locale aspects of the applications you were engaged with. Or your work might not have required you to use JDBC. Or you've always worked on single-threaded programs, so multithreaded programming might be new to you. Moreover, OCPJP 7 emphasizes Java 7, and you might not have been exposed yet to such Java 7 topics as NIO.2, new concurrency APIs, and enhancements such as try-with-resource statements.

- *You may not remember the unusual aspects or corner cases.* No matter how experienced you are, there is always an element of surprise involved when you program. The OCPJP 7 exam tests not just your knowledge and skills in respect of regular features, but also your understanding of unusual aspects or corner cases, such as the behavior of multithreaded code and the use of generics when both overloading and overriding are involved. So you have to bone up on pathological cases that you rarely encounter in your work.

A good way to gauge how much preparation you'll need in the various topics before you can feel confident that you'll pass the OCPJP 7 exam is to take the pre-test in Chapter 2 and the two full-length sample exams in Appendix B and C.

FAQ 14. How do I prepare for the OCPJP 7 exam?

Study this book. In addition,

- *Code, code, code!* Write lots and lots of small programs, experiment with them, and learn from your mistakes.

- *Read, read, read!* Read this book and the tutorial and reference resources on Oracle's site, especially.

- *Oracle's free online Java tutorials*: Access the Java tutorial at
  `http://docs.oracle.com/javase/tutorial/` and the OCPJP 7 tutorial at `http://docs.oracle.com/javase/tutorial/extra/certification/javase-7-programmer2.html`.

- *Java documentation*: The Java API documentation is a mine of information. This
  documentation is available online (see `http://docs.oracle.com/javase/7/docs/api/`)
  and is shipped as part of the Java SDK. If you don't have immediate Internet access, you
  may find javac's `-Xprint` option handy. To print the textual representation of `String`
  class, type the fully qualified name, as in

  ```
  javac -Xprint java.lang.String
  ```

  This will print the list of members in `String` class in console.

- *Read, code, read, code!* Cycle back and forth between your reading and coding so that your
  book knowledge and its practical application are mutually reinforcing. This way, you'll not just
  know a concept, but you'll also *understand* it.

- *Focus most on the topics you're least comfortable with.* Grade yourself on each of the topics in
  OCPJP 7 exam on an ascending scale from 1 to 10. Do remedial preparation in all topics for
  which you rate yourself 8 or less.

FAQ 15. How do I know when I'm ready to take the OCPJP 7 exam?

Take the two full-length OCPJP 7 sample exams given in Appendix B under actual exam conditions: stick to the
2.5-hour time limit; don't take any breaks; and don't refer any books or web sites. If you score 75% or above (the actual
exam pass scores for 1Z0-804 and 1Z0-805 are 65% and 60%, respectively), you'll probably pass the actual exam.

Taking the OCPJP 7 Exam

FAQ 16. What are my options to register for the exam?

You have three registration options for the OCPJP 7 exam:

- Register and pay at the Pearson VUE web site.

- Buy an exam voucher from Oracle and then register yourself in Pearson VUE web site.

- Register and pay at the Oracle Testing Center (OTC), if you have one in your region.

FAQ 17. How do I register for the exam, schedule a day and time for taking the exam, and appear for the exam?

Option 1: Register and pay on the Pearson VUE web site by the following steps:

Step 1. Go to `www.pearsonvue.com/oracle/` (you will be directed here if you click the first
option from Oracle Certification page). Click on "Schedule online" in "Schedule an
exam" section.

Step 2. Select "Sign In." Click on "proctored" in the "what type of exam you are planning to
take" section. Select this exam as `"Information Technology (IT)"` ➤ `"Oracle"` ➤
`"Proctored."` Then you'll be asked to sign in.

Step 3. Log in to your web account on the Pearson site. If you don't have one, create one; you will get the user name and password by the e-mail you provide. When you log in first time, you need to change your password and set security questions and their answers. When you are done with this, you're ready to schedule your exam.

Step 4. Once logged in, you'll get the list of Oracle exams to select from. Select one of the following:

- 1Z0-803, Java SE 7 Programmer I (aka OCAJP 7 exam)

- 1Z0-804, Java SE 7 Programmer II (aka OCPJP 7 exam)

- 1Z0-805, Upgrade to Java SE 7 Programmer (aka OCPJP 7 exam)

These exams are in English. (You can choose another language if you wish and if it is available in the list). This page will also show you the cost of the exam. Select relevant exam from the list, say, "1Z0-804 (Java SE 7 Programmer II)," and click Next.

Step 5. Now you need to select your test location. Choose Country ➤ City ➤ State/Province, and you'll be shown test locations close to your place. Each center will have an icon for information: click it for address and directions. Select up to four centers near to your location and click Next.

Step 6. Select a test center and select date and time for appointments. The page will indicate the available dates and time slots; choose the one most convenient for you. If you have an exam voucher or Oracle University coupon or Oracle promotion code, enter it here.

Step 7. Select from the available payment options (the usual way is to pay using your credit card) and pay your exam fees. Make sure that you have selected the right exam, appropriate test center, and date/time before paying the fees.

Step 8. Done! You will get an appointment confirmation payment receipt by e-mail.

Option 2: Buy an exam voucher from Oracle and register on the Pearson VUE web site.
You can buy a generic exam voucher from Oracle and use it at Pearson site. It costs US$300 if you are living in US and is denominated in an appropriate currency if you live elsewhere. To buy the voucher from Oracle, select "OU Java, Solaris, and other Sun Technology Exam eVoucher." You will be asked to create an Oracle account if you do not have one. Once the account is created, confirm customer type, customer contact information, and pay. Once you pay the fees, you can use the eVoucher at the Pearson VUE site.

Option 3: Register and pay online to take the exam in person at an Oracle Testing Center (OTC).
You can choose this option if a physical exam session is scheduled in your vicinity. It costs US$300 or the local equivalent.

FAQ 18. What are the key things I need to remember before taking the exam and on the day of exam?

Before the exam day:

- You'll get an e-mail from Pearson confirming your appointment and payment. Check the details on what you should bring when you go to the exam center. Note that you'll need at least two photo IDs.

- Before the exam, you'll get a call from the Pearson exam center where you've booked your appointment (albeit, it depends on the exam center).

On the exam day:

- Go to the exam center at least 30 minutes before the exam starts. Your exam center will have lockers for storing your belongings.

- Show your exam schedule information and IDs and then complete the exam formalities, such as signing the documents.

- You'll be taken to a computer in the exam room and will log in to the exam-taking software.

Taking the exam:

- You will see the following on the exam-taking software screen:

    - A timer ticking in one corner showing the time left

    - The current question number you are attempting

    - A check box to select if you want to review the question later

    - The button (labeled "Review") for going to a review screen where you can revisit the questions before completing the exam.

- Once you start, you'll get questions displayed one by one. You can choose the answers by selecting them in the check box. If you are unsure of an answer, select the Review button so that you can revisit it at any point during the exam.

- You may not consult any person or print or electronic materials or programs during the exam.

After the exam:

- Once you're done with the exam, you will get an email after half-an-hour or so containing the details for accessing your score.

- Irrespective of passing or failing the exam, topics from questions you've answered incorrectly will be supplied with your score. You will not, however, be shown the correct answers to the questions you missed.

- If you've passed the OCPJP 7 exam *and* you've also satisfied the applicable prerequisites for certification (e.g., OCAJP certification as the prerequisite of OCPJP 7 certification via the 1Z0-804 exam), a printable certificate can be downloaded from Oracle's CertView web site (`https://education.oracle.com/certview.html`).

- If you failed the exam, you may register and pay again to retake it after a 14-day waiting period.

CHAPTER 2

Pretest

The prospect of taking the OCPJP 7 exam raises many questions in the candidate's mind.

- "What types of questions are asked in the exam?"

- "What topics do the exams cover?"

- "How hard are the questions?"

- "How do I know if I'm ready to take the exam?"

- "Which topics will I need to focus my preparations on in order to pass the exam?"

This chapter presents a *pretest* designed to answer all of your preliminary questions concretely and measurably. Use this pretest as a mental dip-stick to gauge how likely you would be to pass the OCPJP 7 exam if you were to take it today. The questions in this pretest closely mimic the actual questions you will encounter on the OCPJP 7 exam. And they are distributed among the 12 topics in the 1Z0-804 exam syllabus. The post-pretest answer key and evaluation tool at the end of this chapter will enable you to identify precisely those topics on which you will need to focus your preparations to ensure success when you take the actual exam.

The only significant difference between the following pretest and the OCPJP 7 exam is the number of questions and duration. This pretest is configured exactly like an OCPJP 7 exam, only half as long: you will answer 45 questions in 1 hour 15 minutes (rather than 90 questions in 2 hrs 30 minutes).

So let's get started. Simulate real test conditions. Find a quiet place where you can take this pretest without interruption or distraction. Mark your start and finish times. Observe closed-book rules: do not consult the answer key or any other any print, human, or web resources before or during this pretest.

The OCPJP 7 Exam: Pretest

Time: 1 hour 15 minutes   *No. of questions:* 45

---

1.   **Consider the following program:**

```java
class StrEqual {
        public static void main(String []args) {
                String s1 = "hi";
                String s2 = new String("hi");
                String s3 = "hi";

                if(s1 == s2) {
                        System.out.println("s1 and s2 equal");
                } else {
                        System.out.println("s1 and s2 not equal");
                }

                if(s1 == s3) {
                        System.out.println("s1 and s3 equal");
                } else {
                        System.out.println("s1 and s3 not equal");
                }
        }
}
```

Which one of the following options provides the output of this program when executed?

a)
s1 and s2 equal
s1 and s3 equal
b)
s1 and s2 equal
s1 and s3 not equal
c)
s1 and s2 not equal
s1 and s3 equal
d)
s1 and s2 not equal
s1 and s3 not equal

---

2.   **Consider the following program:**

```java
class Point2D {
        private int x, y;
        public Point2D(int x, int y) {
                x = x;
        }

        public String toString() {
                return "[" + x + ", " + y + "]";
        }
```

```
        public static void main(String []args) {
                Point2D point = new Point2D(10, 20);
                System.out.println(point);
        }
}
```

Which one of the following options provides the output of this program when executed?

a) point
b) Point
c) [0, 0]
d) [10, 0]
e) [10, 20]

---

3. **Consider the following program:**

```
class Increment {
        public static void main(String []args) {
                Integer i = 10;
                Integer j = 11;
                Integer k = ++i;            // INCR
                System.out.println("k == j is " + (k == j));
                System.out.println("k.equals(j) is " + k.equals(j));
        }
}
```

Which one of the following options correctly describes the behavior of this program?

a) When executed, this program prints
   k == j is false
   k.equals(j) is false
b) When executed, this program prints
   k == j is true
   k.equals(j) is false
c) When executed, this program prints
   k == j is false
   k.equals(j) is true
d) When executed, this program prints
   k == j is true
   k.equals(j) is true
e) When compiled, the program will result in a compiler error in the line marked with the comment INCR.

---

4. **Consider the following program:**

```
class ArrayCompare {
        public static void main(String []args) {
                int []arr1 = {1, 2, 3, 4, 5};
                int []arr2 = {1, 2, 3, 4, 5};
                System.out.println("arr1 == arr2 is " + (arr1 == arr2));
                System.out.println("arr1.equals(arr2) is " + arr1.equals(arr2));
```

13

```
                    System.out.println("Arrays.equals(arr1, arr2) is " +
                                java.util.Arrays.equals(arr1, arr2));
            }
    }
```

Which one of the following options provides the output of this program when executed?

a) arr1 == arr2 is false
   arr1.equals(arr2) is false
   Arrays.equals(arr1, arr2) is true
b) arr1 == arr2 is true
   arr1.equals(arr2) is false
   Arrays.equals(arr1, arr2) is true
c) arr1 == arr2 is false
   arr1.equals(arr2) is true
   Arrays.equals(arr1, arr2) is true
d) arr1 == arr2 is true
   arr1.equals(arr2) is true
   Arrays.equals(arr1, arr2) is false
e) arr1 == arr2 is true
   arr1.equals(arr2) is true
   Arrays.equals(arr1, arr2) is true

---

5. **Consider the following program:**

```
class NullInstanceof {
        public static void main(String []args) {
                String str = null;
                if(str instanceof Object)    // NULLCHK
                        System.out.println("str is Object");
                else
                        System.out.println("str is not Object");
        }
}
```

Which one of the following options correctly describes the behavior of this program?

a) This program will result in a compiler error in line marked with comment NULLCHK.
b) This program will result in a NullPointerException in line marked with comment NULLCHK.
c) When executed, this program will print the following: str is Object.
d) When executed, this program will print the following: str is not Object.

---

6. **Consider the following program:**

```
interface Side { String getSide(); }

class Head implements Side {
        public String getSide() { return "Head "; }
}

class Tail implements Side {
```

```
                public String getSide() { return "Tail "; }
        }

        class Coin {
                public static void overload(Head side) { System.out.print(side.getSide()); }
                public static void overload(Tail side) { System.out.print(side.getSide()); }
                public static void overload(Side side) { System.out.print("Side "); }
                public static void overload(Object side) { System.out.print("Object "); }

                public static void main(String []args) {
                        Side firstAttempt = new Head();
                        Tail secondAttempt = new Tail();
                        overload(firstAttempt);
                        overload((Object)firstAttempt);
                        overload(secondAttempt);
                        overload((Side)secondAttempt);
                }
        }
```

What is the output of this program when executed?

a) Head Head Tail Tail
b) Side Object Tail Side
c) Head Object Tail Side
d) Side Head Tail Side

---

7. **Consider the following program:**

```
        class Overloaded {
                public static void foo(Integer i) { System.out.println("foo(Integer)"); }
                public static void foo(short i) { System.out.println("foo(short)"); }
                public static void foo(long i) { System.out.println("foo(long)"); }
                public static void foo(int ... i) { System.out.println("foo(int ...)"); }
                public static void main(String []args) {
                        foo(10);
                }
        }
```

Which one of the following options correctly describes the output of this program?

a) foo(Integer)
b) foo(short)
c) foo(long)
d) foo(int ...)

---

8. **Consider the following program:**

```
        class Base {
                public static void foo(Base bObj) {
                        System.out.println("In Base.foo()");
                        bObj.bar();
                }
```

```
            public void bar() {
                    System.out.println("In Base.bar()");
            }
    }

    class Derived extends Base {
            public static void foo(Base bObj) {
                    System.out.println("In Derived.foo()");
                    bObj.bar();
            }
            public void bar() {
                    System.out.println("In Derived.bar()");
            }
    }

    class OverrideTest {
            public static void main(String []args) {
                    Base bObj = new Derived();
                    bObj.foo(bObj);
            }
    }
```

What is the output of this program when executed?

a)
In Base.foo()
In Base.bar()
b)
In Base.foo()
In Derived.bar()
c)
In Derived.foo()
In Base.bar()
d)
In Derived.foo()
In Derived.bar()

---

9. **Consider the following program:**

```
    class CannotFlyException extends Exception {}

    interface Birdie {
            public abstract void fly() throws CannotFlyException;
    }

    interface Biped {
            public void walk();
    }

    abstract class NonFlyer {
            public void fly() { System.out.print("cannot fly ");  }        // LINE A
    }
```

```
class Penguin extends NonFlyer implements Birdie, Biped {          // LINE B
        public void walk() { System.out.print("walk "); }
}

class PenguinTest {
        public static void main(String []args) {
                Penguin pingu = new Penguin();
                pingu.walk();
                pingu.fly();
        }
}
```

Which one of the following options correctly describes the behavior of this program?

a) Compiler error in line with comment LINE A because fly() does not declare to throw CannotFlyException.
b) Compiler error in line with comment LINE B because fly() is not defined and hence need to declare it abstract.
c) It crashes after throwing the exception CannotFlyException.
d) When executed, the program prints "walk cannot fly".

---

10. **Consider the following program:**

```
class TestSwitch {
        public static void main(String []args) {
                String [] cards = { "Club", "spade", " diamond ", "hearts" };
                for(String card : cards) {
                        switch(card) {
                        case "Club" : System.out.print(" club "); break;
                        case "Spade" :  System.out.print(" spade "); break;
                        case "diamond" :  System.out.print(" diamond "); break;
                        case "heart" :  System.out.print(" heart "); break;
                        default: System.out.print(" none ");
                        }
                }
        }
}
```

Which one of the following options shows the output of this program?

a) none none none none
b) club none none none
c) club spade none none
d) club spade diamond none
e) club spade diamond heart

---

11. **Consider the following program:**

```
class Outer {
        static class Inner {
                public final String text = "Inner";
        }
}
```

```
class InnerClassAccess {
        public static void main(String []args) {
                System.out.println(/*CODE HERE*/);
        }
}
```

Which one of the following expressions when replaced for the text in place of the comment /*CODE HERE*/ will print the output "Inner" in console?

a) `new Outer.Inner().text`
b) `Outer.new Inner().text`
c) `Outer.Inner.text`
d) `new Outer().Inner.text`

---

12. **Consider the following enumeration definition:**

```
enum Cards { CLUB, SPADE, DIAMOND, HEARTS };

class CardsEnumTest {
        public static void main(String []args) {
                /* TRAVERSE */
        }
}
```

Which one of the following will you replace in place of the comment /* TRAVERSE */ to traverse the `Cards` **enumeration and print the output "CLUB SPADE DIAMOND HEARTS"?**

a) `for(Cards card : Cards.values())`
       `System.out.print(card + " ");`
b) `for(Cards card : Cards.iterator())`
       `System.out.print(card + " ");`
c) `for(Cards card : Cards.enums())`
       `System.out.print(card + " ");`
d) `for(Cards card : Cards.items())`
       `System.out.print(card + " ");`
e) There is no way to print the string names of this enumeration. The `toString()` method of enumeration returns the ordinal value of the enumeration, which is equivalent to calling `card.ordinal().toString();`.

---

13. **Given these three definitions**

```
interface I1 {}
interface I2 {}
abstract class C {}
```

which one of the following will compile without errors?

a) `class CI12 extends C, I1, I2 {}`
b) `class CI12 implements C extends I1, I2 {}`
c) `class CI12 implements C, I1, I2 {}`
d) `class CI12 extends C implements I1, I2 {}`
e) `class CI12 extends C implements I1 implements I2 {}`
f) `class CI12 implements C extends I1 extends I2 {}`

14. **Given these two definitions**

```
interface I1 {}
interface I2 {}
```

which one of the following will compile without errors?

```
a) interface II implements I1, I2 {}
b) interface II implements I1 implements I2 {}
c) interface II implements I1 extends I2 {}
d) interface II extends I1, I2 {}
```

15. **Consider the following program:**

```
abstract class AbstractBook {
        public String name;
}

interface Sleepy {
        public String name = "undefined";
}

class Book extends AbstractBook implements Sleepy {
        public Book(String name) {
                this.name = name;              // LINE A
        }
        public static void main(String []args) {
                AbstractBook philosophyBook = new Book("Principia Mathematica");
                System.out.println("The name of the book is " + philosophyBook.name); // LINE B
        }
}
```

Which one of the following options correctly describes the behavior of this program?

a) The program will print the output "The name of the book is Principia Mathematica".

b) The program will print the output "The name of the book is undefined".

c) The program will not compile and result in a compiler error "ambiguous reference to name" in line marked with comment LINE A.

d) The program will not compile and result in a compiler error "ambiguous reference to name" in line marked with comment LINE B.

16. **Which one of the following relationships describes the OO design concept of "composition"?**

a) is-a

b) is-a-kind-of

c) has-a

d) is-implemented-in-terms-of

e) composed-as

f) DAO

17. Consider the following program:

```java
import java.util.Arrays;

class DefaultSorter {
        public static void main(String[] args) {
                String[] brics = {"Brazil", "Russia", "India", "China"};
                Arrays.sort(brics, null);         // LINE A
                for(String country : brics) {
                        System.out.print(country + " ");
                }
        }
}
```

Which one of the following options correctly describes the behavior of this program?

a) This program will result in a compiler error in line marked with comment LINE A.

b) When executed, the program prints the following: Brazil Russia India China.

c) When executed, the program prints the following: Brazil China India Russia.

d) When executed, the program prints the following: Russia India China Brazil.

e) When executed, the program throws a runtime exception of NullPointerException when executing the line marked with comment LINE A.

f) When executed, the program throws a runtime exception of InvalidComparatorException when executing the line marked with comment LINE A.

---

18. Consider the following program:

```java
import java.util.*;

class DequeTest {
        public static void main(String []args) {
                Deque<Integer> deque = new ArrayDeque<>();
                deque.addAll(Arrays.asList(1, 2, 3, 4, 5));
                System.out.println("The removed element is: " + deque.remove()); // ERROR?
        }
}
```

Which one of the following correctly describes the behavior of this program?

a) When executed, this program prints the following: "The removed element is: 5".

b) When executed, this program prints the following: "The removed element is: 1".

c) When compiled, the program results in a compiler error of "remove() returns void" for the line marked with the comment ERROR.

d) When executed, this program throws InvalidOperationException.

---

19. Consider the following program:

```java
import java.util.*;

class Diamond {
        public static void main(String[] args) {
                List list1 = new ArrayList<>(Arrays.asList(1, "two", 3.0));  // ONE
```

```
                List list2 = new LinkedList<>
                        (Arrays.asList(new Integer(1), new Float(2.0F), new Double(3.0))); // TWO
                list1 = list2;   // THREE
                for(Object element : list1) {
                        System.out.print(element + " ");
                }
        }
    }
```

Which one of the following describes the expected behavior of this program?

a) The program results in compiler error in line marked with comment ONE.
b) The program results in compiler error in line marked with comment TWO.
c) The program results in compiler error in line marked with comment THREE.
d) When executed, the program prints 1 2.0 3.0.
e) When executed, this program throws a ClassCastException.

---

20. **Consider the following program:**

```
class SimpleCounter<T> {
        private static int count = 0;
        public SimpleCounter() {
                count++;
        }
        static int getCount() {
                return count;
        }
}

class CounterTest {
        public static void main(String []args) {
                SimpleCounter<Double> doubleCounter = new SimpleCounter<Double>();
                SimpleCounter<Integer> intCounter = null;
                SimpleCounter rawCounter = new SimpleCounter();      // RAW
                System.out.println("SimpleCounter<Double> counter is "
                        + doubleCounter.getCount());
                System.out.println("SimpleCounter<Integer> counter is " + intCounter.getCount());
                System.out.println("SimpleCounter counter is " + rawCounter.getCount());
        }
}
```

Which one of the following describes the expected behavior of this program?

a) This program will result in a compiler error in the line marked with comment RAW.
b) When executed, this program will print
   SimpleCounter<Double> counter is 1
   SimpleCounter<Integer> counter is 0
   SimpleCounter counter is 1
c) When executed, this program will print
   SimpleCounter<Double> counter is 1
   SimpleCounter<Integer> counter is 1
   SimpleCounter counter is 1

d) When executed, this program will print
   SimpleCounter<Double> counter is 2
   SimpleCounter<Integer> counter is 0
   SimpleCounter counter is 2
e) When executed, this program will print
   SimpleCounter<Double> counter is 2
   SimpleCounter<Integer> counter is 2
   SimpleCounter counter is 2

---

21. **Consider the following program:**

```
class UsePrintf{
        public static void main(String []args) {
                int c = 'a';
                float f = 10;
                long ell = 100L;
                System.out.printf("char val is %c, float val is %f, long int val is %ld \n", c, f, ell);
        }
}
```

Which one of the following options best describes the behavior of this program when executed?

a) The program prints the following: char val is a, float val is 10.000000, long int val is 100.
b) The program prints the following: char val is 65, float val is 10.000000, long int val is 100.
c) The program prints the following: char val is a, float val is 10, long int val is 100L.
d) The program prints the following: char val is 65, float val is 10.000000, long int val is 100L.
e) The program prints the following: char val is 65, float val is 10, long int val is 100L.
f) The program throws an exception of java.util.UnknownFormatConversionException: Conversion = 'l'.

---

22. **Consider the following program:**

```
import java.util.regex.Pattern;

class Split {
        public static void main(String []args) {
                String date = "10-01-2012"; // 10th January 2012 in dd-mm-yyyy format
                String [] dateParts = date.split("-");
                System.out.print("Using String.split method: ");
                for(String part : dateParts) {
                        System.out.print(part + " ");
                }
                System.out.print("\nUsing regex pattern: ");
                Pattern datePattern = Pattern.compile("-");
                dateParts = datePattern.split(date);
                for(String part : dateParts) {
                        System.out.print(part + " ");
                }
        }
}
```

Which one of the following options correctly provides the output of this program?

a)
Using String.split method: 10-01-2012
Using regex pattern: 10 01 2012
b)
Using String.split method: 10 01 2012
Using regex pattern: 10 01 2012
c)
Using String.split method: 10-01-2012
Using regex pattern: 10-01-2012
d)
Using String.split method:
Using regex pattern: 10 01 2012
e)
Using String.split method: 10 01 2012
Using regex pattern:
f)
Using String.split method:
Using regex pattern:

---

23. **Consider the following program:**

```java
import java.util.regex.Pattern;

class Regex {
        public static void main(String []args) {
                String pattern = "a*b+c{3}";
                String []strings = { "abc", "abbccc", "aabbcc", "aaabbbccc" };
                for(String str : strings) {
                        System.out.print(Pattern.matches(pattern, str) + " ");
                }
        }
}
```

Which one of the following options correctly shows the output of this program?

a) true true true true
b) true false false false
c) true false true false
d) false true false true
e) false false false true
f) false false false false

---

24. **Consider the following program:**

```java
class MatchCheck {
        public static void main(String []args) {
                String[]strings = {"Severity 1", "severity 2", "severity3",
"severity five"};
                for(String str : strings) {
                        if(!str.matches("^severity[\\s+][1-5]")) {
```

```
                                System.out.println(str + " does not match");
                        }
                }
        }
}
```

Which one of the following options correctly shows the output of this program?

a)
Severity 1 does not match
severity 2 does not match
severity five does not match
b)
severity3 does not match
severity five does not match
c)
Severity 1 does not match
severity 2 does not match
d)
Severity 1 does not match
severity3 does not match
severity five does not match

---

25. **Consider the following program:**

```
import java.lang.*;

class InvalidValueException extends IllegalArgumentException {}
class InvalidKeyException extends IllegalArgumentException {}

class BaseClass {
        void foo() throws IllegalArgumentException {
                throw new IllegalArgumentException();
        }
}

class DeriClass extends BaseClass {
        public void foo() throws IllegalArgumentException {
                throw new InvalidValueException();
        }
}

class DeriDeriClass extends DeriClass {
        public void foo() {              // LINE A
                throw new InvalidKeyException();
        }
}
```

```
class EHTest {
        public static void main(String []args) {
                try {
                        BaseClass base = new DeriDeriClass();
                        base.foo();
                } catch(RuntimeException e) {
                        System.out.println(e);
                }
        }
}
```

Which one of the following options correctly describes the behavior of this program?

a) The program prints the following: `InvalidKeyException`.
b) The program prints the following: `RuntimeException`.
c) The program prints the following: `IllegalArgumentException`.
d) The program prints the following: `InvalidValueException`.
e) When compiled, the program will result in a compiler error in line marked with comment Line A due to missing throws clause.

---

26. **Consider the following program:**

```
class EHBehavior {
        public static void main(String []args) {
                try {
                        int i = 10/0; // LINE A
                        System.out.print("after throw -> ");
                } catch(ArithmeticException ae) {
                        System.out.print("in catch -> ");
                        return;
                } finally {
                        System.out.print("in finally -> ");
                }
                System.out.print("after everything");
        }
}
```

Which one of the following options best describes the behavior of this program?

a) The program prints the following: in catch -> in finally -> after everything.
b) The program prints the following: after throw -> in catch -> in finally -> after everything.
c) The program prints the following: in catch -> in finally -> after everything.
d) The program prints the following: in catch -> after everything.
e) The program prints the following: in catch -> in finally ->.
f) When compiled, the program results in a compiler error in line marked with comment in LINE A for divide-by-zero.

27. **Consider the following program:**

```java
class AssertionFailure {
        public static void main(String []args) {
                try {
                        assert false;
                } catch(RuntimeException re) {
                        System.out.println("RuntimeException");
                } catch(Exception e) {
                        System.out.println("Exception");
                } catch(Error e) {    // LINE A
                        System.out.println("Error" + e);
                } catch(Throwable t) {
                        System.out.println("Throwable");
                }
        }
}
```

This program is invoked in command line as follows:

```java
java AssertionFailure
```

Choose one of the following options describes the behavior of this program:

a) Compiler error at line marked with comment LINE A
b) Prints "RuntimeException" in console
c) Prints "Exception"
d) Prints "Error"
e) Prints "Throwable"
f) Does not print any output on console

28. **Consider the following program:**

```java
import java.io.*;

class CreateFilesInFolder {
        public static void main(String []args) {
                String[] fileList = { "/file1.txt", "/subdir/file2.txt", "/file3.txt" };
                for (String file : fileList) {
                        try {
                                new File(file).mkdirs();
                        }
                        catch (Exception e) {
                                System.out.println("file creation failed");
                                System.exit(-1);
                        }
                }
        }
}
```

Assume that underlying file system has necessary permissions to create files, and that the program executed successfully without printing the message "file creation failed." (In the answers, note that the term "current directory" means the directory from which you execute this program, and the term "root directory" in Windows OS means the root path of the current drive from which you execute this program.) What is the most likely behavior when you execute this program?

a) This program will create file1.txt and file3.txt files in the current directory, and file2.txt file in the subdir directory of the current directory.
b) This program will create file1.txt and file3.txt directories in the current directory and the file2.txt directory in the "subdir" directory in the current directory.
c) This program will create file1.txt and file3.txt files in the root directory, and a file2.txt file in the "subdir" directory in the root directory.
d) This program will create file1.txt and file3.txt directories in the root directory, and a file2.txt directory in the "subdir" directory in the root directory.

---

29. **Which of the following two statements is true regarding object serialization in Java?**

a) A serializable interface declares two methods, readObject() and writeObject(). To support serialization in your class, you need to implement the Serializable interface and define these two methods.
b) When serializing an object that has references to other objects, the serialization mechanism also includes the referenced objects as part of the serialized bytes.
c) When an object is serialized, the class members that are declared as transient will not be serialized (and hence their values are lost after deserialization).
d) The Externalizable interface is a marker interface; in other words, it's an empty interface that does not declare any methods.
e) If you attempt to serialize or persist an object that does not implement the Externalizable interface, you'll get a NotExternalizableException.

---

30. **Consider the following program:**

```java
import java.util.*;

class Separate {
        public static void main(String []args) {
                String text = "<head>first program </head> <body>hello world</body>";
                Set<String> words = new TreeSet<>();
                try ( Scanner tokenizingScanner = new Scanner(text) ) {
                        tokenizingScanner.useDelimiter("\\W");
                        while(tokenizingScanner.hasNext()) {
                                String word = tokenizingScanner.next();
                                if(!word.trim().equals("")) {
                                        words.add(word);
                                }
                        }
                }
                for(String word : words) {
                        System.out.print(word + " ");
                }
        }
}
```

Which one of the following options correctly provides the output of this program?

a) hello body program head first world
b) body first head hello program world
c) head first program head body hello world body
d) head first program body hello world
e) < </ >

---

31. **Consider the following code snippet:**

```
Path wordpadPath = Paths.get("C:\\Program Files\\Windows NT\\Accessories\\wordpad.exe");
System.out.println(wordpadPath.subpath(beginIndex, endIndex));
```

What are the values of the integer values beginIndex and endIndex in this program that will result in this code segment printing the string "Program Files" as output?

a) beginIndex = 1 and endIndex = 2
b) beginIndex = 0 and endIndex = 1
c) beginIndex = 1 and endIndex = 1
d) beginIndex = 4 and endIndex = 16

---

32. **Consider the following program:**

```
import java.io.IOException;
import java.nio.file.*;

class Matcher {
        public static void main(String []args) {
                Path currPath = Paths.get(".");
                try (DirectoryStream<Path> stream =
                        Files.newDirectoryStream(currPath, "*o*?{java,class}")) {
                        for(Path file : stream) {
                                System.out.print(file.getFileName() + " ");
                        }
                } catch (IOException ioe) {
                        System.err.println("An I/O error occurred... exiting ");
                }
        }
}
```

Assume that the current path in which the program is run has the following files: Copy.class, Copy.java, Dir.class, Dir.java, Hello.class, hello.html, Matcher.class, Matcher.java, OddEven.class, and PhotoCopy.java. **Assuming that the program ran without throwing** IOException. **Which one of the following options correctly describes the behavior of this program when it is executed?**

a) Prints the following: Copy.class Copy.java Hello.class hello.html OddEven.class PhotoCopy.java
b) Prints the following: Copy.class Copy.java PhotoCopy.java
c) Prints the following: Hello.class hello.html OddEven.class PhotoCopy.java
d) Prints the following: Copy.class Copy.java Hello.class OddEven.class PhotoCopy.java
e) Prints the following: PhotoCopy.java
f) Does not print any output in console
g) Throws the exception java.util.regex.PatternSyntaxException because the pattern is invalid.

33. **Which one of the following options is a correct way to create a watch service for watching a directory for changes?**

a) `Watchable watch = FileSystems.getDefault().newWatchable();`
b) `WatchService watcher = FileSystems.getDefault().newWatchService();`
c) `DirectoryWatchService dirWatcher = FileSystems.getDefault().newDirectoryWatchService();`
d) `FileWatchService fileWatcher = FileSystems.getNewFileWatchService();`
e) `FileDirectoryWatchService fileDirWatcher = WatchService.getNewFileDirectoryWatchService();`

34. **Which of the following two statements are true regarding Statement and its derived types?**

a) Objects of type `Statement` can handle IN, OUT, and INOUT parameters.
b) `PreparedStatement` is used for executing stored procedures.
c) You can get an instance of `PreparedStatement` by calling `preparedStatement()` method in the `Connection` interface.
d) `CallableStatement` extends the `PreparedStatement` class; `PreparedStatement` in turn extends the `Statement` class.
e) The interface `Statement` and its derived interfaces implement the `AutoCloseable` interface, hence it can be used with try-with-resources statement.

35. **Consider the following sequence of statements when using JDBC API. Assume that you've a TempSensor table with the column name temp.**

```
// assume that connection is successfully established to the database
connection.setAutoCommit(true);
Statement statement = connection.createStatement(ResultSet.TYPE_SCROLL_SENSITIVE,
ResultSet.CONCUR_UPDATABLE);
resultSet = statement.executeQuery("SELECT * FROM TempSensor");

// assume that the initial value of temp is "0" in the table

resultSet.moveToInsertRow();
resultSet.updateString("temp", "100");
resultSet.insertRow();
Savepoint firstSavepoint = connection.setSavepoint();

resultSet.moveToInsertRow();
resultSet.updateString("temp", "200");
resultSet.insertRow();
Savepoint secondSavepoint = connection.setSavepoint();

resultSet.moveToInsertRow();
resultSet.updateString("temp", "300");
resultSet.insertRow();
Savepoint thirdSavepoint = connection.setSavepoint();

connection.rollback(secondSavepoint);
connection.commit();
```

Which one of the following options correctly describes the behavior of this program?

a) temp value will be set to "100" in the table TempSensor.
b) temp value will be set to "200" in the table TempSensor.
c) temp value will be set to "300" in the table TempSensor.
d) temp value will be set to "0" in the table TempSensor.
e) The program will result in throwing a SQLException because auto-commit is true.

---

36. **Which one of the following options correctly creates a JdbcRowSet object?**

a) `RowSetProvider rowSetProvider = RowSetFactory.newProvider();`
   `JdbcRowSet rowSet = rowSetProvider.createJdbcRowSet();`
b) `RowSetFactory rowSetFactory = RowSetProvider.newFactory();`
   `JdbcRowSet rowSet = rowSetFactory.createJdbcRowSet();`
c) `JdbcRowSet rowSet = RowSetProvider.newFactory().getJdbcRowSetInstance();`
d) `JdbcRowSet rowSet = RowSetFactory.newProvider().getInstance(connection, "JdbcRowSet");`

---

37. **Consider the following program:**

```
class Worker extends Thread {
        public void run()  {
                System.out.println(Thread.currentThread().getName());
        }
}

class Master {
        public static void main(String []args) throws InterruptedException {
                Thread.currentThread().setName("Master ");
                Thread worker = new Worker();
                worker.setName("Worker ");
                worker.start();
                Thread.currentThread().join();
                System.out.println(Thread.currentThread().getName());
        }
}
```

Which one of the following options correctly describes the behavior of this program?

a) When executed, the program prints the following: "Worker Master ".
b) When executed, the program prints "Worker ", and after that the program hangs (i.e., does not terminate).
c) When executed, the program prints "Worker " and then terminates.
d) When executed, the program throws IllegalMonitorStateException.
e) The program does not compile and fails with multiple compiler errors.

---

38. **Which of the following two statements are true regarding the sleep() method defined in Thread class?**

a) The sleep() method takes milliseconds as an argument for the time to sleep.
b) The sleep() method takes microseconds as an argument for the time to sleep.
c) The sleep() method relinquishes the lock when the thread goes to sleep and reacquires the lock when the thread wakes up.
d) The sleep() method can throw InterruptedException if it is interrupted by another thread when it sleeps.

39. **Consider the following program:**

```java
class Waiter extends Thread {
        public static void main(String[] args) {
                new Waiter().start();
        }
        public void run() {
                try {
                        System.out.println("Starting to wait");
                        wait(1000);
                        System.out.println("Done waiting, returning back");
                }
                catch(InterruptedException e) {
                        System.out.println("Caught InterruptedException ");
                }
                catch(Exception e) {
                        System.out.println("Caught Exception ");
                }
        }
}
```

Which one of the following options correctly describes the behavior of this program?

a) The program prints
   Starting to wait
   Done waiting, returning back
b) The program prints
   Starting to wait
   Caught InterruptedException
c) The program prints
   Starting to wait
   Caught Exception
d) The program prints
   Starting to wait
   After that, the program gets into an infinite wait and deadlocks

---

40. **Consider the following program:**

```java
import java.util.*;
import java.util.concurrent.*;

class SetTest {
        public static void main(String []args) {
                List list = Arrays.asList(10, 5, 10, 20);    // LINE A
                System.out.println(list);
                System.out.println(new HashSet(list));
                System.out.println(new TreeSet(list));
                System.out.println(new ConcurrentSkipListSet(list));
        }
}
```

Which one of the following options correctly describes the behavior of this program?

a) The program prints
   [10, 5, 10, 20]
   [20, 5, 10]
   [5, 10, 20]
   [5, 10, 20]
b) The program prints
   [10, 5, 10, 20]
   [5, 10, 20]
   [5, 10, 20]
   [20, 5, 10]
c) The program prints
   [5, 10, 20]
   [5, 10, 20]
   [5, 10, 20]
   [5, 10, 20]
d) The program prints
   [10, 5, 10, 20]
   [20, 5, 10]
   [5, 10, 20]
   [20, 5, 10]
e) The program prints
   [10, 5, 10, 20]
   [5, 10, 10, 20]
   [5, 10, 20]
   [10, 5, 10, 20]
f) Compiler error in line marked by the comment LINE A since List is not parameterized with the type <Integer>.

---

41. **Consider the following program:**

```java
import java.util.concurrent.*;
import java.util.*;

class COWArrayListTest {
        public static void main(String []args) {
                ArrayList<Integer> aList = new CopyOnWriteArrayList<Integer>(); // LINE A
                aList.addAll(Arrays.asList(10, 20, 30, 40));
                System.out.println(aList);
        }
}
```

Which one of the following options correctly describes the behavior of this program?

a) When executed the program prints the following: [10, 20, 30, 40].
b) When executed the program prints the following: CopyOnWriteArrayList.class.
c) The program does not compile and results in a compiler error in line marked with comment LINE A.
d) When executed the program throws a runtime exception ConcurrentModificationException.
e) When executed the program throws a runtime exception InvalidOperationException.

42. Consider the following program:

```java
import java.util.concurrent.*;
import java.util.*;

class Blocking {
        Deque<String> gangOfFour = new LinkedBlockingDeque<String>();
        class Producer extends Thread {
                String []authors = { "E Gamma", "R Johnson", "R Helm", "J Vlissides" };
                public void run() {
                        for(String author : authors) {
                                gangOfFour.add(author);
                                try {
                                        // take time to add
                                        Thread.sleep(1000);
                                }
                                catch(InterruptedException ie) {
                                        // ignore it
                                }
                        }
                }
        }

        class Consumer extends Thread {
                int numOfAuthors = 4;
                int processedAuthors = 0;
                public void run() {
                        while(processedAuthors < 4) {
                                while (gangOfFour.isEmpty()) { /*wait till an entry is inserted*/ }

                                System.out.println(gangOfFour.remove());
                                processedAuthors++;
                        }
                }
        }

        public static void main(String []args) {
                Blocking blocking = new Blocking();
                blocking.new Producer().start();
                blocking.new Consumer().start();
        }
}
```

Which one of the following options correctly describes the behavior of this program?

a) Prints
   E Gamma
   and then the program terminates.
b) Prints
   E Gamma
   R Johnson
   R Helm
   J Vlissides
   and then the program enters a deadlock and never terminates.

33

c) Prints

E Gamma

R Johnson

R Helm

J Vlissides

and then the program terminates.

d) Prints

J Vlissides

R Helm

R Johnson

E Gamma

and then the program terminates.

e) The program does not print any output, enters a deadlock, and never terminates.

---

43. **For localization, resource bundle property files are created that consist of key-value pairs. Which one of the following is a valid key value pair as provided in a resource bundle property file for some strings mapped to German language?**

a)
```
<pair> <key>from</key> <value>von</value> </pair>
<pair> <key>subject</key> <value> betreff </value> </pair>
```
b)
```
from=von
subject=betreff
```
c)
```
key=from; value=von
key=subject; value=betreff
```
d)
```
pair<from,von>
pair<subject,betreff>
```

---

44. **Assume that you've the following resource bundles in your classpath:**

```
ResourceBundle.properties
ResourceBundle_ar.properties
ResourceBundle_en.properties
ResourceBundle_it.properties
ResourceBundle_it_IT_Rome.properties
```

Also assume that the default locale is English (US), where the language code is en and country code is US. Which one of these five bundles will be loaded for the call
```
loadResourceBundle("ResourceBundle", new Locale("fr", "CA", ""));?
```

a) `ResourceBundle.properties`
b) `ResourceBundle_ar.properties`
c) `ResourceBundle_en.properties`
d) `ResourceBundle_it.properties`
e) `ResourceBundle_it_IT_Rome.properties`

---

45. **Which one of the following is the correct implementation of a custom time formatter implementation that prints the current time in the format 10:42:30 where 10 is hours (value in range 1–12), 42 is minutes, and 30 is seconds?**

a) System.out.println(new SimpleDateFormat("hh:mm:ss").format(new Date()));
b) System.out.println(new CustomDateFormat("hh:mm:ss").format(new Date()));
c) System.out.println(new SimpleTimeFormat("hh:mm:ss").format(new Date()));
d) System.out.println(new CustomDateTimeFormat("HH:MM:SS").format(new Date()));

Answer sheet

Q.No	Answer	Q.No	Answer
1		24	
2		25	
3		26	
4		27	
5		28	
6		29	
7		30	
8		31	
9		32	
10		33	
11		34	
12		35	
13		36	
14		37	
15		38	
16		39	
17		40	
18		41	
19		42	
20		43	
21		44	
22		45	
23			

Answers with Explanations

1. c)

   s1 and s2 not equal
   s1 and s3 equal

   JVM sets a constant pool in which it stores all the string constants used in the type. If two references are declared with a constant, then both refer to the same constant object. The == operator checks the similarity of objects itself (and not the values in it). Here, the first comparison is between two distinct objects, so we get s1 and s2 not equal. On the other hand, since references of s1 and s3 refer to the same object, we get s1 and s3 equal.

2. c) [0, 0]

   The assignment x = x; inside the construct reassigns the passed parameter; it does *not* assign the member x in Point2D. The correct way to perform the assignment is this.x = x;. Field y is not assigned, so its value remains 0.

3. d) When executed, this program prints

   k == j is true
   k.equals(j) is true

   The Integer objects are immutable objects. If there is an Integer object for a value that already exists, then it does not create a new object again. In other words, Java uses sharing of immutable Integer objects, so two Integer objects are equal if their values are equal (no matter if you use == operators to compare the references or use equals() method to compare the contents).

4. a) arr1 == arr2 is false

   arr1.equals(arr2) is false
   Arrays.equals(arr1, arr2) is true

   The first comparison between two array objects is carried out using the == operator, which compares object similarity so it returns false here. The equals() method, which compares this array object with the passed array object, does not compare values of the array since it is inherited from the Object class. Thus we get another false. On the other hand, the Arrays class implements various equals() methods to compare two array objects of different types; hence we get true from the last invocation.

5. d) When executed, this program will print the following: str is not Object.

   The variable str was declared but not instantiated; hence the instanceof operator returns false.

6. b) Side Object Tail Side

   Overloading is based on the static type of the objects (while overriding and runtime resolution resolves to the dynamic type of the objects). Here is how the calls to the overload() method are resolved:

   - overload(firstAttempt); --> firstAttempt is of type Side, hence it resolves to overload(Side).

   - overload((Object)firstAttempt); -> firstAttempt is casted to Object, hence it resolves to overload(Object).

- overload(secondAttempt); -> secondAttempt is of type Tail, hence it resolves to overload(Tail).
- overload((Side)secondAttempt); -> secondAttempt is casted to Side, hence it resolves to overload(Side).

7. c) foo(long)

For an integer literal, the JVM matches in the following order: int, long, Integer, int.... In other words, it first looks for an int type parameter; if it is not provided, then it looks for long type; and so on. Here, since the int type parameter is not specified with any overloaded method, it matches with foo(long).

8. b)

```
In Base.foo()
In Derived.bar()
```

A static method is resolved statically. Inside the static method, a virtual method is invoked, which is resolved dynamically.

9. d) When executed, the program prints "walk cannot fly".

In order to override a method, it is not necessary for the overridden method to specify an exception. However, if the exception is specified, then the specified exception must be the same or a subclass of the specified exception in the method defined in the super class (or interface).

10. b) club none none none

Here is the description of matches for the four enumeration values:

- "club" matches with the case "Club".
- For "Spade", the case "spade" does not match because of the case difference (switch case match is case sensitive).
- does not match with "diamond" because case statements should exactly match and there are extra whitespaces in the original string.
- "hearts" does not match the string "heart".

11. a) new Outer.Inner().text

The correct way to access fields of the static inner class is to use the inner class instance along with the outer class, so new Outer.Inner().text will do the job.

12. a) for(Cards card : Cards.values())
        System.out.print(card + " ");

The values() method of an enumeration returns the array of enumeration members.

13. d) class CI12 extends C implements I1, I2 {}

A class inherits another class using the extends keyword and inherits interfaces using the implements keyword.

14. d) interface II extends I1, I2 {}

It is possible for an interface to extend one or more interfaces. In that case, we need to use the extends keyword and separate the list of super-interfaces using commas.

15. c) The program will not compile and will result in a compiler error "ambiguous reference to name" in LINE A.

Since name is defined in both the base interface and the abstract class, any reference to the member name is ambiguous. The first reference to name is in the line marked with comment LINE A, so the error is flagged in this line by the compiler.

16. c) has-a

Composition is a design concept that refers to the has-a relationship.

17. c) When executed, the program prints the following: Brazil China India Russia.

When null is passed as a second argument to the Arrays.sort() method, it means that the default Comparable (i.e., natural ordering for the elements) should be used. The default Comparator results in sorting the elements in ascending order. The program does not result in a NullPointerException or any other exceptions or a compiler error.

18. b) When executed, this program prints the following: "The removed element is: 1".

The remove() method is equivalent to the removeFirst() method, which removes the first element (head of the queue) of the Deque object.

19. d) When executed, the program prints the following: 1 2.0 3.0.

The List is a generic type that is used here in raw form; hence it allows us to put different types of values in list2. Therefore, it prints the following: 1 2.0 3.0.

20. e) When executed, this program will print

```
SimpleCounter<Double> counter is 2
SimpleCounter<Integer> counter is 2
SimpleCounter counter is 2
```

Count is a static variable, so it belongs to the class and not to an instance. Each time constructor is invoked, count is incremented. Since two instances are created, the count value is two.

21. f) The program throws an exception for java.util.UnknownFormatConversionException: Conversion = 'l'

There is no format specifier for long int, and the same %d format specifier for int is used for long as well. So, the format specifier %ld results in a runtime exception UnknownFormatConversionException.

22. b)

```
Using String.split method: 10 01 2012
Using regex pattern: 10 01 2012
```

Using str.split(regex) is equivalent to using Pattern.compile(regex).split(str).

23. d) false true false true

Here are the following regular expression matches for the character x:

- x* means matches with x for zero or more times.
- x+ means matches with x for one or more times.
- x{n} means match x exactly n times.

The pattern a*b+c{3} means match a zero or more times, followed by b one or more times, and c exactly three times.

So, here is the match for elements in the strings array:

- For "abc", the match fails, resulting in false.

- For "abbccc", the match succeeds, resulting in true.

- For "aabbcc", the match fails, resulting in false.

- For "aaabbbccc", the match succeeds, resulting in true.

24. d) Severity 1 does not match.
    severity3 does not match.
    severity five does not match.

Here is the meaning of the patterns used:

[^xyz]	Any character except x, y, or z (i.e., negation)
\s	A whitespace character
[a-z]	from a to z

So the pattern "^severity[\\s+][1-5]" matches the string "severity" followed by whitespace followed by one of the letters 1 to 5.
For this pattern,

- "Severity 1" does not match because of the capital S in "Severity".

- "severity 2" matches.

- "severity3" does not match since there is no whitespace between severity and 3.

- "severity five" does not match since "five" does not match a numeral from 1 to 5.

25. a) The program prints the following: InvalidKeyException.

It is not necessary to provide an Exception thrown by a method when the method is overriding a method defined with an exception (using the throws clause). Hence, the given program will compile successfully and it will print InvalidKeyException.

26. e) The program prints the following: in catch -> in finally ->.

The statement println("after throw -> "); will never be executed since the line marked with the comment LINE A throws an exception. The catch handles ArithmeticException, so println("in catch -> "); will be executed. Following that, there is a return statement, so the function returns. But before the function returns, the finally statement should be called, hence the statement println("in finally -> "); will get executed. So, the statement println("after everything"); will never get executed.

27. f) Does not print any output on the console

By default, assertions are disabled. If -ea (or the -enableassertions option to enable assertions), then the program would have printed "Error" since the exception thrown in the case of assertion failure is java.lang.AssertionError, which is derived from the Error class.

28. d) This program will create file1.txt and file3.txt directories in the root directory, and a file2.txt directory in the "subdir" directory in the root directory.

The mkdirs() method creates a directory for the given name. Since the file names have / in them, the method creates directories in the root directory (or root path for the Windows drive based on the path in which you execute this program).

29. b) When serializing an object that has references to other objects, the serialization mechanism also includes the referenced objects as part of the serialized bytes.
and
c) When an object is serialized, the class members that are declared as transient will not be serialized (and hence their values are lost after deserialization).

Option b) and c) are true regarding object serialization.

Option a) is wrong because the Serializable interface is a marker interface; in other words, the Serializable interface is an empty interface and it does not declare any methods in it.
Option d) is wrong because the Externalizable interface declares two methods, writeExternal() and readExternal().
Option e) is wrong because there is no such exception as NotExternalizableException.

30. b) Body first head hello program world

TreeSet<String> orders the strings in default alphabetical ascending order and removes duplicates. The delimiter \W is non-word, so the characters such as < act as separators.

31. b) beginIndex = 0 and endIndex = 1

In the Path class's method subpath(int beginIndex, int endIndex), beginIndex is the index of the first element (inclusive of that element) and endIndex is the index of the last element (exclusive of that element). Note that *the name that is closest to the root in the directory hierarchy has index 0.* Here, the string element "Program Files" is the closest to the root C:\, so the value of beginIndex is 0 and endIndex is 1.

32. d) Prints the following: Copy.class Copy.java Hello.class OddEven.class PhotoCopy.java.

In the Glob pattern "*o*?{java,class,html}", the character * matches any number of characters, so *o* matches any string that has "o" in it. The ? matches exactly one character. The pattern {java,class} matches files with the suffixes of "java" or "class". Hence, from the given files, the matching file names are Copy.class, Copy.java, Hello.class, OddEven.class, PhotoCopy.java.

33. b) WatchService watcher = FileSystems.getDefault().newWatchService();

The getDefault() method in FileSystems returns the reference to the underlying FileSystem object. The method newWatchService() returns a new watch service that may be used to watch registered objects for changes and events in files or directories.

34. The correct options are

c) You can get an instance of PreparedStatement by calling the preparedStatement() method in the Connection interface.
e) The interface Statement and its derived interfaces implement the AutoCloseable interface, hence they can be used with a try-with-resources statement.

Option c) and e) are correct statements. The other three are incorrect for the following reasons:

- Option a) Objects of type Statement can handle IN, OUT, and INOUT parameters; you need to use objects of CallableStatement type for that.

- Option b) `PreparedStatement` is used for pre-compiled SQL statements; the `CallableStatement` type is used for stored procedures.

- Option d) `CallableStatement` implements the `PreparedStatement` interface; `PreparedStatement` in turn implements the `Statement` interface. These three types are not classes.

35. e) The program will result in throwing a `SQLException` because auto-commit is true.

    If you call methods such as `commit()` or `rollback()` when the auto-commit mode is set to true, the program will a `SQLException`.

36. b) `RowSetFactory rowSetFactory = RowSetProvider.newFactory();`
    `JdbcRowSet rowSet = rowSetFactory.createJdbcRowSet();`

37. b) When executed, the program prints `"Worker"` and then the program hangs (i.e., does not terminate).

    The statement `Thread.currentThread()` in the `main()` method refers to the "Master" thread. Calling the `join()` method on itself means that the thread waits itself to complete, which would never happen, so this program hangs (and does not terminate).

38. Options a) and d) are true:

    a) Takes milliseconds as the argument for time to sleep.
    d) Can throw the `InterruptedException` if it is interrupted by another thread when it sleeps.

    In option b), the `sleep()` method takes milliseconds as an argument, not microseconds.
    In option), the `sleep()` method does not relinquish the lock when it goes to sleep; it holds the lock.

39. c) The program prints
    Starting to wait
    Caught Exception

    In this program, the `wait()` method is called without acquiring a lock; hence it will result in throwing an `IllegalMonitorStateException`, which will be caught in the catch block for the `Exception`.

40. a) The program prints
    [10, 5, 10, 20]
    [20, 5, 10]
    [5, 10, 20]
    [5, 10, 20]

    Here is the description of the containers that explain the output:

    - `List` is unsorted.

    - `HashSet` is unsorted and retains unique elements.

    - `TreeSet` is sorted and retains unique elements.

    - `ConcurrentSkipListSet` is sorted and retains unique elements.

CHAPTER 2 ■ PRETEST

41. c) The program does not compile and results in a compiler error in the line marked with comment LINE A.

The class CopyOnWriteArrayList does not inherit from ArrayList, so an attempt to assign a CopyOnWriteArrayList to an ArrayList reference will result in a compiler error (the ArrayList suffix in the class named CopyOnWriteArrayList could be misleading as these two classes do not share an is-a relationship).

42. c) Prints
    E Gamma
    R Johnson
    R Helm
    J Vlissides
    and then the program terminates.

The producer class puts an author on the list and then sleeps for some time. In the meantime, the other thread (consumer) keeps checking whether the list is non-empty or not. If it is non-empty, the consumer thread removes the item and prints it. Hence, all four author names get printed.

43. b)
```
from=von
subject=betreff
```

In the resource bundle property files, the key values are separated using the = symbol, with each line in the resource file separated by a newline character.

44. c) ResourceBundle_en.properties

Java looks for candidate locales for a base bundle named ResourceBundle and locale French (Canada), and checks for the presence of the following property files:

```
ResourceBundle_fr_CA.properties
ResourceBundle_fr.properties
```

Since both of them are not there, Java searches for candidate locales for the base bundle named ResourceBundle and a default locale (English - United States):

```
ResourceBundle_en_US.properties
ResourceBundle_en.properties
```

Java finds that there is a matching resource bundle, ResourceBundle_en.properties. Hence it loads this resource bundle.

45. a) System.out.println(new SimpleDateFormat("hh:mm:ss").format(new Date()));

In the format hh:mm:ss, h is for the hour in am/pm (with values in 1–12 range), m is for minutes, and s is for seconds. The class for creating and using custom date or time pattern strings is SimpleDateFormat. The expression new Date() creates a Date object with the current date and time value.

Post-Pretest Evaluation

The 45 questions in this pretest are selected and grouped to represent the 12 topics in the syllabus of the Oracle 1Z0-804 exam. The order of the topics in this pretest replicates the order of the topics in the 1Z0-804 syllabus.

Table 2-1 is your post-pretest evaluation tool. In the rightmost column, fill in the number of your correct pretest answers in each topic from your answer sheet. Wherever your number of correct answers is *less than or equal to* the expected number of correct answers shown in the adjacent column, you will need to focus your preparations for the OPCJP 7 exam on that exam topic and its corresponding chapter in this book.

Table 2-1. *Post-Pretest Evaluation Tool*

Pretest Question Numbers	1Z0-804 Exam Topic	Pertinent Chapter in This Book	Expected No. of Correct Answers	My No. of Correct Answers
1 – 5	OCAJP Basics	–	4	
6 – 9	Java Class Design	3	3	
10 – 12	Advanced Class Design	4	2	
13 – 16	Object-Oriented Design Principles	5	3	
17 – 20	Generics and Collections	6	3	
21 – 24	String Processing	7	3	
25 – 27	Exceptions and Assertions	11	2	
28 – 30	Java I/O Fundamentals	8	2	
31 – 33	Java File I/O (NIO.2)	9	2	
34 – 36	Building Database Applications with JDBC	10	2	
37 – 39	Threads	13	2	
40 – 42	Concurrency	14	2	
42 – 45	Localization	12	2	

CHAPTER 3

■ ■ ■

Java Class Design

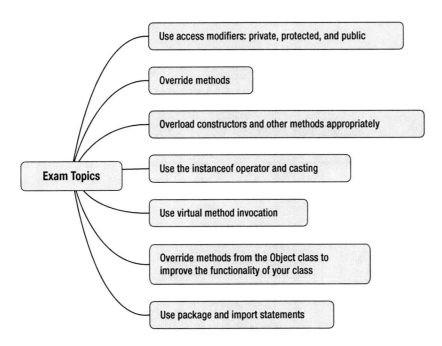

Exam Topics

- Use access modifiers: private, protected, and public
- Override methods
- Overload constructors and other methods appropriately
- Use the instanceof operator and casting
- Use virtual method invocation
- Override methods from the Object class to improve the functionality of your class
- Use package and import statements

Java is an *object-oriented programming* (OOP) language. Object orientation helps a developer to achieve a *modular, extensible, maintainable,* and *reusable* system. To write good-quality programs, a programmer must have a firm command of OOP concepts.

Object-oriented programming revolves around the concept of an *object*, which *encapsulates* data and behavior acting on the data together. An object provides its services through a well-defined *interface*. This interface specifies "what" the object offers, *abstracting* "how" (actual implementation). Object orientation provides support for modeling solutions at a higher level of abstraction in terms of *classes*, a hierarchy of related classes (*inheritance*), association among classes, and dynamic binding (*dynamic polymorphism*).

For any OCPJP exam, you are expected to know essential OOP concepts. The first section of this chapter covers foundations of OOP: abstraction, encapsulation, inheritance, and polymorphism. The second section covers concepts related to classes, in which we cover *constructors* and *access modifiers* in detail. The third section reviews *method overloading* and *constructor overloading*. The fourth section is on inheritance and covers the *is-a relationship, method overriding,* and *type casting*. The final section of this chapter deals with Java *packages* and *import statements*.

Essentials of OOP

To get a sense of the world of object-oriented programming, take a mental stroll around the television department of your local consumer electronics retailer. A television is an abstraction that offers certain functionality through the proper interface (a TV remote). As a viewer, you need not understand how the TV works; the TV abstracts all the finer-grain details of its operation from the viewer (*abstraction*). A television object encapsulates properties of the television (such as brightness, channel number, and volume) and associated behavior to control these properties in a single entity (*encapsulation*). In other words, the access to these properties is restricted to the associated operations. There are different types of televisions, such as CRT television, LED television, and LCD television; they belong to a single family forming an *inheritance hierarchy*. Although all types of televisions support "display" functionality, the internal technology enabling the display of content may differ (*polymorphism*).

With this television analogy in mind and with the help of the programming example introduced in the next section, let's review the essential OOP concepts.

FunPaint Application: An Example

Let's assume that you are implementing a simple drawing program for children called FunPaint (Figure 3-1). Users can drag and drop basic shapes like circles and squares, color them, and create drawings using those shapes.

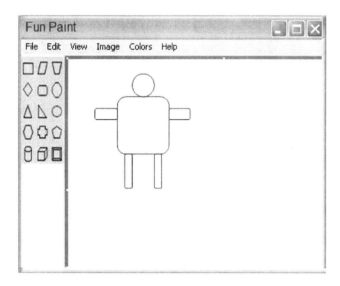

Figure 3-1. *A children's drawing application implemented using OOP concepts*

We'll use this example throughout this chapter to illustrate how OOP concepts can be used effectively for real-world programming and problem solving. For now, assume that the shapes such as Circle and Square are implemented as classes. A user can click on the circle icon and draw a circle in the drawing pane. With a circle, you need to remember associated information like center of the circle, radius of the circle, etc. To enable the user to color a circle, you need to calculate its area. Next you'll look at how OOP concepts can be used to implement FunPaint functionality.

Foundations of OOP

Object orientation is built on the foundations of encapsulation, abstraction, inheritance, and polymorphism. The following sections refresh your understanding of each of these four concepts.

Abstraction

The Latin root of *abstraction* means "taking away"—you take away everything except the specific aspect you wish to focus on. In other words, abstraction means hiding lower-level details and exposing only the essential and relevant details to the users.

For example, in order to drive a car, it is sufficient for a driver to have an essential repertoire of skills enabling her to interface with the car's steering, gear shifting, dashboard, braking, and accelerator systems. For the driver, it is superfluous to know the internal implementation details, such as how fuel is injected into the combustion chamber or how batteries are charged indirectly by the engine. The driver as such is concerned only about using the car and not about how the car works and provides functionality to the driver. In other words, a car *abstracts* the internal details and exposes to the driver only those details that are relevant to the interaction of the driver with the car.

In the FunPaint example, you define operations such as draw() and fillColor(). The user of the class Circle does not need to know how the class is drawing a circle or filling the circle with a specific color. In other words, you are abstracting the details of the class by hiding the implementation details.

Encapsulation

Structured programming *decomposes* the program's functionality into various procedures (*functions*), without much concern about the data each procedure can work with. Functions are free to operate and modify the (usually global and unprotected) data.

In OOP, data and functions operating on that data are combined together to form a single unit, which is referred to as a *class*. The term *encapsulation* refers to combining data and associated functions as a single unit. For example, in the Circle class, radius and center are defined as *private fields*. Now you can adduce methods draw() and fillColor() along with fields radius and center, since the fields and methods are closely related to each other. All the data (fields) required for the methods in the class are available inside the class itself. In other words, the class *encapsulates* its fields and methods together.

 Encapsulation combines data (fields) and logically-related operations (methods). Abstraction hides internal implementation level details and exposes only the relevant details of the class to the users. Abstraction is achieved *through* encapsulation.

Inheritance

Inheritance is a reusability mechanism in object-oriented programming in which the common properties of various objects are exploited to form relationships with each other. The abstract and common properties are provided in the *superclass*, which is available to the more specialized *subclasses*. For example, a color printer and a black-and-white printer are kinds of a printer (*single inheritance*); an all-in-one printer is a printer, scanner, and photocopier (*multiple inheritance*). It should be noted that Java does *not* support multiple inheritance but does support *multiple-interface inheritance* (discussed in detail in Chapters 4 and 5).

When we say that a class B is inherited from another class A, then class B is referred to as a *derived class* (or *subclass*) and class A is called as a *base class* (or *superclass*). By inheritance, the derived class receives the behavior of the base class, such that all the visible member methods and variables of the base class are available in the derived class. Apart from the inherited behavior, the derived class specializes its behavior by adding to or overriding base class behavior.

In FunPaint, the user can draw different shapes. Though the shapes are different, all shapes support similar functionality—for instance, color-filling and finding the area of the shape. Since these methods are common to all the shape classes, you can have a *base class* called Shape and declare these methods in this class. Other classes such as Circle and Triangle inherit from Shape and implement their specialized behavior.

Polymorphism

The Greek roots of the term *polymorphism* refer to the "several forms" of an entity. In the real world, every message you communicate has a context. Depending on the context, the meaning of the message may change and so may the response to the message. Similarly in OOP, a message can be interpreted in multiple ways (polymorphism), depending on the object.

For example, in *function overloading* (one of the polymorphic constructs in Java), you can provide methods with the same name but with different numbers of arguments or types of arguments. The concept is simple, yet it provides a lot of power and flexibility to the programmer. In FunPaint, you can fill the shapes with different colors. Methods like fillColor() can either take the color argument as RGB (Red, Green, Blue) values or as HSB (Hue, Saturation, Brightness) values. The call for the same method, fillColor(), behaves differently based on the provided arguments; this is an example of *compile-time polymorphism*.

Let's assume that you have a method named area() in the Shape base class. The area() method returns the area of the drawn shape. Hence, area() is implemented (*overridden*) in all the derived classes of Shape. A Shape reference can point to any derived class object. When you call the area() method from the Shape reference, it results in calling the area() method of the actual object type (i.e. the dynamic type of the object). This dynamic behavior is known as *runtime polymorphism*.

We packed a lot of concepts and terminology into one simple example. Don't worry if you don't quite digest them all at once. You'll be learning more about them throughout this book.

Class Fundamentals

A *class* is a fundamental abstraction entity and building block in OOP. A class encapsulates *state* (data) and *behavior* (operations) of an entity. For example, a Circle class defines a blueprint for individual circle objects. This Circle class might have state information such as radius and operations such as area() and fillColor(). The Circle class encapsulates state and operations of the circle in a single entity and provides a new abstraction. From an object-oriented programming point of view, it is important to understand that a class defines a new type that could be used by other classes in a program.

Let's look at an example of a class and analyze its various parts (Figure 3-2). This example declares the class Circle, which has the member-variables x, y, and radius of type Integer and the two member-methods, area() and fillColor().

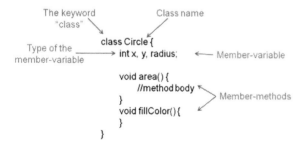

Figure 3-2. *A sample class Circle and its various parts*

 A class is a template (or blueprint), and an object is an instance of a class.

Object Creation

You create classes to use them in your programs. You can create an *instance* (an object using the services of a class). At a high level, there are three steps to using an object in a program.

- **Declaration:** You need to provide a variable declaration that consists of the *type-name* (the class you want to use) and the *object-name*. For example, following statement declares a variable circleObj of type Circle:

  ```
  Circle circleObj;
  ```

- **Instantiation:** You use the keyword new to create an instance; the keyword allocates required memory for the object. In this example, you *instantiate* the circle object by using the following statement:

  ```
  Circle circleObj = new Circle ();
  ```

- **Initialization:** A special method, which you call as a *constructor*, is invoked automatically. The constructor initializes the newly created object.

Constructors

Each time you create an object, a constructor of that class gets called. You can make use of the constructor to initialize the newly created object by setting the initial state of the object, and you can acquire some resources (such as file handles). The main rule of constructors is that they should have the same name as the class. A class can have more than one constructor.

 Every class has a constructor. If you do not explicitly write a constructor for a class, the Java compiler provides a default constructor (without any parameter) for that class.

Assume that you are implementing the Circle class in the FunPaint application. A Circle should remember its center and its radius, so you have three fields: xPos, yPos, and radius.

```
class Circle {
        int xPos, yPos, radius;
}
```

What happens when you create a new Circle object? The values of xPos, yPos, and radius will be initialized to the value 0 by default since they are of type Integer. However, this is not desirable for creating proper Circle objects. Let's define default values for the variables xPos, yPos, and radius, in a *default constructor*:

```
public Circle() {
        xPos = 20; // assume some default values for xPos and yPos
        yPos = 20;
        radius = 10; // default radius
}
```

49

As you can see here, a constructor has the same name as the class and doesn't have any return type. A default constructor does not have any arguments. A default constructor gets invoked when you create a new object without passing any arguments.

Let's check whether this default constructor gets invoked or not when you try to instantiate an object of Circle. For that you'll implement toString() method for printing the values of the Circle members (Listing 3-1). (Note: You don't have to call toString() method explicitly as in this code—it will get called automatically. You'll learn more about it in the "Runtime Polymorphism" section of this chapter).

Listing 3-1. Circle.java

```java
// A 2D Circle class with xPos and yPos fields to store the coordinates for center point
// and radius field to store the radius value of the circle
class Circle {
        private int xPos, yPos, radius;
        // default constructor initializing all the three fields
        public Circle() {
                xPos = 20; // assume some default values for xPos and yPos
                yPos = 20;
                radius = 10; // default radius
        }
        // overridden toString method to print info on Circle object in string form
        public String toString() {
                return "center = (" + xPos + "," + yPos + ") and radius = " + radius;
        }
        public static void main(String[]s) {
                // Passing a object to println automatically invokes the toString method
                System.out.println(new Circle());
        }
}
```

It prints

```
center = (20,20) and radius = 10
```

Yes, your default constructor is working. Got it?

Now, can you see what's wrong with this constructor?

```java
public void Circle() {
        xPos = 20; // assume some default values for xPos and yPos
        yPos = 20;
        radius = 10; // default radius
}
```

A constructor does not have a return type, and here you've given a void return type. This is not a constructor, but it is a method named Circle in this class! Beware: Java allows you to declare methods with same name as the class name, but it is not a good practice to make use of this feature (since it will confuse the programmers reading your code).

 A constructor does not have a return type. If you define a return type, it is not a constructor, but a method! Beware and avoid making this common mistake.

Access Modifiers

The OCPJP exam includes both direct questions on access modifiers and indirect questions that require an underlying knowledge of access modifiers. Hence it is important to understand the various access modifiers supported in Java.

Access modifiers determine the level of visibility (and therefore access) for a Java entity (a class, method, or field). Access modifiers enable you to enforce effective encapsulation. If all member variables of a class can be accessed from anywhere, then there is no point putting these variables in a class and no purpose in encapsulating data and methods together in a class.

Java supports four types of access modifiers:

- Public

- Private

- Protected

- Default (no access modifier specified)

To illustrate the four types of access modifiers, let's assume that you have one more class in the FunPaint application: Canvas. The Shape, Circle, and Circles classes are in one package (graphicshape) and the Canvas class is in another package (appcanvas).

```
// Shape.java
package graphicshape;

class Shape {
        // class definition
}

// Circle.java
package graphicshape;

public class Circle extends Shape {
        // class definition
}

//Circles.java
package graphicshape;

class Circles {
        //class definition
}

// Canvas.java
package appcanvas;
import graphicshape.Circle;

class Canvas {
        //class definition
}
```

For the time being, let's pass over the statements package graphicshape, ...extends Shape, and import graphicshape.Circle and consider them in detail in later sections.

Public Access Modifier

The public access modifier is the most liberal one. If a class or its members are declared as *public*, they can be accessed from any other class regardless of the package boundary. It is comparable to a public place in the real world, such as a company cafeteria that all employees can use irrespective of their department.

In the FunPaint example, let's assume that the class Circle has a public method area(). This method can be accessed from anywhere, even from another package, as shown in the Listing 3-2 snippet.

Listing 3-2. Circle.java

```java
// Shape.java
package graphicshape;

class Shape {
        // class definition elided
}

// Circle.java
package graphicshape;

public class Circle extends Shape {
        public void area() {    //public method
                // code for area method elided
        }
}

// Circles.java
package graphicshape;

class Circles {
        void getArea() {
                Circle circle = new Circle();
                circle.area();  //call to public method area(), within package
        }
}

// Canvas.java
package appcanvas;
import graphicshape.Circle;

class Canvas {
        void getArea() {
                Circle  circle = new Circle();
                circle.area();  //call to public method area(), outside package
        }
}
```

As shown in Listing 3-2, the public method area() is accessible within the same package (in the Circles class), as well as outside of the package (in the Canvas class).

A *public method* in a class is accessible to the outside world only if the class is declared as public. If the class does not specify any access modifier, then the public method is accessible only within the containing package.

Private Access Modifier

The private access modifier is the most stringent access modifier. A *private* class member cannot be accessed from outside the class; only members of the same class can access these private members. It's comparable to a safe deposit box room in a bank, which can only be accessed by a set of authorized personnel and safe deposit box owners.

Let's add the attribute radius to the class Circle as a private member. In this case, the attribute can be assessed by—and only by—the members of the Circle class, as shown in Listing 3-3.

Listing 3-3. Circle.java

```java
// Shape.java
package graphicshape;

class Shape {
        //class definition
}

//Circle.java
package graphicshape;

public class Circle extends Shape {
        private int radius;     //private field
        public void area() {    //public method
                // access to private field radius inside the class
                System.out.println("area:"+3.14*radius*radius);
        }
}

// Circles.java
package graphicshape;

class Circles {
        void getArea() {
                Circle  circle = new Circle();
                circle.area();  //call to public method area(), within package
        }
}

// Canvas.java
package appcanvas;
import graphicshape.Circle;
```

```
class Canvas {
      void getArea() {
            Circle  circle = new Circle();
            circle.area();  // call to public method area(), outside package
      }
}
```

In this example, radius is accessible only inside the Circle class and not in any other class, regardless of the enclosing package.

Protected and Default Access Modifier

Protected and *default access modifiers* are quite similar to each other. If a member method or field is declared as protected or default, then the method or field can be accessed within the package. Note that there is no explicit keyword to provide default access—in fact, when no access modifier is specified, the member has default access. Also, note that default access is also known as *package-protected* access. Protected and default accesses are comparable to the situation in an office where a conference room is accessible only to one department.

What is the difference between protected and default access? One significant difference between these two access modifiers arises when we talk about a subclass belonging to another package than its superclass. In this case, protected members are accessible in the subclass, whereas default members are not.

Let's say the class Shape has the protected member variable color and the class Circle has another method fillColor() declared with default access modifier, as in the snippet in Listing 3-4.

Listing 3-4. Circle.java

```
// Shape.java
package graphicshape;

class Shape {
      protected int color;
}

// Circle.java
package graphicshape;

public class Circle extends Shape {
      private int radius;      // private field
      public void area() {     // public method
            // access to private field radius inside the class
            System.out.println("area:"+3.14*radius*radius);
      }
      void fillColor() {
            System.out.println("color:" + color); //access to protected field, in subclass
      }
}

// Circles.java
package graphicshape;
```

```
class Circles {
        void getArea() {
                Circle  circle = new Circle();
                circle.area();  // call to public method area() within package
                circle.fillColor();      // call to a method with default access modifier
within package
        }
}

// Canvas.java
package appcanvas;
import graphicshape.Circle;

class Canvas {
        void getArea() {
                Circle  circle = new Circle();
                circle.area();  // call to public method area(), outside package
        }
}
```

As the example shows, the protected field color is accessed in the class Circle and the default method fillColor() is called from the class Circles.

The visibility offered by various access modifiers is summarized in Table 3-1.

Table 3-1. *Access Modifiers and Their Visibility*

Access modifiers/ accessibility	Within the same class	Subclass inside the package	Subclass outside the package	Other class inside the package	Other class outside the package
Public	Yes	Yes	Yes	Yes	Yes
Private	Yes	No	No	No	No
Protected	Yes	Yes	Yes	Yes	No
Default	Yes	Yes	No	Yes	No

 It is important to note that a class (or interface) cannot be declared as private or protected. Furthermore, member methods or fields of an interface cannot be declared as private or protected.

Overloading

Now let's enlarge on the concept of polymorphism introduced in the "Polymorphism" section above.

Polymorphism can be of two forms: *static* and *dynamic*. When different forms of a single entity are resolved at compile time (*early binding*), such polymorphism is called *static polymorphism*. When different forms of a single entity are resolved during runtime (*late binding*), such polymorphism is called *dynamic polymorphism*. *Overloading* is an example of static polymorphism.

Method Overloading

In a class, how many methods can you define with the same name? Many! In Java, you can define multiple methods with the same name, provided the argument lists differ from each other. In other words, if you provide different types of arguments, different numbers of arguments, or both, then you can define multiple methods with the same name. This feature is called *method overloading*. The compiler will resolve the call to a correct method depending on the actual number and/or types of the passed parameters.

In the FunPaint application, you can draw and color a shape. Say you want to color a circle. How would you define a method that can implement this functionality? (Please note that any color can be specified using one of these two approaches.)

1. By combining the basic colors of red, green, and blue. This approach is known as RGB scheme. By convention, each of the color values is typically given in the range 0 to 255.

2. By giving hue, saturation, and brightness values. This approach is known as HSB scheme. By convention, each of the values is typically given in the range 0.0 to 1.0.

Let's implement a method in the Circle class called fillColor() that takes RGB or HSB values. Since RGB values are integer values and HSB values are floating point values, how about supporting both these schemes for calling fillColor() method? See Listing 3-5.

Listing 3-5. Circle.java

```java
class Circle {
        // other members
        public void fillColor (int red, int green, int blue) {
                /* color the circle using RGB color values - actual code elided */
        }

        public void fillColor (float hue, float saturation, float brightness) {
                /* color the circle using HSB values - actual code elided */
        }
}
```

As you can see, both fillColor() methods have exactly the same name and both take three arguments; however, the argument types are different. Based on the type of arguments used while calling fillColor() method on Circle, the compiler will decide exactly which method to call. For instance, consider following method calls:

```java
Circle c1 = new Circle(10, 20, 10);
c1.fillColor(0, 255, 255);

Circle c2 = new Circle(50, 100, 5);
c2.fillColor(0.5f, 0.5f, 1.0f);
```

In this code, for the c1 object, the call to fillColor() has integer arguments 0, 255, and 255. Hence, the compiler resolves this call to the method fillColor (int red, int green, int blue). For the c2 object, the call to fillColor() has arguments 0.5f, 0.5f, and 1.0f; hence it resolves the call to fillColor (float hue, float saturation, float brightness).

In the above example, method fillColor() is an overloaded method. The method has same name and the same number of arguments, but the types of the arguments differ. It is also possible to overload methods with different numbers of arguments.

Such overloaded methods are useful for avoiding repeating the same code in different functions. Let's look at a simple example in Listing 3-6.

Listing 3-6. HappyBirthday.java

```java
class HappyBirthday {
        // overloaded wish method with String as an argument
        public static void wish(String name) {
                System.out.println("Happy birthday " + name + "!");
        }

        // overloaded wish method with no arguments; this method in turn invokes wish(String) method
        public static void wish() {
                wish("to you");
        }

        public static void main(String []args) {
                wish();
                wish("dear James Gosling");
        }
}
```

It prints:

```
Happy birthday to you!
Happy birthday dear James Gosling!
```

Here, the method wish(String name) is meant for wishing "Happy Birthday" when the name of the person is known. The default method wish() is for wishing "Happy Birthday" to anyone. As you can see, you don't have to write System.out.println again in the wish() method; you can just reuse the wish(String) method definition by passing the default value "to you" as argument to wish(). Such reuse is effective for large and related method definitions since it saves time writing and testing the same code.

Constructor Overloading

A default constructor is useful for creating objects with a default initialization value. When you want to initialize the objects with different values in different instantiations, you can pass them as the arguments to constructors. And yes, you can have multiple constructors in a class—which is *constructor overloading*. In a class, the default constructor can initialize the object with default initial values, while another constructor can accept arguments that need to be used for object instantiation.

In the FunPaint application, the user can just drag and drop the Circle template in the screen to create a Circle object. In that case, you must set the xPos and yPos values for that dropped position and assume a default value for radius (Listing 3-7).

Listing 3-7. Circle.java

```java
// a Circle object can be created by dragging and dropping a circle template
// the x, and y positions need to be set in that case, but a default radius value can be assumed
public Circle(int x, int y) {
        xPos = x;
        yPos = y;
        radius = 10; // default radius
}
```

Let's retain the toString() method that was defined in the previous section on default constructors:

```java
public String toString() {
        return "center = (" + xPos + "," + yPos + ") and radius = " + radius;
}
```

While creating the object, you can pass the arguments, as in the following statement:

```java
System.out.println(new Circle(50, 100).toString());
```

The above statement prints

```
center = (50,100) and radius = 10
```

Now, can you see what is wrong with the following constructor implementation?

```java
public Circle(int xPos, int yPos) {
        xPos = xPos;
        yPos = yPos;
        radius = 10; // default radius
}
```

```java
System.out.println(new Circle(50, 100));
```

It prints

```
center = (0, 0) and radius = 10
```

What happened? You just changed the name of arguments in the constructor given in the previous example, and it doesn't work!

The statement xPos = xPos; is the culprit. What you wanted was to assign the member xPos to the passed argument value xPos. However, this statement *reassigns* the passed argument value xPos! A passed argument is treated just like a local variable (a variable confined to local scope). If there is a local variable with same name as the field, the local variable *hides* the field.

 In order to avoid subtle bugs, refrain from reusing the same variable names across scopes.

How can you solve this issue? You can rename the argument instead of using xPos, say x. Or you can use this to qualify the use of xPos, as in

```java
public Circle(int xPos, int yPos) {
        this.xPos = xPos;
        this.yPos = yPos;
        radius = 10; // default radius
}
```

In the statement this.xPos = xPos;, you explicitly qualify the variable xPos with this, so the LHS (left-hand side) of the statement refers to the field and the RHS (right-hand side) of the statement refers to the parameter name.

Use the explicit this qualifier when accessing fields inside instance methods or constructors to avoid ambiguity in referring to variable names.

Create another constructor of Circle by passing more parameters. You'll also pass the radius value.

```
public Circle(int x, int y, int r) {
        xPos = x;
        yPos = y;
        radius = r;
}
```

Now you'll write the main() method, and you'll create some Circle objects in it. You'll implement the toString() method to print the center position and the radius (see Listing 3-8).

Listing 3-8. Circle.java

```
public class Circle {
        private int xPos;
        private int yPos;
        private int radius;

        // three overloaded constructors for Circle
        public Circle(int x, int y, int r) {
                xPos = x;
                yPos = y;
                radius = r;
        }

        public Circle(int x, int y) {
                xPos = x;
                yPos = y;
                radius = 10; // default radius
        }

        public Circle() {
                xPos = 20; // assume some default values for xPos and yPos
                yPos = 20;
                radius = 10; // default radius
        }

        public String toString() {
                return "center = (" + xPos + "," + yPos + ") and radius = " + radius;
        }
```

```
        public static void main(String[]s) {
                System.out.println(new Circle());
                System.out.println(new Circle(50, 100));
                System.out.println(new Circle(25, 50, 5));
        }
}
```

This program prints

```
center = (20,20) and radius = 10
center = (50,100) and radius = 10
center = (25,50) and radius = 5
```

As you can see, the compiler has resolved the constructor calls depending on the number of arguments. Did you notice that you are duplicating the code inside the three constructors? To avoid that code duplication—and reduce your typing effort—you can invoke one constructor from another constructor. Of the three constructors, the constructor taking x-position, y-position, and radius is the most general constructor. The other two constructors can be rewritten in terms of calling the three argument constructors, like so:

```
public Circle(int x, int y, int r) {
        xPos = x;
        yPos = y;
        radius = r;
}

public Circle(int x, int y) {
        this(x, y, 10); // passing default radius 10
}

public Circle() {
        this(20, 20, 10);
        // assume some default values for xPos, yPos and radius
}
```

The output is exactly the same as for the previous program, but this program is shorter; you used the this keyword to call one constructor from another constructor of the same class.

Overload resolution

When you define overloaded methods, how does the compiler know which method to call? Can you guess the output of the code in Listing 3-9?

Listing 3-9. Overloaded.java

```
class Overloaded {
        public static void aMethod (int val)       { System.out.println ("int");    }
        public static void aMethod (short val)     { System.out.println ("short");  }
        public static void aMethod (Object val)    { System.out.println ("object"); }
        public static void aMethod (String val )   { System.out.println ("String"); }
```

```
        public static void main(String[] args) {
                byte b = 9;
                aMethod(b);      // first call
                aMethod(9);      // second call
                Integer i = 9;
                aMethod(i);      // third call
                aMethod("9");    // fourth call
        }
}
```

It prints

```
short
int
object
String
```

Here is how the compiler resolved these calls:

- In the first method call, the statement is aMethod(b) where the variable b is of type byte. There is no aMethod definition that takes byte as an argument. The closest type (in size) is short type and not int, so the compiler resolves the call aMethod(b) to aMethod(short val) definition.

- In the second method call, the statement is aMethod(9). The constant value 9 is of type int. The closest match is aMethod(int), so the compiler resolves the call aMethod(9) to aMethod(int val) definition.

- The third method call is aMethod(i), where the variable i is of type Integer. There is no aMethod definition that takes Integer as an argument. The closest match is aMethod(Object val), so it is called. Why not aMethod(int val)? For finding the closest match, the compiler allows implicit upcasts, not downcasts, so aMethod(int val) is not considered.

- The last method call is aMethod("9"). The argument is a String type. Since there is an exact match, aMethod(String val) is called.

This process of the compiler trying to *resolve* the method call from given overloaded method definitions is called *overload resolution*. For resolving a method call, it first looks for the *exact* match—the method definition with exactly same number of parameters and types of parameters. If it can't find an exact match, it looks for the *closest match* by using upcasts. If the compiler can't find any match, then you'll get a compiler error, as in Listing 3-10.

Listing 3-10. More Overloaded.java

```
class Overloaded {
        public static void aMethod (byte val )  { System.out.println ("byte");  }
        public static void aMethod (short val ) { System.out.println ("short"); }

        public static void main(String[] args) {
                aMethod(9);
        }
}
```

Here is the compiler error:

```
Overloaded.java:6: cannot find symbol
symbol  : method aMethod(int)
location: class Overloaded
                aMethod(9);
                ^
```

`1 error`

The type of constant 9 is int, so there is no matching definition for aMethod for the call aMethod(9). As you saw earlier with respect to the overload resolution, the compiler can do upcasts (e.g., byte to int) for the closest match, but it does not consider downcasts (e.g., int to byte or int to short, as in this case). Hence, the compiler does not find any matches and throws you an error.

What if the compiler finds two matches? It will also become an error! Listing 3-11 shows an example.

Listing 3-11. Two Matches in Overloaded.java

```
class Overloaded {
        public static void aMethod (long val1, int val2) {
                System.out.println ("long, int");
        }

        public static void aMethod (int val1, long val2) {
                System.out.println ("int, long");
        }

        public static void main(String[] args) {
                aMethod(9, 10);
        }
}
```

Here is the compiler error:

```
Overloaded.java:6: reference to aMethod is ambiguous, both method aMethod(long,java.lang.Integer) in
Overloaded and method aMethod(java.lang.Integer,long) in Overloaded match
                aMethod(9, 10);
                ^
```

`1 error`

Why did this call become an "ambiguous" call? The constants 9 and 10 are ints. There are two aMethod definitions: one is aMethod(long, int) and another is aMethod(int, long). So there is no exact match for the call aMethod(int, int). An integer can be implicitly upcasted to both long as well as Integer. Which one will the compiler choose? Since there are two matches, the compiler complains with an error that the call is ambiguous.

Overload resolution fails (with a compiler error) if there are no matches or ambiguous matches.

Points to Remember

Here are some interesting rules regarding method overloading that will help you when taking the OCPJP exam:

- Overload resolution takes place entirely at compile time. In the next section, you'll learn about *runtime polymorphism* where the method call is resolved at runtime.

- You cannot overload methods with the methods differing in return types alone.

- You cannot overload methods with the methods differing in exception specifications alone.

- For overload resolution to succeed, you need to define methods such that the compiler finds one exact match. If the compiler finds no matches for your call or if the matching is ambiguous, the overload resolution fails and the compiler issues an error.

The *signature* of a method is made up of the method name, number of arguments, and types of arguments. You can overload methods with same name but with different signatures. Since return type and exception specification are not part of the signature, you cannot overload methods based on return type or exception specification alone.

Inheritance

An important feature supported by object-oriented programming is the hierarchical classification of knowledge using inheritance. Hierarchical models are easy to understand. For example, you can logically categorize vehicles as two-wheelers, three-wheelers, four-wheelers, etc. In the four-wheelers category, there are cars, vans, buses, trucks, etc. In the cars category, there are hatch-backs, sedans, SUVs, etc. When you categorize hierarchically, it becomes easy to understand, model, and write programs. In OOP, you can create such hierarchies easily using inheritance.

Consider a simple example used in earlier sections: class Shape is a base class while Circle and Square are derived classes. In other words, a Circle is a Shape; similarly, a Square is a Shape. Therefore, an inheritance relationship can be referred to as an *is-a relationship*.

In the Java library, you can see extensive use of inheritance. Figure 3-3 shows a partial inheritance hierarchy from java.lang library. The Number class abstracts various numerical (reference) types such as Byte, Integer, Float, Double, Short, and BigDecimal.

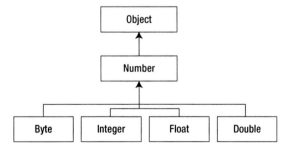

Figure 3-3. *A partial inheritance hierarchy in java.lang package*

The class Number has many common methods that are inherited by the derived classes. The derived classes do not have to implement the common methods implemented by the Number class. Also, you can supply a derived type where the base type is expected. For instance, a Byte is a Number, which means you can provide an object of Byte where an object of Number is expected. You can write general purpose methods (or algorithms) when you write methods for the base type. Listing 3-12 shows a simple example.

Listing 3-12. TestNumber.java

```java
public class TestNumber {
        // take an array of numbers and sum them up
        public static double sum(Number []nums) {
                double sum = 0.0;
                for(Number num : nums) {
                        sum += num.doubleValue();
                }
                return sum;
        }

        public static void main(String []s) {
                // Create a Number array
                Number []nums = new Number[4];
                // assign derived class objects
                nums[0] = new Byte((byte)10);
                nums[1] = new Integer(10);
                nums[2] = new Float(10.0f);
                nums[3] = new Double(10.0f);
                // pass the Number array to sum and print the result
                System.out.println("The sum of numbers is: " + sum(nums));
        }
}
```

This program prints

```
The sum of numbers is: 40.0
```

In the main() method, you declare nums as a Number[]. A Number reference can hold any of its derived type objects. You are creating objects of type Byte, Integer, Float, and Double with initial value 10; the nums array holds these elements. (Note that you needed an explicit cast in new Byte((byte) 10) instead of plain Byte(10) because Byte takes a byte argument and 10 is an int.)

The sum method takes a Number[] and returns the sum of the Number elements. The double type can hold the largest range of values, so you use double as the return type of the sum method. Number has a doubleValue method and this method returns the value held by the Number as a double value. The for loop traverses the array, adds the double values, and then returns the sum once you're done.

As you can see, the sum() method is a general method that can handle any Number[]. A similar example can be given from the Java standard library where java.lang.Arrays class has a static method binarySearch():

```java
static int binarySearch(Object[] a, Object key, Comparator c)
```

This method searches a given key (an Object type) in the given array of Objects. Comparator is an interface declaring the equals and compare methods. You can use binarySearch for objects of any class type that implements this Comparator interface. As you can see, inheritance is a powerful and useful feature for writing general-purpose methods.

In the FunPaint example, there is an inheritance relationship between base type Shape and its derived types such as Circle and Square. What is the advantage of associating these classes by inheritance?

Assume that a FunPaint user can choose the refresh (i.e., redraw) option from the menu for refreshing the shapes. If the Shape base class declares a refresh() method, all the derived classes can implement the refresh() method. Once all derived classes implement the refresh() method, refreshing all the shapes becomes easy.

```
void refreshAll(Shapes[]shapes) {
        for(Shape shape: shapes)          // for all shapes
                shape.refresh();          // call refresh
}
```

Now if you call the refreshAll() method and pass the array containing all Shapes drawn in the screen, the whole drawing will be refreshed. Writing such a generic method is possible only because of the is-a relationship.

Runtime Polymorphism

You just learned that a base class reference can refer to a derived class object. You can invoke methods from the base class reference; however, the actual method invocation depends on the dynamic type of the object pointed to by the base class reference. The type of the base class reference is known as the *static type* of the object and the actual object pointed by the reference at runtime is known as the *dynamic type* of the object.

When the compiler sees the invocation of a method from a base class reference and if the method is an overridable method (a non-static and non-final method), the compiler defers determining the exact method to be called to runtime (late binding). At runtime, based on the actual dynamic type of the object, an appropriate method is invoked. This mechanism is known as *dynamic method resolution* or *dynamic method invocation*.

An Example

Consider that you have the area() method in Shape class. Depending on the derived class—Circle or Square, for example—the area() method will be implemented differently, as shown in Listing 3-13.

Listing 3-13. TestShape.java

```
// Shape.java
class Shape {
        public double area() { return 0; } // default implementation
        // other members
}

// Circle.java
class Circle extends Shape {
        private int radius;
        public Circle(int r) { radius = r; }
        // other constructors
        public double area() { return Math.PI * radius * radius; }
        // other declarations
}

// Square.java
class Square extends Shape {
        private int side;
        public Square(int a) { side = a; }
        public double area() { return side * side; }
        // other declarations
}
```

```
// TestShape.java
class TestShape {
        public static void main(String []args) {
                Shape shape1 = new Circle(10);
                System.out.println(shape1.area());
                Shape shape2 = new Square(10);
                System.out.println(shape2.area());
        }
}
```

This program prints

```
314.1592653589793
100.0
```

This program illustrates how the area() method is called based on the dynamic type of the Shape. In this code, the statement shape1.area(); calls the Circle's area() method while the statement shape2.area(); calls Square's area() method and hence the result.

Now, let's ask a more fundamental question: Why do you need to override methods? In OOP, the fundamental idea in inheritance is to provide a default or common functionality in the base class; the derived classes are expected to provide more specific functionality. In this Shape base class and the Circle and Square derived classes, the Shape provided the default implementation of the area() method. The derived classes of Circle and Square defined their version of the area() method that overrides the base class area() method. So, depending on the type of the derived object you create, from base class reference, calls to area() method will be resolved to the correct method. Overriding (i.e., runtime polymorphism) is a simple yet powerful idea for extending functionality.

Let's look at another example of overriding the Object's toString() method in the Point class. But before doing so, let's explore what happens if you *don't* override the toString() method, as in Listing 3-14.

Listing 3-14. Point.java

```
class Point {
        private int xPos, yPos;

        public Point(int x, int y) {
                xPos = x;
                yPos = y;
        }

        public static void main(String []args) {
                // Passing a Point object to println automatically invokes the toString method
                System.out.println(new Point(10, 20));
        }
}
```

It prints

```
Point@19821f
```

The toString() method is defined in the Object class, which is inherited by all the classes in Java. Here is the overview of the toString() method as defined in the Object class:

```
public String toString()
```

The toString() method takes no arguments and returns the String representation of the object. The default implementation of this method returns ClassName@hex version of the object's hashcode. That is why you get this unreadable output. Note that this hexadecimal value will be different for each instance, so if you try this program, you'll get a different hexadecimal value as output. For example, when we ran this program again, we got this output: Point@affc70.

When you create new classes, you are expected to override this method to return the desired textual representation of your class. Listing 3-15 shows an improved version of the Point class with the overridden version of the toString() method.

Listing 3-15. Improved Point.java

```
// improved version of the Point class with overridden toString method
class Point {
        private int xPos, yPos;

        public Point(int x, int y) {
                xPos = x;
                yPos = y;
        }

        // this toString method overrides the default toString method implementation
        // provided in the Object base class
        public String toString() {
                return "x = " + xPos + ", y = " + yPos;
        }

        public static void main(String []args) {
                System.out.println(new Point(10, 20));
        }
}
```

This program now prints

```
x = 10, y = 20
```

This is much cleaner, as you would expect. To make it clear, here is a slightly different version of the main() method in this Point class implementation:

```
public static void main(String []args) {
        Object obj = new Point(10, 20);
        System.out.println(obj);
}
```

It prints

```
x = 10, y = 20
```

Here, the static type of the obj variable is Object class, and the dynamic type of the object is Point. The println statement invokes the toString() method of the obj variable. Here, the method toString() of the derived class—the Point's toString() method—is invoked due to runtime polymorphism.

Overriding Issues

While overriding, you need to be careful about the access levels, the name of the method, and its signature. Here is the toString() method in the Point class just discussed:

```java
public String toString() {
        return "x = " + xPos + ", y = " + yPos;
}
```

How about using the protected access specifier instead of public in this method definition? Will it work?

```java
protected String toString() {
        return "x = " + xPos + ", y = " + yPos;
}
```

No, it doesn't. For this change, the compiler complains

```
Point.java:8: toString() in Point cannot override toString() in java.lang.Object; attempting to
assign weaker access privileges; was public
```

While overriding, you can provide stronger access privilege, not weaker access; otherwise it will become a compiler error.

Here is another slightly modified version of toString() method. Will it work?

```java
public Object toString() {
        return "x = " + xPos + ", y = " + yPos;
}
```

You get the following compiler error:

```
Point.java:8: toString() in Point cannot override toString() in java.lang.Object; attempting to use
incompatible return type. Found: java.lang.Object. Required: java.lang.String.
```

In this case, you got a compiler error for mismatch because the return type in the overriding method should be exactly the same as the base class method.

Here is another example:

```java
public String ToString() {
        return "x = " + xPos + ", y = " + yPos;
}
```

Now the compiler doesn't complain. But this is a new method named ToString and it has nothing to do with the toString method in Object. Hence, this ToString method *does not* override the toString method in Object.

Keep the following points in mind for correct overriding. The overriding method

- Should have the *same argument list types (or compatible types)* as the base version.

- Should have *the same return type.*

  - But from Java 5 onwards, the return type can be a subclass–covariant return types (which you'll learn shortly).

- Should *not* have a more restrictive access modifier than the base version.

  - But it may have a less restrictive access modifier.

- Should *not* throw new or broader checked exceptions.

  - But it may throw fewer or narrower checked exceptions, or any unchecked exception.

- And, oh yes, the names should exactly match!

Remember that you cannot override a method if you do not inherit it. Private methods cannot be overridden because they are not inherited.

The signatures of the base method and overriding method should be compatible for overriding to take place.

Incorrect overriding is a common source of bugs in Java programs. In questions related to overriding, look for mistakes or problems in overriding when answering the questions.

COVARIANT RETURN TYPES

You know that the return types of the methods should exactly match when overriding methods. However, with the covariant return types feature introduced in Java 5, you can provide the derived class of the return type in the overriding method. Well, that's great, but why do you need this feature? Check out these overridden methods with the same return type:

```java
abstract class Shape {
    // other methods...
    public abstract Shape copy();
}

class Circle extends Shape {
    // other methods...
    public Circle(int x, int y, int radius) { /* initialize fields here */ }
    public Shape copy() { /* return a copy of this object */ }
}

class Test {
    public static void main(String []args) {
        Circle c1 = new Circle(10, 20, 30);
        Circle c2 = c1.copy();
    }
}
```

This code will give a compiler error of "Type mismatch: cannot convert from Shape to Circle". This is because of the lack of an explicit downcast from Shape to Circle in the assignment "Circle c2 = c1.copy();".

Since you know clearly that you are going to assign a Circle object returned from Circle's copy method, you can give an explicit cast to fix the compiler error:

```
Circle c2 = (Circle) c1.copy();
```

Since it is tedious to provide such downcasts (which are more or less meaningless), Java provides covariant return types where you can give the derived class of the return type in the overriding method. In other words, you can change the definition of copy method as follows:

```
public Circle copy() { /* return a copy of this object */ }
```

Now the assignment in the main method Circle c2 = c1.copy(); is valid and no explicit downcast is needed (which is good).

Overriding: Deeper Dive

It is important to understand method overriding in depth, so let's explore it in more detail. Let's use the override equals method in the Point class. Before that, here is the signature of the equals() method in the Object class:

```
public boolean equals(Object obj)
```

The equals() method in the Object class is an overridable method that takes the Object type as an argument. It checks if the contents of the current object and the passed obj argument are equal. If so, the equals() returns true; otherwise it returns false.

Now, let's see whether the Point class is overriding the equals() method correctly in Listing 3-16.

Listing 3-16. Point.java

```
public class Point {
        private int xPos, yPos;

        public Point(int x, int y) {
                xPos = x;
                yPos = y;
        }

        // override the equals method to perform
        // "deep" comparison of two Point objects
        public boolean equals(Point other){
                if(other == null)
                        return false;
                // two points are equal only if their x and y positions are equal
                if( (xPos == other.xPos) && (yPos == other.yPos) )
                        return true;
                else
                        return false;
        }
```

```
        public static void main(String []args) {
                Point p1 = new Point(10, 20);
                Point p2 = new Point(50, 100);
                Point p3 = new Point(10, 20);
                System.out.println("p1 equals p2 is " + p1.equals(p2));
                System.out.println("p1 equals p3 is " + p1.equals(p3));
        }
}
```

This prints

```
p1 equals p2 is false
p1 equals p3 is true
```

The output is as expected, so is this equals() implementation correct? No! Let's make the following slight modification in the main() method:

```
public static void main(String []args) {
        Object p1 = new Point(10, 20);
        Object p2 = new Point(50, 100);
        Object p3 = new Point(10, 20);
        System.out.println("p1 equals p2 is " + p1.equals(p2));
        System.out.println("p1 equals p3 is " + p1.equals(p3));
}
```

Now it prints

```
p1 equals p2 is false
p1 equals p3 is false
```

Why? Both main() methods are equivalent. However, this newer main() method uses the Object type for declaring p1, p2, and p3. The dynamic type of these three variables is Point, so it should call the overridden equals() method. However, the overriding is wrong, so the main() method calls the base version, which is the default implementation of Point in Object class!

 If the name or signature of the base class method and the overriding method don't match, you will cause subtle bugs. So ensure that they are exactly the same.

The equals() method should have Object as the argument instead of the Point argument! The current implementation of the equals() method in the Point class *hides* (*not* overrides) the equals() method of the Object class.

In order to overcome the subtle problems of overloading, you can use @Override annotation, which was introduced in Java 5. This annotation explicitly expresses to the Java compiler the intention of the programmer to use method overriding. In case the compiler is not satisfied with your overridden method, it will issue a complaint, which is a useful alarm for you. Also, the annotation makes the program more understandable, since the @Override annotation just before a method definition helps you understand that you are overriding a method.

Here is the code with @Override annotation for the equals method:

```java
@Override
public boolean equals(Point other) {
        if(other == null)
                        return false;
        // two points are equal only if their x and y positions are equal
        if( (xPos == other.xPos) && (yPos == other.yPos) )
                        return true;
        else
                return false;
}
```

You'll get a compiler error now for this code: "The method equals(Point) of type Point must override or implement a supertype method". How can you fix it? You need to pass the Object type to the argument of the equals method. Listing 3-17 shows the program with the fixed equals method.

Listing 3-17. Fixed Point.java

```java
public class Point {
        private int xPos, yPos;

        public Point(int x, int y) {
                xPos = x;
                yPos = y;
        }

        // override the equals method to perform "deep" comparison of two Point objects
        @Override
        public boolean equals(Object other) {
                if(other == null)
                        return false;

                // check if the dynamic type of 'other' is Point
                // if 'other' is of any other type than 'Point', the two objects cannot be
                // equal if 'other' is of type Point (or one of its derived classes), then
                // downcast the object to Point type and then compare members for equality
                if(other instanceof Point) {
                        Point anotherPoint = (Point) other;
                        // two points are equal only if their x and y positions are equal
                        if( (xPos == anotherPoint.xPos) && (yPos == anotherPoint.yPos) )
                        return true;
                }
                return false;
        }

        public static void main(String []args) {
                Object p1 = new Point(10, 20);
                Object p2 = new Point(50, 100);
                Object p3 = new Point(10, 20);
                System.out.println("p1 equals p2 is " + p1.equals(p2));
                System.out.println("p1 equals p3 is " + p1.equals(p3));
        }
}
```

Now this program prints

```
p1 equals p2 is false
p1 equals p3 is true
```

This is the expected output and with the correct implementation of the `equals` method implementation.

Invoking Superclass Methods

It is often useful to call the base class method inside the overridden method. To do that, you can use the `super` keyword. In derived class constructors, you can call the base class constructor using the `super` keyword. Such a call should be the *first statement* in a constructor if it is used. You can use the `super` keyword for referring to the base class members also. In those cases, it need not be the first statement in the method body. Let's look at an example.

You implemented a `Point` class that is a 2D-point: it had x and y positions. You can also implement a 3D-point class with x, y, and z positions. For that you do not need to start implementing it from scratch: you can extend the 2D-point and add the z position in the 3D-point class. First, you'll rename the simple implementation of `Point` class to `Point2D`. Then you'll create the `Point3D` class by extending this `Point2D` (see Listing 3-18).

Listing 3-18. Point3D.java

```java
// Point2D.java
class Point2D {
        private int xPos, yPos;
        public Point2D(int x, int y) {
                xPos = x;
                yPos = y;
        }

        public String toString() {
                return "x = " + xPos + ", y = " + yPos;
        }

        public static void main(String []args) {
                System.out.println(new Point2D(10, 20));
        }
}

//Point3D.java

// Here is how we can create Point3D class by extending Point2D class
public class Point3D extends Point2D {
        private int zPos;

        // provide a public constructors that takes three arguments (x, y, and z values)
        public Point3D(int x, int y, int z) {
                // call the  superclass constructor with two arguments
                // i.e., call Point2D(int, int) from Point2D(int, int, int) constructor)
                super(10, 20); // note that super is the first statement in the method
                zPos = z;
        }
```

```
        // override toString method as well
        public String toString() {
                return super.toString() + ", z = " + zPos;
        }

        // to test if we extended correctly, call the toString method of a Point3D object
        public static void main(String []args) {
                System.out.println(new Point3D(10, 20, 30));
        }
}
```

In the class Point2D, the class members xPos and yPos are private, so you cannot access them directly to initialize them in the Point3D constructor. However, you can call the superclass constructor using super keyword and pass the arguments. Here, super(10, 20); calls the base class constructor Point2D(int, int). This call to the superclass constructor should be the first statement; if you call it after zPos = z;, you'll get a compiler error:

```
public Point3D(int x, int y, int z) {
        zPos = z;
        super(10, 20);
}

Point3D.java:19: call to super must be first statement in constructor
                super(10, 20);
```

Similarly, you can invoke the toString() method of the base class Point2D in the toString() implementation of the derived class Point3D using the super keyword.

Type Conversions

Java is a *strongly-typed* language: it performs strict type checking to ensure that you are doing only valid conversions. If you perform some obvious invalid casts, the compiler will give a compiler error. If the compiler doesn't catch an invalid cast, it will result in a runtime problem or exception. As a result, you need to be careful when performing type conversions.

Upcasts and Downcasts

You can assign derived objects to base type references without performing any explicit casts: this is *upcasting*. Conversely, if you need to put it back to the derived ones, you will need an explicit cast: this is *downcasting*. Let's examine these two types of casts in detail using simple examples.

In Java, every class derives from the Object base class. Therefore, you can put any object into an Object reference and it will never fail.

```
String str1 = "Hello world";
Object obj = str1; // no explicit cast needed - such conversions will never fail
```

But if you convert from the Object reference to some derived type—say String—it can fail. Why? Because, in general, an Object reference can hold an object of any type and it might not be the type you are downcasting to.

```
String str2 = obj;
```

For this statement, you'll get this error:

```
compiler error - incompatible types
found   : java.lang.Object
required: java.lang.String
```

To fix this, you need to use an explicit downcast to String, like so:

```
String str2 = (String) obj;
```

When you are performing such explicit type casts (downcasts), it is your responsibility to ensure that the downcast is valid. Otherwise, you'll get a runtime exception. Consider the program in Listing 3-19. Can you tell its output?

Listing 3-19. Downcast.java

```
// Code to understand how downcast can fail
class Downcast {
        public static void main(String []args) {
                Integer i = new Integer(10);
                // upcast - its fine and will always succeed
                Object obj = i;
                // downcast - will it succeed? What will happen when it fails?
                String str = (String) obj;
        }
}
```

This program crashes with a runtime exception of

```
Exception in thread "main" java.lang.ClassCastException: java.lang.Integer cannot be cast to
java.lang.String
        at Downcast.main(Downcast.java:6)
```

In this program, you first made the Integer variable i to point to a variable obj of type Object. Such a type conversion is an upcast, so it is fine because such a conversion will always succeed. Now, when you try to convert the Object type variable to String type, it is a downcast. The compiler does not know about the dynamic type of the object pointed to by the obj variable (you know that the dynamic type of the variable pointed to by obj is of type Integer). With an explicit typecast, you force the compiler to make the conversion from Object type to String type. Because an Integer type cannot be converted to String type, the downcast fails by throwing a ClassCastException.

 Upcasts will always succeed, so you don't have to worry about them. However, downcasts may fail with runtime exception, so you need to be careful when downcasting.

Unlike downcasts, invalid casts can be detected by the compiler itself. We'll discuss this topic next.

Casting Between Inconvertible Types

Both String and StringBuffer inherit from Object class. But you cannot directly cast from String to StringBuffer and vice versa. For example, someone can write a code like the following by mistake:

```
Object obj = new StringBuffer("Hello");
String str2 = (String) obj;
```

The compilation succeeds, but this cast fails at runtime:

```
'Exception in thread "main" java.lang.ClassCastException: java.lang.StringBuffer cannot be cast to
java.lang.String'.
```

In this case, you first put a StringBuffer object into an Object type and then tried casting back to String. How about a direct conversion from StringBuffer to String? Will it lead to a compiler error/warning or a runtime exception?

```
String str = (String) new StringBuffer("Hello");
```

You get a compiler error because it is not possible to cast from StringBuffer to String:

```
Cast.java:4: inconvertible types found : java.lang.StringBuffer required: java.lang.String
```

Now how about this statement where the target type is StringBuffer but the intermediate cast is String?

```
StringBuffer str = (String) new StringBuffer("Hello");
```

You still get the same compiler error because it is not possible to cast from StringBuffer to String. This brings us to an important question. How do you know if an invalid cast results in a compiler error or a runtime exception?

If the compiler can use only the static type information of the source and target types and thus infer it as an invalid cast, it becomes a compiler error. If the success/failure of the cast depends on the dynamic type of the object, the compiler cannot predict the result of the cast. In those cases, it becomes a runtime exception.

Using "instanceof" for Safe Downcasts

If a ClassCastException is thrown while executing a program, and if there are no exception handlers for that, the program will terminate. So, how about providing an exception handler like this?

```
try {
        StringBuffer str = new StringBuffer("Hello");
        Object obj = str;
        String strBuf = (String) obj;
}
catch(ClassCastException e) {
        // ignore exception - we don't want program to crash because of this!!!
}
```

Yes, this will work and the program will not crash. But this is a *really* bad idea! There are two main problems in this code.

1. Providing exception handlers for RuntimeExceptions like this create an illusion that the program is working perfectly fine, when it is not!

2. Runtime exceptions like ClassCastException indicate programming errors and should not be caught using exception handlers.

Okay, so what do you do now? Before downcasting, check for the dynamic type of the object and then downcast.

```
StringBuffer str = new StringBuffer("Hello");
Object obj = str;
if(obj instanceof String) {
        String strBuf = (String) obj;
}
```

This is an effective and proper way to achieve downcasting. Using the instanceof operator checks the dynamic type of obj, which helps you to decide whether to downcast it to a String object.

Coming back to the example of FunPaint, you have the abstract base class Shape and many derived objects like Square, Circle, etc. You might need to perform typecasting in order to execute conversions between the base type and the derived types. Here is an example:

```
Shape shape = canvas.getHighlightedShape();
Circle circle = (Circle) shape;
circle.redraw();
```

Here, assume that there is a method called getHighlightedShape() that returns the current highlighted Shape on the canvas. In the statement Circle circle = (Circle) shape;, you are downcasting from the Shape type to the Circle type. However, this is dangerous because if Shape holds a Square object, then this downcast will fail. To avoid that, you need to use operator *instanceof* before downcasting, like so:

```
Shape shape = drawingWindow.getHighlightedShape();
if(shape instanceof Circle) {
        Circle circle = (Circle) shape;
        circle.redraw();
}
```

 It is a bad practice to handle runtime exceptions like ClassCastExceptions. Instead, it is better to introduce defensive programming checks to avoid such exceptions at runtime.

Java Packages

When the size of your application grows, you need an effective mechanism to manage all your source files. Java supports the concept of *package*, which is a scoping construct to organize your classes and to provide namespace management. All closely related classes can be put together in a single entity: a package. A package not only reduces the complexity of a big application but also provides access protection.

In essence, here are the advantages of using packages:

- Packages reduce complexity by facilitating categorization of similar classes.

- Packages provide namespace management. For example, two developers can define the same type name without ending up in a name clash by putting the name in different packages.

- Packages offer access protection (recall the discussion of the default access modifier).

The Java SDK is categorized in various packages. For example, java.lang provides basic language functionality and fundamental types, and java.io can be used to carry out file-related operations.

How can you create your own packages and use (or import) classes from them in other packages? We'll discuss that next.

Working with Packages

When you want to include a class in a package, you just need to declare it in the class using the package statement. In the FunPaint application, you have the class Circle. If you want to include this class in package graphicshape, then the following declaration would work:

```
// Circle.java
package graphicshape;

public class Circle {
        //class definition
}
```

Now, let's say that you want to use this Circle class in your Canvas class (which is in a different package); see Listing 3-20.

Listing 3-20. Canvas.java

```
// Canvas.java
package appcanvas;

public class Canvas {
        public static void main(String[] args) {
                Circle circle = new Circle();
                circle.area();
        }
}
```

This code results in the following error message from the compiler: "Circle cannot be resolved to a type". Well, you can remove this error by providing the fully qualified class name, as shown:

```
// Canvas.java
package appcanvas;

public class Canvas {
        public static void main(String[] args) {
                graphicshape.Circle circle = new graphicshape.Circle();
                circle.area();
        }
}
```

Another and more convenient way to resolve the error is to use the import statement. The import statement directs the compiler where to search for the definition of the used type. In this example, you will import from the graphicshape package:

```
// Canvas.java
package appcanvas;
import graphicshape.Circle;

public class Canvas {
        public static void main(String[] args) {
                Circle circle = new Circle();
                circle.area();
        }
}
```

You need to remember that package statement should appear first, followed by import statement(s). Obviously, you can have only one package statement in a java source file.

Let's assume that you wanted to use various shapes like Circle, Square, Triangle, etc. (belonging to graphicshape package) in the Canvas implementation. You can use one import statement for each graphicshape class (such as import graphicshape.Circle; and import graphicshape.Square;). In such cases, a more convenient way to use the import statement is to use import with a wildcard symbol "*", which means "include all classes in that package," as shown:

```
import graphicshape.*;
```

Note that physical hierarchy (the direct structure in your file system) should reflect the package hierarchy.

You do not need to import java.lang to use the basic functionality of the language. This is the only package that is implicitly imported, and the classes in this package are available for use in all programs.

Static Import

Recollect the implementation of the area() method in Listing 3-13, which is reproduced here:

```
public double area() {
        return Math.PI * radius * radius;
}
```

The implementation uses a static member PI of the Math package; that's why we used PI with package reference. Java 5 introduced a new feature—*static import*—that can be used to import the static members of the imported package or class. You can use the static members of the imported package or class as if you have defined the static member in the current class. To avail yourself of the feature, you must use "static" in the import declaration. Let's reimplement the area() method with a static import:

```
import static java.lang.Math.PI;

// class declaration and other members
public double area() {
        return PI * radius * radius;
}
```

You can also use wildcard character "*" to import all static members of a specified package of class.

Always remember that static import only imports static members of the specified package or class.

A word of caution: Although it is quite convenient to use static imports, it may introduce confusion for any developer who is reading later, especially if the current class also defines similar members. It might become difficult to distinguish between a statically imported definition and a locally specified definition.

NAMING CONVENTIONS FOR JAVA PACKAGES

Oracle recommends the following naming conventions for Java packages:

- A hierarchical structure is used normally to define packages and subpackages.

- All Java packages usually use lowercase letters.

- A product may use an organization structure to define a package hierarchy. For instance, a company (say COMP) has many products, one of which is PROD; one of the features in this product is FTUR; and one of the packages in this feature is PCKG. In this case, the package hierarchy would be comp.prod.ftur.pckg.

- A reversed internet domain name may also serve the purpose of a package hierarchy, such as com.company.feature.

- If the product name or company name has a hyphen or any other special character, employ the underscore symbol in place of the hyphen and other special character.

QUESTION TIME!

In the FunPaint application, you can color objects. You need the class Color to implement this functionality. This class should use RGB (red, green, blue) color scheme. These three color component values should be stored as int values in three fields. The class should implement a default constructor setting the color values to zero and another constructor that takes these three component values as arguments.

1. What will be the output of this program?

```java
class Color {
    int red, green, blue;

    void Color() {
        red = 10;
        green = 10;
        blue = 10;
    }
```

```
        void printColor() {
                System.out.println("red: " + red + " green: " + green + " blue: " + blue);
        }

        public static void main(String [] args) {
                Color color = new Color();
                color.printColor();
        }
}
```

A. Compiler error: no constructor provided for the class.

B. Compiles without errors, and when run, it prints the following: red: 0 green: 0 blue: 0.

C. Compiles without errors, and when run, it prints the following: red: 10 green: 10 blue: 10.

D. Compiles without errors, and when run, crashes by throwing NullPointerException.

Answer: B. Compiles without errors, and when run, it prints the following: red: 0 green: 0 blue: 0.

(Remember that a constructor does not have a return type; if a return type is provided, it is treated as a method in that class. In this case, since Color had void return type, it became a method named Color() in the Color class, with the default Color constructor provided by the compiler. By default, data values are initialized to zero, hence the output.)

2. Look at the following code and predict the output:

```
class Color {
        int red, green, blue;

        Color() {
                Color(10, 10, 10);
        }

        Color(int r, int g, int b) {
                red = r;
                green = g;
                blue = b;
        }

        void printColor() {
                System.out.println("red: " + red + " green: " + green + " blue: " +
blue);
        }

        public static void main(String [] args) {
                Color color = new Color();
                color.printColor();
        }
}
```

    A.   Compiler error: cannot find symbol.

    B.   Compiles without errors, and when run, it prints the following: red: 0 green: 0 blue: 0.

    C.   Compiles without errors, and when run, it prints the following: red: 10 green: 10 blue: 10.

    D.   Compiles without errors, and when run, crashes by throwing `NullPointerException`.

Answer: A. Compiler error: cannot find symbol.

(The compiler looks for the method `Color()` when it reaches this statement: `Color(10, 10, 10);`. The right way to call another constructor is to use the `this` keyword as follows: `this(10, 10, 10);`).

3.   In the FunPaint application, you need to code classes to draw rectangles. A rectangle can have plain or rounded edges. You also need to color a (plain or rounded) rectangle. How will you define classes for creating these plain, colored, and rounded rectangles? You can use is-a relationships as needed.

Look at the following option to implement the required functionality:

```
class Rectangle { /* */ }
class ColoredRectangle extends Rectangle { /* */ }
class RoundedRectangle extends Rectangle { /* */ }
class ColoredRoundedRectangle extends ColoredRectangle, RoundedRectangle { /* */ }
```

Choose an appropriate option:

    A.   Compiler error: '{' expected cannot extend two classes.

    B.   Compiles without errors, and when run, crashes with the exception `MultipleClassInheritanceException`.

    C.   Compiles without errors, and when run, crashes with the exception `NullPointerException`.

    D.   Compiles without errors, and when run, crashes with the exception `MultipleInheritanceError`.

Answer: A. Compiler error: '{' expected – cannot extend two classes.

(This program will result in a compilation error since Java does not support multiple inheritance.)

4.   In the FunPaint application, you can fill colors to various shape objects. To implement it, you need to implement a `Color` class. The `Color` class has three members, `m_red`, `m_green`, and `m_blue`. Focus on the `toString()` method and check if it works fine.

Choose the best option based on the following program:

```
class Color {
        int red, green, blue;

        Color() {
                this(10, 10, 10);
        }
```

```java
        Color(int r, int g, int b) {
                red = r;
                green = g;
                blue = b;
        }
        public String toString() {
            return "The color is: " + red + green + blue;
        }

        public static void main(String [] args) {
                // implicitly invoke toString method
                System.out.println(new Color());
        }
    }
```

A. Compiler error: incompatible types.

B. Compiles without errors, and when run, it prints the following: The color is: 30.

C. Compiles without errors, and when run, it prints the following: The color is: 101010.

D. Compiles without errors, and when run, it prints the following: The color is: red green blue.

Answer: C. Compiles without errors, and when run, it prints the following: The color is: 101010.

(The toString() implementation has the expression "The color is: " + red + blue + green. Since the first entry is String, the + operation becomes the string concatenation operator with resulting string "The color is: 10". Following that, again there is a concatenation operator + and so on until finally it prints "The color is: 101010").

5. Choose the best option based on the following program:

```java
    class Color {
        int red, green, blue;

        Color() {
                this(10, 10, 10);
        }

        Color(int r, int g, int b) {
                red = r;
                green = g;
                blue = b;
        }

        String toString() {
                return "The color is: " + " red = " + red + " green = " + green +
    " blue = " + blue;
        }

        public static void main(String [] args) {
                // implicitly invoke toString method
                System.out.println(new Color());
        }
    }
```

A.   Compiler error: attempting to assign weaker access privileges; `toString` was public in `Object`.

B.   Compiles without errors, and when run, it prints the following: The color is: red = 10 green = 10 blue = 10.

C.   Compiles without errors, and when run, it prints the following: The color is: red = 0 green = 0 blue = 0.

D.   Compiles without errors, and when run, it throws `ClassCastException`.

Answer: A. Compiler error: attempting to assign weaker access privileges; `toString` was public in `Object`. (No access modifier is specified for the `toString()` method. `Object`'s `toString()` method has a public access modifier; you cannot reduce the visibility of the method. Hence, it will result in a compiler error).

Summary

Foundations of OOP

- *Encapsulation*: Combining data and the functions operating on it as a single unit.

- *Abstraction*: Hiding lower-level details and exposing only the essential and relevant details to the users.

- *Inheritance*: Creating hierarchical relationships between related classes.

- *Polymorphism*: Interpreting the same message (i.e., method call) with different meanings depending on the context.

Class Foundations

- A *"class"* is a template (or blueprint) and an *"object"* is an instance of a class.

- A *constructor* does not have a return type.

- You cannot access the *private* methods of the base class in the derived class.

- You can access the *protected* method either from a class in the same package (just like package private or default) as well as from a derived class.

- You can also access a method with a *default access modifier* if it is in the same package.

- You can access *public* methods of a class from any other class.

Overloading

- *Method overloading*: Creating methods with same name but different types and/or numbers of parameters.

- You can have *overloaded constructors*. You can call a constructor of the same class in another constructor using the `this` keyword.

- *Overload resolution* is the process by which the compiler looks to resolve a call when overloaded definitions of a method are available.

Inheritance

- *Inheritance* is also called an *"is-a" relationship.*

- Resolving a method call based on the dynamic type of the object is referred to as *runtime polymorphism.*

- In *overriding*, the name of the method, number of arguments, types of arguments, and return type should match exactly.

- In *covariant return types*, you can provide the derived class of the return type in the overriding method.

- You use the super keyword to call base class methods.

- Overloading is an example of *static polymorphism* (*early binding*) while overriding is an example of *dynamic polymorphism* (*late binding*).

- You don't need to do an explicit cast for doing an *upcast*. An upcast will always succeed.

- You need to do an explicit cast for doing a *downcast*. A downcast may fail. So you can use the instanceof operator to see if a downcast is valid.

Java Packages

- A *package* is a scoping construct to categorize your classes and to provide namespace management.

CHAPTER 4

Advanced Class Design

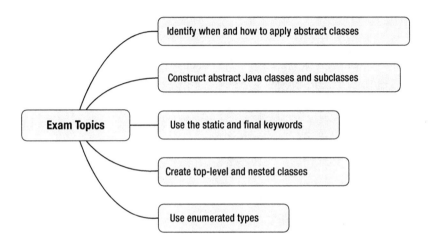

Identify when and how to apply abstract classes

Construct abstract Java classes and subclasses

Exam Topics — Use the static and final keywords

Create top-level and nested classes

Use enumerated types

You learned the basic concepts of OOP and used them to build Java programs in the preceding chapter. In this chapter, you will learn advanced concepts in OOP, support from the Java language, and the nitty-gritty of these concepts.

In the opening section, you will learn about abstract classes and their uses in practical situations. The second and third sections cover two useful and frequently used keywords, `final` and `static`. The fourth section explores the variant flavors of nested classes: static nested classes, inner classes, local inner classes, and anonymous inner classes. The final section discusses enum data types, which were introduced in Java 5.

Some of the concepts in this chapter, especially nested classes and their variants, are not easy to understand on first reading. Although we endeavor to present the more difficult concepts such as anonymous classes and nested interfaces in an easy-to-understand manner, the best way for you to get the hang of them is to write programs using them.

For the OCPJP 7 exam, you need to know all these concepts inside out. This chapter serves to deepen your knowledge of the Java language and directly prepare you for the OCPJP 7 exam.

Abstract Classes

In many programming situations, you want to specify an abstraction without specifying implementation-level details. In such cases, you can use either *abstract classes* or *interfaces* supported by the Java platform. Abstract classes are used in cases when you want to define an abstraction with some common functionality. We will discuss interfaces in detail in the next chapter and will focus only on abstract classes in this section.

You cannot create instances of an abstract class. Then, you may ask, why should I use an abstract class? Abstract classes are quite useful in OOP and are recommended strongly for the following reasons:

- Abstract classes define an abstraction and leave concrete implementation details to subclasses. An abstract type may have various flavors and hence different implementations; abstract classes provide the right platform for subclasses to achieve it. If an abstract type and its subclasses (concrete implementations) are well defined, then the users of such classes can employ runtime polymorphism. Runtime polymorphism is desirable since it introduces loose coupling among objects.

- Another reason to favor abstract classes is their ability to offer default implementation. Subclasses of the abstract class may specialize the default implementation if required.

- Abstract classes are the perfect placeholder for common functionality required in almost all of the subclasses of the abstract class.

Recall the FunPaint application you developed in the last chapter. The Shape class provides an abstraction of the different shapes you can draw in the FunPaint application. You can create objects of Shapes such as Square and Circle, but does it make sense to create an object of Shape class itself directly? No, there is no real-world object named Shape. In fact, Shape is a general-purpose abstraction that can be replaced by any proper shape like Circle.

The Shape class can be rewritten as an abstract class:

```
abstract class Shape {
        public double area() { return 0; } // default implementation
        // other members
}
```

You prefix the abstract keyword before the class definition to declare the class as an abstract class. Let's try creating an object of Shape:

```
Shape shape = new Shape();
```

For this statement, the compiler gives an error of "Shape is abstract; cannot be instantiated". In the Shape class definition, there is a method called area() that returns the area of a particular shape. This method is applicable for all shapes, and that's why it's in this base class Shape. However, what should the implementation of the area() method in the Shape class be? You cannot provide a default implementation; implementing this method as return 0; is a bad solution, although the compiler would happily accept it. A better solution is to declare it as an abstract method, like so:

```
public abstract double area(); // note: no implementation (i.e., no method body definition)
```

Similarly to declaring a class abstract, you declare the method area() as abstract by prefixing the method with the abstract keyword. The main difference between a normal method and an abstract method is that you don't provide a body for an abstract method. If you provide a body, it will become an error, like so:

```
public abstract double area() { return 0; } // compiler error!
```

You get a compiler error for this definition: "abstract methods cannot have a body". Okay, fine! You cannot provide a body of the abstract method, but then what is the significance of an abstract method? An abstract class promises certain functionality through abstract methods to all its clients (users of this abstraction). An abstract method declaration forces all the subclasses to provide an implementation of that abstract method. If a derived class does not implement all the abstract methods defined in the base class, then that derived class should be declared as an abstract class, as in the following example:

```
abstract class Shape {
        public abstract double area(); // no implementation
        // other members
}

class Rectangle extends Shape { }
```

This snippet results in a compiler error of "Rectangle is not abstract and does not override abstract method area() in Shape". To fix this, you need to declare the derived class abstract or provide a definition of the area() method in the derived class. It does not make sense to declare Rectangle as abstract; so you can define the area() method like so:

```
class Rectangle extends Shape {
        private int length, height;
        public double area() { return length * height; }
        // other members ...
}
```

Now let's discuss another scenario where a common functionality needs to be supported by all the shape objects. For instance, each object could be drawn inside another shape object, which means each shape object has a parent (i.e., containing) object. As pointed out earlier, abstract classes are the best place to put a common functionality.

```
public abstract class Shape {
        abstract double area();
        private Shape parentShape;
        public void setParentShape(Shape shape){
                parentShape = shape;
        }
        public Shape getParentShape(){
                return parentShape;
        }
}
```

This abstract class defines an attribute and two methods that will be available for all its subclasses. Useful, isn't it?

Points to Remember

Master the following points about abstract classes and abstract methods, as they might well come up in the OCPJP 7 exam:

- The abstract keyword can be applied to a class or a method but not to a field.

- An abstract class cannot be instantiated. You can, however, create reference variables of an abstract class type. In fact, you can create objects of the classes derived from an abstract class and make the abstract class references refer to the created derived class objects.

- An abstract class can extend another abstract class or can implement an interface.

- An abstract class can be derived from a concrete class! Although the language allows it, it is not a good idea to do so.

- An abstract class need not declare an abstract method, which means it is not necessary for an abstract class to have methods declared as abstract. However, if a class has an abstract method, it should be declared as an abstract class.

- A subclass of an abstract class needs to provide implementation of all the abstract methods; otherwise you need to declare that subclass as an abstract class.

- An abstract class may have methods or fields declared static.

Using the "final" Keyword

For the OCPJP 7 exam, you need to know the uses of the final keyword. In this section, you'll learn how to use the final keyword with classes, methods, and variables.

Final Classes

A final class is a *non-inheritable class*—that is to say, if you declare a class as final, you cannot subclass it. In general, OOP suggests that a class should be open for extension but closed for modification (Open/Closed Principle). However, in some cases you don't want to allow a class to be subclassed. Two important reasons are

1. *To prevent a behavior change by subclassing.* In some cases, you may think that the implementation of the class is complete and should not change. If overriding is allowed, then the behavior of methods might be changed. You know that a derived object can be used where a base class object is required, and you may not prefer it in some cases. By making a class final, the users of the class are assured the unchanged behavior.

2. *Improved performance.* All method calls of a final class can be resolved at compile time itself. As there is no possibility of overriding the methods, it is not necessary to resolve the actual call at runtime for final classes, which translates to improved performance. For the same reason, final classes encourage the inlining of methods. If the calls are to be resolved at runtime, they cannot be inlined.

In the Java library, many classes are declared as final; for example, the String (java.lang.String) and System (java.lang.System) classes. These classes are used extensively in almost all Java programs. For example, if you use a System.out.println() statement, you are using both the System class (in which the output stream and println methods are present) as well as the String class since println takes String as an argument. If these two classes are not declared final, it is possible for someone to change the behavior of these classes by subclassing and then the whole program can start behaving differently. To avoid such a problem, widely used classes like these and wrapper classes such as Integer are made final in the Java library.

 The performance gain from making a class final is modest; the focus should be on using final where it is appropriate. The OCPJP 7 exam will mainly check whether you know the correct uses of the final keyword.

In the FunPaint example, you have a canvas for dragging and dropping shapes to create pictures. Assume that you have a Canvas class for implementing that functionality. Further, you want to ensure that the behavior does not change by inheriting from Canvas. In other words, you want to make Canvas a final class.

```
final class Canvas { /* members */ }

class ExtendedCanvas extends Canvas { /* members */ }
```

If you try to extend a final class, as you just tried to do, you'll get the compiler error "cannot inherit from final Canvas".

Final Methods and Variables

In a class, you may declare a method final. The final method cannot be overridden. Therefore, if you have declared a method as final in a non-final class, then you can extend the class but you cannot override the final method. However, other non-final methods in the base class can be overridden in the derived class implementation.

In the FunPaint application, for instance, one method is final (setParentShape()) and another method is non-final (getParentShape()), as shown in Listing 4-1.

Listing 4-1. Shape.java

```
public abstract class Shape {
        //class members...
        final public void setParentShape(Shape shape){
                //method body
        }
        public Shape getParentShape(){
                //method body
        }
}
```

In this case, the Circle class (subclass of Shape) can override only getParentShape(); if you try to override the final method, you will get following error: "Cannot override the final method from Shape".

Finally, we mention *final variables*. Final variables are like CD-ROMs: once you write something on them, you cannot write again. In programming, universal constants such as PI can be declared as final since you don't want anyone to modify the value of such constants. Final variables can be assigned only once. If you try to change a final variable after initialization, you will get a complaint from your Java compiler.

Points to Remember

Master the following points, as they might well come up in the OCPJP 7 exam:

- The final modifier can be applied to a class, method, or variable. All methods of a final class are implicitly final (hence non-overridable).

- A final variable can be assigned only once. If a variable declaration defines a variable as final but did not initialize it, then it is referred to as *blank final*. You need to initialize a blank final all the constructors you have defined in the class; otherwise the compiler will complain.

- The keyword final can even be applied to parameters. The value of a final parameter cannot be changed once assigned. Here, it is important to note that the "value" is implicitly understood for primitive types. However, the "value" for an object refers to the object reference, not its state. Therefore, you can change the internal state of the passed final object, but you cannot change the reference itself.

Using the "static" Keyword

Suppose that you wanted a write a simple class that counts the number of objects of its class type created so far. Will the program in Listing 4-2 work?

Listing 4-2. Counter.java

```
// Counter class should count the number of instances created from that class
public class Counter {
        private int count; // variable to store the number of objects created
        // for every Counter object created, the default constructor will be called;
        // so, update the counter value inside the default constructor
        public Counter() {
                count++;
        }
        public void printCount() { // method to print the counter value so far
                System.out.println("Number of instances created so far is: " + count);
        }
        public static void main(String []args) {
                Counter anInstance = new Counter();
                anInstance.printCount();
                Counter anotherInstance = new Counter();
                anotherInstance.printCount();
        }
}
```

The output of the program is

```
Number of instances created so far is: 1
Number of instances created so far is: 1
```

Oops! From the output, it is clear that the class does not keep track of the number of objects created. What happened?

You've used an *instance variable* count to keep track of the number of objects created from that class. Since every instance of the class has the value count, it always prints 1! What you need is a variable that can be shared across all its instances. This can be achieved by declaring a variable static. A static variable is associated with its class rather than its object; hence they are known as *class variables*. A static variable is initialized only once when execution of the program starts. A static variable shares its state with all instances of the class. You access a static variable using its class name (instead of an instance). Listing 4-3 shows the correct implementation of the Counter class with both the count variable and the printCount method declared static.

Listing 4-3. Counter.java

```
// Counter class should count the number of instances created from that class
public class Counter {
        private static int count; // variable to store the number of objects created
        // for every Counter object created, the default constructor will be called;
        // so, update the counter value inside the default constructor
        public Counter() {
                count++;
        }
```

```java
        public static void printCount() { // method to print the counter value so far
                System.out.println("Number of instances created so far is: " + count);
        }
        public static void main(String []args) {
                Counter anInstance = new Counter();
                // note how we call printCount using the class name instead of instance variable name
                Counter.printCount();
                Counter anotherInstance = new Counter();
                Counter.printCount();
        }
}
```

This program prints

```
Number of instances created so far is: 1
Number of instances created so far is: 2
```

Here, the static variable count is initialized when the execution started. At the time of first object creation, the count is incremented to one. Similarly, when second object got created, the value of the count became 2. As the output of the program shows, both objects updated the same copy of the count variable.

Note how we changed the call to printCount() to use class name Counter, as in Counter.printCount(). The compiler will accept the previous two calls of anInstance.printCount() and anotherInstance.printCount() as there is no semantic difference between calling a static method using a class name or instance variable name. However, to use instance variables to call static methods is not recommended. It is conventional practice to call instance methods using instance variables and to call static methods using class names.

A static method can only access static variables and can call only static methods. In contrast, an instance method (non-static) may call a static method or access a static variable.

Static Block

Apart from static variables and methods, you can also define a *static block* in your class definition. This static block will be executed by JVM when it loads the class into memory. For instance, in the previous example, you can define a static block to initialize the count variable to default 1 instead of the default value 0, as shown in Listing 4-4.

Listing 4-4. Counter.java

```java
public class Counter {
        private static int count;
        static {
                // code in this static block will be executed when JVM loads the class into memory
                count = 1;
        }
        public Counter() {
                count++;
        }
        public static void printCount() {
                System.out.println("Number of instances created so far is: " + count);
        }
        public static void main(String []args) {
                Counter anInstance = new Counter();
                Counter.printCount();
```

```
                    Counter anotherInstance = new Counter();
                    Counter.printCount();
        }
}
```

This program prints

```
Number of instances created so far is: 2
Number of instances created so far is: 3
```

Do not confuse a static block with a constructor. A constructor will be invoked when an instance of the class is created, while the static block will be invoked when the program initializes.

Points to Remember

- The main() method, where the main execution of the program starts, is always declared static. Why? If it were an instance method, it would be impossible to invoke it. You'd have to start the program to be able to create an instance and then call the method, right?

- You cannot override a static method provided in a base class. Why? Based on the instance type, the method call is resolved with runtime polymorphism. Since static methods are associated with a class (and not with an instance), you cannot override static methods, and runtime polymorphism is not possible with static methods.

- A static method cannot use the this keyword in its body. Why? Remember that static methods are associated with a class and not an instance. Only instance methods have an implicit reference associated with them; hence class methods do not have a this reference associated with them.

- A static method cannot use the super keyword in its body. Why? You use the super keyword for invoking the base class method from the overriding method in the derived class. Since you cannot override static methods, you cannot use the super keyword in its body.

- Since static methods cannot access instance variables (non-static variables), they are most suited for utility functions. For example, all methods in the java.util.math library are static.

- Calling a static method is considered to be slightly more efficient compared to calling an instance method. This is because the complier need not pass the implicit this object reference while calling a static method, unlike an instance method.

Flavors of Nested Classes

Classes defined within the body of another class (or interface) are known as *nested classes*. Normally you define a class, which is a top-level class directly belonging to a package. In contrast, nested classes are classes contained within another class or interface.

What is the benefit of creating classes inside another class or interface? There are several benefits. First, you can put related classes together as a single logical group. Second, nested classes can access all class members of the enclosing class, which might be useful in certain cases. Third, nested classes are sometimes useful for specific purposes. For example, anonymous inner classes are useful for writing simpler event-handling code with AWT/Swing (which is not relevant to the OCPJP 7 exam, and hence not covered in this book). For now, you can take our word for it that nested classes are useful in some situations, so it is worth learning about them.

There are four types or *flavors* of nested classes in Java:

- Static nested class

- Inner class

- Local inner class

- Anonymous inner class

The distinctions among these four flavors are not evident at first sight, and it doesn't help matters that alternative terms are often substituted for them. To help clarify the confusion, we represent the four flavors of nested classes schematically in Figure 4-1.

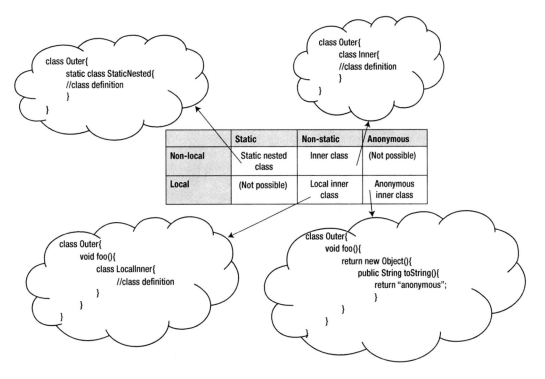

Figure 4-1. *Types of nested classes with examples*

Study this figure. A *local class* is defined within a code block (whether a method, constructor, or initialization block), whereas a *non-local class* is defined inside a class. A *static class* is qualified using the static keyword, whereas a *non-static class* does not use this static keyword with the class definition. In an *anonymous class*, you don't provide the name of the class; you just define its body!

As you can see in Figure 4-1, *static nested classes* are static and non-local, whereas *inner classes* are non-static and non-local. A non-static and local nested class is a *local inner class*, and a local and anonymous nested class is an *anonymous inner class*. A glance back at this figure will serve to refresh your memory of the essential distinctions among the four flavors of nested classes.

Now, let's discuss each of these four flavors in more detail.

Static Nested Classes (or Interfaces)

You can define a class (or interface) as a static member inside another class (or interface). Since the outer type can be a class or an interface and the inner ones can also be a class or interface, there are four combinations. The following are examples of these four types so that you can see their syntax:

```
class Outer {          // an outer class has a static nested class
    static class Inner {}
}

interface Outer {      // an outer interface has a static nested class
    static class Inner {}
}

class Outer {          // an outer class has a static nested interface
    static interface Inner {}
}

interface Outer {      // an outer interface has a static nested interface
    static interface Inner {}
}
```

You don't have to explicitly use the static keyword with a nested interface, since it is implicitly static. Now, let's look at an example that creates as well as uses static nested classes.

Recall the FunPaint example in Chapter 3 that implements a Color class with fields of m_red, m_green, and m_blue. Since all shapes can be colored, you can define the Color class within the Shape class, as shown in Listing 4-5.

Listing 4-5. TestColor.java

```
abstract class Shape {
    public static class Color {
        int m_red, m_green, m_blue;
        public Color() {
            // call the other overloaded Color constructor by passing default values
            this(0, 0, 0);
        }
        public Color(int red, int green, int blue) {
            m_red = red; m_green = green; m_blue = blue;
        }
        public String toString() {
            return " red = " + m_red + " green = " + m_green + " blue = " + m_blue;
        }
        // other color members elided
    }
    // other Shape members elided
}

public class TestColor {
    public static void main(String []args) {
        // since Color is a static nested class,
        // we access it using the name of the outer class, as in Shape.Color
        // note that we do not (and cannot) instantiate Shape class for using Color class
```

```
                    Shape.Color white = new Shape.Color(255, 255, 255);
                    System.out.println("White color has values:" + white);
            }
}
```

It prints

```
White color has:  red = 255 green = 255 blue = 255
```

What do you observe in this code? The Shape class is declared abstract. You can see the Color class defined as a public static class defined within the Shape class. The TestColor class uses the syntax Shape.Color to refer to this class. Other than this minor difference, the Color class looks no different from defining the Color class outside the Shape class. Yes, that is a good observation. So, let's repeat it to make it clear: a static nested class is as good as a class defined as an outer class with one difference—it is physically defined inside another class!

Points to Remember

Here are some notable aspects of static nested classes (and interfaces) that will help you on the OCPJP 7 exam:

- The accessibility (public, protected, etc.) of the static nested class is defined by the outer class.

- The name of the static nested class is expressed with OuterClassName.NestedClassName syntax.

- When you define an inner nested class (or interface) inside an interface, the nested class is declared implicitly public and static. This point is easy to remember: any field in an interface is implicitly declared public and static, and static nested classes have this same behavior.

- Static nested classes can be declared abstract or final.

- Static nested classes can extend another class or it can be used as a base class.

- Static nested classes can have static members. (As you'll see shortly, this statement does not apply to other kinds of nested classes.)

- Static nested classes can access the members of the outer class (only static members, obviously).

- The outer class can also access the members (even private members) of the nested class through an object of nested class. If you don't declare an instance of the nested class, the outer class cannot access nested class elements directly.

Inner Classes

You can define a class (or an interface) as a non-static member inside another class. How about declaring a class or an interface inside an interface? As you just saw in the third bullet above about static inner classes, when you define a class or an interface inside an interface, it is implicitly static. So, it is not possible to declare a non-static inner interface! That leaves two possibilities:

```
class Outer {          // an outer class has an inner class
        class Inner {}
}
```

```
class Outer {              // an outer class has an inner interface
        interface Inner {}
}
```

Let's create a Point class to implement the center of a Circle. Since you want to associate each Circle with a center Point, it is a good idea to make Point an inner class of Circle, as shown in Listing 4-6.

Listing 4-6. Circle.java

```
public class Circle {
        // define Point as an inner class within Circle class
        class Point {
                private int xPos;
                private int yPos;
                // you can provide constructor for an inner class like this
                public Point(int x, int y) {
                        xPos = x;
                        yPos = y;
                }
                // the inner class is like any other class - you can override methods here
                public String toString() {
                        return "(" + xPos + "," + yPos + ")";
                }
        }

        // make use of the inner class for declaring a field
        private Point center;
        private int radius;
        public Circle(int x, int y, int r) {
                // note how to make use of the inner class to instantiate it
                center = this.new Point(x, y);
                radius = r;
        }

        public String toString() {
                return "mid point = " + center + " and radius = " + radius;
        }

        public static void main(String []s) {
                System.out.println(new Circle(10, 10, 20));
        }
        // other methods such as area are elided
}
```

This implementation of Circle and Point is very similar to what you saw earlier, with the only major difference being that you have defined Point as a private member of Circle here. You are instantiating the inner class like so:

```
center = this.new Point(x, y);
```

You might be wondering why you cannot use the usual new statement:

```
center = new Point(x, y);
```

You need to prefix the object reference of the outer class to create an instance of the inner class. In this case, it is a this reference, so you are prefixing it with this before the new operator.

 Every inner class is associated with an instance of the outer class. In other words, an inner class is always associated with an enclosing object.

The outer and inner classes share a special relationship, like friends or members of same family. Member accesses are valid irrespective of the access specifiers such as private. However, there is subtle difference. You can access members of an outer class within an inner class without creating an instance; but this is not the case with an outer class. You need to create an instance of inner class in order to access the members (*any* members, including private members) of the inner class.

One limitation of inner classes is that you cannot **declare** static members in an inner class, like this:

```
class Outer {
        class Inner {
                static int i = 10;
        }
}
```

If you try to do so, you'll get the following compiler error:

```
Outer.java:3: inner classes cannot have static declarations
                static int i = 10;
```

Points to Remember

Here are some important rules about inner classes and interfaces that might prove useful in the OCPJP 7 exam:

- The accessibility (public, protected, etc.) of the inner class is defined by the outer class.

- Just like top-level classes, an inner class can extend a class or can implement interfaces. Similarly, an inner class can be extended by other classes, and an inner interface can be implemented or extended by other classes or interfaces.

- An inner class can be declared final or abstract.

- Inner classes can have inner classes, but you'll have a hard time reading or understanding such complex nesting of classes. (Meaning: Avoid them!)

Local Inner Classes

A *local inner class* is defined in a code block (say, in a method, constructor, or initialization block). Unlike static nested classes and inner classes, local inner classes are not members of an outer class; they are just local to the method or code in which they are defined.

Here is an example of the general syntax of a local class:

```
class SomeClass {
      void someFunction() {
              class Local { }
      }
}
```

As you can see in this code, Local is a class defined within someFunction. It is not available outside of someFunction, not even to the members of the SomeClass. Since you cannot declare a local variable static, you also cannot declare a local class static.

Since you cannot define methods in interfaces, you cannot have local classes or interfaces inside an interface. Nor can you create local interfaces. In other words, you cannot define interfaces inside methods, constructors, and initialization blocks.

Now that you understand the syntax, let's jump into a practical example. In the FunPaint application, you implemented the Color class as a static nested class. Here is the code you saw in that discussion:

```
abstract class Shape {
      public static class Color {
              int m_red, m_green, m_blue;
              public Color() {
                      this(0, 0, 0);
              }
              public Color(int red, int green, int blue) {
                      m_red = red; m_green = green; m_blue = blue;
              }
              public String toString() {
                      return " red = " + m_red + " green = " + m_green + " blue = " + m_blue;
              }
              // other color members elided
      }
      // other Shape members elided
}
```

Now, this toString() method displays a string representation of Color. Assume that you need to display help messages at the bottom of the screen in the FunPaint application. For that you need descriptive messages. Displaying messages in this cryptic format is not very helpful to the reader. So, you want to display the Color string in the following format: "You selected a color with RGB values red = 0 green = 0 blue = 0". For that, you must define a method named getDescriptiveColor() in the class StatusReporter. In getDescriptiveColor(), you must create a derived class of Shape.Color in which the toString method returns this descriptive message. Listing 4-7 is an implementation using local classes.

Listing 4-7. StatusReporter.java

```
class StatusReporter {
        // important to note that the argument "color" is declared final
        // otherwise, the local inner class DescriptiveColor will not be able to use it!!
        static Shape.Color getDesciptiveColor(final Shape.Color color) {
                // local class DescriptiveColor that extends Shape.Color class
                class DescriptiveColor extends Shape.Color {
```

```
                    public String toString() {
                            return "You selected a color with RGB values " + color;
                    }
            }
            return new DescriptiveColor();
    }

    public static void main(String []args) {
            Shape.Color descriptiveColor =
                    StatusReporter.getDesciptiveColor(new Shape.Color(0, 0, 0));
            System.out.println(descriptiveColor);
    }
}
```

The main method checks if the StatusReporter works fine. This program prints

```
You selected a color with RGB values  red = 0 green = 0 blue = 0
```

Let's see how the local class was defined. The getDescriptiveColor() method takes the plain Shape.Color class object and returns a Shape.Color object. Inside the getDescriptiveColor() method, you have defined the class DescriptiveColor, which is local to this method. This DescriptiveColor is a derived class of Shape.Color. Inside the DescriptiveColor class, the only method defined is the toString() method, which overrides the base class Shape.Color toString() method. After the definition of the DescriptiveColor class, the getDescriptiveColor class creates an object of the DescriptiveColor class and returns it.

In the Test class, you can see a main() method that just calls the StatusReporter.getDescriptiveColor() method and stores the result in a Shape.Color reference. You will notice that the getDescritiveColor() method returns a DescriptiveColor object, which derives from Shape.Color, so the descriptiveColor variable initialization works fine. In the println, the dynamic type of descriptiveColor is a DescriptiveColor object, and hence the detailed description of the color object is printed.

Did you notice another feature in the getDescriptiveColor() method? Its argument is declared final. What if you remove the final qualifier, as in the following code?

```
static Shape.Color getDesciptiveColor(Shape.Color color)
```

Well, you'll get the following compiler error:

```
StatusReporter.java:24: local variable color is accessed from within inner class; needs to be
declared final
        return "You selected a color with RGB values " + color;
                                                          ^
```

```
1 error
```

Why? One thing you need to remember about local classes is that you can pass only final variables to a local class.

You can pass only **final** variables to a local inner class.

Points to Remember

The following points about local classes are apt to come up in the OCPJP 7 exam:

- You can create a non-static local class inside a body of code. Interfaces cannot have local classes, and you cannot create local interfaces.

- Local classes are accessible only from the body of the code in which the class is defined. The local classes are completely inaccessible outside the body of the code in which the class is defined.

- You can extend a class or implement interfaces while defining a local class.

- A local class can access all the variables available in the body of the code in which it is defined. You can pass only final variables to a local inner class.

Anonymous Inner Classes

As the name implies, an *anonymous inner class* does not have a name. The declaration of the class automatically derives from the instance-creation expression. They are also referred to simply as *anonymous classes*.

An anonymous class is useful in almost all situations where you can use local inner classes. A local inner class has a name, whereas an anonymous inner class does not—and that's the main difference! An additional difference is that an anonymous inner class cannot have any explicit constructors. A constructor is named after the name of the class, and since an anonymous class has no name, it follows that you cannot define a constructor!

(Before we proceed, just a note: there are no such things as "anonymous interfaces.")

Here is an example just to address the syntax of a local class:

```
class SomeClass {
        void someFunction() {
                new Object() { };
        }
}
```

This code looks cryptic, doesn't it? What is going on here? In the statement new Object() { };, you are declaring a derived class of Object directly using the new keyword. It doesn't define any code and returns an instance of that derived object. The created object is not used anywhere, so it is ignored. The new expression invokes the default constructor here; you could choose to invoke a multiple argument constructor of the base class by passing arguments in the new expression. When defining an anonymous class, it implicitly extends the base class (which is Object base class here).

Don't worry if you didn't understand this example. You'll look now at a more practical example, and the usage of anonymous classes will become clearer.

Previously you saw the DescriptiveColor class (Listing 4-7) inside the getDescriptiveColor method in the StatusReporter class. You can simplify the code by converting the local class into an anonymous class, as shown in Listing 4-8.

Listing 4-8. StatusReporter.java

```
class StatusReporter {
        static Shape.Color getDesciptiveColor(final Shape.Color color) {
                // note the use of anonymous inner classes here -- specifically, there is no name
                // for the class and we construct and use the class "on the fly" in the return
                // statement!
                return new Shape.Color() {
```

```
                        public String toString() {
                                return "You selected a color with RGB values " + color;
                        }
                };
        }
        public static void main(String []args) {
                Shape.Color descriptiveColor =
                        StatusReporter.getDesciptiveColor(new Shape.Color(0, 0, 0));
                System.out.println(descriptiveColor);
        }
}
```

It prints

```
You selected a color with RGB values  red = 0 green = 0 blue = 0
```

That's nice. The rest of the program, including the main() method, remains the same and the getDescriptiveColor() method became simpler! You did not explicitly create a class with a name (which was DescriptiveColor); instead you just created a derived class of Shape.Color "on the fly" in the return statement. Note that the keyword class is also not needed.

Points to Remember

These points about anonymous classes concern questions that might be asked on the OPCJP 7 exam:

- Anonymous classes are defined in the new expression itself, so you cannot create multiple objects of an anonymous class.

- You cannot explicitly extend a class or explicitly implement interfaces when defining an anonymous class.

Enum Data Types

There are many situations where you want to restrict the user to providing input from a predefined list. For instance, you might want the user to choose from a set of constants defining several printer types:

```
public static final int DOTMATRIX = 1;
public static final int INKJET = 2;
public static final int LASER = 3;
```

The solution works. In this case, however, you could pass any other integer (say 10), and compiler would happily take it. Therefore, this solution is not a *typesafe solution*.

To avoid this condition, you may define you own class (say PrinterType) and allow only legitimate values. However, you need to define the class and its attributes manually. That's where formerly you could have employed Joshua Bloch's *typesafe enumeration patterns*. But don't worry—you don't need to learn those patterns anymore. Java 5 introduced the data type *enum* to help you in such situations.

Listing 4-9 defines an enum class (yes, enums are special classes) for the above example.

Listing 4-9. EnumTest.java

```java
// define an enum for classifying printer types
enum PrinterType {
        DOTMATRIX, INKJET, LASER
}

// test the enum now
public class EnumTest {
        PrinterType printerType;

        public EnumTest(PrinterType pType) {
                printerType = pType;
        }

        public void feature() {
                // switch based on the printer type passed in the constructor
                switch(printerType){
                case DOTMATRIX:
                        System.out.println("Dot-matrix printers are economical and almost obsolete");
                        break;
                case INKJET:
                        System.out.println("Inkjet printers provide decent quality prints");
                        break;
                case LASER:
                        System.out.println("Laser printers provide best quality prints");
                        break;
                }
        }

        public static void main(String[] args) {
                EnumTest enumTest = new EnumTest(PrinterType.LASER);
                enumTest.feature();
        }
}
```

It prints

```
Laser printers provide best quality prints
```

Let's probe the Listing 4-9 example in more detail.

- In a switch-case statement, you do not need to provide the fully qualified name for enum elements. This is because switch takes an instance of the enum type, and hence switch-case understands the context (type) in which you are specifying enum elements.

- You cannot provide any input while creating an instance of enumTest other than that specified in the enum definition. That makes enum typesafe.

Note that you can declare an enum (PrinterType in this case) in a separate file, just like you can declare any other normal Java class.

Now that you understand the basic concept of enum data type, let's look at a more detailed example in which you define member attributes and methods in an enum data type. Yes, you can define methods or fields in an enum definition, as shown in Listing 4-10.

Listing 4-10. PrinterType.java

```java
public enum PrinterType {
        DOTMATRIX(5), INKJET(10), LASER(50);

        private int pagePrintCapacity;

        private PrinterType(int pagePrintCapacity) {
                this.pagePrintCapacity = pagePrintCapacity;
        }

        public int getPrintPageCapacity() {
                return pagePrintCapacity;
        }
}
// EnumTest.java
public class EnumTest {
        PrinterType printerType;

        public EnumTest(PrinterType pType) {
                printerType = pType;
        }

        public void feature() {
                switch (printerType) {
                case DOTMATRIX:
                        System.out.println("Dot-matrix printers are economical");
                        break;
                case INKJET:
                        System.out.println("Inkjet printers provide decent quality prints");
                        break;
                case LASER:
                        System.out.println("Laser printers provide the best quality prints");
                        break;
                }
                System.out.println("Print page capacity per minute: " +
                        printerType.getPrintPageCapacity());
        }

        public static void main(String[] args) {
                EnumTest enumTest1 = new EnumTest(PrinterType.LASER);
                enumTest1.feature();
                EnumTest enumTest2 = new EnumTest(PrinterType.INKJET);
                enumTest2.feature();
        }
}
```

The output of the above program is given below:

```
Laser printers provide the best quality prints
Print page capacity per minute: 50
Inkjet printers provide decent quality prints
Print page capacity per minute: 10
```

Well, what do you observe in this new version of enum example program? You defined a new attribute, a new constructor, and a new method for the enum class. The attribute pagePrintCapacity is set by the initial values specified with enum elements (such as LASER(50)), which calls the constructor of the enum class. However, the enum class cannot have a public constructor, or the compiler will complain with following message: "Illegal modifier for the enum constructor; only private is permitted."

A constructor in an enum class can only be specified as private.

Points to Remember

- Enums are implicitly declared public, static, and final, which means you cannot extend them.

- When you define an enumeration, it implicitly inherits from java.lang.Enum. Internally, enumerations are converted to classes. Further, enumeration constants are instances of the enumeration class for which the constant is declared as a member.

- You can apply the valueOf() and name() methods to the enum element to return the name of the enum element.

- If you declare an enum within a class, then it is by default static.

- You cannot use the new operator on enum data types, even inside the enum class.

- You can compare two enumerations for equality using == operator.

- When an enumeration constant's toString() method is invoked, it prints the name of the enumeration constant.

- The static values() method in the Enum class returns an array of the enumeration constants when called on an enumeration type.

- Enumeration constants cannot be cloned. An attempt to do so will result in a CloneNotSupportedException.

- If enumeration constants are from two different enumerations, the equals() method does not return true.

Enum avoids magic numbers, which improves readability and understandability of the source code. Also, enums are typesafe constructs. Therefore, you should use enums wherever applicable.

QUESTION TIME!

1.   Which of the following statements is true?

   A.   You cannot extend a concrete class and declare that derived class abstract.

   B.   You cannot extend an abstract class from another abstract class.

   C.   An abstract class must declare at least one abstract method in it.

   D.   You can create instantiate of a concrete subclass of an abstract class but cannot create instance of an abstract class itself.

   Answer: D. You can create instantiate of a concrete subclass of an abstract class but cannot create instance of an abstract class itself.

2.   Choose the best answer based on the following class definition:

```
public  abstract final class Shape { }
```

   A.   Compiler error: a class must not be empty.

   B.   Compiler error: illegal combination of modifiers abstract and final.

   C.   Compiler error: an abstract class must declare at least one abstract method.

   D.   No compiler error: this class definition is fine and will compile successfully.

   Answer: B. Compiler error: illegal combination of modifiers abstract and final.

   (You cannot declare an abstract class final since an abstract class must to be extended. Class can be empty in Java, including abstract classes. An abstract class can declare zero or more abstract methods.)

3.   Look at the following code and choose the right option for the word <access-modifier>:

```
// Shape.java
public class Shape {
    protected void display() {
            System.out.println("Display-base");
    }
}

// Circle.java
public class Circle extends Shape {
    <access-modifier> void display(){
            System.out.println("Display-derived");
    }
}
```

A. Only protected can be used.

B. Public and protected both can be used.

C. Public, protected, and private can be used.

D. Only public can be used.

Answer: B. Public and protected both can be used.

(You can provide only a less restrictive or same-access modifier when overriding a method.)

4. Consider this program to answer the following question:

```
class Shape {
    public Shape() {
            System.out.println("Shape constructor");
    }
    public class Color {
            public Color() {
                    System.out.println("Color constructor");
            }
    }
}

class TestColor {
    public static void main(String []args) {
            Shape.Color black = new Shape().Color(); // #1
    }
}
```

What will be the output of the program?

A. Compile error: the method Color() is undefined for the type Shape.

B. Compile error: invalid inner class.

C. Works fine: Shape constructor, Color constructor.

D. Works fine: Color constructor, Shape constructor.

Answer: A. Compile error: The method Color() is undefined for the type Shape.

(You need to create an instance of outer class Shape in order to create an inner class instance).

5. If you replace the Color class instantiation statement (tagged as #1 inside a comment in the program given in the previous questions) with the following statement, what would be the output of the program?

```
Shape.Color black = new Shape().new Color();
```

A. Works fine and will print this output:

Shape constructor
Color constructor

B. Works fine and will print this output:

Color constructor
Shape constructor

C. Compiler error: The method Color() is undefined for the type Shape.

D. Compile without error but results in a runtime exception.

Answer: A. Works fine and will print this output:

Shape constructor
Color constructor

6. What will be the output of the given program?

```java
class Shape {
    private boolean isDisplayed;
    protected int canvasID;
    public Shape() {
            isDisplayed = false;
            canvasID = 0;
    }
    public class Color {
            public void display() {
                    System.out.println("isDisplayed: "+isDisplayed);
                    System.out.println("canvasID: "+canvasID);
            }
    }
}

class TestColor {
    public static void main(String []args) {
            Shape.Color black = new Shape().new Color();
            black.display();
    }
}
```

A. Compiler error: an inner class can only access public members of the outer class.

B. Compiler error: an inner class cannot access private members of the outer class.

C. Runs and prints this output:

isDisplayed: false
canvasID: 0

D. Compiles fine but crashes with a runtime exception.

Answer: C. Runs and prints this output:

isDisplayed: false
canvasID: 0

(An inner class can access all members of an outer class, including the private members of the outer class).

7. Look at this program and predict the output:

```java
public class EnumTest {
    PrinterType printerType;

    enum PrinterType {INKJET, DOTMATRIX, LASER};
    public EnumTest(PrinterType pType) {
        printerType = pType;
    }

    public static void main(String[] args) {
        PrinterType pType = new PrinterType();
        EnumTest enumTest = new EnumTest(PrinterType.LASER);
    }
}
```

A. Prints the output printerType:LASER.

B. Compiler Error: enums must be declared static.

C. Compiler Error: cannot instantiate the type EnumTest.PrinterType.

D. This program will compile fine, and when run, will crash and throw a runtime exception.

Answer: C. Compiler Error: cannot instantiate the type EnumTest.PrinterType.

(You cannot instantiate an enum type using new.)

8. Is the enum definition given below correct?

```java
public enum PrinterType {
    private int pagePrintCapacity;        // #1
    DOTMATRIX(5), INKJET(10), LASER(50);  // #2

    private PrinterType(int pagePrintCapacity) {
        this.pagePrintCapacity = pagePrintCapacity;
    }

    public int getPrintPageCapacity() {
        return pagePrintCapacity;
    }
}
```

A. Yes, this enum definition is correct and will compile cleanly without any warnings or errors.

B. No, this enum definition is incorrect and will result in compile error(s).

C. No, this enum definition will result in runtime exception(s).

D. Yes, this enum definition is correct but will compile with warnings.

Answer: B. No, this enum definition is incorrect and will result in compile error(s).

(You need to define enum elements first before any other attribute in an enum class. In other words, this enum definition will compile cleanly if you interchange the statements marked with "#1" and "#2" within comments in this code.)

9. Consider the following code snippet:

```
public class EnumTest {
    public EnumTest() {
            System.out.println("In EnumTest constructor ");
    }
    public void printType() {
            enum PrinterType { DOTMATRIX, INKJET, LASER }
    }
}
```

A. This code will compile cleanly without any compiler warnings or errors, and when used, will run without any problems.

B. This code will compile cleanly without any compiler warnings or errors, and when used, will generate a runtime exception.

C. It will produce a compiler error: enum types must not be local.

D. It will give compile-time warnings but not any compiler errors.

Answer: C. It will produce a compiler error: enum types must not be local.

(An enum can only be defined inside of a top-level class or interface and not within a method).

Summary

Abstract Classes

- An abstraction specifying functionality supported without disclosing finer level details.

- You cannot create instances of an abstract class.

- Abstract classes enable runtime polymorphism, and runtime polymorphism in turn enables loose coupling.

Using the "final" Keyword

- A final class is a non-inheritable class (i.e., you cannot inherit from a final class).

- A final method is a non-overridable method (i.e., subclasses cannot override a final method).

- All methods of a final class are implicitly final (i.e., non-overridable).

- A final variable can be assigned only once.

Using the "static" Keyword

- There are two types of member variables: class variables and instance variables. All variables that require an instance (object) of the class to access them are known as *instance variables*. All variables that are shared among all instances and are associated with a class rather than an object are referred to as *class variables* (declared using the static keyword).

- All static members do not require an instance to call/access them. You can directly call/access them using the class name.

- A static member can call/access only a static member.

Flavors of Nested Classes

- Java supports four types of nested classes: static nested classes, inner classes, local inner classes, and anonymous inner classes.

- Static nested classes may have static members, whereas the other flavors of nested classes can't.

- Static nested classes and inner classes can access members of an outer class (even private members). However, static nested classes can access only static members of outer class.

- Local classes (both local inner classes and anonymous inner classes) can access all variables declared in the outer scope (whether a method, constructor, or a statement block).

Enums

- Enums are a typesafe way to achieve restricted input from users.

- You cannot use new with enums, even inside the enum definition.

- Enum classes are by default final classes.

- All enum classes are implicitly derived from java.lang.Enum.

CHAPTER 5

■ ■ ■

Object-Oriented Design Principles

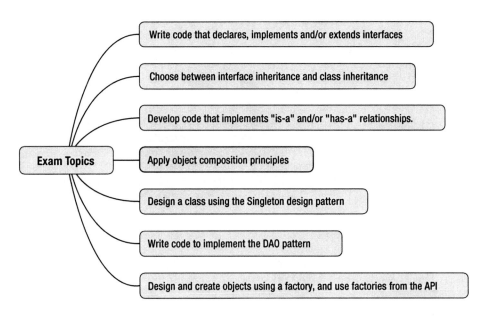

We covered object-oriented programming basics in Chapter 3 and more advanced OOP topics in Chapter 4. In this chapter, we delve still more deeply into OOP concepts.

The chapter begins with an in-depth investigation of *interfaces*. We will discuss how interfaces are different from abstract classes and which construct to use in a given situation. In the second section, we introduce you to the *object composition* principle that says "favor composition over inheritance." The third and fourth sections cover one of most popular topics in OOP: *design patterns*. You will learn the basic concepts behind design patterns and how they relate to OOP. We'll focus on the *singleton, factory, abstract factory*, and *data access object* (DAO) design patterns.

Interfaces

In general, an *interface* refers to a common boundary or interconnection between two entities (which could be human beings, systems, concepts, machines, etc.). For instance, a keyboard in a computer system provides an interface between a human being and the computer. A natural language such as English is an interface between two humans that allows them to exchange their views.

In Java, an interface is a set of abstract methods that defines a protocol (i.e., a contract for conduct). Classes that implement an interface must implement the methods specified in the interface. An interface defines a protocol, and a class implementing the interface honors the protocol. In other words, an interface promises a certain functionality to its clients by defining an abstraction. All the classes implementing the interface provide their own implementations for the promised functionality.

Let's elucidate Java interfaces with an example. Consider the `java.lang.Comparable` interface that specifies the following protocol:

```
public interface Comparable{
        public int compareTo(Object o);
        // Intent is to compare this object with the specified object
        // The return type is integer. Returns negative,
        // zero or a positive value when this object is less than,
        // equal to, or greater than the specified object
}
```

Unrelated classes can provide their own implementations when they implement `Comparable`. These unrelated classes have one aspect in common: they all follow the specification given by `Comparable`, and it is left to the implementation of these individual classes to implement `compareTo()` accordingly. Data structures supported in the `java.util` package implement this interface. If you want to use the general algorithms provided in the library, you have to implement this interface. For example, consider the sample implementation of `max()` method in `java.util.Collections`. It is meant for finding the maximum element in a collection. It uses the `Comparable` interface, and the elements in the collection must provide the implementation for the `compareTo()` method.

The algorithms (i.e., clients of the interface) are completely ignorant about how the `compareTo()` method is implemented. But the clients know the contract that insures the availability of the `compareTo()` method, hence clients can use it. This confers a very important advantage: when a method takes an interface as an argument, you can pass any object that implements that interface (due to runtime polymorphism).

Conceptually, a class and an interface are two different constructs used for two different purposes. A class combines the state and the behavior of a real object, whereas an interface specifies the behavior of an abstract entity.

Declaring and Using Interfaces

Now it's time to implement your own interface for shape objects. Some circular shaped objects (such as `Circle` and `Ellipse`) can be *rolled* to a given degree. You can create a `Rollable` interface and declare a method named `roll()` where

```
interface Rollable {
        void roll(float degree);
}
```

As you can see, you define an interface using the `interface` keyword. You can declare methods in that interface; here it is the `roll()` method. The method takes one argument: the degree for rolling. Now let's implement the interface for `Circle`, which is `Rollable`.

```
class Circle implements Rollable {
        public void roll(float degree) {
        /* implement rolling functionality here */
        }
}
```

You use the `implements` keyword for implementing an interface. Note that the method name, its argument, and the return type in the class definition should exactly match the one given in the interface; if they don't match, the class is not considered to implement that interface.

If you are implementing an interface in an abstract class, the abstract class does not need to define the method.

```
interface Rollable {
        void roll(float degree);
}

abstract class CircularShape implements Rollable extends Shape { }
```

In this case, `CircularShape` implements a `Rollable` interface and extends the `Shape` abstract class (as you saw in Chapters 3 and 4). Now the concrete classes like `Circle` and `Ellipse` can extend this abstract class and define the `roll()` method.

The `Rollable` example you saw has only one method—`roll()`. However, it is common for interfaces to have multiple methods. For example, `java.util` defines the `Iterable` interface as follows:

```
public interface Iterator<E> {
        boolean hasNext();
        E next();
        void remove();
}
```

This interface is meant for traversing a collection. (Don't worry about the "`<E>`" in `Iterator<E>`. It refers to the element type and falls under *generics*, which we cover in detail in the next chapter). It declares three methods: `hasNext()`, `next()`, and `remove()`.

In fact, a class can implement multiple interfaces at the same time—both directly and indirectly through its base classes. For example, the `Circle` class can also implement the standard `Cloneable` interface (for creating copies of the `Circle` object) and the `Serializable` interface (for storing the object in files to recreate the object later, etc.), like so:

```
class Circle extends CircularShape implements Cloneable, Serializable {
        /* definition of methods such as clone here */
}
```

Points to Remember

Here are some key rules about interfaces that will help you in the OCPJP 7 exam:

- An interface cannot be instantiated.

- An interface can extend another interface. Use the `extends` (and *not* the `implements`) keyword for this.

- Interfaces cannot contain instance variables. If you declare a data member in an interface, it should be initialized, and all such data members are implicitly treated as "`public static final`" members.

- An interface cannot declare static methods. It can only declare instance methods.

- You cannot declare members as `protected` *or* `private`. Only `public` access is allowed for members of an interface.

- All methods declared in an interface are implicitly considered to be abstract. If you want, you can explicitly use the `abstract` qualifier for the method.

- You can only declare (and not define) methods in an interface.

- An interface can be declared with empty body (i.e., an interface without any members. Such interfaces are known as *tagging interfaces* (or *marker interfaces*). Such interfaces are useful for defining a common parent, so that runtime polymorphism can be used. For example, `java.util` defines the interface `EventListner` without a body.

- An interface can be declared within another interface or class; such interfaces are known as *nested interfaces*.

- Unlike top-level interfaces that can have only public or default access, a nested interface can be declared as public, protected, or private.

Abstract Classes vs. Interfaces

Abstract classes and interfaces have a lot in common. For example, both can declare methods that all the deriving classes should define. They are also similar in the respect that you can create instances neither of an abstract class nor of an interface.

So, what are the differences between abstract classes and interfaces? Table 5-1 lists some syntactical differences, and Table 5-2 lists some semantic and usage differences.

Table 5-1. *Abstract Classes and Interfaces: Syntactical Differences*

	Abstract Classes	Interfaces
Keyword(s) used	Use the `abstract` and `class` keywords to define a class.	Use the `interface` keyword to define an interface.
Keyword used by the implementing class	Use the `extends` keyword to inherit from an abstract class.	Use the `implements` keyword to implement an interface.
Default implementation	An abstract class can provide default implementation of methods.	You cannot define methods in an interface; you can only declare them.
Fields	An abstract class can have static and non-static fields.	You cannot have any fields (instance variables) in an interface.
Constants	An abstract class can have both static and non-static constants.	Interfaces can have only static constants. If you declare a field, it must be initialized. All fields are implicitly considered to be declared as `public static` and `final`.
Constructors	You can define a constructor in an abstract class (which is useful for initializing fields, for example).	You cannot declare/define a constructor in an interface.
Access specifiers	You can have private and protected members in an abstract class.	You cannot have any private or protected members in an interface; all members are public by default.
Single vs. multiple inheritance	A class can inherit only one class (which can be either an abstract or a concrete class).	A class can implement any number of interfaces.

Table 5-2. *Abstract Classes and Interfaces: Semantic and Usage Differences*

	Abstract Classes	Interfaces
is-a relationship vs. following a protocol	An abstract base class provides a protocol; in addition, it serves as a base class in an is-a relationship.	An interface provides only a protocol. It specifies functionality that must be implemented by the classes implementing it.
Default implementation of a method	An abstract class can provide a default implementation of a method. So, derived class(es) can just use that definition and need not define that method.	An interface can only declare a method. All classes implementing the interface must define that method.
Difficulty in making changes	It is possible to make changes to the implementation of an abstract class. For example, you can add a method with default implementation and the existing derived classes will not break.	If there are already many classes implementing an interface, you cannot easily change that interface. For example, if you declare a new method, all the classes implementing that interface will stop compiling since they do not define that method.

Choosing Between an Abstract Class and an Interface

Now let's compare abstract classes and interfaces. Hmm, interesting...they look quite similar, don't they? How do you choose between them? When should you choose abstract classes, and when should you choose interfaces?

- If you are identifying a base class that abstracts common functionality from a set of related classes, you should use an abstract class. If you are providing common method(s) or protocol(s) that can be implemented even by unrelated classes, this is best done with an interface.

- If you want to capture the similarities among the classes (even unrelated) without forcing a class relationship, you should use interfaces. On the other hand, if there exists an is-a relationship between the classes and the new entity, you should declare the new entity as an abstract class.

Let's look at an example of choosing between abstract classes and interfaces in the FunPaint application. You can have Shape as an abstract base class for all shapes (like Circle, Square, etc.); this is an example of an is-a relationship. Also, common implementations, such as parent shape (as discussed in Chapter 4), can be placed in Shape. Hence, Shape as an abstract class is the best choice in this case.

In FunPaint, the user can perform various actions on shape objects. For example, a few shapes can be rotated, and a few can be rolled. A shape like Square can be rotated and a shape like Circle can be rolled. So, it does not make sense to have rotate() or roll() in the Shape abstract class. The implementation of rotate() or roll() differs with the specific shape, so default implementation could not be provided. In this case, it is best to use interfaces rather than an abstract class. You can create Rotatable and Rollable interfaces that specify the protocol for rotate() and roll() individually, as shown in Listing 5-1.

Listing 5-1. Shape.java

```
// Shape.java
// Shape is the base class for all shape objects; shape objects that are associated with
// a parent shape object is remembered in the parentShape field
public abstract class Shape {
        abstract double area();
        private Shape parentShape;
        public void setParentShape(Shape shape) {
                parentShape = shape;
        }
```

```java
        public Shape getParentShape() {
                return parentShape;
        }
}


// Rollable.java
// Rollable interface can be implemented by circular shapes such as Circle and Ellipse
public interface Rollable {
        void roll(float degree);
}


// Rotatable.java
// Rotable interface can be implemented by shapes such as Square, Rectangle, and Rhombus
public interface Rotatable {
        void rotate(float degree);
}


// Circle.java
// Circle is a concrete class that is-a subtype of Shape; you can roll it and hence implements
Rollable
public class Circle extends Shape implements Rollable {
        private int xPos, yPos, radius;
        public Circle(int x, int y, int r) {
                xPos = x;
                yPos = y;
                radius = r;
        }
        public double area() { return Math.PI * radius * radius; }
        @Override
        public void roll(float degree) {
                // implement rolling functionality here
        }
        public static void main(String[] s) {
                Circle circle = new Circle(10,10,20);
                circle.roll(45);
        }
}


// Rectangle.java
// Rectangle is a concrete class and is-a Shape; it can be rotated and hence implements Rotatable
public class Rectangle extends Shape implements Rotatable {
        private int length, height;
        public Rectangle(int l, int h) {
                length = l;
                height = h;
        }
        public double area() { return length * height; }
        @Override
        public void rotate(float degree) {
                // implement rotating functionality here
        }
}
```

Object Composition

You have learned how to define abstractions in the form of concrete classes, abstract classes, and interfaces. Individual abstractions offer certain functionalities that need to be combined with other objects to represent a bigger abstraction: a composite object that is made up of other smaller objects. You need to make such composite objects to solve real-life programming problems. In such cases, the composite object shares has-a relationships with the containing objects, and the underlying concept is referred to as *object composition.*

By way of analogy, a computer is a composite object containing other objects such as CPU, memory, and a hard disk. In other words, the computer object shares a has-a relationship with other objects.

Let's recollect the FunPaint application in which you defined the Circle class. The class definition is given as follows:

```java
public class Circle {
        private int xPos;
                private int yPos;
                private int radius;

                public Circle(int x, int y, int r) {
                xPos = x;
                        yPos = y;
                        radius = r;
                }
                // other constructors elided ...

        public String toString() {
                return "mid point = (" + xPos + "," + yPos + ") and radius = " + radius;
        }
        // other members (suchas area method) are elided
}
```

In this simple implementation, you use xPos and yPos to define the center of a Circle. Instead of defining these variables as members of class Circle, let's define a class Point, which can be used to define Circle's center. Check the definition of Point class in Listing 5-2.

Listing 5-2. Circle.java

```java
// Point is an independent class and here we are using it with Circle class
class Point {
        private int xPos;
        private int yPos;
        public Point(int x, int y) {
                xPos = x;
                yPos = y;
        }
        public String toString() {
                return "(" + xPos + "," + yPos + ")";
        }
}
```

```java
// Circle.java
public class Circle {
        private Point center;    // Circle "contains" a Point object
        private int radius;
        public Circle(int x, int y, int r) {
                center = new Point(x, y);
                radius = r;
                }
        public String toString() {
                return "center = " + center + " and radius = " + radius;
        }

        public static void main(String []s) {
                System.out.println(new Circle(10, 10, 20));
        }
        // other members (constructors, area method, etc) are elided ...
}
```

This is a better solution than having independent integer members xPos and yPos. Why? You can reuse the functionality provided by the Point class. Note the rewriting of the toString() method in the Circle class by simplifying it:

```java
public String toString() {
        return "center = " + center + " and radius = " + radius;
}
```

Here, the use of the variable center expands to center.toString(). In this example, Circle has a Point object. In other words, Circle and Point share a has-a relationship; in other words, Circle is a composite object containing a Point object.

Composition vs. Inheritance

You are now equipped with a knowledge of composition as well as inheritance (which we covered in detail in Chapter 4). In some situations, it's difficult to choose between the two. It's important to remember that nothing is a silver bullet—you cannot solve all problems with one construct. You need to analyze each situation carefully and decide which construct is best suited for it.

A rule of thumb is to use has-a and is-a phrases for composition and inheritance, respectively. For instance,

- A computer has-a CPU.

- A circle is-a shape.

- A circle has-a point.

- A laptop is-a computer.

- A vector is-a list.

This rule can be useful for identifying wrong relationships. For instance, the relationship of car is-a tire is completely wrong, which means you cannot have an inheritance relationship between the classes Car and Tire. However, the car has-a tire (meaning car has one or more tires) relationship is correct—you can compose a Car object containing Tire objects.

Class inheritance implies an is-a relationship, interface inheritance implies an is-like-a relationship, and composition implies a has-a relationship.

In real scenarios, the relationship distinctions can be non-trivial. You learned that you can make a base class and put the common functionality of many classes in it. However, many people ignore a big caution sign suspended over this practice—always check whether the is-a relationship exists between the derived classes and the base class. If the is-a relationship does not hold, it's better to use composition instead of inheritance.

For example, take a set of classes—say, DynamicDataSet and SnapShotDataSet—which require a common functionality—say, sorting. Now, one could derive these data set classes from a sorting implementation, as given in Listing 5-3.

Listing 5-3. Sorting.java

```java
import java.awt.List;

public class Sorting {
        public List sort(List list) {
                // sort implementation
                return list;
        }
}

class DynamicDataSet extends Sorting {
        // DynamicDataSet implementation
}

class SnapshotDataSet extends Sorting {
        // SnapshotDataSet implementation
}
```

Do you think this is a good solution? No, it's not a good solution for the following reasons:

- The rule of thumb does not hold here. DynamicDataSet is not a Sorting type. If you make such mistakes in class design, it can be very costly—and you might not be able to fix them later if a lot of code has accumulated that makes the wrong use of inheritance relationships. For example, Stack extends Vector in the Java library. Yet a stack clearly is not a vector, so it could not only create comprehension problems but also lead to bugs. When you create an object of Stack class provided by the Java library, you can add or delete items from anywhere in the container because the base class is Vector, which allows you to delete from anywhere in the vector.

- What if these two types of data set classes have a genuine base class, DataSet? In that case, either Sorting will be the base class of DataSet or one could put the class Sorting in between DataSet and two types of data sets. Both solutions would be wrong.

- • There is another challenging issue: what if one DataSet class wants to use one sorting algorithm (say, MergeSort) and another data set class wants to use a different sorting algorithm (say, QuickSort)? Will you inherit from two classes implementing two different sorting algorithms? First, you cannot directly inherit from multiple classes, since Java does not support multiple class inheritance. Second, even if you were able to somehow inherit from two different sorting classes (MergeSort extends QuickSort, QuickSort extends DataSet), that would be an even worse design.

In this case it is best to use composition—in other words, use a has-a relationship instead of an is-a relationship. The resultant code is given in Listing 5-4.

Listing 5-4. Sorting.java

```java
import java.awt.List;

interface Sorting {
        List sort(List list);
}

class MergeSort implements Sorting {
        public List sort(List list) {
                // sort implementation
                return list;
        }
}

class QuickSort implements Sorting {
        public List sort(List list) {
                // sort implementation
                return list;
        }
}

class DynamicDataSet {
        Sorting sorting;
        public DynamicDataSet() {
                sorting = new MergeSort();
        }
        // DynamicDataSet implementation
}

class SnapshotDataSet {
        Sorting sorting;
        public SnapshotDataSet() {
                sorting = new QuickSort();
        }
        // SnapshotDataSet implementation
}
```

Use inheritance when a subclass specifies a base class, so that you can exploit dynamic polymorphism. In other cases, use composition to get code that is easy to change and loosely coupled. In summary, **favor composition over inheritance**.

Points to Remember

Here are some design principles and terminological nuances you should have under your belt when you take the OCPJP 7 exam:

- Adhere to the OO design principle of "favor composition over inheritance." Composition encourages you to follow another useful OO design principle: "program to an interface, not to an implementation." This second injunction means that the functionality of a class should depend only on the interface of another abstraction and not on the specific implementation details of that abstraction. In other words, implementation of a class should not depend on the internal implementation aspects of the other class. Wherever suitable, composition is the technique of choice.

- In OOP, there are many terms related to composition, such as association and aggregation. *Association* is the most general form of a relationship between two objects, whereas *composition* and *aggregation* are special forms of association. In general, the terms *aggregation* and *composition* are used interchangeably. Although these two terms are very similar, they do have a subtle difference. In composition, the lifetime of the contained object and the container object is the same, whereas that is not the case with aggregation. For example, a computer object and a CPU object share a composition relationship, while a library object and a book object share an aggregation relationship.

Design Patterns

In the object-oriented world, the concepts behind design patterns are well established. As an object-oriented programming language developer and as a candidate for OCPJP 7 exam certification, you must know about design patterns and related concepts.

The literal meaning of *design pattern* in programming is a repeatable solution applicable to solve a generic design problem. Experienced programmers and designers learn from their experience and formulate solutions to frequently recurring design problems. Design patterns capture and replicate the experience of experienced software designers.

"Design patterns are descriptions of communicating objects and classes that are customized to solve a general design problem in a particular context." —*Design Patterns: Elements of Reusable Object-Oriented Software* [Aside: This classic 1994 book popularized design patterns. Four authors (Erich Gamma, Richard Helm, Ralph Johnson, and John Vlissides) wrote this book and for this reason it became known as the "Gang of Four" (GoF) book. The patterns covered in this chapter are mostly GoF patterns.]

A clarification before we delve into various design patterns: design patterns are *design solutions*. They are not ready-made solutions like code in a library, which you can take off the shelf and use as needed when you program. Design patterns instead provide template solutions that need to be fine-tuned based on the given context.

Let's consider an example of a design pattern to get an initial sense of the importance and usability of design patterns. In the FunPaint application, let's assume that a class (say ShapeArchiver) is responsible for archiving information about all the drawn shapes. Similarly, another class (say Canvas) is responsible for displaying all drawn shapes. Whenever any change in shapes takes place, you need to inform these two classes as to the changed information. So, how you would like to implement this notification? Listing 5-5 shows a possible implementation.

Listing 5-5. Test.java

```java
// Circle.java
// Circle class "informs" (i.e., "notifies") Canvas and ShapeArchiver whenever it gets "changed"
// by calling the update method of these two classes
public class Circle {
        private Point center;
        public void setCenter(Point center) {
                this.center = center;
                canvas.update(this);
                shapeArchiver.update(this);
        }
        public void setRadius(int radius) {
                this.radius = radius;
                canvas.update(this);
                shapeArchiver.update(this);
        }
        private ShapeArchiver shapeArchiver;
        public void setShapeArchiver(ShapeArchiver shapeArchiver) {
                this.ShapeArchiver = shapeArchiver;
        }
        protected Canvas canvas;
        public void setCanvas(Canvas canvas) {
                this.canvas = canvas;
        }
        private int radius;
        public Circle(int x, int y, int r) {
                center = new Point(x, y);
                radius = r;
        }
        public String toString() {
                return "center = " + center + " and radius = " + radius;
        }
}

// Point.java
class Point {
        private int xPos;
        private int yPos;
        public Point(int x, int y) {
                xPos = x;
                yPos = y;
        }
        public String toString() {
                return "(" + xPos + "," + yPos + ")";
        }
}
```

```java
// ShapeArchiver.java
public class ShapeArchiver {
        public void update(Circle circle) {
                System.out.println("ShapeArchiver::update");
                // update implementation
        }
}

// Canvas.java
public class Canvas {
        public void update(Circle circle) {
                System.out.println("Canvas::update");
                //update implementation
        }
}

// Test.java
public class Test {
        public static void main(String []s) {
                Circle circle = new Circle(10, 10, 20);
                System.out.println(circle);
                circle.setCanvas(new Canvas());
                circle.setShapeArchiver(new ShapeArchiver());
                circle.setRadius(50);
                System.out.println(circle);
        }
}
```

This program prints the following:

```
center = (10,10) and radius = 20
Canvas::update
ShapeArchiver::update
center = (10,10) and radius = 50
```

Well, this implementation works as intended—but there is a problem. There is a tight coupling between the subject (Circle class) and both of the observers (ShapeArchiver and Canvas). Here are the consequences of a tightly coupled design:

- The subject class (Circle) knows about the specific observer classes. As a result, if you change observer classes, you need to change subject class, too. (Hmm, not so good.)

- If you want to add or remove an observer, you cannot do it without changing the subject.

- You cannot reuse either the subject or the observer classes independently.

Okay, there are some problems in the previous implementation. Is there a way to eliminate these problems? Check out the new implementation in Listing 5-6.

Listing 5-6. Test.java

```java
// Circle.java
import java.util.Observable;

public class Circle extends Observable {
        private Point center;
        public void setCenter(Point center) {
                this.center = center;
                setChanged();
                notifyObservers();
        }
        public void setRadius(int radius) {
                this.radius = radius;
                setChanged();
                notifyObservers();
        }
        private int radius;
        public Circle(int x, int y, int r) {
                center = new Point(x, y);
                radius = r;
        }
        public String toString() {
                return "center = " + center + " and radius = " + radius;
        }
}

// Point.java
class Point {
        private int xPos;
        private int yPos;
        public Point(int x, int y) {
                xPos = x;
                yPos = y;
        }
        public String toString() {
                return "(" + xPos + "," + yPos + ")";
        }
}

// Canvas.java
import java.util.Observable;
import java.util.Observer;

public class Canvas implements Observer {
        @Override
        public void update(Observable arg0, Object arg1) {
                System.out.println("Canvas::update");
                // actual update code elided ...
        }
}
```

```
// ShapeArchiver.java
import java.util.Observable;
import java.util.Observer;

public class ShapeArchiver implements Observer{
        @Override
        public void update(Observable arg0, Object arg1) {
                System.out.println("ShapeArchiver::update");
                // actual update code elided ...
        }
}

// Test.java
public class Test {
        public static void main(String []s) {
                Circle circle = new Circle(10, 10, 20);
                System.out.println(circle);
                circle.addObserver(new Canvas());
                circle.addObserver(new ShapeArchiver());
                circle.setRadius(50);
                System.out.println(circle);
        }
}
```

This program prints the following:

```
center = (10,10) and radius = 20
ShapeArchiver::update
Canvas::update
center = (10,10) and radius = 50
```

Well, the output is the same as for the previous version. Did you achieve anything better? Yes, you did. This new implementation is a *loosely coupled* implementation. The subject—Circle class—does not know about the concrete observer classes, and the observers do not know about the concrete subject. Consequently, both the subject and observers can now be used independently and changed independently. Furthermore, you can add and remove observers from the subject without changing the subject class.

This example is an implementation of the Observer design pattern. This design pattern is useful in cases in which you have a subject to be monitored by a couple of observers. These observers need to be informed whenever the subject gets changed. The Observer design pattern creates loose coupling between the subject and the observers.

Java supports an abstract class with the name Observable and an interface named Observer (both provided in the java.util package) to implement the Observer design pattern. The Circle class is extended from Observable, which tags the Circle class as a subject. The Canvas and ShapeArchiver classes implement the Observer interface, and hence implement the update() method. Whenever the state of subject is changed, you call the setChanged() method followed by notifyObservers(), which is implemented in the Observable class. The notifyObservers() method calls all observers registered earlier for that subject.

We hope that this example gives you a good handle on design patterns. In the rest of this chapter, we will explore in detail several more important design patterns.

TYPES OF DESIGN PATTERNS

Broadly, GoF design patterns can be classified into the following three categories:

- **Creational patterns** offer the flexibility to decide who is responsible for object creation, how the object will be created, which object will be created, and when the creation will take place. In essence, creational patterns provide an abstraction for object instantiation.

  Examples: Singleton, Factory, Abstract Factory, and Prototype.

- **Structural patterns** are focused on how related classes (and objects) are composed together to form a larger structure.

  Examples: Composite, Decorator, Proxy, and Façade.

- **Behavioral patterns** define the communication among the objects and control the flow within the participating objects.

  Examples: Mediator, Chain of Responsibility, Observer, State, and Strategy.

The Singleton Design Pattern

There are many situations in which you want to make sure that only one instance is present for a particular class. For example, assume that you defined a class that modifies registry, or you implemented a class that manages printer spooling, or you implemented a thread-pool manager class. In all these situations, you might want to avoid hard-to-find bugs by instantiating no more than one object of such classes. In these situations, you could employ the *singleton design pattern*.

The singleton design pattern is meant to ensure that only one instance of the class is created. The pattern implementation provides a single point of access to the class. This pattern is a *creational design pattern*, which means it controls instantiation of the object. In Java SDK, the pattern is used in many places, such as `java.lang.Runtime`.

Figure 5-1 shows the class diagram of the singleton pattern. It comprises a single class, the class that you want to make as a singleton. It has a private constructor and a static method to get the singleton object.

Singleton
-mySingleton : Singleton
- Singleton() + getSingleton() : Singleton

Figure 5-1. *UML class diagram of singleton design pattern*

The singleton design pattern offers two things: one and only one instance of the class, and a global single point of access to that object.

Assume that the FunPaint application requires a logger that you want to implement as a singleton. Listing 5-7 shows a possible implementation.

Listing 5-7. Logger.java

```
// Logger class must be intantiated only once in the application; it is to ensure that the
// whole of the application makes use of that same logger instance
public class Logger {
        // declare the constructor private to prevent clients
        // from instantiating an object of this class directly
        private Logger() {       }
        public static Logger myInstance;        // by default, this field is initialized to null
        // the static method to be used by clients to get the instance of the Logger class
        public static Logger getInstance() {
                if(myInstance == null) {
                        // this is the first time this method is called, and that's why myInstance
                        is null
                        myInstance = new Logger();
                }
                // return the same object reference any time and every time getInstance is called
                return myInstance;
        }
        public void log(String s) {
                // a trivial implementation of log where we pass the string to be logged to console
                System.err.println(s);
        }
}
```

Look at the singleton implementation of the Logger class. The constructor of the class is declared as private, so you cannot simply create a new instance of the Logger class using the new operator. The only way to get an instance of this class is to call the static member method of the class via the getInstance() method. This method checks whether a Logger object already exists or not. If not, it creates a Logger instance and assigns it to the static member variable. In this way, whenever you call the getInstance() method, it will always return the same object of the Logger class.

 Listing 5-7 used lazy initialization. You could employ early initialization if your singleton constructor is not computationally expensive.

Ensuring That Your Singleton Is Indeed a Singleton

You might be wondering what we are talking about, but it is really important (as well as really difficult) to ensure that your singleton pattern implementation allows only instance of the class.

For instance, the implementation provided in Listing 5-7 works only if your application is single-threaded. In the case of multiple threads, trying to get a singleton object may result in creation of multiple objects, which of course defeats the purpose of implementing a singleton.

Listing 5-8 shows a version of the Logger class that implements the singleton design pattern in a multi-threaded environment.

Listing 5-8. Logger.java

```java
public class Logger {
        private Logger() {
                // private constructor to prevent direct instantiation
        }
        public static Logger myInstance;
        public static synchronized Logger getInstance() {
                if(myInstance == null)
                        myInstance = new Logger();
                return myInstance;
        }
        public void log(String s){
                // log implementation
                System.err.println(s);
        }
}
```

Note the use of the keyword synchronized in this implementation. This keyword is a Java concurrency mechanism to allow only one thread at a time into the synchronized scope. You will learn more about this keyword in Chapter 13.

So, you made the whole method synchronized in order to make it accessible by only a thread at a time. This makes it a correct solution, but there is a problem: poor performance. You wanted to make this method synchronized only at the first time the method is called, but since you declared the whole method as synchronized, all subsequent calls to this method make it a performance bottleneck.

Okay, fine. What if you synchronize only the new statement? See Listing 5-9.

Listing 5-9. Logger.java

```java
public class Logger {
        private Logger() {
                // private constructor
        }
        public static Logger myInstance;
        public static Logger getInstance() {
                if(myInstance == null) {
                        synchronized (Logger.class) {
                                myInstance = new Logger();
                        }
                }
                return myInstance;
        }
        public void log(String s) {
                // log implementation
                System.err.println(s);
        }
}
```

It's a nice try, but this solution does not work either. The synchronization does not prevent the accidental creation of two singleton objects. Now, implement the famous *double-checked locking* (see Listing 5-10).

Listing 5-10. Logger.java

```java
public class Logger {
        private Logger() {
                // private constructor
        }
        public static Logger myInstance;
        public static Logger getInstance() {
                if(myInstance == null) {
                        synchronized (Logger.class) {
                                if(myInstance == null) {
                                        myInstance = new Logger();
                                }
                        }
                }
                return myInstance;
        }
        public void log(String s) {
                // log implementation
                System.err.println(s);
        }
}
```

Well, this implementation is also not a foolproof solution for a multi-threaded application. It creates a problem due to erroneous out-of-order writes allowed by the Java memory model. Although the memory model problem was reportedly fixed in Java 5, we do not encourage you to use this solution.

Listing 5-11 shows another implementation of the Logger class that is based on the "initialization on demand holder" idiom. This idiom uses inner classes and does not use any synchronization construct (recall the discussion of inner classes in Chapter 4). It exploits the fact that inner classes are not loaded until they are referenced.

Listing 5-11. Logger.java

```java
public class Logger {
        private Logger() {
                // private constructor
        }
        public static Logger myInstance;
        public static class LoggerHolder {
                public static Logger logger = new Logger();
        }
        public static Logger getInstance() {
                return LoggerHolder.logger;
        }
        public void log(String s) {
                // log implementation
                System.err.println(s);
        }
}
```

Hmm...at last you've found an efficient working solution. However, before we close this discussion of the singleton design pattern, two parting words of caution. First, use the singleton pattern wherever it is appropriate, but do not overuse it. Second, make sure that your singleton implementation ensures the creation of only one instance even if your code is multi-threaded.

The Factory Design Pattern

In real life, factories are manufacturing units that produce multiple instances of a product (or flavors of a product). For instance, a car factory produces cars of specific types and models. The main responsibility of the factory is to keep producing cars of the required type and model. Here, one important thing to observe is that a car may have different variants and the car factory should be able to manufacture on demand the required variants of the same car.

Similarly, you can implement a factory that returns the required type of object(s) on demand in OOP. In this case, the factory decides which class(es) to instantiate to create the required object(s) and exactly how to create them.

Figure 5-2 shows the UML class diagram of the factory pattern. Client invokes ProductFactory to get an appropriate object from the product hierarchy. ProductFactory creates one of the Products from the Product hierarchy based on the provided information. Client uses the product object without knowing which actual product it is using or how ProductFactory created this product object.

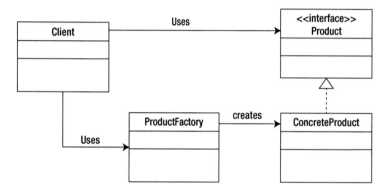

Figure 5-2. *UML class diagram of factory design pattern*

Let's consider an example. In the FunPaint application, there are different types of shapes, such as Circle and Rectangle. Now, the Canvas object might not want to know about the concrete shape that gets created. Assume that the Canvas object receives a shape identifier from the front end based on which corresponding shape object needs to be created. Here, you can have a ShapeFactory that can create the required shape object and return it to the Canvas object. Listing 5-12 shows the implementation of this pattern.

Listing 5-12. Test.java

```java
// Shape.java
public interface Shape {
        public void draw();
        public void fillColor();
}

// Circle.java
public class Circle implements Shape {
        private int xPos, yPos;
        private int radius;
        public Circle(int x, int y, int r) {
                xPos = x;
                yPos = y;
                        radius = r;
                        System.out.println("Circle constructor");
        }
```

```java
        @Override
        public void draw() {
                System.out.println("Circle draw()");
                // draw() implementation
        }
        @Override
        public void fillColor() {
                // fillColor() implementation
        }
}

// Rectangle.java
public class Rectangle implements Shape {
        public Rectangle(int length, int height) {
                this.length = length;
                this.height = height;
                System.out.println("Rectangle constructor");
        }
        private int length, height;
        @Override
        public void draw() {
                System.out.println("Rectangle draw()");
                // draw() implementation
        }
        @Override
        public void fillColor() {
                // fillColor() implementation
        }
}

// ShapeFactory.java
public class ShapeFactory {
         public static Shape getShape(String sourceType) {
                switch(sourceType) {
                case "Circle":
                        return new Circle(10, 10, 20);
                case "Rectangle":
                        return new Rectangle(10, 20);
                }
                return null;
        }
}

// Canvas.java
import java.util.ArrayList;
import java.util.Iterator;
```

```java
public class Canvas {
        private ArrayList<Shape> shapeList = new ArrayList<Shape>();
        public void addNewShape(String shapeType) {
                Shape shape = ShapeFactory.getShape(shapeType);
                shapeList.add(shape);
        }
        public void redraw() {
                Iterator<Shape> itr = shapeList.iterator();
                while(itr.hasNext()) {
                        Shape shape = itr.next();
                        shape.draw();
                }
        }
}

// Test.java
public class Test {
        public static void main(String[] args) {
                Canvas canvas = new Canvas();
                canvas.addNewShape("Circle");
                canvas.addNewShape("Rectangle");
                canvas.redraw();
        }
}
```

It prints the following:

```
Circle constructor
Rectangle constructor
Circle draw()
Rectangle draw()
```

Let's analyze this implementation. You define a Shape interface, which defines two public methods, draw() and fillColor(). Classes Circle and Rectangle implement this interface and provide implementation of interface methods. Class Canvas maintains a list of shapes drawn on canvas, and it offers a method addNewShape() to allow the front-end of the application to create a new instance of requested shape. From the main() method, you invoke the addnewShape() method of Canvas class. In turn, this method calls the getShape() method of ShapeFactory class. The getShape() method examines the requested type of shape, creates a new instance based on the requested type, and returns it to Canvas.

The following insights may be drawn from the above example:

- The Canvas class does not need to know how to create concrete shape objects. This transparency becomes very useful in case concrete object creation is expensive and complicated.

- The Canvas class does not need to know the exact concrete shape types. You can observe from the Canvas implementation that Canvas is only aware of the Shape interface. Therefore, if you add another concrete shape (say Square), you do not need to change the Canvas implementation.

Java SDK defines many such factories. For example, java.util.Calendar is an implementation of the factory design pattern. Listing 5-13 uses the Calendar class.

Listing 5-13. mainClass.java

```java
import java.util.Calendar;

public class MainClass {
        public static void main(String[] args) {
                Calendar calendar = Calendar.getInstance();
                System.out.println(calendar);
        }
}
```

This program prints the following:

```
java.util.GregorianCalendar [...]
```

The output of Listing 5-13 contains all the fields of the calendar object (shown here as [...] to save the space). There are many other examples in Java SDK where the factory pattern is used, including the following:

- `createStatement()` of `java.sql.Connection` interface, which creates a new `Statement` to communicate to database.

- `createSocket()` of `java.rmi.server.RmiClientSocketFactory` interface, which returns a new client `Socket`.

Differences Between Factory and Abstract Factory Design Patterns

Both *factory design patterns* and *abstract factory design patterns* belong to the *creational design pattern* category. As explained in preceding section, a factory design pattern creates (or manufactures) the requested type of object on demand. By contrast, the abstract factory is basically a factory of factories. In other words, the abstract factory design pattern introduces one more indirection to create a specified object. A client of the abstract factory design pattern first requests a proper factory from the abstract factory object, and then it requests an appropriate object from the factory object.

Another very important difference between these two patterns is their applicability: when you have only one type of object to be created, you can use a factory design pattern; when you have a family of objects to be created, you can use an abstract factory design pattern.

Let's explore the abstract factory pattern by reference to its class diagram (Figure 5-3). Assume that there are two product hierarchies, `ProductA` and `ProductB`, along with their concrete product classes. You want to create either `ConcreteProductA1` and `ConcreteProductB1` (as a group) or `ConcreteProductA2` and `ConcreteProductB2`. In this situation, you define an abstract `ProductFactory` with two subclasses, `ProductFactory1` and `ProductFactory2`. `ProductFactory1` creates `ConcreteProductA1` and `ConcreteProductB1` and `ProductFactory2` creates `ConcreteProductA2` and `ConcreteProductB2`. Hence, based on the requirement, you create a required factory object; the selected factory object gives you the required concrete product objects.

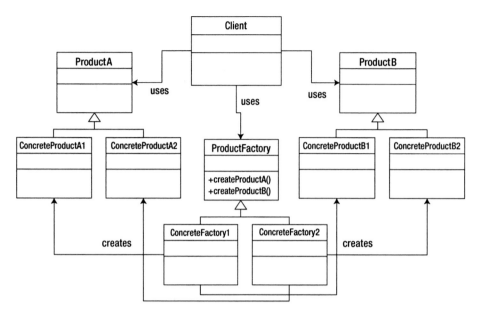

Figure 5-3. *UML class diagram for abstract factory design pattern*

Let's work out an example now. In Listing 5-12, you implemented the factory design pattern. Now, let's assume that shapes can be of two types: `DisplayFriendly` and `PrinterFriendly`. Hence, now there are two flavors available for your `Circle` class (as well as for your `Rectangle` class, *mutatis mutandis*): `DisplayFriendlyCircle` and `PrinterFriendlyCircle`. Now, obviously you want to create only one type of objects: either display-friendly or printer-friendly. Well, you've established that when you want to create a family of objects you should use the abstract factory design pattern. Listing 5-14 shows the implementation.

Listing 5-14. Test.java

```
// Shape.java
public interface Shape {
       public void draw();
}

// PrinterFriendlyShape.java
public interface PrinterFriendlyShape extends Shape {
}

// DisplayFriendlyShape.java
public interface DisplayFriendlyShape extends Shape {
}

// DisplayFriendlyCircle.java
public class DisplayFriendlyCircle implements DisplayFriendlyShape {
private int xPos, yPos;
       private int radius;
       public DisplayFriendlyCircle(int x, int y, int r) {
               xPos = x;
               yPos = y;
```

```java
                radius = r;
                System.out.println("DisplayFriendlyCircle constructor");
        }
        @Override
        public void draw() {
                System.out.println("DisplayFriendlyCircle draw()");
                // draw() implementation
        }
}

// DisplayFriendlyRectangle.java
public class DisplayFriendlyRectangle implements DisplayFriendlyShape {
        public DisplayFriendlyRectangle(int length, int height) {
                this.length = length;
                this.height = height;
                System.out.println("DisplayFriendlyRectangle constructor");
        }
        private int length, height;
        @Override
        public void draw() {
                System.out.println("DisplayFriendlyRectangle draw()");
                // draw() implementation
        }
}

// PrinterFriendlyCircle.java
public class PrinterFriendlyCircle implements PrinterFriendlyShape{
        private int xPos, yPos;
        private int radius;
        public PrinterFriendlyCircle(int x, int y, int r) {
                xPos = x;
                yPos = y;
                radius = r;
                System.out.println("PrinterFriendlyCircle constructor");
        }
        @Override
        public void draw() {
                System.out.println("PrinterFriendlyCircle draw()");
                // draw() implementation
        }
}

// PrinterFriendlyRectangle.java
public class PrinterFriendlyRectangle implements PrinterFriendlyShape {
        public PrinterFriendlyRectangle(int length, int height) {
                this.length = length;
                this.height = height;
                System.out.println("PrinterFriendlyRectangle constructor");
        }
        private int length, height;
        @Override
```

```java
        public void draw() {
                System.out.println("PrinterFriendlyRectangle draw()");
                // draw() implementation
        }
}

// ShapeFactory.java
public interface ShapeFactory {
        public Shape getShape(String sourceType);
}

// DisplayFriendlyFactory.java
public class DisplayFriendlyFactory implements ShapeFactory {
        @Override
        public Shape getShape(String sourceType) {
                switch(sourceType){
                case "Circle":
                        return new DisplayFriendlyCircle(10, 10, 20);
                case "Rectangle":
                        return new DisplayFriendlyRectangle(10, 20);
                }
                return null;
        }
}

// PrinterFriendlyFactory.java
public class PrinterFriendlyFactory implements ShapeFactory {
        @Override
        public Shape getShape(String sourceType) {
                switch(sourceType) {
                        case "Circle":
                                return new PrinterFriendlyCircle(10, 10, 20);
                        case "Rectangle":
                                return new PrinterFriendlyRectangle(10, 20);
                }
                return null;
        }
}

// Test.java
public class Test {
        public static void main(String[] args) {
                Canvas canvas = new Canvas();
                canvas.addNewShape("Circle", "DisplayFriendly");
                canvas.addNewShape("Rectangle", "DisplayFriendly");
                canvas.redraw();
        }
}
```

Don't be scared by the lengthy code—you can understand it. In this code, there are two major features to grasp:

- **Product hierarchy:** Shape is the base interface extended by DisplayFriendlyShape and PrinterFriendlyShape. Two flavors of the Circle and Rectangle classes are defined for each: display-friendly and printer-friendly shape.

- **Abstract factory implementation:** Made up of ShapeFactory as the base interface, and PrinterFriendlyFactory and DisplayFriendlyFactory as the concrete factories. PrinterFriendlyFactory creates only PrinterFriendlyCircle and PrinterFriendlyRectangle; similarly, DisplayFriendlyFactory creates DisplayFriendlyCircle and DisplayFriendlyRectangle.

The rest of the code is quite similar to the factory version of the program in Listing 5-12.

Java SDK employs the abstract factory pattern at numerous places. You would do well, for example, to check out and understand the following:

- `javax.xml.transform.TransformerFactory`

- `javax.xml.xpath.XPathFactory`

Parenthetical Note: For the OCPJP 7 exam, you need to understand the factory design pattern, by which the factory creates new instances of a product hierarchy based on the provided input. Outside the scope of the OCPJP 7 exam but nevertheless noteworthy is another way to implement the factory: *reflection*. The main advantage of using reflection to implement the factory is that you can extend your product hierarchy without changing the implementation of factory or compromising the factory's ability to create newly added classes.

The Data Access Object (DAO) Design Pattern

Suppose that you are at a multicultural fair with your family and you decide to take a ride on the carousel. You see a big panel with many buttons for operating the carousel. You ask the operator to start the carousel, adjust its speed, and stop it. The operator, who knows how to use the panel, follows your instructions. He is providing you an abstraction from the complicated control panel. In fact, if you go to different carousel at the other end of the fair, you can instruct its operator in the same way and that operator will follow your instructions in the same way even though his panel is different from that of the first carousel. In essence, your family can take a ride on any carousel without understanding its operating panel because the knowledge to operate the machine is abstracted by the operator. The *Data Access Object (DAO)* design pattern provides you abstractions in an analogous way.

In real-life projects, you will encounter situations in which you want to make your data persist. You might use flat files (i.e., data files on your native OS), XML files, OODBMS, RDBMS, etc. In such situations, you can use the DAO design pattern. This design pattern abstracts the details of the underlying persistence mechanism and offers you an easy-to-use interface for implementing the persistence feature in your application. The DAO pattern hides the implementation details of the data source from its clients, thereby introducing loose coupling between your core business logic and your persistence mechanism. This loose coupling enables you to migrate from one type of persistence mechanism to another without any big-bang change.

A DAO design pattern essentially separates your core business logic from your persistence logic.

Let's examine the structure of the pattern, which is shown in Figure 5-4. DataSource represents a concrete persistence implementation such as a RDBMS, XML database, or even another system/repository. DAO provides an abstraction for the DataSource, hides the specific implementation level details, and provides a single interface for all different types of data sources. A Client is a user of DAO pattern that uses DataSource through DAO, and TransferObject is a data transfer object used as a medium to transfer the core objects.

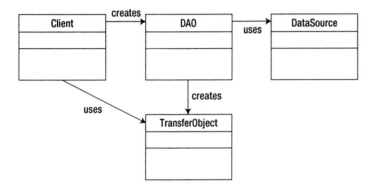

Figure 5-4. *UML class diagram of DAO design pattern*

Apart from the above-mentioned participants (Client, DAO, TransferObject, and DataSource), there could be one more participant for this pattern—DAOFactory. You may have multiple DAO objects, corresponding to all the different types of objects you want to store. You may define a factory (using the factory design pattern, as you did in the preceding section), which can have one method for each DAO object. Don't worry...you're going to implement a factory in your next example.

Assume that you want to implement the DAO design pattern in the FunPaint application. Here, you have a Circle class that you want to store in a persistent data store. Listing 5-15 shows the implementation of the pattern.

Listing 5-15. Test.java

```java
// Circle.java
public class Circle {
        private int xPos, yPos;
        private int radius;
        public Circle(int x, int y, int r) {
                xPos = x;
                yPos = y;
                radius = r;
        }
        public String toString() {
                return "center = (" + xPos + "," + yPos + ") and radius = " + radius;
        }
```

```java
        public CircleTransfer getCircleTransferObject() {
                CircleTransfer circleTransfer = new CircleTransfer();
                circleTransfer.setRadius(radius);
                circleTransfer.setxPos(xPos);
                circleTransfer.setyPos(yPos);
                return circleTransfer;
        }
        // other members
}

// CircleDAO.java
public interface CircleDAO {
        public void insertCircle(CircleTransfer circle);
        public CircleTransfer findCircle(int id);
        public void deleteCircle(int id);
}

// RDBMSDAO.java
public class RDBMSDAO implements CircleDAO {
        @Override
        public void insertCircle(CircleTransfer circle) {
                // insertCircle implementation
                System.out.println("insertCircle implementation");
        }
        @Override
        public CircleTransfer findCircle(int id) {
                // findCircle implementation
                return null;
        }
        @Override
        public void deleteCircle(int id) {
                // deleteCircle implementation
        }
}

// DAOFactory.java
public class DAOFactory {
         public static CircleDAO getCircleDAO(String sourceType) {
                // This is a simple example, so we have listed only "RDBMS" as the only source type
                // In a real-world application, you can provide more source types
                switch(sourceType){
                case "RDBMS":
                        return new RDBMSDAO();
                }
                return null;
        }
}

// CircleTransfer.java
import java.io.Serializable;
```

```java
public class CircleTransfer implements Serializable {
        private int xPos;
        private int yPos;
        private int radius;
        public int getxPos() {
                return xPos;
        }
        public void setxPos(int xPos) {
                this.xPos = xPos;
        }
        public int getyPos() {
                return yPos;
        }
        public void setyPos(int yPos) {
                this.yPos = yPos;
        }
        public int getRadius() {
                return radius;
        }
        public void setRadius(int radius) {
                this.radius = radius;
        }
}

// Test.java
public class Test {
        public static void main(String[] args) {
                Circle circle = new Circle(10, 10, 20);
                System.out.println(circle);
                CircleTransfer circleTransfer = circle.getCircleTransferObject();
                CircleDAO circleDAO = DAOFactory.getCircleDAO("RDBMS");
                circleDAO.insertCircle(circleTransfer);
        }
}
```

Well, that's quite a big program. Let's go through it step by step. The Circle class belongs to your core business logic; apart from the other usual members, the Circle class contains a method—getCircleTransferObject()—that returns the CircleTransfer object with the required data. You define the CircleDAO interface with three methods commonly used with data sources. The RDBMSDAO implements CircleDAO with a concrete implementation to access the RDBMS data source. The CircleTransfer object plays a data carrier role between the main() method (which is acting as a Client) and DAO implementation (i.e., the RDBMSDAO class).

One more feature to be noted in the Listing 5-15 implementation is the use of the factory design pattern. In an application, there might be many DAO objects. For instance, in the FunPaint application you might have CircleDAO, RectangleDAO, SquareDAO, etc. You may define *getter methods* to get corresponding DAO object in a single DAO factory. In each method, you may return an appropriate DAO object based on the provided type, as you do in this example with the RDBMS type.

Here are the benefits of the DAO design pattern:

- The pattern introduces an abstraction: the DAO hides the implementation details of the actual data source from the core business logic. The business logic need not know about the nitty-gritty of the data source, which results in easy-to-understand, less complicated code.

- The pattern separates the persistence mechanism from rest of the application code and puts it together in one class specific to one data source. This centralization enables easier maintenance and easier bug-tracing.

- It is quite easy to extend support for other data sources using this pattern. For instance, if you want to provide support for the XML-based repository in the FunPaint application, this can be achieved by defining a new class (say XMLDAO). This new class will implement your CircleDAO interface, such that you do not need to change the way you access the data source. The only thing that needs to be changed is the parameter you pass to DAOFactory to create a DAO. Easy, isn't it?

Points to Remember

Here are points to remember for the OCPJP 7 exam:

- You saw the factory design pattern implementation in the DAO design pattern. You may also employ abstract factory design pattern if you have multiple DAO objects and you have multiple persistence mechanisms.

- Note that you declared TransferObject (e.g., CircleTransfer) as *serializable*. Any idea why you did that? Well, if you are using the transfer object between two JVMs, then the transfer object has to be serializable.

- In OOP, a useful and important design principle is "separation of concerns." This principle states that *concerns* (or features) should be *separated* (to attain minimum overlap) in order to overcome the inherent complexity involved with software design. The DAO design pattern helps you comply with this design principle. If you are not using DAO, then your business logic will be exposed to the concrete implementation details of the persistence mechanisms—an undesirable state of affairs. Use of the DAO design pattern ensures that you separate your core logic from your persistence mechanism.

QUESTION TIME!

1. Which of the following statements is true?

    A. A class can extend multiple base classes.

    B. You can implement only one interface since Java does not support multiple inheritance.

    C. You can implement multiple interfaces.

    D. You can either extend a class or implement an interface (but not both) at a time.

    Answer: C

2. Consider the following interface declaration:

```
public interface Rotatable {
    void rotate(float degree);
    // insert code
}
```

Now, consider following options which could be replaced with "// insert code":

```
  I.  public  final float degree = 0;

 II.  public  static final float degree = 0;

III.  public  final static float degree = 0;

 IV.  public  final float degree;

  V.  public float degree;

 VI.  float degree = 0;
```

Choose the correct option:

    A. Options I, II, III, and VI will compile without errors.

    B. Options I, II, and III will compile without errors.

    C. Options I will compile without errors.

    D. Options IV, and V will compile without errors.

    E. All options will compile without errors.

Answer: A

3. Consider following example:

```java
public interface xyz {
   void abc() throws IOException;
}
public interface pqr {
   void abc() throws FileNotFoundException;
}
public class Implementation implements xyz, pqr {
   // insert code
   { /*implementation*/ }
}
```

Which of the following statement(s) can you insert in place of "// insert code" comment?

    A. public void abc() throws IOException

    B. public void abc() throws FileNotFoundException

    C. public void abc() throws FileNotFoundException, IOException

    D. public void abc() throws IOException, FileNotFoundException

Answer: B

(Since FileNotFoundException is a subtype of IOException, it satisfies both methods).

4. Consider the following three classes: University, Department, and CSE_Department (CSE stands for Computer Science and Engineering). The University and Department classes are related with relation R1, and the Department and CSE_Department classes are related with relation R2. Which combination of these relations is appropriate?

   A. R1: inheritance, R2: inheritance

   B. R1: composition, R2: inheritance

   C. R1: inheritance, R2: composition

   D. R1: composition, R2: composition

   Answer: B

(A university has many departments, so they share a has-a relationship between them, a composition relationship. CSE_Department is a department, so these two share a is-a relationship between them, an inheritance relationship.)

5. You need to model a file system where there could be subfolders and files in a folder. What is the most appropriate design choice in this case to represent the relationship between Folder and File classes?

   A. Use composition to model the relationship of "a Folder object consists of File objects."

   B. Use composition to model the relationship of "a Folder object consists of File objects or Folder objects."

   C. Use inheritance to define a superclass (say FolderItem) and make Folder and File classes subclasses to this class. Use composition to model the relationship "a Folder object consists of FolderItem objects."

   D. Use inheritance between Folder and File classes to model the relationship "a Folder is of type File."

   Answer: C

(In fact, this arrangement is referred to as a composite design pattern)

Summary

Interfaces

- An interface is a set of abstract methods that defines a protocol.

- An interface cannot be instantiated; however, an interface can extend another interface.

- All methods declared in an interface are implicitly considered to be abstract.

- Abstract class and interface are quite similar concepts. However, you should be careful to use the appropriate construct based on the context.

Object Composition

- Inheritance implies is-a, interface implies is-like-a, and composition implies has-a relationships.

- Favor composition over inheritance whenever feasible.

- Program to an interface, not to an implementation.

Design Patterns

- Design patterns are reusable solutions of frequently recurring design problems.

- The observer design pattern improves loose coupling between subject and observers.

- The singleton design pattern ensures that only one instance of the class is created.

- Making sure that an intended singleton implementation is indeed singleton is a non-trivial task, especially in a multi-threaded environment.

- The factory design pattern "manufactures" the required type of product on demand.

- You should consider using the abstract factory design pattern when you have a family of objects to be created.

- A DAO design pattern essentially separates your core business logic from your persistence logic.

CHAPTER 6

Generics and Collections

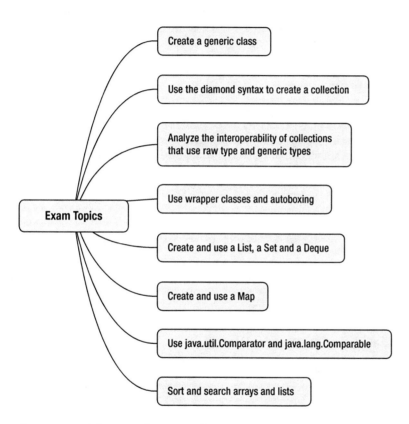

Every non-trivial Java application makes use of data structures and algorithms. The Java collections framework provides a large set of readily usable general-purpose data structures and algorithms. These data structures and algorithms can be used with any suitable data type in a type-safe manner; this is achieved through the use of a language feature known as generics.

Since data structures and algorithms are implemented using generics, these two complementary topics are combined together as a single topic in the 1Z0-804 exam syllabus. In this chapter, we first introduce generics, which are useful for defining reusable data structures and algorithms. We discuss how generics offer more type safety than Object type containers. We also explore other aspects of generics such as wildcard parameters in generics and subtyping in generics.

In the collections part of this chapter, you'll learn how to use the readily available data structures (implemented using generics) provided as part of the Java library. We'll discuss some interfaces and concrete classes in the collections framework that are important from the OPCJP 7 exam perspective.

Generics

Generics are a language feature introduced to Java in Version 1.5. Generics help you write code for one type (say T) that is applicable for all types, instead of writing separate classes for each type. Before generics were introduced in Java, the Object base class was used as an alternative to generics. However, using the Object class for storing elements in a container results in type safety issues—that is, using such a container allows type errors that cannot be identified by the Java compiler and result in runtime exceptions. If you don't understand this description of type safety, don't worry because we're going to explain the type safety problem in detail with a few examples. Understanding type safety is important. In fact, the main motivation for adding generics to the language was because legacy container classes were not type-safe.

Using Object Type and Type Safety

Before the introduction of generics in Java, data structures were implemented by storing and processing elements using the Object base class. We'll discuss an example to understand why those containers are not type-safe. Consider the program in Listing 6-1, which uses the Vector class (you can think of Vector as a "dynamically growing array" where you can add or remove elements similar to an array). Can you predict the output of this program?

Listing 6-1. OldContainerTest.java

```
import java.util.Vector;

// This program demonstrate the lack of type-safety in containers (based on Object type).
class OldContainerTest {
        public static void main(String []args) {
                Vector floatValues = new Vector();
                floatValues.add(10.0f);
                floatValues.add(100.0);
                for(int i = 0; i < floatValues.size(); i++) {
                        System.out.println(floatValues.get(i));
                }
        }
}
```

It prints the following:

```
10.0
100.0
```

Now let's make only one change to this program: instead of directly printing the values returned from Vector's get method, you first store it in a temporary variable of Float type and then print that temporary value using println:

```
Float temp = (Float) floatValues.get(i);
System.out.println(temp);
```

Now this is the output:

```
10.0
Exception in thread "main" java.lang.ClassCastException: java.lang.Double cannot be cast to
java.lang.Float at OldContainerTest.main(OldContainerTest.java:9)
```

Why? What happened? The Vector container is capable of holding any object (i.e., it holds values of the Object type). When you try to put a primitive type, however, it is "boxed" automatically and the wrapper object is put into the container (using the autoboxing feature in Java). For 10.0, the corresponding primitive type is float (note the suffix "f"!), and so a wrapper object of type Float is created and that object is put into the Vector. For 100.0, the primitive type is Double (real numbers, if not given with explicit suffix, are assumed of type Double by default). So, the wrapper object of type Double is created and that object is put into the Vector.

So far, so good. In the original program, there were no casts, so the floating point values were directly printed using the toString() method in println. However, when you try to cast it using the Float type, you get into trouble. You cannot convert the Double value 100.0 into Float type. (Float type can be casted to Double type—but Float type cannot be casted to Double type!) So you get a ClassCastException at runtime.

In other words, a Vector is implemented in terms of Object type. So, you can put an object of any type into a Vector object. You cannot enforce that only elements of certain type can be inserted to the container *at compile time*. In fact, while compiling the program, the compiler does warn you about using *raw type* Vector (see Figure 6-1). We'll discuss more about these raw types (i.e., non-generic types) in the "Interoperability of Raw Types and Generic Types" section of this chapter.

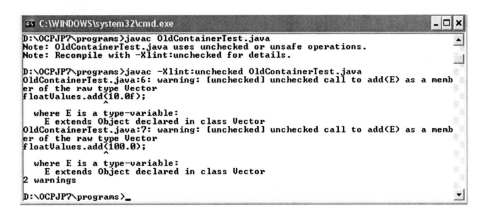

Figure 6-1. *Compiler warning about the use of raw type Vector*

The Vector container that uses the Object base class for storing elements allows you to add elements of any type, while your application logic requires that only strings should be added. With generics, you can specify to the compiler that only elements of a certain type can be added to a container. Generics will ensure that any attempts to add elements of types other than the specified type(s) will be caught at compile time itself. In other words, the use of data structures implemented using generics is checked for type safety at compile time, so those data structures are type-safe.

Using the Object Class vs. Generics

In the previous section, we focused our discussion on type safety issues in using existing data structures that were implemented using the Object base class. In this section, we'll turn our focus to *defining your own data structures*. With an example of a container class definition using the Object base class, you'll understand why such containers are not type-safe. After that, we'll introduce the concept of generics and show you how using generics can help define type-safe containers.

Container Implementation Using the Object Class

Assume that you want to print the object's value within square brackets. For example, to print an Integer object with value 10, instead of printing "10" to the console, you want to print the value inside a "box" like this: "[10]". The default toString() method just gives the String representation of the object's value; you want an enhanced toString() method that will print "[" and "]" before and after the value. How can you do that? You can write a BoxPrinter class that overrides the toString() method. You'll use Object for storing the value since it is the common base class for all types (see Listing 6-2).

Listing 6-2. BoxPrinterTest1.java

```
// The program demonstrates "Object" based implementation and associated lack of type safety
class BoxPrinter {
        private Object val;
        public BoxPrinter(Object arg) {
                val = arg;
        }
        public String toString() {
                return "[" + val + "]";
        }
}

class BoxPrinterTest1 {
        public static void main(String []args) {
                BoxPrinter value1 = new BoxPrinter(new Integer(10));
                        System.out.println(value1);
                BoxPrinter value2 = new BoxPrinter("Hello world");
                System.out.println(value2);
        }
}
```

It works fine and prints the following:

```
[10]
[Hello world]
```

You can pass object of any type, and this code will print its contents within "[" and "]" correctly. This is the same mechanism in which the legacy containers (like Vector) are implemented. So, what is the problem? Well, here is a scenario: assume that you want to add a method named getValue() that gets the value stored in BoxPrinter. How do you get back the original type you put in while creating the BoxPrinter object? This is where the problem starts. Listing 6-3 contains an example.

Listing 6-3. BoxPrinterTest2.java

```java
// The program demonstrates "Object" based implementation and associated lack of type safety
class BoxPrinter {
        private Object val;
        public BoxPrinter(Object arg) {
                val = arg;
        }
        public String toString() {
                return "[" + val + "]";
        }
        public Object getValue() {
                return val;
        }
}

class BoxPrinterTest2 {
        public static void main(String []args) {
                BoxPrinter value1 = new BoxPrinter(new Integer(10));
                System.out.println(value1);
                Integer intValue1 = (Integer) value1.getValue();

                BoxPrinter value2 = new BoxPrinter("Hello world");
                System.out.println(value2);
                        // OOPs! by mistake, we did (Integer) cast instead of (String)
                        Integer intValue2 = (Integer) value2.getValue();
        }
}
```

Here is the output:

```
[10]
[Hello world]
Exception in thread "main" java.lang.ClassCastException: java.lang.String cannot be cast to
java.lang.Integer at BoxPrinterTest2.main(Main.java:22)
```

In the line

```java
Integer intValue2 = (Integer) value2.getValue();
```

by mistake you performed a downcast from Object to Integer instead of Object to String. There is no way for the compiler to detect the mistake that you are trying to convert the value from String to Integer. What you remember as value is of Object type, and the only way to check the correct type before doing the downcast is to check for the type using the instanceof operator. In this case, you can do an instanceof check for String and make sure that the cast is done correctly. In general, however, when you don't know the type of object stored in BoxPrinter, you can never perform an instanceof check in the code to do a downcast! This is the reason why the old Java container classes (which used the Object class for storing elements) are not type-safe.

Container Implementation Using Generics

Listing 6-4 contains a generic version of the BoxPrinter class you saw in the preceding section.

Listing 6-4. BoxPrinterTest3.java

```java
// This program shows container implementation using generics
class BoxPrinter<T> {
        private T val;
        public BoxPrinter(T arg) {
                val = arg;
        }
        public String toString() {
                return "[" + val + "]";
        }
}

class BoxPrinterTest3 {
        public static void main(String []args) {
                BoxPrinter<Integer> value1 = new BoxPrinter<Integer>(new Integer(10));
                System.out.println(value1);

                BoxPrinter<String> value2 = new BoxPrinter<String>("Hello world");
                System.out.println(value2);
        }
}
```

It prints the following:

```
[10]
[Hello world]
```

There are many things you need to note here.

1. See the declaration of BoxPrinter:

   ```
   class BoxPrinter<T>
   ```

You gave the BoxPrinter class a *type placeholder* <T>—the type name T within angle brackets "<" and ">" following the class name. You can use this type name inside the class to indicate that it is a placeholder for the actual type to be provided later. (Note that you've given an unusually short identifier name of T to indicate the type name: this is intentional, and you'll see the naming conventions for generic types a bit later in this chapter.)

2. Inside the class you first use T in field declaration:

   ```
   private T val;
   ```

You are declaring val of the *generic type*—the actual type will be specified later when you use BoxPrinter. In main(), you declare a variable an Integer like this:

```
BoxPrinter<Integer> value1
```

Here, you are specifying that T is of type Integer—identifier T (a placeholder) is replaced with the type Integer. So, the val inside BoxPrinter becomes Integer because T gets replaced with Integer.

3.   Now, here is another place where you use T:

```
public BoxPrinter(T arg) {
        val = arg;
}
```

Similar to the declaration of val with type T, you are saying that the argument for BoxPrinter constructor is of type T. Later in the main() method, when the constructor is called in new, you specify that T is of type Integer:

```
new BoxPrinter<Integer>(new Integer(10));
```

Now, inside the BoxPrinter constructor, arg and val *should be of same type* since both are of type T. For example, if you change the constructor as follows:

```
new BoxPrinter<String>(new Integer(10));
```

the BoxPrinter is of type String, and the argument passed is of type Integer, so you'll get a compiler error for type mismatch in using the generics (which is good because you'll find the problem earlier).

Now, let's add the getValue() method to return the value contained in the BoxPrinter class. Listing 6-5 contains the enhanced version.

Listing 6-5. BoxPrinterTest4.java

```
// This program demonstrates the type-safety feature of generics
class BoxPrinter<T> {
        private T val;
        public BoxPrinter(T arg) {
                val = arg;
        }
        public String toString() {
                return "[" + val + "]";
        }
        public T getValue() {
                return val;
        }
}

class BoxPrinterTest4 {
        public static void main(String []args) {
                BoxPrinter<Integer> value1 = new BoxPrinter<Integer>(new Integer(10));
                System.out.println(value1);
                Integer intValue1 = value1.getValue();

                BoxPrinter<String> value2 = new BoxPrinter<String>("Hello world");
                System.out.println(value2);
                // OOPs! by mistake, we did put String in an Integer
                Integer intValue2 = value2.getValue();
        }
}
```

This is the line where you made a mistake and tried to put a String in an Integer:

```
Integer intValue2 = value2.getValue();
```

And you get the following compiler error:

```
BoxPrinterTest.java:23: incompatible types
found    : java.lang.String
required: java.lang.Integer
                Integer intValue2 = value2.getValue();
```

That's good, isn't it? Instead of a ClassCastException in the case of using an Object class in BoxPrinter, you got a compiler error (incompatible types). Now, you can fix this error and the program will work correctly.

 Generics offer generic implementation with type safety.

On the basis of this simple introduction, let's learn more about generics using a few examples.

Creating Generic Classes

Let's create a Pair generic class that can hold objects of two different types, T1 and T2 (see Listing 6-6). Don't worry too much about how useful this is for real-world problem solving; just try to understand how to write generics of your own.

Listing 6-6. PairTest.java

```
// It demonstrates the usage of generics in defining classes
class Pair<T1, T2> {
        T1 object1;
        T2 object2;
        Pair(T1 one, T2 two) {
                object1 = one;
                object2 = two;
        }
        public T1 getFirst() {
                return object1;
        }
        public T2 getSecond() {
                return object2;
        }
}
```

```
class PairTest {
        public static void main(String []args) {
                Pair<Integer, String> worldCup = new Pair<Integer, String>(2010, "South Africa");
                System.out.println("World cup " +  worldCup.getFirst() +
                        " in " + worldCup.getSecond());
        }
}
```

This program prints the following:

```
World cup 2010 in South Africa
```

Here T1 and T2 are type holders. You give these type placeholders inside angle brackets: <T1, T2>. When using the Pair class, you must specify which specific types you are going to use in place of T1 and T2. For example, you use Integer and String for Pair, as in Pair<Integer, String> in the main() method. Now, think of the Pair class as if it has this body:

```
// how Pair<Integer, String> can be treated internally
class Pair {
        Integer object1;
        String object2;
        Pair(Integer one, String two) {
                object1 = one;
                object2 = two;
        }
        public Integer getFirst() {
                return object1;
        }
        public String getSecond() {
                return object2;
        }
}
```

In other words, try manually doing a find-and-replace for the type placeholders and replace them with actual types in the code. This will help you understand how generics actually work. With this, you can understand how the getFirst() and getSecond() methods return Integer and String values in the main() method.

In the statement

```
Pair<Integer, String> worldCup = new Pair<Integer, String>(2010, "South Africa");
```

note that the types match exactly. If you try

```
Pair<Integer, String> worldCup = new Pair<String, String>(2010, "South Africa");
```

you'll get the following compiler error:

```
TestPair.java:20: cannot find symbol
symbol  : constructor Pair(int,java.lang.String)
location: class Pair<java.lang.String,java.lang.String>
```

Now, how about trying this statement?

```
Pair<Integer, String> worldCup = new Pair<Number, String>(2010, "South Africa");
```

You'll get another compiler error because of the type mismatch in the declared type of worldCup and the type given in the initialization expression:

```
TestPair.java:20: incompatible types
found   : Pair<java.lang.Number,java.lang.String>
required: Pair<java.lang.Integer,java.lang.String>
```

Now modify the generic Pair class. Pair<T1, T2> stores objects of type T1 and T2. How about a generic pair class that takes a type T and stores two objects of that type T? Obviously, one way to do that is to instantiate Pair<T1, T2> with same type, say Pair<String, String>, but it is not a good solution. Why? There is no way to ensure that you are instantiating the Pair with same types! Listing 6-7 is a modified version of Pair—let's call it PairOfT—that takes ones type placeholder T.

Listing 6-7. PairOfT.java

```java
// This program shows how to use generics in your programs

class PairOfT<T> {
        T object1;
        T object2;
        PairOfT(T one, T two) {
                object1 = one;
                object2 = two;
        }
        public T getFirst() {
                return object1;
        }
        public T getSecond() {
                return object2;
        }
}
```

Now, will this statement work?

```
PairOfT<Integer, String> worldCup = new PairOfT<Integer, String>(2010, "South Africa");
```

No, because PairOfT takes one type parameter and you have given two type parameters here. So, you'll get a compiler error. So, how about this statement?

```
PairOfT<String> worldCup = new PairOfT<String>(2010, "South Africa");
```

No, you still get a compiler error:

```
TestPair.java:20: cannot find symbol
symbol  : constructor PairOfT(int,java.lang.String)
location: class PairOfT<java.lang.String>
        PairOfT<String> worldCup = new PairOfT<String>(2010, "South Africa");
```

The reason is that 2010—when boxed—is an Integer and you should give a String as argument. How about this statement?

```
PairOfT<String> worldCup = new PairOfT<String>("2010", "South Africa");
```

Yes, it compiles and will work fine.

Diamond Syntax

In the previous section, we discussed how to create generic type instances, as in the following statement:

```
Pair<Integer, String> worldCup = new Pair<Integer, String>(2010, "South Africa");
```

We also discussed how a compiler error will result if these types don't match, as in the following statement, which will not compile:

```
Pair<Integer, String> worldCup = new Pair<String, String>(2010, "South Africa");
```

See how tedious it is to ensure that you provide same type parameters in both the declaration type (Pair<Integer, String> in this case) and the new object creation expression (new Pair<String, String>() in this case)?

To simplify your life, Java 7 has introduced the *diamond* syntax, in which the type parameters may be omitted: you can just leave it to the compiler to infer the types from the type declaration. So, the declaration can be simplified as

```
Pair<Integer, String> worldCup = new Pair<>(2010, "South Africa");
```

To make it clear, Listing 6-8 contains the full program making use of this diamond syntax.

Listing 6-8. Pair.java

```
// This program shows the usage of the diamond syntax while using generics
class Pair<T1, T2> {
        T1 object1;
        T2 object2;
        Pair(T1 one, T2 two) {
                object1 = one;
                object2 = two;
        }
        public T1 getFirst() {
                return object1;
        }
        public T2 getSecond() {
                return object2;
        }
}
```

```
class TestPair {
        public static void main(String []args) {
                Pair<Integer, String> worldCup = new Pair<>(2010, "South Africa");
                System.out.println("World cup " + worldCup.getFirst() +
                        " in " + worldCup.getSecond());
        }
}
```

This program will compile cleanly and print the following statement:

```
World cup 2010 in South Africa
```

Note that it is a common mistake to forget the diamond operator < > in the initialization expression, as in

```
Pair<Integer, String> worldCup = new Pair (2010, "South Africa");
```

Figure 6-2 shows the compiler warning when you forget to use the diamond syntax. Since Pair is a generic type and you forgot to use the < > or provide the type parameters explicitly, the compiler treats it as a raw type with Pair taking two Object type parameters. Though this behavior did not cause any problem in this particular code segment, it is dangerous and can cause bugs, as the next section shows.

Figure 6-2. *Compiler warning when you forget to use diamond syntax*

Interoperability of Raw Types and Generic Types

A generic type can be used without specifying its associated type; in that case, the type is referred to as *raw type*. For instance, List<T> should be used along with an associated type (i.e., List<String>); however, it can be used without specifying the accompanied type (i.e., List). In the latter case, the List is referred to as raw type.

When you use a raw type, you lose the advantage of type safety afforded by generics. For instance, the type Vector in Listing 6-1 is a raw type. At the time of compilation, the compiler generates a warning, as shown in Figure 6-1. Raw types bypass the type checking at compile time; however, they might throw runtime exceptions (for instance, ClassCastException). Therefore, it is not recommended to use raw types in new code.

Okay, now you understand that you should not use raw types. But, you may ask, why does the compiler itself deny such type declarations? The answer is *backward compatibility*. Java generics were introduced in Java SDK 5. Java supports raw types in order to make the generics-based code compatible with legacy code. However, it is strongly recommended that you should not use raw types going forward.

Why? What will happen if you use raw types along with generics? Let's use both types in Listing 6-9 and examine the effect.

Listing 6-9. RawTest.java

```java
//This program demonstrates usage of raw types along with generics
class RawTest{
        public static void main(String []args) {
                List list = new LinkedList();
                list.add("First");
                list.add("Second");
                List<String> strList = list;   //#1
                for(Iterator<String> itemItr = strList.iterator(); itemItr.hasNext();)
                        System.out.println("Item : " + itemItr.next());

                List<String> strList2 = new LinkedList<>();
                strList2.add("First");
                strList2.add("Second");
                List list2 = strList2;   //#2
                for(Iterator<String> itemItr = list2.iterator(); itemItr.hasNext();)
                        System.out.println("Item : " + itemItr.next());
        }
}
```

What you expect from the above program? Do you think it will compile/execute properly? Well, yes—it will compile (with warnings) and execute without any problem. It prints the following:

```
Item : First
Item : Second
Item : First
Item : Second
```

Listing 6-10 introduces a couple of changes; observe the output.

Listing 6-10. RawTest2.java

```java
// This program demonstrates usage of raw types along with generics
class RawTest{
        public static void main(String []args) {
                List list = new LinkedList();
                list.add("First");
                list.add("Second");
                List<String> strList = list;
                strList.add(10);          //#1: generates compiler error
                for(Iterator<String> itemItr = strList.iterator(); itemItr.hasNext();)
                System.out.println("Item : " + itemItr.next());
```

```
                    List<String> strList2 = new LinkedList<>();
                    strList2.add("First");
                    strList2.add("Second");
                    List list2 = strList2;
                    list2.add(10);  //#2: compiles fine, results in runtime exception
                    for(Iterator<String> itemItr = list2.iterator(); itemItr.hasNext();)
                        System.out.println("Item : " + itemItr.next());
        }
}
```

In the above example, you added two statements. The first statement is as follows:

```
strList.add(10);        //#1: generates compiler error
```

You are trying to add an integer item in a List<String> type list, so you get a compile-time error. As discussed earlier, this type checking at the compiler level is good, as without it in a runtime exception might have resulted later on. Here is the second statement you added:

```
list2.add(10);        //#2: compiles fine, results in runtime exception
```

Here, the list2 linked-list (raw type) is initialized with a generic type List<String>. After the initialization, you added an integer in the list raw type. This is allowed since list2 is a raw type. However, it will result in a ClassCastException.

What can you learn from these two examples? The lesson is to avoid mixing raw types and generic types in your programs, since it might result in erroneous behavior at runtime. If you need to use both in a program, make sure you add a single type of items in the containers and retrieve using the same type.

 Avoid mixing raw types with generic types.

Generic Methods

Similarly to generic classes, you can create generic methods—that is, methods that take generic parameter types. Generic methods are useful for writing methods that are applicable to a wide range of types while the functionality remains the same. For example, there are numerous generic methods in the java.util.Collections class.

Let's implement a simple method named fill(). Given a container, the fill() method fills all the container elements with value val. Listing 6-11 contains the implementation of the fill() method in the Utilities class.

Listing 6-11. Utilities.java

```
// This program demonstrates generic methods
class Utilities {
        public static <T> void fill(List<T> list, T val) {
                for(int i = 0; i < list.size(); i++)
                        list.set(i, val);
        }
}
```

```
class UtilitiesTest {
        public static void main(String []args) {
                List<Integer> intList = new ArrayList<Integer>();
                intList.add(10);
                intList.add(20);
                System.out.println("The original list is: " + intList);
                Utilities.fill(intList, 100);
                System.out.println("The list after calling Utilities.fill() is: " + intList);
        }
}
```

It prints the following:

```
The original list is: [10, 20]
The list after calling Utilities.fill() is: [100, 100]
```

Let's look step-by-step at this code:

1. You create a method named fill() in the Utilities class with this declaration:

    ```
    public static <T> void fill(List<T> list, T val)
    ```

You declare the generic type parameter T in this method. After the qualifiers public and static, you put <T> and then followed it by return type, method name, and its parameters. This declaration is different from generic classes—you give the generic type parameters after the class name in generic classes.

2. In the body, you write the code as if it's a normal method.

    ```
    for(int i = 0; i < list.size(); i++)
            list.set(i, val);
    ```

You loop over the list from 0 until it's sized and set each of the elements to value val in each iteration. You use the set() method in List, which takes the index position in the container as the first argument and the actual value to be set as the second argument.

3. In the main() method in the UtilitiesTest class, this is how you call the fill() method:

    ```
    Utilities.fill(intList, 100);
    ```

Note that you didn't give the generic type parameter value explicitly. Since intList is of type Integer and 100 is boxed to type Integer, the compiler inferred that the type T in the fill() method is of type Integer.

 It is a common mistake to import List from java.awt instead of java.util. Your program may not compile (or it may produce warnings) if you are not using the correct import. Remember, List from java.util is a generic type while List from java.awt is not.

We've discussed the static generic methods. How about non-static generic methods? Hmm, well, there is almost no difference when it comes to non-static methods. Obviously, you need to create an instance of the class in which the non-static method is defined in order to use the non-static method.

Generics and Subtyping

Here is a pop quiz.

Question: Only *one* of the following assignments is correct and compiles without errors. Which one is it? (Note: List is an abstract class, ArrayList extends List; similarly, Number is an abstract class and Integer extends Number).

1. `List<Integer> intList = new List<Integer>();`

2. `List<Integer> intList = new ArrayList<Integer>();`

3. `List<Number> intList = new ArrayList<Integer>();`

4. `List<Integer> intList = new ArrayList<Number>();`

Answer: Only the second assignment will compile without errors.
Why? Let's discuss each of the options.

1. You are trying to assign intList of List<Integer> type to an object of type List<Integer>. But List is an abstract class. You cannot instantiate an abstract class, so you get a compiler error.

2. You are trying to assign intList of List<Integer> type with an object of type ArrayList<Integer>. Since ArrayList extends List, this is valid assignment and you don't get a compiler error.

3. You are trying to assign intList of List<Number> type with an object of type ArrayList<Integer>. ArrayList extends List—that is okay—but the generic parameter should be of the same type in the declaration as well as the initialization. So, you'll get a compiler error (type mismatch).

4. Same reason as in option 3.

You can assign a derived type object to its base type reference; this is what you mean by *subtyping*. However, for generics, the type parameters should match exactly—otherwise you'll get a compiler error. In other words, *subtyping does not work for generic parameters*. Yes, this is a difficult rule to remember, so let's discuss in more detail why subtyping doesn't work for generic type parameters.

For class types, subtyping works. You can assign a derived type object to its base type reference.
For generic type parameters, however, subtyping does not work. You cannot assign a derived generic type parameter to a base type parameter.

Why doesn't subtyping work for generic type parameters? Let's look at what can go wrong if you assume that you can use subtyping for generic type parameters.

```
// illegal code - assume that the following intialization is allowed
List<Number> intList = new ArrayList<Integer>();
intList.add(new Integer(10)); // okay
intList.add(new Float(10.0f)); // oops!
```

The `intList` of `List<Number>` type is supposed to hold an `ArrayList<Number>` object. However, you are storing an `ArrayList<Integer>`. This looks reasonable since `List` extends `ArrayList` and `Integer` extends `Number`. However, you can end up inserting a `Float` value in the `intList`! Recall that the dynamic type of `intList` is the `ArrayList<Integer>` type—so you are violating type safety here (and thus will get the compiler error of incompatible types). Since generics are designed to avoid type-safety mistakes like this, you cannot assign a derived generic type parameter to a base type parameter.

As you can see, subtyping for generic parameter types is not allowed because it is unsafe—but still it is an inconvenient limitation. Fortunately, Java supports *wildcard parameter types* in which you can use subtyping. We'll explore that capability now.

 Type parameters for generics have a limitation: generic type parameters should match exactly for assignments. To overcome this subtyping problem, you can use wildcard types.

Wildcard Parameters

You saw in the preceding section that subtyping doesn't work for generic type parameters. So,

```
List<Number> intList = new ArrayList<Integer>();
```

gives the compiler error of

```
WildCardUse.java:6: incompatible types
found    : java.util.ArrayList<java.lang.Integer>
required: java.util.List<java.lang.Number>
                List<Number> numList = new ArrayList<Integer>();
```

If you slightly change the statement to use wildcard parameter, it will compile

```
List<?> wildCardList = new ArrayList<Integer>();
```

What does a *wildcard* mean? Just like the wildcard you use for substituting for any card in a card game (ah, it's so fun to play card games!), you can use a wildcard to indicate that it can match for any type. With `List<?>`, you mean that it is a `List` of any type—in other words, you can say it is a "list of unknowns!"

But wait a minute…when you want a type indicating "any type," you use the `Object` class, don't you? How about the same statement, but using the `Object` type parameter?

```
List<Object> numList = new ArrayList<Integer>();
```

No luck—you get the same error you got above using List<Number>!

```
WildCardUse.java:6: incompatible types
found    : java.util.ArrayList<java.lang.Integer>
required: java.util.List<java.lang.Object>
              List<Object> numList = new ArrayList<Integer>();
```

In other words, you are still trying to use subtyping for generic parameters—and it still doesn't work. As you can see, List<Object> is not same as List<?>. In fact, List<?> is a supertype of any List type, which means you can pass List<Integer>, or List<String>, or even List<Object> where List<?> is expected.

Let's use the wildcard in an example and see whether it'll work (see Listing 6-12).

Listing 6-12. WildCardUse.java

```java
// This program demonstrates the usage of wild card parameters
class WildCardUse {
        static void printList(List<?> list){
                for(Object l:list)
                        System.out.println("[" + l + "]");
        }

        public static void main(String []args) {
                List<Integer> list = new ArrayList<>();
                list.add(10);
                list.add(100);
                printList(list);
                List<String> strList = new ArrayList<>();
                strList.add("10");
                strList.add("100");
                printList(strList);
        }
}
```

This program prints the following:

```
[10]
[100]
[10]
[100]
```

Well, it works, and the list using wildcard can be passed list of integers as well as list of strings. This happens because of the parameter type of printList() method—List<?>. That's great!

Limitations of Wildcards

Let's consider the following snippet, which tries to add an element and print the list:

```java
List<?> wildCardList = new ArrayList<Integer>();
wildCardList.add(new Integer(10));
System.out.println(wildCardList);
```

You get the following compiler error:

```
WildCardUse.java:7: cannot find symbol
symbol  : method add(java.lang.Integer)
location: interface java.util.List<capture#145 of ? extends java.lang.Number>
               wildCardList.add(new Integer(10));
```

Why? You are absolutely sure that the add() method exists in the List interface. Then why doesn't the compiler find the method?

The problem requires some detailed explanation. When you use wildcard type <?>, you say to the compiler that you are *ignoring* the type information, so <?> stands for unknown type. Every time you try to pass arguments to a generic type, the java compiler tries to infer the type of the passed argument as well as the type of the generics and to justify the type safety. Now, you are trying to use the add() method to insert an element in the list. Since wildCardList doesn't know which type of objects it holds, it is risky to add elements to it. You might end up adding a string—"hello", for example—instead of an integer value. To avoid this problem (remember, generics was introduced in the language to ensure type safety!), the compiler doesn't allow you to call methods that modify the object. Since the add method modifies the object, you get an error! The error message also looks confusing, as in <capture#145 of ? extends java.lang.Number>.

 In general, when you use wildcard parameters, you cannot call methods that modify the object. If you try to modify, the compiler will give you confusing error messages. However, you can call methods that access the object.

Bounded Wildcards

Here is a quick recap on wildcards to understand why you need *bounded wildcards*. You get a compiler error when you try generic types differing in their parameter types, as in

```
// compiler error:
List<Number> numList = new ArrayList<Integer>();
```

You use wildcard types to avoid this compiler error:

```
// now works:
List<?> numList = new ArrayList<Integer>();
```

Assume you want to be able to store only the list of numbers in the numList. However, you might end up storing a list of any type with wildcards, as in

```
List<?> numList = new ArrayList<Integer>();
numList = new ArrayList<String>();
```

Yes, it compiles without any errors. How do you restrict numList to refer to only to Number and its derived classes like Integer, Double, etc.? You do it by using bounded wildcards, like so:

```
List<? extends Number> numList = new ArrayList<Integer>();
numList = new ArrayList<String>();
```

You get the following compiler error:

```
BoundedWildCardUse.java:7: incompatible types
found    : java.util.ArrayList<java.lang.String>
required: java.util.List<? extends java.lang.Number>
                numList = new ArrayList<String>();
```

How about this code?

```
List<? extends Number> numList = new ArrayList<Integer>();
numList = new ArrayList<Double>();
```

Yes, it compiles fine! What is going on here? In List<? extends Number>, the wildcard (?) is bounded with extends Number. This means that any type you substitute for wildcard (?) should satisfy the condition extends Number. For example, in ? extends Number, if you substitute ? with type Integer, you get Integer extends Number—which is logically true. So the compilation will succeed for such substitution. But, in ? extends Number, if you substitute ? with type String, you get String extends Number, which is logically false (remember that String is *not* a Number). So, you get a compiler error. In other words, you limit or bound the wildcard so that the substituted type must be of the extend Number class.

You can use bounded wildcards in method arguments, return types, etc. Here's a simple method that uses bounded wildcards:

```
public static Double sum(List<? extends Number> numList) {
        Double result = 0.0;
        for(Number num : numList) {
                result += num.doubleValue();
        }
        return result;
}
```

Here is a step-by-step description of this method:

1. The method sum() is meant for taking a list of Numbers and returning the sum of the elements in that list.

2. Since the List is to be limited (bounded) by Number, you declare List as List<? Extends Number>.

3. Since you don't know the exact type of the list elements (Integer, Double, etc.), you want to use double as the return type for sum. Since primitive types like int and double are implicitly boxed/unboxed when used with collections, you declare the return type as Double, which is more convenient than using the primitive type double.

4. Coming to the body of the method, since the sum of elements is going to be a Double value, you declare the result variable Double and initialize it with zero.

5. In the for-each loop, you use Number as the loop type. Since the wildcard is bounded by Number, you know that (no matter which List object is actually passed as argument) the element type is going to be a Number.

6. You get the double value from the Number type using the doubleValue method.

7. You return the sum of the elements once you are done.

Listing 6-13 contains the main() method to test the sum() method.

Listing 6-13. BoundedWildCardUse.java

```java
// This program demonstrates the usage of bounded wild cards

import java.util.*;

class BoundedWildCardUse {
        public static Double sum(List<? extends Number> numList) {
                Double result = 0.0;
                for(Number num : numList) {
                        result += num.doubleValue();
                }
                return result;
        }

        public static void main(String []args) {
                List<Integer> intList = new ArrayList<Integer>();
                List<Double> doubleList = new ArrayList<Double>();

                for(int i = 0; i < 5; i++) {
                        intList.add(i);
                        doubleList.add((double) (i * i));
                }
                System.out.println("The intList is: " + intList);
                System.out.println("The sum of elements in intList is: " + sum(intList));

                System.out.println("The doubleList is: " + doubleList);
                System.out.println("The sum of elements in doubleList is: " + sum(doubleList));
        }
}
```

It prints the following:

```
The intList is: [0, 1, 2, 3, 4]
The sum of elements in intList is: 10.0
The doubleList is: [0.0, 1.0, 4.0, 9.0, 16.0]
The sum of elements in doubleList is: 30.0
```

Let's go over the code step-by-step:

1. You create two ArrayLists, one of type Integer and another of type Double.

2. In a for loop, you insert five elements each into the lists. For intList, you insert the values 0 to 4. For doubleList, you insert the square of the values 0 to 4 (0 to 16). Since the doubleList expects the value to be double values, to make it explicit, you use an explicit cast—((double) (i * i)); if you want, you can remove that explicit cast.

3. You print the contents of the intList and doubleList and also print the sum of elements by calling the sum() method you wrote; from the output you can see that the sum() method worked correctly for both types Integer and Double.

Similarly to using the extends keyword with wildcards, as in <? extends Number>, you can use the super keyword, as in <? super Integer>. The expression <? super X> means that you can use any super type (class or interface) including the type X. For instance, the following code snippet compiles well. You may observe that <? super Integer> does not only mean super types of Integer; this expression allows Integer, too.

```
List<? super Integer> intList = new ArrayList<Integer>();
System.out.println("The intList is: " + intList);
```

In the bounded wildcard, <? extends X>, X may be a class or an interface (note that even for interfaces you use the extends keyword). The valid substitution for ? is not just any of its derived classes and interfaces; you can substitute ? for X itself! This is also applicable with <? super X> expressions.

Wildcards in the Collections Class

The collections framework uses wildcards extensively. To understand some more features of bounded wildcards and how wildcards are used in practice, here are some examples from the Collections class.

The first example is the nCopies method:

```
static <T> List<T> nCopies(int num, T obj)
```

The nCopies method returns a read-only List of num elements with value obj. Here is an example:

```
System.out.println("List of 5 elements filled with values 10: " + Collections.nCopies(5, 10));
```

It prints the following:

```
List of 5 elements filled with values 10: [10, 10, 10, 10, 10]
```

The next example is the reverse method:

```
static void reverse(List<?> list);
```

The reverse() method reverses the order of elements in the passed list. You can pass elements of any type; the Collections class just uses the wildcard <?> for the List type.

Here's another example:

```
static <T> void fill(List<? super T> list, T obj)
```

This method fills the whole of the list with values obj. Here you use <? super T>. Why? Here is an example:

```
List<Object> objList = new ArrayList<Object>();
objList.add(new Object());
objList.add(new Object());

Collections.fill(objList, "hello");
System.out.println("The objList is: " + objList);
```

It prints the following:

```
The objList is: [hello, hello]
```

Here, you create a List<Object> that points to an ArrayList<Object>. You create two dummy Objects and insert objList. Then you fill the objList with the String "hello" and it works. As you can see, for the fill() method you can pass a base type List as the first argument.

And for now the final (and rather tough) example: the copy() method. Its declaration:

```
static <T> void copy(List<? super T> dest, List<? extends T> src);
```

The copy() method copies all the elements from src List to dest List. Here is an example to understand why dest is <? super T> and src is <? extends T>:

```
List<? extends Number> intList = Collections.nCopies(5, new Integer(10));
List<Object> objList = new ArrayList<Object>();
for(int i = 0; i < 5; i++) {
        objList.add(new Object());
}

Collections.copy(objList, intList);
System.out.println("The objList is: " + objList);
```

It prints the following:

```
The objList is: [10, 10, 10, 10, 10]
```

Here is a step-by-step description of what's happening in this code:

1. You first create a list intList of type List<? extends Number>. You initialize it with a List filled with five instances of Integer object with value 10 (i.e. new Integer(10);). This is the source List type you are going to use for the Collections.copy method.

2. You create another list objList of type List<Object> and initialize it with an ArrayList<Object>. You initialize objList with five dummy Object instances. You are going to use this List as the target for Collections.copy. Why didn't you use the nCopies method just like what you did for intList? Because the List returned by nCopies is a read-only list and if you use that List as a target for the copy() method, you'll get an UnsupportedOperationException.

3. You use objList as the destination (target) and intList as the source for the Collections.copy method. Now, the type T inferred is Number. As you can see, the src is of type <? extends T> (i.e., for intList); when you substitute Integer as in <Integer extends Number>, the compilation succeeds. Similarly, the dest is of type <? extends T> (i.e., for objList); when you substitute Object as in <Object super Number>, the compilation succeeds.

4. You print the copied integer values in objList.

When you use (or want to use) `<T>`, `<?>`, `<? extends T>`, or `<? super T>` with a specific type, substitute the T with the actual type and visualize how the replaced type would look. This is the easiest way to understand the correct usage of generics with wildcards in collection classes.

Points to Remember

Here are some pointers that might prove valuable in your OCPJP 7 exam:

- It's possible to define or declare generic methods in an interface or a class even if the class or the interface itself is not generic.

- A generic class used without type arguments is known as a *raw type*. Of course, raw types are not type safe. Java supports raw types so that it is possible to use the generic type in code that is older than Java 5 (note that generics were introduced in Java 5). The compiler generates a warning when you use raw types in your code. You may use `@SuppressWarnings({ "unchecked" })` to suppress the warning associated with raw types.

- `List<?>` is a supertype of any `List` type, which means you can pass `List<Integer>`, or `List<String>`, or even `List<Object>` where `List<?>` is expected.

- Implementation of generics is static in nature, which means that the Java compiler interprets the generics specified in the source code and replaces the generic code with concrete types. This is referred to as *type erasure*. After compilation, the code looks similar to what a developer would have written with concrete types. Essentially, the use of generics offers two advantages: first, it introduces an abstraction, which enables you to write generic implementation; second, it allows you to write generic implementation with type safety.

- There are many limitations of generic types due to type erasure. A few important ones are as follows:

    - You cannot instantiate a generic type using new operator. For example, assuming mem is a field, the following statement will result in a compiler error:

      ```
      T mem = new T();          // wrong usage - compiler error
      ```

    - You cannot instantiate an array of a generic type. For example, assuming mem is a field, the following statement will result in a compiler error:

      ```
      T[] amem = new T[100];    // wrong usage - compiler error
      ```

    - You can declare non-static fields of type T, but not of static fields of type T. For example,

      ```
      class X<T> {
        T instanceMem;          // okay
        static T statMem;       // wrong usage - compiler error
      }
      ```

- It is not possible to have generic exception classes; as a result, the following will not compile:

```
class GenericException<T> extends Throwable { } // wrong usage - compiler error
```

- You cannot instantiate a generic type with primitive types—in other words, List<int> cannot be instantiated. However, you can use boxed primitive types.

- The meaning of "extends" and "super" changes in the context of generics. For instance, when you say <? extends X>, you refer to all types that extend X and the type X itself.

The Collections Framework

In the first part of the chapter, we discussed generics in detail. The main use of generics is to be able to write reusable (and type-safe) data structures and algorithms. The Java library has a collections framework that makes extensive use of generics and provides a set of containers and algorithms.

In this section, we will focus on how to use the collections framework. To use collections correctly, you must understand certain related topics. To use collections like HashSet, you must override the hashCode() and equals() methods correctly. To compare objects and store them in collections, you must learn how to use Comparator, Comparable, etc. Since the collections framework uses generics extensively, you'll revisit some of the topics related to generics in the context of the collections framework to gain a better understanding of generics.

Why Reusable Classes?

Assume that you want to write a simple program to get the extension number of a colleague in your company. For that, you have to keep a list of your colleague's names and their extension numbers. In this simple directory you will rarely add or delete entries, but you will frequently look up entries—so the lookup should be very fast.

To implement this simple directory, you must implement a class that *maps* the name (a string) and an extension number (an integer or a string). You must implement methods like adding and deleting entries, looking up extension numbers given the name, etc. Additionally, you can implement methods like getting all the colleagues names, all extension numbers, etc. Implementing a class with all these features—and implementing them correctly and testing these features—takes a lot of time.

Fortunately, Java has data structures like this already implemented in the java.util package. You can just (re) use java.util.HashMap to implement your simple directory. You'll see examples of implementations like this later, but it's important to know that you can just use the data structures readily available in the Java library rather than implementing them yourself.

Basic Components of the Collections Framework

The Java collections framework has three main components:

- **Abstract classes and interfaces:** The collections framework has many abstract classes and interfaces providing general functionality. By learning them, you'll know the offered functionality in terms of public methods.

- **Concrete classes:** These are the actual instances of containers that you'll be using in the programs.

- **Algorithms:** The java.util.Collections implements commonly require functionality like sorting, searching, etc. These methods are *generic*: you can use these methods on different containers.

Plese note that *collection(s)* is a generic term, while `Collection` and `Collections` are the specific APIs of the `java.util` package. `Collections`—as in `java.util.Collections`–is a utility class that contains only static methods. The general term *collection(s)* refers to a container like map, stack, queue, etc. We'll use the term *container(s)* when referring to these *collection(s)* in this chapter to avoid confusion.

Abstract Classes and Interfaces

The type hierarchy in the `java.util` library consists of numerous abstract classes and interfaces that provide generic functionality. Table 6-1 and Figure 6-3 list and display a few important types in this hierarchy. We'll cover some of these types in more detail in later sections of this chapter.

Table 6-1. *Important Abstract Classes and Interfaces in the Collections Framework*

Abstract Class/Interface	Short Description
`Iterable`	A class implementing this interface can be used for iterating with a `for each` statement.
`Collection`	Common base interface for classes in the collection hierarchy. When you want to write methods that are very general, you can pass the `Collection` interface. For example, `max()` method in `java.util.Collections` takes a `Collection` and returns an object.
`List`	Base interface for containers that store a sequence of elements. You can access the elements using an index, and retrieve the same element later (so that it maintains the insertion order). You can store duplicate elements in a `List`.
`Set, SortedSet, NavigableSet` `Queue, Deque`	Interfaces for containers that don't allow duplicate elements. `SortedSet` maintains the set elements in a sorted order. `NavigableSet` allows searching the set for the closest matches.
	`Queue` is a base interface for containers that holds a sequence of elements for processing. For example, the classes implementing `Queue` can be LIFO (last in, first out— as in stack data structure) or FIFO (first in, first out—as in queue data structure). In a `Deque` you can insert or remove elements from *both* the ends.
`Map, SortedMap, NavigableMap`	Base class for containers that map keys to values. In `SortedMap`, the keys are in a sorted order. A `NavigableMap` allows you to search and return the closest match for given search criteria. Note that `Map` hierarchy does *not* extend the `Collection` interface.
`Iterator, ListIterator`	You can traverse over the container in the forward direction if a class implements the `Iterator` interface. You can traverse in both forward and reverse directions if a class implements the `ListIterator` interface.

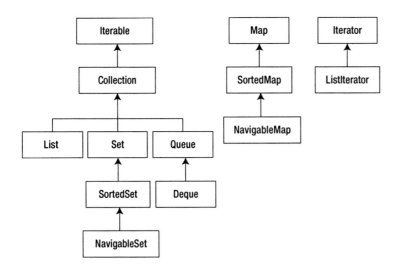

Figure 6-3. *Important high-level java.util interfaces and their inheritance relationships*

Those are quite a few base types, but don't get overwhelmed by them. You'll see specific concrete classes and use some of these base types. We'll only cover the Collection interface and then move on to cover concrete classes by covering each part in this collection hierarchy.

The Collection Interface

The Collection interface provides methods such as add() and remove() that are common to all containers. Table 6-2 lists the most important methods in this interface. Take a look at them before you use them.

Table 6-2. *Important Methods in the Collection Interface*

Method	Short description
boolean add(Element elem)	Adds elem into the underlying container.
void clear()	Removes all elements from the container.
boolean isEmpty()	Checks whether the container has any elements or not.
Iterator<Element> iterator()	Returns an Iterator<Element> object for iterating over the container.
boolean remove(Object obj)	Removes the element if obj is present in the container.
int size()	Returns the number of elements in the container.
Object[] toArray()	Returns an array that has all elements in the container.

Methods such as add() and remove() can fail depending on the underlying container. For example, if the container is read-only, you will not be able to add or remove elements. Apart from these methods, there are many methods in the Collection interface that apply to multiple elements in the container (Table 6-3).

Table 6-3. *Methods in the Collection Interface That Apply to Multiple Elements*

Method	Short Description
`boolean addAll(Collection<? extends Element> coll)`	Adds all the elements in `coll` into the underlying container.
`boolean containsAll(Collection<?> coll)`	Checks if all elements given in `coll` are present in the underlying container.
`boolean removeAll(Collection<?> coll)`	Removes all elements from the underlying container that are also present in `coll`.
`boolean retainAll(Collection<?> coll)`	Retains elements in the underlying container only if they are also present in `coll`; it removes all other elements.

Concrete Classes

Numerous interfaces and abstract classes in the `Collection` hierarchy provide the common methods that specific concrete classes implement/extend. The concrete classes provide the actual functionality, and you'll have to learn only a handful of them to be properly prepared for the OCPJP 7 exam. Table 6-4 summarizes the features of the classes you should know.

Table 6-4. *Important Concrete Classes in Collection Framework*

Concrete Class	Short Description
`ArrayList`	Internally implemented as a resizable array. This is one of the most widely used concrete classes. Fast to search, but slow to insert or delete. Allows duplicates.
`LinkedList`	Internally implements a doubly-linked list data structure. Fast to insert or delete elements, but slow for searching elements. Additionally, `LinkedList` can be used when you need a stack (LIFO) or queue (FIFO) data structure. Allows duplicates.
`HashSet`	Internally implemented as a hash-table data structure. Used for storing a set of elements—it does not allow storing duplicate elements. Fast for searching and retrieving elements. It does *not* maintain any order for stored elements.
`TreeSet`	Internally implements a red-black tree data structure. Like `HashSet`, `TreeSet` does not allow storing duplicates. However, unlike `HashSet`, it stores the elements in a sorted order. It uses a tree data structure to decide where to store or search the elements, and the position is decided by the sorting order.
`HashMap`	Internally implemented as a hash-table data structure. Stores key and value pairs. Uses hashing for finding a place to search or store a pair. Searching or inserting is very fast. It does *not* store the elements in any order.
`TreeMap`	Internally implemented using a red-black tree data structure. Unlike `HashMap`, `TreeMap` stores the elements in a sorted order. It uses a tree data structure to decide where to store or search for keys, and the position is decided by the sorting order.
`PriorityQueue`	Internally implemented using heap data structure. A `PriorityQueue` is for retrieving elements based on priority. Irrespective of the order in which you insert, when you remove the elements, the highest priority element will be retrieved first.

There are many old `java.util` classes (now known as legacy collection types) that were superceded by new collection classes. Some of them are (with newer types in parentheses): `Enumeration` (`Iterator`), `Vector` (`ArrayList`), `Dictionary` (`Map`), and `Hashtable` (`HashMap`). In addition, `Stack` and `Properties` are legacy classes that do not have direct replacements.

The Iterator Interface

Let's discuss `Iterator` first since we will be using `Iterator` to illustrate other concrete classes. The `Iterator` interface is a simple interface with only three methods: `hasNext()`, `next()`, and `remove()` (see Table 6-5).

Table 6-5. *Methods in the Iterator Interface*

Method	Short Description
boolean hasNext()	Checks if the iterator has more elements to traverse.
E next()	Moves the iterator to the next element and returns that (next) element.
void remove()	Removes the last visited element from the underlying container. `next()` should have been called before calling `remove()`; otherwise it will throw an `IllegalStateException`.

List Classes

`List`s are used for storing a sequence of elements. You can insert an element of the container in a specific position using an index, and retrieve the same element later (i.e., it maintains the insertion order). You can store duplicate elements in a list. There are two concrete classes that you need to know: `ArrayList` and `LinkedList`.

ArrayList Class

`ArrayList` implements a resizable array. When you create a native array (say, new `String[10];`), the size of the array is known (fixed) at the time of creation. However, `ArrayList` is a *dynamic array*: it can grow in size as required. Internally, an `ArrayList` allocates a block of memory and grows it as required. So, accessing array elements is very fast in an `ArrayList`. However, when you add or remove elements, internally the rest of the elements are copied; so addition/deletion of elements is a costly operation.

Here's a simple example to visit elements in an `ArrayList`. You take an `ArrayList` and use the `for-each` construct for traversing a collection:

```
ArrayList<String> languageList = new ArrayList<>();
languageList.add("C");
languageList.add("C++");
languageList.add("Java");
for(String language : languageList) {
    System.out.println(language);
}
```

It prints the following:

```
C
C++
Java
```

This for-each is equivalent to the following code, which explicitly uses an Iterator:

```
for(Iterator<String> languageIter = languageList.iterator(); languageIter.hasNext();) {
        String language = languageIter.next();
        System.out.println(language);
}
```

This code segment will also print the same output as the previous for-each loop code. Here is a step-by-step description of how this for loop works:

1. You use the iterator() method to get the iterator for that container. Since languageList is an ArrayList of type <String>, you should create Iterator with String. Name it languageIter.

2. Before entering the loop, you check if there are any elements to visit. You call the hasNext() method for checking that. If it returns true, there are more elements to visit; if it returns false, the iteration is over and you exit the loop.

3. Once you enter the body of the loop, the first thing you have to do is call next() and move the iterator. The next() method returns the iterated value. You capture that return value in the language variable.

4. You print the language value, and then the loop continues.

This *iteration idiom*—the way you call iterator(), hasNext(), and next() methods—is important to learn; we'll be using either the for-each loop or this idiom extensively in our examples.

Note that you create ArrayList<String> and Iterator<String> instead of just using ArrayList or Iterator (i.e., you provide type information along with these classes). The Collection classes are generic classes; therefore you need to specify the type parameters to use them. Here you are storing/iterating a list of strings, so you use <String>.

You can remove elements while traversing a container using iterators. Let's create an object of ArrayList<Integer> type with ten elements. You'll iterate over the elements and remove all of them (instead of using the removeAll() method in ArrayList). Listing 6-14 shows the code. Will it work?

Listing 6-14. TestIterator.java

```
// This program shows the usage of Iterator

import java.util.*;

class TestIterator {
    public static void main(String []args) {
        ArrayList<Integer> nums = new ArrayList<Integer>();
        for(int i = 1; i < 10; i++)
            nums.add(i);
        System.out.println("Original list " + nums);
        Iterator<Integer> numsIter = nums.iterator();
        while(numsIter.hasNext()) {
                numsIter.remove();
        }
        System.out.println("List after removing all elements" + nums);
    }
}
```

It prints the following:

```
Original list [1, 2, 3, 4, 5, 6, 7, 8, 9]
Exception in thread "main" java.lang.IllegalStateException
        at java.util.AbstractList$Itr.remove(AbstractList.java:356)
        at TestIterator.main(Main.java:12)
```

Oops! What happened? The problem is that you haven't called next() before calling remove(). Checking hasNext() in the while loop condition, moving to the element using next(), and calling remove() is the correct idiom for removing an element. If you don't follow it correctly, you can get into trouble (i.e., you'll get IllegalStateException). Similarly, if you call remove() twice without sandwiching a next() between the statements, you'll get this exception.

Let's fix this program by calling next() before calling remove(). Here is the relevant part of the code:

```
Iterator<Integer> numsIter = nums.iterator();
while(numsIter.hasNext()) {
        numsIter.next();
                numsIter.remove();
}
System.out.println("List after removing all elements " + nums);
```

It prints the list with no elements, as expected:

```
List after removing all elements []
```

Remember that next() needs to be called before calling remove() in an Iterator; otherwise, you'll get an IllegalStateException. Similarly, calling remove() in subsequent statements without calling next() between these statements will also result in this exception. Basically, any modifications to the underlying container while an iterator is traversing through the container will result in this exception.

The ListIterator Interface

You should understand ListIterator first before you look at LinkedList. The ListIterator interface extends the Iterator interface, so it inherits the methods hasNext(), next(), and remove(). Additionally, ListIterator has many other methods (see Table 6-6). Using these methods, you can traverse in the reverse direction, get the previous or next index position, and set or add new elements to the underlying container.

Table 6-6. *Methods in the ListIterator Interface (in Addition to Iterator Methods)*

Method	Short Description
boolean hasPrevious()	Checks if the iterator has more elements to traverse in reverse direction.
Element previous()	Moves the iterator to the next element and returns that (next) element in reverse direction.
int nextIndex()	Returns the index of the next element in the iteration in forward direction.
int previousIndex()	Returns the index of the next element in the iteration in reverse direction.
void set(Element)	Sets the last element visited (using next or previous); it replaces the existing element.
void add(Element)	Adds the element into the list at the current iteration position.

The LinkedList Class

The LinkedList class internally uses a doubly-linked list. So, insertion and deletion is very fast in LinkedList. However, accessing an element entails traversing the nodes one-by-one, so it is slow. When you want to add or remove elements frequently in a list of elements, it is better to use a LinkedList. You'll see an example of LinkedList together with the ListIterator interface.

A *palindrome* is a word or phrase that reads the same forward and backward. A *palindrome string* "abcba" reads the same in both directions. Given a string, how can you determine whether the string is a palindrome or not?

Well, you can determine whether an input string is a palindrome or not by storing the input string in a String and using the charAt() method in a for loop to compare characters (one from the start and another from the end). To show you how to use ListIterator and LinkedList, see Listing 6-15 for a contrived solution that does the same thing.

Listing 6-15. ListIterator.java

```java
// This program demonstrates the usage of ListIterator

import java.util.*;

class ListIteratorTest {
        public static void main(String []args) {
                String palStr = "abcba";
                List<Character> palindrome = new LinkedList<Character>();

                for(char ch : palStr.toCharArray())
                        palindrome.add(ch);

                System.out.println("Input string is: " + palStr);
                ListIterator<Character> iterator = palindrome.listIterator();
                ListIterator<Character> revIterator = palindrome.listIterator (palindrome.size());

                boolean result = true;
                while(revIterator.hasPrevious() && iterator.hasNext()) {
                        if(iterator.next() != revIterator.previous()){
                                result = false;
                                break;
                        }
                }
                if (result)
                        System.out.print("Input string is a palindrome");
                else
                        System.out.print("Input string is not a palindrome");
        }
}
```

It prints the following:

```
Input string is: abcba
Input string is a palindrome
```

In this program, you use a LinkedList of Characters to store each character in the input string. Why LinkedList<Character> instead of LinkedList<char>? The container classes store references to objects, so you cannot use primitive types with any of the collection classes. Since you have wrapper classes and auto-boxing, it is not a big problem—that is why you use Character instead of char here.

Also note how you assign LinkedList<Character> to List<Character>. Since the LinkedList class implements the List interface, you can do this assignment. Using Collection interfaces instead of concrete class types for holding references is a good programming practice, since—if you want to change LinkedList to an ArrayList in future—the change is very easy if you use the List interface for reference. Now back to the program.

The method toCharArray() in String returns a char[], and you use a for each loop to traverse each character in that array. As the loop executes, you put the characters into the linked list. Now how do you traverse the linked list in both directions?

You can use the methods hasNext() and next() to traverse the forward and methods of hasPrevious() and previous() in ListIterator for moving in the reverse direction. How do you get the ListIterator from the LinkedList? You have a method listIterator() and listIterator(index) in the List interface. Since you want to traverse the LinkedList in both directions, you use both listIterator() and listIterator(index) methods. In the first case, you get the iterator referring to beginning of the container; in another case, you pass the length of the string as an argument to the listIterator method to get the reverse iterator. Once you get both the iterators, it is straightforward to use hasNext() and next() on the first iterator and the hasPrevious() and previous() methods on the second iterator.

The Set Interface

Set, as we studied in our math classes in high school, contains no duplicates. Unlike List, a Set doesn't remember where you inserted the element (i.e., it doesn't remember the insertion order).

There are two important concrete classes for Set: HashSet and TreeSet. A HashSet is for quickly inserting and retrieving elements; it does *not* maintain any sorting order for the elements it holds. A TreeSet stores the elements in a sorted order (and it implements the SortedSet interface).

The HashSet Class

Given a sentence, how can you remove repeated words in that sentence? Set does not allow duplicates, and HashSet can be used for quick insertion and search. So you can use a HashSet for solving this problem (see Listing 6-16).

Listing 6-16. RemoveDuplicates.java

```java
// This program demonstrates the usage of HashSet class

import java.util.*;

class RemoveDuplicates {
        public static void main(String []args) {
                String tongueTwister = "I feel, a feel, a funny feel, a funny feel I feel,
                if you feel the feel  I feel, I feel the feel you feel";
                Set<String> words = new HashSet<>();

                // split the sentence into words and try putting them in the set
                for(String word : tongueTwister.split("\\W+"))
                        words.add(word);
```

```
                System.out.println("The tongue twister is: " + tongueTwister);
                System.out.print("The words used were: ");
                System.out.println(words);
        }
}
```

It prints the following:

```
The tongue twister is: I feel, a feel, a funny feel, a funny feel I feel, if you
feel the feel I feel, I feel the feel you feel
The words used were: [feel, if, a, funny, you, the, I]
```

In this example, the tongue twister sentence has only two word separators—comma and white space. You split the string using these separators by using the split() method. The split() method takes a regular expression as an argument (regular expressions are covered in Chapter 7). The regular expression \\W+ means it is for splitting on word boundaries. So, the string is separated into words, ignoring the punctuation marks like commas.

You try to insert each word into the set. If the word already exists, the add() method fails and returns false (you are not storing this return value). Once you insert all elements in the HashSet, you print them one by one and find that the tongue twister with 25 words used only 7 words!

The TreeSet Class

Given a sentence, how can you sort the letters used in that sentence into alphabetical order? A TreeSet puts the values in a sorted order, so you can use a TreeSet container for solving this problem (see Listing 6-17).

Listing 6-17. TreeSetTest.java

```
// This program demonstrates the usage of TreeSet class

import java.util.*;

class TreeSetTest {
        public static void main(String []args) {
                String pangram = "the quick brown fox jumps over the lazy dog";
                Set<Character> aToZee = new TreeSet<Character>();
                for(char gram : pangram.toCharArray())
                        aToZee.add(gram);
                System.out.println("The pangram is: " + pangram);
                System.out.print("Sorted pangram characters are: " + aToZee);
        }
}
```

It prints the following:

```
The pangram is: the quick brown fox jumps over the lazy dog
Sorted pangram characters are: [ , a, b, c, d, e, f, g, h, i, j, k, l, m, n, o, p, q, r, s, t, u, v,
w, x, y, z]
```

A *pangram* is a sentence that uses all letters in the alphabet at least once. You want to store characters of a pangram in the set. Since you need to use reference types for containers, you've created a TreeSet of Characters.

Now, how to get the characters from a String? Remember that array indexing doesn't work for Strings. For example, to get the first character "t", if you use pangram[0] in the program, you'll get a compiler error. Fortunately, String has a method called toCharArray() that returns a char[]. So, you use this method for traversing over the string and get all the characters. As you add the characters into the TreeSet, the characters are stored in a sorted order. So, you get all the lowercase letters when you print the set.

Note in the output that there is one leading comma. Why? The pangram string has many whitespace characters. One whitespace also gets stored in the set, so it also gets printed!

The Map Interface

A Map stores key and value pairs. The Map interface does *not* extend the Collection interface. However, there are methods in the Map interface that you can use to get classes in the Collection to work around this problem. Also, the method names in Map are very similar to the methods in Collection, so it is easy to understand and use Map. There are two important concrete classes of Map that we'll cover: HashMap and TreeMap.

A HashMap uses a hash table data structure internally. In HashMap, searching (or looking up elements) is a fast operation. However, HashMap neither remembers the order in which you inserted elements nor keeps elements in any sorted order.

A TreeMap uses a red-black tree data structure internally. Unlike HashMap, TreeMap keeps the elements in sorted order (i.e., sorted by its keys). So, searching or inserting is somewhat slower than the HashMap.

The HashMap Class

Assume that you are implementing a simple spell checker. Given an input string, the spell checker looks for words that are usually misspelled; if there is a match, it prints the correct spelling. So, the spell checker should maintain a list of frequently misspelled words and their correct spellings. How can you implement this?

Given a key, you can look out for a value using a Map. Now, which map to use, HashMap or a TreeMap? There is no *need* (though you are able) to keep the misspelled words in sorted order, and the lookup for misspelled words should be very fast. So, HashMap is suitable for solving this problem.

Listing 6-18 is a simple program showing how to implement a spell checker.

Listing 6-18. SpellChecker.java

```
// This program shows the usage of HashMap class
public class SpellChecker {
    public static void main(String []args) {
        Map<String, String> misspeltWords = new HashMap<String, String>();
        misspeltWords.put("calender", "calendar");
        misspeltWords.put("tomatos", "tomatoes");
        misspeltWords.put("existance", "existence");
        misspeltWords.put("aquaintance", "acquaintance");
        String sentence = "Buy a calender for the year 2013";
        System.out.println("The given sentence is: " + sentence);
        for(String word : sentence.split("\\W+")) {
            if(misspeltWords.containsKey(word)) {
                System.out.println("The correct spelling for " + word
                        + " is: " + misspeltWords.get(word));
            }
        }
    }
}
```

It prints the following:

```
The given sentence is: Buy a calender for the year 2013
The correct spelling for calender is: calendar
```

First, you need to create a table of misspelled words and their correct spellings. Since both key and value are Strings, you create a HashMap<String, String> object. You insert four misspelled words and their correct spellings in the HashMap. The misspelled word is the key and the correct spelling is the value. You use the put() method (instead of the add() method you use in Container) for inserting a pair (a key and its value) into the Map.

You use the simple approach of separating the words in a sentence—you use String's split() method. For each word, you check if the word is an exact match for the misspelled word; if so, you print the value matching that key. You use the containsKey() method for checking if the key exists in the map; it returns a Boolean value. You use the get() method to return the value from the map given the key as argument. Since the given sentence has one word misspelled ("calender"), you print the correct spelling for that word.

Now, let's look at the keys in the misspeltWords HashMap. You can get all the keys in the HashMap using the keySet() method. Since you have HashMap<String, String>, the returned set is of type Set<String>.

```
Set<String> keys = misspeltWords.keySet();
System.out.print("Misspelt words in spellchecker are: ");
System.out.println(keys);
```

It prints the following:

```
Mispelled words in spellcheker are: [calender, existance, aquaintance, tomatos]
```

Similarly, you can use valueSet() method to get the values available in the map.

Overriding the hashCode() Method

Overriding the equals and hashCode methods correctly is important for using the classes with containers (particularly, HashMap and HashSet). Listing 6-19 is a simple Circle class example so you can understand what can go wrong.

Listing 6-19. TestCircle.java

```java
// This program shows the importance of equals() and hashCode() methods

import java.util.*;

class Circle {
        private int xPos, yPos, radius;
        public Circle(int x, int y, int r) {
                xPos = x;
                yPos = y;
                radius = r;
        }

        public boolean equals(Object arg) {
                if(arg == null) return false;
                if(this == arg) return true;
                if(arg instanceof Circle) {
                        Circle that = (Circle) arg;
```

```
                   if( (this.xPos == that.xPos) && (this.yPos == that.yPos)
                       && (this.radius == that.radius )) {
                       return true;
                   }
               }
               return false;
           }
}

class TestCircle {
        public static void main(String []args) {
                Set<Circle> circleList = new HashSet<Circle>();
                circleList.add(new Circle(10, 20, 5));
                System.out.println(circleList.contains(new Circle(10, 20, 5)));
        }
}
```

It prints false (not true)! Why? The Circle class overrides the equals() method, but it doesn't override the hashCode() method. When you use objects of Circle in standard containers, it becomes a problem. For fast lookup, the containers compare hashcode of the objects. If the hashCode() method is not overridden, then—even if an object with same contents is passed—the container will not find that object! So you need to override the hashCode() method.

Okay, how do you override the hashCode() method? In the ideal case, the hashCode() method should return unique hash codes for different objects.

The hashCode() method *should* return the same hash value if the equals() method returns true. What if the objects are different (so that the equals() method returns false)? It is better (although not required) for the hashCode() to return different values if the objects are different. The reason is that it is difficult to write a hashCode() method that gives unique value for every different object.

The methods hashCode() and equals() need to be consistent for a class. For practical purposes, ensure that you follow this one rule: the hashCode() method should return the same hash value for two objects if the equals() method returns true for them.

When implementing the hashCode() method, you can use the values of the instance members of the class to create a hash value. Here is a simple implementation of the hashCode() method of the Circle class:

```
public int hashCode() {
        // use bit-manipuation operators such as ^ to generate close to unique hash codes
        // here we are using the magic numbers 7, 11 and 53, but you can use any numbers,
preferably primes        return (7 * xPos) ^ (11 * yPos) ^ (53 * yPos);
}
```

Now if you run the main() method, it prints "true". In this implementation of the hashCode() method, you multiply the values by a prime number as well as bit-wise operation. You can write complex code for hashCode() if you want a better hashing function, but this implementation is sufficient for practical purposes.

183

You can use bitwise operators for int values. What about other types, like floating-point values or reference types? To give you an example, here is hashCode() implementation of java.awt.Point2D, which has floating point values x and y. The methods getX() and getY() return the x and y values respectively:

```
public int hashCode() {
        long bits = java.lang.Double.doubleToLongBits(getX());
        bits ^= java.lang.Double.doubleToLongBits(getY()) * 31;
        return (((int) bits) ^ ((int) (bits >> 32)));
}
```

This method uses the doubleToLongBits() method, which takes a double value and returns a long value. For floating-point values x and y (returned by the getX and getY methods), you get long values in bits and you use bit-manipulation to get hashCode().

Now, how do you implement the hashCode method if the class has reference type members? For example, consider using an instance of Point class as a member instead of xPos and yPos, which are primitive type fields:

```
class Circle {
        private int radius;
        private Point center;
        // other members...
}
```

In this case, you can use call the hashCode() method of Point to implement Circle's hashCode method:

```
public int hashCode() {
        return center.hashCode() ^ radius;
}
```

> If you're using an object in containers like HashSet or HashMap, make sure you override the hashCode() and equals() methods correctly. If you don't, you'll get nasty surprises (bugs) while using these containers!

The NavigableMap Interface

The NavigableMap interface extends the SortedMap interface. In the Collection hierarchy, the TreeMap class is the widely used class that implements NavigableMap. As the name indicates, with NavigableMap, you can navigate the Map easily. It has many methods that make Map navigation easy. You can get the nearest value matching the given key, all values less than the given key, all values greater than the given key, etc. Let's look at an example: Lennon, McCartney, Harrison, and Starr have taken an online exam. In that exam, the maximum they can score is 100, with a passing score of 40. If you want to find details such as who passed the exam, and sort the exam scores in ascending or descending order, NavigableMap is very convenient (see Listing 6-20).

Listing 6-20. NavigableMapTest.java

```java
// This program demonstrates the usage of navigable tree interface and TreeMap class

import java.util.*;

public class NavigableMapTest {
        public static void main(String []args) {
                NavigableMap<Integer, String> examScores = new TreeMap<Integer, String>();

                examScores.put(90, "Sophia");
                examScores.put(20, "Isabella");
                examScores.put(10, "Emma");
                examScores.put(50, "Olivea");

                System.out.println("The data in the map is: " + examScores);
                System.out.println("The data descending order is: " + examScores.descendingMap());
                System.out.println("Details of those who passed the exam: " +
        examScores.tailMap(40));
                System.out.println("The lowest mark is: " + examScores.firstEntry());
        }
}
```

It prints the following:

```
The data in the map is: {10=Emma, 20=Isabella, 50=Olivea, 90=Sophia}
The data descending order is: {90=Sophia, 50=Olivea, 20=Isabella, 10=Emma}
Details of those who passed the exam: {50=Olivea, 90=Sophia}
The lowest mark is: 10=Emma
```

In this program, you have a NavigableMap<Integer, String> that maps the exam score and the name of the person. You create a TreeMap<String, String> to actually store the exam scores. By default, a TreeMap stores data in ascending order. If you want the data in descending order, it's easy: you just have to use the descendingMap() method (or descendingKeySet() if you are only interested in the keys).

Given the passing score is 40, you might want to get the map with data of those who failed in the exam. For that, you can use the headMap() method with the key value 40 (since the data is in ascending order, you want to get the "head" part of the map from the given position). Similarly, to get the data of those who passed the exam, you can use the tailMap() method.

If you want the immediate ones above and below the passing score, you can use the higherEntry() and lowerEntry() methods, respectively. The firstEntry() and lastEntry() methods give the entries with lowest and highest key values. So, when you use the firstEntry() method on examScores, you get Emma with 10 marks. If you use lastEntry(), you get Sophia, who has score 90.

The Queue Interface

A Queue follows FIFO mechanism: the first inserted element will be removed first. For getting a queue behavior, you can create a LinkedList object and refer it through a Queue reference. When you call the methods from Queue reference, the object behaves like a Queue. Listing 6-21 shows an example and it will become clear. Lennon, McCartney, Harrison, and Starr are taking an online exam. Let's see how you can remember the sequence in which they logged in to take the exam (see Listing 6-21).

Listing 6-21. QueueTest.java

```
// This program shows the key characteristics of Queue interface

import java.util.*;

class QueueTest {
        public static void main(String []args) {
                Queue<String> loginSequence = new LinkedList<String>();

                loginSequence.add("Harrison");
                loginSequence.add("McCartney");
                loginSequence.add("Starr");
                loginSequence.add("Lennon");
                System.out.println("The login sequence is: " + loginSequence);
                while(!loginSequence.isEmpty())
                        System.out.println("Removing " + loginSequence.remove());
        }
}
```

This prints the following:

```
The login sequence is: [Harrison, McCartney, Starr, Lennon]
Removing Harrison
Removing McCartney
Removing Starr
Removing Lennon
```

In this example, you create a Queue<String> to point it to a LinkedList<String> object. Then you add four elements (names in the sequence in which they logged in) to the queue. After the elements are inserted, you print the queue by (implicitly) calling the toString() method on loginSequence. You call the remove() method to remove one element of the queue. The remove() method removes an element from the head of the queue and returns the extracted element. You got the same sequence as output as you inserted in the queue.

The Deque Interface

Deque (Doubly ended queue) is a data structure that allows you to insert and remove elements from both the ends. The Deque interface was introduced in Java 6 in java.util.collection package. The Deque interface extends the Queue interface just discussed. Hence, all methods provided by Queue are also available in the Deque interface. Let's examine the commonly used methods of the Deque interface, summarized in Table 6-7.

Table 6-7. *Commonly Used Methods in the Deque Interface*

Method	Short Description
void addFirst(Element)	Adds the Element to the front of the Deque.
void addLast(Element)	Adds the Element to the last of the Deque.
Element removeFirst()	Removes an element from the front of the Deque and returns it.
Element removeLast()	Removes an element from the last of the Deque and returns it.
Element getFirst()	Returns the first element from the Deque, does not remove.
Element getLast()	Returns the last element from the Deque, does not remove.

All methods listed in Table 6-7 raise appropriate exceptions if they fail. There is another set of methods, listed in Table 6-8, that achieves the same functionality. However, they do not raise exception on failure; instead they return a special value. For instance, the method getFirst() returns the first element from the Deque but does not remove it. If the Deque is empty, it raises the exception, NoSuchElementException. At the same time, the peekFirst() method also carry out the same functionality. However, it returns null if the Deque is empty. When the Deque is created with predefined capacity, the methods listed in Table 6-8 are preferred over the methods listed in Table 6-7.

Table 6-8. *Commonly Used Methods in the Deque Interface (Returns Special Value)*

Method	Short Description
boolean offerFirst(Element)	Adds the Element to the front of the Deque if it is not violating capacity constraint.
boolean offerLast(Element)	Adds the Element to the end of the Deque if it is not violating capacity constraint.
Element pollFirst()	Removes an element from the front of the Deque and returns it; if the Deque is empty, it returns null.
Element pollLast()	Removes an element from the end of the Deque and returns it; if the Deque is empty, it returns null.
Element peekFirst()	Returns the first element from the Deque but does not remove it; returns null if Deque is empty.
Element peekLast()	Returns the last element from the Deque but does not remove it; returns null if Deque is empty.

You just observed that the methods in Table 6-8 return null if they fail. What if you are storing null as an element? Well, it is not recommended that you store null as an argument, since there are methods in the Deque interface that return null, and it would be difficult for you to distinguish between the success or failure of the method call.

There are three concrete implementations of the Deque interface: LinkedList, ArrayDeque, and LinkedBlockingDeque. Let's use ArrayDeque to understand the features of the Deque interface.

It is evident from the list of methods supported by Deque that it is possible to realize the standard behavior of a queue, stack, and deque. Let's implement a special queue (say, to pay utility bill) where a customer can be added only at the end of the queue and can be removed either at the front of the queue (when the customer paid the bill) or from the end of the queue (when the customer gets frustrated from the long line and leaves the queue himself). Listing 6-22 shows how to do this.

Listing 6-22. SplQueueTest.java

```
// This program shows the usage of Deque interface

import java.util.*;

class SplQueue {
        private Deque<String> splQ = new ArrayDeque<>();
        void addInQueue(String customer){
                splQ.addLast(customer);
        }
        void removeFront(){
                splQ.removeFirst();
        }
        void removeBack(){
                splQ.removeLast();
        }
        void printQueue(){
                System.out.println("Special queue contains: " + splQ);
        }
}

class SplQueueTest {
        public static void main(String []args) {
                SplQueue splQ = new SplQueue();
                splQ.addInQueue("Harrison");
                splQ.addInQueue("McCartney");
                splQ.addInQueue("Starr");
                splQ.addInQueue("Lennon");

                splQ.printQueue();
                splQ.removeFront();
                splQ.removeBack();
                splQ.printQueue();
        }
}
```

It prints the following:

```
Special queue contains: [Harrison, McCartney, Starr, Lennon]
Special queue contains: [McCartney, Starr]
```

You first define a class—SplQueue—that defines a container splQ of type ArrayDeque with basic four operations. The method addInQueue() adds a customer at the end of the queue, the method removeBack() removes a customer from the end of the queue, the method removeFront() removes a customer from the front of the queue, and the method printQueue() simply prints all elements of the queue. You simply use the addLast(), removeFront(), and removeLast() methods from the Deque interface to realize the methods of the SplQueue class. In your main() method, you instantiate the SplQueue and called the addInQueue() method of the SplQueue class. After it, you remove one customer from the front and one from the end, and print the contents of the queue before and after this removal. Well, it is working as you expected.

Comparable and Comparator Interfaces

As their names suggest, Comparable and Comparator interfaces are used to compare similar objects (for example, while performing searching or sorting). Assume that you have a container containing a list of Person object. Now, how you compare two Person objects? There are any number of comparable attributes, such as SSN, name, driving-license number, and so on. Two objects can be compared on SSN as well as person's name; this depends on the context. Hence, the criterion to compare the Person objects cannot be predefined; a developer has to define this criterion. Java defines Comparable and Comparator interfaces to achieve the same.

The Comparable class has only one method compareTo(), which is declared as follows:

```
int compareTo(Element that)
```

Since you are implementing the compareTo() method in a class, you have this reference available. You can compare the current element with the passed Element and return an int value. What should the int value be? Well, here are the rules for returning the integer value:

```
return 1 if current object > passed object
return 0 if current object == passed object
return -1 if current object < passed object
```

Now, an important question: what does >, < or == mean for an Element? Hmm, it is left to you to decide how to compare two objects! But the meaning of comparison should be a natural one; in other words, the comparison should mean *natural ordering*. For example, you saw how Integers are compared with each other, based on a *numeric order*, which is the natural order for Integer types. Similarly, you compare Strings using *lexicographic comparison*, which is the natural order for Strings. For user-defined classes, you need to find the natural order in which you can compare the objects. For example, for a Student class, StudentId might be the natural order for comparing Student objects. Listing 6-23 implements a simple Student class now.

Listing 6-23. ComparatorTest.java

```
// This program shows the usage of Comparable interface

import java.util.*;

class Student implements Comparable<Student> {
        String id;
        String name;
        Double cgpa;
        public Student(String studentId, String studentName, double studentCGPA) {
                id = studentId;
                name = studentName;
                cgpa = studentCGPA;
        }
        public String toString() {
                return " \n " + id + " \t " + name + " \t " + cgpa;
        }
```

```
        public int compareTo(Student that) {
                return this.id.compareTo(that.id);
        }
}

class ComparatorTest {
        public static void main(String []args) {
                Student []students = {  new Student("cs011", "Lennon  ", 3.1),
                        new Student("cs021", "McCartney", 3.4),
                        new Student("cs012", "Harrison ", 2.7),
                        new Student("cs022", "Starr ", 3.7) };

                System.out.println("Before sorting by student ID");
                System.out.println("Student-ID \t  Name \t  CGPA (for 4.0) ");
                System.out.println(Arrays.toString(students));

                Arrays.sort(students);

                System.out.println("After sorting by student ID");
                System.out.println("Student-ID \t  Name \t  CGPA (for 4.0) ");
                System.out.println(Arrays.toString(students));
        }
}
```

It prints the following:

```
Before sorting by student ID
Student-ID        Name     CGPA (for 4.0)
[
 cs011            Lennon          3.1,
 cs021            McCartney       3.4,
 cs012            Harrison        2.7,
 cs022            Starr           3.7]
After sorting by student ID
Student-ID        Name     CGPA (for 4.0)
[
 cs011            Lennon          3.1,
 cs012            Harrison        2.7,
 cs021            McCartney       3.4,
 cs022            Starr           3.7]
```

You have implemented the Comparable<Student> interface. When you call the sort() method, it calls the compareTo() method to compare Student objects by their IDs. Since Student IDs are unique, it is a natural comparison order that works well.

Now, you may need to arrange students based on the cumulative grade point average (CGPA) they got. You may even need to compare Students based on their names. If you need to implement two or more alternative ways to compare two similar objects, then you may implement the Comparator class. Listing 6-24 is an implementation (there is no change in the Student class, so we are not producing it here again).

Listing 6-24. ComparatorTest2.java

```java
// This program shows the implementation of Comparator interface

import java.util.*;

class CGPAComparator implements Comparator<Student> {
        public int compare(Student s1, Student s2) {
                return (s1.cgpa.compareTo(s2.cgpa));
        }
}

class ComparatorTest {
        public static void main(String []args) {
                Student []students = {  new Student("cs011", "Lennon  ", 3.1),
                        new Student("cs021", "McCartney", 3.4),
                        new Student("cs012", "Harrison ", 2.7),
                        new Student("cs022", "Starr ", 3.7) };

                System.out.println("Before sorting by CGPA ");
                System.out.println("Student-ID \t  Name \t  CGPA (for 4.0) ");
                System.out.println(Arrays.toString(students));

                Arrays.sort(students, new CGPAComparator());

                System.out.println("After sorting by CGPA");
                System.out.println("Student-ID \t  Name \t  CGPA (for 4.0) ");
                System.out.println(Arrays.toString(students));
        }
}
```

It prints the following:

```
Before sorting by CGPA
Student-ID       Name     CGPA (for 4.0)
[
 cs011           Lennon          3.1,
 cs021           McCartney       3.4,
 cs012           Harrison        2.7,
 cs022           Starr           3.7]
After sorting by CGPA
Student-ID       Name     CGPA (for 4.0)
[
 cs012           Harrison        2.7,
 cs011           Lennon          3.1,
 cs021           McCartney       3.4,
 cs022           Starr           3.7]
```

Yes, the program prints the Student data sorted by their CGPA. You didn't change the Student class; the class still implements the Comparable<String> interface and defines the compareTo() method, but you don't use the compareTo() method in your program. You create a separate class named CGPAComparator and implement the Comparator<Student> interface. You define the compare() method, which takes two Student objects as arguments.

You compare the CGPA of the arguments s1 and s2 by (re)using the compareTo() method from the Double class. You didn't change anything in the main() method except for the way you call the sort() method. You create a new CGPAComparator() object and pass as the second argument to the sort() method. By default sort() uses the compareTo() method; since you are passing a Comparator object explicitly, it now uses the compare() method defined in the CGPAComparator. So, the Student objects are now compared and sorted based on their CGPA.

You've learned quite a lot about the differences between the Comparable and Comparator interfaces, summarized in Table 6-9.

Table 6-9. *Differences between Implementing Comparable and Comparator Interfaces*

Comparable Interface	Comparator Interface
Used when the objects need to be compared in their *natural order*.	Used when the objects need to be compared in custom user-defined order (*other* than the natural order).
You do not create a separate class just to implement the Comparable interface.	You create a separate class just to implement the Comparator interface.
For a given class type, you have only that class (and that class alone) implementing the Comparable interface.	You can have many separate (i.e., independent) classes implementing the Comparator interface, with each class defining different ways to compare objects.
The method in the Comparable interface is declared as int compareTo(ClassType type);.	The method in the Comparator interface is declared as int compare(ClassType type1, ClassType type2);.

Most classes have a natural order for comparing objects, so implement the Comparable interface for your classes in those cases. If you want to compare the objects other than the natural order or if there is no natural ordering present for your class type, then create separate classes implementing the Comparator interface.

Algorithms (Collections Class)

You've seen two important components of the collections framework: abstract classes/interfaces and the concrete class implementations. The collections framework also has a utility class named Collections (note the suffix "s" in the class name). It provides algorithms that are useful for manipulating data structures provided in the collections framework. You'll see important methods like sort(), binarySearch(), reverse(), shuffle(), etc., in this short section (check Table 6-10).

Table 6-10. *Important Algorithms (Static Methods in the Collections Class)*

Method	Short Description
int binarySearch(List<? extends Comparable<? super T>> list, T key)	Looks for the key in List. If found, it returns a value >= 0; otherwise it returns a negative value. It has an overloaded version that also takes a Comparator object for comparing elements.
void copy(List<? super T> dest, List<? extends T> src)	Copies all the elements from src List to dest List.
void fill(List<? super T> list, T obj)	Fills the whole list with the value obj.
T max(Collection<? extends T> coll)	Returns the max element in the list. It has an overloaded version that also takes a Comparator object for comparing elements.
T min(Collection<? extends T> coll)	Returns the min element in the list. It has an overloaded version that also takes a Comparator object for comparing elements.
boolean replaceAll(List<T> list, T oldVal, T newVal)	Replaces all occurrences of oldVal with newVal in list.
void reverse(List<?> list)	Reverses all the elements in the given list.
void rotate(List<?> list, int distance)	Rotates the list given by the value distance.
void shuffle(List<?> list)	Shuffles elements in the list randomly.
void sort(List<T> list)	Sorts the list in its natural order (i.e., by using the compareTo() method). It has an overloaded version that also takes a Comparator object for comparing elements.
void swap(List<?> list, int i, int j)	Swaps the elements in the positions i and j in the list.

Assume that you are creating a playlist of your favorite Michael Jackson songs. There are many things that you can do with a playlist: you can sort, shuffle, search, reverse, or replay songs. Let's do all these in a PlayList program (see Listing 6-25).

Listing 6-25. PlayList.java

```java
// This program demonstrates some of the useful methods in Collections class

import java.util.*;

class PlayList {
        public static void main(String []args) {
                // let's create a list of some Michael Jackson's songs
                List<String> playList = new LinkedList<String>();
                playList.add("Rock With You - 1979");
                playList.add("Billie Jean - 1983");
                playList.add("Man In the Mirror - 1988");
                playList.add("Black Or White - 1991");

                System.out.println("The original playlist of MJ's songs");
                System.out.println(playList);
```

```
                System.out.println("\nThe reversed playlist");
                Collections.reverse(playList);
                System.out.println(playList);

                System.out.println("\nNow after shuffling the playlist");
                Collections.shuffle(playList);
                System.out.println(playList);

                System.out.println("\nSort the songs by their names ");
                Collections.sort(playList);
                System.out.println(playList);

                System.out.println("\nIs my most favourite song Black Or White - 1991
present in the list?");
                String backOrWhiteSong = "Black Or White - 1991";
                int index = Collections.binarySearch(playList, backOrWhiteSong);
                if(index >= 0)
                        System.out.printf("Yes, its the %d song \n", (index + 1));
                else
                        System.out.printf("No, its not there in the playlist \n");

                System.out.println("\nLet me forward by two songs (rotate the list) ");
                Collections.rotate(playList, 2);
                System.out.println(playList);
        }
}
```

It prints the following:

```
The original playlist of MJ's songs
[Rock With You - 1979, Billie Jean - 1983, Man In the Mirror - 1988, Black Or
White - 1991]

The reversed playlist
[Black Or White - 1991, Man In the Mirror - 1988, Billie Jean - 1983, Rock With
You - 1979]

Now after shuffling the playlist
[Black Or White - 1991, Man In the Mirror - 1988, Rock With You - 1979, Billie J
ean - 1983]

Sort the songs by their names
[Billie Jean - 1983, Black Or White - 1991, Man In the Mirror - 1988, Rock With
You - 1979]

Is my most favourite song Black Or White - 1991 present in the list?
Yes, its the 2 song

Let me forward by two songs (rotate the list)
[Man In the Mirror - 1988, Rock With You - 1979, Billie Jean - 1983, Black Or
White - 1991]
```

Just spend a couple of minutes looking at the output against the program and make sure you understand it. Okay, let's see what's happening.

1. You create a LinkedList<String> with four MJ songs.

2. You print the contents of the list; it prints the songs in the order in which you inserted them.

3. The Collections.reverse() method reverses the contents of the given List. So, you have the songs in the reverse order.

4. Next, you shuffle the List using Collections.shuffle()—the songs are in different positions now. You sort the songs by their names. Since the songs are Strings, the songs are now sorted in alphabetical order.

5. You search for your favorite song in the playlist using the Collections.binarySearch() method. This method takes two arguments, the List and the key you are searching for. If the key is found, the int value will be >= 0 and that value is the index of the key in the List. If it is negative, it means the value is not found. You found the song you searched for.

6. You rotate the sorted play list by two positions using the Collections.rotate() method. It takes two arguments, the List and an int value, to tell how many positions you need to move the values.

The Arrays Class

Similar to Collections, Arrays is also a utility class (i.e., the class has only static methods). Methods in Collections are also very similar to methods in Arrays. The Collections class is for container classes; the Arrays class is for native arrays (i.e., arrays with [] syntax).

Methods in the Arrays Class

Listing 6-26 is a trivial example to show why the Arrays class is very useful for working with native arrays. Can you tell what this program prints?

Listing 6-26. PrintArray.java

```
// This code implements a simple integer array

class PrintArray {
        public static void main(String []args) {
                int [] intArray = {1, 2, 3, 4, 5};
                System.out.println("The array contents are:      " + intArray);
        }
}
```

It prints the following:

```
The array contents are:      [I@3e25a5
```

What went wrong? The println() implicitly calls the toString() method of the native int[] array. Native arrays are not classes, though they inherit the Object class, so it is not possible to override methods like toString(). (Remember that overriding can be done only in classes.) In other words, intArray.toString() is called where the toString() method is inherited from Object. So, how do you print the contents of a native array?

Fortunately, you have the Arrays utility class that has methods like toString(). Listing 6-27 is the correct program for printing the contents of a native array.

Listing 6-27. PrintArray2.java

```java
// This program demonstrates the usage of Arrays class

import java.util.*;

class PrintArray {
        public static void main(String []args) {
                int [] intArray = {1, 2, 3, 4, 5};
                System.out.println("The array contents are:  " + Arrays.toString(intArray));
        }
}
```

Now the output is as expected:

```
The array contents are:  [1, 2, 3, 4, 5]
```

Use the Arrays.toString() method to print the contents of the array instead of using Object's toString() method! As you can see, the methods in the Arrays class can be handy. Now, you'll look at methods like sort(), binarySearch(), etc. Table 6-11 lists important methods in the Arrays class.

Table 6-11. *Important (Static) Methods in the Arrays Class*

Method	Description
List<T> asList(T ... a)	Creates a fixed-size List out of the given array.
int binarySearch(Object[] objArray, Object key)	Search for key in objArray. Returns an int value >= (index of the key) if found; otherwise it returns a negative value. Overloads available for primitive types like int[], byte[], etc. Also, overload available for taking a Comparator object.
boolean equals(Object[] objArray1, Object[] objArray2)	Checks if the contents of objArray1 and objArray2 are equal. Overloads available for primitive type arrays like int[], byte[], etc.
void fill(Object[] objArray, Object val)	Fills the objArray with value val. Overloads available for primitive type arrays like int[], byte[], etc.
void sort(Object[] objArray)	Sorts the objArray based on the natural order (i.e., using the compareTo() method). Overloads available for primitive type arrays like int[], byte[], etc. Also an overload is available for taking a Comparator object.
String toString(Object[] a)	Returns the String representation of the given objArray. Overloads available for primitive type arrays like int[], byte[], etc.

The Arrays.sort(Object []) calls the compareTo() method to compare the elements. So, the array elements passed to sort must implement the Comparable interface. The sort method is overloaded for primitive types (like byte[], int[] etc). For the elements, the sorting is done in ascending numeric order. Listing 6-28 calls the sort() method on a String array and an int array.

Listing 6-28. CollectionsTest.java

```
// It demonstrates sorting on Arrays
class CollectionsTest {
        public static void  main(String []args) {
                String [] strArr = { "21", "1", "111", "12", "123" };
                Arrays.sort(strArr);
                System.out.println(Arrays.toString(strArr));

                int [] intArr = { 21, 1, 111, 12, 123 };
                Arrays.sort(intArr);
                System.out.println(Arrays.toString(intArr));
        }
}
```

It prints the following:

```
[1, 111, 12, 123, 21]
[1, 12, 21, 111, 123]
```

The contents of the arrays look similar, but the output looks different. Why? This shows the difference in the sort done for strings and primitive types. The String's compareTo() method does *lexicographic comparison*—the string contents are compared character-by-character. This makes sense, for example, if you have strings like "john", "johannes", "johann", "johnny", etc. However, for numbers, you need to compare values. For this reason, after "1" comes "111" and then "12" and so on with Strings, but 1, 12, 21, and so on with integers.

 Be aware how the values are compared when using the sort() method. For example, numeric comparison is done for integers whereas lexicographic comparison is done for Strings.

You've tried sorting. Now you'll attempt searching values in an array. What does the program in Listing 6-29 print?

Listing 6-29. BinarySearchTest.java

```
// This program shows the usage of binary search

import java.util.*;

class BinarySearchTest {
        public static void  main(String []args) {
                String [] strArr = { "21", "22", "11", "12", "13" };
                System.out.println("The given strArr is: " + Arrays.toString(strArr));
```

```
                int index = Arrays.binarySearch(strArr, "22");
                System.out.println("The index value is: " + index);
        }
}
```

It prints the following:

```
The index value is: -6
```

What went wrong? The binarySearch method takes two arguments: the first is the array to be searched and the second is the key value to be searched. If it succeeds, it returns the index of the key element in the array. If the key value is not found, it returns a negative value. Now, the binarySearch() method expects that it is called on an already sorted array. Here, you forgot to call sort() before doing binary search, so the method failed. Listing 6-30 shows the improved code.

Listing 6-30. BinarySearchTest2.java

```
// This program shows the usage of binary search

import java.util.*;

class BinarySearchTest {
        public static void  main(String []args) {
                String [] strArr = { "21", "22", "11", "12", "13" };
                System.out.println("The given strArr is: " + Arrays.toString(strArr));
                Arrays.sort(strArr);
                System.out.println("strArr after sorting is: " + Arrays.toString(strArr));
                int index = Arrays.binarySearch(strArr, "22");
                System.out.println("The index value is: " + index);
        }
}
```

It prints the following:

```
The given strArr is: [21, 22, 11, 12, 13]
strArr after sorting is: [11, 12, 13, 21, 22]
The index value is: 4
```

Note that array index starts from zero, so the index position of 22 is 4 (i.e., strArr[4] == "22").

 Make sure you always call binarySearch() on a sorted array/container. Otherwise, you'll get unpredictable results.

Array as a List

Assume that you have temperatures recorded in your place for a week's time. How can you write a simple program that prints the maximum and minimum temperatures recorded?

For storing temperatures, you can use an array. However, the Arrays class does not have the max() or min() methods. One way to avoid writing your own method is to convert the array into List using the asList method, and use the max() and min() methods in the Collections class (see Listing 6-31). Remember that the array should be a reference type (you cannot use the asList method for primitive type arrays).

Listing 6-31. ArrayAsList.java

```java
// This program demonstrates the usage of arrays as list

import java.util.*;

public class ArrayAsList {
        public static void main(String []args) {
                Double [] weeklyTemperature = {31.1, 30.0, 32.5, 34.9, 33.7, 27.8};
                List<Double> temperatures = Arrays.asList(weeklyTemperature);
                System.out.println("Maximum temperature recorded was: " +
Collections.max(temperatures));
                System.out.println("Minimum recorded was: " + Collections.min(temperatures));
        }
}
```

This prints the following:

```
Maximum temperature recorded was: 34.9
Minimum recorded was: 27.8
```

Yes, it works. But you made a simple logical mistake. In this program, you have given temperatures of only six and not seven days. You can add one more value in the array, but shall you try adding it directly to the List<Double> that you got? Here is the code segment that tries to add an element in the List:

```java
List<Double> temperatures = Arrays.asList(weeklyTemperature);
temperatures.add(32.3);
```

Now you get the following:

```
Exception in thread "main" java.lang.UnsupportedOperationException
        at java.util.AbstractList.add(AbstractList.java:131)
        at java.util.AbstractList.add(AbstractList.java:91)
        at ArrayAsList.main(ArrayAsList.java:13)
```

You cannot add elements to the list returned by the asList() method. A solution is to create a new List type object (say, an ArrayList object) yourself and add elements to that List, as in Listing 6-32.

Listing 6-32. ArrayAsList2.java

```java
// This program demonstrates the usage of arrays as list

import java.util.*;

class ArrayAsList{
        public static void main(String []args) {
                Double [] temperatureArray = {31.1, 30.0, 32.5, 34.9, 33.7, 27.8};
                System.out.println("The original array is:     " + Arrays.toString(temperatureArray));
```

199

```
                    List<Double> temperatureList = new ArrayList<Double>(Arrays.asList(temperatureArray));
                    temperatureList.add(32.3);
                    System.out.println("The new List with an added element is: " + temperatureList);
        }
}
```

It prints the following:

```
The original array is:    [31.1, 30.0, 32.5, 34.9, 33.7, 27.8]
The new List with an added element is: [31.1, 30.0, 32.5, 34.9, 33.7, 27.8, 32.3]
```

Yes, it works now.

Points to Remember

Here are some interesting facts that might prove useful on your OCPJP exam:

- The difference between an ArrayList and ArrayDeque is that you can add an element anywhere in an array list using an index; however, you can add an element only either at the front or end of the array deque. That makes insertion in array deque much efficient than array list; however, navigation in an array deque becomes more expensive than in an array list.

- There is one more thing you need to remember about using the List returned from the Arrays.asList() method. Though you cannot add elements to the List returned by the asList() method, you can modify the List! Also, the modifications you make through the List are reflected in the original array. For example, if you modify the temperature of the first day from 31.1 to 35.2 in the List, the original array gets modified, as shown in Listing 6-33.

Listing 6-33. ArrayAsList3.java

```java
import java.util.*;

class ArrayAsList3 {
  public static void main(String []args) {
        Double [] temperatureArray = {31.1, 30.0, 32.5, 34.9, 33.7, 27.8};
        System.out.println("The original array is: " + Arrays.toString(temperatureArray));
            List<Double> temperatureList = Arrays.asList(temperatureArray);
            temperatureList.set(0, 35.2);
        System.out.println("The modified array is: " + Arrays.toString(temperatureArray));
        }
}
```

It prints the following:

```
The original array is: [31.1, 30.0, 32.5, 34.9, 33.7, 27.8]
The modified array is: [35.2, 30.0, 32.5, 34.9, 33.7, 27.8]
```

The Arrays class provides only limited functionality and you will often want to use methods in the Collections class. To achieve that, calling the Arrays.asList() method is a useful technique.

Remember that you cannot add elements to the List returned by the Arrays.asList() method. But, you can make changes to the elements in the returned List, and the changes made to that List are reflected back in the array.

QUESTION TIME!

1. Predict the output of this program:

```java
import java.util.*;

class UtilitiesTest {
    public static void main(String []args) {
        List<int> intList = new ArrayList<>();
        intList.add(10);
        intList.add(20);
        System.out.println("The list is: " + intList);
    }
}
```

A. It prints the following: The list is: [10, 20].

B. It prints the following: The list is: [20, 10].

C. It results in a compiler error.

D. It results in a runtime exception.

Answer: C.   It results in a compiler error.

(You cannot specify primitive types along with generics, so List<int> needs to be changed to List<Integer>).

2. Predict the output of this program:

```java
import java.util.*;

class UtilitiesTest {
    public static void main(String []args) {
        List<Integer> intList = new LinkedList<>();
        List<Double> dblList = new LinkedList<>();
        System.out.println("First type: " + intList.getClass());
        System.out.println("Second type:" + dblList.getClass());
    }
}
```

A. It prints the following:

First type: class java.util.LinkedList

Second type:class java.util.LinkedList

201

B. It prints the following:

First type: class java.util.LinkedList<Integer>

Second type:class java.util.LinkedList<Double>

C. It results in a compiler error.

D. It results in a runtime exception.

Answer: A. It prints the following:

First type: class java.util.LinkedList

Second type:class java.util.LinkedList

(Due to type erasure, after compilation both types are treated as same LinkedList type).

3. Which statement is true with respect to List<?> and List<Object>?

A. Both are same, just two different ways to express a same thing.

B. List<?> is a homogenous list of elements of a same unknown type and
List<Object> is a heterogeneous list of elements of different types.

C. List<?> is a heterogeneous list of elements of different types and List<Object> is
a homogenous list of elements of a same unknown type.

Answer: B. List<?> is a homogenous list of elements of a same unknown type and
List<Object> is a heterogeneous list of elements of a same unknown type.

4. Predict the output of this program:

```java
import java.io.*;

class LastError<T> {
    private T lastError;
    void setError(T t){
        lastError = t;
        System.out.println("LastError: setError");
    }
}

class StrLastError<S extends CharSequence> extends LastError<String>{
    public StrLastError(S s) {
    }
    void setError(S s){
        System.out.println("StrLastError: setError");
    }
}

class Test {
    public static void main(String []args) {
        StrLastError<String> err = new StrLastError<String>("Error");
        err.setError("Last error");
    }
}
```

    A.   It prints the following: StrLastError: setError.

    B.   It prints the following: LastError: setError.

    C.   It results in a compilation error.

    D.   It results in a runtime exception.

    Answer: C.   It results in a compilation error.

(It looks like the setError() method in StrLastError is overriding setError() in the LastError class. However, it is not the case. At the time of compilation, the knowledge of type S is not available. Therefore, the compiler records the signatures of these two methods as setError(String) in superclass and setError(S_extends_CharSequence) in subclass—treating them as overloaded methods (not overridden). In this case, when the call to setError() is found, the compiler finds both the overloaded methods matching, resulting in the ambiguous method call error. Here is the error message

```
Test.java:22: error: reference to setError is ambiguous, both method setError(T) in LastError
and method setError(S) in StrLastError match
              err.setError("Last error");
          ^
```

where T and S are type-variables:

T extends Object declared in class LastError.

S extends CharSequence declared in class StrLastError).

Summary

Generics

- Generics will ensure that any attempts to add elements of types other than the specified type(s) will be caught at compile time itself. Hence, generics offer generic implementation with type safety.

- Java 7 introduced *diamond* syntax where the type parameters (after new operator and class name) can be omitted. The compiler will infer the types from the type declaration.

- Generics are not covariant. That is, subtyping doesn't work with generics; you cannot assign a derived generic type parameter to a base type parameter.

- The <?> specifies an unknown type in generics and is known as a wildcard. For example, List<?> refers to list of unknowns.

- Wildcards can be bounded. For example, <? extends Runnable> specifies that ? can match any type as long as it is Runnable or any of its derived types. Note that extends is inclusive, so you can replace X in ? extends X. However, in <? super Runnable>, ? would match only the super types of Runnable, and Runnable itself will not match (i.e., it is an exclusive clause).

- You use the extends keyword for both class type as well as an interface when specifying bounded types in generics. For specifying multiple base types, you use the & symbol. For example, in List<? extends X & Y>, ? will match types, extending *both* the types X and Y.

Collections Framework

- Avoid mixing raw types with generic types. In other cases, make sure of the type safety manually.

- The terms Collection, Collections, and collection are different. Collection— java.util.Collection<E>—is the root interface in the collection hierarchy. Collections—java.util.Collections—is a utility class that contains only static methods. The general term *collection(s)* refers to containers like map, stack, queue, etc.

- The container classes store references to objects, so you cannot use primitive types with any of the collection classes.

- The methods hashCode() and equals() need to be consistent for a class. For practical purposes, ensure that you follow this one rule: the hashCode() method should return the same hash value for two objects if the equals() method returns true for them.

- If you're using an object in containers like HashSet or HashMap, make sure you override the hashCode() and equals() methods correctly.

- The Map interface does not extend the Collection interface.

- It is not recommended that you store null as an argument, since there are methods in the Deque interface that return null, and it would be difficult for you to distinguish between the success or failure of the method call.

- Implement the Comparable interface for your classes where a natural order is possible. If you want to compare the objects other than the natural order or if there is no natural ordering present for your class type, then create separate classes implementing the Comparator interface. Also, if you have multiple alternative ways to decide the order, then go for the Comparator interface.

CHAPTER 7

■ ■ ■

String Processing

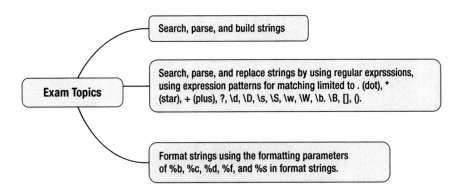

String objects are extensively used in writing Java applications. Java programs use strings not only in business logic but also to implement utility functionality such as logging. Therefore, it is useful and important to understand strings and related concepts.

Apart from the common operations, searching and parsing are two useful operations that are performed on strings. Java provides extensive support to achieve these operations efficiently and easily. Starting from Version 4, Java supports regular expressions and offers two useful classes to exploit the power of regular expressions. From Version 5 on, Java also supports C-like printf() style for formatting strings.

The OCAJP7 exam has three topics related to strings: "Create and manipulate strings;" "Manipulate data using the StringBuilder class and its methods;" and "Test equality between strings and other objects using == and equals()". On the assumption that you have the prerequisites for OCPJP 7 certification and are already comfortable with using strings, we proceed directly to the topics covered in the OCPJP7 exam.

As an OCPJP7 exam candidate, you are expected to be familiar with searching, parsing, and building strings; regular expressions and their usage; and string formatting and format specifiers. In this chapter, we will cover all these topics in detail.

Processing Strings

In this section, you will learn how to process character data stored within a String object.

String Searching

When working with strings, you often need to search within a given string. There are several overloaded versions of the method indexOf() available in the String class for searching a string forward, the lastIndexOf() method for searching a string backward, and the regionMatches() method for comparing a "region" of text within a string. We'll discuss each of these methods in turn.

The IndexOf() Method

How do you search for a particular character within a string and, if it occurs, at what position? For example, which index position does the character J occupy in the string "OCPJP"? Listing 7-1 contains the code that uses the indexOf() method to answer this question.

Listing 7-1. SearchString1.java

```java
// Demonstrates searching a character in a string
public class SearchString1 {
        public static void main(String[] s) {
                String str = "OCPJP";
                System.out.println("Character J occurs at index: " + str.indexOf('J'));
        }
}
```

It prints the following:

```
Character J occurs at index 3
```

Quite easy, right? The indexOf() method searches the specified character— here it is, the character J— and returns the first occurrence of the character (note that the index starts from 0, not 1!). Now, let's search a substring within in a given string. The indexOf() method is overloaded, and one definition of the method takes a string as a search argument. Listing 7-2 shows an example.

Listing 7-2. SearchString2.java

```java
// Demonstrates searching a substring within a string using indexOf() method
public class SearchString2 {
        public static void main(String[] s){
                String str = "I am preparing for OCPJP";
                System.out.println("Substring \"for\" occurs at index: " + str.indexOf("for"));
        }
}
```

This program prints the following:

```
Substring "for" occurs at index: 15
```

(Please note that we used the escape character, \, to print "for" within double quotes.)

What will happen if the search string does not exist in the string? For instance, if you search "fort" instead of "for" in above example, you'll get this result:

```
Substring "for" occurs at index: -1
```

Well, a failed indexOf search results in the value –1, indicating "not found."

These two were simple problems; now let's try a slightly harder one. Given a big string, how can you find how many times a given string (say "am") occurs within that string? Not to worry—in this case there is another version of the indexOf() method. In this method you can specify an index from which the search should commence. Listing 7-3 shows the implementation.

Listing 7-3. SearchString3.java

```
// This example demonstrates how to search multiple occurences of a search string
public class SearchString3 {
        public static void main(String[] s) {
                String str = "I am a student. I am preparing for OCPJP";
                int fromIndex = 0;
                while(str.indexOf("am", fromIndex) > -1) {
                        fromIndex = str.indexOf("am", fromIndex);
                        System.out.println("Substring \"am\" occurs at index: " + fromIndex);
                        fromIndex++;
                }
        }
}
```

The example prints the following:

```
Substring "am" occurs at index: 2
Substring "am" occurs at index: 18
```

It uses a while loop to check whether more occurrences of the search string exist in the input string. It also maintains an index (fromIndex) from which you search ahead. It increments the fromIndex variable after each occurrence of the search string so that the next occurrence of the search string can be found.

If you want to search the last occurrence of the search string, you can use the overloaded versions of the lastIndexOf() method defined in the String class. The String class also has simple methods to check for beginnings or ending of strings, and these methods are given in Table 7-1.

Table 7-1. *Methods to Check for Matching Prefix or Suffix in a String*

Method	Description
boolean startsWith(String prefixString, int offset)	Starting from offset, check if this string has prefixString.
boolean startsWith(String prefixString)	Check if this string has prefixString; equivalent to startsWith(prefixString, 0);
boolean endsWith(String suffixString)	Check if this string has the suffixString.

The regionMatches() Method

Consider the string "Tarzan: Hi Jane, wanna ride an elephant? \n Jane: No thanks! I'm preparing for OCPJP now!" How can you check if the string " Jane: No thanks!" is present as the first part in Jane's response? (Note: Jane's response is the region of text that comes after the newline character "\n".)

There are many ways to solve this problem, and you'll use the regionMatches() method here in order to learn how to use it. Table 7-2 lists the two overloaded methods of the regionMatches() method. To solve the problem in the given string, you can first look for the character "\n" and then from that index position, you can search for the string " Jane: No thanks! ", as shown in Listing 7-4.

Table 7-2. *The regionMatches() Methods and Descriptions*

Method	Description
boolean regionMatches(int start, String matchingStr, int matchStartOffset, int matchLen)	Starting from start in this String object, check if the region of text given by matchingStr matches. In matchStr, check for matchLen characters starting from matchStartOffset.
boolean regionMatches(boolean ignoreCase, int start, String matchingStr, int matchStartOffset, int matchLen)	Same as the previous method, but with the additional first argument, which ignores the case differences.

Listing 7-4. MatchRegionInString.java

```java
// This example demonstrates how to search a "region" of text within a string
public class MatchRegionInString {
        public static void main(String[] s) {
                String chat = "Tarzan: Hi Jane, wanna ride an Elephant? \n Jane: No thanks! I'm
preparing for OCPJP now!";
                String matchString = " Jane: No thanks!";
                // first get the index of the position from which the search region starts
                int startIndex = chat.indexOf('\n');
                System.out.println("Jane's response starts at the index: " + startIndex);
                // if '\n' found, then try matching for the string " Jane: No thanks!" from there
                if(startIndex > -1) {
                        // remember that the index starts from 0 and not 1, so add 1 to startIndex
                        boolean doesMatch = chat.regionMatches(startIndex + 1, matchString, 0,
matchString.length());
                        if(doesMatch)
                                System.out.println("Jane's response matches with the string" +
matchString);
                }
        }
}
```

This program prints the following output, as you expected:

```
Jane's response starts at the index: 41
Jane's response matches the string Jane: No thanks!
```

String Parsing

Parsing is an interesting and useful operation on strings. (The word *parse* means "to analyze to break down into constituent parts based on an assumed structure.") We will introduce you to the basic parsing operation in this section; we will discuss advanced parsing topics later in this chapter when discussing regular expressions.

String Conversions

In your programs, you'll find it is often necessary to convert strings to and from primitive types such as floats, ints, and booleans. To convert from a primitive type value to String type, you can use the overloaded valueOf() method from the String class.

Let's start with converting an integer value 10 to String. Here's how to do it:

```
String str1 = String.valueOf(10);        // right way to convert from an integer to String
```

Note that direct assignments or casts will result in compiler error, such as these two statements:

```
String str1 = 10;              // compiler error-cannot convert from int to String
String str1 = (String) 10;     // compiler error-cannot convert from int to String
```

How about the conversion the other way around: if a string has value of some primitive type (say an integral value), how can you perform the conversion? Obviously, the following two statements, which attempt to directly assign or change type through an explicit cast, will result in compiler errors:

```
int i = "10";            // compiler error-cannot convert from String to int
int i = (int) "10";      // compiler error-cannot convert from String to int
```

To make this type conversion, you need to use the parseInt() static method available in the Integer class, like so:

```
int i = Integer.parseInt("10"); // right way to convert from a String to an int
```

This parseInt() method is an overloaded method. There is another parseInt() method that takes an additional argument: the base (or radix) of the integral value such as octal and hexadecimal. The wrapper classes Byte, Short, Long, Float, and Double have the equivalent parse methods to convert a string to the corresponding primitive type value. What if you pass an invalid argument to one of these parse methods? For example,

```
float f = Float.parseFloat("no such value");
```

For this code, you'll get a runtime exception of java.lang.NumberFormatException since the string "no such value" cannot be converted to float type value.

The Split() Method

Listing 7-5 shows an example of how to split a sentence and print all words in the string using the split() method of the String class.

Listing 7-5. ParseString1.java

```java
// this example demonstrates the usage of split() method
public class ParseString1 {
    public static void main(String[] s) {
        String quote = "Never lend books-nobody ever returns them!";
        String [] words = quote.split(" "); // split strings based on the delimiter " "
(space)
        for (String word : words) {
            System.out.println(word);
        }
    }
}
```

It prints the following:

```
Never
lend
books-nobody
ever
returns
them!
```

The split() method takes a delimiter as a regular expression (you will explore regular expression later in this chapter). In this example, you provide a whitespace as a delimiter, so you are able to extract all the words in the sentence. Note how the characters "-" and "!" are part of the strings "books-nobody" and "them!" since you did not specify any punctuation characters as delimiters. You'll revisit this problem shortly when you learn about regular expressions.

The argument of the split() method is a delimiter string, which is a regular expression. If the regular expression you pass has invalid syntax, you'll get a PatternSyntaxException exception.

Now, let's assume that you have a string containing the path of a folder, and you want to parse this string and print individual folder names. Listing 7-6 shows the implementation.

Listing 7-6. ParseString2.java

```java
public class ParseString2 {
    public static void main(String[] args) {
        String str = "c:\\work\\programs\\parser";
        String [] dirList = str.split("\\\\");
        for (int i=0; i<dirList.length; i++) {
            System.out.println(dirList[i]);
        }
    }
}
```

It prints the following:

```
c:
work
programs
parser
```

In this example, two things may surprise you.

- First, the use of "\\" instead of "\" is interesting. In order to show special characters in a string, you need to use the escape sequence for such special characters. For instance, if you want to put a new line character, you have to use "\n"; similarly you have to use "\t" for a tab symbol. Here, you want to use a backslash, which can be shown in a string as "\\".

- The second thing is the delimiter used with the split() method. Well, a regular expression was used here to parse the path using "\" as a delimiter. We will soon discuss the usage of four consecutive backslashes instead of one when we discuss regular expressions.

Regular Expressions

A *regular expression* defines a search pattern that can be used to execute operations such as string search and string manipulation. A regular expression is nothing but a sequence of predefined symbols specified in a predefined syntax that helps you search or manipulate strings. A regular expression is specified as a string and applied on another string from left to right.

You may wonder why you need a *regex* (short for REGular EXpression) when you can directly perform a search using the string function, as you did in last section using indexOf(), for example. Well, the answer is quite simple. You can use the indexOf() method (or any other similar method) when you know the exact string to be searched. However, in cases where you know only the pattern of a string but not a specific string, you need to use regex. Regex is a much more powerful tool than simple search methods for searching and manipulating strings. For example, say you want to search all e-mail addresses in a given string. You cannot achieve this using the indexOf() method since you don't know the exact e-mail address; however, you can use a regex to specify a pattern that will find all the e-mail addresses in the string.

Understanding regex Symbols

We will now focus on understanding the syntax and semantics of symbols used to specify regular expressions. Table 7-3 shows commonly used symbols to specify regex.

Table 7-3. *Commonly Used Symbols to Specify regex*

Symbol	Description
^expr	Matches expr at beginning of line.
expr$	Matches expr at end of line.
.	Matches any single character (except the newline character).
[xyz]	Matches either x, y, or z.
[p-z]	Specifies a range. Matches any character from p to z.
[p-z1-9]	Matches either any character from p to z or any digit from 1 to 9 (remember, it won't match p1).
[^p-z]	'^' as first character inside a bracket negates the pattern; it matches any character except characters p to z.
Xy	Matches x followed by y.
x|y	Matches either x or y.

You can use the symbols given in Table 7-3 and specify regex. For example, you can write "[0-9]" to match all digit characters or "[\t\r\f\n]" to match all whitespaces. Also, you can also use certain predefined *metasymbols* to ease the regex specification. For instance, you can specify "\d" instead of "[0-9]" to match digits, or "\s" instead of "[\t\r\f\n]" to match all whitespaces. Table 7-4 summarizes a list of commonly used metasymbols.

Table 7-4. *Commonly Used Metasymbols to Specify regex*

Symbol	Description
\d	Matches digits (equivalent to [0–9]).
\D	Matches non-digits.
\w	Matches word characters.

(continued)

Table 7-4. (*continued*)

Symbol	Description
\W	Matches non-word characters.
\s	Matches whitespaces (equivalent to [\t\r\f\n]).
\S	Matches non-whitespaces.
\b	Matches word boundary when outside bracket. Matches backslash when inside bracket.
\B	Matches non-word boundary.
\A	Matches beginning of string.
\Z	Matches end of string.

Okay, so far so good. But what if you want to specify a regex when the match involves an occurrence count of characters? Well, for such situations you can use *quantifier symbols*, provided in Table 7-5.

Table 7-5. *Commonly Used Quantifier Symbols*

Symbol	Description
expr?	Matches 0 or 1 occurrence of expr (equivalent to expr{0,1}).
expr*	Matches 0 or more occurrences of expr (equivalent to expr{0,}).
expr+	Matches 1 or more occurrences of expr (equivalent to expr{1,}).
expr{x}	Matches x occurrences of expr.
expr{x, y}	Matches between x and y occurrences of expr.
expr{x,}	Matches x or more occurrences of expr.

Regex Support in Java

Java 1.4 SDK introduced regex support in Java. The package java.util.regex supports regex. It consists of two important classes, Pattern and Matcher. Pattern represents a regex in a compiled representation, and Matcher interprets a regex and matches the corresponding substring in a given string.

At this point, you may ask why is regex supported by dedicated classes such as Matcher and Pattern when other methods such as split() in the String class already support regex? The single word answer for this question is: performance. The Pattern and Matcher classes are optimized for performance while methods like split() in String are not.

 Use the Pattern and Matcher classes whenever you are performing search or replace on strings heavily; they are more efficient than split() in String or other methods.

Now, let's see how you can use the Pattern and Matcher classes. You first need to call a static method compile() in the Pattern class to get an instance of a pattern. The first argument of this method is a regex. Then, you need to call another static method called matcher() from the Pattern class to get an instance of the Matcher class. The matcher() method returns a Matcher object. This object is then used to execute the required operation on the input string.

Let's look at how to use the Pattern and Matcher classes. Let's assume that you have a string consisting of personal details (such as name, address, phone number) of a set of people. You will use the following string for the examples covered in rest of this section:

```
String str = "Danny Doo, Flat no 502, Big Apartment, Wide Road, Near Huge Milestone, Hugo-city
56010, Ph: 9876543210, Email: danny@myworld.com. Maggi Myer, Post bag no 52, Big bank post office,
Big bank city 56000, ph: 9876501234, Email: maggi07@myuniverse.com.";
```

 You need to specify regex using the backslash (\); do not use the forward slash (/) instead. The compiler will not give any error if you use the forward slash; however, you won't get the desired output.

Searching and Parsing with regex

Let's start with a simple example. You need to write code to print all words of the string str. How can you do this? Well, do you remember metacharacter "\w", which matches with all symbols forming a word? You are going to use "\w" along with the quantifier "+" to make "\w+", which means you want to search all words of length one or more; see Listing 7-7.

Listing 7-7. Regex1.java

```java
import java.util.regex.Matcher;
import java.util.regex.Pattern;

public class Regex1 {
    public static void main(String[] args) {
        String str = "Danny Doo, Flat no 502, Big Apartment, Wide Road, Near Huge Milestone,
Hugo-city 56010, Ph: 9876543210, Email: danny@myworld.com. Maggi Myer, Post bag no 52, Big bank post
office, Big bank city 56000, ph: 9876501234, Email: maggi07@myuniverse.com.";
        Pattern pattern = Pattern.compile("\\w+");
        Matcher matcher = pattern.matcher(str);
        while(matcher.find()) {
            System.out.println(matcher.group());
        }
    }
}
```

It prints the following:

```
Danny
Doo
Flat
no
502
...
maggi07
myuniverse
com
```

(Note that we have truncated the results with . . . to save space.) However, you can see that the regular expression searched all words consisting at least one character. What happened here was that you invoked the compile() method along with a regex of the Pattern class to get an instance of Pattern. After that, you got an instance of the Matcher class by calling the matcher() method on pattern instance. And finally you got the result using the group() and find() methods of the Matcher class. The method find() returns true if there exists any search result. The group() method returns a search result occurrence as a string.

Note that we used two backslashes in the regex ("\\w+") specified in Listing 7-7 because backslash is a escape character in regex. However, backslash is also a escape character in Java strings, which means literal "\\" is interpreted as a single backslash. This translates to an interesting outcome: we write "\\" as a single backslash in a regex, which will be written as "\\\\" in a Java program if we want to specify a single backslash.

In the same way, you can search all the numbers using the "\d+" regex. Now, let's say you want to search and print all ZIP codes (postal code) appeared in the string. Assume that the ZIP code length is always 5. Can you achieve this using regex? Will the program in Listing 7-8 work?

Listing 7-8. Regex2.java

```
import java.util.regex.Matcher;
import java.util.regex.Pattern;

// This program demonstrates how we can search numbers of a specified length
public class Regex2 {
        public static void main(String[] args) {
                String str = "Danny Doo, Flat no 502, Big Apartment, Wide Road, Near Huge Milestone,
Hugo-city 56010, Ph: 9876543210, Email: danny@myworld.com. Maggi Myer, Post bag no 52, Big bank post
office, Big bank city 56000, ph: 9876501234, Email: maggi07@myuniverse.com.";
                Pattern pattern = Pattern.compile("\\d{5}");
                Matcher matcher = pattern.matcher(str);
                while(matcher.find()) {
                        System.out.println(matcher.group());
                }
        }
}
```

You used "\d{5}" as the regex string. Let's see what this program prints:

```
56010
98765
43210
56000
98765
01234
```

Oops! It has printed two ZIP codes but also printed three partial phone numbers, which was unexpected. Hmm, to get only the ZIP codes, you must specify the regex more properly. Try again with Listing 7-9.

Listing 7-9. Regex3.java

```java
import java.util.regex.Matcher;
import java.util.regex.Pattern;

// This program demonstrates how we can search numbers of a specified length
public class Regex3 {
    public static void main(String[] args) {
        String str = "Danny Doo, Flat no 502, Big Apartment, Wide Road, Near Huge Milestone,
Hugo-city 56010, Ph: 9876543210, Email: danny@myworld.com. Maggi Myer, Post bag no 52, Big bank post
office, Big bank city 56000, ph: 9876501234, Email: maggi07@myuniverse.com.";
        Pattern pattern = Pattern.compile("\\D\\d{5}\\D");
        Matcher matcher = pattern.matcher(str);
        while(matcher.find()) {
            System.out.println(matcher.group());
        }
    }
}
```

It prints the following:

```
 56010,
 56000,
```

This time you used "\D\d{5}\D" and it worked well. What you essentially did was specify that a non-digit character is preceded and followed by a six-digit number. Easy, right! Well, there is a problem in this solution. The program is printing one whitespace just before the six-digit number and a comma just after the six-digit number (both matched by "\D"). Can you get rid of these unwanted characters? Yes, there is an elegant solution to this: you can use "\b" (used to detect word boundaries) here. See if this works by trying the code in Listing 7-10.

Listing 7-10. RegexDemo.java

```java
import java.util.regex.Matcher;
import java.util.regex.Pattern;

// This program demonstrates how we can search numbers of a specified length
public class Regex4 {
    public static void main(String[] args) {
        String str = "Danny Doo, Flat no 502, Big Apartment, Wide Road, Near Huge Milestone,
Hugo-city 56010, Ph: 9876543210, Email: danny@myworld.com. Maggi Myer, Post bag no 52, Big bank post
office, Big bank city 56000, ph: 9876501234, Email: maggi07@myuniverse.com.";
        Pattern pattern = Pattern.compile("\\b\\d{5}\\b");
        Matcher matcher = pattern.matcher(str);
        while(matcher.find()) {
            System.out.println(matcher.group());
        }
    }
}
```

It prints the following:

```
56010
56000
```

That's perfect. Similarly, you can also search all phone numbers, since the length of the phone numbers in the example string length is 10.

Now, let's try to do something little more difficult: searching e-mail addresses. In an e-mail address, the first part is a word (which can be specified by "\w+"), followed by a "@", followed by another word, and suffixed by ".com" (for the sake of simplicity, let's ignore other suffixes such as ".edu"). Hence, the regex for searching e-mail address in the example-string is "\w+@\w+\.com". Will this regex string work? Try the code in Listing 7-11.

Listing 7-11. Regex5.java

```java
import java.util.regex.Matcher;
import java.util.regex.Pattern;

// This program demonstrates how we can search email addresses
public class Regex5 {
        public static void main(String[] args) {
                String str = "Danny Doo, Flat no 502, Big Apartment, Wide Road, Near Huge Milestone,
Hugo-city 56010, Ph: 9876543210, Email: danny@myworld.com. Maggi Myer, Post bag no 52, Big bank post
office, Big bank city 56000, ph: 9876501234, Email: maggi07@myuniverse.com.";
                Pattern pattern = Pattern.compile("\\w+@\\w+\\.com");
                Matcher matcher = pattern.matcher(str);
                while(matcher.find()) {
                        System.out.println(matcher.group());
                }
        }
}
```

It prints the following:

```
danny@myworld.com
maggi07@myuniverse.com
```

That worked!

Replacing Strings with regex

In the previous section, you tried searching and parsing strings with regex. You can also manipulate (modify) strings with regex. Let's try replacing strings now.

In the string in your example, currently all phone numbers are represented as a string of consecutive 10 digits. Now you want to change this phone number format to XXX-XXXXXXX format—in other words, you want to insert a dash (–) after the third digit of the phone number. Listing 7-12 shows how to achieve this.

Listing 7-12. Regex6.java

```java
import java.util.regex.Matcher;
import java.util.regex.Pattern;

// This program demonstrates how we can manipulate text
public class Regex6 {
        public static void main(String[] args) {
                String str = "Danny Doo, Flat no 502, Big Apartment, Wide Road, Near Huge Milestone,
Hugo-city 56010, Ph: 9876543210, Email: danny@myworld.com. Maggi Myer, Post bag no 52, Big bank post
office, Big bank city 56000, ph: 9876501234, Email: maggi07@myuniverse.com.";
```

```
            Pattern pattern = Pattern.compile("(\\D)(\\d{3})(\\d{7})(\\D)");
            Matcher matcher = pattern.matcher(str);
            String newStr = matcher.replaceAll("$1$2-$3$4");
            System.out.println(newStr);
        }
}
```

The output of this program is the following:

Danny Doo, Flat no 502, Big Apartment, Wide Road, Near Huge Milestone, Hugo-city 56010, Ph: 987-6543210, Email: danny@myworld.com. Maggi Myer, Post bag no 52, Big bank post office, Big bank city 56000, ph: 987-6501234, Email: maggi07@myuniverse.com.

Good, it worked as expected. But how did you achieve this? One very evident observation is that you used replaceAll() of the Matcher class. However, there is one more important concept that you need to understand to grasp the above example.

You can form groups within a regex. These groups can be used to specify quantifiers on a desired subset of the whole regex. These groups can also be used to specify back-reference. Each group can be referred to as $n where n is an integer—so, for example, the first group can be referred to as $1, the second group can be referred to as $2, and so on.

Here, you formed four groups, and while replacing, you inserted a dash between second and third group. That's how your replacement works.

Now, let's do something different. Let's implement a method to validate an IP address. Can you suggest a regex to match an IP address?

Did you say "\b\d{1,3}\.\d{1,3}\.\d{1,3}\.\d{1,3}\b", where "\b" is used to match word boundaries and "\d{1,3}" is used to specify that you expect three digit number here. Well, it's a nice try but it's wrong!

A valid IP address consists of 4 numbers separated by dots, where each number can be between 0 and 255 (both inclusive). That means any number greater than 255 will result in an invalid IP address. However, in the above regex you can write any three-digit number (even greater than 255) and the regex will match. Hence, it is wrong.

Listing 7-13 shows the correct implementation of the regex for an IP address.

Listing 7-13. Regex7.java

```
import java.util.regex.Pattern;

// This program demonstrates how we can validate an IP address
public class Regex7 {
        void validateIP(String ipStr) {
                String regex = "\\b((25[0-5]|2[0-4]\\d|[01]?\\d\\d?)(\\.)){3}(25[0-5]|2[0-4]\\
d|[01]?\\d\\d?)\\b";
                System.out.println(ipStr + " is valid? " + Pattern.matches(regex, ipStr));
        }
        public static void main(String[] args) {
                String ipStr1 = "255.245.188.123";      // valid IP address
                String ipStr2 = "255.245.188.273";      // invalid IP address - 273 is greater than 255
                Regex7 validator = new Regex7();
                validator.validateIP(ipStr1);
                validator.validateIP(ipStr2);
        }
}
```

This snippet prints the following:

```
255.245.188.123 is valid? True
255.245.188.273 is valid? False
```

The first string (ipStr1) is a valid IP address and the second string (ipStr2) is not a valid IP address. The regex specified by you successfully identified the valid IP address. Don't be alarmed at the lengthy regex; it will be easy once you understand it.

Let's begin with the start and end symbols—"\b" is a boundary marker, as you saw earlier. Now, let's look at the first group, "((25[0-5]|2[0-4]\d|[01]?\d\d?)(\.))", which has two parts: the first part specifies the regex for a number less than 256 and second part specifies a dot. The first part of the first group has 3 subexpressions. The first subexpression specifies that the number could be in the range between 250 and 255. The second subexpression specifies that the number could be 200 to 249, and the third subexpression specifies that the number could be 0 to 199. You want to repeat this first group three times, so you place "{3}" immediately after the first group. The second group is nothing but the first group without a dot.

String Formatting

So far we have discussed how to search or parse a String object. What if you would like to format a string in a predefined template? For example, let's assume that you are computing the area of a circle and you want to print the computed area with only two fractional digits. If you try the usual System.out.println method, it will print a quite big float number. As another example, say you want to separate the digits of a big number with separator such as a comma to print it to the end user. In such cases, you can use the C-style printf() (print formatted) method that was introduced in Java 5.

The method printf() uses string-formatting flags to format strings. It is quite similar to the printf() function provided in the library of the C programming language. The printf() method is provided as part of the PrintStream class. Here is its signature:

```
PrintStream printf(String format, Object... args)
```

The first parameter of the printf() method is a format string. A format string may contain string literals and *format specifiers*. The actual arguments are passed as the second arguments (args parameter here). This method can throw IllegalFormatException if the passed format is not correct.

Format specifiers are the crux of the string formatting concepts. They define the placeholder for a specific data type and its format (such as alignment and width). The remaining parameters of the printf() method are the variables (or literals) that provide the actual data to fill in the placeholders in sequence of the format specifiers.

Format Specifiers

Let's investigate the template of format specifiers in the printf() method:

```
%[flags][width][.precision]datatype_specifier
```

As you can see, each format specifier starts with % sign followed by flags, width, and precision information and ends with data type specifier. In this string, the flags, width, and precision information is optional while the % sign and data type specifiers are mandatory.

Flags are single-character symbols that specify characteristics such as alignment and filling character. For instance, flag "-" specifies left alignment, "^" specifies center alignment, and "0" pads the number with leading zeroes.

The width specifier indicates the minimum number of characters that will span in the final formatted string. If the input data is shorter than the specified width, then it is padded with spaces by default. In case the input data is bigger than the specified width, the full data appears in the output string without trimming.

The *precision field* specifies the number of precision digits in output string. This optional field is particularly useful with floating point numbers.

Finally, the *data type specifier* indicates the type of expected input data. The field is a placeholder for the specified input data. Table 7-6 provides a list of commonly used data type specifiers.

Table 7-6. *Commonly Used Data Type Specifiers*

Symbol	Description
%b	Boolean
%c	Character
%d	Decimal integer (signed)
%e	Floating point number in scientific format
%f	Floating point numer in decimal format
%g	Floating point numer in decimal or scientific format (depending on the value passed as argument)
%h	Hashcode of the passed argument
%n	Line separator (new line character)
%o	Integer formatted as an octal value
%s	String
%t	Date/time
%x	Integer formatted as an hexadecimal value

Let's use the `printf()` method to format the output of the `area()` method of a `Circle` class. By default, the `area()` method calculates the area of the circle and prints using the `System.out.println()` method. However, you want to control the format of the output. More specifically, you want to print the area with only two precision points. Listing 7-14 shows how to achieve this.

Listing 7-14. Circle.java

```java
// This program shows the usage of formatting string in printf() method
class Circle {
        private int x, y, radius;
        public Circle(int x, int y, int radius) {
                this.x = x;
                this.y = y;
                this.radius = radius;
        }
        void area() {
                double tempArea = Math.PI * radius * radius;
                System.out.println("Cirle area using default formatting with println: " + tempArea);
                System.out.printf("Circle area using format specifier with printf: %.2f", tempArea);
        }
        public static void main(String[] str) {
                Circle circle = new Circle(10,10,5);
                circle.area();
        }
}
```

This program produces following output:

```
Cirle area using default formatting with println: 78.53981633974483
Circle area using format specifier with printf: 78.54
```

Well, you can see that the first line contains the unformatted long output while the second line contains formatted output using formatting string in `printf()` method.

Let's use more formatting options in an example. Suppose that you want to print a table of soccer players along with their names, played matches, scored goals, and goals per match information. However, there are a few constraints:

- You want to print the name of players to the left (left aligned).

- You want to specify at least 15 characters for the name of the players.

- You want to print each column at a distance of a tab-stop.

- You want to specify only one precision point in goals per match info.

Listing 7-15 shows how to implement this.

Listing 7-15. FormattedTable.java

```java
// This program demonstrates the use of format specifiers in printf
class FormattedTable {
        static void line() {
                System.out.
println("-----------------------------------------------------------------");
        }
        static void printHeader() {
                System.out.printf("%-15s \t %s \t %s \t %s \n",
                        "Player", "Matches", "Goals", "Goals per match");

        }
        static void printRow(String player, int matches, int goals) {
                System.out.printf("%-15s \t %5d \t\t %d \t\t %.1f \n",
                        player, matches, goals, ((float)goals/(float)matches));
        }
        public static void main(String[] str) {
                FormattedTable.line();
                FormattedTable.printHeader();
                FormattedTable.line();
                FormattedTable.printRow("Demando", 100, 122);
                FormattedTable.printRow("Mushi", 80, 100);
                FormattedTable.printRow("Peale", 150, 180);
                FormattedTable.line();
        }
}
```

This program produces following output:

```
------------------------------------------------------------------------
Player          Matches        Goals        Goals per match
------------------------------------------------------------------------
Demando         100            122          1.2
Mushi            80            100          1.3
Peale           150            180          1.2
------------------------------------------------------------------------
```

Let's analyze the format string specified in the printRow() method. The first part of the format string is "%-15s". Here, the expression starts with %, which indicates the start of a format-specifier string. The next symbol is '-', which is used to make the string left aligned. The number "15" specifies the width of the string and finally data type specifier of "s" indicates the input data type as String. The next format specifier string is "%5d", which signifies it expects an integer that will be displayed in the minimum 5 digits. The last format specifier string is "%.1f", which expects a floating point number that will be displayed with one precision digit. All format specifier strings are separated with one or more "\t"s (tab stops) to make space between the columns.

Points to Remember

Here are some points that might prove useful on your OCPJP exam:

- If you do not specify any string formatting specifier, the printf() method will not print anything from the given arguments!

- Flags such as "-", "^", or "0" make sense only when you specify width with the format specifier string.

- You can also print the % character in a format string; however, you need to use an escape sequence for it. In format specifier strings, % is an escape character—which means you need to use %% to print a single %.

- If you do not provide the intended input data type as expected by the format string, then you can get an IllegalFormatConversionException. For instance, if you provide a string instead of an expected integer in your printRow() method implementation, you will get following exception:

  ```
  Exception in thread "main" java.util.IllegalFormatConversionException:
  d != java.lang.String at java.util.Formatter$FormatSpecifier.failConversion
  (Unknown Source)
  ```

- If you want to form a string and use it later rather than just printing it using the printf() method, you can use a static method in the String class—format(). We have reimplemented the printRow() method used in the last example using the format() method, as shown:

  ```java
  void printRow(String player, int matches, int goals){
      String str = String.format("%-15s \t %5d \t\t %d \t\t %.1f \n",
              player, matches, goals, ((float)goals/(float)matches));
      System.out.print(str);
  }
  ```

QUESTION TIME!

1. Consider this program, which intends to print the word delimited by the characters '*' in its both ends:

```java
public class SearchString {
    public static void main(String[] args) {
            String quote = "An *onion* a day keeps everyone away!";
            // match the word delimited by *'s
            int startDelimit = quote.indexOf('*');
            int endDelimit = quote.lastIndexOf("*");
            System.out.println(quote.substring(startDelimit, endDelimit));
    }
}
```

This program will print one of the following options:

A. *onion

B. *onion*

C. onion

D. *onio

E. nion*

Answer: A. *onion

(The substring (beginIndex, endIndex) consists of characters beginning from the character at beginIndex till the character at the endIndex − 1.)

2. Predict the outcome of the following program:

```java
public class ParseString1 {
    public static void main(String[] s) {
            String quote = "Never lend books-nobody ever returns them!";
            String [] words = quote.split(" ", 2);
            // split strings based on the delimiter " " (space)
            for (String word : words) {
                    System.out.println(word);
            }
    }
}
```

A. It will result in a compile-time error.

B. It will result in a runtime exception.

C. It will print the following output when executed

    Never

    lend

D. It will print the following output when executed

Never

lend books-nobody ever returns them!

Answer: D. It will print the following output when executed

Never

Lend books-nobody ever returns them!

(The second parameter of the split() method specifies the total number of strings that the split() method needs to generate. In the last string (here, in the second string), the split() method puts the remaining part of the string.)

3. Listing 7-11 used the regex "\w+@\w+\.com" to match e-mail addresses in a string where the e-mail addresses end with a ".com" domain. Can you replace the regex with the following: "\w+@\w+.com"?

A. Yes, it will work perfectly and will only match valid e-mail addresses.

B. No, it will result in a compile-time error.

C. No, it will result in a runtime exception.

D. No, it will produce wrong matches and will match invalid e-mail addresses.

Answer: D. No, it will produce wrong matches and will match invalid e-mail addresses.

(It will produce wrong matches. For instance, it will match to "abc@xyz!com" also, since "." works here as a single character wildcard, which could match any character.)

4. Which of the following regular expressions is the correct expression for matching a mobile number stored in following format: +YY-XXXXXXXXXX (YY is the country code, the rest of the number is a mobile number)?

A. "\+\d{2}-\d{10}"

B. "\b\+\d{2}-\d{10}\b"

C. "+\d{2}-\d{10}"

D. "\b+\d{2}-\d{10}\b"

Answer: A. "\+\d{2}-\d{10}"

(You need to provide a backslash as an escape character for "+". Another important point is that you cannot use "\b" in starting and ending if the first or last character of the string is not a word character.)

5. You want to write a regex to match an e-mail address. The e-mail address should not start with a digit and should end with ".com". Which one of the following regex will satisfy this requirement?

A. "\b\w+@\w+\.com\b"

B. "\b\D\w*@\w+\.com\b"

C. "\b\D\w+@\w+\.com\b"

D. None of the above

Answer: B. "b\D\w*@\w+\.com\b"

("\b" is used to mark word boundaries, "\D" is used to match any non-digit number, and "\w*" is used to match any word of length zero or more. The remaining part is similar to that used earlier.)

6. What kind of strings will the regex "\d*[02468]" match?

    A.   Any number containing at least one of the 0, 2, 4, 6, or 8 digits.

    B.   Any number starting from one of the 0, 2, 4, 6, or 8 digits.

    C.   Any number containing all the specified (0, 2, 4, 6, 8) digits at the end of the number.

    D.   Any number ending with one of the specified (0, 2, 4, 6, 8) digits.

    Answer: D. Any number ending with one of the specified (0, 2, 4, 6, 8) digits.

    (All even numbers.)

Summary

Searching, Parsing, and Building Strings

- You can use the overloaded versions of the method indexOf() in the String class for forward searching in a string, lastIndexOf() for backward searching a string, and regionMatches() for comparing a "region" of text within a string.

- To convert from a primitive type value to String type object, you can make use of the overloaded valueOf() method, which takes a primitive type value as an argument and returns the String object. To convert from the String type object to a primitive type value, you can make use of the parse methods available for primitive types in the corresponding wrapper types of the primitive types.

- For parsing a string, you can use the split() method available in the String class. It takes a delimiter as an argument, and this argument is a regular expression.

Regular Expressions

- A regular expression defines a search pattern that can be used to execute operations such as string search and string manipulation.

- Use the Pattern and Matcher classes whenever you are performing search or replace on strings heavily; they are more efficient and faster than any other way to perform search/replace in Java.

- You can form groups within a regex. These groups can be used to specify quantifiers on a desired subset of the whole regex. These groups can also be used to specify back reference.

String Formatting

- The method printf() (and the method format() in the String class) uses string formatting flags to format strings.

- Each format specifier starts with the % sign; followed by flags, width, and precision information; and ending with a data type specifier. In this string, the flags, width, and precision information are optional but the % sign and data type specifier are mandatory.

CHAPTER 8

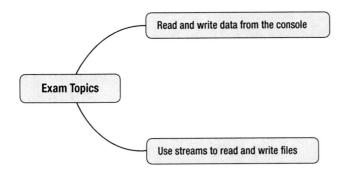

Java I/O Fundamentals

In this chapter, we'll introduce you to the fundamentals of Java I/O programming. We'll cover two topics: how to read and write data from console, and then how to use (file) streams to read and write data.

Programming with I/O involves writing some exception-handling code as well. If you're not familiar with the basics of exception handling, such as how to use try-catch-finally blocks or try-with-resources statements, we recommend that you to read the first three sections in the chapter on exception handling and assertions (Chapter 11) and then return to this chapter.

The support for file manipulation is provided in the java.io and java.nio packages. In the initial part of this chapter, we'll focus only on the java.io package; later, we'll focus on reading and writing data using streams (but none of the other features provided in the java.io package. The java.nio package provides comprehensive support for file I/O, and we cover it in Chapter 9). You can use printf-style formatting with the Console class, and this formatting API is covered in detail in Chapter 7.

Reading and Writing from Console

In this section, we'll discuss reading and writing from the console.

Understanding the Console Class

Using the Console class (which was introduced in Java 1.6) will considerably simplify reading the data from the console and writing the data on the console. Note that the word "console" here refers to the character input device (typically a keyboard), and the character display device (typically the screen display). You can obtain a reference to the console using the System.console() method; if the JVM is not associated with any console, this method will return null.

Your first exercise is to implement a simple Echo command that prints back the line of text typed as input when you run this program (Listing 8-1).

Listing 8-1. Echo.java

```java
import java.io.Console;

// simple implementation of Echo command
class Echo {
        public static void main(String []args) {
                // get the System console object
                Console console = System.console();
                if(console == null) {
                        System.err.println("Cannot retrive console object - are you running your
application from an IDE? Exiting the application ... ");
                        System.exit(-1); // terminate the application
                }
                // read a line and print it through printf
                console.printf(console.readLine());
        }
}
```

Here is how the program behaves for different output:

```
D:\>java Echo
hello world
hello world

D:\>java Echo
^Z
Exception in thread "main" java.lang.NullPointerException
        at java.util.regex.Matcher.getTextLength(Matcher.java:1234)
        ... [this part of the stack trace elided to save space]
        at Echo.main(Echo.java:14)
```

For normal text input, this program works fine. If you type no input and try terminating the program with ^z or ^d (Ctrl+Z or Ctrl+D key combinations), then the program receives no input, so the readLine() method returns null; when printf takes a null argument, it throws a NullReferenceException.

Note that you ran this program from the command line. The method System.console() will succeed if the JVM is invoked from a command line without redirecting input or output streams since the JVM will be associated with a console (typically a keyboard and display screen). If the JVM is invoked indirectly by IDE, or if the JVM is invoked from a background process, then the method call System.console() will fail and return null. For example, Figure 8-1 shows what happened when we ran this program from the Eclipse IDE.

Figure 8-1. System.console() returns null when invoked from Eclipse IDE

In this case, the JVM is not associated with a console (like a command line) since it is invoked from an IDE, so the program failed.

If the JVM is invoked indirectly by IDE, or if the JVM is invoked from a background process, then the method call `System.console()` will fail and return null.

Some of the important methods available in the `Console` class are listed in Table 8-1.

Table 8-1. Important Methods in the Console Class

Method	Short description
`Reader reader()`	Returns the `Reader` object associated with this `Console` object; can perform read operations through this returned reference.
`PrintWriter writer()`	Returns the `PrintReader` object associated with this `Console` object; can perform write operations through this returned reference.
`String readLine()`	Reads a line of text `String` (and this returned string object does not include any line termination characters); returns null if it fails (e.g., the user pressed Ctrl+Z or Ctrl+D in the console)
`String readLine(String fmt, Object... args)`	Same as the `readLine()` method, but it first prints the string `fmt`.
`char[] readPassword()`	Reads a password text and returns as a char array; echoing is disabled with this method, so nothing will be displayed in the console when the password is typed by the user.
`char[] readPassword(String fmt, Object... args)`	Same as the `readPassword()` method, but it first prints the string given as the format string argument before reading the password string.
`Console format(String fmt, Object... args)`	Writes the formatted string (created based on values of `fmt` string and the `args` passed) to the console.
`Console printf(String fmt, Object... args)`	Writes the formatted string (created based on values of `fmt` string and the `args` passed) to the console. This `printf` method is the same as the `format` method: This is a "convenience method"—the method `printf` and the format specifiers are familiar to most C/C++ programmers, so this method is provided in addition to the format method.
`void flush()`	Flushes any of the data still remaining to be printed in the console object's buffer.

Formatted I/O with the Console Class

The Console class supports formatted I/O in the methods printf() and format() plus the overloaded methods of readPassword() and readLine(). We will not cover the printf() and format() methods in this chapter; they are covered in detail in the "String Formatting" section of Chapter 7.

In the methods readPassword() and readLine(), the first argument is the format specifier string, and the following arguments are the values that will be passed to the format specifier string. These two methods return the character data read from the console. What's the difference between the readLine() and readPassword() methods? The main difference is that the readPassword() does not display the typed string in the console (for the obvious reason of not displaying the secret password), whereas readLine() displays the input you type in the console. Another minor difference is that the readLine() method returns a String whereas readPassword() returns a char array. See Listing 8-2.

Listing 8-2. Login.java

```java
import java.io.Console;
import java.util.Arrays;

// code to illustrate the use of readPassword method
class Login {
        public static void main(String []args) {
                Console console = System.console();
                if(console != null) {
                        String userName = null;
                        char[] password = null;
                        userName = console.readLine("Enter your username: ");
                        // typed characters for password will not be displayed in the screen
                        password = console.readPassword("Enter password: ");
                        // password is a char[]: convert it to a String first before comparing contents
                        if(userName.equals("scrat") && new String(password).equals("nuts")) {
                                // we're hardcoding username and password here for
                                // illustration, don't do such hardcoding in pratice!
                                console.printf("login successful!");
                        }
                        else {
                                console.printf("restart application and try again");
                        }
                        // "empty" the password since its use is over
                        Arrays.fill(password, ' ');
                }
        }
}
```

Here is an instance of running this program typing the correct username and password:

```
D:\>java Login
Enter your username: scrat
Enter password:
login successful!
```

Note that nothing was displayed in the console when typing the password. Why is `Arrays.fill(password, ' ');` in this program? It is a recommended practice to "empty" the read password string once its use is over; here you use `Array`'s `fill()` method for this purpose. This is a secure programming practice to avoid malicious reads of program data to discover password strings. In fact, unlike the `readLine()` method, which returns a `String`, the `readPassword()` method returns a char array. With a char array, as soon as the password is validated, it is possible to empty it and remove the trace of the password text from memory; with a `String` object, which is garbage collected, it is not as easy as with a char array.

Special Character Handling in the Console Class

Writing text through `Console`'s `printf()` or `format()` methods has the advantage that these methods handle special characters better than printing text through `PrintStream`. (We'll discuss `streams` in more detail in the next section.) Listing 8-3 shows an example.

Listing 8-3. SpecialCharHandling.java

```java
import java.io.Console;

// better to print thro' Console object - it handles "special characters" better
class SpecialCharHandling {
        public static void main(String []args) {
                // string has three Scandinavian characters
                String scandString = "å, ä, and ö";
                // try printing scandinavian characters directly with println
                System.out.println("Printing scands directly with println: " + scandString);
                // now, get the Console object and print scand characters thro' that
                Console console = System.console();
                console.printf("Printing scands thro' console's printf method: " + scandString);
        }
}
```

Here is what this program prints:

```
Printing scands directly with println: •, •, and ÷
Printing scands thro' console's printf method: å, ä, and ö
```

As you can see from this output, `Console`'s `printf()` method (and other methods) have better support for special characters.

Using Streams to Read and Write Files

What are streams? Streams are ordered sequences of data. Java deals with input and output in terms of streams. For example, when you read a sequence of bytes from a binary file, you're reading from an *input stream*; similarly, when you write a sequence of bytes to a binary file, you're writing to an *output stream*. Note how we referred to reading or writing *bytes* from *binary files*, but what about reading or writing *characters* from *text files*? Java differentiates between processing text and binary data. Before delving deeper into streams and reading or writing data from files, you must first understand the difference between the character streams and byte streams, which is essential for understanding the rest of the chapter.

Character Streams and Byte Streams

Consider the difference between Java source files and class files generated by the compiler. The Java source files have extension of .java and are meant to be read by humans as well as programming tools such as compilers. However, the Java class files have extension of .class and are not meant to be read by humans; they are meant to be processed by low-level tools such as a JVM (executable java.exe in Windows) and Java disassember (executable javap.exe in Windows). We refer to human-readable files containing text (or characters) as *text files*; we refer to the machine readable or low-level data storage files as *binary files*. Naturally, how you interpret what is inside text files vs. binary files is different. For example, in text files, you can interpret the data read from the file and differentiate between a tab character, whitespace character, newline character, etc. However, you don't deal with data from binary files like that; they are low-level values. To give another example, consider a .txt file you create with a text editor such as Notepad in Windows; it contains human-readable text. Now, consider storing your photo in a .bmp or .jpeg file; these files are certainly not human readable. They are meant for processing by photo editing or image manipulation software, and the files contain data in some pre-determined low-level format.

The java.io package has classes that support both character streams and byte streams. You can use character streams for text-based I/O. Byte streams are used for data-based I/O. Character streams for reading and writing are called *readers* and *writers*, respectively (represented by the abstract classes of Reader and Writer). Byte streams for reading and writing are called *input streams* and *output streams*, respectively (represented by the abstract classes of InputStream and OutputStream). Table 8-2 summarizes the differences between character streams and byte streams for your quick reference.

Table 8-2. *Differences Between Character Streams and Byte Streams*

Character streams	Byte streams
Meant for reading or writing to character- or text-based I/O such as text files, text documents, XML, and HTML files.	Meant for reading or writing to binary data I/O such as executable files, image files, and files in low-level file formats such as .zip, .class, .obj, and .exe.
Data dealt with is 16-bit Unicode characters.	Data dealt with is bytes (i.e., units of 8-bit data).
Input and output character streams are called *readers* and *writers*, respectively.	Input and output byte streams are simply called *input streams* and *output streams*, respectively.
The abstract classes of Reader and Writer and their derived classes in the java.io package provide support for character streams.	The abstract classes of InputStream and OutputStream and their derived classes in the java.io package provide support for byte streams.

 If you try using a byte stream when a character stream is needed and vice versa, you'll get a nasty surprise in your programs. For example, a bitmap (.bmp) image file must be processed using a byte stream; if you try using character stream, your program won't work. So don't mix up the streams!

Character Streams

In this section, you'll explore I/O with character streams. You'll learn how to read from and write to text files plus some optional features such as buffering to speed up the I/O. For reading and writing text files, you can use the classes derived from the Reader and Writer abstract classes, respectively. For character streams, Figure 8-2 shows important Reader classes, and Table 8-3 provides a short description of these classes. Figure 8-3 shows important Writer classes, and Table 8-4 provides a short description of these classes. Note that we'll cover only a few important classes in this class hierarchy in this chapter.

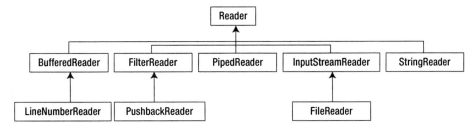

Figure 8-2. *Important classes deriving from the Reader class*

Table 8-3. *Important Classes Deriving from the Reader Class*

Class name	Short description
StringReader	A character stream that operates on strings.
InputStreamReader	This class is a bridge between character streams and byte streams.
FileReader	Derived class of InputStreamReader that provides support for reading character files.
PipedReader	The PipedReader and PipedWriter classes form a pair for "piped" reading/writing of characters.
FilterReader	Abstract base class for streams that support a filtering operation applied on data as characters are read from the stream.
PushbackReader	Derived class of FilterReader that allows read characters to be pushed back into the stream.
BufferedReader	Adds buffering to the underlying character stream so that there is no need to access the underlying file system for each read and write operation.
LineNumberReader	Derived class of BufferedReader that keeps track of line numbers as the characters are read from the underlying character stream.

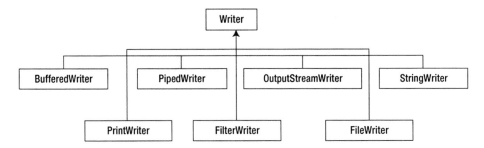

Figure 8-3. *Important classes deriving from the Writer class*

Table 8-4. *Important Classes Deriving from the Writer Class*

Class name	Short description
StringWriter	A character stream that collects the output in a string buffer, which can be used for creating a string.
OutputStreamWriter	This class is a bridge between character streams and byte streams.
FileWriter	Derived class of InputStreamWriter that provides support for writing character files.
PipedWriter	The PipedReader and PipedWriter classes form a pair for "piped" reading/writing of characters in character stream.
FilterWriter	Abstract base class for streams that supports a filtering operation applied on data as characters when writing them to a character stream.
PrintWriter	Supports formatted printing of characters to the output character stream.
BufferedWriter	Adds buffering to the underlying character stream so that there is no need to access the underlying file system for each read and write operation.

Reading Text Files

Reader classes read the contents in the stream and try interpreting them as characters, such as a tab, end-of-file, newline, etc. Listing 8-4 implements a simplified version of the type command in Windows. The type command displays the contents of the file(s) passed as command-line arguments.

Listing 8-4. Type.java

```java
import java.io.FileNotFoundException;
import java.io.FileReader;
import java.io.IOException;

// implements a simplified version of "type" command provided in Windows given
// a text file name(s) as argument, it prints the content of the text file(s) on console
class Type {
        public static void main(String []files) {
                if(files.length == 0) {
                        System.err.println("pass the name of the file(s) as argument");
                        System.exit(-1);
                }
                // process each file passed as argument
                for(String file : files) {
                        // try opening the file with FileReader
                        try (FileReader inputFile = new FileReader(file)) {
                                int ch = 0;
                                // while there are characters to fetch, read, and print the
                                // characters when EOF is reached, read() will return -1,
                                // terminating the loop
                                while( (ch = inputFile.read()) != -1) {
                                        // ch is of type int - convert it back to char
                                        // before printing
                                        System.out.print( (char)ch );
                                }
```

```
                } catch (FileNotFoundException fnfe) {
                        // the passed file is not found ...
                        System.err.printf("Cannot open the given file %s ", file);
                }
                catch(IOException ioe) {
                        // some IO error occurred when reading the file ...
                        System.err.printf("Error when processing file %s... skipping it", file);
                }
                // try-with-resources will automatically release FileReader object
            }
        }
}
```

For a sample text file, here is the output for the type command in Windows and our Type program:

```
D:\> type SaturnMoons.txt
Saturn has numerous icy moons in its rings. Few large moons of Saturn are - Mimas, Enceladus,
Tethys, Dione, Rhea, Titan, Iapetus, and Hyperion.

D:\> java Type SaturnMoons.txt
Saturn has numerous icy moons in its rings. Few large moons of Saturn are - Mimas, Enceladus,
Tethys, Dione, Rhea, Titan, Iapetus, and Hyperion.
```

It works as expected. In this program, you are instantiating the FileReader class and pass the name of the file to be opened. If the file is not found, the FileReader constructor will throw a FileNotFoundException.

Once the file is open, you use the read() method to fetch characters in the underlying file. You are reading character by character. Alternatively, you can use methods such as readLine() to read line by line.

Note that the read() method returns an int instead of a char—it's because when read() reaches End-Of-File (EOF), it returns –1, which is outside the range of char. So, the read() method returns an int to indicate that the end of file has been reached and that you should stop attempting to read any more characters from the underlying stream.

In this program, you only read a text file; you'll now try to read from as well as write to a text file.

Reading and Writing Text Files

In the previous example (Listing 8-4) of reading a text file, you created the character stream as follows:

```
FileReader inputFile = new FileReader(file);
```

This uses unbuffered I/O, which is less efficient when compared to buffered I/O. In other words, the read characters are directly passed instead of using a temporary (internal) buffer, which would speed up the I/O. To programmatically use buffered I/O, you can pass the FileReader reference to a BufferedReader object, as in the following:

```
BufferedReader inputFile = new BufferedReader(new FileReader(file);
```

In the same way, you can also use BufferedWriter for buffered output. (In case of byte streams, you can use BufferedInputStream and BufferedOutputStream, which we'll discuss later in this chapter).

You'll now use buffered I/O to read from and write to a text file. Listing 8-5 contains a simplified version of the copy command in Windows.

233

Listing 8-5. Copy.java

```java
import java.io.BufferedReader;
import java.io.BufferedWriter;
import java.io.FileNotFoundException;
import java.io.FileReader;
import java.io.FileWriter;
import java.io.IOException;

// implements a simplified version of "copy" command provided in Windows
// syntax: java Copy SrcFile DstFile
// copies ScrFile to DstFile; over-writes the DstFile if it already exits
class Copy {
        public static void main(String []files) {
                if(files.length != 2) {
                        System.err.println("Incorrect syntax. Correct syntax: Copy SrcFile DstFile");
                        System.exit(-1);
                }
                String srcFile = files[0];
                String dstFile = files[1];
                // try opening the source and destination file
                // with FileReader and FileWriter
                try (BufferedReader inputFile = new BufferedReader(new FileReader(srcFile));
                BufferedWriter outputFile = new BufferedWriter(new FileWriter(dstFile))) {
                        int ch = 0;
                        // while there are characters to fetch, read the characters from
                        // source stream and write them to the destination stream
                        while( (ch = inputFile.read()) != -1) {
                                // ch is of type int - convert it back to char before
                                // writing it
                                outputFile.write( (char)ch );
                        }
                        // no need to call flush explicitly for outputFile - the close()
                        // method will first call flush before closing the outputFile stream
                } catch (FileNotFoundException fnfe) {
                        // the passed file is not found ...
                        System.err.println("Cannot open the file " + fnfe.getMessage());
                }
                catch(IOException ioe) {
                        // some IO error occurred when reading the file ...
                        System.err.printf("Error when processing file; exiting ... ");
                }
                // try-with-resources will automatically release FileReader object
        }
}
```

Let's first check if this program works. Copy this Java source program itself (Copy.java) into another file (DuplicateCopy.java). You can use the fc (file compare) command provided in Windows to make sure that the contents of the original file and the copied file are same, to ensure that the program worked correctly.

```
D:\> java Copy Copy.java DuplicateCopy.java
D:\> fc Copy.java DuplicateCopyjava
Comparing files Copy.java and DuplicateCopy.java
FC: no differences encountered
```

Yes, it worked correctly. What if you give it a source file name that does not exist?

```
D:\> java Copy Cpy.java DuplicateCopyjava
Cannot open the file Cpy.java (The system cannot find the file specified)
```

You typed Cpy.java instead of Copy.java and the program terminates with a readable error message, as expected.

Here's how this program works. In the try-with-resources statement, you opened srcFile for reading and dstFile for writing. You wanted to use buffered I/O, so you passed FileReader and FileWriter references to BufferedReader and BufferedWriter, respectively.

```
try (BufferedReader inputFile = new BufferedReader(new FileReader(srcFile));
        BufferedWriter outputFile = new BufferedWriter(new FileWriter(dstFile)))
```

You're using the try-with-resources statement, and the close() method for BufferedWriter will first call the flush() method before closing the stream.

 When you're using buffered I/O in your programs, it's a good idea to call the flush() method explicitly in places where you want to ensure that all pending characters or data is flushed (i.e., written to the underlying file).

"Tokenizing" Text

In the last two examples (Listings 8-4 and 8-5), you just read or wrote to text files. However, in real-world programs, you may want to perform some processing when reading or writing files. For example, you may want to look out for certain patterns, search for some specific strings, replace one sequence of characters with another sequence of characters, filter out specific words, format the output in a certain way, etc. You can use existing APIs such as regular expressions (covered in Chapter 7), Scanner, etc. for such purposes.

For illustration, consider that you want to list all the words in a given text file and eliminate all unnecessary whitespaces, punctuation characters, etc. Also, you need to print the resulting words in alphabetical order. To solve this problem, you can use a Scanner and pass the regular expression that you want to match or delimit (see Listing 8-6).

Listing 8-6. Tokenize.java

```
import java.io.FileNotFoundException;
import java.io.FileReader;
import java.util.Scanner;
import java.util.Set;
import java.util.TreeSet;

// read the input file and convert it into "tokens" of words;
// convert the words to same case (lower case), remove duplicates, and print the words
```

```
class Tokenize {
        public static void main(String []args) {
                // read the input file
                if(args.length != 1) {
                        System.err.println("pass the name of the file to be read as an argument");
                        System.exit(-1);
                }
                String fileName = args[0];
                // use a TreeSet<String> which will automatically sort the words
                // in alphabetical order
                Set<String> words = new TreeSet<>();
                try ( Scanner tokenizingScanner = new Scanner(new FileReader(fileName)) ) {
                        // set the delimiter for text as non-words (special characters,
                        // white-spaces, etc), meaning that all words other than punctuation
                        // characters, and white-spaces will be returned
                        tokenizingScanner.useDelimiter("\\W");
                        while(tokenizingScanner.hasNext()) {
                                String word = tokenizingScanner.next();
                                if(!word.equals("")) { // process only non-empty strings
                                        // convert to lowercase and then add to the set
                                        words.add(word.toLowerCase());
                                }
                        }
                        // now words are in alphabetical order without duplicates,
                        // print the words separating them with tabs
                        for(String word : words) {
                                System.out.print(word + '\t');
                        }
                } catch (FileNotFoundException fnfe) {
                        System.err.println("Cannot read the input file - pass a valid file name");
                }
        }
}
```

Let's see if it works:

```
D:\> type limerick.txt
There was a young lady of Niger
Who smiled as she rode on a tiger.
They returned from the ride
With the lady inside
And a smile on the face of the tiger.

D:\> java Tokenize limerick.txt
a       and     as      face    from    inside lady     niger    of      on returned     ride
rode    she     smile   smiled the      there  they tiger   was      who     with                 young
```

Yes, it does work correctly. Now let's see what this program does. The program first opens the file
using a FileReader and passes it to the Scanner object. The program sets the delimiter for Scanner with
useDelimiter("\\W"); the "\W" matches for non-words, so any non-word characters will become delimiters.

(Note that you're setting the delimiter and not the pattern that you want to match). The program makes use of a TreeSet<String> to store the read strings. The program reads words from the underlying stream, checks if it is a non-empty string, and adds the lower-case versions of the string to the TreeSet. Since the data structure is a TreeSet, it removes duplicates; remember that it's a Set, which does not allow duplicates. Further, it is also an ordered data structure, meaning that it maintains an "ordering" of values inserted, which in this case is an alphabetical ordering of Strings. Hence the program correctly prints the words from given text file that contained a limerick.

Byte Streams

In this section, you'll explore I/O with byte streams. You'll first learn how to read and write data files, and also how to stream objects, store them in files and then read them back. The class of OutputStream and its derived classes are shown in Figure 8-4; InputStream and its derived classes are shown in Figure 8-5.

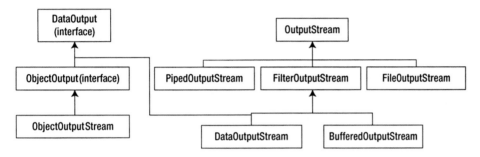

Figure 8-4. *Important classes deriving from the OutputStream abstract class*

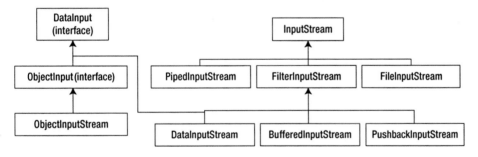

Figure 8-5. *Important classes deriving from the InputStream abstract class*

Table 8-5 summarizes the important classes of InputStream and OutputStream.

Table 8-5. *Important Classes Deriving from the InputStream and OutputStream Classes*

Class name	Short description
PipedInputStream, PipedOutputStream	PipedInputStream and PipedOutputStream create a communication channel on which data can be sent and received. PipedOutputStream sends the data and PipedInputStream receives the data sent on the channel.
FileInputStream, FileOutputStream	FileInputStream receives a byte stream from a file, FileOutputStream writes a byte stream into a file.
FilterInputStream, FilterOutputStream	These filtered streams are used to add functionalities to plain streams. The output of an InputStream can be filtered using FilterInputStream. The output of an OutputStream can be filtered using FilterOutputStream.
BufferedInputStream, BufferedOutputStream	BufferedInputStream adds buffering capabilities to an input stream. BufferedOutputStream adds buffering capabilities to an output stream.
PushbackInputStream	A subclass of FilterInputStream, it adds "pushback" functionality to an input stream.
DataInputStream, DataOutputStream	DataInputStream can be used to read java primitive data types from an input stream. DataOutputStream can be used to write Java primitive data types to an output stream.

Reading a Byte Stream

Byte streams are used for processing files that do not contain human-readable text. For example, a Java source file has human readable content, but a .class file does not. A .class file is meant for processing by the JVM, hence you must use byte streams to process the .class file.

The contents of a .class file are written in a specific file format, described in the specification of the Java Virtual Machine. Don't worry; you're not going to understand this complex file format, but you'll just check its "magic number." Each file format has a magic number used to quickly check the file format. For example ".MZ" is the magic number (or more properly, magic string) for .exe files in Windows. Similarly, the .class files have the magic number "0xCAFEBABE", written as a hexadecimal value. These magic numbers are typically written as first few bytes of a variable length file format.

To understand how byte streams work, you'll just check if the given file starts with the magic number "0xCAFEBABE" (Listing 8-7). If so, it could be a valid .class file; if not, it's certainly not a .class file.

Listing 8-7. ClassFileMagicNumberChecker.java

```
import java.io.FileInputStream;
import java.io.FileNotFoundException;
import java.io.IOException;
import java.util.Arrays;

// check if the passed file is a valid .class file or not.
// note that this is an elementary version of a checker that checks if the given file
// is a valid file that is written according to the JVM specification
// it checks only the magic number
class ClassFileMagicNumberChecker {
      public static void main(String []args) {
            if(args.length != 1) {
                  System.err.println("Pass a valid file name as argument");
                  System.exit(-1);
            }
```

```
String fileName = args[0];
// create a magicNumber byte array with values for four bytes in 0xCAFEBABE
// you need to have an explicit down cast to byte since
// the hex values like 0xCA are of type int
byte []magicNumber = {(byte) 0xCA, (byte)0xFE, (byte)0xBA, (byte)0xBE};
try (FileInputStream fis = new FileInputStream(fileName)) {
        // magic number is of 4 bytes -
        // use a temporary buffer to read first four bytes
        byte[] u4buffer = new byte[4];
        // read a buffer full (4 bytes here) of data from the file
        if(fis.read(u4buffer) != -1) { // if read was successful
                // the overloaded method equals for two byte arrays
                // checks for equality of contents
                if(Arrays.equals(magicNumber, u4buffer)) {
                        System.out.printf("The magic number for passed file %s
matches that of a .class file", fileName);
                }
                else {
                        System.out.printf("The magic number for passed file %s does
not match that of a .class file", fileName);
                }
        }
    } catch(FileNotFoundException fnfe) {
            System.err.println("file does not exist with the given file name ");
    } catch(IOException ioe) {
            System.err.println("an I/O error occurred while processing the file");
    }
  }
}
```

Let's first see if it works by passing the source (.java) file and the .class file for the same program.

```
D:> java ClassFileMagicNumberChecker ClassFileMagicNumberChecker.java
The magic number for passed file ClassFileMagicNumberChecker.java does not match that of a .class file
D:\> java ClassFileMagicNumberChecker ClassFileMagicNumberChecker.class
The magic number for passed file ClassFileMagicNumberChecker.class matches that of a .class file
```

Yes, it works. The classes InputStream and OutputStream form the base of the hierarchies for byte streams. You perform file I/O, so open the given file as a FileInputStream. You need to check the first four bytes, so you read four bytes in a temporary buffer. You need to compare the contents of this buffer against the sequence of bytes 0xCA, 0xFE, 0xBA, and 0xBE. If the contents of these two arrays are not equal, then the passed file is not a .class file.

In this program, you directly manipulate the underlying byte stream using a FileInputStream. In case you need to speed up the program when you read large number of bytes, you can use a buffered output stream, as in

```
BufferedInputStream bis = new BufferedInputStream(new FileInputStream(fileName));
```

Similar to these input streams, you can use output streams to write sequence of bytes to a data file. You can use FileOutputStream and BufferedOutputStream for that.

After reading this program, didn't you think that reading an array of four bytes and comparing the contents of the byte arrays was awkward (instead of directly comparing the contents of an integer)? In other words, 0xCAFEBABE is an integer value, and you could read this value directly as an integer value and compare it against the read integer value. For this, you need to use data streams, which provide methods like readInt(), which we'll discuss now.

Data Streams

To understand how to write or read with byte streams, let's write a simple program that writes and then reads constant values to a data file (see Listing 8-8). To keep the problem simple, you will write only the values 0 to 9 in the form of the following primitive type values: byte, short, int, long, float, and double.

Listing 8-8. DataStreamExample.java

```
import java.io.DataInputStream;
import java.io.DataOutputStream;
import java.io.FileInputStream;
import java.io.FileNotFoundException;
import java.io.FileOutputStream;
import java.io.IOException;


// A simple class to illustrate data streams; write constants 0 and 1 in different data type values
// into a file and read the results back and print them
class DataStreamExample {
        public static void main(String []args) {
                // write some data into a data file with hard-coded name "temp.data"
                try (DataOutputStream dos =
                        new DataOutputStream(new FileOutputStream("temp.data"))) {
                        // write values 1 to 10 as byte, short, int, long, float and double
                        // omitting boolean type because an int value cannot
                        // be converted to boolean
                        for(int i = 0; i < 10; i++) {
                                dos.writeByte(i);
                                dos.writeShort(i);
                                dos.writeInt(i);
                                dos.writeLong(i);
                                dos.writeFloat(i);
                                dos.writeDouble(i);
                        }
                } catch(FileNotFoundException fnfe) {
                        System.err.println("cannot create a file with the given file name ");
                        System.exit(-1); // don't proceed - exit the program
                } catch(IOException ioe) {
                        System.err.println("an I/O error occurred while processing the file");
                        System.exit(-1); // don't proceed - exit the program
                }
                // the DataOutputStream will auto-close, so don't have to worry about it
                // now, read the written data and print it to console
                try (DataInputStream dis = new DataInputStream(new FileInputStream("temp.data"))) {
                        // the order of values to read is byte, short, int, long, float and
                        // double
                        // since we've written from 0 to 0, the for loop has to run 10 times
```

```
                        for(int i = 0; i < 10; i++) {
                                // %d is for printing byte, short, int or long
                                // %f, %g, or %e is for printing float or double
                                // %n is for printing newline
                                System.out.printf("%d %d %d %d %g %g %n",
                                                dis.readByte(),
                                                dis.readShort(),
                                                dis.readInt(),
                                                dis.readLong(),
                                                dis.readFloat(),
                                                dis.readDouble());
                        }
                } catch(FileNotFoundException fnfe) {
                        System.err.println("cannot create a file with the given file name ");
                } catch(IOException ioe) {
                        System.err.println("an I/O error occurred while processing the file");
                } // the DataOutputStream will auto-close, so don't have to worry about it
        }
}
```

First, let's see if it works by executing the program.

```
D:> java DataStreamExample
0 0 0 0 0.000000 0.000000
1 1 1 1 1.000000 1.000000
2 2 2 2 2.000000 2.000000
3 3 3 3 3.000000 3.000000
4 4 4 4 4.000000 4.000000
5 5 5 5 5.000000 5.000000
6 6 6 6 6.000000 6.000000
7 7 7 7 7.000000 7.000000
8 8 8 8 8.000000 8.000000
9 9 9 9 9.000000 9.000000
```

Yes, it works. Now, as mentioned earlier, the contents of data files are not human-readable. In this case, you're writing values 0 to 9 as various primitive type values into the temporary file write named temp.data. If you try to open this data file and see the contents, you won't be able to recognize or understand what it contains. Here's an example of its contents:

```
D:>type temp.data
                                  • •   •       •?Ç  ?•      • •   •        •@   @
• •   •           •@@      • •   •       •@Ç  @•      • •   •         •@á  @¶
• •   •     •@•  @•                @•  @•        A   @
            A•  @"
```

The typed contents of the file temp.data look like garbage values because the primitive type values like the integer values 0 or 9 are stored in terms of bytes. However, the type command in Windows tries to convert these bytes into human-readable characters, hence the output does not make any sense. The data will make sense only if we know the format of the data stored in the file and read it according to that format.

Now let's get back to the program and see how it works. The program writes to the data file with a hard-coded file named `temp.data` in the current directory from which the program is run. This program first writes the data, so it opens the file as an output stream. What does the following statement within the first try block mean?

```
DataOutputStream dos = new DataOutputStream(new FileOutputStream("temp.data"))
```

You can directly perform binary I/O with `OutputStream` and its derived class of `FileOutputStream`, but to process data formats such as primitive type values, you need to use `DataOutputStream`, which acts as a wrapper over the underlying `FileOutputStream`. So, you use the `DataOutputStream` here, which provides methods such as `writeByte` and `writeShort`. You use these methods to write the primitive type values 0 to 9 into the data file. Note that you don't have to close the streams explicitly since you opened the `DataOutputStream` in a try-with-resources statement, hence the `close()` method on dos reference will automatically be invoked. The `close()` method also flushes the underlying stream; this `close()` method will also close the underlying reference to the `FileOutputStream`.

Once the file is written, you read the data file in a similar way. You open a `FileInputStream` and wrap it with a `DataInputStream`. You read the data from the stream and print it in console. You used format specifiers such as `%d` (which is a common format specifier for printing integral values like `byte`, `short`, `int`, or `long`) as well as `%f`, `%g`, or `%e` specifiers for printing floating point values of type `float` or `double`; `%n` is for printing a newline character.

In this program, you wrote and read primitive type values. What about reference type objects, such as Objects, Maps, etc.? Reading and writing objects is achieved through object streams, which we'll discuss now.

Writing to and Reading from Object Streams: Serialization

The classes `ObjectInputStream` and `ObjectOutputStream` support reading and writing Java objects that you use in the program. For example, if you are creating an online e-commerce web site for making purchases, you can choose to write objects such as customers, purchase requests made, etc., to an RDBMS (we'll cover JDBC in Chapter 10), or alternatively, store the objects directly in *flat files*. In such cases, you must know how to read or write objects into streams.

Let's introduce some terms related to this topic before we go ahead. The process of converting objects in memory into sequence of bytes is known as *serialization*. The mechanism of storing objects in memory into files is known as *persistence*. Often these concepts are clubbed together and referred as serialization only.

Listing 8-9 contains a simple example of writing the contents of a `Map` data structure to a file and reading it back to illustrate the use of the classes `ObjectInputStream` and `ObjectOutputStream` to read or write objects. You store the details of the last three US presidents in this map.

Listing 8-9. ObjectStreamExample.java

```java
import java.io.FileInputStream;
import java.io.FileNotFoundException;
import java.io.FileOutputStream;
import java.io.IOException;
import java.io.ObjectInputStream;
import java.io.ObjectOutputStream;
import java.util.HashMap;
import java.util.Map;

// A simple class to illustrate object streams: fill a data structure, write it to a
// temporary file and read it back and print the read data structure
class ObjectStreamExample {
        public static void main(String []args) {
                Map<String, String> presidentsOfUS = new HashMap<>();
                presidentsOfUS.put("Barack Obama", "2009 to --, Democratic Party, 56th term");
                presidentsOfUS.put("George W. Bush", "2001 to 2009, Republican Party, 54th and 55th terms");
```

```
                presidentsOfUS.put("Bill Clinton", "1993 to 2001, Democratic Party, 52nd
and 53rd terms");
                try (ObjectOutputStream oos = new ObjectOutputStream(new
FileOutputStream("object.data"))) {
                        oos.writeObject(presidentsOfUS);
                } catch(FileNotFoundException fnfe) {
                        System.err.println("cannot create a file with the given file name ");
                } catch(IOException ioe) {
                        System.err.println("an I/O error occurred while processing the file");
                } // the ObjectOutputStream will auto-close, so don't have to worry about it

                try (ObjectInputStream ois = new ObjectInputStream(new
FileInputStream("object.data"))) {
                        Object obj = ois.readObject();
                        // first check if obj is of type Map
                        if(obj != null && obj instanceof Map) {
                                Map<String, String> presidents = (Map<String, String>) obj;
                                System.out.println("President name \t Description \n");
                                for(Map.Entry<String, String> president : presidents.entrySet()) {
                                        System.out.printf("%s \t %s %n", president.getKey(),
president.getValue());
                                }
                        }
                } catch(FileNotFoundException fnfe) {
                        System.err.println("cannot create a file with the given file name ");
                } catch(IOException ioe) {
                        System.err.println("an I/O error occurred while processing the file");
                } catch(ClassNotFoundException cnfe) {
                        System.err.println("cannot recognize the class of the object - is the file
corrupted?");
                }
        }
}
```

Before discussing how the program works, let's check if it works.

```
D:\> java ObjectStreamExample
President name    Description

Barack Obama     2009 to --, Democratic Party, 56th term
Bill Clinton     1993 to 2001, Democratic Party, 52nd and 53rd terms
George W. Bush   2001 to 2009, Republican Party, 54th and 55th terms
```

The serialization process converts contents of the objects in memory with the description of the contents (known as *metadata*). When the object has references to other objects, the serialization mechanism also includes them as part of the serialized bytes. If you try to open the file in which the object is persisted, you cannot read these serialized and then persisted objects. For example, if you try to read the object.data file, you'll see numerous unreadable characters.

Now, let's get back to the program and see how it works. In this program, you fill the HashMap container with details of last three US presidents. Then, you open an output stream as follows:

```
ObjectOutputStream oos = new ObjectOutputStream(new FileOutputStream("object.data"))
```

The FileOutputStream opens a temporary file named object.data in the current directory. The ObjectOutputStream is a wrapper over this underlying FileOutputStream. Inside this try-with-resources block, you've only one statement, oos.writeObject(presidentsOfUS), which writes the object to the object.data file.

Reading the object requires a bit more work than writing the object. The readObject() method in ObjectInputStream returns an Object type. You need to convert it back to Map<String, String>. Before downcasting it to this specific type, you check if the obj is of type Map. Note that you don't have to check if it's Map<String, String> because these generic types are lost in the process known as *type erasure* (see Chapter 6 for a discussion on this topic). Once the downcast succeeds, you can read the values of the contents in this object.

Serialization: Some More Details

It is relevant for us to elaborate more on the topic of serialization. As illustrated in the last section, serialization is a process of converting an object to a sequence of bytes. You can write a serialized object to a file as you did in last example or you can put it on a socket to send it over the network.

The last example illustrated how to write objects to streams; that is nothing but serialization with persistence. In the last example, you created an instance of HashMap and then serialized and deserialized it. What if you want to serialize an object of a class you created (instead of serializing HashMap). Well, you can serialize objects of all classes provided the classes implement the Serializable interface. In other words, a class is not serializable by default; you need to implement the Serializable interface to make it serializable. In the last example, the HashMap class also implements the Serializable interface.

 You need to implement the Serializable interface in a class if you want to make the objects of the class serializable.

Now, let's assume that you want to serialize an object that contains an unserializable class member (say Thread or Socket). Or, think of a situation where you do not want to serialize a member variable. For such situations, Java offers a keyword known as transient. You can declare a member variable as transient and that variable will not be serialized by the JVM. Let's look at an example to understand it better. Assume that you have an USPresident class that stores name of a US president, his period, and term of office. You want to serialize the objects of this class, so this class implements the Serializable interface. However, you do not want to serialize one field, say term. Listing 8-10 shows how to achieve this.

Listing 8-10. TransientSerialization.java

```java
import java.io.FileInputStream;
import java.io.FileNotFoundException;
import java.io.FileOutputStream;
import java.io.IOException;
import java.io.ObjectInputStream;
import java.io.ObjectOutputStream;
import java.io.Serializable;

class USPresident implements Serializable{
        private static final long serialVersionUID = 1L;
        @Override
        public String toString() {
                return "US President [name=" + name + ", period=" + period + ", term=" + term + "]";
        }
```

```
        public USPresident(String name, String period, String term) {
                this.name = name;
                this.period = period;
                this.term = term;
        }
        private String name;
        private String period;
        private transient String term;
}
class TransientSerialization {
        public static void main(String []args) {
                USPresident usPresident = new USPresident("Barack Obama", "2009 to --", "56th term");
                System.out.println(usPresident);

                //Serialize the object
                try (ObjectOutputStream oos = new ObjectOutputStream(new
FileOutputStream("USPresident.data"))){
                        oos.writeObject(usPresident);
                }
                catch(FileNotFoundException fnfe) {
                        System.err.println("cannot create a file with the given file name ");
                } catch(IOException ioe) {
                        System.err.println("an I/O error occurred while processing the file");
                } // the ObjectOutputStream will auto-close, so don't have to worry about it

                //De-serialize the object
                try(ObjectInputStream ois = new ObjectInputStream(new
FileInputStream("USPresident.data"))){
                        Object obj = ois.readObject();
                        if(obj != null && obj instanceof USPresident){
                                USPresident presidentOfUS = (USPresident)obj;
                                System.out.println(presidentOfUS);
                        }
                }catch(FileNotFoundException fnfe) {
                        System.err.println("cannot create a file with the given file name ");
                } catch(IOException ioe) {
                        System.err.println("an I/O error occurred while processing the file");
                } catch(ClassNotFoundException cnfe) {
                        System.err.println("cannot recognize the class of the object - is the
file corrupted?");
                }
        }
}
```

It prints the following:

```
US President [name=Barack Obama, period=2009 to --, term=56th term]
US President [name=Barack Obama, period=2009 to --, term=null]
```

This program is very simple. First, you create an instance of a USPresident class with all required fields. Then, you print the contents of the object. After that, you serialize the object and then deserialize it. You print the contents of the object again. What you can observe from the output is that the value of the field term is not stored by the program. Why? Because you declared term as a transient field. All class members declared as transient are not serialized, so their values are lost after deserialization.

One more thing requires attention here—serialVersionUID. In this example, it's set it to 1. If you are implementing Serializable and not defining serialVersionUID, you will get a warning message. In fact, if you don't define it, JVM will define it for you; JVM will compute it based on the class behavior. But why it is required? Well, it is there to prevent mistakenly loading a wrong version of a class while deserializing. Also, defining serialVersionUID enables the serialized program to work across different JVM implementations seamlessly (which might not be a case when you are not defining it explicitly). The bottom line: whenever you make a change in a serialized class, do not forget to change the serialVersionUID also.

Points to Remember

Here are the noteworthy points to help you grasp Java I/O concepts:

- When you use buffered streams, you should call flush() once you are done with data transmission. The internal buffer might be holding some data that will be cleared and sent to the destination once you call flush(). However, the method close() on the stream will automatically call flush().

- You might have observed that you can combine stream objects. You can create an object of BufferedInputStream that takes a FileInputStream object. In this way, the output of one stream is chained to the filtered stream. This is the important, useful, and beautiful way to customize the stream in a desired way.

- The Serializable interface is a marker interface. That means the Serializable interface does not declare any method inside it.

- If you want to customize the process of serialization, you can implement readObject() and writeObject(). Note that both of these methods are private methods, which means you are not overriding or overloading these methods. JVM checks the implementation of these methods and calls them instead of the usual methods. It sounds weird but it is the way the customization of serialization process is implemented in the JVM.

- As discussed in earlier sections, a serialized object can be communicated over the network and deserialized on another machine. However, the class file of the object must be in the path of the destination machine, otherwise only the state of the object will be restored—not the whole object (i.e., you cannot invoke a method on the restored object).

- You can create your own protocol for serialization. For that, you just need to implement the Externalizable interface instead of the Serializable interface.

- When you are not specifying serialVersionUID in a serialized class, JVM computes it for you. However, each JVM implementation has different mechanism to compute it; hence, it is not guaranteed that your serialized class will work on two different JVMs when you have not specified the serialVersionUID explicitly. Therefore, it is strongly recommended that you provide serialVersionUID in a class implementing the Serializable interface.

QUESTION TIME!

1. Consider the following code snippet:

```
USPresident usPresident = new USPresident("Barack Obama", "2009 to --", 56);
try (ObjectOutputStream oos = new ObjectOutputStream(new
FileOutputStream("USPresident.data"))){
    oos.writeObject(usPresident);
    usPresident.setTerm(57);
    oos.writeObject(usPresident);
    }
```

If you deserialize the object and print the field term (term is declared as int and is not a transient), what it will print?

A. 56

B. 57

C. null

D. Compiler error

E. Runtime exception

Answer: A. 56

(Yes, it will print 56 even though you changed the term using its setter to 57 and serialized again. This happens due to serialVersionUID, which is checked by the JVM at the time of serialization. If a class is already serialized and you try to serialize it again, the JVM will not serialize it.)

2. Consider the following code segment:

```
OutputStream os = new FileOutputStream("log.txt");
System.setErr(new PrintStream(os)); // SET SYSTEM.ERR
System.err.println("Error");
```

Which one of the following statements is true regarding this code segment?

A. The line with comment SET SYSTEM.ERR will not compile and will result in a compiler error.

B. The line with comment SET SYSTEM.ERR will result in throwing a runtime exception since System.err cannot be programmatically redirected.

C. The program will print the text "Error" in console since System.err by default sends the output to console.

D. This code segment redirects the System.err to the log.txt file and will write the text "Error" to that file.

Answer: D. This code segment redirects the System.err to the log.txt file and will write the text "Error" to that file.

(Note that you can redirect the System.err programmatically using the setErr() method. System.err is of type PrintStream, and the System.setErr() method takes a PrintStream as an argument. Once the error stream is set, all writes to System.err will be redirected to it. Hence, this program will create log.txt with the text "Error" in it.)

3. Which one of the following definitions of the AResource class implementation is correct so that it can be used with try-with-resources statement?

A. ```
class AResource implements Closeable {
        protected void close() /* throws IOException */ {
                // body of close to release the resource
        }
}
```

B. ```
class AResource implements Closeable {
        public void autoClose() /* throws IOException */ {
                // body of close to release the resource
        }
}
```

C. ```
class AResource implements AutoCloseable {
        void close() /* throws IOException */ {
                // body of close to release the resource
        }
}
```

D. ```
class AResource implements AutoCloseable {
        public void close() throws IOException {
                // body of close to release the resource
        }
}
```

Answer:

D. ```
class AResource implements AutoCloseable {
        public void close() throws IOException {
                // body of close to release the resource
        }
}
```

(AutoCloseable is the base interface of the Closeable interface; AutoCloseable declares close as void close() throws Exception; In Closeable, it is declared as public void close() throws IOException;. For a class to be used with try-with-resources, it should both implement Closeable or AutoCloseable and correctly override the close() method. Option A declares open() protected; since the close() method is declared public in the base interface, you cannot reduce its visibility to protected, so this will result in a compiler error. Option B declares autoClose(); a correct implementation
```

would define the `close()` method. Option C declares `close()` with default access; since the close method is declared public in the base interface, you cannot reduce its visibility to default accesses, so it will result in a compiler error. Option D is a correct implementation of the `AResource` class that overrides the `close()` method.)

4. Consider the following code segment:

```
FileInputStream findings = new FileInputStream("log.txt");
DataInputStream dataStream = new DataInputStream(findings);
BufferedReader br = new BufferedReader(new InputStreamReader(dataStream));
String line;
while ((line = br.readLine()) != null) {
        System.out.println(line);
}
br.close();
```

Which two options are true regarding this code segment?

A. `br.close()` statement will close only the `BufferedReader` object, and `findings` and `dataStream` will remain unclosed.

B. The `br.close()` statement will close the `BufferedReader` object and the underlying stream objects referred by `findings` and `dataStream`.

C. The `readLine()` method invoked in the statement `br.readLine()` can throw an `IOException`; if this exception is thrown, `br.close()` will not be called, resulting in a resource leak.

D. The `readLine()` method invoked in the statement `br.readLine()` can throw an `IOException`; however, there will not be any resource leaks since Garbage Collector collects all resources.

E. In this code segment, no exceptions can be thrown calling `br.close()`, so there is no possibility of resource leaks.

Answer: B and C. The `br.close()` statement will close the `BufferedReader` object and the underlying stream objects referred to by `findings` and `dataStream`. The `readLine()` method invoked in the statement `br.readLine()` can throw an `IOException`;if this exception is thrown, `br.close()` will not be called, resulting in a resource leak. Note that Garbage Collector will only collect unreferenced memory resources; it is the programmer's responsibility to ensure that all other resources such as stream objects are released.

Summary

Reading and Writing Data to Console

- You can obtain a reference to the console using the `System.console()` method; if the JVM is not associated with any console, this method will fail and return null.

- Many methods are provided in `Console`-support formatted I/O. You can use the `printf()` and `format()` methods available in the `Console` class to print formatted text; the overloaded `readLine()` and `readPassword()` methods take format strings as arguments.

- Use the readPassword() method for reading secure strings such as passwords. It is recommended to use Array's fill() method to "empty" the password read into the character array (to avoid malicious access to the typed passwords).

- The methods in the Console class have better support for special characters compared to printing text through PrintStreams.

Read and Write to Files with Streams

- The java.io package has classes supporting both character streams and byte streams.

- You can use character streams for text-based I/O. Byte streams are used for data-based I/O.

- Character streams for reading and writing are called *readers* and *writers* respectively (represented by the abstract classes of Reader and Writer).

- Byte streams for reading and writing are called *input streams* and *output streams* respectively (represented by the abstract classes of InputStream and OutputStream).

- You should only use character streams for processing text files (or human-readable files), and byte streams for data files. If you try using one type of stream instead of another, your program won't work as you would expect; even if it works by chance, you'll get nasty bugs. So don't mix up streams, and use the right stream for a given task at hand.

- For both byte and character streams, you can use buffering. The buffer classes are provided as wrapper classes for the underlying streams. Using buffering will speed up the I/O when performing bulk I/O operations.

- For processing data with primitive data types and strings, you can use data streams.

- *Serialization*: The process of converting the objects in memory into a series of bytes.

- *Persistence*: The mechanism of storing objects in memory into files.

- You can use object streams for object persistence (i.e., reading and writing objects in memory to files and vice versa).

■ ■ ■

Java File I/O (NIO.2)

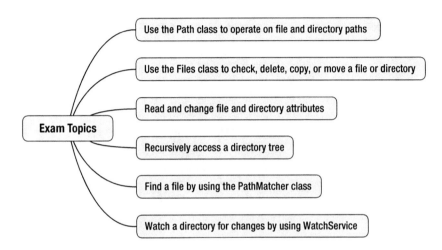

We covered I/O fundamentals in the last chapter, where you learned how to read and write from console and how to use streams to read and write to files. In this chapter, you will learn how to work with file systems—for example, how to save a file/directory; create a file/directory; navigate directories; copy, move, or delete a file/directory; and so on. As a Java programmer, you should be aware how to programmatically achieve these file/directory operations.

Java offers a rich set of APIs to manipulate files and directories. In fact, Java 7 introduces a new set of I/O APIs called NIO.2 that offer convenient ways to perform operations related to a file system. In this chapter, you will explore how to perform various file operations such as create, move, copy, and delete. You will also learn how to search files in a directory structure and how to get/set properties of files/directories.

A Quick History of I/O APIs

Initially, Java offered the File class (in the `java.io` package) to access file systems. This class represents a file/directory in the file system and allows you to perform operations such as checking the existence of a file/directory, getting the properties, and deleting a file/directory. However, the first version of the API was not sufficient to meet the needs of developers, and a need for improved I/O APIs was felt. In brief, the following shortcomings were noticed in the first version of the Java I/O APIs:

- The File class lacked the significant functionality required to implement even commonly used functionality. For instance, it lacked a copy method to copy a file/directory.

- The File class defined many methods that returned a Boolean value. Thus, in case of an error, false was returned, rather than throwing an exception, so the developer had no way of knowing why that call failed.

- The File class did not provide good support for handling symbolic links.

- The File class handled directories and paths in an inefficient way (it did not scale well).

- The File class provided access to a very limited set of file attributes, which was insufficient in many situations.

To overcome these problems, Java introduced *NIO (New IO)* in Java 4. The key features of NIO were:

- **Channels and Selectors:** NIO offered support for various types of channels. A *channel* is an abstraction over lower-level file system features (such as memory-mapped files and file locking) that lets you transfer data at a faster speed. Channels are non-blocking, so Java provides another feature—a *selector*—to select a ready channel for data transfer. A *socket* is a blocking feature whereas a channel is a non-blocking feature.

- **Buffers:** Java 4 introduced buffering for all primitive classes (except for Boolean). It provided the Buffer class that offers operations such as clear, flip, mark, reset, and rewind. Concrete classes (subclasses of the Buffer base class) offers getters and setters for setting and getting data to and from a buffer.

- **Charset:** Java 4 also introduced charset (java.nio.charset), encoders, and decoders to map bytes and Unicode symbols.

With SE 7 version, Java has introduced comprehensive support for I/O operations. Java 7 introduces the java.nio.file package for better support for handling symbolic links, to provide comprehensive attribute access, and to support the extended file system through interfaces or classes such as Path, Paths, and Files. You will explore these topics in more detail in the rest of this chapter.

Using the Path Interface

File systems usually form a tree. The file system starts with a root directory that contains files and directories (directories are also called *folders* in Windows). Each directory, in turn, may have subdirectories or hold files. To locate a file, you just need to put together the directories from the root directory to the immediate directory containing the file, along with a file separator, trailing with the file name. For instance, if the myfile.txt file resides in a mydocs directory, which resides in root directory C:\, then the path of the file is C:\mydocs\myfile.txt. Every file has a unique path to locate it (apart from symbolic links).

A path could be an *absolute path* (such as C:\mydocs\myfile.txt), which starts from a root element. On the other hand, a path could be specified as a *relative path*. When you try to compile a Java program, you just write something like javac programFileName.java; here, you have specified the Java source file path relative to the currently selected directory, so this path is a relative path. You need a reference path (such as current directory path in this case) to interpret a relative path.

Before we proceed further, it is relevant to talk about *symbolic links*. A symbolic link is like a pointer or reference for the actual file. In general, symbolic links are transparent to the applications, which means the operations are performed directly on the actual files rather than these links (except, of course, for the symbolic link-specific operations).

Java 7 introduces a new programming abstraction for path, namely the Path interface. This Path abstraction is used in new features and APIs throughout NIO.2, so it is an important interface to understand. A path object contains the names of directories and files that make the full path of the file/directory represented by the Path object; the Path abstraction provides methods to extract path elements, manipulate them, and append them. In fact, you will see later that almost all of the methods that access files/directories to get information about them or manipulate them use Path objects. Before you see a few examples illustrating how to use the Path interface, Table 9-1 quickly summarizes important methods in this interface.

Table 9-1. *Important Methods in the Path Interface*

Method	Description
Path getRoot()	Returns a Path object representing the root of the given path, or null if the path does not have a root.
Path getFileName()	Returns the file name or directory name of the given path. Note that the file/directory name is the last element or name in the given path.
Path getParent()	Returns the Path object representing the parent of the given path, or null if no parent component exists for the path.
int getNameCount()	Returns the number of file/directory names in the given path; returns 0 if the given path represents the root.
Path getName(int index)	Returns the ith file/directory name; the index 0 starts from closest name to the root.
Path subpath(int beginIndex, int endIndex)	Returns a Path object that is part of this Path object; the returned Path object has a name that begins at beginIndex till the element at index *endIndex - 1*. In other words, beginIndex is inclusive of the name in that index and exclusive of the name in endIndex. This method may throw IllegalArgumentException if beginIndex is >= number of elements, or endIndex <= beginIndex, or endIndex is > number of elements.
Path normalize()	Removes redundant elements in path such as . (dot symbol that indicates current directory) and .. (double dot symbol that indicates parent directory).
Path resolve(Path other) Path resolve(String other)	Resolves a path against the given path. For example, this method could combine the given path with the other path and return the resulting path.
Boolean isAbsolute()	Returns true if the given path is an absolute path; returns false if not (when the given path is a relative path, for example).
Path startsWith(String path) Path startsWith(Path path)	Returns true if this Path object starts with the given path, or else returns false.
Path toAbsolutePath()	Returns the absolute path.

Getting Path Information

Let's create a Path object and retrieve the basic information associated with the object. Listing 9-1 shows how to create a Path object and get information about it.

Listing 9-1. PathInfo1.java

```java
import java.nio.file.*;

// Class to illustrate how to use Path interface and its methods
public class PathInfo1 {
        public static void main(String[] args) {
                // create a Path object by calling static method get() in Paths class
                Path testFilePath = Paths.get("D:\\test\\testfile.txt");

                // retrieve basic information about path
                System.out.println("Printing file information: ");
                System.out.println("\t file name: " + testFilePath.getFileName());
                System.out.println("\t root of the path: " + testFilePath.getRoot());
                System.out.println("\t parent of the target: " + testFilePath.getParent());

                // print path elements
                System.out.println("Printing elements of the path: ");
                for(Path element : testFilePath) {
                        System.out.println("\t path element: " + element);
                }
        }
}
```

The program prints the following:

```
Printing file information:
        file name: testfile.txt
        root of the path: D:\
        parent of the target: D:\test
Printing elements of the path:
        path element: test
        path element: testfile.txt
```

The output is self explanatory. Let's understand the program.

- First, you create a Path instance using the get() method of the Paths class. The get() method expects a string representing a path as an input. This is the easiest way to create a Path object.

- Note that you use an escape character, \, in Paths.get("D:\\test\\testfile.txt"). Without that, \t would mean a tab character, and if you run the program, you'll get a java.nio.file.InvalidPathException since you cannot have tab characters in path names.

- Then, you extract the file name represented by this Path object using the getFilename() method of the Path object.

- You also use getRoot() to get the root element of the Path object and parent directory of the target file using the getParent() method.

- You iterate the elements in the path using a foreach loop. Alternatively, you can use getNameCount() to get the number of elements or names in the path and use getName(index) to iterate and access elements/names one by one.

Now, let's try another example. In this example, you will explore some interesting aspects of a Path object such as how to get an absolute path from a relative path and how you can *normalize* a path.

Before looking at the example, you need to first understand the methods used in the example:

- The toUri() method returns the URI (a path that can be opened from a browser) from the path.

- The toAbsolutePath() method returns the absolute path from a given relative path. In case the input path is already an absolute path, the method returns the same object.

- The normalize() method performs normalization on the input path. In other words, it removes unnecessary symbols (such as "." and "..") from the Path object.

- toRealPath() is an interesting method. It returns an absolute path from the input path object (as toAbsolutePath()). Also, it normalizes the path (as in normalize()). Further, if linking options are chosen properly, it resolves symbolic links also. However, to succeed with this method, it is necessary that the target file/directory exists in the file system, which is *not* a prerequisite for other Path methods.

Now, let's take a look at the example in Listing 9-2. Assume that the file name Test does not exist in your file system.

Listing 9-2. PathInfo2.java

```java
import java.io.IOException;
import java.nio.file.*;

// To illustrate important methods such as normalize(), toAbsolutePath(), and toReativePath()
class PathInfo2 {
        public static void main(String[] args) throws IOException {
                //get a path object with relative path
                Path testFilePath = Paths.get(".\\Test");
                System.out.println("The file name is: " + testFilePath.getFileName());
                System.out.println("It's URI is: " + testFilePath.toUri());
                System.out.println("It's absolute path is: " + testFilePath.toAbsolutePath());
                System.out.println("It's normalized path is: " + testFilePath.normalize());

                // get another path object with normalized relative path
                Path testPathNormalized = Paths.get(testFilePath.normalize().toString());
                System.out.println("It's normalized absolute path is: " +
testPathNormalized.toAbsolutePath());
                System.out.println("It's normalized real path is: " +
                        testFilePath.toRealPath (LinkOption.NOFOLLOW_LINKS));
        }
}
```

In our machine it printed the following:

```
The file name is: Test
It's URI is: file:///D:/OCPJP7/programs/NIO2/./Test
It's absolute path is: D:\OCPJP7\programs\NIO2\.\Test
It's normalized path is: Test
```

```
It's normalized absolute path is: D:\OCPJP7\programs\NIO2\Test
Exception in thread "main" java.nio.file.NoSuchFileException: D:\OCPJP7\programs\NIO2\Test
        at sun.nio.fs.WindowsException.translateToIOException(WindowsException.java:79)
        [... stack trace elided ...]
        at PathInfo2.main(PathInfo2.java:16)
```

Depending on the directory in which you run this program, the directory path will be different for you. In this program you instantiated a Path object using a relative path. The method getFileName() returns the target file name, as you just saw in the last example. The getUri() method returns the URI, which can be used with browsers, and the toAbsolutePath() method returns the absolute path of the given relative path. (Note that we are executing the program from the "D:/OCPJP7/programs/NIO2/" folder, hence it becomes the current working directory and therefore it appears in the absolute path and URI.)

You call the normalize() method to remove redundant symbols from the path, so the normalize() method removes the leading dot (In many operating systems, the "." (single dot) symbol represents the current directory and ".." (double dot) represents parent directory). You then instantiate another Path object using normalized output and print the absolute path again. Finally, you try to call toRealpath(); however, you get an exception (NoSuchFileException). Why? Because, you have not created the Test directory in the current working directory.

Now, let's create a Test directory in the D:/OCPJP7/programs/NIO2/ directory and run this example again. We got the following output:

```
The file name is: Test
It's URI is: file:///D:/OCPJP7/programs/NIO2/./Test/
It's absolute path is: D:\OCPJP7\programs\NIO2\.\Test
It's normalized path is: Test
It's normalized absolute path is: D:\OCPJP7\programs\NIO2\Test
It's normalized real path is: D:\OCPJP7\programs\NIO2\Test
```

Now, the last call toRealPath() works fine and returns the absolute normalized path.

Path provides many other useful methods, and some of them are listed in Table 9-1. To give an example, here's how to use the resolve() method:

```
Path dirName = Paths.get("D:\\OCPJP7\\programs\\NIO2\\");
Path resolvedPath = dirName.resolve("Test");
System.out.println(resolvedPath);
```

This code segment prints the following:

```
D:\OCPJP7\programs\NIO2\Test
```

This resolve() method considers the given path to be a directory and joins (i.e., resolves) the passed path with it, as shown in this example.

The toPath() method in the java.io.File class returns the Path object; this method was added in Java 7. Similarly, you can use the toFile() method in the Path interface to get a File object.

Comparing Two Paths

The Path interface provides two methods to compare two Path objects: equals() and compareTo(). The equals() method checks the equality of two Path objects and returns a Boolean value when compareTo() compares two Path objects character by character and returns an integer: 0 if both Path objects are equal; a negative integer if this path is lexicographically less than the parameter path; and a positive integer if this path is lexicographically greater than the parameter path.

Listing 9-3 contains a small program to understand these methods.

Listing 9-3. PathCompare1.java

```java
import java.nio.file.*;

// illustrates how to use compareTo and equals and also shows the difference between the two methods
class PathCompare1 {
        public static void main(String[] args) {
                Path path1 = Paths.get("Test");
                Path path2 = Paths.get("D:\\OCPJP7\\programs\\NIO2\\Test");
                // comparing two paths using compareTo() method
                System.out.println("(path1.compareTo(path2) == 0) is: " + (path1.compareTo(path2) == 0));

                //comparing two paths using equals() method
                System.out.println("path1.equals(path2) is: " + path1.equals(path2));

                // comparing two paths using equals() method with absolute path
                System.out.println("path2.equals(path1.toAbsolutePath()) is "
                                + path2.equals(path1.toAbsolutePath()));
        }
}
```

Intentionally, we have taken one path as relative path and another one as absolute path. Can you guess the output of the program? It printed the following:

```
(path1.compareTo(path2) == 0) is: false
path1.equals(path2) is: false
path2.equals(path1.toAbsolutePath()) is true
```

Let's understand the program step by step.

- You first compare two paths using the compareTo() method, which compares paths character by character and returns an integer. In this case, since one path is a relative path and another one is an absolute path, it is expected to get first a message that says both paths are not equal.

- Then you compare both paths using equals(). The result is the same, which means even if two Path objects are pointing to the same file/directory, it is possible that equals() returns false. You need to make sure that both paths are absolute paths.

- In the next step, you convert the relative path to an absolute path and then compare them using equals(). This time both paths match.

Even if two `Path` objects point to the same file/directory, it is not guaranteed that you will get true from the `equals()` method. You need to make sure that both are absolute and normalized paths for an equality comparison to succeed for paths.

Using the Files Class

The previous section discussed how to create a `Path` instance and extract useful information from it. Now you will use `Path` objects to manipulate files/directories. Java 7 offers a new `Files` class (in the `java.nio.file` package) that you can use to perform various file-related operations on files or directories. Note that `Files` is a utility class, meaning that it is a final class with a private constructor and consists only of static methods. So you can make use of the `Files` class by calling the static methods it provides, such as `copy()` to copy files. This class provides a wide range of functionality. With this class you can create directories, files, or symbolic links; create streams such as directory streams, byte channels, or input/output streams; examine the attributes of the files; walk the file tree; or perform file operations such as read, write, copy, or delete. Table 9-2 provides a sample of the important methods in the `Files` class.

Table 9-2. *Some Methods Related to File Attributes in the Files Class*

Method	Description

`Path createDirectory(Path dirPath, FileAttribute<?>... dirAttrs)`
 	
`Path createDirectories(Path dir, FileAttribute<?>... attrs)`
	Creates a file given by the `dirPath`, and sets the attributes given by `dirAttributes`. May throw exceptions such as `FileAlreadyExistsException` or `UnsupportedOperationException` (e.g., when the file attributes cannot be set as given by `dirAttrs`). The difference between `createDirectory` and `createDirectories` is that `createDirectories` creates intermediate directories given by `dirPath` if they are not already present.

`Path createTempFile(Path dir, String prefix, String suffix, FileAttribute<?>... attrs)`	Creates a temporary file with given prefix, suffix, and attributes in the directory given by `dir`.
`Path createTempDirectory(Path dir, String prefix, FileAttribute<?>... attrs)`	Creates a temporary directory with the given prefix, directory attributes in the path specified by `dir`.
`Path copy(Path source, Path target, CopyOption... options)`	Copy the file from source to target. `CopyOption` could be REPLACE_EXISTING, COPY_ATTRIBUTES, or NOFOLLOW_LINKS. Can throw exceptions such as `FileAlreadyExistsException`.
`Path move(Path source, Path target, CopyOption... options)`	Similar to the copy operation except that the source file is removed; if the source and target are in the same directory, it is a file rename operation.
`boolean isSameFile(Path path, Path path2)`	Checks if the two `Path` objects are located the same file or not.
`boolean exists(Path path, LinkOption... options)`	Checks if a file/directory exists in the given path; can specify LinkOption.NOFOLLOW_LINKS to not to follow symbolic links.

(continued)

Table 9-2. (*continued*)

Method	Description
`Boolean isRegularFile(Path path, LinkOption...)`	Returns true if the file represented by path is a regular file.
`Boolean isSymbolicLink(Path path)`	Returns true if the file presented by path is a symbolic link.
`Boolean isHidden(Path path)`	Return true if the file represented by path is a hidden file.
`long size(Path path)`	Returns the size of the file in bytes represented by path.
`UserPrincipal getOwner(Path path, LinkOption...)`, `Path setOwner(Path path, UserPrincipal owner)`	Gets/sets the owner of the file.
`FileTime getLastModifiedTime(Path path, LinkOption...)`, `Path setLastModifiedTime(Path path, FileTime time)`	Gets/sets the last modified time for the specified time.
`Object getAttribute(Path path, String attribute, LinkOption...)`, `Path setAttribute(Path path, String attribute, Object value, LinkOption...)`	Gets/sets the specified attribute of the specified file.

Checking File Properties and Metadata

In the last section on the `Path` interface, you tried to figure out whether two paths are pointing to the same file or not (see Listing 9-3). There is another way to find out the same thing. You can use the `isSameFile()` method from the `Files` class. Listing 9-4 shows how to do it.

Listing 9-4. PathCompare2.java

```
import java.io.IOException;
import java.nio.file.*;

// illustrates how to use File class to compare two paths
class PathCompare2 {
        public static void main(String[] args) throws IOException {
                Path path1 = Paths.get("Test");
                Path path2 = Paths.get("D:\\OCPJP7\\programs\\NIO2\\Test");

                System.out.println("Files.isSameFile(path1, path2) is: "
                                + Files.isSameFile(path1, path2));
        }
}
```

The program prints the following:

```
Files.isSameFile(path1, path2) is: true
```

In this case, you create the `Test` directory in the path `D:\OCPJP7\programs\NIO2\` and it worked fine.

However, if the `Test` file/directory does not exist in the given path, you'll get a `NoSuchFileException`. But how can you figure out if a file/directory exists in the given path? The `Files` class offers the `exists()` method to do that.

In fact, you can distinguish between a file and a directory using another method called isDirectory() from the Files class. Listing 9-5 uses these methods.

Listing 9-5. PathExists.java

```java
import java.nio.file.*;

class PathExists {
        public static void main(String[] args) {
                Path path = Paths.get(args[0]);

                if(Files.exists(path, LinkOption.NOFOLLOW_LINKS)) {
                        System.out.println("The file/directory " + path.getFileName() + " exists");
                        // check whether it is a file or a directory
                        if(Files.isDirectory(path, LinkOption.NOFOLLOW_LINKS)) {
                                System.out.println(path.getFileName() + " is a directory");
                        }
                        else {
                                System.out.println(path.getFileName() + " is a file");
                        }
                }
                else {
                        System.out.println("The file/directory " + path.getFileName() + " does not exist");
                }
        }
}
```

In this program, you are accepting a file/directory name from the command line and creating a Path object. Then, you are using the exists() method from the Files class to find out whether the file/directory exists or not. The second parameter of the exists() method is link-option, which is used to specify whether you want to follow symbolic links or not; in this case, you are not following symbolic links. If the file/directory associated with the input path exists, then you are checking whether the input path is indicating a file or a directory using the isDirectory() method of the Files class.

We ran this program with two different command line arguments and we got the following output:

```
D:\OCPJP7\programs\NIO2\src>java PathExists PathExists.java
The file/directory PathExists.java exists
PathExists.java is a file

D:\OCPJP7\programs\NIO2\src>java PathExists D:\OCPJP7\
The file/directory OCPJP7 exists
OCPJP7 is a directory

D:\OCPJP7\programs\NIO2\src>java PathExists D:\
The file/directory null exists
null is a directory
```

In these outputs, you may have noticed the behavior when the root name (drive name in Windows in this case) is given as an argument. A root name is a directory, but path.getFileName() returns null if the path is a root name, hence the output.

Existing files might not allow you to read, write, or execute based on your credentials. You can check the ability of a program to read, write, or execute programmatically. The Files class provides the methods isReadable(), isWriteable(), and isExecutable() to do that. Listing 9-6 uses these methods in a small example.

Listing 9-6. FilePermissions.java

```java
import java.nio.file.*;

class FilePermissions {
        public static void main(String[] args) {
                Path path = Paths.get(args[0]);
                System.out.printf( "Readable: %b, Writable: %b, Executable: %b ",
                        Files.isReadable(path), Files.isWritable(path), Files.isExecutable(path));
        }
}
```

Let's execute this program with two different inputs; here is the output:

```
D:\OCPJP7\programs\NIO2\src>java FilePermissions readonly.txt
Readable: true, Writable: false, Executable: true
D:\OCPJP7\programs\NIO2\src>java FilePermissions FilePermissions.java
Readable: true, Writable: true, Executable: true
```

For the readonly.txt file, the permissions are readable, and executable, but not writable. The file FilePermissions.java itself has all the three permissions: readable, writable, and executable.

There are many other methods that can be used to fetch file properties. Let's use the getAttribute() method to get some attributes of a file. The method takes variable number of parameters: first, a Path object; second, an attribute name; and subsequently, the link options (see Listing 9-7).

Listing 9-7. FileAttributes.java

```java
import java.io.IOException;
import java.nio.file.*;

class FileAttributes {
        public static void main(String[] args) {
                Path path = Paths.get(args[0]);
                try {
                        Object object = Files.getAttribute(path, "creationTime",
LinkOption.NOFOLLOW_LINKS);
                        System.out.println("Creation time: " + object);

                        object = Files.getAttribute(path, "lastModifiedTime",
LinkOption.NOFOLLOW_LINKS);
                        System.out.println("Last modified time: " + object);

                        object = Files.getAttribute(path, "size", LinkOption.NOFOLLOW_LINKS);
                        System.out.println("Size: " + object);

                        object = Files.getAttribute(path, "dos:hidden", LinkOption.NOFOLLOW_LINKS);
                        System.out.println("isHidden: " + object);
```

```
                              object = Files.getAttribute(path, "isDirectory", LinkOption.NOFOLLOW_LINKS);
                              System.out.println("isDirectory: " + object);
                    } catch (IOException e) {
                              e.printStackTrace();
                    }
          }
}
```

Let's first execute this program by giving the name of this program itself and then look at what happens:

```
D:\> java FileAttributes FileAttributes.java
Creation time: 2012-10-06T10:20:10.34375Z
Last modified time: 2012-10-06T10:21:54.859375Z
Size: 914
isHidden: false
isDirectory: false
```

The tricky part of the example is the second parameter of the getAttribute() method. You need to provide a correct attribute name to extract the associated value. The expected string should be specified in view:attribute format, where view is the type of FileAttributeView and attribute is the name of the attribute supported by view. If no view is specified, the view is assumed as basic. In this case, you specified all attributes belonging to a basic view except one attribute from dos view. If you do not specify the correct view name, you will get an UnsupportedOperationException, and if you mess up with the attribute name, you will get an IllegalArgumentException.

For example, if you type sized instead of size, you'll get this exception:

Exception in thread "main" java.lang.IllegalArgumentException: 'sized' not recognized
[...stack trace elided...]

Well, you now know how to read metadata associated with files using the getAttribute() method. However, if you want to read many attributes in one shot, then calling the getAttribute() method for each attribute might not be a good idea (from a performance standpoint). In this case, Java 7 offers a solution: an API— readAttributes()–to read the attributes in one shot. The API comes in two flavors:

```
Map<String,Object> readAttributes(Path path, String attributes, LinkOption... options)
```

```
<A extends BasicFileAttributes> A readAttributes(Path path, Class<A> type, LinkOption... options)
```

The first method returns a Map of attribute value pairs and takes variable length parameters. The attributes parameter is the key parameter where you need to specify what you want to retrieve. This parameter is similar to what you used in the getAttribute() method; however, here you can specify a list of attributes you want, and you can also use '*' to specify all attributes. For instance, using "*" means all attributes of the default FileAttributeView, such as BasicFileAttributes (specified as basic-file-attributes). Another example is: dos:*, which refers to all attributes of dos file attributes.

The second method uses generics syntax (Chapter 6). The second parameter here takes a class from the BasicFileAttributes hierarchy. We'll talk about the hierarchy shortly. The method returns an instance from the BasicFileAttributes hierarchy.

The file attributes hierarchy is shown in Figure 9-1. The BasicFileAttributes is the base interface from which DosFileAttributes and PosixFileAttributes are derived. Note that these attribute interfaces are provided in the java.nio.file.attribute package.

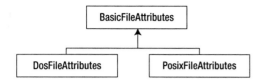

Figure 9-1. *The hierarchy of BasicFileAttributes*

As you can observe, the BasicFileAttributes interface defines the basic attributes supported by all common platforms. However, specific platforms define their own file attributes, which are captured by DosFileAttributes and PosixFileAttributes. You can specify any one of these interfaces to retrieve associated file attributes. Listing 9-8 contains a program to retrieve all attributes of a file using BasicFileAttributes.

Listing 9-8. FileAttributes2.java

```
import java.io.IOException;
import java.nio.file.*;
import java.nio.file.attribute.*;

class FileAttributes2 {
        public static void main(String[] args) {
                Path path = Paths.get(args[0]);
                try {
                        BasicFileAttributes fileAttributes = Files.readAttributes(path,
BasicFileAttributes.class);
                        System.out.println("File size: " + fileAttributes.size());
                        System.out.println("isDirectory: " + fileAttributes.isDirectory());
                        System.out.println("isRegularFile: " + fileAttributes.isRegularFile());
                        System.out.println("isSymbolicLink: " + fileAttributes.isSymbolicLink());
                        System.out.println("File last accessed time: " +
fileAttributes.lastAccessTime());
                        System.out.println("File last modified time: " +
fileAttributes.lastModifiedTime());
                        System.out.println("File creation time: " + fileAttributes.creationTime());
                } catch (IOException e) {
                        e.printStackTrace();
                }
        }
}
```

The following is a sample output of the program:

```
D:\>java FileAttributes2 FileAttributes2.java
File size: 904
isDirectory: false
isRegularFile: true
isSymbolicLink: false
File last accessed time: 2012-10-06T10:28:29.0625Z
File last modified time: 2012-10-06T10:28:22.4375Z
File creation time: 2012-10-06T10:26:39.1875Z
```

You use the `readAttribute()` method along with `BasicFileAttributes` to retrieve basic file properties. Similarly, you can retrieve attributes associated with a file in a DOS or UNIX environment using `DosFileAttributes` and `PosixFileAttributes`, respectively.

Copying a File

Now let's try copying a file/directory from one location to another location. This task is easy to accomplish: just call `Files.copy()` to copy the file from source to target. Here is the signature of this method:

```
Path copy(Path source, Path target, CopyOption... options)
```

Listing 9-9 uses this method to write a simple file copy program.

Listing 9-9. FileCopy.java

```java
import java.io.IOException;
import java.nio.file.*;

public class FileCopy {
        public static void main(String[] args) {
                if(args.length != 2){
                        System.out.println("usage: FileCopy <source-path> <destination-path>");
                        System.exit(1);
                }
                Path pathSource = Paths.get(args[0]);
                Path pathDestination = Paths.get(args[1]);
                try {
                        Files.copy(pathSource, pathDestination);
                        System.out.println("Source file copied successfully");
                } catch (IOException e) {
                        e.printStackTrace();
                }
        }
}
```

Let's execute it and see whether it works.

```
D:\> java FileCopy FileCopy.java Backup.java
Source file copied successfully
```

Yes, it's working. Let's try running it again with same arguments.

```
D:\OCPJP7\programs\NIO2\src>java FileCopy FileCopy.java Backup.java
java.nio.file.FileAlreadyExistsException: Backup.java
        at sun.nio.fs.WindowsFileCopy.copy(Unknown Source)
        [...stack trace elided...]
```

Oops! What happened? When you tried copying the file for the second time, you got a `FileAlreadyExistsException` since the destination file already exists. So, what if you want to overwrite the existing file? The solution: you need to tell the copy() method that you would like to overwrite an existing file. In Listing 9-9, change the copy() method as follows:

```
Files.copy(pathSource, pathDestination, StandardCopyOption.REPLACE_EXISTING);
```

In this change, you are specifying an additional argument (since the copy() method supports variable arguments) to tell the method that you want to overwrite a file if it already exists. So, let's run this program and see whether it works.

```
D:\>java FileCopy FileCopy.java Backup.java
Source file copied successfully

D:\>java FileCopy FileCopy.java Backup.java
Source file copied successfully
```

Yes, it works. Now, try to copy a file to a new directory.

```
D:\OCPJP7\programs\NIO2\src>java FileCopy FileCopy.java bak\Backup.java
java.nio.file.NoSuchFileException: FileCopy.java -> bak\Backup.java
        [...stack trace elided ...]
```

Well, here you tried to copy a file to back directory that does not exist. For this, you got the NoSuchFileException. Note that not just the given directory but all intermediate directories in a path must exist for the copy() method to succeed.

 All the directories (except the last one if you are copying a directory) in the specified path must exist to avoid NoSuchFileException.

What if you try copying a directory? It will work, but remember that it will only copy the top-level directory, not the not the files/directories contained within that directory.

 If you copy a directory using the copy() method, it will not copy the files/directories contained in the source directory; you need to explicitly copy them to the destination folder.

You will revisit this topic later in this chapter when you implement a copy program that can copy a directory into another directory along with the contained files/directories.

Moving a File

Moving a file is quite similar to copying a file; for this purpose, you can use the Files.move() method. The signature of this method is

```
Path move(Path source, Path target, CopyOption... options)
```

Listing 9-10 contains a small program that uses this method.

Listing 9-10. FileMove.java

```java
import java.io.IOException;
import java.nio.file.*;

public class FileMove {
        public static void main(String[] args) {
                if(args.length != 2){
                        System.out.println("usage: FileMove <source-path> <destination-path>");
                        System.exit(-1);
                }
                Path pathSource = Paths.get(args[0]);
                Path pathDestination = Paths.get(args[1]);
                try {
                        Files.move(pathSource, pathDestination, StandardCopyOption.REPLACE_EXISTING);
                        System.out.println("Source file moved successfully");
                } catch (IOException e) {
                        e.printStackTrace();
                }
        }
}
```

This basic implementation works fine. However, here are some observations peculiar to the move() method:

- As is the case with the copy() method, the move() method also does not overwrite the existing destination file unless you specify it to do so using REPLACE_EXISTING.

- If you move a symbolic link, the link itself will be moved, not the target file of the link. It is important to note that in the case of the copy() method, if you specify a symbolic link, the target of the link is copied, not the link itself.

- A non-empty directory can be moved if moving the directory does not require moving the containing files/directories. For instance, moving a directory from one physical drive to another might be unsuccessful (an IOException will be thrown). If moving a directory operation is successful, then all the contained files/directories will also be moved.

- You can specify a move() operation as an atomic operation using the ATOMIC_MOVE copy option. If move() is performed as a non-atomic operation and it fails in between, the state of both files is unknown and undefined.

Deleting a File

The Files class provides a delete() method to delete a file/directory/symbolic link. Listing 9-11 contains a simple program to delete a specified file.

Listing 9-11. FileDelete.java

```java
import java.io.IOException;
import java.nio.file.*;

public class FileDelete {
        public static void main(String[] args) {
```

```
            if(args.length != 1){
            System.out.println("usage: FileDelete <source-path>");
                    System.exit(1);
            }
            Path pathSource = Paths.get(args[0]);
            try {
                    Files.delete(pathSource);
                    System.out.println("File deleted successfully");
            } catch (IOException e) {
                    e.printStackTrace();
            }
        }
}
```

It prints the following when executed:

```
D:\> java FileDelete log.txt
File deleted successfully
```

There are a few points to remember when using the Files.delete() method. In the case of a directory, the delete() method should be invoked on an empty directory; otherwise the method will fail. In the case of a symbolic link, the link will be deleted, not the target file of the link. The file you intend to delete must exist; otherwise you will get a NoSuchFileException. If you silently delete a file and do not want to be bothered about this exception, then you may use the deleteIfExists() method, which will not complain if the file does not exist and deletes it if the file exists.

Walking a File Tree

In various situations, you need to walk through the file tree. For instance, when you want to search a specific file/ directory, you need to walk the file tree. Another example of when you need to walk a file tree is when you want to copy the whole directory containing files/subdirectories.

The Files class provides two methods that let you walk a file tree; the signatures of these methods are given here:

```
Path walkFileTree(Path start, FileVisitor<? super Path> visitor)

Path walkFileTree(Path start, Set<FileVisitOption> options, int maxDepth, FileVisitor<?
super Path> visitor)
```

Both methods take a path from which the file tree walk will start and an instance of FileVisitor that will govern what you to do while walking a file tree. (We will talk about FileVisitor in detail shortly.) In addition, the second method takes two more parameters: file visit options and maximum depth. The maximum depth parameter specifies the depth of the file tree you wish to visit; a 0 value indicates only the specified file and a MAX_VALUE indicates that all levels of directories must be visited.

Note that you need to supply a FileVisitor instance to the walkFileTree() methods. The FileVisitor interface allows you to perform certain operations at certain key junctures. For instance, the interface provides a visitFile()method that you can implement to specify exactly what needs to be done when the FileVisitor instance visits a file. Similarly, it also provides three more useful methods, which can be customized based on your needs: preVisitDirectory(), postVisitDirectory(), and visitFileFailed(). Table 9-3 provides a short summary of these methods.

Table 9-3. *Methods Supported by the FileVisitor Interface*

Method	Description
FileVisitResult preVisitDirectory(T dir, BasicFileAttributes attrs)	Invoked just before the elements of the directory are accessed.
FileVisitResult visitFile(T file, BasicFileAttributes attrs)	Invoked when a file is visited.
FileVisitResult postVisitDirectory(T dir, IOException exc)	Invoked when all the elements of the directory are accessed.
FileVisitResult visitFileFailed(T file, IOException exc)	Invoked when the file cannot be accessed.

You need to implement the `FileVisitor` interface so that you can create an instance of your implementation and pass it to the `walkFileTree()` methods. However, if you do not want to implement all four methods in the `FileVisitor` interface, you can simply extend your implementation from the `SimpleFileVisitor` class. In this way, you can simply override those methods that you want to customize.

Listing 9-12 contains an example so you can understand this more clearly. Assume that you want to print the file tree from a specific point.

Listing 9-12. FileTreeWalk.java

```java
import java.io.IOException;
import java.nio.file.*;
import java.nio.file.attribute.BasicFileAttributes;

class MyFileVisitor extends SimpleFileVisitor<Path> {
        public FileVisitResult visitFile(Path path, BasicFileAttributes fileAttributes){
                System.out.println("file name:" + path.getFileName());
                return FileVisitResult.CONTINUE;
        }
        public FileVisitResult preVisitDirectory(Path path, BasicFileAttributes fileAttributes){
                System.out.println("----------Directory name:" + path + "----------");
                return FileVisitResult.CONTINUE;
        }
}

public class FileTreeWalk {
        public static void main(String[] args) {
                if(args.length != 1) {
                        System.out.println("usage: FileWalkTree <source-path>");
                        System.exit(-1);
                }
                Path pathSource = Paths.get(args[0]);
                try {
                        Files.walkFileTree(pathSource, new MyFileVisitor());
                } catch (IOException e) {
                        e.printStackTrace();
                }
        }
}
```

Let's first execute this program and then understand how it works.

```
D:\> java FileTreeWalk ch9-13
----------Directory name: ch9-13----------
file name:.classpath
file name:.project
----------Directory name: ch9-13\.settings----------
file name:org.eclipse.jdt.core.prefs
----------Directory name: ch9-13\bin----------
file name:FileTreeWalk.class
file name:MyFileVisitor.class
----------Directory name: ch9-13\bin\Test----------
file name:log.txt
----------Directory name: ch9-13\src----------
file name:FileTreeWalk.class
file name:FileTreeWalk.java
file name:MyFileVisitor.class
----------Directory name: ch9-13\src\Test----------
file name:log.txt
```

We have executed this program with one directory. It printed all the files and directories contained in the given input directory. Now, here's how it works:

- You define a FileVisitor, MyFileVisitor, in which you overrode two methods, visitFile() and preVisitDirectory(), of the SimpleFileVisitor class. In these methods you just printed the name (along with path in case of directory) of the file/directory.

- You then invoked walkFileTree() with an instance of MyFileVisitor.

- The walkFileTree() method starts from the specified input path. It invokes the visitFile() method when it visits a file, preVisitDirectory() just before it starts visiting the elements of a directory, postVisitDirectory() immediately after it finishes visiting all the elements of the directory, and visitFileFailed() in case any file/directory is not accessible.

- Here, since you have overridden two methods, you are able to print the file names and the path of the directories visited.

- One more thing that requires attention here is the FileVisitReturn value. You can control the flow of the walk using FileVisitReturn values. There are four types of different return values:

  - **CONTINUE**: It indicates that the walk through the file tree should continue.

  - **TERMINATE**: It indicates that the walk through the file tree should be terminated immediately.

  - **SKIP_SUBTREE**: It indicates that the rest of the subtree should be skipped for the walking file tree.

  - **SKIP_SIBLINGS**: It indicates that walking file tree should be stopped for the current directory and its sibling directories. If it is returned from the preVisitDirectory(), then the containing files/directories are not visited and the postVisitDirectory() is also not visited. If it is returned from visitFile(), then no further file in the directory is visited. If it is returned from the postVisitDirectory(), then siblings of the directory are not visited.

Revisiting File Copy

You saw how to copy a file from one location to another. However, you couldn't perform a copy on an entire directory (and its files/subdirectories). Now you can walk through the file tree, making it easier to implement a copy program that can copy the entire directory along with containing elements. Listing 9-13 shows the program to do so.

Listing 9-13. FileTreeWalkCopy.java

```java
import java.io.IOException;
import java.nio.file.*;
import java.nio.file.attribute.*;

// Our File visitor implementation that performs copy
class MyFileCopyVisitor extends SimpleFileVisitor<Path> {
        private Path source, destination;

        public MyFileCopyVisitor(Path s, Path d) {
                source = s;
                destination = d;
        }
        public FileVisitResult visitFile(Path path, BasicFileAttributes fileAttributes) {
                Path newd = destination.resolve(source.relativize(path));
                try {
                        Files.copy(path, newd, StandardCopyOption.REPLACE_EXISTING);
                } catch (IOException e) {
                        e.printStackTrace();
                }
                return FileVisitResult.CONTINUE;
        }
        public FileVisitResult preVisitDirectory(Path path, BasicFileAttributes fileAttributes) {
                Path newd = destination.resolve(source.relativize(path));
                try {
                        Files.copy(path, newd, StandardCopyOption.REPLACE_EXISTING);
                }catch (IOException e) {
                        e.printStackTrace();
                }
                return FileVisitResult.CONTINUE;
        }
}

public class FileTreeWalkCopy {
        public static void main(String[] args) {
                if(args.length != 2) {
                        System.out.println("usage: FileTreeWalkCopy <source-path> <destination-path>");
                        System.exit(1);
                }
                Path pathSource = Paths.get(args[0]);
                Path pathDestination = Paths.get(args[1]);
                try {
                        Files.walkFileTree(pathSource, new MyFileCopyVisitor(pathSource, pathDestination));
                        System.out.println("Files copied successfully!");
```

```
        } catch (IOException e) {
                e.printStackTrace();
        }
    }
}
```

Let's execute this program and see whether it works:

```
D:\> java FileTreeWalkCopy Test Test2
Files copied successfully!
```

Well, the program copied the Test directory along with the files contained in the Test directory to the Test2 directory. Essentially, what you are doing is quite simple: in the preVisitDirectory() method, you are copying the directory (which is being visited). To retrieve the new destination path, you are using the relativize() method from the Path class. Similarly, you get a new destination path each time you visit a file, which is used to copy the file to the destination directory. That's it. You're done.

Finding a File

Once you understand how to walk through the file tree, it is very straightforward and easy to find a desired file. For instance, if you are looking for a particular file/directory, then you may try to match the file/directory name you are looking for with the visitFile() or preVisitDirectory() method. However, if you are looking for all files matching a particular pattern (for instance, all Java source files or xml files) in a file tree, you can use glob or regex to match the names of files. The PathMatcher interface is useful in this context as it will match a path for you once you specified the desired pattern. The PathMatcher interface is implemented for each file system, and you can get an instance of it from the FileSystem class using the getPathMatcher() method.

Before looking at a detailed example, let's first understand Glob patterns. Glob is a pattern-specifying mechanism where you can specify file matching patterns as strings. Table 9-4 summarizes the supported patterns by the glob syntax.

Table 9-4. Patterns Supported by Glob Syntax

Pattern	Description
*	Matches any string of any length, even zero length.
**	Similar to "*", but it crosses directory boundaries.
?	Matches to any single character,
[xyz]	Matches to either x, y, or z.
[0-5]	Matches to any character in the range 0 to 5.
[a-z]	Matches to any lowercase letter.
{xyz, abc}	Matches to either xyz or abc.

Hence, you can specify syntax such as File*.java to match all Java source files that start with the letters "File" or you can have syntax such as program[0-9].class, which will match files such as program0.class, program1.class, and so on.

Let's try an example that takes a path (a starting path) and a pattern (to find matching files) and then prints the list of files that match the specified pattern. The program is given in Listing 9-14.

Listing 9-14. FileTreeWalkFind.java

```java
import java.io.IOException;
import java.nio.file.*;
import java.nio.file.attribute.*;

class MyFileFindVisitor extends SimpleFileVisitor<Path> {
        private PathMatcher matcher;

        public MyFileFindVisitor(String pattern){
                try {
                        matcher = FileSystems.getDefault().getPathMatcher(pattern);
                } catch(IllegalArgumentException iae) {
                        System.err.println("Invalid pattern; did you forget to prefix \"glob:\"?
(as in glob:*.java)");
                        System.exit(-1);
                }

        }
        public FileVisitResult visitFile(Path path, BasicFileAttributes fileAttributes){
                find(path);
                return FileVisitResult.CONTINUE;
        }
        private void find(Path path) {
                Path name = path.getFileName();
                if(matcher.matches(name))
                        System.out.println("Matching file:" + path.getFileName());
        }
public FileVisitResult preVisitDirectory(Path path, BasicFileAttributes fileAttributes){
                find(path);
                return FileVisitResult.CONTINUE;
        }
}

public class FileTreeWalkFind {
        public static void main(String[] args) {
                if(args.length != 2){
System.out.println("usage: FileTreeWalkFind <start-path> <pattern to search>");
                        System.exit(-1);
                }
                Path startPath = Paths.get(args[0]);
                String pattern = args[1];
```

```
            try {
                    Files.walkFileTree(startPath, new MyFileFindVisitor(pattern));
                    System.out.println("File search completed!");
            } catch (IOException e) {
                    e.printStackTrace();
            }

        }
}
```

Let's execute it first and then understand how it works.

```
d:\> java FileTreeWalkFind ch9-15 glob:File*.java
Matching file:FileTreeWalkFind.java
File search completed!

d:\> java FileTreeWalkFind ch9-15 glob:File*
Matching file:FileTreeWalkFind.class
Matching file:FileTreeWalkFind.class
Matching file:FileTreeWalkFind.java
File search completed!
```

Here's how it works:

- You define your `FileVisitor`, `MyFileFindVisitor`, which overrides two methods, `visitFile()` and `preVisitDirectory()`.

- In the constructor of your visitor class, you retrieve a `PathMatcher` instance using a `FileSystem` instance.

- The overridden methods call a method of `find()`; this method creates a `Path` object from the file name of the passed `Path` object. This is necessary since you want matcher to match only the file name, not the whole path.

- You start walking through the file tree using the method `walkFileTree()`; you specify an instance of `MyFileFindVisitor` as the `FileVisitor`.

- If the current visiting file/directory matches the pattern, you print the file name. The process of matching the specified pattern is carried out by a `PathMatcher` instance.

Watching a Directory for Changes

Let's assume that you have implemented a simple IDE to work on Java programs. You have loaded a Java source file in it and you are working on it. What happens if some other program changes the source file you are working on? You might want to ask the user whether he wants to reload the source file. In fact, many IDEs and other programs shows a message to the user and ask permission from the user to reload the files (see Figure 9-2). However, the key point is: how do you get notified that the file you are working on was modified by some other program?

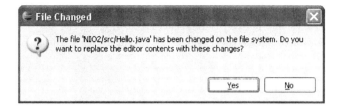

Figure 9-2. *File change notification shown in Eclipse IDE*

Java 7 offers a directory watch service that can achieve exactly the same result. You can register a directory using this service to change event notification, and whenever any change happens in the directory (such as new file creation, file deletion, and file modification) you will get an event notification about the change. The watch service is a convenient, scalable, and an easy way to keep track of the changes in a directory.

Let's look at a program in Listing 9-15 first and then see how the watch service API works. Assume that you want to monitor the src directory of your current project. You are interested in file modification events, such that any change in any file of the directory results in an event notification to your program.

Listing 9-15. KeepAnEye.java

```
import java.io.IOException;
import java.nio.file.*;

public class KeepAnEye {
        public static void main(String[] args) {
                Path path = Paths.get("..\\src");
                WatchService watchService = null;
                try {
                        watchService = path.getFileSystem().newWatchService();
                        path.register(watchService, StandardWatchEventKinds.ENTRY_MODIFY);
                } catch (IOException e1) {
                        e1.printStackTrace();
                }

                //infinite loop
                for(;;){
                        WatchKey key = null;
                        try {
                                key = watchService.take();
                        } catch (InterruptedException e) {
                                e.printStackTrace();
                        }
                        // iterate for each event
                        for(WatchEvent<?> event:key.pollEvents()){
                                switch(event.kind().name()){
                                case "OVERFLOW":
                                        System.out.println("We lost some events");
                                        break;
                                case "ENTRY_MODIFY":
```

```
                                    System.out.println("File " + event.context() + " is changed!");
                                    break;
                            }
                    }
                    //resetting the key is important to receive subsequent notifications
                    key.reset();
            }
    }
}
```

Execute this program and meanwhile try to change the source file as well as the class file in the src directory. You may get results like this:

```
d:\workspace\ch9-16\src>java KeepAnEye
File KeepAnEye.java is changed!
File KeepAnEye.java is changed!
File KeepAnEye.java is changed!
File KeepAnEye.class is changed!
File KeepAnEye.class is changed!
```

Well, that's great—it's working as intended. Now, let's understand the program step by step:

- The first thing you need to do is to get an instance of WatchService. You can get a watch service instance using the FileSystem class. Here, you are getting a FileSystem instance using a path instance, and then you are requesting an instance of watch service from the FileSystem. You may also get an instance of the FileSystem from FileSystems (FileSystems.getDefault()).

- Once you have an instance of the watch service, the next step is to register the directory to the watch service. The Path object provides two methods for registration: the first register() method takes variable arguments (first an instance of watch service and subsequently the kind of watch event in which you are interested). The second register() method takes one additional parameter—the watch event modifier. Here, you are using the first register() method.

- You want to receive an event notification only when a file is modified; thus you specify ENTRY_MODIFY (belonging to StandardWatchEventKinds). Other kinds watch events include ENTRY_CREATE, ENTRY_DELETE, and OVERFLOW. The first three kinds are self-explanatory; OVERFLOW specifies that a few event notifications are discarded or missed. These event kinds can be specified based on the requirements.

- Once the registration is done, you are ready to receive event notifications. You can implement an infinite loop in which you wait for the suitable event to happen.

- In the loop, you need to wait for the event to happen. Here, you can ask the watch service to notify this program when an event occurs. You can do this using three methods:

  - The poll() method returns a queued key if available; otherwise it returns immediately.

  - The poll(long, TimeUnit) method returns a queued key if available; otherwise it waits for the specified time (the long value) and for the specified time unit. The method returns after the specified time limit is elapsed.

- The take() method returns a queued key if available; otherwise it waits until a key is available.

  - The key difference between the poll() and take() methods is that poll() is a non-blocking call and take() is a blocking call.

- When a key is returned, one or more events might be queued; that's why you put in another for loop to iterate through all the available events.

- You can get the kind of event using the kind() method and the name of the file for which the event has occurred using the context() method.

- Once you are done with event processing, you need to reset the key using the reset() method on the key.

Points to Remember

Here are the concepts you need to understand in order to pass this section of the OCPJP exam.

- Do not confuse File with Files, Path with Paths, and FileSystem with FileSystems: they are different. *File* is an old class (Java 4) that represents file/directory path names, while *Files* was introduced in Java 7 as a utility class with comprehensive support for I/O APIs. The *Path* interface represents a file/directory path and defines a useful list of methods. However, the *Paths* class is a utility class that offers only two methods (both to get the Path object). *FileSystems* offer a list of factory methods for the class FileSystem, whereas *FileSystem* provides a useful set of methods to get information about a file system.

- The file or directory represented by a Path object might not exist.

- You learned how to perform a copy for files/directories. However, it is not necessary that you perform copy on two files/directories only. You can take input from an InputStream and write to a file, or you can take input from a file and copy to an OutputStream. Methods copy(InputStream, Path, CopyOptions...) and copy(Path, OutputStream, CopyOptions...) could be used here.

- You must be careful about performing an operation when walking a file tree. For instance, if you are performing a recursive delete, you should first delete all the containing files before deleting the directory that is holding these containing files.

- The Visitor design pattern is used to enable walking through a file tree.

- In the context of a watch service, a state is associated with a watch key. A watch key might be in ready state (ready to accept events), in signed state (when one or more events are queued), or in invalid state (when the watch key is not valid). If the key is in the signed state, it is required to call the reset() method; otherwise the state of the key will not change to ready state and you will not receive any further event notification.

- Your program may receive an OVERFLOW event even if the program is not registered for this event.

- If you are watching a directory using the watch service offered by Java 7, then only files contained in that directory will be watched—and not the files contained in the subdirectories of that directory. If you intend to watch the whole subtree of the file system, you need to recursively register each directory in the subtree.

QUESTION TIME!

1. Consider the following program:

```java
import java.nio.file.*;

public class PathInfo {
    public static void main(String[] args) {
        Path aFilePath = Paths.get("D:\\dir\\file.txt");         // FILEPATH

        while(aFilePath.iterator().hasNext()) {
            System.out.println("path element: " + aFilePath.iterator().next());
        }
    }
}
```

Assume that the file `D:\dir\file.txt` exists in the underlying file system. Which one of the following options correctly describes the behavior of this program?

A) The program gives a compiler error in the line marked with the comment `FILEPATH` because the checked exception `FileNotFoundException` is not handled.

B) The program gives a compiler error in the line marked with the comment `FILEPATH` because the checked exception `InvalidPathException` is not handled.

C) The program gets into an infinite loop printing "path element: dir" forever.

D) The program prints the following:

   path element: dir

   path element: file.txt

Answer: C) The program gets into an infinite loop printing "path element: dir" forever.

(In the `while` loop, you use `iterator()` to get a temporary iterator object. So, the call to `next()` on the temporary variable is lost, so the `while` loop gets into an infinite loop. In other words, the following loop will terminate after printing the "dir" and "file.txt" parts of the path:

```java
Iterator<Path> paths = aFilePath.iterator();
while(paths.hasNext()) {
    System.out.println("path element: " + paths.next());
}
```

Option A) is wrong because the `Paths.get` method does not throw `FileNotFoundException`.

Option B) is wrong because `InvalidPathException` is a `RuntimeException`. Also, since the file path exists in the underlying file system, this exception will not be thrown when the program is executed.

Option D) is wrong because the program will get into an infinite loop).

2. Which **two** of the following statements are correct regarding the `SimpleFileVisitor` interface?

A) The `postVisitDirectory` method, declared in `SimpleFileVisitor`, will be invoked after all the entries (i.e., files and subdirectories) of the directory have been visited.

B) The `visitFile` method, declared in `SimpleFileVisitor`, will be invoked when a file is visited.

C) The `visitFileOrDirectory` method, declared in `SimpleFileVisitor`, will be invoked when a file or subdirectory is visited.

D) The `walkFileTree` method, declared in `SimpleFileVisitor`, will walk the file tree.

Answer: A) and B) are correct statements.

(Regarding option C), there is no such method as `visitFileOrDirectory` in `SimpleFileVisitor` interface. Regarding option D), the `walkFileTree` method is a static method defined in the `Files` class that will walk the file tree. The `walkFileTree` method is not declared in `SimpleFileVisitor`. In fact, `FileVisitor` is one of the arguments this method takes for which you can pass a `SimpleFileVisitor` object as an argument.)

3. Consider the following program:

```
import java.nio.file.*;

class Relativize {
    public static void main(String []args) {
            Path javaPath =
Paths.get("D:\\OCPJP7\\programs\\NIO2\\src\\Relativize.java").normalize();
            Path classPath =
Paths.get("D:\\OCPJP7\\programs\\NIO2\\src\\Relativize.class").normalize();
            Path result = javaPath.relativize(classPath);
            if(result == null) {
                    System.out.println("relativize failed");
            } else if(result.equals(Paths.get(""))) {
                    System.out.println("relative paths are same, so relativize
returned empty path");
            } else {
                    System.out.println(result);
            }
    }
}
```

Which of the following options correctly shows the output of this program?

A) The program prints the following: relativize failed.

B) The program prints the following: relative paths are same, so relativize returned empty path.

C) The program prints the following: ..\Relativize.class.

D) The program prints the following: ..\Relativize.java.

Answer: C) The program prints the following: ..\Relativize.class.

(The `relativize()` method constructs a relative path between this path and a given path. In this case, the paths for both the files are the same and they differ only in the file names (`Relativize.java` and `Relativize.class`). The relative comparison of paths is performed from the given path to the passed path to the relativize method, so it prints ..\Relativize.class.

Note: The `normalize()` method removes any redundant name elements in a path. In this program, there are no redundant name elements, so it has no impact on the output of this program.)

4. Consider the following program:

```
import java.nio.file.*;

class SubPath {
    public static void main(String []args) {
Path aPath = Paths.get("D:\\OCPJP7\\programs\\..\\NIO2\\src\\.\\SubPath.java");
            aPath = aPath.normalize();
            System.out.println(aPath.subpath(2, 3));
    }
}
```

This program prints the following:

A) ..

B) src

C) NIO2

D) NIO2\src

E) ..\NIO2

Answer: B) src

(The normalize() method removes redundant name elements in the given path, so after the call to the normalize() method, the aPath value is D:\OCPJP7\NIO2\src\SubPath.java.

The subpath(int beginIndex, int endIndex) method returns a path based on the values of beginIndex and endIndex. The name that is closest to the root has index 0; note that the root itself (in this case D:\) is not considered as an element in the path. Hence, the name elements "OCPJP7", "NIO2", "src", "SubPath.java" are in index positions 0, 1, 2, and 3, respectively.

Note that beginIndex is the index of the first element, inclusive of that element; endIndex is the index of the last element, exclusive of that element. Hence, the subpath is "sub", which is at index position 2 in this path.)

5. Assuming that the variable path points to a valid Path object, which one of the following statements is the correct way to create a WatchService?

A) WatchService watchService = WatchService.getInstance(path);

B) WatchService watchService = FileSystem.newWatchService();

C) WatchService watchService = path.getFileSystem().newWatchService();

D) WatchService watchService = FileSystem("default").getWatchService(path);

Answer: C) WatchService watchService = path.getFileSystem().newWatchService();

(The newWatchService() method is an abstract method defined in the FileSystem class. To get a WatchService instance associated with a given path object, you need to first get the associated FileSystem object and call the newWatchService() method on that FileSystem object. Hence, option C) is the right answer.)

Summary

Working with the Path Class

- A Path object is a programming abstraction to represent a path of a file/directory.

- You can get an instance of Path using the get() method of the Paths class.

- Path provides two methods to use to compare Path objects: equals() and compareTo(). Even if two Path objects point to the same file/directory, it is not guaranteed that you will get true from the equals() method.

Performing Operations on Files/Directories

- You can check the existence of a file using the exists() method of the Files class.

- The Files class provides the methods isReadable(), isWriteable(), and isExecutable() to check the ability of the program to read, write, or execute programmatically.

- You can retrieve attributes of a file using the getAttributes() method.

- You can use the readAttributes() method of the Files class to read attributes of a file in bulk.

- The method copy() can be used to copy a file from one location to another. Similarly, the method move() can be used to move a file from one location to another.

- While copying, all the directories (except the last one if you are copying a directory) in the specified path must exist to avoid NoSuchFileException.

- Use the delete() method to delete a file; use the deleteIfExists() method to delete a file only if it exists.

Walking a File Tree

- The Files class provides two flavors of walkFileTree() to enable you to walk through a file system.

- The FileVisitor interface allows you to perform certain operations at certain key junctures.

- If you do not want to implement all four methods in the FileVisitor interface, you can simply extend your implementation from the SimpleFileVisitor class.

Finding a File

- The PathMatcher interface is useful when you want to find a file satisfying a certain pattern. You can specify the pattern using glob or regex.

Watching a Directory for Changes

- Java 7 offers a directory watch service that can notify you when the file you are working on is changed by some other program.

- You can register a Path object using a watch service along with certain event types. Whenever any file in the specified directory changes, an event is sent to the registered program.

CHAPTER 10

■ ■ ■

Building Database Applications with JDBC

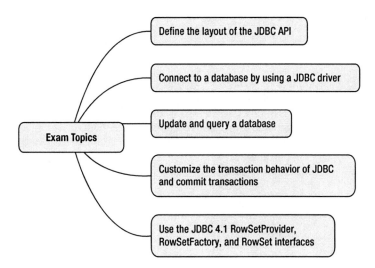

JDBC (Java DataBase Connectivity) is an important Java API that defines how a client accesses a database. As such, it is critical in building large-scale enterprise Java solutions. As an Oracle certified programmer, it is expected that you understand JDBC and its related features. You can use JDBC to perform database operations such as inserting, updating, and creating database entities as well as executing SQL queries. Using JDBC support, you can also perform transactions on the database.

This chapter discusses JDBC features in terms of ResultSet, Connection, and Statement implementations. JDBC 4.1 introduces RowSet and its related utility classes such as RowSetFactory and RowSetProvider, which are also discussed in this chapter.

The JDBC classes are part of the packages java.sql.* and javax.sql.*. In this chapter, we assume that you're already familiar with SQL queries and have some basic understanding of database concepts.

Introduction to JDBC

When you write applications for solving real-world problems, you routinely come upon requirements where you need to store, navigate, and modify data. In an enterprise environment, you need to work with DBMSs (Database Management Systems) to handle the large amounts of data you have. However, interacting with DBMSs (henceforth, we simply refer to DBMSs as *databases*) is not really trivial or straightforward. Numerous enterprise and open source database systems are available today and they differ from each other: DB2, SQL Server, MySQL, Oracle, and many more. This heterogeneity of popular databases makes it difficult write code that can be used with any database. To solve these problems and to make your life easy, Java offers JDBC. JDBC is a set of APIs provided by Java to programmatically interact with various databases.

At a high level, interacting with a database involves the following steps:

- Establishing a connection to a database.

- Executing SQL queries to retrieve, create, or modify a database.

- Closing the connection to the database.

Java provides a set of APIs (i.e., JDBC) to carry out these activities with databases. In other words, you can use JDBC to establish a connection to a database, execute your SQL query, and close the connection with the database. The beauty of JDBC is that you are not writing a program for a specific database. JDBC creates loose coupling between your Java program and the type of database used. For instance, databases may differ in how they establish a connection (for instance, the API name may differ with databases). JDBC hides all the heterogeneity of these databases and offers a single set of APIs to interact with all types of databases.

The Architecture of JDBC

Let's examine the vital components of JDBC and how these components work together to achieve seamless integration with databases. A simplified architecture of JDBC is graphically represented in Figure 10-1. A Java application uses JDBC APIs to interact with databases. JDBC APIs interact with the JDBC driver manager to transparently connect and perform various database activities with different types of databases. The JDBC driver manager uses various JDBC drivers to connect to their specific DBMSs.

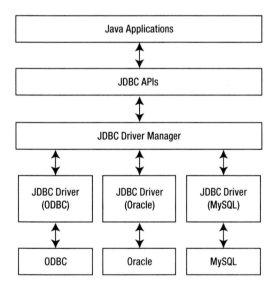

Figure 10-1. *JDBC architecture*

In this context, JDBC drivers and the driver manager play a key role in realizing the objective of JDBC. JDBC drivers are specifically designed to interact with their respective DBMSs. The driver manager works as a directory of JDBC drivers—in other words, it maintains a list of available data sources and their drivers. The driver manager chooses an appropriate driver to communicate to the respective DBMS. It can manage multiple concurrent drivers connected to their respective data sources.

You can observe here that the complexity of heterogeneous interactions is delegated to the JDBC driver manager and JDBC drivers; hence all the details and complications are hidden by the JDBC API from the application developer.

Two-Tier and Three-Tier JDBC Architecture

Broadly, JDBC architectures can be seen in two major configurations: two-tier and three-tier. In a two-tier configuration, a Java application along with a JDBC driver constitutes the first tier as a client. On the other hand, the database works as a server that fulfills the requirements sent from the clients. Typically, the database resides on a different machine connected through the network.

The first tier in a three-tier configuration is a lightweight Java application (an applet, for instance) that communicates to the application server (the second tier). The application server in turn forwards the request to the database (the third tier). In this configuration, the middle tier plays a vital role since the behavior of the configuration can be fine-tuned based on the requirements (for instance, enforcing access control).

Types of JDBC Drivers

There are a number of types of JDBC drivers that have emerged, and they are being used by the industry based on preference and needs. They can be categorized based on the technology used to communicate to the actual respective DBMS. The type of these drivers can play a critical role when selecting an appropriate DBMS for a Java application. There are four types of JDBC drivers:

- **JDBC-ODBC bridge drivers (type 1):** You may already know about ODBC (Open Database Connectivity), which is a portable middleware API written in C for accessing databases. The first category belongs to the drivers that are designed to work with ODBC drivers; they play the role of a bridge from a Java application to an ODBC driver. Such drivers are useful especially in cases when the ODBC driver for the DBMS is available. The JDBC driver calls the ODBC native calls using Java Native Interface (JNI). The drivers from this category might not be suitable for applets since often client-side software and an ODBC driver are required for this bridge to work properly.

- **Native-API driver (type 2):** The database drivers belonging to this category use client-side libraries of a specific database and convert JDBC calls to native database calls. Mostly, these drivers are not written entirely in Java, and hence are not portable. These drivers are not suitable for Java applets since they require proprietary client software installed on client machines. However, these drivers are typically faster than type 1 drivers.

- **The network-protocol driver (type 3):** This type of database driver implements a three-tier architecture where JDBC calls are converted to native database calls via a middleware implementation. In other words, the driver calls database middleware and the middleware actually converts JDBC calls to database specific native calls. Typically, the driver is implemented in Java, which does not require any other client implementation at client side; hence they could be employed in Internet-based applications. However, these drivers are typically slower than type 2 drivers.

- **Native-protocol driver (type 4):** Such drivers are implemented in Java completely, so they are platform independent. Drivers belonging to this category directly make database specific calls over the network without any support of additional client side libraries. These drivers are the most flexible database drivers among all other database types. These drivers perform better than other driver types. However, these drivers may be lacking in covering the security aspects of database access.

For an enterprise application, you need to select an appropriate driver based on the requirements.

Setting Up the Database

Before you start exploring JDBC APIs and their usage with the help of examples, first you must configure a database with which you will work. The database needs to be configured properly before you start writing JDBC programs. You can use any widely available database. In this chapter, we will use MySQL to explain various aspects of JDBC APIs since this database is free and widely available. Hence, we are showing steps to set up a MySQL database on your machine assuming that you use Windows (if you are using another operating system, these steps will slightly differ):

- The first step is to download the appropriate installer for your platform. For MySQL database, you may download the latest installer from the MySQL download page (www.mysql.com/downloads/mysql/).

- Once the installer gets downloaded, the next step is to install it. You must have admin privileges in your machine to install the software. You need to invoke the installer and follow all the steps shown by the installation wizard. Keep the default values and complete the installation. The installer will ask you to provide a root password; remember it because it will be used in these examples.

- The next step is to download the database connector. The database connector only will allow you to connect to the database. You can download the connector for MySQL from its connector download page (http://dev.mysql.com/downloads/connector/j/).

- Do not forget to add the path of the connector to the classpath. If the connector name is mysql-connector-java-5.1.21-bin.jar stored in C:\mysql-connector-java-5.1.21, then add c:\ mysql-connector-java-5.1.21\mysql-connector-java-5.1.21-bin.jar to the classpath.

- Invoke the command-line client of MySQL (in our case, it is "MySQL 5.5 Command Line Client" shown in start menu). You will get a MySQL prompt once you provide the root password, as shown here:

```
Enter password: ********
Welcome to the MySQL monitor. Commands end with ; or \g.
Your MySQL connection id is 1
Server version: 5.5.27 MySQL Community Server (GPL)

Copyright (c) 2000, 2011, Oracle and/or its affiliates. All rights reserved.

Oracle is a registered trademark of Oracle Corporation and/or its affiliates. Other names may be
trademarks of their respective owners.

Type 'help;' or '\h' for help. Type '\c' to clear the current input statement.

mysql> /* Let's create a database for our use.*/

mysql> create database addressBook;
Query OK, 1 row affected (0.01 sec)

mysql> /* Now, let's create a table in this database and insert two records for our use later. */

mysql> use addressBook;
Database changed

mysql> create table contact (id int not null auto_increment, firstName varchar(30) Not null,
lastName varchar(30), email varchar(30), phoneNo varchar(13), primary key (id));
Query OK, 0 rows affected (0.20 sec)
```

```
mysql> insert into contact values (default, 'Michael', 'Taylor', 'michael@abc.com',
'+919876543210');
Query OK, 1 row affected (0.10 sec)

mysql> insert into contact values (default, 'William', 'Becker', 'william@abc.com',
'+449876543210');
Query OK, 1 row affected (0.03 sec)

mysql> /* That's it. Our database is ready to use now.*/
```

Connecting to a Database Using a JDBC Driver

In this section, we will discuss how to programmatically connect to a database using a JDBC driver. Before that we'll briefly cover the Connection interface.

The Connection Interface

The Connection interface of the java.sql package represents a connection from application to the database. It is a channel through which your application and the database communicate. Table 10-1 lists important methods in the Connection interface. All these methods will throw SQLExceptions so we won't mention it again in the table. We list transaction-related methods of the Connection interface in Table 10-3.

Table 10-1. *Important Methods in the Connection Interface*

Method	Description
Statement createStatement()	Creates a Statement object that can be used to send SQL statements to the database.
PreparedStatement prepareStatement(String sql)	Creates a PreparedStatement object that can contain SQL statements. The SQL statement can have IN parameters; they may contain '?' symbol(s), which are used as placeholders for passing actual values later.
CallableStatement prepareCall(String sql)	Creates a CallableStatement object for calling stored procedures in the database. The SQL statement can have IN or OUT parameters; they may contain '?' symbol(s), which are used as placeholders for passing actual values later.
DatabaseMetaData getMetaData()	Gets the DataBaseMetaData object. This metadata contains useful information, such as database schema information, table information, etc., which is especially useful when you don't know the underlying database.
Clob createClob()	Returns a Clob object (Clob is the name of the interface). CLOB (Character Large Object) is a built-in type in SQL; it can be used to store a column value in a row of a database table.
Blob createBlob()	Returns a Blob object (Blob is the name of the interface). BLOB (Binary Large Object) is a built-in type in SQL; it can be used to store a column value in a row of a database table.
void setSchema(String schema)	When passed the schema name, it sets this Connection object to the database schema to access.
String getSchema()	Returns the schema name of the database associated with this Connection object; returns null if no schema is associated with it.

Connecting to the Database

The first step to communicate with your database is to set up a connection between your application and the database server. Listing 10-1 shows a simple application to acquire a connection.

Listing 10-1. DbConnect.java

```java
import java.sql.*;

// The class attempts to acquire a connection with the database
class DbConnect {
        public static void main(String[] args) {
                // url points to jdbc protocol : mysql subprotocol; localhost is the address
                // of the server where we installed our DBMS (i.e. on local machine) and
                // 3306 is the port on which we need to contact our DBMS
                String url = "jdbc:mysql://localhost:3306/";
                // we are connecting to the addressBook database we created earlier
                String database = "addressBook";
                // we login as "root" user with password "mysql123"
                String userName = "root";
                String password = "mysql123";
                try (Connection connection = DriverManager.getConnection
                        (url + database, userName, password)){
                        System.out.println("Database connection: Successful");
                } catch (Exception e) {
                        System.out.println("Database connection: Failed");
                        e.printStackTrace();
                }
        }
}
```

Let's analyze the program step by step:

1. The URL of `jdbc:mysql://localhost:3306/` indicates that `jdbc` is the protocol and `mysql` is a subprotocol; `localhost` is the address of the server where we installed our DBMS (i.e., on local machine), and 3306 is the port on which we need to contact our DBMS. (Note that this port number will be different when you use some other database. In fact, we used the default port number provided by the MySQL database, which can be changed if required. Additionally, if you are using some other database, the subprotocol will also change.) You need to use the `addressBook` database with `root` credentials.

2. You can get a connection object by invoking the `DriverManager.getConnection()` method; the method expects the URL of the database along with a database name, user name, and password.

3. You need to close it before coming out of the program. This example uses a try-with-resources statement; hence the `close()` method for `connection` will be automatically called.

4. If anything goes wrong, you will get an exception. In that case, it will print the stack trace of the exception.

Okay, now run this program. Here is the output:

```
Database connection: Failed
java.sql.SQLException: No suitable driver found for jdbc:mysql://localhost:3306/addressBook
        at java.sql.DriverManager.getConnection(DriverManager.java:604)
        at java.sql.DriverManager.getConnection(DriverManager.java:221)
        at DbConnect.main(DbConnect.java:16)
```

Oops! What happened? Why did you get this SQLException? Well, it is a common mistake to forget to add the path of the jar in the classpath environment variable. In this case, the JDBC API will not be able to locate the JDBC driver and so will throw this exception. Remember, entering only the path of the jar is not enough; you need to add the jar name along with the full path also of the classpath variable.

You need to put the full path of the jar file of your JDBC driver to avoid getting an exception for "no suitable driver found." In fact, entering only the path of the jar is not enough; you need to add the jar name along with the full path to the classpath variable.

Okay, let's update the classpath variable and then try again. If you attempt the same program; you might get another exception:

```
Database connection: Failed
java.sql.SQLException: Access denied for user 'root'@'localhost' (using password: YES)
        at com.mysql.jdbc.SQLError.createSQLException(SQLError.java:1074)
        [... rest of the stack trace elided ...]
```

In this program, we've given the username "root" and password "mysql123". If you've set the root user password to something else, you'll get this exception with the message "access denied for user." There are two ways to fix this problem. The first way is to change the program to give your password instead of the "mysql123" we've used in this program. The second way is to reset the password in your database. For MySQL, you can reset your password as follows for the user "root":

```
UPDATE mysql.user SET Password=PASSWORD('mysql123') WHERE User='root';
FLUSH PRIVILEGES;
```

Here is the output if this program runs successfully:

```
Database connection: Successful
```

When you see this output, it means that you are able to establish a connection with the database. If you want to try out the programs in the rest of this chapter, you should get this program working in your system; you need to establish a connection to query or update the database.

You've already seen two examples of SQLException thrown from the JDBC API. When you get a SQLException, you can rarely do anything in the program to recover from it. What you can do in a real-world application is to wrap it as a higher-level exception and rethrow it to the calling component. To save space in code segments, we'll just print the stack trace of the exception and ignore it in the programs in this chapter.

Listing 10-1 contains the following code to get the connection (given within a try-with-resources statement) where you don't explicitly load the JDBC driver:

```
Connection connection = DriverManager.getConnection(url + database, userName, password);
```

Prior to JDBC 4.0, you would have to explicitly load the JDBC driver using the Class.forName() statement, as in the following:

```
Class.forName("com.mysql.jdbc.Driver").newInstance();
Connection connection = DriverManager.getConnection(url + database, userName, password);
```

In other words, in JDBC 4.0 and later, there is no need to explicitly load the driver as the JDBC API will automatically load the driver when you call getConnection(). This code is *backward-compatible*—meaning that, even if you provide the explicit Class.forName() call in your code in JDBC 4.0 or later, the statement will be ignored and your code will work as before.

Querying and Updating the Database

Once you establish a connection to the desired database, you intend to perform the actual task—you query or update of the database. You can perform a query using a SELECT SQL statement and an update using one of the INSERT, UPDATE, or DELETE SQL statements. JDBC provides two important interfaces to support queries: Statement and Resultset. We will discuss these interfaces briefly in the next two subsections.

Statement

As the name suggests, Statement is a SQL statement that can be used to communicate a SQL statement to the connected database and receive results from the database. You can form SQL queries using Statement and execute it using APIs provided in Statement (or one of its derived) interfaces. Statement comes in three flavors: Statement, PreparedStatement, and CallableStatement, which are shown in the inheritance hierarchy in Figure 10-2.

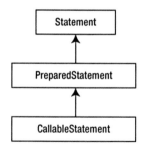

Figure 10-2. *The Statement interface and its subinterfaces*

How do you choose from these three Statement interfaces for a given situation? What are the differences among these different flavors of Statements? Here's more information about these Statements:

- **Statement:** You need to use Statement when you need to send a SQL statement to the database without any parameter. In normal cases, you need to use this interface only. You can create an instance of Statement using the createStatement() method in the Connection interface.

- **PreparedStatement:** PreparedStatement represents a *precompiled SQL statement* that can be customized using IN parameters. Usually, it is more efficient than a Statement object; hence, it is used to improve the performance, especially if a SQL statement is executed multiple times. You can get an instance of PreparedStatement by calling the preparedStatement() method in the Connection interface.

- **CallableStatement:** CallableStatement is used to execute *stored procedures.* CallableStatement instances can handle IN as well as OUT and INOUT parameters. You need to call the prepareCall() method in the Connection interface to get an instance of this class.

Once you have created an appropriate Statement object, you are ready to execute a SQL statement using the Statement object. The Statement interface provides three execute methods: executeQuery(), executeUpdate(), and execute(). You can use one of these execute methods to execute your SQL statement. If your SQL statement is a SELECT query, you can use the executeQuery() method, which returns a ResultSet (defined in the next section). When you want to update a database using one of the INSERT, UPDATE, or DELETE statements, you should use the executeUpdate() method, which returns an integer reflecting the updated number of rows. If you don't know the type of SQL statement, you can use the execute() method, which may return multiple resultsets or multiple update counts or a combination of both.

Choose the proper execute method based on the type of the SQL statement. Remember that each execute method returns different output. The method executeQuery() returns a resultset, executeUpdate() returns an update count, and the execute() method may return multiple resultsets, or multiple update counts, or a combination of both.

ResultSet

Relational databases contain tables. Each table has a set of attributes (properties of an object modeled by the table) that are represented by columns; rows are records containing values for those properties. When you query a database, it results in tabular data: a certain number of rows containing the columns requested by the query. This tabular data is referred to as ResultSet. In summary, a ResultSet is a table with column headings and associated values requested by the query.

A ResultSet maintains a *cursor* pointing to the current row. At one time you can read only one row, so you must change the position of the cursor to read/navigate through the whole ResultSet. *Initially, the cursor is set to just before the first row.* You need to call the next() method on the ResultSet to advance the cursor position by one row. This method returns a boolean value; hence you can use it in a while loop to iterate the whole ResultSet. Table 10-2 shows other methods supported by ResultSet for moving the cursor.

Table 10-2. *Useful Methods of ResultSet to Move the Cursor*

Method	Description
void beforeFirst()	Sets the cursor just before the first row in the ResultSet.
void afterLast()	Sets the cursor just after the last row of the ResultSet.
boolean absolute(int rowNumber)	Sets the cursor to the requested row number absolutely.
boolean relative(int rowNumber)	Sets the cursor to the requested row number relatively.
boolean next()	Sets the cursor to the next row of the ResultSet.
boolean previous()	Sets the cursor to the previous row of the ResultSet.

ResultSet also provides a set of methods to read the value at the desired column in the current row. In general, these methods come in two flavors: the first flavor takes column number as the input and the second flavor accepts column name as the input. For instance, the methods to read a double value are double getDouble(int columnNumber) and double getDouble(String columnName). In a similar way, ResultSet provides get() methods for all basic types.

Similarly, ResultSet provides a set of methods to update values at the desired column in the selected row. These methods also come in two variants: void updateXXX(int columnNumber, XXX x) and void updateXXX(String columnName, XXX x), where the update methods are defined for various data types represented as XXX.

Querying the Database

Now you know all the necessary interfaces that will be used to execute a simple SQL query on a database: Connection, Statement, and ResultSet. Let's query a database and print the output. Recollect that you have created a database named addressBook and a table named contact within this database, and inserted two rows within the table. Assume that you want to print the table contents; Listings 10-2 and 10-3 contain the program to do so.

Listing 10-2. DbConnector.java

```java
import java.sql.*;

// Utility class with method connectToDb() that will be used by other programs in this chapter
public class DbConnector {
        public static Connection connectToDb() throws SQLException {
                String url = "jdbc:mysql://localhost:3306/";
                String database = "addressBook";
                String userName = "root";
                String password = "mysql123";
                return DriverManager.getConnection(url + database, userName, password);
        }
}
```

Listing 10-3. DbQuery.java

```java
import java.sql.*;

// Program to illustrate how to query a database
class DbQuery {
        public static void main(String[] args) {
                // Get connection, execute query, get the result set
                // and print the entries from the result rest
                try (Connection connection = DbConnector.connectToDb();
                        Statement statement = connection.createStatement();
                        ResultSet resultSet = statement.executeQuery("SELECT * FROM contact")){
                        System.out.println("ID \tfName \tlName \temail \t\tphoneNo");
                        while (resultSet.next()) {
                                System.out.println(resultSet.getInt("id") + "\t"
                                + resultSet.getString("firstName") + "\t"
                                + resultSet.getString("lastName") + "\t"
                                + resultSet.getString("email") + "\t"
                                + resultSet.getString("phoneNo"));
                        }
                }
```

```
        catch (SQLException sqle) {
                sqle.printStackTrace();
                System.exit(-1);
        }
    }
}
```

The output of the program is

```
ID      fName    lName    email               phoneNo
1       Michael  Taylor   michael@abc.com     +919876543210
2       William  Becker   william@abc.com     +449876543210
```

Let's have a look at what is happening in this code snippet step by step.

- In the main() method, there is a try-with-resources statement. The first statement is a call to the connectToDb() method, which is defined in the program. The connectToDb() method simply connects to the database (which you saw in the last example) and returns a Connection object if it succeeds.

- In the next statement, you create a Statement object from the connection.

- The Statement object is now used to execute a query. You want to fetch all the columns in the contact table; hence you write SELECT * FROM contact as a SQL query. You execute the query using the executeQuery() method of the statement object. The outcome of the query is stored in a ResultSet object.

- Now this ResultSet object is used to print the fetched data. You read all column values in the current row and you do the same for each row in the ResultSet object.

- Since you've created the Connection, Statement, and ResultSet objects within a try-with-resources statement, there is no need to explicitly call close() on these resources. However, if you are not using try-with-resources, you need to release them explicitly in a finally block.

Here, you are using column names to read the associated values. You can use column numbers instead to do the same job. Here is the modified code inside the while loop to use column numbers instead:

```
while (resultSet.next()) {
        System.out.println(resultSet.getInt(1)
                + "\t" + resultSet.getString(2)
                + "\t" + resultSet.getString(3)
                + "\t" + resultSet.getString(4)
                + "\t" + resultSet.getString(5));
}
```

This code produces exactly the same result as the last example. However, one important thing to observe here is that *column index starts from 1, not from 0.*

The column index in the ResultSet object starts from 1, not from 0.

Here, while referring to columns by column index, if you refer to a column by an index that is more than the total number of columns, you will get an exception. For instance, if you change one of the column indices used in the last example to 6, you will get the following exception:

```
java.sql.SQLException: Column Index out of range, 6 > 5.
        at com.mysql.jdbc.SQLError.createSQLException(SQLError.java:1074)
        [... this part of the stack trace elided ...]
        at DbQuery.main(DbQuery.java:18)
```

Hence, you should be careful and always provide the correct column indices.

In this example, you know the number of columns as well as the data types in columns. What if you neither know the number of columns in each row nor the data types in the columns? You can use the getMetaData() method and use the getColumnCount() method to get the column count. When you don't know the data type of a column entry, you can just use the getObject() method on the ResultSet object. Here is the modified code that makes use of these methods:

```
// from resultSet metadata, find out how many columns are there and then read the column entries
int numOfColumns = resultSet.getMetaData().getColumnCount();
while (resultSet.next()) {
        // remember that the column index starts from 1 not 0
        for(int i = 1; i <= numOfColumns; i++) {
                // since we do not know the data type of the column, we use getObject()
                System.out.print(resultSet.getObject(i) + "\t");
        }
        System.out.println("");
}
```

The output of the program remains the same, so we haven't shown the resulting output here.

Okay, let's carry out another exercise. This time you just want to print the name and e-mail address where the first name matches to "Michael." See Listing 10-4.

Listing 10-4. DbQuery4.java

```
import java.sql.*;

class DbQuery4 {
        public static void main(String[] args) throws SQLException {
                try (Connection connection = DbConnector.connectToDb();
                        Statement statement = connection.createStatement();
                        ResultSet resultset = statement.executeQuery("SELECT firstName,
email FROM contact WHERE firstName=\"Michael\"")) {
                        System.out.println("fName \temail");
                        while (resultset.next()){
                                System.out.println(resultset.getString("firstName") + "\t"
                                                + resultset.getString("email"));
                        }
                } catch (SQLException e) {
                        e.printStackTrace();
                        System.exit(-1);
                }
        }
}
```

It prints:

```
fName    email
Michael  michael@abc.com
```

Updating the Database

Now let's update the database. You can update a database in two ways: you can use SQL queries to update the database directly, or you can fetch a ResultSet using a SQL query and then you can change the ResultSet and the database. JDBC supports both of these methods. Let's focus on retrieving the ResultSet and modifying the ResultSet and the database.

In order to modify the ResultSet and the database, the ResultSet class provides a set of update methods for each data type. Also, there are other supporting methods such as updateRow() and deleteRow() to make the task simpler. It's time to get your hands dirty: assume that one of your contacts in your addressBook database has changed his phone number, so you are now going to update his phone number in your database using a JDBC program.

Listing 10-5. DbUpdate.java

```java
import java.sql.*;

// To illustrate how we can update a database
class DbUpdate {
        public static void main(String[] args) throws SQLException {
                try (Connection connection = DbConnector.connectToDb();
                        Statement statement = connection.createStatement();
                        ResultSet resultSet = statement.executeQuery("SELECT * FROM contact
WHERE firstName=\"Michael\"")) {
                                // first fetch the data and display it before the update operation
                                System.out.println("Before the update");
                                System.out.println("id \tfName \tlName \temail \t\tphoneNo");
                                while (resultSet.next()) {
                                        System.out.println(resultSet.getInt("id") + "\t"
                                                + resultSet.getString("firstName") + "\t"
                                                + resultSet.getString("lastName") + "\t"
                                                + resultSet.getString("email") + "\t"
                                                + resultSet.getString("phoneNo"));
                                }
                                // now update the resultSet and display the modified data
                                resultSet.absolute(1);
                                resultSet.updateString("phoneNo", "+919976543210");
                                System.out.println("After the update");
                                System.out.println("id \tfName \tlName \temail \t\tphoneNo");
                                resultSet.beforeFirst();
                                while (resultSet.next()) {
                                        System.out.println(resultSet.getInt("id") + "\t"
                                                + resultSet.getString("firstName") + "\t"
                                                + resultSet.getString("lastName") + "\t"
                                                + resultSet.getString("email") + "\t"
                                                + resultSet.getString("phoneNo"));
                                }
```

```
                    } catch (SQLException e) {
                            e.printStackTrace();
                            System.exit(-1);
                    }
            }
}
```

Let's pick out the nitty-gritty of the program step by step:

- You establish the connection using the DbConnector.connectToDb() method.

- After creating a Statement object, you execute a query on the database to find out the record associated with *Michael*. (For the sake of simplicity we are assuming that the ResultSet will contain exactly one record.)

- You print the retrieved record.

- You use the absolute() method to move the cursor to the first row in the ResultSet object; then you update the phone number using the updateString() method.

- And finally you print the modified resultset.

Well, that looks straightforward. Now, execute it and see what this program prints:

```
Before the update
id      fName   lName   email           phoneNo
1       Michael Taylor  michael@abc.com +919876543210
com.mysql.jdbc.NotUpdatable: Result Set not updatable.(...rest of the text elided)
        at com.mysql.jdbc.ResultSetImpl.updateString(ResultSetImpl.java:8618)
        at com.mysql.jdbc.ResultSetImpl.updateString(ResultSetImpl.java:8636)
        at DbUpdate.main(DbUpdate.java:34)
```

Oops, the program crashed after throwing an exception! What happened?

You are trying to update a ResultSet object that is not updatable. In other words, in order to make the update in the ResultSet and the database, you need to make this ResultSet updatable. You can do that by creating a proper Statement object; while calling the createStatement() method you can pass inputs such as whether you want a scrollable ResultSet that is sensitive to changes or you want an updatable ResultSet.

So, make this one single change to the call to the createStatement() method in Listing 10-5:

```
Statement statement = connection.createStatement(ResultSet.TYPE_SCROLL_SENSITIVE, ResultSet.CONCUR_
UPDATABLE);
```

Now run this changed program to see if it works.

```
Before the update
id      fName   lName   email           phoneNo
1       Michael Taylor  michael@abc.com +919876543210
After the update
id      fName   lName   email           phoneNo
1       Michael Taylor  michael@abc.com +919876543210
```

Good, the program did not result in any exception. But wait, the phone number of Michael is not updated! What happened? You forgot a vital statement after the update: the updateRow() method. Every time you make change in ResultSet using the appropriate updateXXX() method, you need to call updateRow() to make sure that all the values are actually updated in the database. Make this change and try again (see Listing 10-6).

Listing 10-6. DbUpdate2.java

```java
import java.sql.*;

// To illustrate how we can update a database
class DbUpdate2 {
        public static void main(String[] args) throws SQLException {
                try (Connection connection = DbConnector.connectToDb();
                        // create a statement from which the created ResultSets
                        // are "scroll sensitive" as well as "updatable"
                        Statement statement =
                        connection.createStatement(ResultSet.TYPE_SCROLL_SENSITIVE,
                        ResultSet.CONCUR_UPDATABLE);
                        ResultSet resultSet = statement.executeQuery("SELECT * FROM
                                contact WHERE firstName=\"Michael\"")) {
                        // first fetch the data and display it before the update operation
                        System.out.println("Before the update");
                        System.out.println("id \tfName \tlName \temail \t\tphoneNo");
                        while (resultSet.next()) {
                                System.out.println(resultSet.getInt("id") + "\t"
                                + resultSet.getString("firstName") + "\t"
                                + resultSet.getString("lastName") + "\t"
                                + resultSet.getString("email") + "\t"
                                + resultSet.getString("phoneNo"));
                        }
                        // now update the resultSet and display the modified data
                        resultSet.absolute(1);
                        resultSet.updateString("phoneNo", "+919976543210");
                        // reflect those changes back to the database by calling updateRow() method
                        resultSet.updateRow();
                        System.out.println("After the update");
                        System.out.println("id \tfName \tlName \temail \t\tphoneNo");
                        resultSet.beforeFirst();
                        while (resultSet.next()) {
                                System.out.println(resultSet.getInt("id") + "\t"
                                + resultSet.getString("firstName") + "\t"
                                + resultSet.getString("lastName") + "\t"
                                + resultSet.getString("email") + "\t"
                                + resultSet.getString("phoneNo"));
                        }
                } catch (SQLException e) {
                        e.printStackTrace();
                        System.exit(-1);
                }
        }
}
```

Now this program prints the following:

```
Before the update
id      fName   lName   email           phoneNo
1       Michael Taylor  michael@abc.com +919876543210
```

```
After the update
id      fName   lName   email             phoneNo
1       Michael Taylor  michael@abc.com   +919976543210
```

Yes, it is working fine now. Now you know the requirements and steps required to update a row in a database.

Always call `updateRow()` after modifying the row contents; otherwise you will lose the changes.

Next, how about inserting a record in the RecordSet and the database? Try the next example, shown in Listing 10-7.

Listing 10-7. DbInsert.java

```java
import java.sql.*;

// To illustrate how to insert a row in a ResultSet and in the database
class DbInsert {
    public static void main(String[] args) throws SQLException {
        try (Connection connection = DbConnector.connectToDb();
        Statement statement = connection.createStatement(
                ResultSet.TYPE_SCROLL_SENSITIVE, ResultSet.CONCUR_UPDATABLE);
        ResultSet resultSet = statement.executeQuery("SELECT * FROM contact")) {
        System.out.println("Before the insert");
        System.out.println("id \tfName \tlName \temail \t\tphoneNo");
        while (resultSet.next()){
                System.out.println(resultSet.getInt("id") + "\t"
                        + resultSet.getString("firstName") + "\t"
                        + resultSet.getString("lastName") + "\t"
                        + resultSet.getString("email") + "\t"
                        + resultSet.getString("phoneNo"));
        }
        resultSet.moveToInsertRow();
        resultSet.updateString("firstName", "John");
        resultSet.updateString("lastName", "K.");
        resultSet.updateString("email", "john@abc.com");
        resultSet.updateString("phoneNo", "+19753186420");
        resultSet.insertRow();
        System.out.println("After the insert");
        System.out.println("id \tfName \tlName \temail \t\tphoneNo");
        resultSet.beforeFirst();
        while (resultSet.next()){
                System.out.println(resultSet.getInt("id") + "\t"
                        + resultSet.getString("firstName") + "\t"
                        + resultSet.getString("lastName") + "\t"
                        + resultSet.getString("email") + "\t"
                        + resultSet.getString("phoneNo"));
        }
```

```
            } catch (SQLException e) {
                    e.printStackTrace();
            }
    }
}
```

What happened in this example? After printing the current records, you call the moveToInsertRow() method. This method sets the cursor to a new record and prepares the ResultSet for the insertion of a row (creates a buffer to hold the column values). After it, you use the updateString() method to modify each column value in the newly added row. And finally, you call insertRow() to finally insert the new row into the ResultSet and the database. One important thing to note here is that you need to provide correct types of values for each column. Also, you cannot leave a column blank (i.e., not provide any value) if the column value can not be left unfilled. In both of these violations, you may get a SQLException.

Let's see what this program prints.

```
Before the insert
id      fName   lName   email           phoneNo
1       Michael Taylor  michael@abc.com +919976543210
2       William Becker  william@abc.com +449876543210
After the insert
id      fName   lName   email           phoneNo
1       Michael Taylor  michael@abc.com +919976543210
2       William Becker  william@abc.com +449876543210
3       John    K.      john@abc.com    +19753186420
```

Looks good! Now let's try another operation: delete a record from the database. Take a look at the program in Listing 10-8.

Listing 10-8. DbDelete.java

```java
import java.sql.*;

// To illustrate how to delete a row in a ResultSet and in the database
class DbDelete {
        public static void main(String[] args) throws SQLException {
                try (Connection connection = DbConnector.connectToDb();
                        Statement statement =
                        connection.createStatement(ResultSet.TYPE_SCROLL_SENSITIVE,
                        ResultSet.CONCUR_UPDATABLE);
                        ResultSet resultSet1 =
                                statement.executeQuery
                                ("SELECT * FROM contact WHERE firstName=\"John\"")) {
                        if(resultSet1.next()){
                                // delete the first row
                                resultSet1.deleteRow();
                        }
                        resultSet1.close();

                        // now fetch again from the database
                        try (ResultSet resultSet2 =
                                statement.executeQuery("SELECT * FROM contact")) {
```

```
                             System.out.println("After the deletion");
                             System.out.println("id \tfName \tlName \temail \t\tphoneNo");
                             while (resultSet2.next()){
                                     System.out.println(resultSet2.getInt("id") + "\t"
                                             + resultSet2.getString("firstName") + "\t"
                                             + resultSet2.getString("lastName") + "\t"
                                             + resultSet2.getString("email") + "\t"
                                             + resultSet2.getString("phoneNo"));
                             }
                     }
             } catch (SQLException e) {
                     e.printStackTrace();
                     System.exit(-1);
             }
     }
}
```

This program simply selects a proper row to delete and calls the deleteRow() method on the current selected row. Here's the output of the program:

```
After the deletion
id      fName   lName   email           phoneNo
1       Michael Taylor  michael@abc.com +919976543210
2       William Becker  william@abc.com +449876543210
```

Well, the program works fine and correctly removes the row where the first name of the person is "John."

You might have remembered that you have created a table named contact in your database to work with. At that time, you created that table from the MySQL command prompt. The same task could have been done through a JDBC program. At this juncture, let's create a new table named familyGroup in the database programmatically (see Listing 10-9). You will use this table later in this chapter.

Listing 10-9. DbCreateTable.java

```java
import java.sql.*;
class DbCreateTable {
     public static void main(String[] args) {
             try (Connection connection = DbConnector.connectToDb();
                     Statement statement = connection.createStatement()){
                     // use CREATE TABLE SQL statement to create table familyGroup
                     int result = statement.executeUpdate("CREATE TABLE familyGroup (id int not
                     null auto_increment, nickName varchar(30) not null, primary key(id));");
                     System.out.println("Table created successfully");

             }
             catch (SQLException sqle) {
                     sqle.printStackTrace();
                     System.exit(-1);
             }
     }
}
```

The program prints the following:

```
Table created successfully
```

The program is working as expected. Here, you connect to the database and get the statement object as you did earlier. Then, you issue a SQL statement using the Update() method. Using the SQL statement, you declare that a table called familyGroup needs to be created along with two columns: id and nickName. Also, you declare that id should be treated as the primary key. That's it; the SQL statement creates a new table in your database.

Note that the syntax of the SQL statement is your responsibility. If you pass a wrong SQL statement, you will get a MySQLSyntaxErrorException belonging to the com.mysql.jdbc.exceptions.jdbc4.MySQLSyntaxErrorException.

Getting the Database Metadata

You can get the metadata from a Connection object to examine the capabilities of the underlying database. You can do this by calling the getMetaData() method in the Connection interface; its return type is DatabaseMetaData. This DatabaseMetaData is a rich class that provides a large number of methods to examine the database details. For example, you can check the kind of transactions the database supports, the maximum number of columns you can have in a table, etc. Listing 10-10 will make it clearer to you.

Listing 10-10. DbConnectionMetaData.java

```java
import java.sql.*;
// To illustrate how to obtain metadata from Collection object
// and examine the metadata for using it in a program
class DbConnectionMetaData {
        public static void main(String []args) throws SQLException {
                Connection connection = DbConnector.connectToDb();
                DatabaseMetaData metaData = connection.getMetaData();
                System.out.println("Displaying some of the database metadata from the
                Connection object");
                System.out.println("Database is: " + metaData.getDatabaseProductName() + " " +
                metaData.getDatabaseProductVersion());
                System.out.println("Driver is: " + metaData.getDriverName() + metaData.
                getDriverVersion());
                System.out.println("The URL for this connection is: " + metaData.getURL());
                System.out.println("User name is: " + metaData.getUserName());
                System.out.println("Maximum no. of rows you can insert is: " + metaData.
                getMaxRowSize());
        }
}
```

It prints the following:

```
Displaying some of the database metadata from the Connection object
Database is: MySQL 5.5.27
Driver is: MySQL-AB JDBC Drivermysql-connector-java-5.1.21 ( Revision: ${bzr.rev
ision-id} )
The URL for this connection is: jdbc:mysql://localhost:3306/addressBook
User name is: root@localhost
Maximum no. of rows you can insert is: 2147483639
```

Points to Remember

Here are a couple of points that could be helpful on your OCPJP exam:

- The boolean absolute(int) method in ResultSet moves the cursor to the passed row number in that ResultSet object. If the row number is positive, it moves to that position from the beginning of the ResultSet object; if the row number is negative, it moves to that position from the end of the ResultSet object. Assume that there are 10 entries in the ResultSet object. Calling absolute(3) will move the cursor to the third row. Calling absolute(-3) will move the cursor to the 10-3, seventh row. If you give out of range values, the cursor will move to either beginning or end.

- In a ResultSet object, calling absolute(1) is equivalent to calling first(), and calling absolute(-1) is equivalent to calling last().

Performing Transactions

A *transaction* is a set of SQL operations that needs to be either executed all successfully or not at all. Failure to perform even one operation leads to an inconsistent and erroneous database.

A database must satisfy the ACID properties (Atomicity, Consistency, Isolation, and Durability) to guarantee the success of a database transaction.

- **Atomicity:** Each transaction should be carried out in its entirety; if one part of the transaction fails, then the whole transaction fails.

- **Consistency:** The database should be in a valid state before and after the performed transaction.

- **Isolation:** Each transaction should execute in complete isolation without knowing the existence of other transactions.

- **Durability:** Once the transaction is complete, the changes made by the transaction are permanent (even in the occurrence of unusual events such as power loss).

A classic example of a transaction is fund transfer through a bank account. If one wants to transfer some money x to another account, the money x should be deducted from the first account and should be added to the other account. In essence, there are two operations to complete the fund transfer (which you can call a transaction). Failing either operation is not acceptable: if money is deducted from the first account and not added to the other account, the first account holder unnecessarily loses x amount of money; if the second account gets x amount of money without deducting from the first account, the bank will definitely have a problem. Hence, either both the operations should be successful or both operations should fail.

 All operations of a transaction must be either successful or not happen at all.

In general, each statement is a transaction in a JDBC environment. What does this mean? When you call methods such as updateRow(), the JDBC immediately updates the underlying database. This behavior of JDBC can be controlled by the setAutoCommit() method; by default it is true, so each update statement changes the database immediately. However, if you set this property to false, it is your responsibility to call the commit() method on the Connection object. The commit() method actually commits all the changes to the database.

Before seeing an example program for a transaction using the Connection interface, you'll first see transaction related methods supported in this class (Table 10-3). (Note that all the methods given in this table may throw SQLException, so we don't mention that explicitly in this table for each method.)

Table 10-3. *Transaction-Related Methods in the Connection Interface*

Method	Description
void setAutoCommit(boolean autoCommit)	Sets the auto-commit mode to true or false. By default, Connection objects have auto-commit set to true, and you can set it to false by calling this method with false as the argument value.
boolean getAutoCommit()	Returns the auto-commit mode value (a true value means auto-commit mode, and a false value means manual commit mode).
Savepoint setSavepoint()	Creates a Savepoint object in the current transaction and returns that object.
Savepoint setSavepoint(String name)	Same as the previous method, except that the Savepoint object has a name associated with it.
void releaseSavepoint(Savepoint savepoint)	Removes the given Savepoint object and the subsequent Savepoint objects from the current transaction.
void rollback(Savepoint savepoint)	Rolls back to the given Savepoint state. In other words, all the changes done after the Savepoint was created will be lost or removed (an undo operation till that Savepoint). Will throw a SQLException if rollback cannot be done (for example, an invalid Savepoint object is passed).
void rollback()	Rolls back (undoes) all the changes made in the current transaction. Will throw a SQLException if rollback fails (e.g., rollback() was called when auto-commit mode is set).
void commit()	Makes (commits) all the changes done so far in the transaction to the database.

Let's understand transactions with the help of an example. As you recall, you have a MySQL database named addressBook in which you have a table named contact. Now, you want to have different groups of contacts; for instance, one such group is familyGroup; you are maintaining another table called familyGroup for family members. Let's imagine now that you want to add a new record in the familyGroup table (you are storing only nicknames of the family members) along with full contact details in the table contact. Imagine a situation where you add the nickname of a family member in familyGroup but could not add the full contact details of your contact! The situation would lead to an inconsistent database. This is an example of a transaction since you want to execute both operations successfully (or don't want to make changes at all, so that you can make an attempt again). Listing 10-11 contains a small program to achieve it.

Listing 10-11. DbTransaction.java

```java
import java.sql.*;

// To illustrate how to do commit or rollback
class DbTransaction {
        public static void main(String[] args) throws SQLException {
                Connection connection = DbConnector.connectToDb();
                ResultSet resultSet1 = null, resultSet2 = null;
                // we're using explicit finally blocks
                // instead of try-with-resources statement in this code
                try {
                        // for commit/rollback we first need to set auto-commit to false
                        connection.setAutoCommit(false);
                        Statement statement = connection.createStatement
                                (ResultSet.TYPE_SCROLL_SENSITIVE, ResultSet.CONCUR_UPDATABLE);
                        resultSet1 = statement.executeQuery("SELECT * FROM familyGroup");
                        resultSet1.moveToInsertRow();
                        resultSet1.updateString("nickName", "Sam Uncle");
                        // updating here... but this change will be lost if a rollback happens
                        resultSet1.insertRow();
                        System.out.println("First table updated...");

                        resultSet2 = statement.executeQuery("SELECT * FROM contact");
                        resultSet2.moveToInsertRow();
                        resultSet2.updateString("firstName", "Samuel");
                        // resultSet2.updateString("firstName",
                        //      "The great Samuel the billionaire from Washington DC");
                        resultSet2.updateString("lastName", "Uncle");
                        resultSet2.updateString("email", "sam@abc.com");
                        resultSet2.updateString("phoneNo", "+119955331100");
                        // updating here... but this change will be lost of a rollback happens
                        resultSet2.insertRow();
                        System.out.println("Both tables updated, committing now.");
                        // we're committing the changes for both the tables only now
                        connection.commit();
                } catch (SQLException e) {
                        System.out.println(
                                "Something gone wrong, couldn't add a contact in family group");
                        // roll back all the changes in the transaction since something has gone wrong
                        connection.rollback();
                        e.printStackTrace();
                }
                finally {
                        if(connection != null) connection.close();
                        if(resultSet1 != null) resultSet1.close();
                        if(resultSet2 != null) resultSet2.close();
                }
        }
}
```

Let's understand the program first. There are basically two operations in the transaction. The first is to add a new row in the table called `familyGroup` for the contact "Sam Uncle." The second is to add the full contact details of "Sam Uncle" in the table called `contact`. Now, look at the key differences: you call the `setAutoCommit()` method with argument `false`; hence, auto commit will not happen. Another difference is that you are calling the method `commit()` with a connection object. Hence, when both the operations are successful, you will update the database (with scheduled updates) by calling the `commit()` method.

Now, let's execute this program and see what it prints.

```
Something gone wrong, couldn't add a contact in family group
com.mysql.jdbc.exceptions.jdbc4.MySQLSyntaxErrorException: Table 'addressbook.familygroup'
doesn't exist
        at sun.reflect.NativeConstructorAccessorImpl.newInstance0(Native Method)
        [... this part of the stack trace elided to save space ...]
        at DbTransaction.main(DbTransaction.java:18)
```

What happened? You haven't created a `familyGroup` table yet. Do it in the MySQL command line.

```
mysql> create table familyGroup (id int not null auto_increment, nickName varchar(30) Not null,
primary key (id));
Query OK, 0 rows affected (0.11 sec)
```

Now try running the program again.

```
First table updated...
Something gone wrong, couldn't add a contact in family group
com.mysql.jdbc.MysqlDataTruncation: Data truncation: Data too long for column 'firstName' at row 1
        at com.mysql.jdbc.MysqlIO.checkErrorPacket(MysqlIO.java:4072)
        [... this part of stack trace elided to save space ...]
        at DbTransaction.main(DbTransaction.java:43)
```

Well, you got a `SQLException` since the string provided for Uncle Sam's name is too long. You can observe that the first table got updated and the exception occurred while executing the second operation. However, you have set the auto commit mode to false; hence, the first table is not changed in the database. Both the tables will actually be changed when you execute the `commit()` method. In other words, if the `commit()` method does not execute in manual commit mode, then there will be no change in the database. In the above example, neither table got changed since the exception occurred before the `commit()` method could execute.

Let's change the name of the Sam uncle in the `updateString()` method (in the above program) and rerun the example. Replace the earlier statement with this new statement:

```
resultSet2.updateString("firstName", "Samuel");
```

Let's see the output of the program this time.

```
First table updated...
Both tables updated, committing now.
```

Perfect! Both operations worked this time, so the transaction is complete.

Rolling Back Database Operations

In the last example (Listing 10-11), you used a method called `rollback()` using a `Connection` object. This method is used to roll back all the uncommitted operations in a transaction.

What happens if you remove the rollback statement from the last example? If your answer is that it will work given a successful condition, but the program will not work in case of an exception (since the `rollback()` method call is missing), you are wrong. The program will work in both conditions. Yes, in both the conditions! Okay, then why are you using the `rollback()` at all? The answer is given in the following three points:

- The above example illustrates a two-operation transaction that is quite simple. In this case, explicit `rollback()` will not change anything. However, in case of a multi-stage transaction where you can define various milestones (in the form of `savepoints`, which we will discuss shortly), rollback plays a vital role. Unfinished or incomplete subtransaction states may cause inconsistencies.

- If your connection object is a pooled connection object, then it makes sense to call `rollback()`. In case of a pooled connection object, the connection object will be reused later, and at that time unfinished operations may cause inconsistencies.

- In general, using the `rollback()` method in failed cases is always recommended.

In case of a large transaction, you can divide the transaction into multiple subtransactions. In other words, you can define multiple milestones to complete the transaction. These milestones are referred to as `savepoints`, and Java abstraction for this concept is `java.sql.Savepoint` interface. Once a transaction completes a certain milestone, that point can be saved as a `Savepoint` and operations performed till that point can be committed. In case a failure occurred later, while executing other database operations, you can rollback the database till your last defined and saved `savepoint`. This way, you need not carry the whole lengthy transaction all over again; you can start from the last saved `savepoint`. Listing 10-12 demonstrates how to use `savepoints`.

Listing 10-12. DbSavepoint.java

```java
import java.sql.*;

// To illustrate how to use savepoints with commits and rollbacks
class DbSavepoint {
        public static void main(String[] args) throws SQLException {
                Connection connection = DbConnector.connectToDb();
                ResultSet resultSet = null;
                // we're using explicit finally blocks
                // instead of try-with-resources statement in this code
                try {
                        // for commit/rollback we first need to set auto-commit to false
                        connection.setAutoCommit(false);
                        Statement statement =
                                connection.createStatement(
                                ResultSet.TYPE_SCROLL_SENSITIVE,
                                ResultSet.CONCUR_UPDATABLE);
                        resultSet = statement.executeQuery("SELECT * FROM familyGroup");

                        System.out.println("Printing the contents of the table before inserting");
                        while(resultSet.next()) {
                                System.out.println(resultSet.getInt("id") + " "
                                        + resultSet.getString("nickName"));
                        }
```

```
            System.out.println("Starting to insert rows");
            // first insert
            resultSet.moveToInsertRow();
            resultSet.updateString("nickName", "Tom");
            resultSet.insertRow();
            System.out.println("Inserted row for Tom");
            // our first savepoint is here...
            Savepoint firstSavepoint = connection.setSavepoint();

            // second insert
            resultSet.moveToInsertRow();
            resultSet.updateString("nickName", "Dick");
            resultSet.insertRow();
            System.out.println("Inserted row for Dick");
            // our second savepoint is here... after we inserted Dick
            // we can give a string name for savepoint
            Savepoint secondSavepoint = connection.setSavepoint("SavepointForDick");

            // third insert
            resultSet.moveToInsertRow();
            resultSet.updateString("nickName", "Harry");
            resultSet.insertRow();
            System.out.println("Inserted row for Harry");
            // our thrid savepoint is here... for "Harry"
            Savepoint thirdSavepoint = connection.setSavepoint("ForHarry");
            System.out.println("Table updation complete...");

            // rollback to the state when Dick was inserted;
            // so the insert for Harry will be lost
            System.out.println(
                    "Rolling back to the state where Tom and Dick were inserted");
            connection.rollback(secondSavepoint);
            // commit the changes now and see what happens to the contents of the table
            connection.commit();
            System.out.println("Printing the contents of the table after commit");
            resultSet = statement.executeQuery("SELECT * FROM familyGroup");
            while(resultSet.next()) {
                    System.out.println(resultSet.getInt("id") + " "
                            + resultSet.getString("nickName"));
            }
    } catch (SQLException e) {
            System.out.println("Something gone wrong, couldn't add a contact in family group");
            // roll back all the changes in the transaction since something has gone wrong
            connection.rollback();
            e.printStackTrace();
    }
```

```
            finally {
                    if(connection != null) connection.close();
                    if(resultSet != null) resultSet.close();
            }
        }
    }
}
```

Run this program first.

```
Printing the contents of the table before inserting
Starting to insert rows
Inserted row for Tom
Inserted row for Dick
Inserted row for Harry
Table updation complete...
Rolling back to the state where Tom and Dick were inserted
Printing the contents of the table after commit
1 Tom
2 Dick
```

Now let's understand the program.

1.   First you get the connection, create a statement, get a ResultSet, and print the contents of the table (which is empty).

2.   You insert three rows, one after another. After inserting each row, you create a Savepoint object in that transaction. The first savepoint is an unnamed Savepoint after inserting "Tom" and the second and third are named savepoints occur after inserting "Dick" and "Harry."

3.   In the statement connection.rollback(secondSavepoint);, you instruct JDBC to roll back the transaction to the second savepoint. Remember that you've created the second savepoint to remember the state after inserting "Tom" and "Dick" but before inserting "Harry." So the rollback is to the state where rows containing "Tom" and "Dick" are inserted.

4.   The commit() method commits the current state of the transaction. Since the rollback is already called, the current state of the transaction is that there are two rows inserted containing the nicknames "Tom" and "Dick." Printing the contents of the table confirms that it is indeed the case.

The RowSet Interface

The interface javax.sql.RowSet extends the ResultSet interface to provide support for the JavaBean component model. The RowSet interface defines getters and setters for different data types.

RowSet also supports methods to add and remove event listeners (since it is a JavaBean component). Other Java objects may use the event notification mechanism supported by RowSet. The RowSet interface implements the Observer design pattern (as a Subject). A Java object that wants to receive event notification from RowSet must implement the RowSetListner interface and must be registered with the RowSet object. RowSet notifies all the registered objects on the occurrence of one of the following events: change in cursor location, change in a row, and change in the entire RowSet object.

Java provides five different flavors of the RowSet interface (see Figure 10-3). The interfaces of these flavors can be found in the javax.sql.rowset package. The five interfaces are JdbcRowSet, JoinRowSet, CachedRowSet, WebRowSet, and FilteredRowSet. Java also offers a default reference implementation of these interfaces that can be found in the com.sun.rowset package. These implementations are JdbcRowSetImpl, JoinRowSetImpl, CachedRowSetImpl, WebRowSetImpl, and FilteredRowSetImpl.

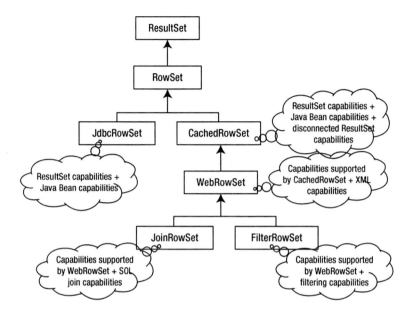

Figure 10-3. *The RowSet hierarchy*

JdbcRowSet is a connected RowSet, which means a JdbcRowSet implementation is always connected to the corresponding database. The other four interfaces are disconnected RowSets, which means an object of any one of these four RowSet implementations (except JdbcRowSet) connects to the database only when they want to read or write; all the other times they are disconnected from the database. This property of implementation of these four interfaces along with the capability of being serializable make them suitable for sending over the network.

Figure 10-3 shows the hierarchical relationship among various RowSet interfaces. As you already know, RowSet is a subinterface of the ResultSet interface. JdbcRowSet is a subinterface of RowSet; JdbcRowSet has all the features ResultSet supports plus Java Bean capabilities. CachedRowSet is also a subinterface of the RowSet interface; it has all the features JdbcRowSet supports plus it has the capabilities of a disconnected ResultSet. WebRowSet adds XML capabilities to the CachedRowSet features. Similarly, JoinRowSet adds SQL join capabilities to WebRowSet, and FilteredRowSet adds result filtering capabilities to WebRowSet.

Let's now discuss the RowSetProvider class and the RowSetFactory interface, which were introduced in Java 7. RowSetProvider provides APIs to get a RowSetFactory implementation that can be used to instantiate a proper RowSet implementation. It provides the following two methods:

- **RowSetFactory newFactory():** This API creates a new instance of a RowSetFactory implementation. So which factory implementation will this method instantiate? It is a good question; the answer is that this API infers the type of factory implementation to instantiate from the environment settings. It first looks in the system property javax.sql.rowset.RowSetFactory. If the API could not infer the factory implementation, then it uses ServiceLoader API to determine the type of the factory implementation to instantiate, and finally it looks for the platform default implementation of the RowSetFactory instance. If the API could not infer the factory implementation type, it raises a SQLException.

- **RowSetFactory newFactory(String factoryClassName, ClassLoader classloader):** If it is unclear which driver will be loaded when you call the plain newFactory() method due to multiple drivers in the scope, you can use the overloaded method newFactory(), which takes the class name of the factory and the class loader and instantiates the appropriate factory.

RowSetFactory defines five methods; each method creates a type of RowSet implementation. So why are RowSetFactory and RowSetProvider required to create a RowSet implementation when you can create them using the traditional plain way? The answer is *flexibility*; you can create the RowSet object without specifying the details that you need to provide during a traditional RowSet object; you can then set other details once the object gets created. How about writing a program to see how to use RowSetFactory and RowSetProvider? See Listing 10-13.

Listing 10-13. DbQuery5.java

```java
import javax.sql.rowset.*;
import java.sql.*;

// To illustrate how to use RowSet, RowSetProvider, and RowSetFactory
class DbQuery5 {
        public static void main(String[] args) {
                String url = "jdbc:mysql://localhost:3306/addressBook";
                String userName = "root";
                String password = "mysql123";
                try {
                        // first, create a factory object for rowset
                        RowSetFactory rowSetFactory = RowSetProvider.newFactory();
                        // create a JDBC rowset from the factory
                        JdbcRowSet rowSet = rowSetFactory.createJdbcRowSet();
                        rowSet.setUrl(url);
                        rowSet.setUsername(userName);
                        rowSet.setPassword(password);
                        rowSet.setCommand("SELECT * FROM contact");
                        rowSet.execute();
                        System.out.println("id \tfName \tlName \temail \t\tphoneNo");
                        while (rowSet.next()){
                                System.out.println(rowSet.getInt("id") + "\t"
                                        + rowSet.getString("firstName") + "\t"
                                        + rowSet.getString("lastName") + "\t"
                                        + rowSet.getString("email") + "\t"
                                        + rowSet.getString("phoneNo"));
                        }
                } catch (SQLException sqle) {
                        sqle.printStackTrace();
                }
        }
}
```

It prints the following:

```
Id      fName   lName   email           phoneNo
1       Michael Taylor  michael@abc.com +919976543210
2       William Becker  william@abc.com +449876543210
3       Samuel  Uncle   sam@abc.com     +119955331100
```

The output of the program is as expected. However, you made use of RowSetProvider and RowSetFactory. You first get the appropriate RowSetFactory and then create JdbcRowSet using the factory. The rest of the program is as you saw in Listing 10-3.

Points to Remember

Here are a few useful points that could be helpful in your OCPJP exam:

- You can use column name or column index with ResultSet methods. The index you use is the index of the ResultSet object, not the column number in the database table.

- A Statement object closes the current ResultSet object if a) the Statement object is closed, b) is re-executed, or c) is made to retrieve the next set of result. That means it is not necessary to call close() explicitly with ResultSet object; however, it is good practice to call close() once you are done with the object.

- You may use the column name of a ResultSet object without worrying about the case: getXXX() methods accept case insensitive column names to retrieve the associated value.

- Think of a case when you have two columns in a ResultSet object with the same name. How you can retrieve the associated values using the column name? If you use a column name to retrieve the value, it will always point to the first column that matches with the given name. Hence, you have to use column index in this case to retrieve values associated with both columns.

- You might remember that the PreparedStatement interface inherits from Statement. However, PreparedStatement overrides all flavors of execute() methods. For instance, the behavior of executeUpdate() might be different from its base method.

- It is your responsibility to issue a correct SQL command; a JDBC Statement will not check for its correctness. For example, if there is a syntax error in the SQL command string, then you will not get a compiler error. Rather, you'll get a MySQLSyntaxErrorException at runtime.

- You may call the appropriate get() method immediately after inserting a row using the insertRow() method. However, the values of the row are undefined.

- You may cancel any update you made using the method cancelRowUpdates(). However, you must call this method before calling the method updateRow(). In all other cases, it has no impact on the row.

- While connecting to the database, you need to specify the correct username and password. If the provided username or password is not correct, you will get a SQLException.

- JDBC 4.1 introduces the capability to use try-with-resources statement to close resources (Connection, ResultSet, and Statement) automatically.

```
QUESTION TIME!
```

1. Consider the following code segment. Assume that the connection object is valid and
    statement.executeQuery() method successfully returns a ResultSet object with a few
    rows in it.

    ```
    Statement statement = connection.createStatement();
    ResultSet resultSet = statement.executeQuery("SELECT * FROM contact")){
    System.out.println("ID \tfName \tlName \temail \t\tphoneNo");
    // from resultSet metadata, find out how many columns are there and then read the
    column entries
    int numOfColumns = resultSet.getMetaData().getColumnCount();
    while (resultSet.next()) {
    // traverse the columns by index values
        for(int i = 0; i < numOfColumns; i++) {
            // since we do not know the data type of the column, we use getObject()
            System.out.print(resultSet.getObject(i) + "\t");
        }
        System.out.println("");
    }
    ```

Which of the following statements is true regarding this code segment?

A. The code segment will successfully print the contents of the rows in the ResultSet
    object.

B. The looping header is wrong. To traverse all the columns, it should be

    ```
    for(int i = 0; i <= numOfColumns; i++) {
    ```

C. The looping header is wrong. To traverse all the columns, it should be

    ```
    for(int i = 1; i <= numOfColumns; i++) {
    ```

D. The looping header is wrong. To traverse all the columns, it should be

    ```
    for(int i = 1; i < numOfColumns; i++) {
    ```

Answer: C. The looping header is wrong. To traverse all the columns, it should be

```
for(int i = 1; i <= numOfColumns; i++) {
```

(Given N columns in a table, the valid column indexes are from 1 to N and not 0 to N - 1.)

2. Assume that you've freshly created this table with the following command in MySQL:

    ```
    create table familyGroup (id int not null auto_increment, nickName varchar(30) Not
    null, primary key (id));
    ```

You've written this program that makes use of this table:

```
import java.sql.Connection;
import java.sql.ResultSet;
import java.sql.SQLException;
import java.sql.Statement;
```

```
class DbTransactionTest {
    public static void main(String[] args) throws SQLException {
            try (Connection connection = DbConnector.connectToDb();
                    Statement statement =
                     connection.createStatement(
                            ResultSet.TYPE_SCROLL_SENSITIVE,
ResultSet.CONCUR_UPDATABLE);
                    ResultSet resultSet =
                            statement.executeQuery("SELECT * FROM familyGroup")) {
                    resultSet.moveToInsertRow();
                    resultSet.updateString("nickName", "Sam");
                    resultSet.insertRow();  // INSERT ROW
                    System.out.println("Table updated with a row...");
                    connection.commit();    // COMMIT STMT
            }
        }
    }
```

What will be the result of executing this program assuming that establishing the connection succeeds?

    A.   The program will successfully insert a row with id = 1 and nickName = "Sam".

    B.   A SQLException will be thrown in the line where the INSERT ROW comment is provided because you cannot insert a row on a read-only ResultSet object.

    C.   A SQLException will be thrown in the line where the COMMIT STMT statement is provided because auto-commit is enabled; hence the commit will fail.

    D.   The program will not insert anything into the familyGroup table.

Answer: C. A SQLException will be thrown in the line where the COMMIT STMT statement is provided because auto-commit is enabled; hence the commit will fail.

(Any attempt to use methods such as commit, rollback, setSavepoint, etc. will result in throwing a SQLException if auto-commit is not disabled.)

    3.   Consider the following sequence of operations in a transaction:

```
// assume that all operations execute in this program successfully without
// throwing any exceptions; also assume that the connection is established
// successfully
connection.setAutoCommit(false);

// insert a row into the table here
// create a savepoint in this transaction here

//insert another row into the table here
//create a named savepoint in this transaction here

//insert the third row into the table here

connection.rollback();
connection.commit();
```

What will be the effect of this sequence of actions after executing the statement `connection.commit()`?

    A.   Three rows will be inserted into the table.

    B.   No rows will be inserted into the table.

    C.   One row will be inserted into the table.

    D.   Two rows will be inserted into the table.

    E.   All three rows will be inserted into the table.

Answer: B. No rows will be inserted into the table.

(Since `connection.rollback();` is called before `connection.commit()`, all operations will be undone and no rows will be inserted into the table.)

4.   Which one of the following statements would be needed in JDBC 3.0?

    A.   `Connection connection = DriverManager.getConnection("jdbc:mysql://`
        `localhost:3306/addressBook", "root", "password"))`

    B.   `Connection connection = DriverManager.createConnection("jdbc:mysql://`
        `localhost:3306/addressBook", "root", "password"))`

    C.   `Class.forName("com.mysql.jdbc.Driver").newInstance();`

    D.   `Class.forName("com.mysql.jdbc.Driver").getInstance();`

Answer: C. `Class.forName("com.mysql.jdbc.Driver").newInstance();`

(You need to explicitly load the JDBC driver using the `Class.forName()` statement in JDBC 3.0. From 4.0 onwards, this statement is not needed and you can directly get the connection. Note that option A) shows how to get the connection for MySQL, and this URI will depend on the specific database used.)

5.   Consider this program and choose the best option describing its behavior (assume that the connection is valid):

```
try (Statement statement = connection.createStatement();
 ResultSet resultSet = statement.executeQuery("SELECT * FROM contact")){
   System.out.println(resultSet.getInt("id") + "\t"
    + resultSet.getString("firstName") + "\t"
    + resultSet.getString("lastName") + "\t"
    + resultSet.getString("email") + "\t"
    + resultSet.getString("phoneNo"));
}
catch (SQLException sqle) {
 System.out.println("SQLException");
}
```

    A.   This program will print the following: `SQLException`.

    B.   This program will print the first row from contact.

    C.   This program will print all the rows from contact.

    D.   This program will report compiler errors.

Answer: A. This program will print the following: `SQLException`.

(The statement while (resultSet.next()) is missing.)

6. Which of the following two statements are correct regarding RowSets in JDBC?

    A. It is possible to use JdbcRowSet as a JavaBeans component.

    B. WebRowSet provides result set in the JSON format.

    C. The filter in a FilteredRowSet object is set at the time of its creation; a filter cannot be set once the FilteredRowSet object is created.

    D. A CachedRowSet object caches data in its memory, which makes it possible to use the CachedRowSet object without always being connected to its data source.

Answer:

A. It is possible to use JdbcRowSet as a JavaBeans component.

D. A CachedRowSet object caches data in its memory, which makes it possible to use the CachedRowSet object without always being connected to its data source.

(Note that B) WebRowSet provides a result set in XML format (not JSON format which is one of the alternatives to XML) and C) The filter in a FilteredRowSet object can be set using the setFilter() method any time).

7. Which of the following interfaces does NOT extend the RowSet interface?

    A. JdbcRowSet

    B. CachedRowSet

    C. WebRowSet

    D. TraversalRowSet

    E. JoinRowSet

Answer: D) TraversalRowSet

(The interfaces deriving from JdbcRowSet are CachedRowSet, WebRowSet, JoinRowSet, and FilteredRowSet.)

Summary
Define the Layout of the JDBC API

- JDBC (Java Database Connectivity) APIs provided by Java are meant for programmatic access to DataBase Management Systems (DBMSs).

- JDBC hides all the heterogeneity of all the DBMSs and offers a single set of APIs to interact with all types of databases.

- The complexity of heterogeneous interactions is delegated to JDBC driver manager and JDBC drivers; hence all the details and complications are hidden by the JDBC API from the application developer.

- There are four types of drivers:

    - **Type 1 (JDBC-ODBC bridge drivers):** JDBC driver calls ODBC (Open Database Connectivity) native calls using the Java Native Interface (JNI).

    - **Type 2 (Native-API drivers):** These drivers use client-side libraries of a specific database and convert JDBC calls to native database calls.

    - **Type 3 (Network-protocol drivers):** These drivers call database middleware and the middleware actually converts JDBC calls to database-specific native calls.

    - **Type 4 (Native-protocol drivers):** The driver directly makes database-specific calls over the network without any support of additional client-side libraries.

Connect to a Database by Using a JDBC driver

- The `java.sql.Connection` interface provides a channel through which the application and the database communicate.

- The `getConnection()` method in the `DriverManager` class takes three arguments: the URL string, username string, and password string.

- The syntax of the URL (which needs to be specified to get the `Connection` object) is `<protocol>:<subprotocol>://<server>:<port>/`. An example of a URL string is `jdbc:mysql://localhost:3306/`. The `<protocol>` `jdbc` is the same for all DBMSs; `<subprotocol>` will differ for each DBMS, `<server>` depends on the location in which you host the database, and each DBMS uses a specific `<port>` number.

- If the JDBC API is not able to locate the JDBC driver, it will throw a `SQLException`. If there are jars for the drivers available, they need to be included in the classpath to enable the JDBC API to locate the driver.

- Prior to JDBC 4.0, you would have to explicitly load the JDBC driver using the `Class.forName()` statement; with JDBC 4.0 and above, this statement is not needed and the JDBC API will load the driver from the details given in the URL string.

Update and Query a Database

- JDBC supports two interfaces for querying and updating: `Statement` and `Resultset`.

- A `Statement` is a SQL statement that can be used to communicate a SQL statement to the connected database and receive results from the database. There are three types of `Statements`:

    - `Statement`: You need to use `Statement` when you need to send a SQL statement to the database without any parameter.

    - `PreparedStatement`: Represents a precompiled SQL statement that can be customized using IN parameters.

    - `CallableStatement`: Used to execute stored procedures; can handle IN as well as OUT and INOUT parameters.

- A `ResultSet` is a table with column heading and associated values requested by the query.

- A `ResultSet` object maintains a cursor pointing to the current row. Initially, the cursor is set to just before the first row; calling the `next()` method advances the cursor position by one row.

- The column index in the ResultSet object starts from 1 (*not* from 0).

- You need to call updateRow() after modifying the row contents in a ResultSet; otherwise changes made to the ResultSet object will be lost.

- By calling the getMetaData() method in the Connection interface, you can examine the capabilities of the underlying database.

Customize the Transaction Behavior of JDBC and Commit Transactions

- A transaction is a set of SQL operations that needs to be either executed all successfully or not at all.

- Transaction-related methods are supported in the Connection interface.

- By default auto-commit mode is set to true, so all changes you make through the connection are committed automatically to the database.

- You can use setAutoCommit(false); to enable manual commits. With auto-commit not enabled, you need to explicitly commit or rollback transactions.

- If the commit() method does not execute in manual commit mode, there will be no change in the database.

- You can divide a big transaction into multiple milestones. These milestones are referred to as savepoints. This way you may save the changes to a database up to a milestone once the milestone is achieved.

Use the JDBC 4.1 RowSetProvider, RowSetFactory, and RowSet Interfaces

- RowSet is a special ResultSet that supports the JavaBean component model.

- JdbcRowSet is a connected RowSet while other subinterfaces of RowSet (i.e., JoinRowSet, CachedRowSet, WebRowSet, and FilteredRowSet) are disconnected RowSets.

- RowSetProvider provides APIs to get a RowSetFactory implementation, which can in turn be used to instantiate a relevant RowSet implementation.

■ ■ ■

Exceptions and Assertions

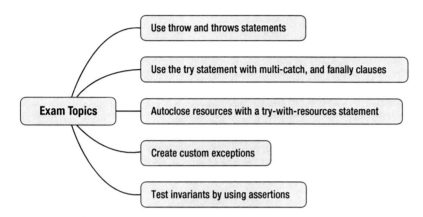

In this chapter, you'll learn about Java's support for exception handling in detail. You'll first learn the basic concepts behind exception handling and then you'll learn how to throw, catch, and rethrow exceptions. You'll also learn about the recently added language features such as try-with-resources and multi-catch statements. Following that, you'll learn how to define your own exception classes (custom exceptions). Finally, we'll discuss the related topic of assertions and teach you how to use them in your programs. Most of the programming examples in this chapter make use of I/O functions (Chapters 8 and 9) to illustrate the concepts of exception handling.

Introduction to Exception Handling

As programmers, we are optimistic—we just write code to solve the problem at hand and expect it to work without any problems. However, things do go wrong (more often than we'd like!), so we should always anticipate errors and exceptions, and write code to handle the exceptional conditions.

Java has built-in support for exceptions. The Java language supports exception handling in the form of the throw, throws, try, catch, and finally keywords. See Figure 11-1 to understand the basic syntax of these keywords.

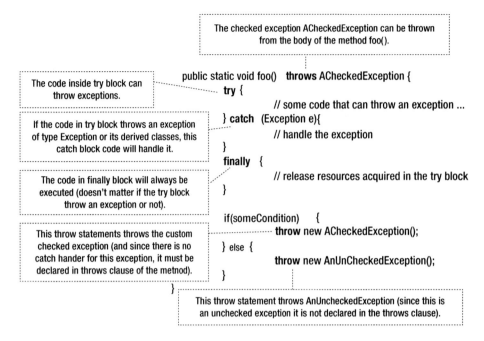

Figure 11-1. *The basic syntax of exception handling-related keywords*

Throwing Exceptions

Listing 11-1 is a very simple programming example in which you want to echo the text typed as command-line arguments back to the user. Assume that the user must type some text as command-line arguments to echo, or else you need to inform the user about the "error condition."

Listing 11-1. Echo.java

```java
// A simple program without exception handling code
class Echo {
        public static void main(String []args) {
                if(args.length == 0) {
                        // no arguments passed - display an error to the user
                        System.out.println("Error: No input passed to echo command... ");
                        System.exit(-1);
                }
                else {
                        for(String str : args) {
                                // command-line arguments are separated and passed as an array
                                // print them by adding a space between the array elements
                                System.out.print(str + " ");
                        }
                }
        }
}
```

In this case, you print the error in the console using a `println()` statement. This is a trivial program and the error occurred in the `main()` method, so the error handling is easy. In this case, you can terminate the program after printing the error message to the console. However, if you are deep within the function calls in a complex application, you need a better way to indicate that an "exceptional condition" has occurred and then inform the caller about that condition. Further, you often need to recover from an error condition instead of terminating the program. So you need to be able to "handle" an exception or "rethrow" that exception further up in the call stack so that a caller can handle that exception. (We'll revisit this topic of rethrowing exceptions later in this chapter.) At present, you'll change the program in Listing 11-1 to throw an exception instead of printing an error message (in a separate program, Echo1.java), like so:

```
if(args.length == 0) {
        // no arguments passed - throw an exception
        throw new IllegalArgumentException("No input passed to echo command");
}
```

This block inside the `if` condition for `args.length == 0` is the only part that needs to be changed within this program. Note the syntax for throwing an exception: the `throw` keyword followed by the exception object. Here you make use of `IllegalArgumentException`, which is already defined in the Java library. Later in this chapter, you'll see how to define your own exceptions.

Now, if you run this program without passing any arguments in the command line, the program will throw an `IllegalArgumentException`.

```
D:\> java Echo1
Exception in thread "main" java.lang.IllegalArgumentException: No input passed to echo command
        at Echo1.main(Echo1.java:5)
```

Since there was no handler for this exception, this uncaught exception terminated the program. In this case, you explicitly threw an exception. Exceptions can also get thrown when you write some code or call Java APIs. You'll look at an example now.

Unhandled Exceptions

Consider the program in Listing 11-2, which attempts to read an integer value that the user types in the console and prints the read integer back to the console. For reading an integer from the console, you make use of the `readInt()` method provided in the `java.util.Scanner` class. To instantiate the `Scanner` class, you pass in `System.in`, which is a reference to the *system input stream*.

Listing 11-2. ScanInt1.java

```
// A simple progam to accept an integer from user

import java.util.*;

class ScanInt {
        public static void main(String [] args) {
                System.out.println("Type an integer in the console: ");
                Scanner consoleScanner = new Scanner(System.in);
                System.out.println("You typed the integer value: " + consoleScanner.nextInt());
        }
}
```

When you run this program and type an integer, say 10, in the console, the program works correctly and prints the integer back to you successfully.

```
D:\> java ScanInt1
Type an integer in the console:
10
You typed the integer value: 10
```

However, what if you (or the user of the program) mistakenly type the string "ten" instead of the integer value "10"? The program will terminate after throwing an exception like this:

```
D:\> java ScanInt1
Type an integer in the console:
ten
Exception in thread "main" java.util.InputMismatchException
        at java.util.Scanner.throwFor(Scanner.java:909)
        at java.util.Scanner.next(Scanner.java:1530)
        at java.util.Scanner.nextInt(Scanner.java:2160)
        at java.util.Scanner.nextInt(Scanner.java:2119)
        at ScanInt.main(ScanInt1.java:7)
```

If you read the documentation of nextInt(), you'll see that this method can throw InputMismatchException " if the next token does not match the Integer regular expression, or is out of range." In this simple program, you assume that you (or the user) will always type an integer value as expected, and when that assumption fails, an exception gets thrown. If there is an exception thrown from a program, and it is left unhandled, the program will terminate abnormally after throwing a stack trace like the ones shown here.

A *stack trace* shows the list of the method (with the line numbers) that was called before the control reached the statement where the exception was thrown. As a programmer, you'll find it useful to trace the control flow for debugging the program and fix the problem that led to this exception.

So, how do you handle this situation? You need to put this code within try and catch blocks and then handle the exception.

Try and Catch Statements

Java provides the try and catch keywords to handle any exceptions that can get thrown in the code you write. Listing 11-3 is the improved version of the program from Listing 11-2.

Listing 11-3. ScanInt2.java

```java
// A simple progam to accept an integer from user in normal case,
// otherwise prints an error message

import java.util.*;

class ScanInt2 {
        public static void main(String [] args) {
                System.out.println("Type an integer in the console: ");
                Scanner consoleScanner = new Scanner(System.in);
                try {
                        System.out.println("You typed the integer value: " + consoleScanner.nextInt());
                } catch(InputMismatchException ime) {
```

```
                        // nextInt() throws InputMismatchException in case anything other
                        than an integer
                        // is typed in the console; so handle it
                        System.out.println("Error: You typed some text that is not
                        an integer value...");
                }
        }
}
```

If anything other than a valid integer is typed in the input, this program prints a readable error message to the user.

```
D:\> java ScanInt2
Type an integer in the console:
ten
Error: You typed some text that is not an integer value...
```

Now let's analyze this code. The block followed by the try keyword limits the code segment for which you expect that some exceptions could be thrown. If any exception gets thrown from the try block, the Java runtime will search for a *matching handler* (which we'll discuss in more detail a bit later). In this case, an exception handler for InputMismatchException is present, which is of exactly the same type as the exception that got thrown. This *exactly matching* catch handler is available just outside the try block in the form of a block preceded by the keyword catch, and this catch block gets executed. In the catch block you caught the exception, so you're handling the exception here. You are providing a human readable error string rather than throwing a raw stack trace (as you did in the earlier program in Listing 11-2), so you're providing a graceful exit for the program.

Programmatically Accessing the Stack Trace

You saw that the stack trace is useful for debugging, so how to get it in the catch block? You can use the printStackTrace() method, which will print the stack trace to the console. Let's add the following statement to the catch block:

```
ime.printStackTrace();
```

Now this statement will print the stack trace:

```
java.util.InputMismatchException
        at java.util.Scanner.throwFor(Scanner.java:909)
        at java.util.Scanner.next(Scanner.java:1530)
        at java.util.Scanner.nextInt(Scanner.java:2160)
        at java.util.Scanner.nextInt(Scanner.java:2119)
        at ScanInt2.main(ScanInt2.java:9)
```

You can also access each of the entries in the stack trace. All exceptions have a method named getStackTrace() that returns an array of StackTraceElements. So, consider that you write these statements in the catch block:

```
System.out.println("The calls in the stack trace are: ");
// access each element in the "call stack" and print them individually
for(StackTraceElement methodCall : ime.getStackTrace())
        System.out.println(methodCall);
```

When you execute this code segment, it will print the following:

```
The calls in the stack trace are:
java.util.Scanner.throwFor(Scanner.java:909)
java.util.Scanner.next(Scanner.java:1530)
java.util.Scanner.nextInt(Scanner.java:2160)
java.util.Scanner.nextInt(Scanner.java:2119)
ScanInt2.main(ScanInt2.java:9)
```

Multiple Catch Blocks

In Listing 11-2, you used a Scanner object to read an integer from the console. Note that you can use a Scanner object to read from a String as well (see Listing 11-4).

Listing 11-4. ScanInt3.java

```java
// A program that scans an integer from a given string

import java.util.*;

class ScanInt3 {
        public static void main(String [] args) {
                String integerStr = "100";
                System.out.println("The string to scan integer from it is: " + integerStr);
                Scanner consoleScanner = new Scanner(integerStr);
                try {
                        System.out.println("The integer value scanned from string is: " +
                                consoleScanner.nextInt());
                } catch(InputMismatchException ime) {
                        // nextInt() throws InputMismatchException in case anything other
                        than an integer
                        // is provided in the string
                        System.out.println("Error: Cannot scan an integer from the given string");
                }
        }
}
```

This program prints the following:

```
The string to scan integer from it is: 100
The integer value scanned from string is: 100
```

What happens if you modify the program in Listing 11-4 so that the string contains a non-integer value, as in

```
String integerStr = "hundred";
```

The try block will throw an InputMismatchException, which will be handled in the catch block, and you'll get this output:

```
The string to scan integer from it is: hundred
Error: Cannot scan an integer from the given string
```

Now, what if you modify the program in Listing 11-4 so that the string contains an empty string, as in

```
String integerStr = "";
```

For this, nextInt() will throw a NoSuchElementException, which is not handled in this program, so this program would crash.

```
The string to scan integer from it is:
Exception in thread "main" java.util.NoSuchElementException
        at java.util.Scanner.throwFor(Scanner.java:907)
        at java.util.Scanner.next(Scanner.java:1530)
        at java.util.Scanner.nextInt(Scanner.java:2160)
        at java.util.Scanner.nextInt(Scanner.java:2119)
        at ScanInt3.main(ScanInt.java:11)
```

Further, if you look at the JavaDoc for Scanner.nextInt() method, you'll find that it can also throw an IllegalStateException (this exception is thrown if the nextInt() method is called on a Scanner object that is already closed). So, let's provide catch handlers for InputMismatchException, NoSuchElementException, and IllegalStateException (see Listing 11-5).

Listing 11-5. ScanInt4.java

```java
// A program that scans an integer from a given string

import java.util.*;

class ScanInt4 {
        public static void main(String [] args) {
                String integerStr = "";
                System.out.println("The string to scan integer from it is: " + integerStr);
                Scanner consoleScanner = new Scanner(integerStr);
                try {
                        System.out.println("The integer value scanned from string is: " +
                                consoleScanner.nextInt());
                } catch(InputMismatchException ime) {
                        System.out.println("Error: Cannot scan an integer from the given string");
                } catch(NoSuchElementException nsee) {
                        System.out.println("Error: Cannot scan an integer from the given string");
                } catch(IllegalStateException ise) {
                        System.out.println("Error: nextInt() called on a closed Scanner object");
                }
        }
}
```

Here is the output when you run this program:

```
The string to scan integer from it is:
Error: Cannot scan an integer from the given string
```

As you can see from the output, since the string is empty, NoSuchElementException gets thrown. It is caught in the catch handler for this exception, and the code provided inside the catch block gets executed to result in a graceful exit.

Note how you provided more than one catch handler by stacking them up: you provided specific (i.e., derived type) exception handlers followed by more general (i.e., base type) exception handlers. If you provide a derived exception type after a base exception type, you get a compiler error. You might not already know, but NoSuchElementException is the base class of InputMismatchException! See what happens when you try to reverse the order of catch handlers for InputMismatchException and NoSuchElementException.

```
try {
        System.out.println("The integer value scanned from string is: "
                + consoleScanner.nextInt());
} catch(NoSuchElementException nsee) {
        System.out.println("Error: Cannot scan an integer from the given string");
} catch(InputMismatchException ime) {
        System.out.println("Error: Cannot scan an integer from the given string");
}
```

This code segment will result in this compiler error:

```
ScanInt4.java:14: error: exception InputMismatchException has already been caught

                } catch(InputMismatchException ime) {
                  ^
1 error
```

When providing multiple catch handlers, handle specific exceptions before handling general exceptions. If you provide a derived class exception catch handler *after* a base class exception handler, your code will not compile.

Multi-Catch Blocks

You just saw that you cannot reverse the order of the catch handlers for InputMismatchException and NoSuchElementException. However, is it possible to combine these two catch handlers together? Java 7 provides a feature named *multi-catch blocks* in which you can combine multiple catch handlers (see Listing 11-6).

Listing 11-6. ScanInt5.java

```
// A program that illustrates multi-catch blocks

import java.util.*;

class ScanInt5 {
        public static void main(String [] args) {
                String integerStr = "";
                System.out.println("The string to scan integer from it is: " + integerStr);
                Scanner consoleScanner = new Scanner(integerStr);
                try {
                        System.out.println("The integer value scanned from string is: " +
                                consoleScanner.nextInt());
```

```
        } catch(NoSuchElementException | IllegalStateException multie) {
                System.out.println("Error: An error occured while attempting to scan
                the integer");
        }
    }
}
```

Note how you combine the catch handlers together using the | (OR) operator here (the same operator you use for performing bit-wise OR operation on integral values) for combining the catch clauses of NoSuchElementException and IllegalStateException.

Unlike the combined catch clauses for NoSuchElementException and IllegalStateException, you cannot combine the catch clauses of NoSuchElementException and InputMismatchException. As we've already discussed, NoSuchElementException is the base class of InputMismatchException, and you cannot catch both of them in the multi-catch block. If you try compiling such a multi-catch clause, you'll get this compiler error:

```
ScanInt5.java:11: error: Alternatives in a multi-catch statement cannot be related by subclassing
        } catch(InputMismatchException | NoSuchElementException exception) {
                                         ^
```

So what is the alternative? When you need such a catch handler for the exceptions where one exception is the base class of another exception class, providing the catch handler for the base class alone is sufficient (since that base class catch handler will handle the derived class exception if it occurs).

 In a multi-catch block, you cannot combine catch handlers for two exceptions that share a base- and derived-class relationship. You can only combine catch handlers for exceptions that do not share the parent-child relationship between them.

How do you know if it is better to combine exception handling blocks or stack them? It is a design choice where you must consider the following aspects: a) Do the exceptions get thrown for similar reason or for different reasons? (b) Is the handling code similar or different? If you answer "similar" for both the questions, it is better to combine them; if you say "different" for either one of these two questions, then it is better to separate them.

How about the specific situation in Listing 11-6? Is it better to combine or separate the handlers for the InputMismatchException and IllegalStateException exceptions? You can see that the exception handling is the same for both of the catch blocks. But the reasons for these two exceptions are considerably different. The InputMismatchException gets thrown if you (or the user) type invalid input in the console. The IllegalStateException gets thrown because of a programming mistake when you call the nextInt() method after calling the close() method on Scanner. So, in this case, it is a better design choice to separate the handlers for these two exceptions.

General Catch Handlers

Did you notice that many exceptions can get thrown when you use APIs related to I/O operations? We just discussed that in order to call just one method, nextInt() of the Scanner class, you need to handle three exceptions: the InputMismatchException, the NoSuchElementException, and the IllegalStateException. If you keep handling specific exceptions such as this that may not actually result in an exceptional condition when you run the program, most of your code will consist of try-catch code blocks! Is there a better way to say "handle all other exceptions"? Yes, you can provide a *general exception handler*.

Here is the code snippet that shows only the try-catch blocks for the class ScanInt3 from Listing 11-4, enhanced with a general exception handler:

```
try {
        System.out.println("You typed the integer value: " + consoleScanner.nextInt());
} catch(InputMismatchException ime) {
        // if something other than integer is typed, we'll get this exception, so handle it
        System.out.println("Error: You typed some text that is not an integer value...");
} catch(Exception e) {
        // catch IllegalStateException here which is unlikely to occur...
        System.out.println("Error: Encountered an exception and could not read an integer from the
        console... ");
}
```

This code provides a catch handler for the base exception of the type Exception. So, if the try block throws any other exception than the InputMismatchException, and if that exception is a derived class of the Exception class, this general catch handler will handle it. It is recommended practice to catch specific exceptions, and then provide a general exception handler to ensure that all other exceptions are handled as well.

CHAINED EXCEPTIONS

When you want to catch an exception and throw another exception, you can "chain" the first exception to the thrown exception. In other words, when throwing an exception, you can associate another exception that caused it.

When creating an exception object you can use a constructor that takes another exception as an argument; this passed argument is the exception chained to the exception object being created. There is also an overloaded constructor that takes a description message as an additional argument. For example, the following are two overloaded constructors of the Exception class:

```
Exception(Throwable cause)
Exception(string detailMsg, throwable cause)
```

Similar constructors are available for other classes such as Throwable, Error, and RuntimeException. The following program illustrates chained exceptions:

```
class ChainedException {
        public static void foo() {
                try {
                        String [] str = { "foo" };
                        System.out.println("About to throw ArrayIndexOutOfBoundsException");
                        // following statement has out-of-bounds access
                        String functionName = str[10];
                } catch(ArrayIndexOutOfBoundsException oob) {
                        System.out.println("Wrapping ArrayIndexOutOfBoundsException into
                        a RuntimeException");
                        throw new RuntimeException(oob);
                }
        }
}
```

```
        public static void main(String []args) {
            try {
                foo();
            } catch(Exception re) {
                System.out.println("The caught exception in main is: " + re.getClass());
                System.out.println("The cause of the exception is: " + re.getCause());
            }
        }
}
```

When executed, this program prints the following:

```
About to throw ArrayIndexOutOfBoundsException
Wrapping ArrayIndexOutOfBoundsException into a RuntimeException
The caught exception in main is: class java.lang.RuntimeException
The cause of the exception is: java.lang.ArrayIndexOutOfBoundsException: 10
```

Methods related to chained exceptions are the getCause() and initCause() methods defined in the Throwable class.

The getCause() method returns a Throwable object. It returns an exception chained to the exception object on which this method is invoked. This chained exception is the original exception that caused this exception. If no exception is chained to this exception, this method returns null.

The initCause(Throwable causeException) method sets the chained exception for the exception object on which this method is called. If the chained exception has already been set when creating the exception object, calling this method will result in throwing an IllegalStateException. This method can be called only once; any attempt to call it more than once will result in throwing an IllegalStateException.

Note that exceptions can be chained to any level of depth.

Finally Blocks

There is a close() method provided in the Scanner class, and you need to close it. In the classes ScanInt1, ScanInt2, and ScanInt3 (Listings 11-2, 11-3, and 11-4, respectively), note that you opened a Scanner object but did not close it. So, these programs have a *resource leak*! The word "resource" refers to any of the classes that acquire some system sources from the underlying operating system, such as network, file, database, and other handles. But how do you know which classes need to be closed? Well, nice question. The answer is that if a class implements java.io.Closeable, then you must call the close() method of that class; otherwise, it will result in a resource leak.

 The garbage collector (GC) is responsible for releasing only memory resources. If you are using any class that acquires system resources, it is your responsibility to release them by calling the close() method on that object.

ScanInt6 (Listing 11-7) calls the close() method of the Scanner object in its main() method; you want to shorten the code, so you'll use a general exception handler for handling all exceptions that can be thrown within the try block.

Listing 11-7. ScanInt6.java

```java
import java.util.*;

class ScanInt6 {
    public static void main(String [] args) {
        System.out.println("Type an integer in the console: ");
        Scanner consoleScanner = new Scanner(System.in);
        try {
            System.out.println("You typed the integer value: " +
                                    consoleScanner.nextInt());
            System.out.println("Done reading the text... closing the Scanner");
                                    consoleScanner.close();
        } catch(Exception e) {
            // call all other exceptions here ...
            System.out.println("Error: Encountered an exception and could not read
            an integer from the console... ");
            System.out.println("Exiting the program - restart and try the program again!");
        }
    }
}
```

Let's see if this program works.

```
D:\> java ScanInt6
Type an integer in the console:
10
You typed the integer value: 10
Done reading the text... closing the Scanner
```

Because the program printed "Done reading the text... closing the Scanner", and completed the execution normally, you can assume that the statement consoleScanner.close(); has executed successfully. What happens if an exception gets thrown?

```
D:\> java ScanInt6
Type an integer in the console:
ten
Error: Encountered an exception and could not read an integer from the console...
Exiting the program - restart and try the program again!
```

As you can see from the output, the program did not print "Done reading the text... closing the Scanner", so the statement consoleScanner.close(); has not executed. How can you fix it? One way is to call consoleScanner. close() in the catch block as well, like this:

```java
try {
    System.out.println("You typed the integer value: " + consoleScanner.nextInt());
    System.out.println("Done reading the text... closing the Scanner");
    consoleScanner.close();
} catch(Exception e) {
    // call all other exceptions here ...
    consoleScanner.close();
```

```
            System.out.println("Error: Encountered an exception and could not read an integer
            from the console... ");
            System.out.println("Exiting the program - restart and try the program again!");
}
```

This solution will work but is not elegant. You know you can have multiple catch blocks and you have to provide calls to consoleScanner.close(); in all the catch blocks! Is there a better way to release the resources? Yes, you can use release resources in a finally block (see Listing 11-8).

Listing 11-8. ScanInt7.java

```java
import java.util.*;

class ScanInt7 {
    public static void main(String [] args) {
        System.out.println("Type an integer in the console: ");
        Scanner consoleScanner = new Scanner(System.in);
        try {
            System.out.println("You typed the integer value: " +
                            consoleScanner.nextInt());
        } catch(Exception e) {
            // call all other exceptions here ...
            System.out.println("Error: Encountered an exception and could not read
            an integer from the console... ");
            System.out.println("Exiting the program - restart and try the program again!");
        } finally {
            System.out.println("Done reading the integer... closing the Scanner");
            consoleScanner.close();
        }
    }
}
```

In this case, a finally block is provided after the catch block. This finally block will be executed whether an exception has occurred or not. So, the finally block is a good place to call the close() method on the Scanner object to ensure that this resource is always released.

 If you call System.exit() inside a method, it will abnormally terminate the program. So, if the calling method has a finally block, it will not be called and resources may leak. For this reason, it is a bad programming practice to call System.exit() to terminate a program.

Now, let's see if the scanner is closed both in the case when the program completes normally (i.e., without throwing an exception) and when the program terminates after throwing an exception.

```
D:\> java ScanInt7
Type an integer in the console:
10
You typed the integer value: 10
Done reading the integer... closing the Scanner
```

```
D:\> java ScanInt7
Type an integer in the console:
ten
Error: Encountered an exception and could not read an integer from the console...
Exiting the program - restart and try the program again!
Done reading the integer... closing the Scanner
```

Yes, the statement "Done reading the integer... closing the Scanner" is called whether an exception is thrown or not. Note that you can have a finally block directly after a try block without a catch block as well; this feature is used rarely, but is nevertheless a useful feature.

Points to Remember

Here are some interesting points related to throwing /handling exceptions and releasing resources in a finally block:

- You can catch exceptions and wrap them into more generic exceptions and throw them higher up in the call stack. When you catch an exception and create a more general exception, you can retain reference to the original exception; this is called *exception chaining*.

```
catch(LowLevelException lle) {
    // wrap the low-level exception to a higher-level exception;
    // also, chain the original exception to the newly thrown exception
    throw new HighLevelException(lle);
}
```

  Chaining exceptions is useful for debugging purposes. When you get a general exception, you can check if there is a chained lower-level exception and try to understand why that lower-level exception occurred.

- The finally statement is always executed irrespective of whether the code in the try block throws an exception or not. Consider the following method. Will it return true or false to the caller?

```
static boolean returnTest() {
    try {
        return true;
    }
    finally {
        return false;
    }
}
```

  This method will always return false because finally is always invoked. In fact, if you use the -Xlint option, you'll get this compiler warning: "finally clause cannot complete normally." (Note that you can have a try block followed by either catch block or finally block or both blocks.)

PRECISE RETHROW

Consider the following program:

```java
class PreciseRethrow {
    public static void main(String []str) {
            try {
                    foo();
            }
            catch(NumberFormatException ife) {
                    System.out.println(ife);
            }
    }

        static private void foo() throws NumberFormatException {
            try {
                    int i = Integer.parseInt("ten");
            }
            catch(Exception e) {
                    throw e;
            }
    }
}
```

If you try this program in Java versions earlier to Java 1.7, you'll get this error:

```
C:\> javac -source 1.6 PreciseRethrow.java
PreciseRethrow.java:16: error: unreported exception Exception; must be caught or
 declared to be thrown
                    throw e;
                    ^
1 error
```

In this program, the `Integer.parseInt()` method can throw a `NumberFormatException`. However, the catch block declares catching the general exception type `Exception`. Inside the catch block, the exception is rethrown. Now, the method `foo()`'s throws clause indicates it can throw the `NumberFormatException`, which is correct because it is the only exception that the `Integer.parseInt()` method can throw. However, since the static type of the rethrown exception is `Exception`, the compiler will complain that the throws clause of the `foo()` method should declare `Exception`.

Java 7 allows you to be more precise when you rethrow an exception. If you rethrow an exception from a catch block, you can throw a type that the try block can throw but no previous catch handles has handled it. Also, the rethrown exception type need not be same as the catch type parameter; it can be a subtype of the catch parameter. Hence the class `PreciseRethrow` given above will compile without warnings or errors. (Of course the program will crash after throwing `NumberFormatException` because the string "ten" is not an integer!)

Try-with-Resources

It is a fairly common mistake by Java programmers to forget releasing resources, even in the finally block. Also, if you're dealing with multiple resources, it is tedious to remember to call the close() method in the finally block. Java 7 introduced a feature named try-with-resources to help make your life easier. Listing 11-9 makes use of this feature; it is an improved version of Listing 11-8.

Listing 11-9. TryWithResources1.java

```java
import java.util.*;

class TryWithResources1 {
        public static void main(String [] args) {
                System.out.println("Type an integer in the console: ");
                try(Scanner consoleScanner = new Scanner(System.in)) {
                        System.out.println("You typed the integer value: " + consoleScanner.nextInt());
                } catch(Exception e) {
                        // catch all other exceptions here ...
                        System.out.println("Error: Encountered an exception and could not read
                        an integer from the console... ");
                        System.out.println("Exiting the program - restart and try the program again!");
                }
        }
}
```

The behavior will be similar to that of the program in Listing 11-7, so we're not running the program and showing the sample output again.

Make sure you take a closer look at the syntax for try-with-resources block.

```java
try(Scanner consoleScanner = new Scanner(System.in)) {
```

In this statement, you have acquired the resources inside the parenthesis after the try keyword, but before the try block. Also, in the example, you don't provide the finally block. The Java compiler will internally translate this try-with-resources block into a try-finally block (of course, the compiler will retain the catch blocks you provide). You can acquire multiple resources in the try-with-resources block; such resource acquisition statements should be separated by semicolons.

Can you provide try-with-resources statements without any explicit catch or finally blocks? Yes! Remember that a try block can be associated with a catch block, finally block, or both. A try-with-resources statement block gets expanded internally into a try-finally block. So, you can provide a try-with-resources statement without explicit catch or finally blocks. Listing 11-10 uses a try-with-resources statement without any explicit catch or finally blocks.

Listing 11-10. TryWithResources2.java

```java
import java.util.*;

class TryWithResources2 {
        public static void main(String [] args) {
                System.out.println("Type an integer in the console: ");
                try(Scanner consoleScanner = new Scanner(System.in)) {
                        System.out.println("You typed the integer value: " + consoleScanner.nextInt());
                }
        }
}
```

Although it is possible to create a try-with-resources statement without any explicit catch or finally, it doesn't mean you should do so! For example, since this code does not have a catch block, if you type some invalid input, the program will crash.

```
D:\> java TryWithResources1
Type an integer in the console:
ten
Exception in thread "main" java.util.InputMismatchException
        at java.util.Scanner.throwFor(Scanner.java:909)
        at java.util.Scanner.next(Scanner.java:1530)
        at java.util.Scanner.nextInt(Scanner.java:2160)
        at java.util.Scanner.nextInt(Scanner.java:2119)
        at TryWithResources1.main(TryWithResources1.java:7)
```

So, the benefit of a try-with-resources statement is that it simplifies your life by not having to provide finally blocks explicitly. However, you still need to provide necessary catch blocks.

Note that for a resource to be usable with a try-with-resources statement, the class of that resource must implement the java.lang.AutoCloseable interface. This interface declares one single method named close(). You already know that the try-with-resources feature was added in Java 7. This AutoCloseable interface was also introduced in Java 7, and the interface is made of the base interface of the Closeable interface. This is to make sure that the existing resource classes work seamlessly with a try-with-resources statement. In other words, you can use all old stream classes with try-with-resources because they implement the AutoCloseable interface.

Closing Multiple Resources

You can use more than one resource in a try-with-resources statement. Here is a code snippet for creating a zip file from a given text file that makes use of a try-with-resources statement:

```
// buffer is the temporary byte buffer used for copying data from one stream to another stream
byte [] buffer = new byte[1024];

// these stream constructors can throw FileNotFoundException
try (ZipOutputStream zipFile = new ZipOutputStream(new FileOutputStream(zipFileName));
        FileInputStream fileIn = new FileInputStream(fileName)) {
        zipFile.putNextEntry(new ZipEntry(fileName));             // putNextEntry can throw
                                                                  // IOException
        int lenRead = 0; // the variable to keep track of number of bytes sucessfully read
        // copy the contents of the input file into the zip file
        while((lenRead = fileIn.read(buffer)) > 0) {             // read can throw IOException
                zipFile.write(buffer, 0, lenRead);               // write can throw IOException
        }
        // the streams will be closed automatically because they are within try-with-
        // resources statement
}
```

In this code, the buffer is a byte array. This array is temporary storage useful for copying raw data from one stream to another stream. In the try-with-resources statement, you open two streams: ZipOutputStream for writing to the zip file and FileInputStream for reading in the text file. (Note: API support for zip (and jar) files is available in java.util.zip library.) You want to read the input text file, zip it, and put that entry in the zip file. For putting a file/directory entry into the zip file, the ZipOutputStream class provides a method named putNextEntry(), which takes a ZipEntry object as an argument. The statement zipFile.putNextEntry(new ZipEntry(fileName)); puts a file entry named fileName into the zipFile.

For reading the contents of the text file, you use the read() method in the FileInputStream class. The read() method takes the buffer array as the argument. The amount of data to read per iteration (i.e., "data chunk size" to read) is given by the size of the passed array; it is 1024 bytes in this code. The read() method returns the number of bytes it read, and if there is no more data to read, it returns –1. The while loop checks if read succeeded (using the > 0 condition) before writing it to the zip file.

For writing data to the zip file, you use the write() method in the ZipOutputStream class. The write() method takes three arguments: the first argument is the data buffer; the second argument is start offset in the data buffer (which is 0 because you always read from the start of the buffer); and the third is the number of bytes to be written.

Now we come to the main discussion. Note how you open two resources in the try block and these two resource acquisition statements are separated by semicolons. You do not have an explicit finally block to release the resources because the compiler will automatically insert calls to the close methods for these two streams in the finally block(s).

Listing 11-11 is the complete program that makes use of this code segment to illustrate the use of try-with-resources statement for auto-closing multiple streams.

Listing 11-11. ZipTextFile.java

```java
import java.util.*;
import java.util.zip.*;
import java.io.*;

// class ZipTextFile takes the name of a text file as input and creates a zip file
// after compressing that text file.

class ZipTextFile {
        public static final int CHUNK = 1024; // to help copy chunks of 1KB
        public static void main(String []args) {
                if(args.length == 0) {
                        System.out.println("Pass the name of the file in the current directory to be
                        zipped as an argument");
                        System.exit(-1);
                }

                String fileName = args[0];
                // name of the zip file is the input file name with the suffix ".zip"
                String zipFileName = fileName + ".zip";

                byte [] buffer = new byte[CHUNK];
                // these constructors can throw FileNotFoundException
                try (ZipOutputStream zipFile = new ZipOutputStream(new FileOutputStream(zipFileName));
                FileInputStream fileIn = new FileInputStream(fileName)) {
                        // putNextEntry can throw IOException
                        zipFile.putNextEntry(new ZipEntry(fileName));
                        int lenRead = 0; // variable to keep track of number of bytes
                                        // successfully read
                        // copy the contents of the input file into the zip file
                        while((lenRead = fileIn.read(buffer)) > 0) {
                                // both read and write methods can throw IOException
                                zipFile.write (buffer, 0, lenRead);
                        }
```

```
                    // the streams will be closed automatically because they are
                    // within try-with-resources statement
            }
            // this can result in multiple exceptions thrown from the try block;
            // use "suppressed exceptions" to get the exceptions that were suppressed!
            catch(Exception e) {
                    System.out.println("The caught exception is: " + e);
                    System.out.print("The suppressed exceptions are: ");
                    for(Throwable suppressed : e.getSuppressed()) {
                            System.out.println(suppressed);
                    }
            }
        }
    }
}
```

We've already discussed the try-with-resources block part. What we have not discussed is *suppressed exceptions*. In a try-with-resources statement, there might be more than one exception that could get thrown; for example, one within the try block, one within the catch block, and another one within the finally block. However, only one exception can be caught, so the other exception(s) will be listed as suppressed exceptions. From a given exception object, you can use the method getSuppressed() to get the list of suppressed exceptions.

Points to Remember

Here are some interesting points about try-with-resources statement that will help you in the OCPJP 7 exam:

- You cannot assign to the resource variables declared in the try-with-resources within the body of the try-with-resources statement. This is to make sure that the same resources acquired in the try-with-resources header are released in the finally block.

- It is a common mistake to close a resource explicitly inside the try-with-resources statement. Remember that try-with-resources expands to calling the close() method in the finally block, so the expanded code will have a double call to the close() method. Consider the following code:

```
try(Scanner consoleScanner = new Scanner(System.in)) {
        System.out.println("You typed the integer value: " + consoleScanner.nextInt());
        consoleScanner.close();
        // explicit call to close() method - remember that try-with-resources
        // statement will also expand to calling close() in finally method;
        // hence this will result in call to close() method in Scanner twice!
}
```

The documentation of the close() method in the Scanner class says that if the scanner object is already closed, then invoking the method again will have no effect. So, you are safe in this case. However, in general, you cannot expect all the resources to have implemented a close() method that is safe to call twice. So, it is a bad practice to explicitly call the close() method inside a try-with-resource statement.

Exception Types

Until now, we have focused on explaining the language constructs related to exceptions: the try, catch, multi-catch, finally, and try-with-resources blocks. Some concepts won't be clear to you yet. For example, you learned the throws clause where you declare that a method can throw certain exceptions. You saw that for some types of exceptions, you don't need to declare them in the throws clause, but for certain other kinds of exceptions, you can declare them in the throws clause. Why? What are these different kinds of exceptions? To answer these questions and get a better idea about the exception handling support in the Java library, we'll discuss types of exceptions in this section.

In Java, you cannot throw any primitive types as exception objects. This does not mean that you can throw any reference type objects as exceptions. The thrown object should be an instance of the class Throwable or one of its subclasses: Throwable is the apex class of the exception hierarchy in Java. Exception handling constructs such as the throw statement, throws clause, and catch clause deal only with Throwable and its subclasses. There are three important subclasses of Throwable that you need to learn in detail: the Error, Exception, and RuntimeException classes. Figure 11-2 provides a high-level overview of these classes.

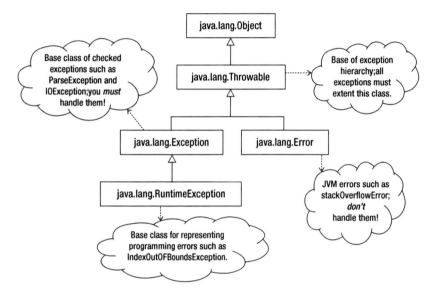

Figure 11-2. *Java's exception hierarchy*

The Exception Class

Exceptions of type Exception are known as *checked exceptions*. If code can throw an Exception, you must handle it using a catch block or declare that the method throws that exception, forcing the caller of that method to handle that exception. Consider Listing 11-12.

Listing 11-12. CheckedExceptionExample1.java

```java
import java.io.*;

class CheckedExceptionExample1 {
        public static void main(String []args) {
                FileInputStream fis = new FileInputStream(args[0]);
        }
}
```

This program results in a compiler error.

```
CheckedExceptionExample1.java:5: error: unreported exception FileNotFoundException; must be caught
or declared to be thrown
                FileInputStream fis = new FileInputStream(args[0]);
                                      ^

1 error
```

The constructor of `FileInputStream` declares that it throws the exception `FileNotFoundException`. This `FileNotFoundException` is derived from the `Exception` class, hence is a checked exception. With checked exceptions, Java forces you to think about failure conditions and how to handle them. Now, think about the code in Listing 11-13: you are trying to open the file given by the string `args[0]`, which may not be present. If you don't want to catch and handle the `FileNotFoundException`, you can declare the `main()` method to throw this exception.

Listing 11-13. CheckedExceptionExample2.java

```java
import java.io.*;

class CheckedExceptionExample2 {
        public static void main(String []args) throws FileNotFoundException {
                FileInputStream fis = new FileInputStream(args[0]);
        }
}
```

This program will compile fine without any errors. However, this code is still not satisfactory: if you pass the name of a file in the command line that does not exist in the search path, the program will crash after throwing this exception:

```
D:\ > java CheckedExceptionExample2 somefile.txt
Exception in thread "main" java.io.FileNotFoundException: somefile.txt (The system cannot find the
file specified)
        at java.io.FileInputStream.open(Native Method)
        at java.io.FileInputStream.<init>(FileInputStream.java:138)
        at java.io.FileInputStream.<init>(FileInputStream.java:97)
        at CheckedExceptionExample2.main(CheckedExceptionExample2.java:5)
```

A better way to handle the situation is to throw an error message to the user and inform her that she has to pass the file name as the first argument to the program, as in Listing 11-14.

Listing 11-14. CheckedExceptionExample3.java

```java
import java.io.*;

class CheckedExceptionExample3 {
        public static void main(String []args) {
                try {
                        FileInputStream fis = new FileInputStream(args[0]);
                } catch(FileNotFoundException fnfe) {
                        System.out.println("Error: There is no file that exists with name "
                        + args[0]);
                        System.out.println("Pass a valid file name as commandline argument!");
                }
        }
}
```

Now, when passed with a name of the file that does not exist, the program will terminate and show this useful error message to the user:

```
D:\ > java CheckedExceptionExample3 somefile.txt
Error: There is no file that exists with name somefile.txt
Pass a valid file name as commandline argument!
```

 If you have some code that can throw a checked exception from a method, you can choose between the two alternatives. You can either handle that exception by providing a catch block or declare that method to throw that exception. If you don't catch or declare the method to throw that exception, your code won't compile.

Table 11-1 summarizes the important subclasses of the Exception class.

Table 11-1. *Important Subclasses of the Exception Class*

Class	Short Description
CloneNotSupportedException	Thrown when the clone() method is invoked on an object whose class does not implement a Cloneable interface.
IOException	Thrown when an Input/Output operation fails (say because of an interrupted call).
EOFException	Thrown when end-of-file (EOF) is reached unexpectedly; subclass of IOException.
FileNotFoundException	Thrown when the runtime is not able to locate or open the given file; derived class of IOException.
ReflectiveOperationException	Thrown when a reflection operation fails; superclass of reflection related exceptions such as NoSuchMethodException and InvocationTargetException.
RuntimeException	Superclass of unchecked exceptions (discussed in the next section in this chapter).
SQLException	Thrown when a database access or related operations fail; superclass of database-related exceptions such as SerialException.
ParseException	Thrown when the parsing fails (for example, while processing locale-sensitive information such as dates and times in the Format class).

The RuntimeException Class

RuntimeException is a derived class of the Exception class. The exceptions deriving from this class are known as *unchecked exceptions*. Let's first discuss an example of a RuntimeException. Recollect Listing 11-14 in the context of FileNotFoundException (we've renamed the class in Listing 11-15).

Listing 11-15. UnCheckedExceptionExample1.java

```java
import java.io.*;

class UnCheckedExceptionExample1 {
    public static void main(String []args) throws FileNotFoundException {
        FileInputStream fis = new FileInputStream(args[0]);
    }
}
```

What happens if you run the program without passing any arguments to this program? It will crash after throwing an ArrayIndexOutOfBoundsException.

```
Exception in thread "main" java.lang.ArrayIndexOutOfBoundsException: 0
        at UnCheckedExceptionExample1.main(UnCheckedExceptionExample1.java:5)
```

In this program, without checking the length of args (to see if it contains any values), you attempt indexing args in the expression args[0]. In other words, you assume that the user will always provide the name of the file to open as a command-line argument, and when no argument is provided, it becomes an exceptional condition. Hence, it is a programming mistake. Note that though the expression args[0] can throw ArrayIndexOutOfBoundsException, you did not catch this exception or declare it in the throws clause of the main() method. This is because ArrayIndexOutOfBoundsException is a RuntimeException, so it is an unchecked exception.

 It is optional to handle unchecked exceptions. If a code segment you write in a method can throw an unchecked exception, it is not mandatory to catch that exception or declare that exception in the throws clause of that method.

How can you fix the problem in Listing 11-15? How about the following change in the program to handle the ArrayIndexOutOfBoundsException (shown in Listing 11-16)?

Listing 11-16. UnCheckedExceptionExample2.java

```java
import java.io.*;

class UnCheckedExceptionExample2 {
    public static void main(String []args) throws FileNotFoundException {
        try {
            FileInputStream fis = new FileInputStream(args[0]);
        } catch (ArrayIndexOutOfBoundsException aioobe) {
            System.out.println("Error: No arguments passed in the commandline!");
            System.out.println("Pass the name of the file to open as commandline argument");
        }
    }
}
```

When run, this program prints the following:

```
D:\> java UnCheckedExceptionExample2
Error: No arguments passed in the commandline!
Pass the name of the file to open as commandline argument
```

Yes, showing the error message and telling the user the right thing to do is good. However, this approach of catching a runtime exception such as ArrayIndexOutOfBoundsException is a *bad practice*! Why? Runtime exceptions such as ArrayIndexOutOfBoundsException indicate likely *programming errors,* and you should fix the code instead of catching and handling the exceptions. So, how do you fix the program here? You can check the length of args before attempting to access the array member (see Listing 11-17).

Listing 11-17. UnCheckedExceptionExample3.java

```java
import java.io.*;

class UnCheckedExceptionExample3 {
    public static void main(String []args) throws FileNotFoundException {
        // if any argument is passed, it would be greater than or equal to one
        if(args.length >= 1) {
            FileInputStream fis = new FileInputStream(args[0]);
        } else {
            System.out.println("Error: No arguments passed in the commandline!");
            System.out.println("Pass the name of the file to open as commandline
            argument");
        }
    }
}
```

The output is the same if no argument is passed to the program, but the code is better: it checks if it is possible to perform array indexing before actually indexing the array and thus is programmed defensively.

 It is a good practice to perform defensive checks and avoid raising unnecessary runtime exceptions.

Table 11-2 summarizes the important subclasses of the RuntimeException class.

Table 11-2. Important Subclasses of the RuntimeException Class

Class	Short Description
ArithmeticException	Thrown when arithmetic errors occur, such as attempting to divide by zero.
BufferOverflowException, BufferUnderflowException	Thrown for an attempt to write beyond a buffer's limits.
ClassCastException	Thrown when an attempt is made to cast between incompatible types (such as String to Integer type or vice versa).
NegativeArraySizeException	Thrown when an attempt is made to create an array of negative size.
NoSuchElementException	Thrown when an attempt is made to use the nextElement() method on an Enumeration when no more values exist to access.
NullPointerException	When an attempt is made to de-reference through a null reference.
UnsupportedOperationException	Thrown when an attempt is made to apply an operation that is not supported or that does not exist (for example, attempting to write to a read-only file system will result in throwing a ReadOnlyFileSystemException, which is a derived class of this exception).
IllegalArgumentException	Thrown when an incorrect or inappropriate argument is passed to a method.
IndexOutOfBoundsException	Thrown when an attempt is made to access the data structure using an index value that is not within the permissible range; base class of ArrayIndexOutOfBoundsException and StringIndexOutOfBoundsException.

The Error Class

When the JVM detects a serious abnormal condition in the program, it raises an exception of type Error. When you get an exception of Error or its subtypes, the exception is not meant for you to handle. The best course of action is to let the program crash! Why? Let's discuss a trivial example to understand this.

Assume that you try to run a program that does not exist! For example, consider the UnCheckedExceptionExample3 class that you saw in Listing 11-16; if you make a mistake in the capitalization of the class name and try to invoke it, you'll get NoClassDefFoundError.

```
D:\ > java UncheckedExceptionExample3
Exception in thread "main" java.lang.NoClassDefFoundError: UncheckedExceptionExample3 (wrong name:
UnCheckedExceptionExample3)
        at java.lang.ClassLoader.defineClass1(Native Method)
        at java.lang.ClassLoader.defineClass(ClassLoader.java:791)
        at java.security.SecureClassLoader.defineClass(SecureClassLoader.java:142)
        at java.net.URLClassLoader.defineClass(URLClassLoader.java:449)
        at java.net.URLClassLoader.access$100(URLClassLoader.java:71)
        at java.net.URLClassLoader$1.run(URLClassLoader.java:361)
        at java.net.URLClassLoader$1.run(URLClassLoader.java:355)
        at java.security.AccessController.doPrivileged(Native Method)
        at java.net.URLClassLoader.findClass(URLClassLoader.java:354)
        at java.lang.ClassLoader.loadClass(ClassLoader.java:423)
        at sun.misc.Launcher$AppClassLoader.loadClass(Launcher.java:308)
        at java.lang.ClassLoader.loadClass(ClassLoader.java:356)
        at sun.launcher.LauncherHelper.checkAndLoadMain(LauncherHelper.java:480)
```

As the helpful part of the stack trace indicates ("wrong name: UnCheckedExceptionExample3"), you have given a class to load that does not exist by the given name (note that names in Java are case-sensitive). So, the JVM responded with a NoClassDefFoundError.

Let's consider a programming example to understand how an error could occur. Assume that you're writing a recursive method to calculate the factorial of a number and forget to put in the right termination condition (see Listing 11-18).

Listing 11-18. NonTerminatingRecursion.java

```java
class NonTerminatingRecursion {
        // factorial is a recursive call
        static int factorial(int n) {
                int result = 0;
                // Assume that the following termination condition statement is missing ...
                // if(n == 0) return 1;
                result = factorial(n - 1) * n;
                return result;
        }
        public static void main(String ... args) {
                System.out.println("factorial of 4 is: " + factorial(4));
        }
}
```

When run, this program crashes after throwing this exception:

```
Exception in thread "main" java.lang.StackOverflowError
        at NonTerminatingRecursion.factorial(NonTerminatingResursion.java:7)
        at NonTerminatingRecursion.factorial(NonTerminatingResursion.java:7)
        [... this at "NonTerminatingRecursion.factorial(NonTerminatingResursion.java:7)" is repeated
        a large number of times...]
```

For each method call, the JVM creates a runtime structure called a *stack frame* in its stack area. Since the recursive call, the JVM keeps creating such stack frames, and after some time, it exhausts the stack area. At this point, the JVM cannot continue its execution, so it throws the StackOverflowError. When you get a StackOverflowError, you can almost be sure that it is a programming error that caused this exception. You need to fix the program to avoid raising this exception.

 Exceptions of type Error indicate an abnormal condition in the program. There is no point in catching this exception and trying to continue execution and pretending nothing has happened. It is a *really* bad practice to do so!

Table 11-3 provides a list of important subclasses of the Error class.

Table 11-3. Important Subclasses of the Error Class

Class	Short Description
AssertionError	Thrown when an assertion fails (discussed later in this chapter).
IOError	Thrown when a serious I/O error occurs.
VirtualMachineError	Thrown when the JVM itself enters an erroneous state (due to a bug) or when the JVM runs out of resources (such as memory).
OutOfMemoryError	Thrown when the JVM cannot allocate memory anymore; a derived class of VirtualMachineError.
LinkageError	Thrown when the linking performed by the JVM fails (for example, due to a circular class hierarchy in which case the ClassCircularityError will be thrown, which is a derived class of LinkageError).
NoClassDefFoundError	Thrown when attempting to load the definition of a class when the class loader cannot find that class.
StackOverflowError	Thrown when the application has a non-terminating recursive call, or when the application makes too many function calls that the JVM cannot handle; a derived class of VirtualMachineError.

The Throws Clause

A method can throw checked exceptions; the clause throws specifies these checked exceptions in the method signature. You had a brief look at the throws keyword in the beginning of this chapter. In the throws clause, you list *checked exceptions* that a method can throw, so understanding checked exceptions is prerequisite for understanding the throws clause. Since we've covered checked exceptions in the previous section on exception types, we'll cover the throws clause now.

Let's try reading an integer stored in a file named integer.txt in the current directory. There is an overloaded constructor of the Scanner class that takes a File object as input, so let's try using it. Listing 11-19 shows the program. Will it work?

Listing 11-19. ThrowsClause1.java

```java
import java.io.*;
import java.util.*;

class ThrowsClause1 {
        public static void main(String []args) {
                System.out.println("Reading an integer from the file 'integer.txt': ");
                Scanner consoleScanner = new Scanner(new File("integer.txt"));
                System.out.println("You typed the integer value: " + consoleScanner.nextInt());
        }
}
```

This code will result in a compiler error of "unreported exception FileNotFoundException; must be caught or declared to be thrown." If you look at the declaration of this Scanner method, you'll see a throws clause:

```java
public Scanner(File source) throws FileNotFoundException {
```

So, any method that invokes this constructor should either handle this exception or add a throws clause to declare that the method can throw this exception. Add a throws clause to the main() method; see Listing 11-20.

Listing 11-20. ThrowsClause2.java

```
import java.io.*;
import java.util.*;

class ThrowsClause2 {
        public static void main(String []args) throws FileNotFoundException {
                System.out.println("Reading an integer from the file 'integer.txt': ");
                Scanner consoleScanner = new Scanner(new File("integer.txt"));
                System.out.println("You typed the integer value: " + consoleScanner.nextInt());
        }
}
```

If you run this program and there is no file named integer.txt, the program will crash after throwing this exception:

```
Reading an integer from the file 'integer.txt':
Exception in thread "main" java.io.FileNotFoundException: integer.txt (The system cannot find the
file specified)
        at java.io.FileInputStream.open(Native Method)
        at java.io.FileInputStream.<init>(FileInputStream.java:138)
        at java.util.Scanner.<init>(Scanner.java:656)
        at ThrowsClause2.main(ThrowsClause2.java:7)
```

Let's now extract the code inside the main() method to a new method named readIntFromFile(). You have defined it as an instance method, so you also create an object of the ThrowsClause3 class to invoke this method from the main() method. Since the code inside readIntFromFile() can throw a FileNotFoundException, it has to either introduce a catch handler to handle this exception or declare this exception in its throws clause (see Listing 11-21).

Listing 11-21. ThrowsClause3.java

```
import java.io.*;
import java.util.*;

class ThrowsClause3 {
        // since this method does not handle FileNotFoundException,
        // the method must declare this exception in the throws clause
        public int readIntFromFile() throws FileNotFoundException {
                Scanner consoleScanner = new Scanner(new File("integer.txt"));
                return consoleScanner.nextInt();
        }

        // since readIntFromFile() throws FileNotFoundException and main() does not handle
        // it, the main() method declares this exception in its throws cause
        public static void main(String []args) throws FileNotFoundException {
                System.out.println("Reading an integer from the file 'integer.txt': ");
                System.out.println("You typed the integer value: " +
                new ThrowsClause3().readIntFromFile());
        }
}
```

The behavior of the program remains the same in both Listings 11-20 and 11-21. However, Listing 11-21 shows how the main() method also must still declare to throw the FileNotFoundException in its throws clause (otherwise, the program will not compile).

Method Overriding and the Throws Clause

When an overridable method has a throws clause, there are many things to consider while overriding that method. Consider the program in Listing 11-22, which implements an interface named IntReader. This interface declares a single method named readIntFromFile() with the throws clause listing a FileNotFoundException.

Listing 11-22. ThrowsClause4.java

```java
import java.io.*;
import java.util.*;

// This interface is meant for implemented by classes that would read an integer from a file
interface IntReader {
        int readIntFromFile() throws IOException;
}

class ThrowsClause4 implements IntReader {
        // implement readIntFromFile with the same throws clause
        // or a more general throws clause
        public int readIntFromFile() throws FileNotFoundException {
                Scanner consoleScanner = new Scanner(new File("integer.txt"));
                return consoleScanner.nextInt();
        }
        // main method elided in this code since the focus here is to understand
        // issues related to overriding when throws clause is present
}
```

In this code, you can observe few important facts. First, you can declare the throws clause for methods declared in interfaces; in fact, you can provide the throws clause for abstract methods declared in abstract classes as well. Second, the method declared in the IntReader interface declares to throw IOException, which is a more general exception than a FileNotFoundException (Figure 11-3). While implementing a method, it is acceptable to either provide the throws clause listing the same exception type as the base method or a more specific type than the base method. In this case, the readIntFromFile() method lists a more specific exception (FileNotFoundException) in its throws clause against the more general exception of IOException listed in the throws clause of the base method declared in the IntReader interface.

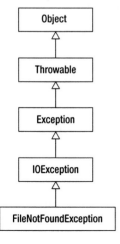

Figure 11-3. Class hierarchy of FileNotFoundException

What if you try changing the throws clause? There are many ways to change the throws clause in the overriding method, including the following:

    a.   Not providing any throws clause.

    b.   Listing more general checked exceptions to throw.

    c.   Listing more checked exceptions in addition to the given checked exception(s) in the base method.

If you attempt any of these three cases, you'll get a compiler error. For example, try not providing the throws clause in the `readIntFromFile()` method in the class that implements the `IntReader` interface.

```
public int readIntFromFile() {
        Scanner consoleScanner = new Scanner(new File("integer.txt"));
        return consoleScanner.nextInt();
}
```

You'll get this compiler error: "unreported exception FileNotFoundException; must be caught or declared to be thrown."

To summarize, the base class method's throws clause is a contract that it provides to the caller of that method: it says that the caller should handle the listed exceptions or declare those exceptions in its throws clause. When overriding the base method, the derived method should also adhere to that contract. The caller of the base method is prepared to handle only the exceptions listed in the base method, so the overriding method cannot throw more general or other than the listed checked exceptions.

However, note that this discussion that the derived class method's throws clause should follow the contract for the base method's throws clause is limited to checked exceptions. Unchecked exceptions can still be added or removed from the contract when compared to the base class method's throws clause. For example, consider the following:

```
public int readIntFromFile() throws IOException, NoSuchElementException {
        Scanner consoleScanner = new Scanner(new File("integer.txt"));
        return consoleScanner.nextInt();
}
```

This is an acceptable throws clause since `NoSuchElementException` can get thrown from the `readIntFromFile()` method. This exception is an unchecked exception, and it gets thrown when the `nextInt()` method could not read an integer from the file. This is a common situation, for example, if you have an empty file named `integer.txt`; an attempt to read an integer from this file will result in this exception.

Points to Remember

Here are some noteworthy points about the throws statement that could help you in the OCPJP 7 exam:

- If a method does not have a throws clause, it does *not* mean it cannot throw any exceptions; it just means it cannot throw any *checked* exceptions.

- It is a good practice to use the `@throws` JavaDoc tag to document the specific situations or cases in which an exception (both checked and unchecked) might be thrown from the method.

- It is a bad practice to use a throws clause to list unchecked exceptions that a method may throw. Why? Since the compiler cannot force the callers to handle unchecked exceptions, it does not make sense to list them in the throws clause. Rather, if a method can throw an unchecked exception, it is better to use the `@throws` clause to document that possibility.

- Static initialization blocks cannot throw any checked exceptions. Why? Remember that static initialization blocks are invoked when the class is loaded, so there is no way to handle the thrown exceptions in the caller. Further, there is no way to declare the checked exceptions in a throws clause.

- Non-static initialization blocks can throw checked exceptions; however, all the constructors should declare those exceptions in their throws clause. Why? The compiler merges the code for non-static initialization blocks and constructors during its code generation phase, hence the throws clause of the constructor can be used for declaring the checked exceptions that a non-static initialization block can throw.

- An overriding method cannot declare more exceptions in the throws clause than the list of exceptions declared in the throws clause of the base method. Why? The callers of the base method see only the list of the exceptions given in the throws clause of that method and will declare or handle these checked exceptions in their code (and not more than that).

- An overriding method can declare more specific exceptions than the exception(s) listed in the throws clause of the base method; in other words, you can declare derived exceptions in the throws clause of the overriding method.

- If a method is declared in two or more interfaces, and if that method declares to throw different exceptions in the throws clause, the implementation should list all of these exceptions.

Custom Exceptions

In most situations, it will be sufficient to throw exceptions that are already provided in the Java library. For example, if you're checking for the validity of the arguments passed to a public function, and you find them to be null or out of expected range, you can throw an IllegalArgumentException. However, for most non-trivial applications, it will be necessary for you to develop your own exception classes (custom exceptions) to indicate exceptional conditions.

How do you define a custom exception? There are two options: you can extend either the Exception or RuntimeException class depending on your need. If you want to force the users of your custom exception to handle the exception, then you can extend your exception class from the Exception class, which will make your custom exception a checked exception. If you want to give flexibility to the users of your custom exception, and leave it to the users of your exception to decide if they want to handle the exception or not, you can derive your exception from the RuntimeException class. So it is a design choice that you make to choose the base class of your custom exception. How about extending the Throwable or Error class for custom exceptions? The Throwable class is too generic to make it the base class of your exception, so it is not recommended. The Error class is reserved for fatal exceptions that the JVM can throw (such as StackOverflowError), so it is not advisable to make this the base class of your exception.

 Custom exceptions should extend either the Exception or RuntimeException class. It is a bad practice to create custom exceptions by extending the Throwable or Error classes.

For extending from a base class, you need to see what methods the base class provides. In this case, you want to create a custom exception by extending the Exception or RuntimeException classes. Since the Exception class is the base class of the RuntimeException class, it is sufficient to know the members of the Exception class. Table 11-4 lists the important methods (including constructors) of the Exception class.

Table 11-4. *Important Methods and Constructors of the Exception Class*

Member	Short description
Exception()	Default constructor of the Exception class with no additional (or detailed) information on the exception.
Exception(String)	Constructor that takes a detailed information string about the constructor as an argument.
Exception(String, Throwable)	In addition to a detailed information string as an argument, this exception constructor takes the cause of the exception (which is another exception) as an argument.
Exception(Throwable)	Constructor that takes the cause of the exception as an argument.
String getMessage()	Returns the detailed message (passed as a string when the exception was created).
Throwable getCause()	Returns the cause of the exception (if any, or else returns null).
Throwable[] getSuppressed()	Returns the list of suppressed exceptions (typically caused when using a try-with-resources statement) as an array.
void printStackTrace()	Prints the stack trace (i.e., the list of method calls with relevant line numbers) to the console (standard error stream). If the cause of an exception (which is another exception object) is available in the exception, then that information will also be printed. Further, if there are any suppressed exceptions, they are also printed.

For illustrating how to create your own exception classes, assume that you want to create a custom exception named InvalidInputException. When you try to read input (read an integer, in this case), and if it fails, you want to throw this InvalidInputException. Listing 11-23 defines this exception class by extending the RuntimeException class.

Listing 11-23. InvalidInputException.java

```java
// a custom "unchecked exception" that is meant to be thrown
// when the input provided by the user is invalid
class InvalidInputException extends RuntimeException {
        // default constructor
        public InvalidInputException() {
                super();
        }

        // constructor that takes the String detailed information we pass while
        // raising an exception
        public InvalidInputException(String str) {
                super(str);
        }

        // constructor that remembers the cause of the exception and
        // throws the new exception
        public InvalidInputException(Throwable originalException) {
                super(originalException);
        }
```

```
            // first argument takes detailed information string created while
            // raising an exception
            // and the second argument is to remember the cause of the exception
            public InvalidInputException(String str, Throwable originalException) {
                    super(str, originalException);
            }
}
```

In this InvalidInputException class, you did not introduce any new fields but you can add any fields if necessary. This is also a simple custom exception where the constructors simply call the base class versions of the same constructor type. The class CustomExceptionTest (see Listing 11-24) shows how to make use of this custom exception.

Listing 11-24. InvalidInputException.java

```
import java.util.*;

// class for testing the custom exception InvalidInputException
class CustomExceptionTest {
        public static int readIntFromConsole() {
                Scanner consoleScanner = new Scanner(System.in);
                int typedInt = 0;
                try {
                        typedInt = consoleScanner.nextInt();
                } catch(NoSuchElementException nsee) {
                        System.out.println("Wrapping up the exception and throwing it...");
                        throw new InvalidInputException("Invalid integer input typed in console", nsee);
                } catch(Exception e) {
                        // call all other exceptions here ...
                        System.out.println("Error: Encountered an exception and could not read
                        an integer from the console... ");
                }
                return typedInt;
        }
        public static void main(String [] args) {
                System.out.println("Type an integer in the console: ");
                try {
                        System.out.println("You typed the integer value: " + readIntFromConsole());
                } catch(InvalidInputException iie) {
                        System.out.println("Error: Invalid input in console... ");
                        System.out.println("The current caught exception is of type: " + iie);
                        System.out.println("The originally caught exception is of type: " +
                        iie.getCause());
                }
        }
}
```

First compile and run this program before reading the discussion of the code.

```
D:\> java CustomExceptionTest
Type an integer in the console:
one
Wrapping up the exception and throwing it...
Error: Invalid input in console...
The current caught exception is of type: InvalidInputException: Invalid integer input typed in
console
The originally caught exception is of type: java.util.InputMismatchException
```

In this code, you use InvalidInputException just like any other exception already defined in the Java library. You are catching the InvalidInputException thrown from the readIntFromConsole() method in the main() method. The following statement invokes the toString() method of the InvalidInputException:

```
System.out.println("The current caught exception is of type: " + iie);
```

You did not override the toString() method, so the InvalidInputException class inherits the default implementation of the toString() method from the RuntimeException base class. This default toString() method prints the name of the exception thrown (InvalidInputException) and it also includes the detailed information string ("Invalid integer input typed in console") that you passed while creating the exception object. The last statement in the main() method is to get the cause of the exception.

```
System.out.println("The originally caught exception is of type: " + iie.getCause());
```

Since the cause of InvalidInputException is InputMismatchException, this exception name is printed in the console as a fully qualified name, java.util.InputMismatchException. You can think of InputMismatchException *causing* InvalidInputException; these two exceptions are known as *chained exceptions.*

Assertions

When creating application programs, you assume many things. However, often it happens that the assumptions don't hold, resulting in an erroneous condition. The assert statement is used to check or test your assumptions about the program.

The keyword assert provides support for assertions in Java. Each assertion statement contains a Boolean expression. If the result of the Boolean expression is true, it means the assumption is true, nothing happens. However, if the Boolean result is false, then the assumption you had about the program holds no more, and an AssertionError is thrown. Remember that the Error class and its derived classes indicate serious runtime errors and are not meant to be handled. In the same way, if an AssertionError is thrown, the best course of action is not to catch the exception and to allow the program to terminate. After that, you need to examine why the assumption did not hold true and then fix the program.

There are many reasons why you should add assertions to the program. One reason is that it helps find the problems early; when you check your assumptions in the program, and when any of them fail, you immediately know where to look out for the problem and what to fix. Also, when other programmers read your code with assertions, they will be in a better position to understand the code because you are making your assumptions explicit using assertions.

Assert Statement

Assert statements in Java are of two forms:

```
assert booleanExpression;
```

```
assert booleanExpression : "Detailed error message string";
```

It is a compiler error if a non-Boolean expression is used within the assert statement. Listing 11-25 contains the first example for assertions.

Listing 11-25. AssertionExample1.java

```
class AssertionExample1 {
        public static void main(String []args) {
                int i = -10;
                if(i < 0) {
                        // if negative value, convert into positive value
                        i = -i;
                }
                System.out.println("the value of i is: " + i);
                // at this point the assumption is that i cannot be negative;
                // assert this condition since its an assumption that will always hold
                assert (i >= 0) : "impossible: i is negative!";
        }
}
```

In this program, you are checking if the value of i is < 0; you are using the expression -i to convert it to a positive value. Once the condition check if (i < 0) is completed, the value of i cannot be negative, or that is your assumption. Such assumptions can be asserted with an assert statement. Here is the assert statement:

```
assert (i >= 0) : "impossible: i is negative!";
```

The program will run fine if the Boolean expression (i >= 0) evaluates to true. However, if it evaluates to false, the program will crash by throwing an AssertionError. Let's check this behavior (you need to use the –ea flag to enable assertions at runtime; we will discuss more about this flag in a moment).

```
D:\>java -ea AssertionExample1
the value of i is: 10
```

Yes, this program executed successfully without throwing any exceptions.

Is there any value of i for which the condition will fail? Yes, there is! If the value of i is a minimum possible value of integer, then it cannot be converted into a positive value. Why? Remember that the range of integers is -2^{31} to $2^{31} - 1$, so the integer values the value of i as –2147483648 to 2147483647. In other words, the positive value 2147483648 is not in the range of integers. So, if the value of i is –2147483648, then the expression -i will *overflow* and again result in the value –2147483648. Thus, your assumption is not true.

In Listing 11-25, change the value of i to the minimum value of an integer, as in the following:

```
int i = Integer.MIN_VALUE;
```

Now, try running this program.

```
D:\> java -ea AssertionExample1
the value of i is: -2147483648
Exception in thread "main" java.lang.AssertionError: impossible: i is negative!
        at AssertionExample1.main(AssertionExample1.java:12)
```

In this output, note how the assertion failed. The application crashes because the program threw the AssertionError, and there is no handler, so the program terminates.

You saw that assertions are disabled at runtime; to enable assertions at runtime, use an -ea switch (or its longer form of -enableasserts). To disable assertions at runtime, use a -da switch. If assertions are disabled by default at runtime, then what is the use of -da switch? There are many uses. For example, if you want to enable assertions for all classes within a given package and want to disable asserts in a specific class in that package, then a -da switch is useful. Table 11-5 lists the important command-line arguments and their meaning. Note that you need not recompile your programs to enable or disable assertions; just use the command-line arguments when invoking the JVM to enable or disable them.

Table 11-5. *Important Command-Line Arguments for Enabling/Disabling Assertions*

Command-Line Argument	Short Description
-ea	Enables assertions by default (except system classes).
-ea:<class name>	Enables assertions for the given class name.
-ea:<package name>...	Enables assertions in all the members of the given package <package name>.
-ea:...	Enable assertions in the given unnamed package.
-esa	Short for -enablesystemsassertions; enables assertions in system classes. This option is rarely used.
-da	Disable assertions by default (except system classes).
-da:<class name>	Disable assertions for the given class name.
-ea:<package name>...	Disables assertions in all the members of the given package <package name>.
-da:...	Disable assertions in the given unnamed package.
-dsa	Short for -disablesystemsassertions; disables assertions in system classes. This option is rarely used.

How Not to Use Asserts

The key to understanding assertions is that they are useful for debugging and testing applications, and assertions are meant to be disabled when the application is deployed to end users.

- Don't use assertions for validating input values or for validating arguments to public methods. For signaling such runtime failures, use exceptions instead.

- Don't use assertions to check conditions that are required for the correct functioning of the application. Since assertions are disabled by default at runtime, the application will not function correctly when the asserted conditions are not present in the code.

- The Boolean expressions given inside assert statements should not have side effects—modifying variable values, printing values to console, etc. In other words, the functioning of the application should remain the same no matter if assertions are enabled or disabled.

QUESTION TIME!

1. Consider the following class hierarchy from the package `java.nio.file` and answer the question.

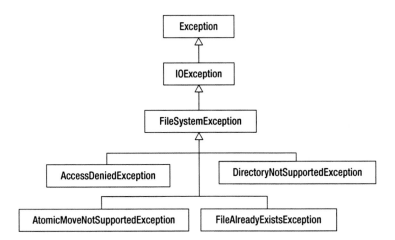

In the following class definitions, the base class `Base` has the method `foo()` that throws a `FileSystemException`; the derived class `Deri` extending the class `Base` overrides the `foo()` definition.

```
class Base {
        public void foo() throws FileSystemException {
                throw new FileSystemException("");
        }
}

class Deri extends Base {
        /* provide foo definition here */
}
```

Which of the following overriding definitions of the `foo()` method in the `Deri` class are compatible with the base class `foo()` method definition? Choose all the `foo()` method definitions that could compile without errors when put in the place of the comment: /* provide foo definition here */

A.
```
    public void foo() throws IOException {
            super.foo();
    }
```

B.
```
    public void foo() throws AccessDeniedException {
            throw new AccessDeniedException("");
    }
```

C.
```
public void foo() throws FileSystemException, RuntimeException {
        throw new NullPointerException();
}
```

D.
```
public void foo() throws Exception {
        throw new NullPointerException();
}
```

Answer: B and C.

(In option A and D, the throws clause declares to throw exceptions IOException and Exception respectively, which are more general than the FileSystemException, so they are not compatible with the base method definition. In option B, the foo() method declares to throw AccessDeniedException, which is more specific than FileSystemException, so it is compatible with the base definition of the foo() method. In option C, the throws clause declares to throw FileSystemException, which is the same as in the base definition of the foo() method. Additionally it declares to throw RuntimeException, which is not a checked exception, so the definition of the foo() method is compatible with the base definition of the foo() method).

2.   Consider the following program:

```
class ChainedException {
        public static void foo() {
                try {
                        throw new ArrayIndexOutOfBoundsException();
                } catch(ArrayIndexOutOfBoundsException oob) {
                        RuntimeException re = new RuntimeException(oob);
                        re.initCause(oob);
                        throw re;
                }
        }
        public static void main(String []args) {
                try {
                        foo();
                } catch(Exception re) {
                        System.out.println(re.getClass());
                }
        }
}
```

When executed, this program prints which of the following?

A.   class java.lang.RuntimeException

B.   class java.lang.IllegalStateException

C.   class java.lang.Exception

D.   class java.lang.ArrayIndexOutOfBoundsException

Answer: B. class java.lang.IllegalStateException

(In the expression new `RuntimeException(oob);`, the exception object `oob` is already chained to the `RuntimeException` object. The method `initCause()` cannot be called on an exception object that already has an exception object chained during the constructor call. Hence, the call `re.initCause(oob);` results in `initCause()` throwing an `IllegalStateException`.)

3.   Consider the following program:

```
class ExceptionTest {
        public static void foo() {
                try {
                        throw new ArrayIndexOutOfBoundsException();
                } catch(ArrayIndexOutOfBoundsException oob) {
                        throw new Exception(oob);
                }
        }
        public static void main(String []args) {
                try {
                        foo();
                } catch(Exception re) {
                        System.out.println(re.getCause());
                }
        }
}
```

Which one of the following options correctly describes the behavior of this program?

A.   java.lang.Exception

B.   java.lang.ArrayIndexOutOfBoundsException

C.   class java.lang.IllegalStateException

D.   This program fails with compiler error(s)

Answer: D. This program fails with compiler error(s)

(The foo() method catches `ArrayIndexOutOfBoundsException` and chains it to an `Exception` object. However, since `Exception` is a checked exception, it must be declared in the throws clause of foo(). Hence this program results in this compiler error:

```
ExceptionTest.java:6: error: unreported exception Exception; must be caught or declared to
be thrown
                        throw new Exception(oob);
                        ^
1 error)
```

4. Consider the following program:

```java
import java.io.*;
import java.sql.*;

class MultiCatch {
        public static void fooThrower() throws FileNotFoundException {
                throw new FileNotFoundException();
        }
        public static void barThrower() throws SQLException {
                throw new SQLException();
        }
        public static void main(String []args) {
                try {
                        fooThrower();
                        barThrower();
                } catch(FileNotFoundException || SQLException multie) {
                        System.out.println(multie);
                }
        }
}
```

Which one of the following options correctly describes the behavior of this program?

A. This program prints the following: java.io.FileNotFoundException.

B. This program prints the following: java.sql.SQLException.

C. This program prints the following: java.io.FileNotFoundException || java.sql.SQLException.

D. This program fails with compiler error(s).

Answer: D. This program fails with compiler error(s).

(For multi-catch blocks, the single pipe (|) symbol needs to be used and not double pipe (||), as provided in this program. Hence this program will fail with compiler error(s).)

5. Consider the following class hierarchy from the package javax.security.auth.login and answer the questions.

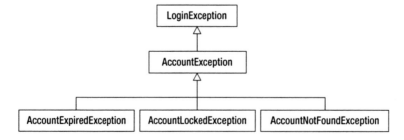

5.1. Which of the following handlers that makes use of multi-catch exception handler feature will compile without errors?

A. `catch (AccountException | LoginException exception)`

B. `catch (AccountException | AccountExpiredException exception)`

C. `catch (AccountExpiredException | AccountNotFoundException exception)`

D. `catch (AccountExpiredException exception1 | AccountNotFoundException exception2)`

Answer: C. `catch (AccountExpiredException | AccountNotFoundException exception)`

(For A and B, the base type handler is provided with the derived type handler, hence the multi-catch is incorrect. For D, the exception name exception1 is redundant and will result in a syntax error. C is the correct option and this will compile fine without errors).

5.2. Consider the following code segment, which makes use of this exception hierarchy:

```
try {
    LoginException le = new AccountNotFoundException();
    throw (Exception) le;
}
catch (AccountNotFoundException anfe) {
    System.out.println("In the handler of AccountNotFoundException");
}
catch (AccountException ae) {
    System.out.println("In the handler of AccountException");
}
catch (LoginException le) {
    System.out.println("In the handler of LoginException");
}
catch (Exception e) {
    System.out.println("In the handler of Exception");
}
```

When executed, which of the following statements will this code segment print?

A. In the handler of AccountNotFoundException

B. In the handler of AccountException

C. In the handler of LoginException

D. In the handler of Exception

Answer: A. In the handler of AccountNotFoundException

(In this code, the created type of the exception is `AccountNotFoundException`. Though the exception object is stored in the variable of type `LoginException` and then type-casted to `Exception`, the dynamic type of the exception remains the same, which is `AccountNotFoundException`. When looking for a catch handler, the Java runtime looks for the exact handler based on the dynamic type of the object. Since it is available immediately as the first handler, this exactly matching catch handler got executed.)

Summary

Introduction to Exception Handling

- When an exception is thrown from a try block, the JVM looks for a matching catch handler from the list of catch handlers in the method call-chain. If no matching handler is found, that unhandled exception will result in crashing the application.

- While providing multiple exception handlers (stacked catch handlers), specific exception handlers should be provided before general exception handlers. Providing base exception handlers before the derived handlers will result in a compiler error.

- You can programmatically access the stack trace using the methods such as printStackTrace() and getStackTrace(), which can be called on any exception object.

- A try block can have multiple catch handlers. If the cause of two or more exceptions is similar, and the handling code is also similar, you can consider combining the handlers and make it into a multi-catch block.

- The code inside a finally block will be executed irrespective of whether a try block has successfully executed or resulted in an exception. This makes a finally block the most suitable place to release resources, such as file handles, data base handles, network streams, etc.

Try-with-Resources

- Forgetting to release resources by explicitly calling the close() method is a common mistake. You can use a try-with-resources statement to simplify your code and auto-close resources. For a resource to be usable in a try-with-resources statement, the class of that resource must implement the java.lang.AutoCloseable interface and define the close() method.

- You can auto-close multiple resources within a try-with-resources statement. These resources need to be separated by semicolons in the try-with-resources statement header.

- Because you can use multiple resources within a try-with-resources statement, the possibility of more than one exception getting thrown from the try block and the finally block is high. If a try block throws an exception, and a finally block also throws exception(s), then the exceptions thrown in the finally block will be added as suppressed exceptions to the exception that gets thrown out of the try block to the caller.

Exception Types

- The class Throwable is the root class of the exception hierarchy. Only Throwable and its derived classes can be used with Java exception handling keywords such as try, catch, and throws.

- The Exception class (except its sub-hierarchy of the RuntimeException class) and its derived classes are known as *checked exceptions*. These exceptions represent exceptional conditions that can be *reasonably expected* to occur when the program executes, hence they must be handled. A method that contains some code segment that can throw a checked exception must either provide a catch handler to handle it or declare that exception in its throws clause.

- The `RuntimeException` and `Error` classes and derived classes are known as *unchecked exceptions*. They can be thrown anywhere in the program (without being declared that the segment of code can throw these exceptions).

- The `RuntimeException` classes and derived classes represent programming mistakes (logical mistakes) and are not *generally* expected to be caught and handled in the program. However, in some cases, it is meaningful to handle these exceptions in catch blocks.

- The `Error` classes and derived classes represent exceptions that arise because of JVM errors; either the JVM has detected a serious abnormal condition or has run out of resources. When an `Error` occurs, the *typical* best course of action is to terminate the program.

- A catch block should either handle the exception or rethrow it. To *hide* or *swallow* an exception by catching an exception and doing nothing is really a bad practice.

Throws Clause

- The throws clause for a method is meant for listing the *checked exceptions* that the method body can throw.

- Static initialization blocks cannot throw any checked exceptions. Non-static initialization blocks can throw checked exceptions; however, all the constructors should declare that exception in their throws clause.

- A method's throws clause is part of the contract that its overriding methods in derived classes should obey. An overriding method can provide the same throw clause as the base method's throws clause or a more specific throws clause than the base method's throws clause. The overriding method cannot provide a more general throws clause or declare to throw additional checked exceptions when compared to the base method's throws clause.

Custom Exceptions

- You can define your own exception classes (known as custom exceptions) in your programs.

- It is recommended that you derive custom exceptions from either the `Exception` or `RuntimeException` class. Creation of custom exceptions by extending the `Throwable` class (too generic) or the `Error` class (exceptions of this type are reserved for JVM and the Java APIs to throw) is not recommended.

- You can wrap one exception and throw it as another exception. These two exceptions become *chained exceptions*. From the thrown exception, you can get the cause of the exception.

Assertions

- Assertions are condition checks in the program and are meant to be used for explicitly checking the assumptions you make while writing programs.

- The `assert` statement is of two forms: one that takes a Boolean argument and one that takes an additional string argument.

- If the Boolean condition given in the assert argument fails (i.e., evaluates to false), the program will terminate after throwing an `AssertionError`. It is not advisable to catch and recover from when an `AssertionError` is thrown by the program.

- By default, assertions are disabled at runtime. You can use the command-line arguments of `-ea` (for enabling asserts) and `-da` (for disabling asserts) and their variants when you invoke the JVM.

CHAPTER 12

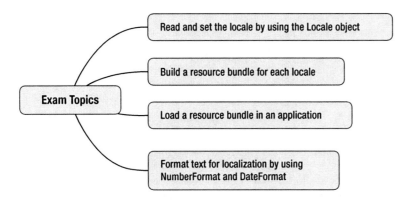

Localization

Exam Topics

- Read and set the locale by using the Locale object
- Build a resource bundle for each locale
- Load a resource bundle in an application
- Format text for localization by using NumberFormat and DateFormat

Computers and software have become so prevalent today that they are used everywhere in the world for human activities. For any software to be relevant and useful to these users, it needs to be localized. The process in which we adapt the software to the local language and customs is known as *localization*. A *locale* represents a country's distinctive assemblage of language, culture, numbers, currency, etc.

Java provides good support for localizing software applications; we'll cover the related topics in detail in this chapter. Although Java supports Unicode, and most computers have the necessary fonts for displaying text in multiple languages, it's our job to consciously adapt the software to different locales. For example, localization does not just mean displaying text for a locale—it can also mean using audio or video clips for a locale. Furthermore, aspects related to displaying date or time or using local currencies also need to be considered.

In this chapter, you'll learn how to localize your software. Localization mainly involves creating *resource bundles* for different locales, as well as making the software culture-aware by adapting it for use in different locales. We'll show you how to create and use these resource bundles in first three sections. In the final section we'll teach you how to handle time and date, numbers, and currencies for different locales.

Introduction

Localization is all about making the software relevant and usable for the users from different cultures—in other words, customizing software for people from different countries or languages. How do you localize a software application? Two important guidelines should be heeded when you localize a software application:

- Do not hardcode text (such as messages to the users, textual elements in GUIs, etc.) and separate them into external files or dedicated classes. With this accomplished there is usually minimal effort to add support for a new locale in your software.

- Handle cultural-specific aspects such as date, time, currency, and formatting numbers with localization in mind. Instead of assuming a default locale, design in such a way that the current locale is fetched and customized.

 Text may not be the only thing that needs to be localized in an application. For example, if your application uses audio sounds to give instructions, they will need to be changed for localization. Similarly, if the software displays some glyphs or pictures for a specific locale, they also need to be transformed.

Locales

A locale is "a place representing a country, language, or culture." Consider the Canada-French locale. French is spoken in many parts of Canada, and this could be a locale. In other words, if you want to sell software that is customized for Canadians who speak French, then you need to facilitate your software for this locale. In Java, this locale is represented by the code fr_CA where fr is short for French and CA is short for Canada; we'll discuss the naming scheme for locales in more detail later in this section.

The Locale Class

In Java, the Locale class provides programming support for locales. Table 12-1 lists important methods in this class.

Table 12-1. *Important Methods in the Locale Class*

Method	Short Description
static Locale[] getAvailableLocales()	Returns a list of available locales (i.e., installed locales) supported by the JVM.
static Locale getDefault()	Returns the default locale of the JVM.
static void setDefault(Locale newLocale)	Sets the default locale of the JVM.
String getCountry()	Returns the country *code* for the locale object.
String getDisplayCountry()	Returns the country *name* for the locale object.
String getLanguage()	Returns the language *code* for the locale object.
String getDisplayLanguage()	Returns the language *name* for the locale object.

(continued)

Table 12-1. (*continued*)

Method	Short Description
String getVariant()	Returns the variant *code* for the locale object.
String getDisplayVariant()	Returns the *name* of the variant code for the locale object.
String toString()	Returns a String composed of the codes for the locale's language, country, variant, etc.

The code in Listing 12-1 detects the default locale and checks the available locales in the JVM.

Listing 12-1. AvailableLocales.java

```
import java.util.Locale;

class AvailableLocales {
    public static void main(String []args) {
        System.out.println("The default locale is: " + Locale.getDefault());
        Locale [] locales = Locale.getAvailableLocales();
        System.out.printf("No. of other available locales is: %d, and they are: %n",
        locales.length);
        for(Locale locale : locales) {
            System.out.printf("Locale code: %s and it stands for %s %n",
            locale, locale.getDisplayName());
        }
    }
}
```

It prints the following:

```
The default locale is: en_US
No. of other available locales is: 156, and they are:
Locale code: ms_MY and it stands for Malay (Malaysia)
Locale code: ar_QA and it stands for Arabic (Qatar)
Locale code: is_IS and it stands for Icelandic (Iceland)
Locale code: sr_RS_#Latn and it stands for Serbian (Latin,Serbia)
Locale code: no_NO_NY and it stands for Norwegian (Norway,Nynorsk)
Locale code: th_TH_TH_#u-nu-thai and it stands for Thai (Thailand,TH)
Locale code: fr_FR and it stands for French (France)
Locale code: tr and it stands for Turkish
Locale code: es_CO and it stands for Spanish (Colombia)
Locale code: en_PH and it stands for English (Philippines)
Locale code: et_EE and it stands for Estonian (Estonia)
Locale code: el_CY and it stands for Greek (Cyprus)
Locale code: hu and it stands for Hungarian
 [...rest of the output elided...]
```

Let's look at the methods in the program before analyzing the output. You use the method getDefault() in Locale to get the code of the default locale. After that you use getAvailableLocales() in the Locale class to get the list of available locales in your JVM. Now, for each locale you print the code for the locale by implicitly calling the toString() method of locale and also print the descriptive name using the getDisplayName() method of Locale.

The program prints the default locale as en_US for this JVM, which means the default is the English language spoken in US. Then it prints a very long list of available locales; to save space, we've shown only small part of the output. From this program, you know that there are many locales available and supported, and there is a default locale associated with every JVM.

There are four different kinds of locale codes in this output:

- Just one code, as in the last entry shown above: hu for Hungarian.

- Two codes separated by underscore, as in the first locale shown, ms_MY, where ms stands for Malaysia and MY stands for Malay.

- Three codes separated by underscores, as in no_NO_NY where no stands for Norway, NO for Norwegian, and NY for Nynorsk.

- Two or three initial codes separated by underscores and the final one by # or _#, as in th_TH_TH_#u-nu-thai, which we'll discuss now. Here is how these locale names are encoded:

```
language + "_" + country + "_" + (variant + "_#" | "#") + script + "-" + extensions
```

For the locale code of th_TH_TH_#u-nu-thai,

- The language code is th (Thai) and it is always written in lowercase.

- The country code is TH (Thailand) and it is always written in uppercase.

- The variant name is TH; here it repeats the country code, but it could be any string.

- The script name is an empty string here; if given, it will be a four-letter string with the first letter in uppercase and the rest in lowercase (e.g., Latn).

- The extension follows the # or _# character; it is u-nu-thai in this example.

This coding scheme is to allow programming variations even within the same language. For example, English is spoken in many countries, and there are variations in the language based on the country in which English is spoken. We all know that American English is different from British English, but there are many such versions. Let's change the loop in Listing 12-1 to list only the locales that are related to English, like so:

```
for(Locale locale : locales) {
        // filter and display only English locales
        if(locale.getLanguage().equals("en")) {
                System.out.printf("Locale code: %s and it stands for %s %n",
                locale, locale.getDisplayName());
        }
}
```

It prints the following:

```
Locale code: en_MT and it stands for English (Malta)
Locale code: en_GB and it stands for English (United Kingdom)
Locale code: en_CA and it stands for English (Canada)
Locale code: en_US and it stands for English (United States)
Locale code: en_ZA and it stands for English (South Africa)
Locale code: en and it stands for English
Locale code: en_SG and it stands for English (Singapore)
Locale code: en_IE and it stands for English (Ireland)
```

```
Locale code: en_IN and it stands for English (India)
Locale code: en_AU and it stands for English (Australia)
Locale code: en_NZ and it stands for English (New Zealand)
Locale code: en_PH and it stands for English (Philippines)
```

The output refers to different locales in English. You use the getLanguage() method in Locale, which returns the locale code. What are other such methods? You'll explore the methods available in the Locale class now.

Getting Locale Details

The getter methods in the Locale class such as getLanguage(), getCountry(), and getVariant() return *codes*, whereas the similar methods getDisplayCountry(), getDisplayLanguage(), and getDisplayVariant() return *names*. Listing 12-2 illustrates how to use these methods for the locale Locale.CANADA_FRENCH.

Listing 12-2. LocaleDetails.java

```java
import java.util.Locale;

public class LocaleDetails {
        public static void main(String args[]) {
                Locale.setDefault(Locale.CANADA_FRENCH);
                Locale defaultLocale = Locale.getDefault();
                System.out.printf("The default locale is %s %n", defaultLocale);
                System.out.printf("The default language code is %s and the name is %s %n",
                        defaultLocale.getLanguage(), defaultLocale.getDisplayLanguage());
                System.out.printf("The default country code is %s and the name is %s %n",
                        defaultLocale.getCountry(), defaultLocale.getDisplayCountry());
                System.out.printf("The default variant code is %s and the name is %s %n",
                        defaultLocale.getVariant(), defaultLocale.getDisplayVariant());
        }
}
```

It prints the following:

```
The default locale is fr_CA
The default language code is fr and the name is français
The default country code is CA and the name is Canada
The default variant code is  and the name is Canada
```

Let's understand the program. The setDefault() method takes a Locale object as argument. In this program, you set the default locale as Locale.CANADA_FRENCH with this statement:

```java
Locale.setDefault(Locale.CANADA_FRENCH);
```

The Locale class has many static Locale objects representing common locales so that you don't have to instantiate them and use them directly in your programs. In this case, Locale.CANADA_FRENCH is a static Locale object. Instead of using this static Locale object, you can choose to instantiate a Locale object. Here is an alternative way to set the default locale by creating a new Canada (French) locale object:

```java
Locale newLocale = new Locale("fr", "CA", "");
Locale.setDefault(newLocale);
```

The getDefault() method in Locale returns the default locale object set in the JVM. The next statement uses methods to get information related to the country. The difference between the getCountry() and getDisplayCountry() methods is that the former method returns the country code (which is not very readable for us), and the latter returns the country name, which is human readable. The country code is a two or three letter code (this code comes from an international standard: ISO 3166).

The behavior of getLanguage() and getDisplayLanguage() is similar to getting country details. The language code consists of two or three letters, and this code comes from another international standard (ISO 639).

There was no variant in this locale, so nothing got printed when you used the getVariant() and getDisplayVariant() methods. However, for some other locale, there could be variant values, and those values would get printed for that locale. The variant could be any extra details such as operating environments (like MAC for Macintosh machine) or name of the company (such as Sun or Oracle).

Other than these, you also have less widely used methods such as getScript(), which returns the script code for the locale.

Resource Bundles

In the last section, we discussed the Locale class and the way to get details of the default locale and the list of available locales. How do you *use* this locale information to customize the behavior of your programs? Let's take a simple example of greeting someone: in English, you say "Hello," but if the locale is different, how do you change this greeting to say, for example, "Ciao" if the locale is Italy (and Italian)?

One obvious solution is to get the default locale, check if the locale is Italy and print "Ciao." It will work, but this approach is neither flexible nor extensible. How about customizing to other locales like Saudi Arabia (Arabic) or India (Hindi)? You have to find and replace all the locale specific strings for customizing for each locale; this task will be a nightmare if your application consists of thousands of such strings spread over a million lines of code.

In Java, resource bundles provide a solution to this problem of how to customize the application to locale-specific needs. So, what is a resource bundle? A resource bundle is a set of classes or property files that help define a set of keys and map those keys to locale specific values.

The abstract class ResourceBundle provides an abstraction of resource bundles in Java. It has two derived classes: PropertyResourceBundle and ListResourceBundle (see Figure 12-1). The two derived classes provide support for resource bundles using two different mechanisms:

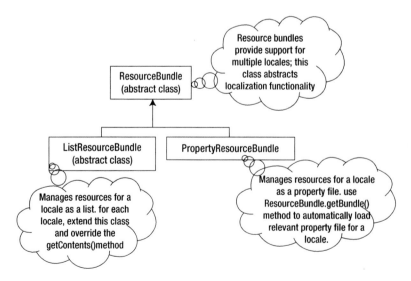

Figure 12-1. *ResourceBundle and its two derived classes*

- **The** `PropertyResourceBundle` **Class:** This concrete class provides support for multiple locales in the form of property files. For each locale, you specify the keys and values in a property file for that locale. For a given locale, if you use the `ResourceBundle.getBundle()` method, the relevant property file will be automatically loaded. Of course, there is no magic in it; you have to follow certain naming conventions for creating the property files, which we'll discuss in the section dedicated to discussing property files. You can use only `String`s as keys and values when you use property files.

- **The** `ListResourceBundle` **Class:** For adding support to a locale, you can extend this abstract class. In your derived class, you have to override the `getContents()` method, which returns an `Object [][]`. This array must have the list of keys and values. The keys must be `String`s. Typically the values are also `String`s, but values can be anything: sound clips, video clips, URLs, or pictures.

Let's take a quick look at the methods supported by the `ResourceBundle` abstract class. Table 12-2 summarizes the important methods of this class. We'll now discuss localization support using these two derived classes of `ResourceBundle`.

Table 12-2. *Important Methods in the ResourceBundle Abstract Class*

Method	Short Description
`Object getObject(String key)`	Returns the value mapped to the given key. Throws a `MissingResourceException` if no object for a given key is found.
`static ResourceBundle getBundle(String baseName),` `static final ResourceBundle getBundle(String baseName, Locale locale)` `final ResourceBundle getBundle(String baseName, Locale targetLocale, Control control)`	Returns the `ResourceBundle` for the given `baseName`, `locale`, and `control`; throws a `MissingResourceException` if no matching resource bundle is found. The `Control` instance is meant for controlling or obtaining info about the resource bundle loading process.
`string getString(String key)`	Returns the value mapped to the given key; equivalent to casting the return value from `getObject()` to `String`. Throws a `MissingResourceException` if no object for a given key is found. Throws `ClassCastException` if the object returned is not a `String`.

Using PropertyResourceBundle

If you design your application with localization in mind using property files, you can add support for new locales to the application *without changing anything in the code*!

We'll now look at an example using resource files and it will become clear to you. Let's start with a very simple program that prints "Hello" to the user. This program has three property file resource bundles:

1. The default resource bundle that assumes the English (US) locale.

2. A resource bundle for the Arabic locale.

3. A resource bundle for the Italian locale.

As discussed above, property files define strings as key value pairs in a file. Here is an example of a classpath that can be mapped to an actual path in your machine: classpath = C:\Program Files\Java\jre7. Property files will usually contain numerous such key value pairs, with each such pair in separate lines, as in the following:

```
classpath = C:\Program Files\Java\jre7
temp = C:\Windows\Temp
windir = C:\Windows
```

In the case of localization, you use property files to map the same key strings to different value strings. In the program, you'll refer the key strings, and by loading the matching property file for the locale, the corresponding values for the keys will be fetched from the property files for use in the program.

The naming of these property files is important (you'll see why soon) and below is the content of these bundles. To keep this example simple, there is only one key-value pair in these property files; in real-world programs, there could be a few hundred or even thousands of pairs present in each property file.

```
D:\>type ResourceBundle.properties
Greeting = Hello

D:\>type ResourceBundle_ar.properties
Greeting = As-Salamu Alaykum

D:\>type ResourceBundle_it.properties
Greeting = Ciao
```

As you can see, the default bundle is named ResourceBundle.properties. The resource bundle for Arabic is named ResourceBundle_ar.properties. Note the suffix _ar, indicating Arabic as a local language. Similarly, the resource bundle for Italian is named ResourceBundle_it.properties, which makes use of the _it suffix to indicate the Italian as the associated language with this property file. Listing 12-3 makes use of these resource bundles.

Listing 12-3. LocalizedHello.java

```java
import java.util.*;

public class LocalizedHello {
    public static void main(String args[]) {
        Locale currentLocale = Locale.getDefault();
        ResourceBundle resBundle =
            ResourceBundle.getBundle("ResourceBundle", currentLocale);
        System.out.printf(resBundle.getString("Greeting"));
    }
}
```

There are two options to run this program in the desired way:

- **Option I:** Change the default locale in the program by calling the setDefault() method:

```java
Locale.setDefault(Locale.ITALY);
```

This option is not recommended since it will require changing the program to set the locale.

- **Option II:** Change the default locale when invoking the JVM from the command line (if you're invoking the JVM from an IDE, provide the command line arguments to the JVM in the IDE settings):

```
D:\>java -Duser.language = it -Duser.region = IT LocalizedHello
```

Let's try the program by setting the locale with Option II (passing arguments to the command line when invoking the JVM).

```
D:\>java LocalizedHello
Hello
D:\>java -Duser.language=it LocalizedHello
Ciao
D:\>java -Duser.language=ar LocalizedHello
As-Salamu Alaykum
```

As you can see, depending on the locale that you explicitly set (Italian or Arabic in this example), or the default locale (US English in this example), the corresponding property file is loaded and the message string is resolved.

If you forget to create property files or they are not in the path, you will get a `MissingResourceException`.

In the program, first you get the current locale in the statement.

```
Locale currentLocale = Locale.getDefault();
```

After that, you load the resource bundle that starts with the name ResourceBundle and pass the locale for loading the resource bundle.

```
ResourceBundle resBundle = ResourceBundle.getBundle("ResourceBundle", currentLocale);
```

Finally, from the resource bundle, you look for the key "Greeting" and use the value of that key based on the loaded resource bundle.

```
System.out.printf(resBundle.getString("Greeting"));
```

Using ListResourceBundle

Support for a new locale can be added using `ListResourceBundle` by extending it. While extending the `ListResourceBundle`, you need to override the abstract method *getContents()*; the signature of this method is

```
protected Object[][] getContents();
```

Note that the keys are Strings, but values can be of any type, hence the array type is Object; further, the method returns a list of key and value pairs. As a result, the getContents() method returns a two-dimensional array of Objects.

Listing 12-4 shows an example of extending the ListResourceBundle, which is supposed to return the largest box-office movie hit for that particular locale. It defines a resource bundle named ResBundle. Since the name of the class does not have any suffix (such as _it or _en_US), it is the default implementation of the resource bundle. When looking for a matching ResBundle for any locale, this default implementation will be used in case no match is found.

Listing 12-4. ResBundle.java

```
import java.util.*;

// default US English version
public class ResBundle extends ListResourceBundle {
        public Object[][] getContents() {
                        return contents;
        }
        static final Object[][] contents = {
                { "MovieName", "Avatar" },
                { "GrossRevenue", (Long) 2782275172L }, // in US dollars
                { "Year", (Integer)2009 }
        };
}
```

Now, let's define a ResBundle for the Italian locale. You give the class the suffix _it_IT. The language code it stands for Italian and the country code IT stands for Italy. See Listing 12-5.

Listing 12-5. ResBundle_it_IT.java

```
import java.util.*;

// Italian version
public class ResBundle_it_IT extends ListResourceBundle {
        public Object[][] getContents() {
                        return contents;
        }
        static final Object[][] contents = {
                { "MovieName", "Che Bella Giornata" },
                { "GrossRevenue", (Long) 43000000L }, // in euros
                { "Year", (Integer)2011 }
        };
}
```

As you can see, the implementations for ResBundle and ResBundle_it_IT are similar except for the values mapped to the keys. Now how do you know if your resource bundles are working or not? Listing 12-6 loads ResBundle for both default and Italian locales.

Listing 12-6. LocalizedHello2.java

```java
import java.util.*;

public class LocalizedHello2 {
        public static void printMovieDetails(ResourceBundle resBundle) {
                String movieName = resBundle.getString("MovieName");
                Long revenue = (Long)(resBundle.getObject("GrossRevenue"));
                Integer year = (Integer) resBundle.getObject("Year");

                System.out.println("Movie " + movieName + "(" + year ")" + " grossed "
                + revenue );
        }
        public static void main(String args[]) {
                // print the largest box-office hit movie for default (US) locale
                Locale locale = Locale.getDefault();
                printMovieDetails(ResourceBundle.getBundle("ResBundle", locale));

                // print the largest box-office hit movie for Italian locale
                locale = new Locale("it", "IT", "");
                printMovieDetails(ResourceBundle.getBundle("ResBundle", locale));
        }
}
```

It prints the following:

```
Movie Avatar (2009) grossed 2782275172
Movie Che Bella Giornata (2011) grossed 43000000
```

It loaded the default and Italian resource bundles successfully. However, there are problems with this output. The value 2782275172 is a US dollar value and the value 43000000 is in Euros. Moreover, the numbers are printed without commas, so it is difficult to make sense of these figures. These values need to be localized as well, and we'll revisit this topic in the last section of this chapter.

Now, consider the following statement from this program:

```
Long revenue = (Long)(resBundle.getObject("GrossRevenue"));
```

This statement returns the value mapping to the key named GrossRevenue in the resource bundle. You have defined it as an integer object in the classes ResBundle and ResBundle_it_IT—so it worked. If you cast the types incorrectly, you'll get a ClassCastException.

Furthermore, note that *the keyname is case sensitive and the key name should exactly match*—or else you'll get a MissingResourceException. For example, in this statement, if you mistype GrossRevenu instead of GrossRevenue as the key name, the program will crash with this exception:

```
The Exception in the thread "main" java.util.MissingResourceException: Can't find resources for
bundle ResBundle, key GrossRevenu
```

You create resource bundles by extending the ListResourceBundle class, whereas with PropertyResourceBundle, you create the resource bundle as property files. Furthermore, when extending ListResourceBundle, you can have any type of objects as values, whereas values in a properties file can only be Strings.

Loading a Resource Bundle

You've already loaded resource bundles in the programs you've written using ResourceBundle or its two derived classes. You need to understand this loading process thoroughly, and we'll cover it in more detail in this section.

The process of finding a matching resource bundle is same for classes extended from ListResourceBundles as for property files defined for PropertyResourceBundles.

For the resource bundles implemented as classes extended from ListResourceBundles, Java uses the reflection mechanism to find and load the class. You need to make sure that the class is public so that the reflection mechanism will find the class.

Naming Convention for Resource Bundles

Java enforces a predefined naming convention to be followed for creating resource bundles. Only through the names of the property bundles does the Java library load the relevant locales. Hence, it is important to understand and follow this naming convention when creating the property bundles for localizing Java applications.

You already saw how a locale name is encoded. Understanding this locale name encoding is important for naming the resource bundles because it makes use of the same encoding scheme. A fully qualified resource bundle has the following form:

```
packagequalifier.bundlename + "_" + language + "_" + country + "_" + (variant + "_#" | "#") + script
+ "-" + extensions
```

Here is the description of the elements in this fully qualified name:

- **packagequalifier**: The name of the package (or the subpackages) in which the resource bundle is provided.

- **bundlename**: The name of the resource bundle that you'll use in the program to refer and load it.

- **language**: A two-letter abbreviation typically given in lowercase for the locale's language (in rare cases, it could be three letters as well).

- **country**: A two letter abbreviation typically given in uppercase for the locale's country (in rare cases, it could be three letters as well).

- **variant**: An arbitrary list of variants (in lowercase or uppercase) to differentiate locales when you need more than one locale for a language and country combination.

We've omitted describing script and extension since they are rarely used.

For example, consider this fully qualified name:

`localization.examples.AppBundle_en_US_Oracle_exam`

In this case, `localization.examples` is the package, `AppBundle` is the name of the resource bundle, `en` is language (which stands for English), `US` is the country, and `Oracle_exam` is the variant.

The two (or sometimes three) letter abbreviations for the locale's language and country are predefined since they are based on international standards. We don't provide the detailed list and there is also no need to know or remember all of them. You can look at the documentation of the `Locale` class to understand that.

On the OCPJP 7 exam, you're not expected to memorize language codes or country codes that are used for naming resource bundles. However, you are expected to *remember the naming convention* and recognize the constituents of a fully qualified resource bundle name.

Given that there could be many resource bundles for a bundle name, what is the search sequence to determine the resource bundle to be loaded? To clarify, we present the sequence as a series of steps. The search starts from Step 1. If at any step the search finds a match, the resource bundle is loaded. Otherwise, the search proceeds to the next step.

- **Step 1:** The search starts by looking for an exact match for the resource bundle with the full name.

- **Step 2:** The last component (the part separated by _) is dropped and the search is repeated with the resulting shorter name. *This process is repeated till the last locale modifier is left.*

- **Step 3:** The search is restarted using the full name of the bundle for the default locale.

- **Step 4:** Search for the resource bundle with just the name of the bundle.

- **Step 5:** The search fails, throwing a `MissingBundleException`.

The search starts with the given locale details and if not found, proceeds with checking for default locale, as in:

```
BundleName + "_" + language + "_" + country + "_" + variant
BundleName + "_" + language + "_" + country
BundleName + "_" + language
BundleName + "_" + defaultLanguage + "_" + defaultCountry
BundleName + "_" + defaultLanguage
```

Consider an example to find out how the matching resource bundle is found, and it will become clear to you. Assume that you have the following five entries in the search path, and your default locale is US English.

```
ResourceBundle.properties              -- Global bundle
ResourceBundle_ar.properties           -- Arabic language bundle
ResourceBundle_en.properties           -- English bundle (assuming en_US is the default locale)
ResourceBundle_it.properties           -- Italian language bundle
ResourceBundle_it_IT_Rome.properties   -- Italian (Italy, Rome, Vatican) bundle
```

The getBundle() method takes a ResourceBundle.Control object as an additional parameter. By extending this ResourceBundle.Control class and passing the instance of that extended class to the getBundle() method, you can change the default resource bundle search process or read from non-standard resource bundle formats (such as XML files).

So, you'll extend this ResourceBundle.Control class and override the getCandidateLocales() method. This is to programmatically list the candidate locales and finally display the matching locale. The program is given in Listing 12-7.

Listing 12-7. CandidateLocales.java

```java
import java.util.*;

// Extend ResourceBundle.Control and override getCandidateLocales method
// to get the list of candidate locales that Java searches for
class TalkativeResourceBundleControl extends ResourceBundle.Control {
        // override the default getCandidateLocales method to print
        // the candidate locales first
        public List<Locale> getCandidateLocales(String baseName, Locale locale) {
                List<Locale> candidateLocales = super.getCandidateLocales(baseName, locale);
                System.out.printf("Candidate locales for base bundle name %s and locale %s %n",
                baseName, locale.getDisplayName());
                for(Locale candidateLocale : candidateLocales) {
                    System.out.println(candidateLocale);
                }
                return candidateLocales;
        }
}

// Use a helper method loadResourceBundle to load a bundle given the bundle name and locale
class CandidateLocales {
        public static void loadResourceBundle(String resourceBundleName, Locale locale) {
                // Pass an instance of TalkativeResourceBundleControl
                // to print candidate locales
                ResourceBundle resourceBundle = ResourceBundle.getBundle(resourceBundleName, locale,
                new TalkativeResourceBundleControl());
                String rbLocaleName = resourceBundle.getLocale().toString();
                // if the resource bundle locale name is empty,
                // it means default property file
                if(rbLocaleName.equals("")) {
                        System.out.println("Loaded the default property file with name: " +
                        resourceBundleName);
                } else {
                        System.out.println("Loaded the resource bundle for the locale: " +
                        resourceBundleName + "." + rbLocaleName);
                }
        }
}
```

```
        public static void main(String[] args) {
                // trace how ResourceBundle_it_IT_Rome.properties is resolved
                loadResourceBundle("ResourceBundle", new Locale("it", "IT", "Rome"));
        }
}
```

It prints the following:

```
Candidate locales for base bundle name ResourceBundle and locale Italian (Italy, Rome)
it_IT_Rome
it_IT
it

Loaded the resource bundle for the locale: ResourceBundle.it_IT_Rome
```

Now, before trying with other locales, consider how the program works. To trace how Java resolves the resource bundle to be finally loaded, you need to get the list of candidate locales. With the ResourceBundle.getBundle() method, you can pass an additional argument that is an instance of the ResourceBundle.Control class. For this reason, you define the TalkativeResourceBundleControl class.

The TalkativeResourceBundleControl class extends the ResourceBundle.Control class and overrides the getCandidateLocales() method. This getCandidateLocales() method returns a List<Locale> instance that contains the list of candidate locales for the given locale. You invoke super.getCandidateLocales() and traverse the resulting List<Locale> object to print the candidate locales so that you can examine the output later. From this overridden getCandidateLocales() method, you simply return this List<Locale> object. So, the behavior of TalkativeResourceBundleControl is identical to ResourceBundle.Control except that the overridden getCandidateLocales() in TalkativeResourceBundleControl prints the candidate locales.

The CandidateLocales class makes use of the TalkativeResourceBundleControl. It has a helper method called loadResourceBundle() that takes the resource bundle name and the name of the locale as arguments. This method simply passes these argument values to the ResourceBundle.getBundle() method; additionally it instantiates TalkativeResourceBundleControl and passes that object as the third argument to this method. The getBundle() method returns a ResourceBundle object. If the locale of the ResourceBundle.getLocale() name is empty, it means Java has loaded the global resource bundle. (Remember that the global resource bundle for that bundle name does not have any associated locale details.) If the name of the locale is not empty, it means Java has resolved to that particular locale.

Now, consider the code in the main() method. It calls loadResourceBundle() for the locale it_IT_Rome. There are three candidate locales and of that it correctly loaded the matching property file for the locale it_IT_Rome. So you know that it loaded the property file ResourceBundle_it_IT_Rome.properties correctly.

To continue this experiment, let's change the code inside the main() method of Listing 12-7 to this code:

```
loadResourceBundle("ResourceBundle", new Locale("fr", "CA", ""));
```

Now the program prints the following:

```
Candidate locales for base bundle name ResourceBundle and locale French (Canada)
fr_CA
fr
Candidate locales for base bundle name ResourceBundle and locale English (United States)
en_US
en
Loaded the resource bundle for the locale: ResourceBundle.en
```

Why does the program print the above output? Note that there is no corresponding property file for the fr_CA locale in the list of property files. So, the search continues to check the property files for the default locale. In this case, the default locale is en_US, and there is a property file for the en (English) locale. So, from the candidate locales, Java resolves to load the property file ResourceBundle_en.properties correctly.

Here is the final example. Replace the code in the main() method with this statement:

```
loadResourceBundle("ResBundl", Locale.getDefault());
```

The program prints the following:

```
Candidate locales for base bundle name ResBundl and locale English (United States)
en_US
en
```

```
The exception in thread "main" java.util.MissingResourceException: Can't find bundle for base name
ResBundl, locale en_US
        [... thrown stack trace elided ...]
```

You don't have any resource bundle named ResBundl and you've given the default locale (en_US in this case). Java searches for the bundle for this locale, and you know that you have not provided any bundle with name ResBundl. So, the program crashes after throwing a MissingResourceException.

Formatting for Local Culture

Text is obviously the main aspect to be localized. However, there are many aspects that are handled differently based on the locale: date and time, numbers, and currencies. We'll discuss each of these topics in detail now.

For localize text, the main approach you need to follow is not to hardcode the strings. The key idea to remember for date, time, currency, and numbers is to use culture-aware formatting to localize them. Figure 12-2 shows how the two important classes we'll discuss in this section—NumberFormat and DateFormat—are both inherited from the Format base class; these classes are part of the java.text package and are useful for making locale-aware software.

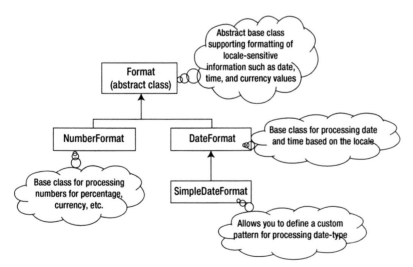

Figure 12-2. *The Format class and its important derived classes*

The NumberFormat Class

The NumberFormat class provides support for processing numbers in a locale-sensitive manner. For example, depending on the locale, how thousands are separated, the punctuation characters used for separating them, printing an amount as a currency value, etc. are different, and the NumberFormat class provides this functionality.

The NumberFormat class provides methods to format or parse numbers. Here "formatting" means converting a numeric value to a string value in a culture-sensitive way; similarly, "parsing" means converting a number back to numeric form. For example, if you want to print the long constant value 10_000_000L into ten million in German locale, you format this value by passing it to the format() method in the NumberFormat class, and this method will return the String "10.000.000" (note the use of dot as a separation character for thousands). Now, if you read the input value 10 million in German locale to convert that value to a long value to use it in the program, you can pass the string to the parse() method. Listing 12-8 shows the steps to perform these conversions.

Listing 12-8. FormatNumber.java

```java
import java.util.*;
import java.text.*;

// class to demonstrate how to format or parse numbers for a particular locale
class FormatNumber {
        public static void main(String []args) {
                long tenMillion = 10_000_000L;
                // first print ten million in German locale
                NumberFormat germanFormat = NumberFormat.getInstance(Locale.GERMANY);
                String localizedTenMillion = germanFormat.format(tenMillion);
                System.out.println("Ten million in German locale is " + localizedTenMillion);

                // now, scan the value ten million given in German locale
                try {
                        Number parsedAmount = germanFormat.parse(localizedTenMillion);
                        if(tenMillion == parsedAmount.longValue()) {
                                System.out.println("Successfully parsed the number for the locale");
                        }
                }
                catch (ParseException pe) {
                        System.err.println("Error: Cannot parse the number for the locale");
                }
        }
}
```

It prints the following:

```
Ten million in German locale is 10.000.000
Successfully parsed the number value back to Number value based on the locale
```

As you can see, the value 10 million is printed in this format in German locale: 10.000.000. To parse such a number in a given locale, you can use the NumberFormat's parse() method, which returns a Number if the parsing is successful—or else the method throws a checked exception, ParseException.

Note that the parse() method is different from the format() method. The parse() method is meant for reading numbers provided as String and trying to convert it to Number. The format() method is used for printing the values according to the values set in the NumberFormat object. Listing 12-9 illustrates the difference between the two.

Listing 12-9. FractionDigits.java

```java
import java.util.*;
import java.text.*;

public class FractionDigits {
        public static void main(String[] args) throws ParseException {
                String[] numbers = {"1.222", "0.12345F"};
                double[] doubles = {1.222, 0.12345F};
                NumberFormat numberFormat = NumberFormat.getInstance();
                numberFormat.setMaximumFractionDigits(2);
                System.out.println("Using format method: ");
                for(double val : doubles) {
                        System.out.println(numberFormat.format(val));
                }
                System.out.println("Using parse method: ");
                for(String number : numbers) {
                        System.out.println(numberFormat.parse(number));
                }
        }
}
```

It prints the following:

```
Using format method:
1.22
0.12
Using parse method:
1.222
0.12345
```

The parse() method reads the values and converts it to Number if it succeeds. So, it does not use the maximum fraction digits set using setMaximumFractionDigits(); however, if it were to use the format() method, which is meant for printing numbers, it would use this maximum fraction digits limit set, which explains the difference between the outputs.

Important methods in the NumberFormat class are listed in Table 12-3. The static methods that start with the "get" prefix and end with the "Instance" suffix—such as getCurrencyInstance()—are factory methods supported by this class.

Table 12-3. *Important Methods in the NumberFormat Class*

Method	Short Description
String format(double number) String format(long number)	Formats the number according to the NumberFormat's locale. The first two overloaded methods use an implicit StringBuffer, whereas the last two use an explicit StringBuffer to build the String.
Number parse(String source)	Parses the number from the given String. It returns a Long or Double instance depending on the value of the number given in source. Throws a ParseException if the parse fails.

(continued)

Table 12-3. (*continued*)

Method	Short Description
static Locale[] getAvailableLocales()	Returns the list of the locales supported by the Java runtime for number formatting.
static NumberFormat getInstance()	Factory method that returns a NumberFormat object for the default locale.
Currency getCurrency()	Returns the currency instance used by this NumberFormat object.
static NumberFormat getCurrencyInstance()	Returns the instance of NumberFormat suitable for currency formatting purposes; an overloaded version of this method takes a Locale as an argument.
static NumberFormat getIntegerInstance()	Returns the instance of NumberFormat suitable for use for formatting integer numbers; an overloaded version of this method takes a Locale as an argument.
static NumberFormat getPercentInstance()	Returns the instance of NumberFormat suitable for use for formatting for percentages; an overloaded version of this method takes a Locale as an argument.

The NumberFormat class supports printing currency values. You can use its getCurrencyInstance() method, which returns a Currency object. Listing 12-10 illustrates how to make use of this method for printing the value 10 million in four different locales (without performing exchange rate conversions).

Listing 12-10. LocalizedCurrency.java

```java
import java.util.*;
import java.text.*;

// Ilustrates how to use NumberFormat class to get Currency instance
class LocalizedCurrency {
        public static void main(String []args) {
                long tenMillion = 10000000L; // this is ten million
                Locale [] locales =
                        { Locale.CANADA, Locale.FRANCE, Locale.GERMANY, Locale.TAIWAN };
                // for each of the four locales,
                // print the currency amount as it looks in that locale
                for(Locale locale : locales) {
                        System.out.println("Ten million in " + locale.getDisplayName() + "
                        is " + NumberFormat.getCurrencyInstance(locale).format(tenMillion));
                }
        }
}
```

It prints:

```
Ten million in English (Canada) is $10,000,000.00
Ten million in French (France) is 10 000 000,00
Ten million in German (Germany) is 10.000.000,00
Ten million in Chinese (Taiwan) is NT$10,000,000.00
```

As you can see, by using the NumberFormat object returned from getCurrencyInstance(Locale), you can format numbers to print them as currency values for a locale. You can also use the Currency class independently of the NumberFormat class, as we'll discuss now.

The Currency Class

Table 12-4 lists important methods the Currency class.

Table 12-4. *Important Methods in the Currency Class*

Method	Short Description
int getNumericCode()	Returns ISO 4217 numeric code for the currency.
int getDefaultFractionDigits()	Returns the default number of digits used with the currency, such as zero for the Japanese Yen and two for the US Dollar.
String getDisplayName()	Returns the readable description of the Currency for the underlying locale, for example, US Dollar.
String getDisplayName(Locale)	Returns the readable description of the Currency for the given locale.
static Currency getInstance(String currencyCode)	Returns the Currency object corresponding to the given currency code.
static Currency getInstance(Locale locale)	Returns the Currency object corresponding to the given Locale object.
static Set < Currency > getAvailableCurrencies()	Get the list of Currency instances available in the JDK.
String getSymbol()	Returns the currency symbol, if any; otherwise, returns the currency code.
String getSymbol(Locale)	Returns the currency symbol for the given Locale object.
String getCurrencyCode()	Returns the currency code (ISO 4217) for locale of the Currency instance.

Listing 12-11 shows how to make use of few of these methods listed in Table 12-4.

Listing 12-11. CurrencyDetails.java

```java
import java.util.*;

// Get the currency details of the default locale (en_US locale)
class CurrencyDetails {
    public static void main(String []args) {
        Locale locale = Locale.getDefault();
        Currency currencyInstance = Currency.getInstance(locale);
        System.out.println(" The currency code for locale " + locale
            + " is: " + currencyInstance.getCurrencyCode()
```

```
                + " \n The currency symbol is " + currencyInstance.getSymbol()
                + " \n The currency name is " + currencyInstance.getDisplayName());
        }
}
```

It prints the following:

```
The currency code for locale en_US is: USD
The currency symbol is $
The currency name is US Dollar
```

The output is self-explanatory. Note that for many locales where there is no symbol involved, getSymbol() will just return the currency code.

The DateFormat Class

The DateFormat class provides support for processing date and time in a locale-sensitive manner (the name simply says DateFormat, but it supports both date and time). Table 12-5 lists some of the important methods in the DateFormat class.

Table 12-5. *Important Methods in the DateFormat Class*

Method	Short Description
String format(Date date)	Formats the given date for the default locale and returns a textual representation. Its overloaded version takes a StringBuffer and position as arguments and returns a StringBuffer object; useful if an existing StringBuffer needs to be formatted for date.
Date parse(String source)	Reads the given String according to the default locale conventions to return a Date object; throws ParseException if it fails. It has an overloaded version that takes ParsePosition (the position from which to parse the String) as an additional argument.
String format(Date date)	Formats the given date for the default locale and returns a textual representation.
static Locale[] getAvailableLocales()	Returns an array of Locales that are supported by the Java runtime for date/time formatting.
static DateFormat getInstance()	Returns the default DateFormat instance that supports *both* date and time; it uses DateFormat.SHORT style for both date and time.
static DateFormat getDateInstance()	Returns the DateFormat instance suitable for processing dates for default locale; its two overloaded versions take style and Locale as additional arguments.
static DateFormat getTimeInstance()	Returns the DateFormat instance suitable for processing time for a default locale; its two overloaded versions take style and Locale as additional arguments.
static DateFormat getDateTimeInstance()	Returns the DateFormat instance suitable for processing both date and time for a default locale; its two overloaded versions take style and Locale as additional arguments.

Depending on the locale, the displayed date or time can be considerably different, as shown from the output of the program in Listing 12-12 for four locales.

Listing 12-12. DatePrint.java

```
import java.util.*;
import java.text.*;

// Class to demonstrate the use of DateFormat class to format the date and print it
class DatePrint {
        public static void main(String[] args) {
                // the default constructor for the Date
                // sets the date/time for current date/time
                Date today = new Date();
                Locale [] locales = { Locale.CANADA, Locale.FRANCE, Locale.GERMANY, Locale.ITALY };
                for(Locale locale : locales) {
                        // DateFormat.FULL refers to the full details of the date
                        DateFormat dateFormat = DateFormat.getDateInstance(DateFormat.FULL, locale);
                        System.out.println("Date in locale " + locale + " is: " + dateFormat.
                        format(today));
                }
        }
}
```

When this program was run on Sept 4, 2012, it printed the following:

```
Date in locale en_CA is: Tuesday, September 4, 2012
Date in locale fr_FR is: mardi 4 septembre 2012
Date in locale de_DE is: Dienstag, 4. September 2012
Date in locale it_IT is: martedì 4 settembre 2012
```

This program gets an instance of the DateFormat class using one of the overloaded versions of the getDateInstance() method. This method takes the *display format style* as the first argument, and the locale to be used for formatting the date as the second argument. What are those display format styles? Listing 12-13 shows the four styles and how the dates look different for these styles.

Listing 12-13. DateStyleFormats.java

```
import java.util.*;
import java.text.*;

// Demonstrates the use of constants in DateFormat that determines the display style
class DateStyleFormats {
        public static void main(String []args) {
                Date now = new Date();
                int [] dateStyleFormats = { DateFormat.SHORT, DateFormat.MEDIUM, DateFormat.LONG,
                DateFormat.FULL, DateFormat.DEFAULT};
                System.out.println("Today's date in different styles are: ");

                // print today's date in all four formats plus
                // the default format in the default Locale
                for(int dateStyleFormat : dateStyleFormats) {
```

```
                    DateFormat dateFormat = DateFormat.getDateInstance(dateStyleFormat);
                    System.out.println(dateFormat.format(now));
            }
        }
}
```

When run on Sept 5, 2012, it printed the following:

```
Today's date in different styles are:
9/5/12
Sep 5, 2012
September 5, 2012
Wednesday, September 5, 2012
Sep 5, 2012
```

As you can see, you can get an instance of DateFormat for a preferred style based on the need. The default style is DateFormat.MEDIUM.

The DateFormat has three overloaded factory methods—getDateInstance(), getTimeInstance(), and getDateTimeInstance()—that return DateFormat instances for processing date, time, and both date and time, respectively. Listing 12-14 shows how to use them.

Listing 12-14. DateTimePrint.java

```java
import java.util.*;
import java.text.*;

// Class to demonstrate the use of DateFormat class to get date, time, or date with time
class DateTimePrint {
        public static void main(String []args) {
                // the default constructor for the Date gets the current time and date
                Date today = new Date();
                Locale [] locales =
                        { Locale.CANADA, Locale.FRANCE, Locale.GERMANY, Locale.ITALY };

                // print the header first
                System.out.printf("%5s \t %10s \t %10s \t %10s %n",
                        "Locale", "Date", "Time", "Date with Time");

                // print the date, time, and date & time for each locale
                for(Locale locale : locales) {
                        // DateFormat.SHORT is for giving the date or
                        // time details in compact format
                        DateFormat dateFormat = DateFormat.getDateInstance(DateFormat.SHORT, locale);
                        DateFormat timeFormat = DateFormat.getTimeInstance(DateFormat.SHORT, locale);

                        // now, for Date & Time, change the styles to MEDIUM and FULL
                        DateFormat dateTimeFormat = DateFormat.getDateTimeInstance(DateFormat.
                        MEDIUM, DateFormat.FULL, locale);
                        System.out.printf("%5s \t %10s \t %10s \t %20s %n", locale,
                        dateFormat.format(today), timeFormat.format(today),
                        dateTimeFormat.format(today));
                }
        }
}
```

When run on Sept 5, 2012 in the afternoon, it printed the following:

```
Locale       Date        Time      Date with Time
en_CA      05/09/12     2:32 PM    5-Sep-2012 2:32:56 o'clock PM GMT + 05:30
fr_FR      05/09/12      14:32     5 sept. 2012 14 h 32 GMT + 05:30
de_DE      05.09.12      14:32     05.09.2012 14:32 Uhr GMT + 05:30
it_IT      05/09/12      14.32     5-set-2012 14.32.56 GMT + 05:30
```

This program shows how to get instances of DateFormat for processing date, time, or both date and time. You can also see the effect of using different styles for different locales.

Until now you have only used DateFormat to process predefined date and time for different locales. If you want to create your own format or pattern for processing the date or time, can you do that? Yes, the SimpleDateFormat class provides this facility.

The SimpleDateFormat Class

SimpleDateFormat extends the DateFormat class. SimpleDateFormat uses the concept of a pattern string to format the date and time. Before you delve deeper into creating pattern strings, first look at a simple example to learn how to create a custom format for printing date and time (Listing 12-15).

Listing 12-15. PatternStringExample.java

```java
import java.util.*;
import java.text.*;

// Use SimpleDateFormat for creating custom date and time formats as a pattern string
class PatternStringExample {
        public static void main(String []args) {
                String pattern = "dd-MM-yy"; /* d for day, M for month, y for year */
                SimpleDateFormat formatter = new SimpleDateFormat(pattern);
                // the default Date constructor initializes to current date/time
                System.out.println(formatter.format(new Date()));
        }
}
```

It prints the date in following format:

```
05-09-12
```

You encode the format of the date or time using letters to form a date or time pattern string. Usually these letters are repeated in the pattern. Note that the uppercase and lowercase letters can have similar or different meanings, so read the documentation carefully when trying to use these letters. For example, in dd-MM-yy, MM refers to month; however, in dd-mm-yy, mm refers to minutes!

In this program, you've given a simple example for creating a custom format for date. Similar letters are available for creating custom date and time pattern strings. Here is the list of important letters and their meanings for creating patterns for dates:

G   Era (BC/AD)
y   Year
Y   Week year
M   Month (in year)
w   Week (in year)

W   Week (in month)
D   Day (in year)
d   Day (in month)
F   Day of week in month
E   Day name in week
u   Day number of week (value range 1-7)

Listing 12-16 is a program that uses simple to difficult pattern strings for creating custom date formats.

Listing 12-16. CustomDatePatterns.java

```
import java.util.*;
import java.text.*;

// Using an example, illustrates the use of "pattern strings" for printing dates
class CustomDatePatterns {
        public static void main(String []args) {
                // patterns from simple to complex ones
                String [] dateFormats = {
                        "dd-MM-yyyy", /* d is day (in month), M is month, y is year */
                        "d '('E')' MMM, YYYY", /*E is name of the day (in week), Y is year*/
                        "w'th week of' YYYY", /* w is the week of the year */
                        "EEEE, dd'th' MMMM, YYYY" /*E is day name in the week */
                };
                Date today = new Date();
                System.out.println("Default format for the date is " +
                DateFormat.getDateInstance().format(today));
                for(String dateFormat : dateFormats) {
                        System.out.printf("Date in pattern \"%s\" is %s %n", dateFormat,
                        new SimpleDateFormat(dateFormat).format(today));
                }
        }
}
```

In a sample run, it printed the following:

```
Default format for the date is Sep 5, 2012
Date in pattern "dd-MM-yyyy" is 05-09-2012
Date in pattern "d '('E')' MMM, YYYY" is 5 (Wed) Sep, 2012
Date in pattern "w'th week of' YYYY" is 36th week of 2012
Date in pattern "EEEE, dd'th' MMMM, YYYY" is Wednesday, 05th September, 2012
```

As you can see, repeating letters result in a longer form for an entry. For example, when you use E (which is the name of the day in the week), it prints Wed, whereas when you use EEEE, it prints the full form of the day name, which is Wednesday.

Another important thing to notice is how to print text within the given pattern string. For that you use text separated by single quotes, as in 'within single quotes' which will be printed as it is by the SimpleDateFormat. For example, '('E')' prints (Wed). If you give an incorrect pattern or forget to use single quotes for separating your text from pattern letters inside the pattern string, you'll get an IllegalArgumentException exception for passing an "Illegal pattern."

Now, look at a similar example for creating custom time pattern strings. Here is the list of important letters useful for defining a custom time pattern:

a Marker for the text am/pm marker
H Hour (value range 0-23)
k Hour (value range 1-24)
K Hour in am/pm (value range 0-11)
h Hour in am/pm (value range 1-12)
m Minute
s Second
S Millisecond
z Time zone (general time zone format)

For more letters and their descriptions, see the JavaDoc for the SimpleDateFormat class. Listing 12-17 is a program that uses simple to difficult pattern strings for creating custom time formats.

Listing 12-17. CustomTimePatterns.java

```java
import java.util.*;
import java.text.*;

// Using an example, illustrates the use of "pattern strings" for constructing custom time formats
class TimePattern {
        public static void main(String []args) {
                // patterns from simple to complex ones
                String [] timeFormats = {
                        "h:mm", /* h is hour in am/pm (1-12), m is minute */
                        "hh 'o''clock'",   /* '' is the escape sequence to print a single quote */
                        "H:mm a", /* H is hour in day (0-23), a is am/pm*/
                        "hh:mm:ss:SS", /* s is seconds, S is milliseconds */
                        "K:mm:ss a, zzzz" /*K is hour in am/pm(0-11), z is time zone */
                };
                Date today = new Date();
                System.out.println("Default format for the time is " +
                DateFormat.getTimeInstance().format(today));
                for(String timeFormat : timeFormats) {
                        System.out.printf("Time in pattern \"%s\" is %s %n", timeFormat,
                        new SimpleDateFormat(timeFormat).format(today));
                }
        }
}
```

It printed the following:

```
Default format for the time is 3:10:05 PM
Time in pattern "hh 'o''clock'" is 03 o'clock
Time in pattern "h:mm" is 3:10
Time in pattern "H:mm a" is 15:10 PM
Time in pattern "hh:mm:ss:SS" is 03:10:05:355
Time in pattern "K:mm:ss a, zzzz" is 3:10:05 PM, GMT + 05:30
```

Note that the output differs based on the pattern string you use in this program.

Points to Remember

Here are some pointers that might prove useful on your exam:

- There are many ways to get or create a Locale object. We list four options here for creating an instance of Italian locale that corresponds to the language code of it.

    Option 1: Use the constructor of the Locale class: Locale(String language, String country, String variant):

    Locale locale1 = new Locale("it", "", "");

    Option 2: Use the forLanguageTag(String languageTag) method in the Locale class:

    Locale locale2 = Locale.forLanguageTag("it");

    Option 3: Build a Locale object by instantiating Locale.Builder and then call setLanguageTag() from that object:

    Locale locale3 = new Locale.Builder().setLanguageTag("it").build();

    Option 4: Use the predefined static final constants for locales in the Locale class:

    Locale locale4 = Locale.ITALIAN;

    You can choose the way to create a Locale object based on your need. For example, the Locale class has only a few predefined constants for locales. If you want a Locale object from one of the predefined ones, you can straightaway use it, or you'll have to check which other option to use.

- Instead of calling Locale's getDisplayCountry() method, which takes no arguments, you can choose the overloaded version of getDisplayCountry(Locale), which takes a Locale object as an argument. This will print the name of the country *as in the passed locale*. For example, for the call Locale.GERMANY.getDisplayCountry(), you'll get the output "Deutschland" (that's how Germans refer to their country); however, for the call Locale.GERMANY. getDisplayCountry(Locale.ENGLISH), you'll get the output "Germany" (that's how British refer to the country name Germany).

QUESTION TIME!

---

1. Consider this program:

```java
import java.text.NumberFormat;
import java.text.ParseException;

public class FractionDigits {
    public static void main(String[] args) {
        String[] numbers = {"1.222", "0.456789F"};
        NumberFormat numberFormat = NumberFormat.getInstance();
        numberFormat.setMaximumFractionDigits(2);
```

```
                for(String number : numbers) {
                        try {
                                System.out.println(numberFormat.parse(number));
                        }
                        catch(ParseException pe) {
                                System.out.println("Failed parsing " + number);
                        }
                }
        }
}
```

This program prints which of the following?

A) 1.22

    0.45

B) 1.22

    0.46

C) 1.222

    0.456789

D) 1.222

    Failed parsing 0.456789

E) Failed parsing 1.222

    0.456789

F) Failed parsing 1.222

    Failed parsing 0.456789

Answer:

C) 1.222

    0.456789

(The parse() method reads the values and converts it to Number if it succeeds. So, it does not use the maximum fraction digits set using setMaximumFractionDigits; however, if it were to use the format() method, which is meant for printing numbers, it will use this maximum fraction digits limit set.)

2. Consider this program:

```
import java.text.SimpleDateFormat;
import java.util.Date;
import java.util.Locale;

// Use SimpleDateFormat for creating custom date and time formats as a "pattern string"
class PatternStringExample {
    public static void main(String []args) {
            String pattern = "EEEE";
            SimpleDateFormat formatter = new SimpleDateFormat(pattern, Locale.US);
```

```
        Date today = new Date();
        System.out.println(formatter.format(today));
    }
}
```

Which of the following is the most likely output (i.e., the output that would match with the string pattern EEEE given in this code segment)?

A) F

B) Friday

C) Sept

D) September

Answer: B) Friday

(E is the day name in the week; the pattern EEEE prints the name of the day in its full format. Fri is a short form which would be printed by the pattern E, but EEEE will print the day of the week in full form, i.e., Friday. Since the locale is us Locale.US, it will print in English. Sept or September is impossible since E refers to the name in the week, not in a month.)

3.   Which one of the following statements makes use of a factory method?

A)   `Locale locale1 = new Locale("it", "", "");`

B)   `NumberFormat.getInstance(Locale.GERMANY);`

C)   `Locale locale3 = new Locale.Builder().setLanguageTag("it").build();`

D)   `Date today = new Date();`

E)   `Locale locale4 = Locale.ITALIAN;`

Answer: B) `NumberFormat.getInstance(Locale.GERMANY);`

(A factory method creates an instance and returns back. Using a constructor directly to create an object is not related to a factory method, so A) and D) are not correct. C) builds a locale and is perhaps an example for the Builder pattern. E) merely accesses the predefined `Locale` object; so it's not a method.)

4.   Which of the following is a correct override for extending the `ListResourceBundle` class?

A)   ```
      public HashMap<String, String> getContents() {
              Map<String, String>contents = new HashMap<>();
              contents.add("MovieName", "Avatar");
              return contents;
      }
      ```

B)    ```
      public Object[] getContents() {
              return new Object[] { { "MovieName" } , { "Avatar" } };
      }
      ```

C)   ```
      public Object[][] getContents() {
              return new Object[][] { { "MovieName", "Avatar" } };
      }
      ```
      ```

```
D)  public String[] getKeysAndValues() {
            return new String[] { { "MovieName" } , { "Avatar" } };
    }
```

```
E)  public String[] getProperties() {
            return new String[] { { "MovieName" }, { "Avatar" } };
    }
```

Answer: C)

```
public Object[][] getContents() {
    return new Object[][] { { "MovieName", "Avatar" } };
}
```

(The return type of the getContents() method is Object[][]. Further, the method should return a new object of type Object [][]. So C) is the correct answer.)

Summary

Read and Set the Locale Using the Locale Object

- A *locale* represents a language, culture, or country; the Locale class in Java provides an abstraction for this concept.

- Each locale can have three entries: the language, country, and variant. You can use standard codes available for language and country to form locale tags. There are no standard tags for variants; you can provide variant strings based on your need.

- The getter methods in the Locale class—such as getLanguage(), getCountry(), and getVariant()—return *codes*; whereas the similar methods of getDisplayCountry(), getDisplayLanguage(), and getDisplayVariant() return *names*.

- The getDefault() method in Locale returns the default locale set in the JVM. You can change this default locale to another locale by using the setDefault() method.

- There are many ways to create or get a Locale object corresponding to a locale:

  - Use the constructor of the Locale class.

  - Use the forLanguageTag(String languageTag) method in the Locale class.

  - Build a Locale object by instantiating Locale.Builder and then call setLanguageTag() from that object.

  - Use the predefined static final constants for locales in the Locale class.

Build a Resource Bundle for Each Locale

- A resource bundle is a set of classes or property files that help define a set of keys and map those keys to locale-specific values.

- The class ResourceBundle has two derived classes: PropertyResourceBundle and ListResourceBundle. You can use ResourceBundle.getBundle() to automatically load a bundle for a given locale.

- The `PropertyResourceBundle` class provides support for multiple locales in the form of property files. For each locale, you specify the keys and values in a property file for that locale. You can use only Strings as keys and values.

- To add support for a new locale, you can extend the `ListResourceBundle` class. In this derived class, you have to override the `Object [][] getContents()` method. The returned array must have the list of keys and values. The keys must be Strings, and values can be any objects.

- When passing the key string to the `getObject()` method to fetch the matching value in the resource bundle, make sure that the passed keys and the key in the resource bundle exactly match (the keyname is case sensitive). If they don't match, you'll get a `MissingResourceException`.

- The naming convention for a fully qualified resource bundle name is
`packagequalifier.bundlename` + `"_"` + `language` + `"_"` + `country` + `"_"` +
`(variant` + `"_#"` | `"#")` + `script` + `"-"` + `extensions`.

Load a Resource Bundle in an Application

- The process of finding a matching resource bundle is same for classes extended from `ListResourceBundles` as for property files defined for `PropertyResourceBundles`.

- Here is the search sequence to look for a matching resource bundle. Search starts from Step 1. If at any step the search finds a match, the resource bundle is loaded. Otherwise, the search proceeds to the next step.

  - **Step 1:** The search starts by looking for an exact match for the resource bundle with the full name.

  - **Step 2:** The last component (the part separated by _) is dropped and the search is repeated with the resulting shorter name. *This process is repeated till the last locale modifier is left.*

  - **Step 3:** The search is restarted using the full name of the bundle for the default locale.

  - **Step 4:** Search for the resource bundle with just the name of the bundle.

  - **Step 5:** The search fails, throwing a `MissingBundleException`.

- The `getBundle()` method takes a `ResourceBundle.Control` object as an additional parameter. By extending this `ResourceBundle.Control` class and passing that object, you can control or customize the resource bundle searching and loading process.

Format Text for Localization Using NumberFormat and DateFormat

- To handle date and time, numbers, and currencies in a culture-sensitive way, you can use the `java.text.Format` class and its two main derived classes `NumberFormat` and `DateFormat` for that.

- The `NumberFormat` class provides support locale-sensitive handling of numbers relating to how thousands are separated, treating a number as a currency value, etc.

- The `NumberFormat` class provides methods to format or parse numbers. "Formatting" means converting a numeric value to a textual form suitable for displaying to users; "parsing" means converting a number back to numeric form for use in the program. The `parse()` method returns a `Number` if successful—otherwise it throws `ParseException` (a checked exception).

- `NumberFormat` has many factory methods: `getInstance()`, `getCurrencyInstance()`, `getIntegerInstance()`, and `getPercentInstance()`.

- The Currency class provides support for handling currency values in a locale-sensitive way.

- The DateFormat class provides support for processing date and time in a locale-sensitive manner.

- The DateFormat has three overloaded factory methods—getDateInstance(), getTimeInstance(), and getDateTimeInstance()—that return DateFormat instances for processing date, time, and both date and time, respectively.

- SimpleDateFormat (derived from DateFormat) uses the concept of a pattern string to support custom formats for date and time.

- You encode the format of the date or time using case-sensitive letters to form a date or time pattern string.

■ ■ ■

CHAPTER 13

Threads

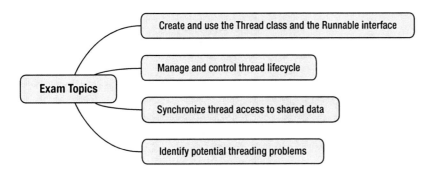

- Create and use the Thread class and the Runnable interface
- Manage and control thread lifecycle

Exam Topics

- Synchronize thread access to shared data
- Identify potential threading problems

These days, when you buy a computer—be it a laptop or a desktop—you can see labels like *dual core*, *quad core*, etc. to describe the type of processor inside the system. Processors these days have multiple cores, which are multiple execution units in the same processor. To make the best use of these multi-cores, we need to run tasks or threads in parallel. In other words, we need to make our programs multi-threaded (or concurrent). In essence, concurrency is gaining importance with more widespread use these days. Fortunately, Java has built-in support for concurrency. In this chapter, you'll learn the basics of multi-threaded programming and how to write concurrent programs and applications. More advanced topics about concurrency are covered in the next chapter.

The Latin root of the word *concurrency* means "running together." In programming, you can have multiple threads running in parallel in a program executing different tasks at the same time. Therefore, it is a powerful and useful feature.

Multiple threads can run in the context of the same process and thus share the same resources. You can use multi-threading for various reasons. In GUI applications or applets, multi-threading improves the responsiveness of the application to the users. For large computation-intensive applications, parallelizing the jobs can improve the performance of the application if it is running on multi-processor or multi-core machine.

Introduction to Concurrent Programming

In a typical application like a word processor, many tasks need to be executed at the same time—say, responding to the user, checking spellings, carrying out formatting and certain associated background tasks, etc. Executing multiple tasks at a time is expected from an interactive application like a word processor. It is possible to do such tasks sequentially; however, the user experience might not remain same. For example, many word processors have an auto-save feature. If the auto-save is invoked every 60 seconds, and if during that time the application will not respond to the user's actions, the user will feel as if the application is hanging. Instead of executing such tasks sequentially, if the auto-save task is automatically executed in the background without disrupting the main activity of responding to the user, the user experience will be much better. A similar scenario is running spell check in a dictionary in the background as the user types some words and then suggesting alternative spelling for misspelled words. Performing such activities in parallel enhances the responsiveness of the application, and thus the user experience. Such parallel activities can be implemented as threads: running multiple threads in parallel at the same time is called *multi-threading* or *concurrency*.

Multi-threading is very useful for Internet applications as well. For example, an applet displaying stock market updates might want to retrieve the latest information and display graphs and text updates. You can write a straightforward infinite loop that will keep waiting for the updates and then refresh the graphics and text. This approach wastes processor cycles; also, the user will feel that the applet hangs when an update occurs. A better approach is to make a thread wait for the updates to occur and inform the main thread when any update happens. Then separate threads can refresh the applet graphics and text.

The `Object` and `Thread` classes and the `Runnable` interface provide the necessary support for concurrency in Java. The `Object` class has methods like `wait()`, `notify()`/`notifyAll()`, etc., which are useful for multi-threading. Since every class in Java derives from the `Object` class, all the objects have some basic multi-threading capabilities. For example, you can acquire a lock on *any* object in Java (don't worry if you don't understand yet what we mean by "acquiring a lock"—we'll discuss it later in this chapter). However, to *create* a thread, this basic support from `Object` is not useful. For that, a class should extend the `Thread` class or implement the `Runnable` interface. Both `Thread` and `Runnable` are in the `java.lang` library, so you don't have to import these classes explicitly for writing multi-threaded programs.

Important Threading-Related Methods

Table 13-1 lists some important methods in the `Thread` class, which you'll be using in this chapter.

***Table 13-1.** Important Methods in the Thread Class*

Method	Method Type	Short Description
`Thread currentThread()`	Static method	Returns reference to the current thread.
`String getName()`	Instance method	Returns the name of the current thread.
`int getPriority()`	Instance method	Returns the priority value of the current thread.
`void join()`, `void join(long)`, `void join(long, int)`	Overloaded instance methods	The current thread invoking join on another thread waits until the other thread dies. You can optionally give the timeout in milliseconds (given in `long`) or timeout in milliseconds as well as nanoseconds (given in `long` and `int`).
`void run()`	Instance method	Once you start a thread (using the `start()` method), the `run()` method will be called when the thread is ready to execute.
`void setName(String)`	Instance method	Changes the name of the thread to the given name in the argument.
`void setPriority(int)`	Instance method	Sets the priority of the thread to the given argument value.
`void sleep(long)` `void sleep(long, int)`	Overloaded static methods	Makes the current thread sleep for given milliseconds (given in `long`) or for given milliseconds and nanoseconds (given in `long` and `int`).
`void start()`	Instance method	Starts the thread; JVM calls the `run()` method of the thread.
`String toString()`	Instance method	Returns the string representation of the thread; the string has the thread's name, priority, and its group.

In this chapter, you'll also be using some threading related methods in the Object class shown in Table 13-2.

Table 13-2. *Important Threading-Related Methods in the Object Class*

Method	Method Type	Short Description
void wait(), void wait(long), void wait(long, int)	Overloaded instance methods	The current thread should have acquired a lock on this object before calling any of the wait methods.
		If wait() is called, the thread waits infinitely until some other thread notifies (by calling the notify()/notifyAll() method) for this lock.
		The method wait(long) takes milliseconds as an argument. The thread waits till it is notified or the timeout happens.
		The wait(long, int) method is similar to wait(long) and additionally takes nanoseconds as an argument.
void notify()	Instance method	The current thread should have acquired a lock on this object before calling notify(). The JVM chooses a *single* thread that is waiting on the lock and wakes it up.
void notifyAll()	Instance method	The current thread should have acquired a lock before calling notifyAll(). The JVM wakes up *all* the threads waiting on a lock.

Creating Threads

A Java thread can be created in two ways: by extending the Thread class or by implementing the Runnable interface. Both of them have a method named run(). The JVM will call this method when a thread starts executing. You can think of the run() method as a starting point for the execution of a thread, just like the main() method, which is the starting point for the execution of a program. You'll first see two examples for creating threads—extend Thread and implement Runnable—before learning the differences between them.

Extending the Thread Class

You'll first consider how to extend the Thread class. You need to override the run() method when you want to extend the Thread class. If you don't override the run() method, the default run() method from the Thread class will be called, which does nothing.

To override the run() method, you need to declare it as public; it takes no arguments and has a void return type—in other words, it should be declared as public void run().

A thread can be created by invoking the start() method on the object of the Thread class (or its derived class). When the JVM schedules the thread, it will move the thread to a *runnable* state and then execute the run() method. (We'll discuss thread states later in this chapter). When the run() method completes its execution and returns, the thread will terminate. Listing 13-1 is the first example of multi-threading.

Listing 13-1. MyThread1.java

```java
class MyThread1 extends Thread {
        public void run() {
                try {
                        sleep(1000);
                }
                catch (InterruptedException ex) {
                        ex.printStackTrace();
                        // ignore the InterruptedException - this is perhaps the one of the
                        // very few of the exceptions in Java which is acceptable to ignore
                }
                System.out.println("In run method; thread name is: "+getName());
        }
        public static void main(String args[])  {
                Thread myThread = new MyThread1();
                myThread.start();
                System.out.println("In main method; thread name is: "+
                        Thread.currentThread().getName());
        }
}
```

This program prints the following:

```
In main method; thread name is: main
In run method; thread name is: Thread-0
```

In this example, the MyThread1 class extends the Thread class. You have overridden the run() method in this class. This run() method will be called when the thread runs. In the main() function, you create a new thread and start it using the start() method. An important note: you do not invoke the run() method directly. Instead you start the thread using the start() method; the run() method is invoked automatically by the JVM. We'll revisit this topic later.

For printing the name of the thread, you can use the instance method getName(), which returns a String. Since main() is a static method, you don't have access to this reference. So you get the current thread name using the static method currentThread() in the Thread class (which returns a Thread object). Now you can call getName on that returned object. As you'll see later, the main() method is also executed as a thread! However, inside the run() method, you can directly call the getName() method: MyThread1 extends Thread, so all base class members are available in MyThread1 also.

The program prints messages from both the main thread and myThread (that you created in main). The name of the thread printed is *Thread-0*. You'll see the default naming conventions for threads a little later.

Figure 13-1 shows how this program executes and prints the output. Note that the main thread and the myThread1 thread execute at the same time (i.e., concurrently), as shown in the diagram. If you try this program a couple of times, you'll either get the output shown above, or the order of these two statements might be reversed (depending on which thread is scheduled first for executing this statement). You'll study this non-deterministic behavior a little later in this chapter.

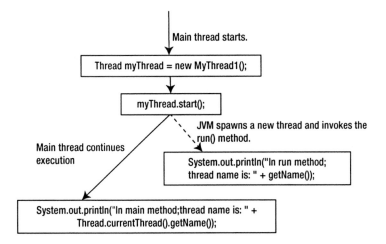

Figure 13-1. *Spawning a new thread from the main method*

Implementing the Runnable Interface

The Thread class itself implements the Runnable interface. Instead of extending the Thread class, you can implement the Runnable interface. The Runnable interface declares a sole method, run().

```
// in java.lang package
public interface Runnable {
        public void run();
}
```

When you implement the Runnable interface, you need to define the run() method. Remember Runnable does not declare the start() method. So, how do you create a thread if you implement the Runnable interface? Thread has an overloaded constructor, which takes a Runnable object as an argument.

```
Thread(Runnable target)
```

You can use this overloaded constructor to create a thread from a class that implements the Runnable interface.

First, let's change the previous program by implementing the Runnable interface. If you change "class MyThread1 extends Thread" to "class MyThread1 implements Runnable" and compile the code, you get two compiler errors:

```
MyThread1.java:3: cannot find symbol
symbol  : method getName()
location: class MyThread1
                System.out.println("In run method; thread name is: " + this.getName());

MyThread1.java:7: incompatible types
found    : MyThread1
required: java.lang.Thread
                Thread myThread=new MyThread1();
```

The getName() method is available in the Thread class, but the MyThread1 class does not extend Thread any more, so it results in a compiler error. Similarly, the start() method is available in the Thread class, and you don't have that method any more since you directly implement Runnable.

Listing 13-2 contains the improved version of the program implementing the Runnable interface after fixing these two compiler errors.

Listing 13-2. MyThread2.java

```java
class MyThread2 implements Runnable {
        public void run() {
                System.out.println("In run method; thread name is: "+
                Thread.currentThread().getName());
        }

        public static void main(String args[]) throws Exception {
                Thread myThread = new Thread(new MyThread2());
                myThread.start();
                System.out.println("In main method; thread name is: "+
                Thread.currentThread().getName());
        }
}
```

It prints the same output as the previous program:

```
In main method; thread name is: main
In run method; thread name is: Thread-0
```

You are implementing the run() method like the previous program. However, to get the name of the string, you must follow a round-about route and get the thread name with Thread.currentThread().getName(), as you did in the case of getting the thread name in the main() method. Similarly, in the main() method, to create a thread you must pass the object of the class to the Thread constructor. It was easy and convenient to just create the MyThread1 object and call the start() method on that while extending the Thread class.

SHOULD YOU EXTEND THE THREAD OR IMPLEMENT THE RUNNABLE?

You can either extend the Thread class or implement the Runnable interface to create a thread. So, which one do you choose?

The Thread class has the default implementation of the run() method, so if you don't provide a definition of the run() method while extending the Thread class, the compiler will not complain. However, the default implementation in the Thread class does *nothing*, so if you want your thread to do some meaningful work, you need to still define it. The Runnable interface declares the run() method, so you *must* define the run() method in your class if you implement the Runnable interface. So it doesn't matter if you implement Runnable or extend Thread. You have to define the run() method for all practical reasons. In summary, that is not a major difference between extending a Thread and implementing Runnable. How about an inheritance relationship?

Since Java supports only single inheritance, if you extend from Thread, you cannot extend from any other class. Since inheritance is an is-a relationship, you will rarely need the class to have an is-a relationship with the Thread class. So OOP purists argue that you should not extend the Thread class. On the other hand, if you implement the Runnable interface, you can still extend some other class. So, many Java experts suggest that it is better to implement the Runnable interface unless there are some strong reasons to extend the Thread class.

However, extending the Thread class is more convenient in many cases. In the example you saw for getting the name of the thread, you had to use Thread.currentThread().getName() when implementing the Runnable interface whereas you just used the getName() method directly while extending Thread since MyThread1 extends Thread. So, extending Thread is a little more convenient in this case.

Both the techniques are useful and mostly equivalent for problem solving. So take a practical perspective here: use either of them as needed for the specific problem you are trying to solve. For the OCPJP 7 exam, you'll have to know how to create classes for threading either by extending the Thread class or implementing the Runnable interface, as well as the difference between the two approaches.

The Start() and Run() Methods

You override the run() method but invoke the start() method. Why can't you directly call the run() method? If you change the previous program by only changing myThread.start() to myThread.run(), what will happen? Listing 13-3 shows the program with this modification (plus changing the name of this class to MyThread3).

Listing 13-3. MyThread3.java

```java
class MyThread3 implements Runnable {
        public void run() {
                System.out.println("In run method; thread name is: "+
                Thread.currentThread().getName());
        }

        public static void main(String args[]) throws Exception {
                Thread myThread=new Thread(new MyThread3());
                myThread.run(); // note run() instead of start() here
                System.out.println("In main method; thread name is : "+
                Thread.currentThread().getName());
        }
}
```

This prints the following:

```
In run method; thread name is: main
In main method; thread name is: main
```

Now the output is different! If you call the run() method directly, it simply *executes as part of the calling thread.* It does not execute as a thread: it doesn't get scheduled and get called by the JVM. That is why the getName() method in the run() method returns "main" instead of "Thread-0." When you call the start() method, the thread gets scheduled and the run() method is invoked by the JVM when it is time to execute that thread.

Never call the run() method directly for invoking a thread. Use the start() method and leave it to the JVM to implicitly invoke the run() method. Calling the run() method directly instead of calling start() is a mistake and is fairly common bug.

Thread Name, Priority, and Group

You need to understand three main aspects associated with each Java thread: its *name, priority,* and the *thread group* to which it belongs.

Every thread has a name, which you can used to identify the thread. If you do not give a name explicitly, a thread will get a default name. The priority can vary from 1, the lowest, to 10, the highest. The priority of the normal thread is by default 5, and you can change this default priority value by explicitly providing a priority value. Every thread is part of a *thread group.* It's a rarely used feature, so we won't cover it in this book. The toString() method of Thread prints these three details, so see Listing 13-4 for a simple program to get these details.

Listing 13-4. SimpleThread.java

```java
class SimpleThread {
        public static void main(String []s) {
                Thread t=new Thread();
                System.out.println(t);
        }
}
```

This program prints the following:

```
Thread[Thread-0,5,main]
```

Thread is the name of the class. Within "[" and "]" is the name of the thread, its priority, and the thread group. You did not give any name to the thread, so the default name Thread-0 was given (as you create more threads, threads will be given names like Thread-1, Thread-2, etc). The default priority is 5. You created the thread in main(), so the default thread group is "main."

Now let's try changing the name and priority of the thread using the setName() and setPriority() methods:

```java
Thread t=new Thread();
t.setName("SimpleThread");
t.setPriority(9);
System.out.println(t);
```

This code segment prints the following:

```
Thread[SimpleThread,9,main]
```

The thread has the name and priority that you gave it. You can change the name of the threads as you wish and it does not change the behavior of the program. However, you need to be careful in changing thread priority since it can affect scheduling of threads. You can programmatically access the minimum, normal, and maximum priority of the threads using the static members MIN_PRIORITY, NORM_PRIORITY, and MAX_PRIORITY , as shown in Listing 13-5.

Listing 13-5. ThreadPriorities.java

```java
class ThreadPriorities {
        public static void main(String []s) {
                System.out.println("Minimum priority of a thread: " + Thread.MIN_PRIORITY);
                System.out.println("Normal priority of a thread: " + Thread.NORM_PRIORITY);
                System.out.println("Maximum priority of a thread: " + Thread.MAX_PRIORITY);
        }
}
```

This program prints the following:

```
Minimum priority of a thread: 1
Normal priority of a thread: 5
Maximum priority of a thread: 10
```

Using the Thread.sleep() Method

Let's say you want to implement a countdown timer for a time bomb that counts from nine to zero pausing 1 second for each count. After reaching zero, it should print "Boom!!!" You can implement this functionality by creating a thread to execute the countdown. In order to pause it for each second, you can call the Thread.sleep method. See Listing 13-6.

Listing 13-6. TimeBomb.java

```java
class TimeBomb extends Thread {
        String [] timeStr ={ "Zero", "One", "Two", "Three", "Four", "Five", "Six", "Seven", "Eight",
        "Nine" };

        public void run() {
                for(int i=9; i>= 0; i--) {
                        try {
                                System.out.println(timeStr[i]);
                                Thread.sleep(1000);
                        }
                        catch(InterruptedException ie) {
                                ie.printStackTrace();
                        }
                }
        }

        public static void main(String []s) {
                TimeBomb timer =new TimeBomb();
                System.out.println("Starting 10 second count down... ");
                timer.start();
                System.out.println("Boom!!!");
        }
}
```

It prints the following with 1 second pause for printing from Nine to Zero:

```
Starting 10 second count down...
Boom!!!
Nine
Eight
Seven
Six
Five
Four
Three
Two
One
Zero
```

The program didn't quite work. The message "Boom!!!" got printed even before the countdown started! Before discussing the cause of this strange behavior, let's go over the basics of the sleep() method.

You use the static method sleep() available in the Thread class for putting the current thread to sleep (or pause) for a certain time period. There are two overloaded static sleep() methods in the Thread class:

```
void sleep(long)
void sleep(long, int)
```

The first version of the sleep() method takes milliseconds as an argument. The second version, in addition to the milliseconds, takes nanoseconds as the second argument.

The sleep() method throws InterruptedException. Since InterruptedException is a checked exception (it extends from the Exception class), you need to provide a try-catch block around sleep() or declare the run() method that throws the exception InterruptedException. However, if you declare void run() throws InterruptedException, you won't be overriding the run() method since the exception specification is different (the run() method does not throw any checked exceptions). So, you must provide a try-catch block to handle this exception within run(). What should you do to handle InterruptedException?

First, you need to understand what InterruptedException means and when it gets thrown. A thread can "interrupt" another thread, say, to request it to stop working. In that case, the thread receiving the interrupt—if it is in sleep() or wait() (which we'll revisit later)—results in throwing an InterruptedException. The thread receiving the interrupt can ignore the interrupt and continue execution (which is not a good idea, but it is possible to do so), or it can stop the execution. You will not interrupt other threads in the multi-threaded programs we cover in this book. So let's assume that your threads will not get any interrupts, and you'll ignore the exception and ask the thread to continue working. In other words, you'll be consciously ignoring the InterruptedException (after calling the printStackTrace() method of the exception); however, in real-world programs, you may need to handle this exception if you use a thread interrupt feature.

Coming back to the program's output, the message "Boom!!!" gets printed just after printing "Starting 10 second count down. . . " and not after counting down to zero. Why did this happen?

The main thread starts the execution of the timer thread by calling timer.start(). The main thread execution is independent of the execution of the timer thread, so it executes the next statement, which is printing "Boom!!!" to the console.

But remember that you want the main() method to wait until the timer thread completes. How do you do that? For that you'll have to learn how to use the join() method provided in the Thread class.

Using Thread's Join Method

The Thread class has the instance method join() for waiting for a thread to "die." In the TimeBomb program, you want the main() thread to wait for the timer thread to complete its execution. You can use the instance method join() in the Thread class to achieve that. Here is the improved version of the TimeBomb program, with changes only in the main() method:

```java
public static void main(String []s) {
        TimeBomb timer = new TimeBomb();
        System.out.println("Starting 10 second count down... ");
        timer.start();
        try {
                timer.join();
        }
        catch(InterruptedException ie) {
                ie.printStackTrace();
        }
        System.out.println("Boom!!!");
}
```

Now the program prints the output as expected:

```
Starting 10 second count down...
Nine
Eight
Seven
Six
Five
Four
Three
Two
One
Zero
Boom!!!
```

The Thread class has three overloaded versions of the join() method:

```
void join();
void join(long);
void join(long, int);
```

If the current thread invokes join() (the first overloaded version listed here) on an instance of another thread, then the current thread waits indefinitely for that other thread to die. The next two overloaded methods take a "timeout" period as an argument; the current thread will wait for the other thread to die only until the timeout period expires. The current thread will continue execution in case the other thread doesn't complete before that timeout period. The second method takes the timeout period in milliseconds (long type value) and the third overloaded version takes both milliseconds as well as nanoseconds (long and int type values).

The join() method also throws InterruptedException; you'll ignore this exception for the same reasons discussed for the sleep() method earlier in this chapter.

Asynchronous Execution

In the previous program, you saw that the main thread and the thread that you created execute independently. In other words, threads run *asynchronously*. Threads do not run sequentially (like function calls), so the order of execution of threads is not predictable—in other words, thread behavior is *non-deterministic* in nature. To understand this, consider Listing 13-7.

Listing 13-7. AsyncThread.java

```
class AsyncThread extends Thread {
        public void run() {
                System.out.println("Starting the thread " + getName());
                for(int i=0; i<3; i++) {
                        System.out.println("In thread " + getName() + "; iteration " + i);
                        try {
                                // sleep for sometime before the next iteration
                                Thread.sleep(10);
                        }
                        catch(InterruptedException ie) {
                                // we're not interrupting any threads
```

```
                                    // - so safe to ignore this exeception
                                    ie.printStackTrace();
                            }
                    }
            }

            public static void main(String args[]) {
                    AsyncThread asyncThread1 = new AsyncThread();
                    AsyncThread asyncThread2 = new AsyncThread();
                    // start both the threads around the same time
                    asyncThread1.start();
                    asyncThread2.start();
            }
}
```

In Listing 13-7, the run() method has a for loop that iterates three times. In the for loop, you print the name of the thread and the iteration number. After printing this info, you force the current thread to sleep for 10 milliseconds.

In one sample run, the output was the following:

```
Starting the thread Thread-0
Starting the thread Thread-1
In thread Thread-1; iteration 0
In thread Thread-0; iteration 0
In thread Thread-1; iteration 1
In thread Thread-0; iteration 1
In thread Thread-0; iteration 2
In thread Thread-1; iteration 2
```

In another sample run, the output was the following:

```
Starting the thread Thread-0
Starting the thread Thread-1
In thread Thread-1; iteration 0
In thread Thread-0; iteration 0
In thread Thread-1; iteration 1
In thread Thread-0; iteration 1
In thread Thread-1; iteration 2
In thread Thread-0; iteration 2
```

As you can see, the output for these two runs is slightly different (see the italicized part in the outputs)! Why?

The threads Thread-0 and Thread-1 are executed independently. The output is not fixed and the execution order of the iterations in the threads is not predictable. A programmer cannot determine the execution order of the threads. The underlying platform may use any one of the multiple processors or time-slice a single processor to allot CPU time for a thread. This cannot be controlled by the JVM or the programmer. This is one of the fundamental and most important concepts to understand in multi-threading.

 You can neither predict nor control the order of execution of threads!

Since behavior of multi-threaded programs is non-deterministic, you must be careful in writing multi-threaded programs. You cannot expect pre-determined output based on the execution order of threads.

The States of a Thread

A thread has various states during its lifetime. It is important to understand the different states of a thread and learn to write robust code based on that understanding. You'll see three thread states—*new, runnable* and *terminated*—which are applicable to almost all threads you will create in this section. We will discuss more thread states later.

A program can access the state of the thread using Thread.State enumeration. The Thread class has the getState() instance method, which returns the current state of the thread; see Listing 13-8 for an example.

Listing 13-8. BasicThreadStates.java

```
class BasicThreadStates extends Thread {
        public static void main(String []s) throws Exception {
                Thread t=new Thread(new BasicThreadStates());
                System.out.println("Just after creating thread; \n" +
                        "        The thread state is: " + t.getState());
                t.start();
                System.out.println("Just after calling t.start(); \n" +
                        "        The thread state is: " + t.getState());
                t.join();
                System.out.println("Just after main calling t.join(); \n" +
                        "        The thread state is: " + t.getState());
        }
}
```

This program prints the following:

```
Just after creating thread;
        The thread state is: NEW
Just after calling t.start();
        The thread state is: RUNNABLE
Just after main calling t.join();
        The thread state is: TERMINATED
```

Just after the creation of the thread and just before calling the start() method on that thread, the thread is in the *new* state. After calling the start() method, the thread is ready to run or is in the running state (which you cannot determine), so it is in *runnable* state. From the main() method, you are calling t.join(). The main() method waits for the thread t to die. So, once the statement t.join() successfully gets executed by the main() thread, it means that the thread t has died or terminated. So, the thread is in the *terminated* state now.

A word of advice: be careful about accessing the thread states using the getState() method. Why? By the time you acquire information on a thread state and print it, the state could have changed! We know the last statement is confusing. To understand the problem with getting thread state information using the getState() method, consider the previous example. In one sample run of the same program, it printed the following:

```
Just after creating thread;
        The thread state is: NEW
Just after calling t.start();
        The thread state is: TERMINATED
Just after main calling t.join();
        The thread state is: TERMINATED
```

Note the italicized part of the output, the statement after printing "Just after calling t.start();". In the initial output, you got the thread state (as expected) as RUNNABLE state. However, in another execution of the same program without any change, it printed the state as TERMINATED. Why? In this case, the thread is dead before you could get a chance to check it and print its status! (Note that you have not implemented the run() method in the BasicThreadStates class, so the default implementation of the run() method does nothing and terminates quickly.)

Every Java thread goes through these three states, as shown in Figure 13-2. Among these, the *runnable* state actually consists of two separate states at the operating system level, which we will discuss now.

Figure 13-2. *Basic states in the life of a thread*

Two States in "Runnable" State

Once a thread makes the state transition from the *new* state to the *runnable* state, you can think of the thread having two states at the OS level: the *ready* state and *running* state. A thread is in the *ready* state when it is waiting for the OS to run it in the processor. When the OS actually runs it in the processor, it is in the *running* state. There might be many threads waiting for processor time. The current thread may end up taking lots of time and finally may give up the CPU voluntarily. In that case, the thread again goes back to the *ready* state. These two states are shown in Figure 13-3.

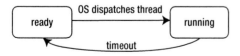

Figure 13-3. *Runnable state implemented as two states in the OS level*

Concurrent Access Problems

Concurrent programming in threads is fraught with pitfalls and problems. We will discuss two main concurrent access problems—*data races* and *deadlocks*—in this section.

Data Races

Threads share memory, and they can concurrently modify data. Since the modification can be done at the same time without safeguards, this can lead to unintuitive results.

When two or more threads are trying to access a variable and one of them wants to modify it, you get a problem known as a *data race* (also called as *race condition* or *race hazard*). Listing 13-9 shows an example of a data race.

Listing 13-9. DataRace.java

```java
// This class exposes a publicly accessible counter
// to help demonstrate data race problem
class Counter {
      public static long count=0;
}

// This class implements Runnable interface
// Its run method increments the counter three times
class UseCounter implements Runnable {
      public void increment() {
              // increments the counter and prints the value
              // of the counter shared between threads
              Counter.count++;
              System.out.print(Counter.count + "  ");
      }
      public void run() {
              increment();
              increment();
              increment();
      }
}

// This class creates three threads
public class DataRace {
      public static void main(String args[]) {
              UseCounter c=new UseCounter();
              Thread t1=new Thread(c);
              Thread t2=new Thread(c);
              Thread t3=new Thread(c);
              t1.start();
              t2.start();
              t3.start();
      }
}
```

In this program, there is a Counter class that has a static variable count. In the run() method of the UseCounter class, you increment the count three times by calling the increment() method. You create three threads in the main() function in the DataRace class and start it. You expect the program to print 1 to 9 sequentially as the threads run and increment the counters. However, when you run this program, it does print nine integer values, but the output looks like garbage! In a sample run, we got these values:

```
3   3   5   6   3   7   8   4   9
```

Note that the values will usually be different every time you run this program; when we ran it two more times, we got these outputs:

```
3   3   5   6   3   4   7   8   9
```

```
3   3   3   6   7   5   8   4   9
```

So, what is the problem?

The expression `Counter.count++` is a write operation, and the next `System.out.print` statement has a read operation for `Counter.count`. When the three threads execute, each of them has a local copy of the value `Counter.count` and when they update the `counter` with `Counter.count++`, they need not immediately reflect that value in the main memory (see Figure 13-4). In the next read operation of `Counter.count`, the local value of `Counter.count` is printed.

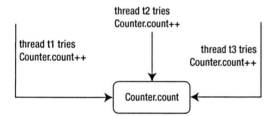

Figure 13-4. *Threads t1, t2, and t3 trying to change Counter.count, causing a data race*

Therefore, this program has a data race problem. To avoid this problem, you need to ensure that a single thread does the write and read operations together (*atomically*). The section of code that is commonly accessed and modified by more than one thread is known as *critical section*. To avoid the data race problem, you need to ensure that the critical section is executed by only one thread at a time.

How do you do that? By acquiring a lock on the object. Only a single thread can acquire a lock on an object at a time, and only that thread can execute the block of code (i.e., the critical section) protected by the lock. Until then, the other threads have to wait. Internally, this is implemented with monitors and the process is called *locking* and *unlocking* (i.e., *thread synchronization*). Let's discuss this in more detail.

Thread Synchronization

Java has a keyword, `synchronized`, that helps in thread synchronization. You can use it in two forms—synchronized blocks and synchronized methods.

Synchronized Blocks

In synchronized blocks, you use the synchronized keyword for a reference variable and follow it by a block of code. A thread has to acquire a lock on the synchronized variable to enter the block; when the execution of the block completes, the thread releases the lock. For example, you can acquire a lock on this reference if the block of code is within a non-static method:

```
synchronized(this) {
        // code segment guarded by the mutex lock
}
```

What if an exception gets thrown inside the synchronized block? Will the lock get released? Yes, no matter whether the block is executed fully or an exception is thrown, the lock will be automatically released by the JVM.

With synchronized blocks, you can acquire a lock on a reference variable only. If you use a primitive type, you will get a compiler error.

```
int i = 10;
synchronized(i) { /* block of code here*/}
```

For this code, you will get the following compiler error:

```
Lock.java:5: int is not a valid type's argument for the synchronized statement
found   : int
required: reference
                synchronized(i) { /* block of code here*/}
```

Here is an improved version of the program discussed in the previous section that performs synchronized access to Counter.count and does both read and write operations on that in a critical section. For that, you need to change only the increment method, as in

```
public void increment() {
        // These two statements perform read and write operations
        // on a variable that is commonly accessed by multiple threads.
        // So, acquire a lock before processing this "critical section"
        synchronized(this) {
                Counter.count++;
                System.out.print(Counter.count + "  ");
        }
}
```

Now the program prints the expected output correctly:

```
1  2  3  4  5  6  7  8  9
```

In the increment() method, you acquire a lock on the this reference before reading and writing to Counter.count. So, it is not possible for more than one thread to execute these statements at the same time. Since only one thread can acquire a lock and execute the "critical section" code block, the counter is incremented by only one thread at a given time; as a result, the program prints the values 1 to 9 correctly (without the data race problem).

Synchronized Methods

An entire method can be declared synchronized. In that case, when the method declared as synchronized is called, a lock is obtained on the object on which the method is called, and it is released when the method returns to the caller. Here is an example:

```
public synchronized void assign(int i) {
        val = i;
}
```

Now the assign() method is a synchronized method. If you call the assign() method, it will acquire the lock on the this reference implicitly and then execute the statement val = i;. What happens if some other thread acquired the lock already? Just like synchronized blocks, if the thread cannot get the lock, it will be *blocked* and the thread will wait until the lock becomes available.

A synchronized method is equivalent to a synchronized block if you enclose the whole method body in a synchronized(this) block. So, the equivalent assign() method using synchronized blocks is

```
public void assign() {
        synchronized(this) {
                val = i;
        }
}
```

You can declare static methods synchronized. However, what is the reference variable on which the lock is obtained? Remember that static methods do not have the implicit this reference. Static synchronized methods acquire locks on the class object. Every class is associated with an object of Class type, and you can access it using ClassName.class syntax. For example,

```
class SomeClass {
        private static int val;
        public static synchronized void assign(int i) {
                val = i;
        }
        // more members ...
}
```

In this case, the assign method acquires a lock on the SomeClass.class object when it is called. Now the equivalent assign() method using synchronized blocks can be written as

```
class SomeClass {
        private static int val;
        public static void assign(int i) {
                synchronized(SomeClass.class) {
                        val = i;
                }
        }
        // more members ...
}
```

You cannot declare constructors synchronized; it will result in a compiler error. For example, for

```
class Synchronize {
      public synchronized Synchronize() { /* constructor body */}
      // more methods
}
```

you get this error:

```
Synchronize.java:2: modifier synchronized not allowed here
      public synchronized Synchronize() { /* constructor body */}
```

Why can't you declare constructors synchronized? The JVM ensures that only one thread can invoke a constructor call (for a specific constructor) at a given point in time. So, there is no need to declare a constructor synchronized. However, if you want, you can use synchronized blocks inside constructors.

Let's get back to the Counter example. The increment() method can be rewritten as a synchronized method also:

```
// declaring the increment synchronized instead of using
// a synchronized statement for a block of code inside the method
public synchronized void increment() {
      Counter.count++;
      System.out.print(Counter.count + "  ");
}
```

Now the program prints the expected output correctly:

```
1  2  3  4  5  6  7  8  9
```

In this case, increment() is an instance method. What about static methods? First, let's look at the data race problem when the increment() method is a static method; see Listing 13-10.

Listing 13-10. DataRace.java

```
class Counter {
      public static long count=0;
}

class UseCounter implements Runnable {
      public static void increment() {
            Counter.count++;
            System.out.print(Counter.count + "  ");
      }
      public void run() {
            increment();
            increment();
            increment();
      }
}
```

```
public class DataRace {
        public static void main(String args[]) {
                UseCounter c = new UseCounter();
                Thread t1 = new Thread(c);
                Thread t2 = new Thread(c);
                Thread t3 = new Thread(c);
                t1.start();
                t2.start();
                t3.start();
        }
}
```

Yes, this program has the data race problem. To fix it, you can declare the static `increment` method as synchronized, as in

```
public static synchronized void increment() {
        Counter.count++;
        System.out.print(Counter.count + "  ");
}
```

With this change, the program does not have the data race problem.

Beginners commonly misunderstand that a synchronized block obtains a lock for a block of code. Actually, the lock is obtained for an object and not for a piece of code. The obtained lock is held until all the statements in that block complete execution.

Synchronized Blocks vs. Synchronized Methods

As you can see from the previous discussion on synchronized blocks and synchronized methods, you can use either of them to solve the data race problem. So which one should you choose? As in other language features, you need to choose between synchronized methods and blocks depending on the needs of a particular situation. Here are some factors for consideration.

If you want to acquire a lock on an object for only a small block of code and not the whole method, then synchronized blocks are sufficient; using synchronized methods is overkill in that case. In general, it is better to acquire locks for small segments of code instead of locking methods unnecessarily, so synchronized blocks are useful there. In synchronized blocks, you can explicitly provide the reference object on which you want to acquire a lock. However, in the case of a synchronized method, you do not provide any explicit reference to acquire a lock on. A synchronized method acquires an implicit lock on the `this` reference (for instance methods) and class object (for static methods).

On the other hand, if you want to acquire a lock on the entire body of a small method, then using synchronized as a method attribute is more elegant and convenient than synchronized blocks. In synchronized methods, while reading the declaration of the method itself, it becomes clear that a method is synchronized; with synchronized blocks, you need to read the documentation or look inside the code to understand that some synchronization is performed.

Deadlocks

Obtaining and using locks is tricky, and it can lead to lots of problems. One of the difficult (and common) problems is known as a *deadlock*. There are other problems such as *livelocks* and *lock starvation*, which we'll briefly discuss in the next section.

A deadlock arises when locking threads result in a situation where they cannot proceed and thus wait indefinitely for others to terminate. Say, one thread acquires a lock on resource r1 and waits to acquire another on resource r2. At the same time, say there is another thread that has already acquired r2 and is waiting to obtain a lock on r1. Neither of the threads can proceed until the other one releases the lock, which never happens—so they are stuck in a deadlock.

Listing 13-11 shows how this situation can arise (using the example from the Cricket game).

Listing 13-11. DeadLock.java

```java
// Balls class has a globally accessible data member to hold the number of balls thrown so far
class Balls {
        public static long balls=0;
}

// Runs class has a globally accessible data member to hold the number of runs scored so far
class Runs {
        public static long runs=0;
}

// Counter is a thread class that has two methods - IncrementBallAfterRun and
// IncrementRunAfterBall.
// For demonstrating deadlock, we call these two methods in the run method,
// so that locking can be requested in opposite order in these two methods
class Counter implements Runnable {
        // this method increments runs variable first and then increments the balls variable
        // since these variables are accessible from other threads,
        // we need to acquire a lock before processing them
        public void IncrementBallAfterRun() {
                // since we're updating runs variable first, lock the Runs.class reference first
                synchronized(Runs.class) {
                        // now acquire lock on Balls.class variable before updating balls variable
                        synchronized(Balls.class) {
                                Runs.runs++;
                                Balls.balls++;
                        }
                }
        }

        public void IncrementRunAfterBall() {
                // since we're updating balls variable first, lock the Balls.class reference first
                synchronized(Balls.class) {
                        // now acquire lock on Runs.class variable before updating runs variable
                        synchronized(Runs.class) {
                                Balls.balls++;
                                Runs.runs++;
                        }
                }
        }
```

413

```
        public void run() {
                // call these two methods which acquire locks in different order
                // depending on thread scheduling and the order of lock acquision,
                // a deadlock may or may not arise
                IncrementBallAfterRun();
                IncrementRunAfterBall();
        }
}

public class DeadLock {
        public static void main(String args[]) throws InterruptedException {
                Counter c = new Counter();
                // create two threads and start them at the same time
                Thread t1 = new Thread(c);
                Thread t2 = new Thread(c);
                t1.start();
                t2.start();
                System.out.println("Waiting for threads to complete execution...");
                t2.join();
                t2.join();
                System.out.println("Done.");
        }
}
```

If you execute this program, the program might run fine, or it might deadlock and never terminate (the occurrence of deadlock in this program depends on how threads are scheduled).

```
D:\>java DeadLock
Waiting for threads to complete execution...
Done.

D:\>java DeadLock
Waiting for threads to complete execution...
Done.

D:\>java DeadLock
Waiting for threads to complete execution...
[deadlock - user pressed ctrl+c to terminate the program]

D:\>java DeadLock
Waiting for threads to complete execution...
Done.
```

In this example, there are two classes, Balls and Runs, with static members called balls and runs. The Counter class has two methods, IncrementBallAfterRun() and IncrementRunAfterBall(). They acquire locks on the Balls.class and Runs.class in the opposite order. The run() method calls these two methods consecutively. The main() method in the Dead class creates two threads and starts them.

When the threads t1 and t2 execute, they invoke the methods IncrementBallAfterRun and IncrementRunAfterBall. In these methods, locks are obtained in opposite order. It might happen that t1 acquires a lock on Runs.class and then waits to acquire a lock on Balls.class. Meanwhile, t2 might have acquired the Balls.class and now will be waiting to acquire a lock on the Runs.class. Therefore, this program can lead to a deadlock (Figure 13-5).

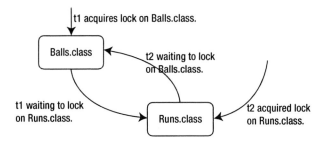

Figure 13-5. *Deadlock between threads t1 and t2*

It cannot be assured that this program will lead to a deadlock every time you execute this program. Why? You never know the sequence in which threads execute and the order in which locks are acquired and released. For this reason, such problems are said to be non-deterministic, and such problems cannot be reproduced consistently.

There are different strategies to deal with deadlocks, such as deadlock prevention, avoidance, or detection. For exam purposes, this is what you need to know about deadlocks:

- Deadlocks can arise in the context of multiple locks.

- If multiple locks are acquired in the same order, then a deadlock will not occur; however, if you acquire them in a different order, then deadlocks may occur.

- Deadlocks (just like other multi-threading problems) are non-deterministic; you cannot consistently reproduce deadlocks.

 Avoid acquiring multiple locks. If you want to acquire multiple locks, make sure that they are acquired in the same order everywhere to avoid deadlocks.

Other Threading Problems

So far we discussed data races and deadlocks with examples. We'll now briefly discuss two more threading problems: livelocks and lock starvation.

Livelocks

To help understand livelocks, let's consider an analogy. Assume that there are two robotic cars that are programmed to automatically drive in the road. There is a situation where two robotic cars reach the two opposite ends of a narrow bridge. The bridge is so narrow that only one car can pass through at a time. The robotic cars are programmed such that they wait for the other car to pass through first. When both the cars attempt to enter the bridge at the same time, the following situation could happen: each car starts to enter the bridge, notices that the other car is attempting to do the same, and reverses! Note that the cars keep moving forward and backward and thus appear as if they're doing lots of work, but there is no progress made by either of the cars. This situation is called a *livelock*.

Consider two threads t1 and t2. Assume that thread t1 makes a change and thread t2 undoes that change. When both the threads t1 and t2 work, it will appear as though lots of work is getting done, but no progress is made. This situation is called a livelock in threads.

The similarity between livelocks and deadlocks is that the process "hangs" and the program never terminates. However, in a deadlock, the threads are stuck in the same state waiting for other thread(s) to release a shared resource; in a livelock, the threads keep executing a task, and there is continuous change in the process states, but the application as a whole does not make progress.

Lock Starvation

Consider the situation in which numerous threads have different priorities assigned to them (in the range of lowest priority, 1, to highest priority, 10, which is the range allowed for priority of threads in Java). When a mutex lock is available, the thread scheduler will give priority to the threads with high priority over low priority. If there are many high-priority threads that want to obtain the lock and also hold the lock for long time periods, when will the low-priority threads get a chance to obtain the lock? In other words, in a situation where low-priority threads "starve" for a long time trying to obtain the lock is known as *lock starvation*.

There are many techniques available for detecting or avoiding threading problems like livelocks and starvation, but they are not within the scope of OCPJP7 exam. From the exam perspective, you are expected to know the different kinds of threading problems that we've already covered in this chapter.

The Wait/Notify Mechanism

In multi-threaded programs, often there is a need for one thread to communicate to another thread. The wait/notify mechanism is useful when threads must communicate in order to provide a functionality.

Let's take the example of a coffee shop. A waiter is using a coffee machine in a coffee shop and delivering coffee to customers. The coffee machine in this coffee shop is an antique machine: it makes one cup of coffee at a time, and it takes five to ten minutes time to make a cup. The waiter does not have to be idle while waiting for the coffee machine to complete making coffee; he can go to customers in the meantime to deliver the coffee prepared earlier. This example is a little contrived, though: assume that coffee machine keeps making the coffee and waiter keeps delivering it.

The method wait() allows the calling thread to wait for the wait object (on which wait() is called). In other words, if you want to make a thread wait for another thread, you can ask it to wait for the wait object using the wait() method. A thread remains in the *wait* state until some another thread calls the notify() or notifyAll() method on the wait object. To understand the wait/notify mechanism, you are going to simulate this coffee shop situation in a program. You can implement the coffee machine as one thread and the waiter as another thread in two different classes. The coffee machine can notify the waiter to take the coffee, and it can wait until the waiter has taken the coffee from the tray. Similarly, the waiter can take the coffee if it is available and notify the coffee machine to make another cup.

Explaining the wait/notify mechanism with an example involves quite a bit of code. But this is an interesting example to illustrate this concept, so read on. Listing 13-12 contains the CoffeeMachine class.

Listing 13-12. CoffeeMachine.java

```java
// The CoffeeMachine class runs as an independent thread.
// Once the machine makes a coffee, it notifies the waiter to pick it up.
// When the waiter asks the coffee machine to make a coffee again,
// it starts all over again, and this process keeps goes on ...
class CoffeeMachine extends Thread {
        static String coffeeMade = null;
        static final Object lock = new Object();
        private static int coffeeNumber = 1;
        void makeCoffee() {
                synchronized(CoffeeMachine.lock) {
                        if(coffeeMade != null) {
```

```
                try {
                        System.out.println("Coffee machine: Waiting for waiter
                        notification to deliver the coffee");
                        CoffeeMachine.lock.wait();
                }
                catch(InterruptedException ie) {
                        ie.printStackTrace();
                }
        }
        coffeeMade = "Coffee No. "+coffeeNumber ++;
        System.out.println("Coffee machine says: Made " + coffeeMade);
        // once coffee is ready, notify the waiter to pick it up
        CoffeeMachine.lock.notifyAll();
        System.out.println("Coffee machine: Notifying waiter to pick the coffee ");
    }
}

public void run() {
        while(true) {
                makeCoffee();
                try {
                        System.out.println("Coffee machine: Making another coffee now");
                        // simulate the time taken to make a coffee by calling sleep method
                        Thread.sleep(10000);
                }
                catch(InterruptedException ie) {
                        // its okay to ignore this exception
                        // since we're not using thread interrupt mechanism
                        ie.printStackTrace();
                }
        }
    }
}
```

The CoffeeMachine object is going to run as a thread, so it extends the Thread class and implements the run() method. The run() method goes on forever and keeps calling the makeCoffee() method. For each iteration, it calls sleep() for ten seconds to simulate the time taken for the coffee machine to make the coffee.

The CoffeeMachine has three static members. The coffeeMade member has the string description for the coffee that it has made. The lock member is for the synchronization between the CoffeeMachine and Waiter threads. The numOfCoffees is used internally by the makeCoffee() method to get the description of the coffee made.

The makeCoffee() method does most of the work. The first thing it does is acquire the lock CoffeeMachine.lock using the synchronized keyword. Inside the block, it checks if the coffeeMade is null or not. The first time the CoffeeMachine thread calls the makeCoffee() method, coffeeMade will be null. In other cases, it is the Waiter thread that makes coffeeMade null and notifies (using the notifyAll() method) the CoffeeMachine thread. If the Waiter thread hasn't cleared it yet, it goes to the wait() state and prints the message, "Waiting for waiter notification to deliver the coffee".

Once the Waiter notifies the CoffeeMachine thread, the machine delivers the next coffee to the waiter; it prints the message notifying the waiter to pick up the coffee. Now let's look at the Waiter class (see Listing 13-13).

Listing 13-13. Waiter.java

```java
// The Waiter runs as an independent thread
// It interacts with the CoffeeMachine to wait for a coffee
// and deliver the coffee once ready and request the coffee machine
// for the next one, and this activity keeps going on forever ...
class Waiter extends Thread {
        public void getCoffee() {
                synchronized(CoffeeMachine.lock) {
                        if(CoffeeMachine.coffeeMade == null) {
                                try {
                                        // wait till the CoffeeMachine says (notifies) that
                                        // coffee is ready
                                        System.out.println("Waiter: Will get orders till
                                                        coffee machine notifies me ");
                                        CoffeeMachine.lock.wait();
                                }
                                catch(InterruptedException ie) {
                                        // its okay to ignore this exception
                                        // since we're not using thread interrupt mechanism
                                        ie.printStackTrace();
                                }
                        }
                        System.out.println("Waiter: Delivering " + CoffeeMachine.coffeeMade);
                        CoffeeMachine.coffeeMade=null;
                        // ask (notify) the coffee machine to prepare the next coffee
                        CoffeeMachine.lock.notifyAll();
                        System.out.println("Waiter: Notifying coffee machine to make another one");
                }
        }

        public void run() {
                // keep going till the user presses ctrl-C and terminates the program
                while(true) {
                        getCoffee();
                }
        }
}
```

The Waiter class also extends the Thread since a Waiter object is going to run as a thread as well. It has a run()
method and it does something very simple: it keeps calling the getCoffee() method forever.

The Waiter class has the getCoffee() method where most of the work is done. The first thing the method does is
try to acquire a lock on CoffeeMachine.lock. Once it gets the lock, it checks if the coffeeMade is null. If the variable
is null, it means the CoffeeMachine thread is still preparing the coffee. In that case, the Waiter thread calls wait()
and then prints the message, "Will get orders till coffee machine notifies me". When the CoffeeMachine thread has
made the coffee, it will set the variable coffeeMade, and it will be non-null then; that thread will also notify the Waiter
thread using notifyAll().

Once the Waiter thread gets notified, it can deliver the coffee to the customer; it prints the message "Delivering
coffee". After that, it clears the coffeeMade variable to null and notifies the CoffeeMachine to make another coffee
("Notifying coffee machine to make another one"). Listing 13-14 shows the CoffeeShop class.

Listing 13-14. CoffeeShop.java

```
// This class instantiates two threads - CoffeeMachine and Waiter threads
// and these two threads interact with each other through wait/notify
// till you terminate the application explicitly by pressing Ctrl-C
class CoffeeShop {
        public static void main(String []s) {
                CoffeeMachine coffeeMachine=new CoffeeMachine();
                Waiter waiter=new Waiter();
                coffeeMachine.start();
                waiter.start();
        }
}
```

What the main() method in the CoffeeShop class does is trivial: it creates CoffeeMachine and Waiter threads and starts them. Now, these two threads communicate with each other and go on forever. The program output looks like this:

```
Coffee machine says: Made Coffee No. 1
Coffee machine: Notifying waiter to pick the coffee
Coffee machine: Making another coffee now
Waiter: Delivering Coffee No. 1
Waiter: Notifying coffee machine to make another one
Coffee machine says: Made Coffee No. 2
Coffee machine: Notifying waiter to pick the coffee
Coffee machine: Making another coffee now
Waiter: Will get orders till coffee machine notifies me
Waiter: Delivering Coffee No. 2
Waiter: Notifying coffee machine to make another one
Coffee machine says: Made Coffee No. 3
Coffee machine: Notifying waiter to pick the coffee
Coffee machine: Making another coffee now
Waiter: Will get orders till coffee machine notifies me
Waiter: Delivering Coffee No. 3
Waiter: Notifying coffee machine to make another one
```

// goes on forever until you press Ctrl-C to terminate the application. . .

SHOULD YOU USE NOTIFY() OR NOTIFYALL()?

You have two methods—notify() and notifyAll()—for notifying (i.e., for waking up a waiting thread in the Thread class). But which one should you use?

Let's examine the subtle difference between these two calls. The notify() method wakes up *one thread* waiting for the lock (the first thread that called wait() on that lock). The notifyAll() method wakes up *all the threads* waiting for the lock; the JVM selects one of the threads from the list of threads waiting for the lock and wakes that thread up.

In the case of a single thread waiting for a lock, there is no significant difference between notify() and notifyAll(). However, when there is more than one thread waiting for the lock, in both notify() and notifyAll(), the exact thread woken up is under the control of the JVM and you cannot programmatically control waking up a specific thread.

At first glance, it appears that it is a good idea to just call notify() to wake up one thread; it might seem unnecessary to wake up all the threads. However, the problem with notify() is that the thread woken up might not be the suitable one to be woken up (the thread might be waiting for some other condition, or the condition is still not satisfied for that thread etc). In that case, the notify() might be lost and no other thread will wake up potentially leading to a type of deadlock (the notification is lost and all other threads are waiting for notification—forever!).

To avoid this problem, it is always better to call notifyAll() when there is more than one thread waiting for a lock (or more than one condition on which waiting is done). The notifyAll() method wakes up all threads, so it is not very efficient. However, this performance loss is negligible in real world applications.

Prefer notifyAll() to notify().

Using notify()/notifyAll() will wake up only threads waiting on the lock on which it is called; it will not wake up any other threads. If by mistake you use wait() on one lock and notify()/notifyAll() on another lock, the waiting thread will never get notified and the program will hang (leading to one kind of deadlock situation)!

Let's Solve a Problem

Since the wait/notify mechanism is important to understand, let's take another example and try to understand it more rigorously.

> **Problem Statement:** *Assume that you need to implement a dice player game. This is a two player game (say the players are "Joe" and "Jane") where the players throw the dice on their turns. When one player throws the dice, another player waits. Once the player completes throwing, he/she informs the other player to play; after that, he/she starts waiting for the other player to throw the dice. You need to implement these two players as two threads working together. The game ends after each player throws 6 times (so there will be a total of 12 throws in the game).*

Since the problem statement says "implement these two players as two threads working together," your solution is a multi-threaded program with each player implemented as a thread. The problem also states that when one player throws the dice, another waits. So, you should perhaps use a wait/notify mechanism. The dice rolling should result in a random value, so you can use the Random class for creating random numbers from 1 to 6.

Here is a solution. First go through the whole program (Listing 13-15), and then you'll see the explanation of how it works.

Listing 13-15. DiceGame.java

```java
import java.util.Random;

// the Gamers class just holds the name of players who roll the dice
class Gamers {
        // prevent instantiating this utility class by making constructor private
        private Gamers() {}
        public static final String JOE = "Joe";
        public static final String JANE = "Jane";
}

// the Dice class abstracts how the dice rolls and who plays it
class Dice {
        // to remember whose turn it is to roll the dice
        private static String turn = null;
        synchronized public static String getTurn() { return turn; }
        synchronized public static void setTurn(String player) { turn = player; }

        // which player starts the game
        public static void setWhoStarts(String name) { turn = name; }

        // prevent instantiating the class by making it private (we've only static members)
        private Dice() { }

        // when we roll the dice, it should give a random result
        private static Random random = new Random();
        // random.nextInt(6) gives values from 0 to 5, so add 1 to result in roll()
        public static int roll() { return random.nextInt(6)+1; }
}

// the class Player abstracts a player playing the Dice game
// each player runs as a separate thread, so Player extends Thread class
class Player extends Thread {
        private String currentPlayer = null;
        private String otherPlayer = null;

        public Player(String thisPlayer) {
                currentPlayer = thisPlayer;
                // we've only two players; we remember them in currentPlayer and otherPlayer
                otherPlayer = thisPlayer.equals(Gamers.JOE) ? Gamers.JANE: Gamers.JOE;
        }

        public void run() {
                // each player rolls the dice 6 times in the game
                for(int i=0; i<6; i++) {
                        // acquire the lock before proceeding
                        synchronized(Dice.class) {
```

```
                        // if its not currentPlayer's turn, then
                        // wait for otherPlayers's notification
                        while(!Dice.getTurn().equals(currentPlayer)) {
                                try {
                                        Dice.class.wait(1000);
                                        System.out.println(currentPlayer +
                                                " was waiting for "+otherPlayer);
                                }
                                catch(InterruptedException ie) {
                                        ie.printStackTrace();
                                }
                        }
                        // its currentPlayer's turn now; throw the dice
                        System.out.println(Dice.getTurn()+" throws " + Dice.roll());
                        // set the turn to otherPlayer, and notify the otherPlayer
                        Dice.setTurn(otherPlayer);
                        Dice.class.notifyAll();
                }
        }
    }
}


// class DiceGame just starts the game by starting player threads
class DiceGame {
        public static void main(String []s) {
                Player player1 = new Player(Gamers.JANE);
                Player player2 = new Player(Gamers.JOE);
                // don't forget to set who starts the game
                Dice.setWhoStarts(Gamers.JOE);
                player1.start();
                player2.start();
        }
}
```

When you run the program, the sample output will be like this:

```
Joe throws 2
Jane was waiting for Joe
Jane throws 5
Joe throws 6
Jane was waiting for Joe
Jane throws 1
Joe throws 2
Jane was waiting for Joe
Jane throws 6
Joe throws 6
Jane was waiting for Joe
Jane throws 5
Joe was waiting for Jane
Joe throws 5
Jane was waiting for Joe
```

```
Jane throws 4
Joe was waiting for Jane
Joe throws 4
Jane was waiting for Joe
Jane throws 5
```

Now, let's look at the code in more detail to understand how it works.

```
// the Gamers class just holds the name of players who roll the dice
class Gamers {
        // prevent instantiating this utility class by making constructor private
        private Gamers() {}
        public static final String JOE = "Joe";
        public static final String JANE = "Jane";
}
```

The class Gamers is just a utility class that holds the name of the players (Joe and Jane). Since there is no need to instantiate the class, you declare the constructor private.

The class Dice abstracts how the dice are rolled; it also remembers the turns that the players take.

```
class Dice {
        // to remember whose turn it is to roll the dice
        private static String turn = null;
        synchronized public static String getTurn() { return turn; }
        synchronized public static void setTurn(String player) { turn = player; }

        // which player starts the game
        public static void setWhoStarts(String name) { turn = name; }

        // prevent instantiating the class by making it private (we've only static members)
        private Dice() { }

        // when we roll the dice, it should give a random result
        private static Random random = new Random();
        // random.nextInt(6) gives values from 0 to 5, so add 1 to result in roll()
        public static int roll() { return random.nextInt(6)+1; }
}
```

You have a member named turn of type String. This variable holds the name of the current player whose turn has come to roll the dice. The method getTurn() and setTurn() are getter and setter methods for this member. When the game starts, you should say who should start the game (you need to set turn to a proper initial value); you do it by calling setWhoStarts. All the members in the class are static, so there is no need to instantiate the class; you enforce this by making the constructor private.

The dice rolling should result in a random value in the range 1 to 6. You can use the Random class in the java.util package to get the random number. The Random class has an instance method of nextInt() that you can use to get the range of values you want. If you pass int value 6 to nextInt, it returns the values from 0 to 5, so you add 1 to get the value ranging from 1 to 6.

The Player class is where you do most of the work. The class Player abstracts a player playing the Dice game. Each player runs as a separate thread, so Player extends the Thread class. Alternatively, you could implement Player by implementing the Runnable interface. Both are equivalent and acceptable solutions.

```
class Player extends Thread {
        private String currentPlayer = null;
        private String otherPlayer = null;
```

423

```
        public Player(String thisPlayer) {
                currentPlayer = thisPlayer;
                // we've only two players; we remember them in currentPlayer and otherPlayer
                otherPlayer = thisPlayer.equals(Gamers.JOE) ? Gamers.JANE: Gamers.JOE;
        }
        // other members
}
```

You create two Player threads for each of the players. So, you remember the values in currentPlayer and otherPlayer; you set these values in the Player constructor.

Here is the Player's run() method:

```
public void run() {
        // each player rolls the dice 6 times in the game
        for(int i=0; i<6; i++) {
                // acquire the lock before proceeding
                synchronized(Dice.class) {
                        // if its not currentPlayer's turn, then
                        // wait for otherPlayers's notification
                        while(!Dice.getTurn().equals(currentPlayer)) {
                                try {
                                        System.out.println(currentPlayer +
                                                " waiting for "+otherPlayer);
                                        Dice.class.wait(1000);
                                }
                                catch(InterruptedException ie) {
                                        ie.printStackTrace();
                                }
                        }
                        // its currentPlayer's turn now; throw the dice
                        System.out.println(Dice.getTurn() +
                        " throws "+Dice.roll());
                        // set the turn to otherPlayer, and notify the otherPlayer
                        Dice.setTurn(otherPlayer);
                        Dice.class.notifyAll();
                }
        }
}
```

The run() method will be called for each Player thread. Each player rolls the dice six times, so you have a for loop with six iterations. In every loop iteration, you check if it's the currentPlayer's turn to roll the dice. If not, you make the player thread wait till the otherPlayer informs the currentPlayer that his/her turn has come. Before going to check the turn, you need to acquire a lock. Any common lock is good, and you use the Dice.class as the lock here. Once the currentPlayer gets the notification, he/she calls the Dice.roll() method. His/her turn is over now, so he/she sets the turn to the other player and calls notifyAll() to wake up the otherPlayer thread. You could have used the notify() method, but it is equally acceptable to use the notifyAll() method, which is better to use.

The DiceGame class does something very simple. It has the main() method and you create the Jane and Joe player objects. You set one of them to start the game. You call the start() methods for these two player threads to start playing.

If you want a mechanism to wait for a particular event to occur, a wait/notify mechanism is the best choice. Sometimes programmers solve this problem by using a sleep call, and they repeatedly check the condition to see if the event has occurred. This is an ineffective solution. Further, calling sleep does not release the lock (unlike wait), so a solution using sleep is prone to deadlocks. Do not use the sleep method when a wait/notify mechanism is the appropriate solution.

More Thread States

Earlier in this chapter we discussed three basic thread states: *new*, *runnable* and *terminated* states. In addition to these states, a thread can also be in *blocked, waiting, timed_waiting* states, which we'll discuss now. Figure 13-6 shows how and when the state transitions typically happen for these six states.

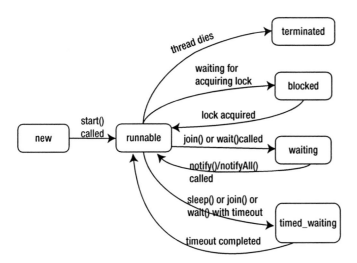

Figure 13-6. *Possible states in the lifetime of a thread*

timed_waiting and blocked States

Listing 13-16 contains a simple example to understand *timed_waiting* and *blocked* states.

Listing 13-16. MoreThreadStates.java

```java
// This Thread class just invokes sleep method after acquiring lock on its class object
class SleepyThread extends Thread {
        public void run() {
                synchronized(SleepyThread.class) {
                        try {
                                Thread.sleep(1000);
                        }
                        catch(InterruptedException ie) {
                                // its okay to ignore this exception since we're not
```

```
                                        // interrupting exceptions in this code
                                        ie.printStackTrace();
                        }
                }
        }
}

// The class creates two threads to show how to these threads will enter into
// TIMED_WAITING and BLOCKED states
class MoreThreadStates {
        public static void main(String []s) {
                Thread t1=new SleepyThread();
                Thread t2=new SleepyThread();
                t1.start();
                t2.start();
                System.out.println(t1.getName()+": I'm in state " + t1.getState());
                System.out.println(t2.getName()+": I'm in state " + t2.getState());
        }
}
```

It prints the following:

```
Thread-0: I'm in state TIMED_WAITING
Thread-1: I'm in state BLOCKED
```

You have the SleepyThread class with a run() method that just acquires a lock and goes to sleep. You're creating two threads, t1 and t2, in the main() method.

When t1 runs, it acquires the lock (SleepyThread.class) and goes to sleep. Remember, when a thread sleeps, it doesn't relinquish the lock: it just holds the lock. So sleep() is called for 1 second (1000 milliseconds; the argument to sleep() is in milliseconds), so the thread t1 is in state TIMED_WAITING.

Meanwhile, the main thread starts t2 thread. When its run() method is called, it finds that it has to acquire the lock (SleepyThread.class). However, you know that the lock is already acquired by thread t1 and the thread is still sleeping (and it is in the *timed_waiting* state). So, thread t2 waits to acquire the lock, hence it is in the *blocking* state. The main() method just prints the state of these two threads by calling the getState() method after spawning the threads.

waiting State

The *waiting* state typically happens when a thread waits for a specific condition to happen by calling the wait() method. Listing 13-17 is a simple example to illustrate the *waiting* state.

Listing 13-17. WaitingThreadState.java

```
// This class has run method which waits forever since there is no other thread to notify it
class InfiniteWaitThread extends Thread {
        static boolean okayToRun = false;
        synchronized public void run() {
                while(!okayToRun) {
                        try {
                                // note the call to wait without any timeout value
                                // so it waits forever for some thread to notify it
                                wait();
                        }
```

```
                        catch(InterruptedException ie) {
                                // its okay to ignore this exception since we're not
                                // interrupting exceptions in this code
                                ie.printStackTrace();
                        }
                }
        }
}

class WaitingThreadState {
        public static void main(String []s) {
                Thread t=new InfiniteWaitThread();
                t.start();
                System.out.println(t.getName()+": I'm in state " + t.getState());
        }
}
```

This program prints the following:

```
Thread-0: I'm in state WAITING
```

You must press Ctrl + C to terminate the thread since the thread waits infinitely for the condition to happen (i.e., okayToRun to become true). In real world programs, you'll also write code to have the condition happen; in other words, you'll write code to set okayToRun to true and then call notify()/notifyAll(). However, since this is a dummy program just to illustrate the *waiting* state, we're leaving out that part.

What if you change the wait statement inside the run statement to, say, wait(1000)? Now the program will print TIMED_WAITING. The state *timed_waiting* happens not just for sleep with timeout that you saw earlier; it also works for the wait() method call with a timeout value.

Using Thread.State enum

The Thread class defines Thread.State enumeration, which has a list of possible thread states. Listing 13-18 is a simple program that prints the value of the states in this enumeration.

Listing 13-18. ThreadStatesEnumeration.java

```
class ThreadStatesEnumeration {
        public static void main(String []s) {
                for(Thread.State state : Thread.State.values()){
                        System.out.println(state);
                }
        }
}
```

It prints the following:

```
NEW
RUNNABLE
BLOCKED
WAITING
TIMED_WAITING
TERMINATED
```

Understanding IllegalThreadStateException

You should be cautious whenever writing code for threads, always keeping in mind the states of the threads. If you don't exercise care about the underlying states, what will happen? Let's look at the simple example in Listing 13-19 first.

Listing 13-19. ThreadStateProblem.java

```
class ThreadStateProblem {
        public static void main(String []s) {
                Thread thread=new Thread();
                thread.start();
                thread.start();
        }
}
```

The program fails with this stack trace:

```
Exception in thread "main" java.lang.IllegalThreadStateException
        at java.lang.Thread.start(Unknown Source)
        at ThreadStateProblem.main(ThreadStateProblem.java:6)
```

Here, you are trying to start a thread that has already started. When you call start(), the thread moves to the *new* state. There is no proper state transition from the *new* state if you call start() again, so the JVM throws an IllegalThreadStateException.

Never call the start() method twice on the same thread.

Can you fix the problem by adding a try-catch block around the second call to start()? That is a bad solution! IllegalThreadStateException is a RuntimeException, meaning that it indicates a programming error. So, you need to fix the problem in the program instead of handling it. Even if you provide a try-catch block, what can you do within the catch block? Nothing; you can leave it empty or just log the exception. Such empty catch blocks are indications of bad code. So, the correct solution in this case is to make sure that start() is not called again for the same thread.

Never write a catch block for handling IllegalThreadStateException. If you get this exception, there is certainly a bug in the code. Fix that bug.

Listing 13-20 contains another example.

Listing 13-20. ThreadStateProblem.java

```java
class ThreadStateProblem extends Thread {
        public void run() {
                try {
                        wait(1000);
                }
                catch(InterruptedException ie) {
                        // its okay to ignore this exception since we're not
                        // interrupting exceptions in this code
                        ie.printStackTrace();
                }
        }

        public static void main(String []s) {
                new ThreadStateProblem().start();
        }
}
```

This program also crashes with IllegalMonitorStateException, like this:

```
Exception in thread "Thread-0" java.lang.IllegalMonitorStateException
        at java.lang.Object.wait(Native Method)
        at ThreadStateProblem.run(ThreadStateProblem.java:4)
```

The wait(int) method (with or without timeout value) should be called only after acquiring a lock: a wait() call adds the thread to the waiting queue of the acquired lock. If you don't do that, there is no proper transition from the *running* state to *timed_waiting* (or *waiting* state, if a timeout value is not given) to happen. So, the program crashes by throwing an IllegalMonitorStateException exception.

The correct fix is to acquire the lock before calling wait(). In this case, you can declare the run() method synchronized:

```java
synchronized public void run() {
        try {
                wait(1000);
        }
        catch(InterruptedException ie) {
                // its okay to ignore this exception since we're not
                // interrupting exceptions in this code
                ie.printStackTrace();
        }
}
```

Since the run() method is synchronized, wait() will add itself to the this object reference lock. Since there is no one calling the notify()/notifyAll() method, after a timeout of 1 second (1000 milliseconds) is over, it will return from the run() method. So, the wait(1000); statement behaves almost like a sleep(1000) statement; the difference is that calling wait() releases the lock on this object when it waits while sleep() call will not release the lock when it sleeps.

Call wait and notify/notifyAll *only* after acquiring the relevant lock.

QUESTION TIME!

1. Here is a class named PingPong that extends the Thread class. Which of the following PingPong class implementations correctly prints "ping" from the worker thread and then prints "pong" from the main thread?

A.
```java
class PingPong extends Thread {
        public void run() {
                System.out.println("ping ");
        }
        public static void main(String []args)  {
                Thread pingPong = new PingPong();
                System.out.print("pong");
        }
}
```

B.
```java
class PingPong extends Thread {
        public void run() {
                System.out.println("ping ");
        }
        public static void main(String []args)  {
                Thread pingPong = new PingPong();
                pingPong.run();
                System.out.print("pong");
        }
}
```

C.
```java
class PingPong extends Thread {
        public void run() {
                System.out.println("ping");
        }
        public static void main(String []args)  {
                Thread pingPong = new PingPong();
                pingPong.start();
                System.out.println("pong");
        }
}
```

D. ```
    class PingPong extends Thread {
            public void run() {
                    System.out.println("ping");
            }
            public static void main(String []args) throws InterruptedException{
                    Thread pingPong = new PingPong();
                    pingPong.start();
                    pingPong.join();
                    System.out.println("pong");
            }
    }
    ```

**Answer:** D.

(The main thread creates the worker thread and waits for it to complete (which prints "ping"). After that it prints "pong". So, this implementation correctly prints "ping pong". Why are the other options wrong?

The main() method creates the worker thread, but doesn't start it. So, this program only prints "pong". The program always prints "ping pong", but it is misleading. This program directly calls the run() method instead of calling the start() method. So, this is a single threaded program. The main thread and the worker thread execute independently without any coordination. So, depending on which thread is scheduled first, you can get "ping pong" or "pong ping" printed.)

2.  Consider the following program and choose the correct option describing its behavior.

```
class ThreadTest {
    public static void main(String []args) throws InterruptedException {
            Thread t1 = new Thread() {
                    public void run() { System.out.print("t1 "); }
            };
            Thread t2 = new Thread() {
                    public void run() { System.out.print("t2 "); }
            };
            t1.start();
            t1.sleep(5000);
            t2.start();
            t2.sleep(5000);
            System.out.println("main ");
    }
}
```

A. t1 t2 main

B. t1 main t2

C. main t2 t1

D. This program results in a compiler error.

E. This program throws a runtime error.

Answer: A. t1 t2 main
```

(When a new thread is created, it is in the *new* state. Then, it moves to the *runnable* state. Only from the *runnable* state can the thread go to the *timed_waiting* state after calling `sleep()`. Hence, before executing `sleep()`, the `run()` method for that thread is called. So, the program prints "t1 t2 main".)

3. You've written an application for processing tasks. In this application, you've separated the critical or urgent tasks from the ones that are not critical or urgent. You've assigned high priority to critical or urgent tasks.

    In this application, you find that the tasks that are not critical or urgent are the ones that keep waiting for an unusually long time. Since critical or urgent tasks are high priority, they run most of the time. Which one of the following multi-threading problems correctly describes this situation?

    A. Deadlock

    B. Starvation

    C. Livelock

    D. Race condition

    Answer: B. Starvation

    (The situation in which low-priority threads keep waiting for a long time to acquire the lock and execute the code in critical sections is known as starvation.)

4. Consider the following program:

```java
class ExtendThread extends Thread {
        public void run() { System.out.print(Thread.currentThread().getName()); }
}

class ThreadTest{
        public static void main(String []args) throws InterruptedException {
                Thread thread1 = new Thread(new ExtendThread(), "thread1 ");
                Thread thread2 = new Thread(thread1, "thread2 ");
                thread1.start();
                thread2.start();
                thread1.start();        // START
        }
}
```

Which one of the following correctly describes the behavior of this program?

A. The program prints the following: thread1 thread2 thread1.

B. The program prints the following: thread1 thread1 thread1.

C. The program prints the following: thread1 thread2.

D. The program results in a compiler error for the statement marked with the comment START.

E. The program throws an `IllegalMonitorStateException` when executing the statement marked with the comment START.

Answer: E. The program throws an `IllegalMonitorStateException` when executing the statement marked with the comment START.

(It is illegal to call the start() method more than once on a thread; in that case, the thread will throw an IllegalMonitorStateException.]

5.   Which of the following two definitions of Sync (when compiled in separate files) will compile without errors?

A.   ```
class Sync {
        public synchronized void foo() {}
}
```

B.   ```
abstract class Sync {
        public synchronized void foo() {}
}
```

C.   ```
abstract class Sync {
        public abstract synchronized void foo();
}
```

D.   ```
interface Sync {
        public synchronized void foo();
}
```

Answer: A. and B.

(Abstract methods (in abstract classes or interfaces) cannot be declared synchronized, hence the options C and D are incorrect.)

Summary

Introduction to Concurrent Programming

- You can create classes that are capable of multi-threading by implementing the Runnable interface or by extending the Thread class.

- Always implement the run() method. The default run() method in Thread does nothing.

- Call the start() method and not the run() method directly in code. (Leave it to the JVM to call the run() method.)

- Every thread has a thread name, priority, and thread-group associated with it; the default toString() method implementation in Thread prints them.

- If you call the sleep() method of a thread, the thread does not release the lock and it holds on to the lock.

- You can use the join() method to wait for another thread to terminate.

- In general, if you are not using the "interrupt" feature in threads, it is safe to ignore InterruptedException; however it's better still to log or print the stack trace if that exception occurs.

- Threads execute asynchronously; you cannot predict the order in which the threads run.

- Threads are also non-deterministic: in many cases, you cannot reproduce problems like deadlocks or data races every time.

Thread States

- There are three basic thread states: *new, runnable,* and *terminated.* When a thread is just created, it is in a *new* state; when it is ready to run or running, it is in a *runnable* state. When the thread dies, it's in *terminated* state.

- The *runnable* state has two states internally (at the OS level): *ready* and *running* states.

- A thread will be in the *blocked* state when waiting to acquire a lock. The thread will be in the *timed_waiting* state when a timeout is given for calls like wait. The thread will be in the *waiting* state when, for example, wait() is called (without a time out value).

- You will get an IllegalThreadStateException if your operations result in invalid thread state transitions.

Concurrent Access Problems

- Concurrent reads and writes to resources may lead to the *data race* problem.

- You must use thread synchronization (i.e., locks) to access shared values and avoid data races. Java provides thread synchronization features to provide protected access to shared resources—namely, synchronized blocks and synchronized methods.

- Using locks can introduce problems such as deadlocks. When a deadlock happens, the process will *hang* and will never terminate.

- A deadlock typically happens when two threads acquire locks in opposite order. When one thread has acquired one lock and waits for another lock, another thread has acquired that other lock and waits for the first lock to be released. So, no progress is made and the program deadlocks.

- To avoid deadlocks, it is better to avoid acquiring multiple locks. When you have to acquire such multiple locks, ensure that they are acquired in the same order in all places in the program.

The Wait/Notify Mechanism

- When a thread has to wait for a particular condition or event to be satisfied by another thread, you can use a wait/notify mechanism as a communication mechanism between threads.

- When a thread needs to wait for a particular condition/event, you can either call wait() with or without a timeout value specified.

- To avoid notifications getting lost, it is better to always use notifyAll() instead of notify().

CHAPTER 14

▓ ▓ ▓

Concurrency

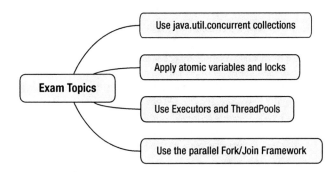

- Use java.util.concurrent collections
- Apply atomic variables and locks
- **Exam Topics**
- Use Executors and ThreadPools
- Use the parallel Fork/Join Framework

From the beginning, Java supported concurrency in the form of low-level threads management, locks, synchronization, and APIs for concurrency. We covered them in the preceding chapter in our discussion of the Thread class, Runnable interface, and synchronized keyword.

Since 5.0, Java also supports high-level concurrency APIs in its java.util.concurrent package. In this chapter, we'll focus on these APIs for concurrent programming. These high-level APIs exploit today's multi-core hardware, in which a single processor has multiple cores. These APIs are also useful for exploiting concurrency in machines that support multiple processors.

Most of the Java concurrency utilities are provided in the java.util.concurrent package. Classes to efficiently update shared variables without using locks are provided in the java.util.concurrent.atomic subpackage. The Lock interface and the classes deriving from it are provided in the java.util.concurrent.locks subpackage.

Using java.util.concurrent Collections

There are many classes in the java.util.concurrent package that provide high-level APIs for concurrent programming. In this section, we will mainly discuss synchronizer classes provided in this package. Following that, we will briefly cover the important concurrent collection classes provided in the java.util.concurrent package.

You already understand the low-level concurrency constructs (such as the use of the synchronized keyword, Runnable interface, and Thread class for creating threads) from the preceding chapter. In the case of a shared resource that needs to be accessed by multiple threads, access and modifications to the shared resource need to be protected. When you use the synchronized keyword, you employ mutexes to synchronize between threads for safe shared access. Threads also often needed to coordinate their executions to complete a bigger higher-level task. The wait/notify pattern discussed in the last chapter is one way to coordinate the execution of multiple threads.

Using APIs for acquiring and releasing locks (using mutexes) or invoking the wait/notify methods on locks are low-level tasks. It is possible to build higher-level abstractions for thread synchronization. These high-level abstractions for synchronizing activities of two or more threads are known as *synchronizers*. Synchronizers internally make use of the existing low-level APIs for thread coordination.

The synchronizers provided in the java.util.concurrent library and their uses are listed here:

- Semaphore controls access to one or more shared resources.

- Phaser is used to support a synchronization barrier.

- CountDownLatch allows threads to wait for a countdown to complete.

- Exchanger supports exchanging data between two threads.

- CyclicBarrier enables threads to wait at a predefined execution point.

Now, we'll discuss each of these synchronizers in turn with the help of examples.

Semaphore

A semaphore controls access to shared resources. A semaphore maintains a counter to specify the number of resources that the semaphore controls. Access to the resource is allowed if the counter is greater than zero, while a zero value of the counter indicates that no resource is available at the moment and so the access is denied.

The methods acquire() and release() are for acquiring and releasing resources from a semaphore. If a thread calls acquire() and the counter is zero (i.e., resources are unavailable), the thread waits until the counter is non-zero and then gets the resource for use. Once the thread is done using the resource, it calls release() to increment the resource availability counter.

Note if the number of resources is 1, then at a given time only one thread can access the resource; in this case, using the semaphore is similar to using a lock. Table 14-1 lists the important methods in the Semaphore class.

Table 14-1. *Important Methods in the Semaphore Class*

Method	Description
Semaphore(int permits)	Constructor to create Semaphore objects with a given number of *permits* (the number of threads that can access the resource at a time). If the permit's value is negative, the given number of release() calls must happen before acquire() calls can succeed.
Semaphore(int permits, boolean fair)	Same as the previous constructor, but this extra fair option indicates that the permits should be allotted on a first-come-first-served basis.
void acquire() void acquire(int permits)	Acquires a permit if available; otherwise, it blocks until a permit becomes available. Can throw an InterruptedException if some other thread interrupts it while waiting to acquire a permit. The overloaded version takes a number of permits as an argument.
void acquireUninterruptibly()	Same as the acquire() method, but this thread cannot be interrupted while waiting to acquire a permit.
boolean tryAcquire() boolean tryAcquire(long timeout, TimeUnit unit)	Acquires a permit from the semaphore if available at the time of the call and returns true; if unavailable, it returns false immediately (without blocking). The overloaded tryAcquire() method additionally takes a time-out argument—the thread blocks to acquire a permit from the semaphore until a given time-out period.
void release() void release(int permits)	Releases a permit from the semaphore. The overloaded version specifies the number of permits to release.

Let's assume that there are two ATM machines available in a ATM machine room. Therefore, only two people are allowed at a time in the room. There are five people waiting outside to use the ATM machines. The situation can be simulated by the code in Listing 14-1, in which each ATM machine is treated as a resource controlled by semaphore.

Listing 14-1. ATMRoom.java

```java
import java.util.concurrent.Semaphore;

// This class simulates a situation where an ATM room has only two ATM machines
// and five people are waiting to access the machine. Since only one person can access
// an ATM machine at a given time, others wait for their turn
class ATMRoom {
        public static void main(String []args) {
                // assume that only two ATM machines are available in the ATM room
                Semaphore machines = new Semaphore(2);

                // list of people waiting to access the machine
                new Person(machines, "Mickey");
                new Person(machines, "Donald");
                new Person(machines, "Tom");
                new Person(machines, "Jerry");
                new Person(machines, "Casper");
        }
}

// Each Person is an independent thread; but their access to the common resource
// (two ATM machines in the ATM machine room in this case) needs to be synchronized.
class Person extends Thread {
        private Semaphore machines;
        public Person(Semaphore machines, String name) {
                this.machines = machines;
                this.setName(name);
                this.start();
        }
        public void run() {
                try {
                        System.out.println(getName() + " waiting to access an ATM machine");
                        machines.acquire();
                        System.out.println(getName() + " is accessing an ATM machine");
                        Thread.sleep(1000); // simulate the time required for withdrawing amount
                        System.out.println(getName() + " is done using the ATM machine");
                        machines.release();
                } catch(InterruptedException ie) {
                        System.err.println(ie);
                }
        }
}
```

Here is the output of the program in one sample run:

```
Mickey waiting to access an ATM machine
Tom waiting to access an ATM machine
```

```
Jerry waiting to access an ATM machine
Donald waiting to access an ATM machine
Casper waiting to access an ATM machine
Tom is accessing an ATM machine
Mickey is accessing an ATM machine
Tom is done using the ATM machine
Mickey is done using the ATM machine
Jerry is accessing an ATM machine
Donald is accessing an ATM machine
Donald is done using the ATM machine
Jerry is done using the ATM machine
Casper is accessing an ATM machine
Casper is done using the ATM machine
```

Now let's analyze how this program works. People waiting to access an ATM machine are simulated by creating a Person class that extends Thread. The run() method in the Thread class acquires a semaphore, simulates withdrawing money from the ATM machine, and releases the semaphore.

The main() method simulates an ATM room with two ATM machines by creating a Semaphore object with two *permits*. People waiting in the queue to access the ATM machine are implemented by just adding them to the Semaphore object.

As you can see from the program output, the semaphore allows only two threads at a time and the other threads keep waiting. When a thread releases the semaphore, another thread acquires it. Cool, isn't it?

CountDownLatch

This synchronizer allows one or more threads to wait for a countdown to complete. This countdown could be for a set of events to happen or until a set of operations being performed in other threads completes. Table 14-2 lists important methods in this class.

Table 14-2. Important Methods in the CountDownLatch Class

Method	Description
CountDownLatch(int count)	Creates an instance of CountDownLatch with the number of times the countDown() method must be called before the threads waiting with await() can continue execution.
void await()	If the current count in CountDownLatch object is zero, it immediately returns; otherwise, the thread blocks until the countdown reaches zero. Can throw an InterruptedException.
boolean await(long timeout, TimeUnit unit)	Same as the previous method, await(), but takes an additional time-out argument. If the thread returns successfully after the count reaches zero, this method returns true; if the thread returns because of time-out, it returns false.
void countDown()	Reduces the number of counts by one in this CountDownLatch object. If the count reaches zero, all the (a)waiting threads are released. If the current count is already zero, nothing happens.
long getCount()	Returns the pending counts in this CountDownLatch object.

When you create a CountDownLatch, you initialize it with an integer, which represents a count value. Threads would wait (by calling the await() method) for this count to reach zero. Once zero is reached, all threads are released; any other calls to await() would return immediately since the count is already zero. The counter value can be decremented by one by calling the countDown() method. You can get the current value of the counter using the getCount() method. See Listing 14-2.

Listing 14-2. RunningRaceStarter.java

```java
import java.util.concurrent.*;

// this class simulates the start of a running race by counting down from 5. It holds
// three runner threads to be ready to start in the start line of the race and once the count down
// reaches zero, all the three runners start running...

class RunningRaceStarter {
        public static void main(String []args) throws InterruptedException {
                CountDownLatch counter = new CountDownLatch(5);
                // count from 5 to 0 and then start the race

                // instantiate three runner threads
                new Runner(counter, "Carl");
                new Runner(counter, "Joe");
                new Runner(counter, "Jack");

                System.out.println("Starting the countdown ");
                long countVal = counter.getCount();
                while(countVal > 0) {
                        Thread.sleep(1000); // 1000 milliseconds = 1 second
                        System.out.println(countVal);
                        if(countVal == 1) {
                                // once counter.countDown(); in the next statement is called,
                                // Count down will reach zero; so shout "Start"
                                System.out.println("Start");
                        }
                        counter.countDown(); // count down by 1 for each second
                        countVal = counter.getCount();
                }
        }
}

// this Runner class simulates a track runner in a 100-meter dash race. The runner waits until the
// count down timer gets to zero and then starts running
class Runner extends Thread {
        private CountDownLatch timer;
        public Runner(CountDownLatch cdl, String name) {
                timer = cdl;
                this.setName(name);
                System.out.println(this.getName() + " ready and waiting for the count down to start");
                start();
        }
```

```
        public void run() {
                try {
                        // wait for the timer count down to reach 0
                        timer.await();
                } catch (InterruptedException ie) {
                        System.err.println("interrupted -- can't start running the race");
                }
                System.out.println(this.getName() + " started running");
        }
}
```

This program prints the following:

```
Carl ready and waiting for the count down to start
Joe ready and waiting for the count down to start
Jack ready and waiting for the count down to start
Starting the countdown
5
4
3
2
1
Start
Joe started running
Carl started running
Jack started running
```

Let's consider how the program works. The class Runner simulates a runner in a running race waiting to start running. It waits for the race to start by calling the await() method on the CountDownLatch object passed through the constructor.

The RunningRaceStarter class creates a CountDownLatch object. This counter object is initialized with the count value 5, which means the countdown is from 5 to 0. In the main() method, you create Runner objects; these three threads wait on the counter object. For each second, you call the countDown() method, which decrements count by 1. Once the count reaches zero, all three waiting threads are released and they automatically continue execution.

Note: In this program, the sequence in which Joe, Carl, or Jack is printed cannot be predicted since it depends on thread scheduling. So, if you run this program, you may get these three names printed in some other order.

Exchanger

The Exchanger class is meant for exchanging data between two threads. What Exchanger does is something very simple: it waits until both the threads have called the exchange() method. When both threads have called the exchange() method, the Exchanger object actually exchanges the data shared by the threads with each other. This class is useful when two threads need to synchronize between them and continuously exchange data.

This class is a tiny class with only one method: exchange(). Note that this exchange() method has an overloaded form where it takes a time-out period as an argument.

Listing 14-3 shows an example simulating silly talk between the Java Duke mascot and the coffee shop. The two threads DukeThread and CoffeeShop threads run independently. However, for a chat to happen, they need to listen when the other is talking. An Exchange object provides a means for them to talk to each other.

Listing 14-3. KnockKnock.java

```java
import java.util.concurrent.Exchanger;

// The DukeThread class runs as an independent thread. It talks to the CoffeeShopThread that
// also runs independently. The chat is achieved by exchanging messages through a common
// Exchanger<String> object that synchronizes the chat between them.
// Note that the message printed are the "responses" received from CoffeeShopThread
class DukeThread extends Thread {
        private Exchanger<String> sillyTalk;

        public DukeThread(Exchanger<String> args) {
                sillyTalk = args;
        }
        public void run() {
                String reply = null;
                try {
                        // start the conversation with CoffeeShopThread
                        reply = sillyTalk.exchange("Knock knock!");
                        // Now, print the response received from CoffeeShopThread
                        System.out.println("CoffeeShop: " + reply);

                        // exchange another set of messages
                        reply = sillyTalk.exchange("Duke");
                        // Now, print the response received from CoffeeShopThread
                        System.out.println("CoffeeShop: " + reply);

                        // an exchange could happen only when both send and receive happens
                        // since this is the last sentence to speak, we close the chat by
                        // ignoring the "dummy" reply
                        reply = sillyTalk.exchange("The one who was born in this coffee shop!");
                        // talk over, so ignore the reply!
                } catch(InterruptedException ie) {
                        System.err.println("Got interrupted during my silly talk");
                }
        }
}

class CoffeeShopThread extends Thread {
        private Exchanger<String> sillyTalk;

        public CoffeeShopThread(Exchanger<String> args) {
                sillyTalk = args;
        }
        public void run() {
                String reply = null;
                try {
                        // exchange the first messages
                        reply = sillyTalk.exchange("Who's there?");
                        // print what Duke said
                        System.out.println("Duke: " + reply);
```

```
                      // exchange second message
                      reply = sillyTalk.exchange("Duke who?");
                      // print what Duke said
                      System.out.println("Duke: " + reply);

                      // there is no message to send, but to get a message from Duke thread,
                      // both ends should send a message; so send a "dummy" string
                      reply = sillyTalk.exchange("");
                      System.out.println("Duke: " + reply);
              } catch(InterruptedException ie) {
                      System.err.println("Got interrupted during my silly talk");
              }
        }
    }
}

// Coordinate the silly talk between Duke and CoffeeShop by instantitaing the Exchanger object
// and the CoffeeShop and Duke threads
class KnockKnock {
              public static void main(String []args) {
                      Exchanger<String> sillyTalk = new Exchanger<String>();
                      new CoffeeShopThread(sillyTalk).start();
                      new DukeThread(sillyTalk).start();
              }
}
```

The program prints the following:

```
Duke: Knock knock!
CoffeeShop: Who's there?
Duke: Duke
CoffeeShop: Duke who?
Duke: The one who was born in this coffee shop!
```

The comments inside the program explain how the program works. The main concept to understand with this example is that Exchanger helps coordinate (i.e., synchronize) exchanging messages between two threads. Both the threads wait for each other and use the exchange() method to exchange messages.

CyclicBarrier

There are many situations in concurrent programming where threads may need to wait at a predefined execution point until all other threads reach that point. CyclicBarrier helps provide such a synchronization point; see Table 14-3 for the important methods in this class.

Table 14-3. *Important Methods in the CyclicBarrier Class*

Method	Description
CyclicBarrier(int numThreads)	Creates a CyclicBarrier object with the number of threads waiting on it specified. Throws IllegalArgumentException if numThreads is negative or zero.
CyclicBarrier(int parties, Runnable barrierAction)	Same as the previous constructor; this constructor additionally takes the thread to call when the barrier is reached.
int await() int await(long timeout, TimeUnit unit)	Blocks until the specified number of threads have called await() on this barrier. The method returns the arrival index of this thread. This method can throw an InterruptedException if the thread is interrupted while waiting for other threads or a BrokenBarrierException if the barrier was broken for some reason (for example, another thread was timed-out or interrupted). The overloaded method takes a time-out period as an additional option; this overloaded version throws a TimeoutException if all other threads aren't reached within the time-out period.
boolean isBroken()	Returns true if the barrier is broken. A barrier is broken if at least one thread in that barrier was interrupted or timed-out, or if a barrier action failed throwing an exception.
void reset()	Resets the barrier to the initial state. If there are any threads waiting on that barrier, they will throw the BrokenBarrier exception.

Listing 14-4 is an example that makes use of CyclicBarrier class.

Listing 14-4. CyclicBarrierTest.java

```java
import java.util.concurrent.*;

// The run() method in this thread should be called only when four players are ready to start the game
class MixedDoubleTennisGame extends Thread {
    public void run() {
        System.out.println("All four players ready, game starts \n Love all...");
    }
}

// This thread simulates arrival of a player.
// Once a player arrives, he/she should wait for other players to arrive
class Player extends Thread {
    CyclicBarrier waitPoint;
    public Player(CyclicBarrier barrier, String name) {
        this.setName(name);
        waitPoint = barrier;
        this.start();
    }
    public void run() {
        System.out.println("Player " + getName() + " is ready ");
```

```
                    try {
                            waitPoint.await(); // await for all four players to arrive
                    } catch(BrokenBarrierException | InterruptedException exception) {
                            System.out.println("An exception occurred while waiting... " + exception);
                    }
            }
    }

// Creates a CyclicBarrier object by passing the number of threads and the thread to run
// when all the threads reach the barrier
class CyclicBarrierTest {
        public static void main(String []args) {
                // a mixed-double tennis game requires four players; so wait for four players
                // (i.e., four threads) to join to start the game
                System.out.println("Reserving tennis court \n As soon as four players arrive,
game will start");
                CyclicBarrier barrier = new CyclicBarrier(4, new MixedDoubleTennisGame());
                new Player(barrier, "G I Joe");
                new Player(barrier, "Dora");
                new Player(barrier, "Tintin");
                new Player(barrier, "Barbie");
        }
}
```

The program prints the following:

```
Reserving tennis court
As soon as four players arrive, game will start
Player G I Joe is ready
Player Dora is ready
Player Tintin is ready
Player Barbie is ready
All four players ready, game starts
 Love all...
```

Now let's see how this program works. In the main() method you create a CyclicBarrier object. The constructor takes two arguments: the number of threads to wait for, and the thread to invoke when all the threads reach the barrier. In this case, you have four players to wait for, so you create four threads, with each thread representing a player. The second argument for the CyclicBarrier constructor is the MixedDoubleTennisGame object since this thread represents the game, which will start once all four players are ready.

Inside the run() method for each Player thread, you call the await() method on the CyclicBarrier object. Once the number of awaiting threads for the CyclicBarrier object reaches four, the run() method in MixedDoubleTennisGame is called.

Phaser

Phaser is a useful feature when few independent threads have to work in phases to complete a task. So, a synchronization point is needed for the threads to work on a part of a task, wait for others to complete other part of the task, and do a sync-up before advancing to complete the next part of the task. Table 14-4 lists important methods in this class.

Table 14-4. *Important Methods in the Phaser class*

Method	Description
`Phaser()`	Creates a `Phaser` object with no registered parties and no parents. The initial phase is set to 0.
`Phaser(int numThreads)`	Creates a `Phaser` object with a given number of threads (parties) to arrive to advance to the next stage; the initial phase is set to 0.
`int register()`	Adds a new thread (party) to this `Phaser` object. Returns the phase current number. Throws an `IllegalStateException` if the maximum supported parties are already registered.
`int bulkRegister(int numThreads)`	Adds numThreads of unarrived parties to this `Phaser` object. Returns the phase current number. Throws an `IllegalStateException` if maximum supported parties are already registered.
`int arrive()`	Arrives at this phase without waiting for other threads to arrive. Returns the arrival phase number. Can throw an `IllegalStateException`.
`int arriveAndDeregister()`	Same as the previous method, but also deregisters from the `Phaser` object.
`int arriveAndAwaitAdvance()`	Arrive at this phase and waits (i.e., blocks) until other threads arrive.
`int awaitAdvance(int phase)`	Waits (i.e., blocks) until this `Phaser` object advances to the given phase value.
`int getRegisteredParties()`	Returns the number of threads (parties) registered with this `Phaser` object.
`int getArrivedParties()`	Returns the number of threads (parties) arrived at the current phase of the `Phaser` object.
`int getUnarrivedParties()`	Returns the number of threads (parties) that have not arrived when compared to the registered parties at the current phase of the `Phaser` object.

Consider the example of processing a delivery order in a small coffee shop. Assume that there are only three workers: a cook, a helper, and an attendant. To simplify the program logic, assume that each delivery order consists of three food items. Completing a delivery order consists of preparing the three orders one after another. To complete preparing a food item, all three workers—the cook, the helper, and the attendant—should do their part of the work. Listing 14-5 shows how this situation can be implemented using the `Phaser` class.

Listing 14-5. ProcessOrder.java

```java
import java.util.concurrent.*;

// ProcessOrder thread is the master thread overlooking to make sure that the Cook, Helper,
// and Attendant are doing their part of the work to complete preparing the food items
// and complete order delivery
// To simplify the logic, we assume that each delivery order consists of exactly three food items
class ProcessOrder {
        public static void main(String []args) throws InterruptedException {
                // the Phaser is the synchronizer to make food items one-by-one,
                // and deliver it before moving to the next item
                Phaser deliveryOrder = new Phaser(1);
```

```java
                System.out.println("Starting to process the delivery order ");

                new Worker(deliveryOrder, "Cook");
                new Worker(deliveryOrder, "Helper");
                new Worker(deliveryOrder, "Attendant");

                for(int i = 1; i <= 3; i++) {
                        // Prepare, mix and deliver this food item
                        deliveryOrder.arriveAndAwaitAdvance();
                        System.out.println("Deliver food item no. " + i);
                }
                // work completed for this delivery order, so deregister
                deliveryOrder.arriveAndDeregister();
                System.out.println("Delivery order completed... give it to the customer");
        }
}


// The work could be a Cook, Helper, or Attendant. Though the three work independently, the
// should all synchronize their work together to do their part and complete preparing a food item
class Worker extends Thread {
        Phaser deliveryOrder;
        Worker(Phaser order, String name) {
                deliveryOrder = order;
                this.setName(name);
                deliveryOrder.register();
                start();
        }
        public void run() {
                for(int i = 1; i <= 3; i++) {
                        System.out.println("\t" + getName() + " doing his work for order no. " + i);
                        if(i == 3) {
                                // work completed for this delivery order, so deregister
                                deliveryOrder.arriveAndDeregister();
                        } else {
                                deliveryOrder.arriveAndAwaitAdvance();
                        }
                        try {
                                Thread.sleep(3000); // simulate time for preparing the food item
                        } catch(InterruptedException ie) {
                                /* ignore exception */
                                ie.printStackTrace();
                        }
                }
        }
}
```

The program prints the following:

```
Starting to process the delivery order
        Cook doing his work for order no. 1
        Attendant doing his work for order no. 1
        Helper doing his work for order no. 1
Deliver food item no. 1
        Helper doing his work for order no. 2
        Attendant doing his work for order no. 2
        Cook doing his work for order no. 2
Deliver food item no. 2
        Helper doing his work for order no. 3
        Cook doing his work for order no. 3
        Attendant doing his work for order no. 3
Deliver food item no. 3
Delivery order completed...give it to the customer
```

In this program, you create a Phaser object to support the synchronizing of three Worker thread objects. You create a Phaser object by calling the default constructor of the Phaser object. When the Worker thread objects are created, they register themselves to the Phaser object. Alternatively, you could have called

```
Phaser deliveryOrder = new Phaser(3); // for three parties (i.e., threads)
```

In this case, you would not need to call the register() method on the Phaser object in the Worker thread constructor.

In this case, you've assumed that a delivery order consists of processing three food items, so the for loop runs three times. For each iteration, you call deliveryOrder.arriveAndAwaitAdvance(). For this statement to proceed, all the three parties (the Cook, Helper, and Attendant) have to complete their part of the work to prepare the food item. You simulate "preparing food" by calling the sleep() method in the run method for these Worker threads. These worker threads call deliveryOrder.arriveAndAwaitAdvance() for preparing each food item. As each food item is prepared (i.e., each phase is completed), the work progresses to the next phase. Once three phases are complete, the delivery order processing is complete and the program returns.

Concurrent Collections

The java.util.concurrent package provides a number of classes that are thread-safe equivalents of the ones provided in the collections framework classes in the java.util package (see Table 14-5). For example, java.util.concurrent.ConcurrentHashMap is a concurrent equivalent to java.util.HashMap. The main difference between these two containers is that you need to explicitly synchronize insertions and deletions with HashMap, whereas such synchronization is built into the ConcurrentHashMap. If you know how to use HashMap, you know how to use ConcurrentHashMap implicitly. From the OCPJP 7 exam perspective, you only need to have an overall understanding of the classes in Table 14-5, so we won't delve into details on how to make use of these classes.

Table 14-5. Some Concurrent Collection Classes in the java.util.concurrent Package

Class/Interface	Short Description
BlockingQueue	This interface extends the Queue interface. In BlockingQueue, if the queue is empty, it waits (i.e., blocks) for an element to be inserted, and if the queue is full, it waits for an element to be removed from the queue.
ArrayBlockingQueue	This class provides a fixed-sized array based implementation of the BlockingQueue interface.
LinkedBlockingQueue	This class provides a linked-list-based implementation of the BlockingQueue interface.
DelayQueue	This class implements BlockingQueue and consists of elements that are of type Delayed. An element can be retrieved from this queue only after its delay period.
PriorityBlockingQueue	Equivalent to java.util.PriorityQueue, but implements the BlockingQueue interface.
SynchronousQueue	This class implements BlockingQueue. In this container, each insert() by a thread waits (blocks) for a corresponding remove() by another thread and vice versa.
LinkedBlockingDeque	This class implements BlockingDeque where insert and remove operations could block; uses a linked-list for implementation.
ConcurrentHashMap	Analogous to Hashtable, but with safe concurrent access and updates.
ConcurrentSkipListMap	Analogous to TreeMap, but provides safe concurrent access and updates.
ConcurrentSkipListSet	Analogous to TreeSet, but provides safe concurrent access and updates.
CopyOnWriteArrayList	Similar to ArrayList, but provides safe concurrent access. When the ArrayList is updated, it creates a fresh copy of the underlying array.
CopyOnWriteArraySet	A Set implementation, but provides safe concurrent access and is implemented using CopyOnWriteArrayList. When the container is updated, it creates a fresh copy of the underlying array.

Listings 14-6 and 14-7 show how a concurrent version differs from its non-concurrent version. Assume that you have a PriorityQueue object shared by two threads. Assume that one thread inserts an element into the priority queue, and the other thread removes an element. If the threads are scheduled such that the inserting an element occurs before removing the element, there is no problem. However, if the first thread attempts to remove an element before the second thread inserts an element, you get into trouble.

Listing 14-6. PriorityQueueExample.java

```java
import java.util.*;

// Simple PriorityQueue example. Here, we create two threads in which one thread inserts an element,
// and another thread removes an element from the priority queue.
class PriorityQueueExample {
    public static void main(String []args) {
        final PriorityQueue<Integer> priorityQueue = new PriorityQueue<>();
        // spawn a thread that removes an element from the priority queue
```

```
            new Thread() {
                    public void run() {
                            // Use remove() method in PriorityQueue to remove the element if available
                            System.out.println("The removed element is: " + priorityQueue.remove());
                    }
            }.start();
            // spawn a thread that inserts an element into the priority queue
            new Thread() {
                    public void run() {
                            // insert Integer value 10 as an entry into the priority queue
                            priorityQueue.add(10);
                            System.out.println("Successfully added an element to the queue ");
                    }
            }.start();
    }
}
```

If you run this program, it throws an exception like this:

```
Exception in thread "Thread-0" java.util.NoSuchElementException
at java.util.AbstractQueue.remove(AbstractQueue.java:117)
at PriorityQueueExample$1.run(QueueExample.java:10)
Successfully added an element to the queue
```

This output indicates that the first thread attempted removing an element from an empty priority queue, and hence it results in a NoSuchElementException.

However, consider a slight modification of this program (Listing 14-7) that uses a PriorityBlockingQueue instead of PriorityQueue.

Listing 14-7. PriorityBlockingQueueExample.java

```
// Illustrates the use of PriorityBlockingQueue. In this case, if there is no element available in
the priority queue
// the thread calling take() method will block (i.e., wait) until another thread inserts an element

import java.util.concurrent.*;

class PriorityBlockingQueueExample {
        public static void main(String []args) {
                final PriorityBlockingQueue<Integer> priorityBlockingQueue
                        = new PriorityBlockingQueue<>();
                new Thread() {
                        public void run() {
                                try {
                                        // use take() instead of remove()
                                        // note that take() blocks, whereas remove() doesn't block
                                        System.out.println("The removed element is: "
                                                + priorityBlockingQueue.take());
                                } catch(InterruptedException ie) {
                                        // its safe to ignore this exception
                                        ie.printStackTrace();
                                }
                        }
```

```
                }.start();
                new Thread() {
                        public void run() {
                                // add an element with value 10 to the priority queue
                                priorityBlockingQueue.add(10);
                                System.out.println("Successfully added an element to the queue ");
                        }
                }.start();
        }
}
```

The program prints the following:

```
Successfully added an element to the queue
The removed element is: 10
```

This program will not result in a crash as in the previous case (Listing 14-6). This is because the take() method will block until an element gets inserted by another thread; once inserted, the take() method will return that value. In other words, if you're using a PriorityQueue object, you need to synchronize the threads such that insertion of an element always occurs before removing an element. However, in PriorityBlockingQueue, the order does not matter, and no matter which operation (insertion or removal of an element) is invoked first, the program works correctly. In this way, concurrent collections provide support for safe use of collections in the context of multiple threads without the need for you to perform explicit synchronization operations.

Apply Atomic Variables and Locks

The java.util.concurrent package has two subpackages: java.util.concurrent.atomic and java.util.concurrent.locks. In this section we discuss these two subpackages. Unlike the rest of this chapter, which discusses high-level concurrency abstractions, both atomic variables and locks are low-level APIs. However, they provide more fine-grained control when you want to write multithreaded code.

Atomic Variables

Have you seen code that acquires and releases locks for implementing primitive/simple operations like incrementing a variable, decrementing a variable, and so on? Such acquiring and releasing of locks for such primitive operations is not efficient. In such cases, Java provides an efficient alternative in the form of atomic variables.

Here is a list of some of the classes in this package and their short description:

- AtomicBoolean: Atomically updatable Boolean value.

- AtomicInteger: Atomically updatable int value; inherits from the Number class.

- AtomicIntegerArray: An int array in which elements can be updated atomically.

- AtomicLong: Atomically updatable long value; inherits from Number class.

- AtomicLongArray: A long array in which elements can be updated atomically.

- AtomicReference<V>: An atomically updatable object reference of type V.

- AtomicReferenceArray<E>: An atomically updatable array that can hold object references of type E (E refers to be base type of elements).

Only AtomicInteger and AtomicLong extend from Number class but not AtomicBoolean. All other classes in the java.util.concurrent.atomic subpackage inherit directly from the Object class.

Of the classes in the java.util.concurrency.atomic subpackage, AtomicInteger and AtomicLong are the most important. Table 14-6 lists important methods in the AtomicInteger class. (The methods in AtomicLong are analogous to these.)

Table 14-6. *Important Methods in the AtomicInteger Class*

Method	Description
AtomicInteger()	Creates an instance of AtomicInteger with initial value 0.
AtomicInteger(int initVal)	Creates an instance of AtomicInteger with initial value initVal.
int get()	Returns the integer value held in this object.
void set(int newVal)	Resets the integer value held in this object to newVal.
int getAndSet(int newValue)	Returns the current int value held in this object and sets the value held in this object to newVal.
boolean compareAndSet (int expect, int update)	Compares the int value of this object to the expect value, and if they are equal, sets the int value of this object to the update value.
int getAndIncrement()	Returns the current value of the integer value in this object and increments the integer value in this object. Similar to the behavior of i++ where i is an int.
int getAndDecrement()	Returns the current value of the integer value in this object and decrements the integer value in this object. Similar to the behavior of i-- where i is an int.
int getAndAdd(int delta)	Returns the integer value held in this object and adds given delta value to the integer value.
int incrementAndGet()	Increments the current value of the integer value in this object and returns that value. Similar to the behavior of ++i where i is an int.
int decrementAndGet()	Decrements the current integer value in this object and returns that value. Similar to behavior of --i where i is an int.
int addAndGet(int delta)	Adds the delta value to the current value of the integer in this object and returns that value.
int intValue() long longValue() float floatValue() doubleValue()	Casts the current int value of the object and returns it as int, long, float, or double values.

Let's try out an example to understand how to use AtomicInteger or AtomicLong. Assume that you have a counter value that is public and accessible by all threads. How do you update or access this common counter value safely without introducing the data race problem (discussed in the previous chapter)? Obviously, you can use the synchronized keyword to ensure that the critical section (the code that modifies the counter value) is accessed by only one thread at a given point in time. The critical section will be very small, as in

```java
public void run() {
        synchronized(SharedCounter.class) {
                SharedCounter.count++;
        }
}
```

However, this code is inefficient since it acquires and releases the lock every time just to increment the value of count. Alternatively, if you declare count as AtomicInteger or AtomicLong (whichever is suitable), then there is no need to use a lock with synchronized keyword. Listing 14-8 gives the full program to show how to use AtomicLong in practice.

Listing 14-8. AtomicVariableTest.java

```java
import java.util.concurrent.atomic.*;

// Class to demonstrate how incrementing "normal" (i.e., thread unsafe) integers and incrementing
// "atomic" (i.e., thread safe) integers are different: Incrementing a shared Integer object without
locks can result
// in a data race; however, incrementing a shared AtomicInteger will not result in a data race.

class AtomicVariableTest {
        // Create two integer objects - one normal and another atomic -  with same initial value
        private static Integer integer = new Integer(0);
        private static AtomicInteger atomicInteger = new AtomicInteger(0);

        static class IntegerIncrementer extends Thread {
                public void run() {
                        System.out.println("Incremented value of integer is: " + ++integer);
                }
        }
        static class AtomicIntegerIncrementer extends Thread {
                public void run() {
                        System.out.println("Incremented value of atomic integer is: "
                                        + atomicInteger.incrementAndGet());
                }
        }
        public static void main(String []args) {
                // create three threads each for incrementing atomic and "normal" integers
                for(int i = 0; i < 5; i++) {
                        new IntegerIncrementer().start();
                        new AtomicIntegerIncrementer().start();
                }
        }
}
```

The actual output depends on thread scheduling. In one run it printed the following:

```
Incremented value of atomic integer is: 1
Incremented value of integer is: 1
Incremented value of integer is: 1
Incremented value of atomic integer is: 2
Incremented value of integer is: 2
Incremented value of atomic integer is: 3
Incremented value of integer is: 3
Incremented value of integer is: 4
Incremented value of atomic integer is: 4
Incremented value of atomic integer is: 5
```

In this output, notice that incrementing the Integer object has resulted in a data race: the final value of Integer after incrementing it 5 times (from initial value 0) is 4. For AtomicInteger, however, it is 5—which is correct.

Let's analyze this program. The AtomicVariableTest has two data members—one of type Integer and the other of type AtomicInteger—with same initial value.

There are two Thread classes. One class increments Integer value in its run() method, and the other increments AtomicInteger in its run() method. In the main() method, you spawn five threads of these two kind of Threads. The output shows that incrementing the Integer value is prone to a data race when it is without a lock, whereas it is safe to increment the AtomicInteger value without any locks.

Locks

In the last chapter, we discussed the synchronized keyword and how it enforces that only one thread executes in a critical section at a time. The java.util.concurrent.locks package provides facilities that are more sophisticated. In this section, we will discuss the Lock interface.

Using a Lock object is similar to obtaining implicit locks using the synchronized keyword. The aim of both constructs is the same: to ensure that only one thread accesses a shared resource at a time. However, unlike the synchronized keyword, Locks also support the wait/notify mechanism along with its support for Condition objects.

 You can think of using synchronized for locking implicitly and using Lock objects for locking explicitly.

The advantage of using the synchronized keyword (implicit locking) is that you don't have to remember to release the lock in a finally block since, at the end of the synchronized block (or method), code will be generated to automatically release the lock. Although this is a useful feature, there are some situations where you may need to control the release of the lock manually (say, for releasing it other than at the end of that block), and Lock objects provide this flexibility. However, it is your responsibility to ensure that you release the lock in a finally block while using Lock objects. The following snippet describes the usage idiom for a Lock:

```
Lock lock = /* get Lock type instance */;
lock.lock();
```

```
try {
        // critical section
}
finally {
        lock.unlock();
}
```

Another difference between implicit locks and explicit Lock objects is that you can do a "non-blocking attempt" to acquire locks with Locks. Well, what does "non-blocking attempt" mean here? You get a lock if that lock is available for locking, or you can back out from requesting the lock using the tryLock() method on a Lock object. Isn't it interesting? If you acquire the lock successfully, then you can carry out the task to be carried out in a critical section; otherwise you execute an alternative action. It is noteworthy that an overloaded version of the tryLock() method takes the timeout value as an argument so that you can wait to acquire the lock for the specified time.

```
tryLock(long time, TimeUnit unit).
```

With tryLock(), the idiom to use the Lock object is:

```
Lock lock = /* get Lock type instance */;
if(tryLock()) {
        try {
                // critical section
        }
        finally {
                lock.unlock();
        }
}
else {

}
```

Using tryLock() helps avoid some of the thread synchronization-related problems discussed in the last chapter, such as deadlocks and livelocks. Table 14-7 lists important methods in the Lock class.

Table 14-7. *Important Methods in the Lock Class*

Method	Description
void lock()	Acquires the lock.
boolean tryLock()	Acquires the lock and returns true if the lock is available; if the lock is not available, it does not acquire the lock and returns false.
boolean tryLock(long time, TimeUnit unit)	Same as the previous method tryLock(), but waits for the given waiting time before failing to acquire the lock and returns false.
void lockInterruptibly()	Acquires a lock; during the process of a acquiring the lock, if another thread interrupts it, this method throws an InterruptedException
Condition newCondition()	Returns a Condition object associated with this Lock object.
void unlock()	Releases the lock.

Let's look at an example of a Lock object. In this example, you use a Lock object and pass it to threads to synchronize them on this Lock object. This program is a simple variation of the program using Semaphores given in Listing 14-1. In Listing 14-9, you simulate accessing an ATM machine, which is a shared resource. Of course, only one person can use an ATM machine at a time, hence the code for accessing the machine is a critical section.

Listing 14-9. ATMRoom.java

```java
import java.util.concurrent.locks.*;

// This class simulates a situation where only one ATM machine is available and
// and five people are waiting to access the machine. Since only one person can
// access an ATM machine at a given time, others wait for their turn
class ATMMachine {
        public static void main(String []args) {
                // A person can use a machine again, and hence using a "reentrant lock"
                Lock machine = new ReentrantLock();

                // list of people waiting to access the machine
                new Person(machine, "Mickey");
                new Person(machine, "Donald");
                new Person(machine, "Tom");
                new Person(machine, "Jerry");
                new Person(machine, "Casper");
        }
}


// Each Person is an independent thread; their access to the common resource
// (the ATM machine in this case) needs to be synchronized using a lock
class Person extends Thread {
        private Lock machine;
        public Person(Lock machine, String name) {
                this.machine = machine;
                this.setName(name);
                this.start();
        }
        public void run() {
                try {
                        System.out.println(getName() + " waiting to access an ATM machine");
                        machine.lock();
                        System.out.println(getName() + " is accessing an ATM machine");
                        Thread.sleep(1000); // simulate the time required for withdrawing amount
                } catch(InterruptedException ie) {
                        System.err.println(ie);
                }
                finally {
                        System.out.println(getName() + " is done using the ATM machine");
                        machine.unlock();
                }
        }
}
```

Here is the output of this program:

```
Donald waiting to access an ATM machine
Jerry waiting to access an ATM machine
Tom waiting to access an ATM machine
Mickey waiting to access an ATM machine
Donald is accessing an ATM machine
Casper waiting to access an ATM machine
Donald is done using the ATM machine
Jerry is accessing an ATM machine
Jerry is done using the ATM machine
Tom is accessing an ATM machine
Tom is done using the ATM machine
Mickey is accessing an ATM machine
Mickey is done using the ATM machine
Casper is accessing an ATM machine
Casper is done using the ATM machine
```

As you can observe from the output, the machine is accessed by only one person at a time, though there may be others waiting to access it. In this program, the class ATMMachine creates a Lock object representing an ATM machine. There are five people waiting to access the machine, which is simulated by creating five instances of the Person class. The Person class extends the Thread and remembers the Lock object on which it has to acquire and release the lock.

The run() method simply acquires the lock, accesses the shared resource, and releases the lock in a finally block. The Lock object (machine variable here) ensures that only one thread accesses it at a given point in time. Other threads block while one thread is accessing the lock.

Note that you may get a different order of people accessing the machine if you try running this program. This is because the access order depends on how the scheduler in the JVM schedules the threads to run.

The ReadWriteLock interface (which extends from the Lock interface) specifies a lock that provides separate locks for read-only access and write access. You can use the readLock() and writeLock() methods to get instances of read and write locks, respectively. The ReentrantReadWriteLock class implements the ReadWriteLock interface.

Conditions

A Condition supports thread notification mechanism. When a certain condition is not satisfied, a thread can wait for another thread to satisfy that condition; that other thread could notify once the condition is met. A condition is bound to a lock. A Condition object offers three methods to support wait/notify pattern: await(), signal(), and signalAll(). These three methods are analogous to the wait(), notify(), and notifyAll() methods supported by the Object class.

A thread can wait for a condition to be true using the await() method, which is an interruptible blocking call. If you want non-interruptible waiting, you can call awaitUninterruptibly(). You can also specify time duration for the waiting using one of the overloaded methods:

- long awaitNanos(long nanosTimeout)

- boolean await(long time, TimeUnit unit)

- boolean awaitUntil(Date deadline)

Now let's look at an example that makes use of Condition objects. Assume that you're waiting for a person named Joe to come on train IC1122, which is from Madrid to Paris. When Joe's train arrives at the station, he informs you; you pick him up and go home.

Assuming that multiple trains can arrive at a railway station, you need to wait for a specific train to arrive. Once the train arrives that you're interested in, you get a "notification" or "signal" from that train. This scenario is a good candidate for using the wait/notify pattern. There are two ways to implement this pattern. The first option is to use implicit locks and make use of the wait() and notifyAll() methods in the Object class. The second option—shown in Listing 14-10—is to use the explicit Lock and Condition objects and use the await() and signalAll() methods in the Condition object.

Listing 14-10. RailwayStation.java

```java
import java.util.concurrent.locks.*;

// This class simulates arrival of trains in a railway station.
class RailwayStation {
        // A common lock for synchronization
        private static Lock station = new ReentrantLock();
        // Condition to wait or notify the arrival of Joe in the station
        private static Condition joeArrival = station.newCondition();

        // Train class simulates arrival of trains independently
        static class Train extends Thread {
                public Train(String name) {
                    this.setName(name);
                }
                public void run() {
                        station.lock();
                        try {
                                System.out.println(getName() + ": I've arrived in station ");
                                if(getName().startsWith("IC1122")) {
                                        // Joe is coming in train IC1122 - he announces it to us
                                        joeArrival.signalAll();
                                }
                        }
                        finally {
                                station.unlock();
                        }
                }
        }

        // Our wait in the railway station for Joe is simulated by this thread. Once we get
notification from Joe
        // that he has arrived, we pick-him up and go home
        static class WaitForJoe extends Thread {
                public void run() {
                        System.out.println("Waiting in the station for IC1122 in which Joe is coming");
                        station.lock();
                        try {
                                // await Joe's train arrival
                                joeArrival.await();
```

```
                            // if this statement executes, it means we got a train arrival signal
                            System.out.println("Pick up Joe and go home");
                    } catch(InterruptedException ie) {
                            ie.printStackTrace();
                    }
                    finally {
                            station.unlock();
                    }
            }
    }

    // first create a thread that waits for Joe to arrive and then create new Train threads
    public static void main(String []args) throws InterruptedException {
            // we are waiting before the trains start coming
            new WaitForJoe().start();
            // Trains are separate threads - they can arrive in any order
            new Train("IC1234 - Paris to Munich").start();
            new Train("IC2211 - Paris to Madrid").start();
            new Train("IC1122 - Madrid to Paris").start();
            new Train("IC4321 - Munich to Paris").start();
    }
}
```

Here is the output of this program:

```
Waiting in the station for IC1122 in which Joe is coming
IC1234 - Paris to Munich: I've arrived in station
IC1122 - Madrid to Paris: I've arrived in station
IC2211 - Paris to Madrid: I've arrived in station
Pick up Joe and go home
IC4321 - Munich to Paris: I've arrived in station
```

Let's analyze how this program works. In the RailwayStation class you have a common Lock object named station. From that station object, you obtain a Condition object (remember that a condition is always associated with a lock) named joeArrival. You used the newCondition() method, so the resulting Condition object is an interruptible condition; you have not specified any time-out, so the awaiting thread will wait forever until it gets the signal.

The Train class is a Thread that simulates arrival of a train in the railway station. The run() method in Train first obtains the lock before announcing that the train has arrived, and it releases before the method exits. Note that if you call await() on the Condition object without acquiring a lock, you'll get an IllegalMonitorStateException. In the run() method, if the Train name is IC1122, it will signal us that Joe has arrived by calling joeArrival.signalAll();.

Your wait in the railway station for Joe is simulated by this WaitForJoe thread. In the run() method, you acquire the lock and wait for the joeArrival condition to be signaled. Once you are notified (i.e., signaled) that he has arrived, you pick him up and go home.

In multithreading, a common need is to wait for a condition to be satisfied by one thread before another thread can proceed. Using polling (i.e., repeatedly checking for a condition using a while loop) is a bad solution because this solution wastes CPU cycles; further, it is also prone to data races. Use guarded blocks using wait/notify or await/signal instead.

Multiple Conditions on a Lock

From the OCPJP 7 exam perspective, it is important to understand locks and conditions. So, we'll discuss one more detailed example that makes use of locks and conditions. In this program, we show how you can get multiple Condition objects on a Lock object.

Assume that you are asked to implement a fixed-size queue with the size of the queue determined at the time of thread creation. In a typical queue, if there are no elements in the queue and if the remove() method is called, it will throw a NoSuchElementException (as you saw in Listing 14-6). However, in this case, you want the thread to block until some other thread inserts an element. Similarly, if you try inserting in a queue that is already full, instead of throwing IllegalStateException to indicate that it is not possible to insert any more elements, the thread should block until an element is removed. In other words, you need to implement a simple blocking queue (see Listing 14-11).

Listing 14-11. BlockerQueue.java

```java
import java.util.concurrent.locks.*;

// this implements a fixed size queue with size determined at the time of creation. I/ if remove()
is called
// when there are no elements, then the queue blocks (i.e., waits) until an element is inserted.
// If insert() is called when the queue is full, then the queue blocks until an element is removed

class BlockerQueue {
        // remember the max size of the queue
        private int size = 0;

        // array to store the elements in the queue
        private Object elements[];

        // pointer that points to the current element in the queue
        private int currPointer = 0;

        // internal lock used for synchronized access to the BlockerQueue
        private Lock internalLock = new ReentrantLock();

        // condition to wait for when queue is empty that makes use of the common lock
        private Condition empty = internalLock.newCondition();

        // condition to wait for when queue is full that makes use of the common lock
        private Condition full =  internalLock.newCondition();

        public BlockerQueue(int size) {
                this.size = size;
                elements = new Object[size];
        }

        // remove an element if available; or if there are no elements in the queue,
        // await insertion of an element. Once an element is inserted, notify to any threads
        // waiting for insertion in a full queue
        public Object remove() {
                Object element = null;
                internalLock.lock();
```

```
                try {
                        if(currPointer == 0) {
                                System.out.println("In remove(): no element to remove, so waiting
for insertion");

                                // cannot remove - no elements in the queue;
                                // so block until an element is inserted
                                empty.await();
                                // if control reaches here, that means some thread completed
                                // calling insert(), so proceed to remove that element
                                System.out.println("In remove(): got notification that an element has
got inserted");
                        }
                        // decrement the currPointer and then get the element
                        element = elements[--currPointer];
                        System.out.println("In remove(): removed the element " + element);

                        // an element is removed, so there is space for insertion
                        // so notify any threads waiting to insert
                        full.signalAll();
                        System.out.println("In remove(): signalled that there is space for insertion");
                } catch(InterruptedException ie) {
                        ie.printStackTrace();
                } finally {
                        internalLock.unlock();
                }
                return element;
        }

        // insert an element if there is space for insertion. if queue is full,
        // await for remove() to be called and get signal to proceed for insertion.
        // after insertion, signal any awaiting threads in case of an empty queue.
        public void insert(Object element) {
                internalLock.lock();
                try {
                        if(currPointer == size) {
                                System.out.println("In insert(): queue is full, so waiting for removal");
                                // cannot insert - the queue is full;
                                // so block until an element is removed
                                full.await();
                                // if control reaches here, that means some thread completed
                                // calling remove(), so proceed to insert this element
                                System.out.println("In insert(): got notification that remove got called,
so proceeding to insert the element");
                        }
                        // get the element and after that decrement the currPointer
                        elements[currPointer++] = element;
                        System.out.println("In insert(): inserted the element " + element);
                        // an element is inserted, so any other threads can remove it...
                        // so notify any threads waiting to remove
                        empty.signalAll();
                        System.out.println("In insert(): notified that queue is not empty");
```

```
                } catch(InterruptedException ie) {
                        ie.printStackTrace();
                } finally {
                        internalLock.unlock();
                }
        }
}
```

Here is test code for this class:

```
class BlockerQueueTest1 {
        public static void main(String []args) {
                final BlockerQueue blockerQueue = new BlockerQueue(2);
                new Thread() {
                        public void run() {
                                System.out.println("Thread1: attempting to remove an item from the queue ");
                                Object o = blockerQueue.remove();
                        }
                }.start();

                new Thread() {
                        public void run() {
                                System.out.println("Thread2: attempting to insert an item to the queue");
                                blockerQueue.insert("one");
                        }
                }.start();
        }
}
```

This test code prints the following:

```
Thread1: attempting to remove an item from the queue
In remove(): no element to remove, so waiting for insertion
Thread2: attempting to insert an item to the queue
In insert(): inserted the element one
In insert(): notified that queue is not empty
In remove(): got notification that an element has got inserted
In remove(): removed the element one
In remove(): signalled that there is space for insertion
```

As you can see from the output, the remove() method got called first, which waits for insert() to be called. Once insert() is complete, the remove() method successfully removes the element from the queue. Now, let's try another test case to test if blocking in the insert() method works:

```
class BlockerQueueTest2 {
        public static void main(String []args) {
                final BlockerQueue blockerQueue = new BlockerQueue(3);
                blockerQueue.insert("one");
                blockerQueue.insert("two");
                blockerQueue.insert("three");
                new Thread() {
```

```
                        public void run() {
                                System.out.println("Thread2: attempting to insert an item to the queue");
                                blockerQueue.insert("four");
                        }
                }.start();

                new Thread() {
                        public void run() {
                                System.out.println("Thread1: attempting to remove an item from the queue ");
                                Object o = blockerQueue.remove();
                        }
                }.start();
        }
}
```

This test code prints the following:

```
In insert(): inserted the element one
In insert(): notified that queue is not empty
In insert(): inserted the element two
In insert(): notified that queue is not empty
In insert(): inserted the element three
In insert(): notified that queue is not empty
Thread2: attempting to insert an item to the queue
In insert(): queue is full, so waiting for removal
Thread1: attempting to remove an item from the queue
In remove(): removed the element three
In remove(): signalled that there is space for insertion
In insert(): got notification that remove got called, so proceeding to insert the element
In insert(): inserted the element four
In insert(): notified that queue is not empty
```

As you can see from the output, when a thread invokes insert on the full queue (you have specified the capacity as 3 elements in this case), the thread blocks. Once another thread removed an element from the queue, the blocked thread resumes and successfully inserts the element.

Use Executors and ThreadPools

You can directly create and manage threads in the application by creating Thread objects. However, if you want to abstract away the low-level details of multi-threaded programming, you can make use of the Executor interface.

Figure 14-1 shows the important classes and interfaces in the Executor hierarchy. In this section, you'll focus on using the Executor interface, ExecutorService, and ThreadPools. We'll cover ForkJoinPool in the next section, "Use the Parallel Fork/Join Framework."

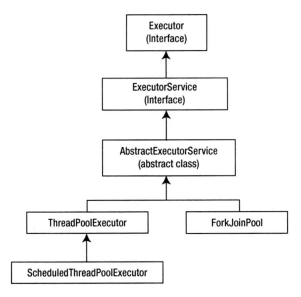

Figure 14-1. *Important classes/interfaces in the Executor hierarchy*

Executor

Executor is an interface that declares only one method: void execute(Runnable). This may not look like a big interface by itself, but its derived classes (or interfaces), such as ExecutorService, ThreadPoolExecutor, and ForkJoinPool, support useful functionality. We will discuss the derived classes of Executor in more detail in the rest of this section. For now, look at Listing 14-12 for a simple example of the Executor interface to understand how to implement this interface and use it in practice.

Listing 14-12. ExecutorTest.java

```
import java.util.concurrent.*;

// This Task class implements Runnable, so its a Thread object
class Task implements Runnable {
        public void run() {
                System.out.println("Calling Task.run() ");
        }
}

// This class implements Executor interface and should override execute(Runnable) method.
// We provide an overloaded execute method with an additional argument 'times' to create and
// run the threads for given number of times
class RepeatedExecutor implements Executor {
        public void execute(Runnable runnable) {
                new Thread(runnable).start();
        }
```

```java
        public void execute(Runnable runnable, int times) {
                System.out.printf("Calling Task.run() thro' Executor.execute() for %d times %n", times);
                for(int i = 0; i < times; i++) {
                        execute(runnable);
                }
        }
}

// This class spawns a Task thread and explicitly calls start() method.
// It also shows how to execute a Thread using Executor
class ExecutorTest {
        public static void main(String []args) {
                Runnable runnable = new Task();
                System.out.println("Calling Task.run() by directly creating a Thread object");
                Thread thread = new Thread(runnable);
                thread.start();
                RepeatedExecutor executor = new RepeatedExecutor();
                executor.execute(runnable, 3);
        }
}
```

Here is the output of this program:

```
Calling Task.run() by directly creating a Thread object
Calling Task.run()
Calling Task.run() thro' Executor.execute() for 3 times
Calling Task.run()
Calling Task.run()
Calling Task.run()
```

In this program, you have a Task class that implements Runnable by providing the definition of the run() method. The class RepeatedExecutor implements the Executor interface by providing the definition of the execute(Runnable) method.

Both Runnable and Executor are similar in the sense that they provide a single method for implementation. In this definition you may have noticed that Exectutor by itself is not a thread, and you must create a Thread object to execute the Runnable object passed in the execute() method. However, the main difference between Runnable and Exectutor is that Executor is meant to abstract how the thread is executed. For example, depending on the implementation of Executor, Exectutor may schedule a thread to run at a certain time, or execute the thread after a certain delay period.

In this program, you have overloaded the execute() method with an additional argument to create and execute threads a certain number of times. In the main() method, you first create a Thread object and schedule it for running. After that, you instantiate RepeatedExectutor to execute the thread three times.

Callable, Executors, ExecutorService, ThreadPool, and Future

Callable is an interface that declares only one method: call(). Its full signature is V call() throws Exception. It represents a task that needs to be completed by a thread. Once the task completes, it returns a value. For some reason, if the call() method cannot execute or fails, it throws an Exception.

To execute a task using the Callable object, you first create a thread pool. A thread pool is a collection of threads that can execute tasks. You create a thread pool using the Executors utility class. This class provides methods to get instances of thread pools, thread factories, etc.

The ExecutorService interface implements the Executor interface and provides services such as termination of threads and production of Future objects. Some tasks may take considerable execution time to complete. So, when you submit a task to the executor service, you get a Future object.

Future represents objects that contain a value that is returned by a thread in the future (i.e., it returns the value once the thread terminates in the "future"). You can use the isDone() method in the Future class to check if the task is complete and then use the get() method to fetch the task result. If you call the get() method directly while the task is not complete, the method blocks until it completes and returns the value once available.

Enough talking—try a simple example to see how these classes work together (Listing 14-13).

Listing 14-13. CallableTest.java

```java
// Factorial implements Callable so that it can be passed to a ExecutorService
// and get executed as a task.
class Factorial implements Callable<Long> {
        long n;
        public Factorial(long n) {
                this.n = n;
        }
        public Long call() throws Exception {
                if(n <= 0) {
                        throw new Exception("for finding factorial, N should be > 0");
                }
                long fact = 1;
                for(long longVal = 1; longVal <= n; longVal++) {
                        fact *= longVal;
                }
                return fact;
        }
}

// Illustrates how Callable, Executors, ExecutorService, and Future are related;
// also shows how they work together to execute a task
class CallableTest {
        public static void main(String []args) throws Exception {
                // the value for which we want to find the factorial
                long N = 20;
                // get a callable task to be submitted to the executor service
                Callable<Long> task = new Factorial(N);
                // create an ExecutorService with a fixed thread pool consisting of one thread
                ExecutorService es = Executors.newSingleThreadExecutor();
                // submit the task to the executor service and store the Future object
                Future<Long> future = es.submit(task);
                // wait for the get() method that blocks until the computation is complete.
                System.out.printf("factorial of %d is %d", N, future.get());
                // done. shutdown the executor service since we don't need it anymore
                es.shutdown();
        }
}
```

The program prints the following:

```
factorial of 20 is 2432902008176640000
```

In this program, you have a `Factorial` class that implements `Callable`. Since the task is to compute the factorial of a number N, the task needs to return a result. You use `Long` type for the factorial value, so you implement `Callable<Long>`. Inside the `Factorial` class, you define the `call()` method that actually performs the task (the task here is to compute the factorial of the given number). If the given value N is negative or zero, you don't perform the task and throw an exception to the caller. Otherwise, you loop from 1 to N and find the factorial value.

In the `CallableTest` class, you first create an instance of the `Factorial` class. You then need to execute this task. For the sake of simplicity, you get a singled-threaded executor by calling the `newSingleThreadExecutor()` method in the `Executors` class. Note that you could use other methods such as `newFixedThreadPool(nThreads)` to create a thread pool with multiple threads depending on the level of parallelism you need.

Once you get an `ExecutorService`, you submit the task for execution. `ExecutorService` abstracts details such as when the task is executed, how the task is assigned to the threads, etc. You get a reference to `Future<Long>` when you call the `submit(task)` method. From this future reference, you call the `get()` method to fetch the result after completing the task. If the task is still executing when you call `future.get()`, this `get()` method will block until the task execution completes. Once the execution is complete, you need to manually release the `ExecutorService` by calling the `shutdown()` method.

Now that you are familiar with the basic mechanism of how to execute tasks, here's a complex example. Assume that your task is to find the sum of numbers from 1 to N where N is a large number (a million in our case). Of course, you can use the formula $[(N * (N + 1)) / 2]$ to find out the sum. Yes, you'll make use of this formula to check if the summation from 1...N is correct or not. However, just for illustration, you'll divide the range 1 to 1 million to N sub-ranges and by spawn N threads to sum up numbers in that sub-range; see Listing 14-14.

Listing 14-14. SumOfN.java

```java
import java.util.*;
import java.util.concurrent.*;

// We create a class SumOfN that sums the values from 1..N where N is a large number.
// We divide the task
// to sum the numbers to 10 threads (which is an arbitrary limit just for illustration).
// Once computation is complete, we add the results of all the threads,
// and check if the calculation is correct by using the formula (N * (N + 1))/2.
class SumOfN {
        private static long N = 1_000_000L;    // one million
        private static long calculatedSum = 0; // value to hold the sum of values in range 1..N
        private static final int NUM_THREADS = 10; // number of threads to create for distributing the effort

        // This Callable object sums numbers in range from..to
        static class SumCalc implements Callable<Long> {
                long from, to, localSum = 0;

                public SumCalc(long from, long to) {
                        this.from = from;
                        this.to = to;
                }
                public Long call() {
                        // add in range 'from' .. 'to' inclusive of the value 'to'
                        for(long i = from; i <= to; i++) {
                                localSum += i;
                        }
                        return localSum;
                }
        }
}
```

```
        // In the main method we implement the logic to divide the summation tasks to
        // given number of threads and finally check if the calculated sum is correct
        public static void main(String []args) {
                // Divide the task among available fixed number of threads
                ExecutorService executorService = Executors.newFixedThreadPool(NUM_THREADS);
                // store the references to the Future objects in a List for summing up together
                List<Future<Long>> summationTasks = new ArrayList<>();
                long nByTen = N/10;        // divide N by 10 so that it can be submitted as 10 tasks
                for(int i = 0; i < NUM_THREADS; i++) {
                        // create a summation task
                        // starting from (10 * 0) + 1 .. (N/10 * 1) to (10 * 9) + 1 .. (N/10 * 10)
                        long fromInInnerRange = (nByTen * i) + 1;
                        long toInInnerRange = nByTen * (i+1);
                        System.out.printf("Spawning thread for summing in range %d to %d %n",
fromInInnerRange, toInInnerRange);
                        // Create a callable object for the given summation range
                        Callable<Long> summationTask =
                                new SumCalc(fromInInnerRange, toInInnerRange);
                        // submit that task to the executor service
                        Future<Long> futureSum = executorService.submit(summationTask);
                        // it will take time to complete, so add it to the list to revisit later
                        summationTasks.add(futureSum);
                }

                // now, find the sum from each task
                for(Future<Long> partialSum : summationTasks) {
                        try {
                                // the get() method will block (i.e., wait) until the computation is over
                                calculatedSum += partialSum.get();
                        } catch(CancellationException | ExecutionException
                                | InterruptedException exception) {
                                // unlikely that you get an exception - exit in case something goes wrong
                                exception.printStackTrace();
                                System.exit(-1);
                        }
                }

                // now calculate the sum using formula (N * (N + 1))/2 without doing the hard-work
                long formulaSum = (N * (N + 1))/2;
                // print the sum using formula and the ones calculated one by one
                // they must be equal!
                System.out.printf("Sum by threads = %d, sum using formula = %d",
                        calculatedSum, formulaSum);
        }
}
```

Here is the output of this program:

```
Spawning thread for summing in range 1 to 100000
Spawning thread for summing in range 100001 to 200000
Spawning thread for summing in range 200001 to 300000
Spawning thread for summing in range 300001 to 400000
```

```
Spawning thread for summing in range 400001 to 500000
Spawning thread for summing in range 500001 to 600000
Spawning thread for summing in range 600001 to 700000
Spawning thread for summing in range 700001 to 800000
Spawning thread for summing in range 800001 to 900000
Spawning thread for summing in range 900001 to 1000000
Sum by threads = 500000500000, sum using formula = 500000500000
```

Let's now analyze how this program works. In this program, you need to find the sum of 1..N where N is one million (a large number). The class SumCalc implements Callable<Long> to sum the values in the range from to to. The call() method performs the actual computation of the sum by looping from from to to and returns the intermediate sum value as a Long value.

In this program, you divide the summation task among multiple threads. You can determine the number of threads based on the number of cores available in your processor; however, for the sake of keeping the program simpler, use ten threads.

In the main() method, you create a ThreadPool with ten threads. You are going to create ten summation tasks, so you need a container to hold the references to those tasks. Use ArrayList to hold the Future<Long> references.

In the first for loop in main(), you create ten tasks and submit them to the ExecutorService. As you submit a task, you get a Future<Long> reference and you add it to the ArrayList.

Once you've created the ten tasks, you traverse the array list in the next for loop to get the results of the tasks. You sum up the partial results of the individual tasks to compute the final sum.

Once you get the computed sum of values from one to one million, you use the simple formula N * (N + 1)/2 to find the formula sum. From the output, you can see that the computed sum and the formula sum are equal, so you can ascertain that your logic of dividing the tasks and combining the results of the tasks worked correctly.

Now, before we move on to discuss the fork/join framework, we'll quickly discuss a few classes that are useful for concurrent programming.

ThreadFactory

ThreadFactory is an interface that is meant for creating threads instead of explicitly creating threads by calling new Thread(). For example, assume that you often create high-priority threads. You can create a MaxPriorityThreadFactory to set the default priority of threads created by that factory to maximum priority (see Listing 14-15).

Listing 14-15. TestThreadFactory.java

```java
import java.util.concurrent.*;

// A ThreadFactory implementation that sets the thread priority to max
// for all the threads it creates
class MaxPriorityThreadFactory implements ThreadFactory {
        private static long count = 0;
        public Thread newThread(Runnable r) {
              Thread temp = new Thread(r);
              temp.setName("prioritythread" + count++);
              temp.setPriority(Thread.MAX_PRIORITY);
              return temp;
        }
}
```

```java
class ARunnable implements Runnable {
        public void run() {
                System.out.println("Running the created thread ");
        }
}

class TestThreadFactory {
        public static void main(String []args) {
                ThreadFactory threadFactory = new MaxPriorityThreadFactory();
                Thread t1 = threadFactory.newThread(new ARunnable());
                System.out.println("The name of the thread is " + t1.getName());
                System.out.println("The priority of the thread is " + t1.getPriority());
                t1.start();
        }
}
```

It prints the following:

```
The name of the thread is prioritythread0
The priority of the thread is 10
Running the created thread
```

With the use of ThreadFactory, you can reduce boilerplate code to set thread priority, name, thread-pool, etc.

The ThreadLocalRandom Class

When you do concurrent programming, you'll find that there is often a need to generate random numbers. Using Math.random() is not efficient for concurrent programming. For this reason, the java.util.concurrent package introduces the ThreadLocalRandom class, which is suitable for use in concurrent programs. You can use ThreadLocalRandom.current() and then call methods such as nextInt() and nextFloat() to generate the random numbers.

TimeUnit Enumeration

You've already seen some methods earlier in this chapter that take TimeUnit as an argument. TimeUnit is an enumeration that is used to specify the resolution of the timing. The unit of time in TimeUnit can be one of DAYS, HOURS, MINUTES, SECONDS, MICROSECONDS, MILLISECONDS, or NANOSECONDS. The enumeration also has useful methods for converting between these time units. For example,

```java
System.out.printf("One day has %d hours, %d minutes, %d seconds",
        TimeUnit.DAYS.toHours(1), TimeUnit.DAYS.toMinutes(1), TimeUnit.DAYS.toSeconds(1));
```

prints

```
One day has 24 hours, 1440 minutes, 86400 seconds
```

Some of the methods in the Java API use specific periods. For example, the sleep() method takes time to sleep in milliseconds. So, what if you want to specify the time for thread sleep in some other time unit, say seconds or days? TimeUnit makes this task easy. See Listing 14-16 for an example.

Listing 14-16. TimeUnitExample.java

```
import java.util.concurrent.TimeUnit;

// A simple example showing how to make use of TimeUnit enumeration
class TimeUnitExample {
    public static void main(String []args) throws InterruptedException {
        System.out.println("Calling sleep() method on main thread for 2 seconds");
        // Thread.sleep takes milli-seconds as argument. By using TimeUnit enumeration,
        // you can specify the time to sleep in other time units such as hours, minutes,
        // seconds, etc.
        Thread.sleep(TimeUnit.SECONDS.toMillis(2));
        System.out.println("main thread wakes up from sleep");
    }
}
```

Use the Parallel Fork/Join Framework

The Fork/Join framework in the java.util.concurrent package helps simplify writing parallelized code. The framework is an implementation of the ExecutorService interface and provides an easy-to-use concurrent platform in order to exploit multiple processors. This framework is very useful for modeling divide-and-conquer problems. This approach is suitable for tasks that can be divided recursively and computed on a smaller scale; the computed results are then combined. Dividing the task into smaller tasks is *forking*, and merging the results from the smaller tasks is *joining*.

The Fork/Join framework uses the work-stealing algorithm: when a worker thread completes its work and is free, it takes (or "steals") work from other threads that are still busy doing some work. Initially, it will appear to you that using Fork/Join is a complex task. Once you get familiar with it, however, you'll realize that it is conceptually easy and that it significantly simplifies your job. The key is to recursively subdivide the task into smaller chunks that can be processed by separate threads.

Briefly, the Fork/Join algorithm is designed as follows:

```
forkJoinAlgorithm() {
    split tasks;
    fork the tasks;
    join the tasks;
    compose the results;
}
```

Here is the pseudo-code of how these steps work:

```
doRecursiveTask(input) {
    if (the task is small enough to be handled by a thread) {
        compute the small task;
        if there is a result to return, do so
    }
    else {
        divide (i.e., fork) the task into two parts
        call compute() on first task, join() on second task, combine both results and return
    }
}
```

Figure 14-2 visualizes how the task is recursively subdivided into smaller tasks and how the partial results are combined. As shown by the figure, a task is split into two subtasks, and then each subtask is again split in two subtasks, and so on until each split subtask is computable by each thread. Once a thread completes the computation, it returns the result for combining it with other results; in this way all the computed results are combined back.

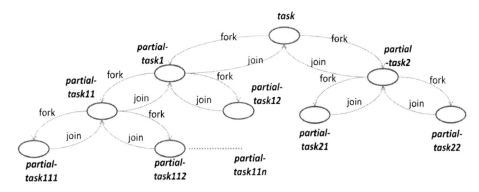

Figure 14-2. *How the Fork/Join framework uses divide-and-conquer to complete the task*

Useful Classes of the Fork/Join Framework

The following classes play key roles in the Fork/Join framework: `ForkJoinPool`, `ForkJoinTask`, `RecursiveTask`, and `RecursiveAction`. Let's consider these classes in more detail.

- `ForkJoinPool` is the most important class in the Fork/Join framework. It is a thread pool for running fork/join tasks—it executes an instance of `ForkJoinTask`. It executes tasks and manages their lifecycle. Table 14-8 lists the important methods belonging to this abstract class.

Table 14-8. *Important Methods in the ForkJoinPool Class*

Method	Description
`void execute(ForkJoinTask<?> task)`	Executes a given task asynchronously.
`<T> T invoke(ForkJoinTask<T> task)`	Executes the given task and returns the computed result.

`<T> List<Future<T>>`
`invokeAll(Collection<? extends`
`            Callable<T>> tasks)`
	Executes all the given tasks and returns a list of future objects when all the tasks are completed.

`boolean isTerminated()`	Returns `true` if all the tasks are completed.
`int getParallelism()`	Status checking methods.
`int getPoolSize()`	
`long getStealCount()`	
`int getActiveThreadCount()` `<T> ForkJoinTask<T> submit(Callable<T> task)`	Executes a submitted task. Overloaded versions take different types of tasks; returns a Task object or a Future object.
`<T> ForkJoinTask<T> submit(ForkJoinTask<T> task)`	
`ForkJoinTask<?> submit(Runnable task)`	
`<T> ForkJoinTask<T> submit(Runnable task, T result)`	

- ForkJoinTask<V> is a lightweight thread-like entity representing a task that defines methods such as fork() and join(). Table 14-9 lists the important methods of this class.

Table 14-9. *Important Methods in the ForkJoinTask Class*

Method	Description
boolean cancel(boolean mayInterruptIfRunning)	Attempts to cancel the execution of the task.
ForkJoinTask<V> fork()	Executes the task asynchronously.
V join()	Returns the result of the computation when the computation is done.
V get()	Returns the result of the computation; waits if the computation is not complete.
V invoke()	Starts the execution of the submitted tasks; waits until computation complete, and returns results.
static <T extends ForkJoinTask<?>> Collection<T> invokeAll(Collection<T> tasks)	
boolean isCancelled()	Returns true if the task is cancelled.
boolean isDone()	Returns true if the task is completed.

- RecursiveTask<V> is a task that can run in a ForkJoinPool; the compute() method returns a value of type V. It inherits from ForkJoinTask.

- RecursiveAction is a task that can run in a ForkJoinPool; its compute() method performs the actual computation steps in the task. It is similar to RecursiveTask, but does not return a value.

Using the Fork/Join Framework

Let's ascertain how you can use Fork/Join framework in problem solving. Here are the steps to use the framework:

- First, check whether the problem is suitable for the Fork/Join framework or not. Remember: the Fork/Join framework is not suitable for all kinds of tasks. This framework is suitable if your problem fits this description:

  - The problem can be designed as a recursive task where the task can be subdivided into smaller units and the results can be combined together.

  - The subdivided tasks are independent and can be computed separately without the need for communication between the tasks when computation is in process. (Of course, after the computation is over, you will need to join them together.)

- If the problem you want to solve can be modeled recursively, then define a task class that extends either RecursiveTask or RecursiveAction. If a task returns a result, extend from RecursiveTask; otherwise extend from RecursiveAction.

- Override the compute() method in the newly defined task class. The compute() method actually performs the task if the task is small enough to be executed; or split the task into subtasks and invoke them. The subtasks can be invoked either by invokeAll() or fork() method (use fork() when the subtask returns a value). Use the join() method to get the computed results (if you used fork() method earlier).

- Merge the results, if computed from the subtasks.

- Then instantiate ForkJoinPool, create an instance of the task class, and start the execution of the task using the invoke() method on the ForkJoinPool instance.

- That's it—you are done.

Now let's try solving the problem of how to sum 1..N where N is a large number. In Listing 14-16, you subdivided the sum computation task iteratively into ten sub-ranges; then you computed the sum for each sub-range and then computed the sum-of-the-partial sums. Alternatively, you can solve this problem rescursively using the Fork/Join framework (Listing 14-17).

Listing 14-17. SumOfNUsingForkJoin.java

```java
import java.util.concurrent.*;

// This class illustrates how we can compute sum of 1..N numbers using fork/join framework.
// The range of numbers are divided into half until the range can be handled by a thread.
// Once the range summation completes, the result gets summed up together.

class SumOfNUsingForkJoin {
        private static long N = 1000_000; // one million - we want to compute sum
                                          // from 1 .. one million
        private static final int NUM_THREADS = 10; // number of threads to create for
                                                   // distributing the effort

        // This is the recursive implementation of the algorithm; inherit from RecursiveTask
        // instead of RecursiveAction since we're returning values.
        static class RecursiveSumOfN extends RecursiveTask<Long> {
                long from, to;
                // from and to are range of values to sum-up
                public RecursiveSumOfN(long from, long to) {
                        this.from = from;
                        this.to = to;
                }
                // the method performs fork and join to compute the sum.
                // if the range of values can be summed by a thread
                // (remember that we want to divide the summation task equally among NUM_THREADS)
                // then, sum the range of numbers from..to using a simple for loop
                // otherwise, fork the range and join the results
                public Long compute() {
                        if( (to - from) <= N/NUM_THREADS) {
                                // the range is something that can be handled by a thread, so do summation
                                long localSum = 0;
                                // add in range 'from' .. 'to' inclusive of the value 'to'
                                for(long i = from; i <= to; i++) {
                                        localSum += i;
                                }
                                System.out.printf("\t Summing of value range %d to %d is %d %n",
from,to, localSum);

                                return localSum;
                        }
```

```
                      else { // no, the range is big for a thread to handle, so fork the computation
                              // we find the mid-point value in the range from..to
                              long mid = (from + to)/2;
                              System.out.printf("Forking computation into two ranges: " +
                                      "%d to %d and %d to %d %n", from, mid, mid, to);
                              // determine the computation for first half with the range from..mid
                              RecursiveSumOfN firstHalf = new RecursiveSumOfN(from, mid);
                              // now, fork off that task
                              firstHalf.fork();
                              // determine the computation for second half with the range mid+1..to
                              RecursiveSumOfN secondHalf = new RecursiveSumOfN(mid + 1, to);
                              long resultSecond = secondHalf.compute();
                              // now, wait for the first half of computing sum to
                              // complete, once done, add it to the remaining part
                              return firstHalf.join() + resultSecond;
                      }
              }
      }

      public static void main(String []args) {
              // Create a fork-join pool that consists of NUM_THREADS
              ForkJoinPool pool = new ForkJoinPool(NUM_THREADS);
              // submit the computation task to the fork-join pool
              long computedSum = pool.invoke(new RecursiveSumOfN(0, N));
              // this is the formula sum for the range 1..N
              long formulaSum = (N * (N + 1)) / 2;
              // Compare the computed sum and the formula sum
              System.out.printf("Sum for range 1..%d; computed sum = %d, formula sum = %d %n", N,
computedSum, formulaSum);
      }
}
```

The program prints the following:

```
Forking computation into two ranges: 0 to 500000 and 500000 to 1000000
Forking computation into two ranges: 0 to 250000 and 250000 to 500000
Forking computation into two ranges: 0 to 125000 and 125000 to 250000
Forking computation into two ranges: 0 to 62500 and 62500 to 125000
        Summing of value range 0 to 62500 is 1953156250
        Summing of value range 62501 to 125000 is 5859406250
Forking computation into two ranges: 125001 to 187500 and 187500 to 250000
        Summing of value range 125001 to 187500 is 9765656250
        Summing of value range 187501 to 250000 is 13671906250
Forking computation into two ranges: 250001 to 375000 and 375000 to 500000
Forking computation into two ranges: 250001 to 312500 and 312500 to 375000
        Summing of value range 250001 to 312500 is 17578156250
        Summing of value range 312501 to 375000 is 21484406250
Forking computation into two ranges: 375001 to 437500 and 437500 to 500000
        Summing of value range 375001 to 437500 is 25390656250
        Summing of value range 437501 to 500000 is 29296906250
Forking computation into two ranges: 500001 to 750000 and 750000 to 1000000
Forking computation into two ranges: 500001 to 625000 and 625000 to 750000
```

```
Forking computation into two ranges: 500001 to 562500 and 562500 to 625000
        Summing of value range 500001 to 562500 is 33203156250
        Summing of value range 562501 to 625000 is 37109406250
Forking computation into two ranges: 625001 to 687500 and 687500 to 750000
        Summing of value range 625001 to 687500 is 41015656250
        Summing of value range 687501 to 750000 is 44921906250
Forking computation into two ranges: 750001 to 875000 and 875000 to 1000000
Forking computation into two ranges: 750001 to 812500 and 812500 to 875000
        Summing of value range 750001 to 812500 is 48828156250
        Summing of value range 812501 to 875000 is 52734406250
Forking computation into two ranges: 875001 to 937500 and 937500 to 1000000
        Summing of value range 875001 to 937500 is 56640656250
        Summing of value range 937501 to 1000000 is 60546906250
Sum for range 1..1000000; computed sum = 500000500000, formula sum = 500000500000
```

Let's analyze how this program works. In this program, you want to compute the sum of the values in the range 1..1,000,000. For the sake of simplicity, you decide to use ten threads to execute the tasks. The class RecursiveSumOfN extends RecursiveTask<Long>. In RecursiveTask<Long>, you use <Long> because the sum of numbers in each sub-range is a Long value. In addition, you chose RecursiveTask<Long> instead of plain RecursiveAction because each subtask returns a value. If the subtask does not return a value, you can use RecursiveAction instead.

In the compute() method, you decide whether to compute the sum for the range or subdivide the task further using following condition:

```
(to - from) <= N/NUM_THREADS)
```

You use this "threshold" value in this computation. In other words, if the range of values is within the threshold that can be handled by a task, then you perform the computation; otherwise you recursively divide the task into two parts. You use a simple for loop to find the sum of the values in that range. In the other case, you divide the range similarly to how you divide the range in a binary search algorithm: for the range from .. to, you find the mid-point and create two sub-ranges from .. mid and mid + 1 .. to. Once you call fork(), you wait for the first task to complete the computation of the sum and spawn another task for the second half of the computation.

In the main() method, you create a ForkJoinPool with number of threads given by NUM_THREADS. You submit the task to the fork/join pool and get the computed sum for 1..1,000,000. Now you also calculate the sum using the formula to sum N continuous numbers.

From the output of the program, you can observe how the task got subdivided into subtasks. You can also verify from the output that the computed sum and sum computed from the formula are the same, indicating that your division of tasks for summing the sub-ranges is correct.

In this program, you arbitrarily assumed the number of threads to use was ten threads. This was to simplify the logic of this program. A better approach to decide the threshold value is to divide the data size length by the number of available processors. In other words,

```
threshold value = (data length size) / (number of available processors);
```

How do you programmatically get the number of available processors? For that you can use the method Runtime.getRuntime().availableProcessors().

In Listing 14-17, you used RecursiveTask; however, if a task is not returning a value, then you should use RecursiveAction. Let's implement a search program using RecursiveAction. Assume that you have a big array (say of 10,000 items) and you want to search a key item. You can use the Fork/Join framework to split the task into several subtasks and execute them in parallel. Listing 14-18 contains the program implementing the solution.

Listing 14-18. SearchUsingForkJoin.java

```java
import java.util.concurrent.*;

//This class illustrates how we can search a key within N numbers using fork/join framework
// (using RecursiveAction).
//The range of numbers are divided into half until the range can be handled by a thread.
class SearchUsingForkJoin {
        private static int N = 10000;
        private static final int NUM_THREADS = 10; // number of threads to create for
                                                   // distributing the effort
        private static int searchKey= 100;
        private static int[] arrayToSearch;

        // This is the recursive implementation of the algorithm;
        // inherit from RecursiveAction
        static class SearchTask extends RecursiveAction {
                private static final long serialVersionUID = 1L;
                int from, to;
                // from and to are range of values to search
                public SearchTask(int from, int to) {
                        this.from = from;
                        this.to = to;
                }

                public void compute() {
                        //If the range is smaller enough to be handled by a thread,
                        //we search in the range
                        if( (to - from) <= N/NUM_THREADS) {
                                // add in range 'from' .. 'to' inclusive of the value 'to'
                                for(int i = from; i <= to; i++) {
                                        if(arrayToSearch[i] == searchKey)
                                                System.out.println("Search key found at index:" +i);
                                }
                        }
                        else {
                                // no, the range is big for a thread to handle,
                                // so fork the computation
                                // we find the mid-point value in the range from..to
                                int mid = (from + to)/2;
                                System.out.printf("Forking computation into two ranges: " +
"%d to %d and %d to %d %n", from, mid, mid, to);
                                //invoke all the subtasks
                                invokeAll(new SearchTask(from, mid),new SearchTask(mid + 1, to));
                        }
                }
        }
```

```
        public static void main(String []args) {
                //intantiate the array to be searched
                arrayToSearch = new int[N];
                //fill the array with random numbers
                for(int i=0; i<N; i++){
                        arrayToSearch[i] = ThreadLocalRandom.current().nextInt(0,1000);
                }
                // Create a fork-join pool that consists of NUM_THREADS
                ForkJoinPool pool = new ForkJoinPool(NUM_THREADS);
                // submit the computation task to the fork-join pool
                pool.invoke(new SearchTask(0, N-1));
        }
}
```

The program prints the following output (which might be different from run to run):

```
Forking computation into two ranges: 0 to 4999 and 4999 to 9999
Forking computation into two ranges: 0 to 2499 and 2499 to 4999
Forking computation into two ranges: 5000 to 7499 and 7499 to 9999
Forking computation into two ranges: 2500 to 3749 and 3749 to 4999
Forking computation into two ranges: 0 to 1249 and 1249 to 2499
Forking computation into two ranges: 2500 to 3124 and 3124 to 3749
Forking computation into two ranges: 7500 to 8749 and 8749 to 9999
Forking computation into two ranges: 5000 to 6249 and 6249 to 7499
Forking computation into two ranges: 8750 to 9374 and 9374 to 9999
Forking computation into two ranges: 5000 to 5624 and 5624 to 6249
Forking computation into two ranges: 7500 to 8124 and 8124 to 8749
Forking computation into two ranges: 3750 to 4374 and 4374 to 4999
Search key found at index:4736
Search key found at index:2591
Forking computation into two ranges: 1250 to 1874 and 1874 to 2499
Search key found at index:1315
Forking computation into two ranges: 0 to 624 and 624 to 1249
Search key found at index:445
Search key found at index:9402
Search key found at index:9146
Forking computation into two ranges: 6250 to 6874 and 6874 to 7499
Search key found at index:6797
Search key found at index:7049
Search key found at index:862
```

The key difference between Listings 14-14 and 14-15 is that you used RecursiveAction in the latter instead of RecursiveTask. You made several changes to extend the task class from RecursiveAction. The first change is that the compute() method is not returning anything. Another change is that you used the invokeAll() method to submit the subtasks to execute. Another obvious change is that you carried out search in the compute() method instead of summation in earlier case. Apart from these changes, the program in Listing 14-17 works much like the program in Listing 14-18.

Points to Remember

Remember these points for your exam:

- It is possible to achieve what the Fork/Join framework offers using basic concurrency constructs such as start() and join(). However, the Fork/Join framework abstracts many lower-level details and thus is easier to use. In addition, it is much more efficient to use the Fork/Join framework instead handling the threads at lower levels. Furthermore, using ForkJoinPool efficiently manages the threads and performs much better than conventional threads pools. For all these reasons, you are encouraged to use the Fork/Join framework.

- Each worker thread in the Fork/Join framework has a work queue, which is implemented using a Deque. Each time a new task (or subtask) is created, it is pushed to the head of its own queue. When a task completes a task and executes a join with another task that is not completed yet, it works smart. The thread pops a new task from the head of its queue and starts executing rather than sleeping (in order to wait for another task to complete). In fact, if the queue of a thread is empty, then the thread pops a task from the tail of the queue belonging to another thread. This is nothing but a work-stealing algorithm.

- It looks obvious to call fork() for both the subtasks (if you are splitting in two subtasks) and call join() two times. It is correct—but inefficient. Why? Well, basically you are creating more parallel tasks than are useful. In this case, the original thread will be waiting for the other two tasks to complete, which is inefficient considering task creation cost. That is why you call fork() once and call compute() for the second task.

- The placement of fork() and join() calls are very important. For instance, let's assume that you place the calls in following order:

```
first.fork();
resultFirst = first.join();
resultSecond = second.compute();
```

This usage is a serial execution of two tasks, since the second task starts executing only after the first is complete. Thus, it is less efficient even than its sequential version since this version also includes cost of the task creation. The take-away: watch your placement of fork/join calls.

- Performance is not always guaranteed while using the Fork/Join framework. One of the reasons we mentioned earlier is the placement of fork/join calls.

QUESTION TIME!

1. Consider the following program:

```
import java.util.concurrent.atomic.*;

class AtomicIntegerTest {
    static AtomicInteger ai = new AtomicInteger(10);
    public static void check() {
        assert (ai.intValue() % 2) == 0;
    }
    public static void increment() {
        ai.incrementAndGet();
    }
```

```
        public static void decrement() {
                ai.getAndDecrement();
        }
        public static void compare() {
                ai.compareAndSet(10, 11);
        }
        public static void main(String []args) {
                increment();
                decrement();
                compare();
                check();
                System.out.println(ai);
        }
}
```

The program is invoked as follows:

```
java -ea AtomicIntegerTest
```

What is the expected output of this program?

A. It prints 11.

B. It prints 10.

C. It prints 9.

D. It crashes throwing an AssertionError.

Answer:

D. It crashes throwing an AssertionError.

(The initial value of AtomicInteger is 10. Its value is incremented by 1 after calling incrementAndGet(). After that, its value is decremented by 1 after calling getAndDecrement(). The method compareAndSet(10, 11) checks if the current value is 10, and if so sets the atomic integer variable to value 11. Since the assert statement checks if the atomic integer value % 2 is zero (that is, checks if it is an even number), the assert fails and the program results in an AssertionError.)

2. Which one of the following options correctly makes use of Callable that will compile without any errors?

A. import java.util.concurrent.Callable;

```
class CallableTask implements Callable {
        public int call() {
                System.out.println("In Callable.call()");
                return 0;
        }
}
```

B. ```java
    import java.util.concurrent.Callable;

    class CallableTask extends Callable {
            public Integer call() {
                    System.out.println("In Callable.call()");
                    return 0;
            }
    }
    ```

C.  ```java
    import java.util.concurrent.Callable;

    class CallableTask implements Callable<Integer> {
            public Integer call() {
                    System.out.println("In Callable.call()");
                    return 0;
            }
    }
    ```

D. ```java
    import java.util.concurrent.Callable;

    class CallableTask implements Callable<Integer> {
            public void call(Integer i) {
                    System.out.println("In Callable.call(i)");
            }
    }
    ```

**Answer:**

C.  ```java
    import java.util.concurrent.Callable;

    class CallableTask implements Callable<Integer> {
            public Integer call() {
                    System.out.println("In Callable.call()");
                    return 0;
            }
    }
    ```

(The `Callable` interface is defined as follows:

```java
public interface Callable<V> {
    V call() throws Exception;
}
```

In option A), the `call()` method has the return type `int`, which is incompatible with the return type expected for overriding the `call` method and so will not compile.

In option B), the `extends` keyword is used, which will result in a compiler (since `Callable` is an interface, the `implements` keyword should be used).

Option C) correctly defines the `Callable` interface providing the type parameter `<Integer>`. The same type parameter `Integer` is also used in the return type of the `call()` method that takes no arguments, so it will compile without errors.

In option D), the return type of call() is void and the call() method also takes a parameter of type Integer. Hence, the method declared in the interface Integer call() remains unimplemented in the CallableTask class and so the program will not compile.)

3. Which one of the following methods return a Future object?

A. The overloaded replace() methods declared in the ConcurrentMap interface

B. The newThread() method declared in the ThreadFactory interface

C. The overloaded submit() methods declared in the ExecutorService interface

D. The call() method declared in the Callable interface

Answer:

C. The overloaded submit() methods declared in ExecutorService interface

Option A) The overloaded replace() methods declared in the ConcurrentMap interface remove an element from the map and return the success status (a Boolean value) or the removed value.

Option B) The newThread() is the only method declared in the ThreadFactory interface and it returns a Thread object as the return value.

Option C) The ExecutorService interface has overloaded submit() method that takes a task for execution and returns a Future representing the pending results of the task.

Option D) The call() method declared in Callable interface returns the result of the task it executed.)

4. You're writing an application that generates random numbers in the range 0 to 100. You want to create these random numbers for use in multiple threads as well as in ForkJoinTasks. Which one of the following options will you use for less contention (i.e., efficient solution)?

A. int randomInt = ThreadSafeRandom.current().nextInt(0, 100);

B. int randomInt = ThreadLocalRandom.current().nextInt(0, 101);

C. int randomInt = new Random(seedInt).nextInt(101);

D. int randomInt = new Random().nextInt() % 100;

Answer:

B. int randomInt = ThreadLocalRandom.current().nextInt(0, 101);

(ThreadLocalRandom is a random number generator that is specific to a thread. From API documentation of this class: "Use of the ThreadLocalRandom rather than shared Random objects in concurrent programs will typically encounter much less overhead and contention."

The method "int nextInt(int least, int bound)" in the ThreadLocalRandom class returns a pseudo-random number that is uniformly distributed between the given least value and the bound value. Note that the value in parameter least is inclusive of that value and the bound value is exclusive. So, the call nextInt(0, 101) returns pseudo-random integers in the range 0 to 100.)

5. In your application, there is a producer component that keeps adding new items to a fixed-size queue; the consumer component fetches items from that queue. If the queue is full, the producer has to wait for items to be fetched; if the queue is empty, the consumer has to wait for items to be added.

Which one of the following utilities is suitable for synchronizing the common queue for concurrent use by a producer and consumer?

A. RecursiveAction

B. ForkJoinPool

C. Future

D. Semaphore

E. TimeUnit

Answer:

D. Semaphore

(The question is a classic producer–consumer problem that can be solved by using semaphores. The objects of the synchronizer class java.util.concurrent.Semaphore can be used to guard the common queue so that the producer and consumer can synchronize their access to the queue. Of the given options, semaphore is the only *synchronizer*; other options are unrelated to providing synchronized access to a queue.

Option A) RecursiveAction supports recursive ForkJoinTask, and option B) ForkJoinPool provides help in running a ForkJoinTask in the context of the Fork/Join framework. Option C) Future represents the result of an asynchronous computation whose result will be "available in the future once the computation is complete." Option E) TimeUnit is an enumeration that provides support for different time units such as milliseconds, seconds, and days.)

Summary

Using java.util.concurrent Collections

- A semaphore controls access to shared resources. A semaphore maintains a counter to specify number of resources that the semaphore controls.

- CountDownLatch allows one or more threads to wait for a countdown to complete.

- The Exchanger class is meant for exchanging data between two threads. This class is useful when two threads need to synchronize between each other and continuously exchange data.

- CyclicBarrier helps provide a synchronization point where threads may need to wait at a predefined execution point until all other threads reach that point.

- Phaser is a useful feature when few independent threads have to work in phases to complete a task.

Applying Atomic Variables and Locks

- Java provides an efficient alternative in the form of atomic variables where one needs to acquire and release a lock just to carry out primitive operations on variables.

- A lock ensures that only one thread accesses a shared resource at a time.

- A Condition supports thread notification mechanism. When a certain condition is not satisfied, a thread can wait for another thread to satisfy that condition; that other thread could notify once the condition is met.

Using Executors and ThreadPools

- The Executors hierarchy abstracts the lower-level details of multi-threaded programming and offers high-level user-friendly concurrency constructs.

- The Callable interface represents a task that needs to be completed by a thread. Once the task completes, the call() method of a Callable implementation returns a value.

- A thread pool is a collection of threads that can execute tasks.

- Future represents objects that contain a value that is returned by a thread in the future.

- ThreadFactory is an interface that is meant for creating threads instead of explicitly creating threads by calling a new Thread().

Using the Parallel Fork/Join Framework

- The Fork/Join framework is a portable means of executing a program with decent parallelism.

- The framework is an implementation of the ExecutorService interface and provides an easy-to-use concurrent platform in order to exploit multiple processors.

- This framework is very useful for modeling divide-and-conquer problems.

- The Fork/Join framework uses the work-stealing algorithm: when a worker thread completes its work and is free, it takes (or "steals") work from other threads that are still busy doing some work.

- The work-stealing technique results in decent load balancing thread management with minimal synchronization cost.

- ForkJoinPool is the most important class in the Fork/Join framework. It is a thread pool for running fork/join tasks—it executes an instance of ForkJoinTask. It executes tasks and manages their lifecycles.

- ForkJoinTask<V> is a lightweight thread-like entity representing a task that defines methods such as fork() and join().

■ ■ ■

OCPJP 7 Quick Refresher

This chapter provides a quick summary to important points to remember from the OCPJP 7 exam perspective. A summarized list of exam tips is also compiled to help you prepare for the exam. Read this chapter the day before taking the exam. Good luck!

EXAM TIPS

- Most questions in the OCPJP 7 exam are about predicting the behavior of the program. In our experience taking the exam, we found that if we read the question and immediately start looking at the answers, the answers confused us in many cases (leading us to selecting the wrong answer!). To avoid this confusion, we suggest an alternative approach: first understand the question and arrive at an answer, and *then* check the options to see if there is a matching answer. This is especially important for questions related to pattern matching (in regex, glob, etc.); if you look at the answers first, they can often mislead you to choosing the wrong answer!

- Questions in the OCPJP 7 exam clearly mention the number of correct options that you should select for a given question. The exam software will *not* warn you if you choose only one option for a question that requires selecting multiple answers and vice versa. So, beware of this pitfall, and ensure that you select only the exact number of answers as explicitly mentioned for each question.

- While taking the OCPJP 7 exam, you can mark the question to revisit later if you're not sure of the answer. The exam software provides a check box at the top right side of the screen.

- There are many questions in the exam that are long or time-consuming. If you're taking too long to read or answer a particular question, mark it for revisiting later.

- Many of the questions ask you to predict the behavior of a program, and most of the options will provide possible output with one of the options mentioning that the prgoram will result in a compiler error (without giving the specific compiler error). It is a common mistake to be "optimistic" and assume that the program will compile without errors! For example, you know that you will get a compiler error if you try to instantiate an abstract class; however, in a question that presents you a 20-25 lines program, it is easy to miss an attempt to instantiate an abstract class if you directly look at the list of answers. To avoid this pitfall, we recommend that you first look for possible compiler errors in the program before checking other options relating to the output of the program.

- Look out for potential exceptions that the program can throw before looking at the answers. For example, check if the program could result in an IllegalThreadStateException for the program relating to thread state transition. Similarly, programs that perform downcasts without checking the type first can result in a ClassCastException. Yes, it is obvious, but in our experience in taking the exam, we found that it was easy to miss out on such common runtime exceptions when answering the questions.

- There are many APIs in which arguments are passed to specify the range. For example, the subpath(int beginIndex, int endIndex) method in the Path interface takes beginIndex and endIndex as arguments. In this case, note that beginIndex is the index of the first name element, *inclusive* of itself, and endIndex is the index of the last name element, *exclusive* of itself. In other words, in *most* Java APIs methods that specify a range (such as the nextInt() method in Random), the first argument is inclusive and the second argument is exclusive. When answering a question whose answer depends on the range, and when you don't know if the arguments are inclusive or not, an educated guess would be to treat the first argument as inclusive and the second argument as exclusive!

- In questions involving assertions, the question will mention if assertions are enabled or disabled by mentioning if the -ea or -da option is passed in the command line (if it is not explicitly mentioned, remember that the assertions are *disabled* in a program by default). Answer questions about the behavior of the program, keeping in mind whether assertions are enabled or disabled.

- For questions relating to passing null to APIs, do not always assume that the API will throw a NullPointerException. For example, the add() method in ArrayList accepts null arguments and does not throw a NullPointerException. In general, while reviewing the behavior of methods in the Java library, give a special attention to the corner cases and the exceptions that the methods can throw.

- While reviewing APIs, understand the differences between similar looking classes or methods (for example, similarities and differences between the Comparable and Comparator interfaces).

- When predicting the output of the programs relating to threads and concurrency, give special attention to how thread scheduling and thread interleaving can affect the output.

- When taking the exam, you may be given an erasable scribble board. You may find it handy for answering certain kinds of questions. For example, we recommend that you to quickly draw the class relationships on the board for selecting the correct option(s) for questions relating to class relationships (such as is-a and has-a relationships).

Chapter 3: Java Class Design

- You cannot access the *private* methods of the base class in the derived class.

- You can access the *protected* method from a class in the same package (just like package private or default) as well as a derived class (even belonging to another package).

- You can have *overloaded constructors*. You can call a constructor of the same class in another constructor using the this keyword.

- *Inheritance* is also called an *is-a relationship*.

- In *overriding*, the name of the method, number of arguments, types of arguments, and return type should match exactly (however, in *covariant return types*, you can provide the derived class of the return type in the overriding method).

- You cannot overload methods that differ in return types alone. Similarly, you cannot overload methods that differ in exception specifications alone.

- For an overload resolution to succeed, you need to define methods such that the compiler finds one exact match. If the compiler finds no matches for your call or finds more than one match, the overload resolution fails and the compiler issues an error.

- Overloading is an example of *static polymorphism* (*early binding*) while overriding is an example of *dynamic polymorphism* (*late binding*).

- You don't need to do an explicit cast to perform an *upcast*. An upcast will always succeed.

- You need to do an explicit cast to perform a *downcast*. A downcast may fail. You can use the `instanceof` operator to see if a downcast is valid.

- A static import only imports static members of the specified package or class.

Chapter 4: Advanced Class Design

- The `abstract` keyword can be applied to a class or a method but not to a field.

- An abstract class cannot be instantiated. You can, however, create reference variables of an abstract class type.

- An abstract class can extend another abstract class or can implement an interface. Further, an abstract class can be derived from a concrete class (though it is not a good practice)!

- An abstract class need not declare an abstract method, which means it is not necessary for an abstract class to have methods declared as abstract. However, if a class has an abstract method, it should be declared as an abstract class.

- A concrete subclass of an abstract class needs to provide implementation of all the abstract methods it inherits; otherwise you need to declare that subclass as an abstract class.

- An abstract class may have methods or fields declared static. A final class is a non-inheritable class (i.e., you cannot inherit from a final class).

- A final method is a non-overridable method (i.e., subclasses cannot override a final method).

- All methods of a final class are implicitly final (i.e., non-overridable).

- A final variable must be initialized. If it's not initialized when it is declared, it must be initialized in all the constructors. Also, a final variable can be assigned only once.

- The keyword `final` can be used for parameters. The value of a `final` parameter cannot be changed once assigned. Here, it is important to note that the value is implicitly understood for primitive types. However, the value for an object refers to the object reference, not its state. Therefore, you can change the internal state of the passed final object, but you cannot change the reference itself.

- All static members do not require an instance of its class to call/access them. You can directly call/access them using the class name.

- A static member can call/access only a static member of its own class.

- A static method cannot use the `this` or `super` keyword in its body.

- Java supports four types of nested classes: static nested classes, inner classes, local inner classes, and anonymous inner classes.

- Static nested classes may have static members, whereas the other flavors of nested classes may not.

- Static nested classes and inner classes can access members of an outer class (even private members). However, static nested classes can access only static members of the outer class.

- Local classes (both local inner classes and anonymous inner classes) can access all variables declared in the outer scope (whether a method, constructor, or a statement block).

- You cannot use `new` with `enum`s, even inside the `enum` definition.

- `Enum`s are implicitly declared public, static, and final, which means you cannot extend them.

- When you define an enumeration, it implicitly inherits from `java.lang.Enum`. Internally, enumerations are converted to classes. Further, enumeration constants are instances of the enumeration class for which the enumeration constants are declared as members.

- If you declare an `enum` within a class, then it is by default static.

- You can compare two enumerations for equality using the `==` operator. When an enumeration constant's `toString()` method is invoked, it prints the name of the enumeration constant.

Chapter 5: Object-Oriented Design Principles

- An interface can extend another interface. Use the `extends` (and *not* the `implements`) keyword for this.

- All methods declared in an interface are implicitly considered to be abstract.

- Interfaces cannot contain instance variables. If you declare a data member in an interface, it should be initialized, and all such data members are implicitly treated as `public static final` members.

- An interface cannot declare static methods. It can only declare instance methods.

- You cannot declare members as `protected` or `private` in an interface. Only `public` access is allowed for members of an interface.

- All methods declared in an interface are implicitly considered to be abstract. You can, however, explicitly use the `abstract` qualifier for the method.

- An interface can be declared with an empty body (i.e., an interface without any members; these interfaces are known as *tagging interfaces* or *marker interfaces*). Such interfaces are useful for defining a common parent, so that runtime polymorphism can be used. For example, `java.util` defines the interface `EventListener` without a body.

- An interface can be declared within another interface or class. Such interfaces are known as nested interfaces.

- Unlike top-level interfaces that can have only public or default access, a nested interface can be declared as public, protected, or private.

- Inheritance implies is-a, interface implies is-like-a, and composition implies has-a relationships.

- Favor composition over inheritance wherever feasible.

- The Singleton design pattern ensures that only one instance of the class is created.

- Making sure that an intended singleton implementation is indeed singleton is a non-trivial task, especially in a multi-threaded environment.

- The factory design pattern "manufactures" the required type of product on demand.

- You should consider using the abstract factory design pattern when you have a family of objects to be created.

- A DAO design pattern essentially separates your core business logic from your persistence logic.

- In a DAO pattern, you may also employ the abstract factory design pattern if you have multiple DAO objects and you have multiple persistence mechanisms.

Chapter 6: Generics and Collections

- Generics will ensure that any attempts to mix elements of types other than the specified type(s) will be caught at compile time itself. Hence, generics offer type safety over using the Object type.

- Java 7 has introduced the "diamond" syntax where the type parameters (given after new operator and class name) can be omitted. The compiler will infer the types from the type declaration.

- Generics are not covariant. That is, subtyping doesn't work with generics. You cannot assign a derived generic type parameter to a base type parameter.

- The <?> specifies an unknown type in generics and is known as a wildcard. For example, List<?> refers to a list of unknown type values.

- Wildcards can be bounded. For example, <? extends Runnable> specifies that ? can match any type as long as it is Runnable or any of its derived types. Note that both extends and super in this context are inclusive clauses, so you can replace X in <? extends X> and <? super X>.

- Use the extends keyword for both class type and interface when specifying bounded types in generics. For specifying multiple base types, use the & symbol. For example, in List<? extends X & Y>, ? will match types, extending *both* the types X and Y.

- In general, when you use wildcard parameters, you cannot call methods that modify the object. If you try to modify, the compiler will give error messages. However, you can call methods that access the object.

- The terms Collection, Collections, and collection are different. Collection— java.util. Collection<E>—is the root interface in the collection hierarchy. Collections—java.util. Collections—is a utility class that contains only static methods. The general term collection(s) refers to containers like map, stack, queue, etc.

- It's possible to define or declare generic methods in an interface or a class even if the class or the interface is not generic.

- A generic class used without its type arguments is known as a *raw type*. Of course, raw types are not type safe. Java supports raw types so that it is possible to use the generic type in code that is older than Java 5 (note that generics were introduced in Java 5). The compiler generates a warning when you use raw types in your code. You may use @SuppressWarnings({ "unchecked" }) to suppress the warning associated with raw types.

- List<?> is a supertype of any List type, which means you can pass List<Integer>, or List<String>, or even List<Object> where List<?> is expected.

- Implementation of generics is static in nature, which means that the Java compiler interprets the generics specified in the source code and replaces the generic code with concrete types. This is referred to as *type erasure*. After compilation, the code looks similar to what a developer would have written with concrete types. Essentially, the use of generics offers two advantages: first, it introduces an abstraction that enables you to write generic implementation; second, it allows you to write generic implementation with type safety.

- There are many limitations of generic types due to type erasure. A few important ones are the following:

  - You cannot instantiate a generic type using a new operator. For example, assuming mem is a field, the following statement will result in a compiler error:

    ```
    T mem = new T(); // wrong usage - compiler error
    ```

  - You cannot instantiate an array of a generic type. For example, assuming mem is a field, the following statement will result in a compiler error:

    ```
    T[] amem = new T[100]; // wrong usage - compiler error
    ```

  - You can declare non-static fields of type T, but not of static fields of type T. For example,

    ```
    class X<T> {
      T instanceMem;  // okay
      static T statMem;         // wrong usage - compiler error
    }
    ```

- It is not possible to have generic exception classes. For example, the following will not compile:

  ```
  class GenericException<T> extends Throwable { } // wrong usage - compiler error
  ```

- You cannot instantiate a generic type with primitive types. For example, List<int> will elicit a compiler error. However, you can use boxed primitive types.

- The methods hashCode() and equals() need to be consistent for a class. For practical purposes, ensure that you follow this rule: the hashCode() method should return the same hash value for two objects if the equals() method returns true for them.

- If you're using an object in containers like HashSet or HashMap, make sure you override the hashCode() and equals() methods correctly.

- In containers, it is not recommended that you store null as an argument since it could be difficult to understand the behavior of methods that return null. For example, there are methods in the Deque interface that return null, and it would be difficult for you to distinguish if the method successfully returned the element value null, or if the method failed and returned null.

- The Figure 15-1 shows important interfaces belonging to the java.util package.

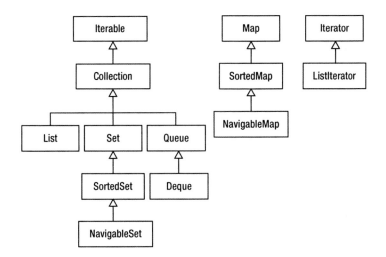

Figure 15-1. *Important high-level java.util interfaces and their inheritance relationships*

- Implement the Comparable interface for your classes when a natural order is possible. If you want to compare the objects other than the natural order or if there is no natural ordering present for your class type, then create separate classes implementing the Comparator interface. Also, if you have multiple alternative ways to decide the order, then go for the Comparator interface.

Chapter 7: String Processing

- A regular expression defines a search pattern that can be used to execute operations such as string search and string manipulation. Table 15-1 summarizes commonly used symbols to specify regex, Table 15-2 lists commonly used metasymbols to specify regex, and Table 15-3 presents commonly used quantifiers with regex.

Table 15-1. *Commonly Used Symbols to Specify Regular Expressions*

Symbol	Description
^expr	Matches the expr at the beginning of line.
expr$	Matches the expr at the end of line.
.	Matches any single character (except newline character).
[xyz]	Matches either x, y, or z.
[p-z]	Specifies a range. Matches any character from p to z.
[p-z1-9]	Matches either any character from p to z or any digit from 1 to 9 (remember, it won't match p1).
[^p-z]	'^' as first character inside a bracket negates the pattern; it matches any character except characters p to z.
Xy	Matches x followed by y.
x | y	Matches either x or y.

Table 15-2. *Commonly Used Metasymbols to Specify Regular Expressions*

Symbol	Description
\d	Matches digits (equivalent to [0–9]).
\D	Matches non-digits.
\w	Matches word characters.
\W	Matches non-word characters.
\s	Matches whitespaces (equivalent to [\t\r\f\n]).
\S	Matches non-whitespaces.
\b	Matches word boundary when outside bracket. Matches backslash when inside bracket.
\B	Matches non-word boundary.
\A	Matches beginning of string.
\Z	Matches end of string.

Table 15-3. *Commonly Used Quantifier Symbols*

Symbol	Description
expr?	Matches 0 or 1 occurrence of expr (equivalent to expr{0,1}).
expr*	Matches 0 or more occurrences of expr (equivalent to expr{0, }).
expr+	Matches 1 or more occurrences of expr (equivalent to expr{1, }).
expr{x}	Matches x occurrences of expr.
expr{x, y}	Matches between x and y occurrences of expr.
expr{x,}	Matches x or more occurrences of expr.

- The argument of the `split()` method is a delimiter string, which is a regular expression. If the regular expression you pass has invalid syntax, you'll get a `PatternSyntaxException` exception.

- Use the `Pattern` and `Matcher` classes whenever you are performing a search or replace on strings heavily; they are more efficient and faster than any other way to perform search/replace in Java.

- You can form groups within a regex. These groups can be used to specify quantifiers on a desired subset of the whole regex. These groups can also be used to specify back reference.

- The method `printf()` (and the method `format()` in the `String` class) uses string formatting flags to format strings.

- Each format specifier starts with the % sign; followed by flags, width, and precision information; and ending with a data type specifier. In this string, the flags, width, and precision information are optional while the % sign and data type specifier are mandatory. Table 15-4 shows the commonly used data type specifier symbols.

Table 15-4. *Commonly Used Data Type Specifiers*

Symbol	Description
%b	Boolean
%c	Character
%d	Decimal integer (signed)
%e	Floating point number in scientific format
%f	Floating point number in decimal format
%g	Floating point number in decimal or scientific format (depending on the value passed as argument)
%h	Hashcode of the passed argument
%n	Line separator (new line character)
%o	Integer formatted as an octal value
%s	String
%t	Date/time
%x	Integer formatted as an hexadecimal value

- If you do not specify any string formatting specifier, the `printf()` method will not print anything from the given arguments!

- Flags such as `'-'`, `'^'`, or `'0'` make sense only when you specify width with the format specifier string.

- You can also print the % character in a format string; however, you need to use an escape sequence for it. In format specifier strings, % is an escape character, which means you need to use %% to print a single %.

- If you do not provide the intended input data type as expected by the format string, you can get an `IllegalFormatConversionException`.

- If you want to form a string and use it later rather than just printing it using the `printf()` method, you can use a static method in the `String` class, `format()`.

Chapter 8: Java I/O Fundamentals

- You can obtain reference to the console using the `System.console()` method; if the JVM is not associated with any console, this method will fail and return null.

- Many methods are provided in `Console`-support formatted I/O. You can use the `printf()` and `format()` methods available in the `Console` class to print formatted text; the overloaded `readLine()` and `readPassword()` methods take format strings as arguments.

- You can use character streams for text-based I/O and byte streams for data-based I/O.

- Character streams for reading and writing are called *readers* and *writers*, respectively (represented by the abstract classes Reader and Writer). Byte streams for reading and writing are called *input streams* and *output streams*, respectively (represented by the abstract classes InputStream and OutputStream).

- You can combine stream objects. You can create an object of BufferedInputStream that takes a FileInputStream object. In this way, the output of one stream is chained to the filtered stream. This is an important, useful, and elegant way to customize the stream based on your needs.

- For processing data with primitive data types and Strings, you can use data streams.

- *Serialization* is the process of converting the objects in memory into a series of bytes. You need to implement the Serializable interface in a class if you want to make the objects of the class serializable.

- The Serializable interface is a marker interface. That means the Serializable interface does not declare any method inside it.

- If you want to customize the process of serialization, you can implement the readObject() and writeObject() methods. Note that both of these methods are private methods, which means you are not overriding or overloading these methods. JVM checks the implementation of these methods and calls them instead of the usual methods. It sounds weird but it is the way the customization of the serialization process is implemented in the JVM.

- A serialized object can be communicated over the network and deserialized on another machine. However, the class file of the object must be in the path of the destination machine, otherwise only the state of the object will be restored, not the whole object (i.e., you cannot invoke a method on the restored object).

- You can create your own protocol for serialization. For that, you need to implement the Externalizable interface instead of the Serializable interface.

- When you are not specifying serialVersionUID in a serialized class, JVM computes it for you. However, each JVM implementation has different mechanism to compute it; hence, it is not guaranteed that your serialized class will work on two different JVMs when you have not specified the serialVersionUID explicitly. Therefore, it is strongly recommended that you provide serialVersionUID in a class implementing the Serializable interface.

Chapter 9: Java File I/O (NIO.2)

- A Path object is a programming abstraction to represent a path of a file/directory.

- Do not confuse File with Files, Path with Paths, and FileSystem with FileSystems; they are different. *File* is an old class (Java 4) that represents file/directory path names, while *Files* was introduced in Java 7 as a utility class with comprehensive support for I/O APIs. The *Path* interface represents a file/directory path and defines a useful set of methods. However, the *Paths* class is a utility class that offers only two methods (both to get the Path object). *FileSystems* offer a list of factory methods for the class FileSystem, whereas *FileSystem* provides a useful set of methods to get information about a file system.

- The file or directory represented by a Path object might not exist.

- Path provides two methods to use to compare Path objects: equals() and compareTo(). Even if two Path objects point to the same file/directory, it is not guaranteed that you will get true from the equals() method. You need to make sure that both are absolute and normalized paths for an equality comparison to succeed for paths.

- You can check the existence of a file using the exists() method of the Files class.

- You can retrieve attributes of a file using the getAttributes() method. You can use the readAttributes() method of the Files class to read attributes of a file in bulk.

- While copying, all the directories (except the last one if you are copying a directory) in the specified path must exist to avoid NoSuchFileException.

- If you copy a directory using the copy() method, it will not copy the files/directories contained in the source directory; you need to explicitly copy them to the destination folder.

- It is not necessary that you perform copy on two files/directories only. You can take input from an InputStream and write to a file; similarly, you can take input from a file and copy to an OutputStream. You can use the methods copy(InputStream, Path, CopyOptions...) and copy(Path, OutputStream, CopyOptions...).

- Use the delete() method to delete a file; use the deleteIfExists() method to delete a file only if it exists.

- If you do not want to implement all four methods in the FileVisitor interface, you can simply extend your implementation from the SimpleFileVisitor class.

- The PathMatcher interface is useful when you want to find a file satisfying a certain pattern. You can specify the pattern using glob or regex. Table 15-5 summarizes the patterns supported by the Glob syntax.

Table 15-5. *Patterns Supported by Glob Syntax*

Pattern	Description
*	Matches any string of any length, even zero length.
**	Similar to "*" but it crosses directory boundaries.
?	Matches to any single character.
[xyz]	Matches to either x, y, or z.
[0-5]	Matches to any character from the range 0 to 5.
[a-z]	Matches to any lowercase letter.
{xyz, abc}	Matches to either xyz or abc.

- Java 7 offers a directory watch service that can notify you when the file you are working on is changed by some other program. You can register a Path object using a watch service along with certain event types. Whenever any file in the specified directory changes, an event is sent to the registered program.

- You must be careful performing an operation while walking a file tree. For instance, if you are performing a recursive delete, then you should first delete all the containing files before deleting the directory that is holding these containing files.

- The Visitor design pattern is used to enable walking through a file tree.

- In the context of a watch service, a state is associated with a watch key. A watch key might be in ready state (ready to accept events), in signed state (when one or more events are queued), or in invalid state (when the watch key is not valid). If the key is in the signed state, it is required to call the reset() method; otherwise the state of the key will not change to ready state and you will not receive any further event notification.

- If you are watching a directory using the watch service offered by Java 7, only files contained in that directory will be watched—and not the files contained in the subdirectories of that directory. If you intend to watch the whole subtree of the file system, you need to recursively register each directory in the subtree.

Chapter 10: Building Database Applications with JDBC

- JDBC (Java DataBase Connectivity) APIs provided by Java are meant for programmatic access to DataBase Management Systems (DBMSs).

- JDBC hides all the heterogeneity of all the DBMSs and offers a single set of APIs to interact with all types of databases. The complexity of heterogeneous interactions is delegated to the JDBC driver manager and JDBC drivers; hence all the details and complications are hidden by the JDBC API from the application developer.

- There are four types of drivers:

  - **Type 1 (JDBC-ODBC bridge drivers):** The JDBC driver calls ODBC (Open Database Connectivity) native calls using the Java Native Interface (JNI).

  - **Type 2 (Native-API drivers):** These drivers use client-side libraries of a specific database and convert JDBC calls to native database calls.

  - **Type 3 (Network-protocol drivers):** These drivers call database middleware, and the middleware actually converts JDBC calls to database-specific native calls.

  - **Type 4 (Native-protocol drivers):** The driver directly makes database-specific calls over the network without any support of an additional client-side library.

- The java.sql.Connection interface provides a channel through which the application and the database communicate. The getConnection() method in the DriverManager class takes three arguments: the URL string, username string, and password string.

- The syntax of the URL (which needs to be specified to get Connection object) is <protocol>:<subprotocol>://<server>:<port>/. An example of URL string is jdbc:mysql://localhost:3306/. The <protocol> jdbc is same for all DBMSs; <subprotocol> will differ for each DBMS, <server> depends on the location in which you host the database, and each DBMS uses a specific <port> number.

- If the JDBC API is not able to locate the JDBC driver, it will throw a SQLException. If there are jars for the drivers available, they need to be included in the classpath to enable the JDBC API to locate the driver.

- Prior to JDBC 4.0, you had to explicitly load the JDBC driver using the Class.forName() statement; with JDBC 4.0 and above, this statement is not needed and JDBC API will load the driver from the details given in the URL string.

- JDBC supports two classes for querying and updating: Statement and Resultset.

- A Statement is a SQL statement that can be used to communicate a SQL statement to the connected database and receive results from the database. There are three types of Statements:

    - Statement: Use Statement when you need to send a SQL statement to the database without any parameter.

    - PreparedStatement: Represents a precompiled SQL statement that can be customized using IN parameters.

    - CallableStatement: Used to execute stored procedures; can handle IN as well as OUT and INOUT parameters.

- Choose the proper execute method based on the type of the SQL statement. Remember that each execute method returns different output. The method executeQuery() returns a resultset; executeUpdate() returns an update count; and the execute() method may return multiple resultsets, or multiple update count, or combination of both.

- A Statement object closes the current ResultSet object if a) the Statement object is closed, b) is re-executed, or c) is made to retrieve the next set of result. That means it is not necessary to call close() explicitly with the ResultSet object; however, it is good practice to call close() once you are done with the object.

- It is your responsibility to issue a correct SQL command; JDBC Statement will not check for its correctness. For example, if there is a syntax error in the SQL command string, you will not get a compiler error. Rather, you'll get a SQLSyntaxErrorException at runtime.

- A ResultSet object maintains a cursor pointing to the current row. Initially, the cursor is set to just before the first row; calling the next() method advances the cursor position by one row.

- You can use column name or column index with ResultSet methods. The index you use is the index of the ResultSet object, not the column number in the database table.

- The column index in the ResultSet object starts from 1 (*not* from 0).

- You may use the column name of a ResultSet object without worrying about the case: getXXX() methods accept case-insensitive column names to retrieve the associated value.

- Think of a case when you have two columns in a ResultSet object with the same name. How you can retrieve the associated values using the column name? If you use column name to retrieve the value, it will always point to the first column that matches with the given name. Hence, you have to use column index in this case to retrieve values associated with the both columns.

- You need to call updateRow() after modifying the row contents in a ResultSet; otherwise changes made to the ResultSet object will be lost.

- You may cancel any update you made using the method cancelRowUpdates(). However, you must call this method before calling the method updateRow(). In all other cases, it has no impact on the row.

- By calling the getMetaData() method in the Connection interface, you can examine the capabilities of the underlying database.

- A transaction is a set of SQL operations that needs to be either executed all successfully or not at all.

- By default auto-commit mode is set to true, so all changes you make through the connection are committed automatically to the database. You can use setAutoCommit(false); to enable manual commits. With auto-commit not enabled, you need to explicitly commit or rollback transactions.

- If the commit() method does not execute in manual commit mode, there will be no change in the database.

- You can divide a big transaction into multiple milestones. These milestones are referred to as Savepoints. This way you may save the changes to database up to a milestone once the milestone is achieved.

- RowSet is a special ResultSet that supports the JavaBean component model. Figure 15-2 summarizes the RowSet hierarchy and associated key capabilities.

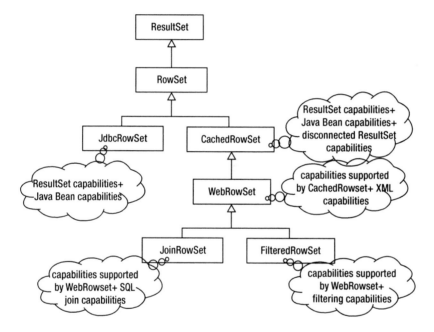

Figure 15-2. *The RowSet hierarchy*

- JdbcRowSet is a connected RowSet while other subinterfaces of RowSet (i.e., JoinRowSet, CachedRowSet, WebRowSet, and FilteredRowSet) are disconnected RowSets.

- RowSetProvider provides APIs to get the RowSetFactory implementation, which can in turn be used to instantiate a relevant RowSet implementation.

- JDBC 4.1 introduces the capability to use try-with-resources statement to close resources (Connection, ResultSet, and Statement) automatically.

Chapter 11: Exceptions and Assertions

- While providing multiple exception handlers ("stacked" catch handlers), specific exception handlers should be provided before general exception handlers. Providing base exception handlers before the derived handlers will result in a compiler error.

- A try block can have multiple catch handlers. If the cause of two or more exceptions is similar and the handling code is also similar, you can consider combining the handlers and make it into a multi-catch block.

- The code inside a finally block will be executed irrespective of whether a try block has successfully executed or resulted in an exception. This makes a finally block the most suitable place to release resources such as file handles, data base handles, network streams, etc.

- In a multi-catch block, you cannot combine catch handlers for two exceptions that share a base- and derived-class relationship. You can only combine catch handlers for exceptions that do not share the parent-child inheritance relationship between them.

- Forgetting to release resources by explicitly calling the close() method is a common mistake. You can use a try-with-resources statement to simplify your code and auto-close resources. For a resource to be usable in a try-with-resources statement, the class of that resource must implement the java.lang.AutoCloseable interface and define the close() method.

- You can auto-close multiple resources within a try-with-resources statement. These resources need to be separated by semicolons in the try-with-resources statement header.

- Because you can use multiple resources within a try-with-resources statement, the possibility of more than one exception getting thrown from both the try block and the finally block is high. If a try block throws an exception, and a finally block also throws exception(s), then the exception(s) thrown in the finally block will be added as *suppressed exceptions* to the exception that gets thrown out of the try block to the caller.

- You cannot assign to the resource variables declared in the try-with-resources within the body of the try-with-resources statement. This is to make sure that the same resources acquired in the try-with-resources header are released in the finally block.

- It is a common mistake to close a resource explicitly inside the try-with-resources statement. Remember that try-with-resources expands to calling the close() method in the finally block, so if you provide an explicit call to the close() method in the finally block, the expanded finally block will effectively have a double call to the close() method.

- The class Throwable is the root class of the exception hierarchy. Only Throwable and its derived classes can be used with Java exception handling keywords such as try, catch, and throws.

- The Exception class (except its subhierarchy of the RuntimeException class) and its derived classes are known as *checked exceptions*. These exceptions represent exceptional conditions that can be "reasonably expected" to occur when the program executes and thus must be handled. A method that contains some code segment that can throw a checked exception must either provide a catch handler to handle it or declare that exception in its throws clause.

- The RuntimeException and Error classes and derived classes are known as *unchecked exceptions*. They can be thrown anywhere in the program (without being declared that the segment of code can throw these exceptions).

- The RuntimeException classes and derived classes represent programming mistakes (logical mistakes) and are not *generally* expected to be caught and handled in the program. However, in some cases it is meaningful to handle these exceptions in catch blocks.

- The `Error` classes and `derived` classes represent exceptions that arise because of JVM errors—either the JVM has detected a serious abnormal condition or has run out of resources. When an `Error` occurs, the *typical* best course of action is to terminate the program.

- A catch block should either handle the exception or rethrow it. To *hide* or *swallow* an exception by catching an exception and doing nothing is really a bad practice.

- The throws clause for a method is meant for listing the *checked exceptions* that the method body can throw.

- Static initialization blocks cannot throw any checked exceptions. Non-static initialization blocks can throw checked exceptions; however, all the constructors should declare that exception in their throws clause.

- A method's throws clause is part of the contract that its overriding methods in derived classes should obey. An overriding method can provide the same throw clause as the base method's throws clause or a more specific throws clause than the base method's throws clause. The overriding method cannot provide a more general throws clause or declare to throw additional checked exceptions when compared to the base method's throws clause.

- If a method does not have a throws clause, it does *not* mean it cannot throw any exceptions—it just means it cannot throw any *checked* exceptions.

- It is a bad practice to use a throws clause to list unchecked exceptions that a method may throw. Why? Since the compiler cannot force the callers to handle unchecked exceptions, it does not make sense to list them in the throws clause. Rather, if a method can throw an unchecked exception, it is better to use the `@throws` clause to document that possibility.

- Non-static initialization blocks can throw checked exceptions; however, all the constructors should declare those exceptions in their throws clause. Why? The compiler merges the code for non-static initialization blocks and constructors during its code generation phase, so the throws clause of the constructor can be used to declare the checked exceptions that a non-static initialization block can throw.

- An overriding method cannot declare more exceptions in the throws clause than the list of exceptions declared in the throws clause of the base method. Why? The callers of the base method see only the list of the exceptions given in the throws clause of that method and will declare or handle these checked exceptions in their code (and not more than that).

- An overriding method can declare more specific exceptions than the exception(s) listed in the throws clause of the base method; in other words, you can declare derived exceptions in the throws clause of the overriding method.

- If a method is declared in two or more interfaces and if that method declares to throw different exceptions in the throws clause, then the implementation should list all these exceptions in its throws clause.

- You can define your own exception classes (known as custom exceptions) in your programs.

- It is recommended that you derive custom exceptions from either the `Exception` or `RuntimeException` class. Creation of custom exceptions by extending the `Throwable` class (too generic) or the `Error` class (exceptions of this type are reserved for JVM and the Java APIs to throw) is not recommended.

- You can wrap one exception and throw it as another exception. These two exceptions become chained exceptions. From the thrown exception, you can get the cause of the exception.

- Assertions are condition checks in the program and are meant to be used to explicitly check the assumptions you make while writing programs.

- The assert statement is of two forms: the one that takes a Boolean argument and the other one that takes an additional string argument.

- If the Boolean condition given in the assert argument fails (i.e., evaluates to false), the program will terminate after throwing an AssertionError. It is not advisable to catch and recover from when an AssertionError is thrown by the program.

- By default, assertions are disabled at runtime. You can use the command-line arguments -ea (for enabling asserts) and -da (for disabling asserts) and their variants when you invoke the JVM.

Chapter 12: Localization

- A *locale* represents a language, culture, or country; the Locale class in Java provides an abstraction for this concept.

- Each locale can have three entries: the language, country, and variant. You can use standard codes available for language and country to form locale tags. There are no standard tags for variants; you can provide variant strings based on your need.

- There are many ways to create or get a Locale object corresponding to a locale:

  - Use the constructor of the Locale class.

  - Use the forLanguageTag(String languageTag) method in the Locale class.

  - Build a Locale object by instantiating Locale.Builder and then calling setLanguageTag() from that object.

  - Use the predefined static final constants for locales in the Locale class.

- A resource bundle is a set of classes or property files that help define a set of keys and map those keys to locale-specific values.

- The class ResourceBundle has two derived classes: PropertyResourceBundle and ListResourceBundle. You can use ResourceBundle.getBundle() to automatically load a bundle for a given locale.

- The PropertyResourceBundle class provides support for multiple locales in the form of property files. For each locale, you specify the keys and values in a property file for that locale. You can use only Strings as keys and values.

- The naming convention for a fully qualified resource bundle name is packagequalifier. bundlename + "_" + language + "_" + country + "_" + (variant + "_#" | "#") + script + "-" + extensions.

- The search sequence to look for a matching resource bundle is presented here. Search starts from Step 1. If at any step the search finds a match, the resource bundle is loaded. Otherwise, the search proceeds to the next step.

  - **Step 1:** The search starts by looking for an exact match for the resource bundle with the full name.

  - **Step 2:** The last component (the part separated by _) is dropped and the search is repeated with the resulting shorter name. *This process is repeated till the last locale modifier is left.*

  - **Step 3:** The search is restarted using the full name of the bundle for the default locale.

  - **Step 4:** Search for the resource bundle with just the name of the bundle.

  - **Step 5:** The search fails, throwing a MissingBundleException.

- For the resource bundles implemented as classes extended from `ListResourceBundles`, Java uses the reflection mechanism to find and load the class. You need to make sure that the class is public so that the reflection mechanism will find the class.

- To handle date and time, numbers, and currencies in a culture-sensitive way, you can use the `java.text.Format` class and its two main derived classes, `NumberFormat` and `DateFormat`. Figure 15-3 shows `Format` and its important derived classes.

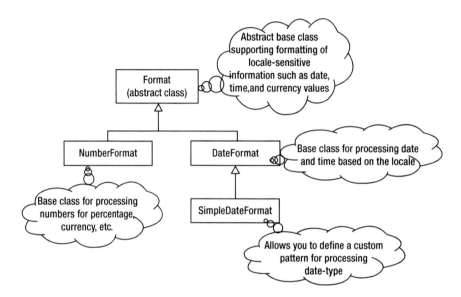

Figure 15-3. *The Format class and its important derived classes*

- The `NumberFormat` class provides methods to format or parse numbers. "Formatting" means converting a numeric value to a textual form suitable for displaying to users; "parsing" means converting a number back to numeric form for use in the program. The `parse()` method returns a `Number` if successful; otherwise it throws `ParseException` (a checked exception).

- `NumberFormat` has many factory methods: `getInstance()`, `getCurrencyInstance()`, `getIntegerInstance()`, and `getPercentInstance()`.

- The `Currency` class provides good support for handling currency values in a locale-sensitive way.

- The `DateFormat` class provides support for processing date and time in a locale-sensitive manner.

- `DateFormat` has three overloaded factory methods—`getDateInstance()`, `getTimeInstance()`, and `getDateTimeInstance()`—that return `DateFormat` instances for processing date, time, and both date and time, respectively.

- `SimpleDateFormat` (derived from `DateFormat`) uses the concept of a *pattern string* to support custom formats for date and time. Here is the list of important letters and their meanings for creating patterns for dates:

G	Era (BC/AD)
y	Year
Y	Week year
M	Month (in year)

w	Week (in year)
W	Week (in month)
D	Day (in year)
d	Day (in month)
F	Day of week in month
E	Day name in week
u	Day number of week (value range 1–7)

- Similarly, here are the important letters useful for defining a custom time pattern:

a	Marker for the text am/pm marker
H	Hour (value range 0–23)
k	Hour (value range 1–24)
K	Hour in am/pm (value range 0–11)
h	Hour in am/pm (value range 1–12)
m	Minute
s	Second
S	Millisecond
z	Time zone (general time zone format)

Chapter 13: Threads

- You can create classes that are capable of multi-threading by implementing the Runnable interface or by extending the Thread class.

- Always implement the run() method. The default run() method in Thread does nothing.

- Call the start() method and not the run() method directly in code. (Leave it to the JVM to call the run() method.)

- Every thread has thread name, priority, and thread-group associated with it; the default toString() method implementation in Thread prints them.

- If you call the sleep() method of a thread, the thread does not release the lock and it holds on to the lock.

- You can use the join() method to wait for another thread to terminate.

- In general, if you are not using the "interrupt" feature in threads, it is safe to ignore the InterruptedException; however it's better still to log or print the stack trace if that exception occurs.

- Threads are non-deterministic: in many cases, you cannot reproduce problems like deadlocks or data races by running the program again.

- There are three basic thread states: *new*, *runnable* and *terminated*. When a thread is just created, it is in *new* state; when it is ready to run or running, it is in *runnable* state. When the thread dies, it's in *terminated* state.

- The runnable state has two states internally (at the OS level): *ready* and *running* states.

- A thread will be in the *blocked* state when waiting to acquire a lock. The thread will be in the *timed_waiting* state when timeout is given for calls like wait. The thread will be in the *waiting* state when, for example, wait() is called (without time out value).

- You will get an IllegalThreadStateException if your operations result in invalid thread state transitions.

- Simultaneous reads and writes to common resources shared by multiple threads may lead to the "data race" (also known as "race condition" and "race hazard") problem.

- You must use thread synchronization (i.e., locks) to access shared values and avoid data races. Java provides thread synchronization features to provide protected access to shared resources—namely, synchronized blocks and synchronized methods.

- Using locks can introduce problems such as deadlocks. When a deadlock happens, the process will hang and will never terminate.

- A deadlock typically happens when two (or more) threads acquire locks in opposite order. When one thread has acquired one lock and waits for another lock, another thread has acquired that other lock and waits for the first lock to be released. So, no progress is made and the program deadlocks.

- To avoid deadlocks, it is better to avoid acquiring multiple locks. When you must acquire such multiple locks, ensure that they are acquired in the same order in all places in the program.

- When a thread has to wait for a particular condition or event to be satisfied by another thread, you can use a wait/notify mechanism as a communication mechanism between threads.

- When a thread needs to wait for a particular condition/event, you can call wait() with or without timeout value specified.

- To avoid notifications getting lost, it is better to always use notifyAll() instead of notify().

Chapter 14: Concurrency

- A semaphore controls access to shared resources. A semaphore maintains a counter to specify number of resources that the semaphore controls.

- CountDownLatch allows one or more threads to wait for a countdown to complete.

- The Exchanger class is meant for exchanging data between two threads. This class is useful when two threads need to synchronize between them and also continuously exchange data.

- CyclicBarrier helps provide a synchronization point where threads may need to wait at a predefined execution point until all other threads reach that point.

- Phaser is a useful feature when a few independent threads have to work in phases to complete a task.

- Instead of acquiring and releasing a lock just to carry out operations on primitive type variables, Java provides an efficient alternative in the form of atomic variables.

- Classes AtomicInteger and AtomicLong extend from the Number class. All other classes in the java.util.concurrent.atomic subpackage inherit directly from the Object class and do not extend the Number class.

- Conditions support thread notification mechanism. When a certain condition is not satisfied, a thread can wait for another thread to satisfy that condition; that other thread could notify once the condition is met.

- The Executors hierarchy abstracts the lower-level details of multi-threaded programming and offers high-level user-friendly concurrency constructs.

- The Callable interface represents a task that needs to be completed by a thread. Once the task completes, the call() method of a Callable implementation returns a value.

- `Future` represents objects that contain a value that is returned by a thread in the future.

- `ThreadFactory` is an interface that is meant for creating threads instead of explicitly creating threads by calling `new Thread()`.

- The Fork/Join framework allows for exploiting parallelism (available in the form of multiple cores) for certain kinds of tasks. A task that can be modeled as a divide-and-conquer problem is suitable to be used with Fork/Join framework.

- The Fork/Join framework is an implementation of the `ExecutorService` interface.

- The Fork/Join framework uses the work-stealing algorithm—in other words, when a `worker` thread completes its work and is free, it takes (or "steals") work from other threads that are still busy doing some work.

- The work-stealing technique results in decent load balancing thread management with minimal synchronization cost.

- In Fork/Join, it looks acceptable to call `fork()` for both the subtasks (if you are splitting in two subtasks) and call `join()` two times. It is correct—but inefficient. Why? In this case, the original thread will be waiting for the other two tasks to complete, which is inefficient considering task creation cost. That is why you call `fork()` once and call `compute()` for the second task.

- `ForkJoinPool` is the most important class for the Fork/Join framework. It is a thread pool for running fork/join tasks—in other words, it executes an instance of `ForkJoinTask`. It executes tasks and manages their lifecycles.

- ForkJoinTask<V> is a lightweight thread-like entity representing a task that defines methods such as `fork()` and `join()`.

■ ■ ■

Exam Topics

This appendix lists the topics for the following two certification exams:

- **Java SE 7 Programmer II** exam (a.k.a. exam number **1Z0-804**):

  OCAJP 7 certification + 1ZO-804 pass = **Oracle Certified Professional, Java SE 7 Programmer (OCPJP 7)** certification

- **Upgrade to Java SE 7 Programmer** exam (a.k.a. exam number **1Z0-805**):

  Earlier version (OCPJP 5 or OCPJP 6 or any SCJP) certification + 1ZO-805 pass = **Oracle Certified Professional, Java SE 7 Programmer (OCPJP 7)** certification

We show how the exam topics map to the chapters in this book (denoted "G&S" for Ganesh and Sharma) in parentheses beside the topic headings below.

OCPJP7 Exam (1Z0-804 a.k.a. Java SE 7 Programmer II) Topics

While preparing the reader equally for the Z10-804 or Z10-805 exam paths to OCPJP 7 certification, this book is organized to mirror the topics of the more comprehensive exam, the 1Z0-804. The exam topics in the 1Z0-804 syllabus map to the chapters in this book in a one-to-one correspondence as indicated in the parentheses below. We wish to thank Oracle Corporation for providing permission to use of their exam topics in this appendix.

1. Java Class Design (G&S Chapter 3)

1.1. Use access modifiers: `private`, `protected`, and `public`.

1.2. Use override methods.

1.3. Use overload constructors and other methods appropriately.

1.4. Use the `instanceof` operator and casting.

1.5. Use virtual method invocation.

1.6. Use override methods from the `Object` class to improve the functionality of your class.

1.7. Use `package` and `import` statements.

2. Advanced Class Design (G&S Chapter 4)

2.1. Identify when and how to apply abstract classes.

2.2. How to construct abstract Java classes and subclasses.

2.3. Use the `static` and `final` keywords.

2.4. Create top-level and nested classes.

2.5. Use enumerated types.

3. Object-Oriented Design Principles (G&S Chapter 5)

3.1. Write code that declares, implements, and/or extends interfaces.

3.2. Choose between interface inheritance and class inheritance.

3.3. Develop code that implements "is-a" and/or "has-a" relationships.

3.4. Apply object composition principles.

3.5. Design a class using the `Singleton` design pattern.

3.6. Write code to implement the DAO pattern.

3.7. Design and create objects using a factory, and use factories from the API.

4. Generics and Collections (G&S Chapter 6)

4.1. Create a generic class.

4.2. Use the diamond syntax to create a collection.

4.3. Analyze the interoperability of collections that use raw type and generic types.

4.4. Use wrapper classes and autoboxing.

4.5. Create and use a `List`, a `Set`, and a `Deque`.

4.6. Create and use a `Map`.

4.7. Use `java.util.Comparator` and `java.lang.Comparable`.

4.8. Sort and search arrays and lists.

5. String Processing (G&S Chapter 7)

5.1. Search, parse, and build strings.

5.2. Search, parse, and replace strings by using regular expressions, using expression patterns for matching limited to . (dot), * (star), + (plus), ?, \d, \D, \s, \S, \w, \W, \b. \B, [], ().

5.3. Format strings using the formatting parameters %b, %c, %d, %f, and %s in format strings.

6. Exceptions and Assertions (G&S Chapter 11)

6.1. Use `throw` and `throws` statements.

6.2. Use the `try` statement with multi-catch and finally clauses.

6.3. Autoclose resources with a try-with-resources statement.

6.4. Create custom exceptions.

6.5. Test invariants by using assertions.

7. Java I/O Fundamentals (G&S Chapter 8)

7.1. Read and write data from the console.

7.2. Use streams to read and write files.

8. Java File I/O (NIO.2) (G&S Chapter 9)

8.1. Use the `Path` class to operate on file and directory paths.

8.2. Use the `Files` class to check, delete, copy, or move a file or directory.

8.3. Read and change file and directory attributes.

8.4. Recursively access a directory tree.

8.5. Find a file by using the `PathMatcher` class.

8.6. Watch a directory for changes by using `WatchService`.

9. Building Database Applications with JDBC (G&S Chapter 10)

9.1. Define the layout of the JDBC API.

9.2. Connect to a database by using a JDBC driver.

9.3. Update and query a database.

9.4. Customize the transaction behavior of JDBC and commit transactions.

9.5. Use the JDBC 4.1 `RowSetProvider`, `RowSetFactory`, and `RowSet` interfaces.

10. Threads (G&S Chapter 13)

10.1. Create and use the `Thread` class and the `Runnable` interface.

10.2. Manage and control thread lifecycle.

10.3. Synchronize thread access to shared data.

10.4. Identify potential threading problems.

11. Concurrency (G&S Chapter 14)

11.1. Use `java.util.concurrent` collections.

11.2. Apply atomic variables and locks.

11.3. Use `Executors` and `ThreadPools`.

11.4. Use the parallel Fork/Join framework.

12. Localization (G&S Chapter 12)

12.1. Read and set the locale by using the `Locale` object.

12.2. Build a resource bundle for each local.

12.3. Load a resource bundle in an application.

12.4. Format text for localization by using `NumberFormat` and `DateFormat`.

OCPJP 7 Exam (1Z0-805, a.k.a. Upgrade to Java SE 7 Programmer) Topics

This book covers all the topics covered on the upgrade exam—the alternative path to OCPJP 7 certification—in the chapters indicated in the parentheses.

1. Language Enhancements (G&S Chapters 6, 11)

1.1. Use `String` in the switch statement.

1.2. Use binary literals and numeric literals with underscores.

1.3. Use try-with-resources.

1.4. Use multi-catch in exception statements.

1.5. Use the diamond operator with generic declarations.

1.6. Use more precise rethrow in exceptions.

2. Design Patterns (G&S Chapter 5)

2.1. Design a class using the `Singleton` design pattern.

2.2. Identify when and how to use composition to solve business problems.

2.3. Write code to implement the `DAO` pattern.

2.4. Design a class that uses the `Factory` design pattern.

3. Database Applications with JDBC (G&S Chapter 10)

3.1. Describe the JDBC API.

3.2. Identify the Java statements required to connect to a database using JDBC.

3.3. Use the JDBC 4.1 `RowSetProvider`, `RowSetFactory`, and new `RowSet` interfaces.

3.4. Use JDBC transactions.

3.5. Use the proper JDBC API to submit queries and read results from the database.

3.6. Use JDBC `PreparedStatement` and `CallableStatement`.

4. Concurrency (G&S Chapters 13, 14)

4.1. Identify potential threading problems.

4.2. Use `java.util.concurrent` collections.

4.3. Use atomic variables and locks.

4.4. Use `Executors` and `ThreadPools`.

4.5. Use the parallel Fork/Join framework.

5. Localization (G&S Chapter 12)

5.1. Describe the advantages of localizing an application.

5.2. Define what a locale represents.

5.3. Read and set the locale by using the `Locale` object.

5.4. Build a resource bundle for each locale.

5.5. Call a resource bundle from an application.

5.6. Select a resource bundle based on locale.

5.7. Format text for localization by using `NumberFormat` and `DateFormat`.

6. Java File I/O (NIO.2) (G&S Chapter 9)

6.1. Use the `Path` class to operate on file and directory paths.

6.2. Use the `Files` class to check, delete, copy, or move a file or directory.

6.3. Read and change file and directory attributes.

6.4. Recursively access a directory tree.

6.5. Find a file by using the `PathMatcher` class.

6.6. Watch a directory for changes by using `WatchService`.

APPENDIX B

■ ■ ■

Mock Test – 1

The questions in this mock test are designed per the requirements of the OCPJP 7 exam pattern and its standard. The questions in the real exam will not be equally distributed based on exam topics and you'll get questions in a random order. Further, when you take the real exam, you'll find that some of the questions are unintuitive or confusing. For instance, you may find questions 22, 23, and 26 to be incomplete or confusing and that is intentional.

Take the test as if it were your real OCPJP 7 exam. Best of luck.

Time: 2 hours 30 minutes   *No. of questions:* 90

1. **Consider the following code snippet:**

    ```
    if(i == 10.0)
        System.out.println("true");
    ```

    Which one of the following declarations of the variable i will compile without errors and print true when the program executes?

    a) int i = 012;

    b) int i = 10.0f;

    c) int i = 10L;

    d) int i = 10.0;

2. **Consider the following program:**

    ```
    import java.math.BigDecimal;

    class NumberTest {
        public static void main(String []args) {
            Number [] numbers = new Number[4];
            numbers[0] = new Number(0);        // NUM
            numbers[1] = new Integer(1);
            numbers[2] = new Float(2.0f);
            numbers[3] = new BigDecimal(3.0);        // BIG
            for(Number num : numbers) {
                System.out.print(num + " ");
            }
        }
    }
    ```

513

Which one of the following options correctly describes the behavior of this program?

a)   Compiler error in line marked with comment NUM because Number cannot be instantiated.

b)   Compiler error in line marked with comment BIG because BigDecimal does not inherit from Number.

c)   When executed, this program prints the following: 0 1 2.0 3.

d)   When executed, this program prints the following: 0.0 1.0 2.0 3.0.

3.   **Consider the following code segment:**

```
StringBuffer strBuffer = new StringBuffer("This, that, etc.!");
System.out.println(strBuffer.replace(12, 15, "etcetera"));
```

Which one of the following options correctly describes the behavior of this code segment?

a)   This code segment: This, that, etcetera.!

b)   This code segment: This, that, etcetera!

c)   This code segment: This, that, etc.

d)   This program throws in an ArrayIndexOutOfBoundsException.

4.   **Consider the following program:**

```
class SBAppend {
        public static void main(String []args) {
                Object nullObj = null;
                StringBuffer strBuffer = new StringBuffer(10);

                strBuffer.append("hello ");
                strBuffer.append("world ");
                strBuffer.append(nullObj);
                strBuffer.insert(11, '!');
                System.out.println(strBuffer);
        }
}
```

Which one of the following options correctly describes the behavior of this program?

a)   This program prints the following: hello world!

b)   This program prints the following: hello world! null

c)   This program throws a NullPointerException.

d)   This program throws an InvalidArgumentException.

e)   This program throws an ArrayIndexOutOfBoundsException.

5.   **Consider the following code segment:**

```
Boolean b = null;
System.out.println(b ? true : false);
```

Which one of the following options correctly describes the behavior of this code segment?

a) This code will result in a compiler error since a reference type (of type Boolean) cannot be used as part of expression for condition check.

b) This code will result in a throwing a NullPointerException.

c) This code will print true in console.

d) This code will print false in console.

6. **What will be the output of the following program?**

```java
class Base {
    public Base() {
            System.out.println("Base");
    }
}

class Derived extends Base {
    public Derived() {
            System.out.println("Derived");
    }
}

class DeriDerived extends Derived {
    public DeriDerived() {
            System.out.println("DeriDerived");
    }
}

class Test {
    public static void main(String []args) {
            Derived b = new DeriDerived();
    }
}
```

a) Base
   Derived
   DeriDerived

b) Derived
   DeriDerived

c) DeriDerived
   Derived
   Base

d) DeriDerived
   Derived

7. **Consider the following code segment:**

```
MODIFIER class SomeClass { }
```

Which three of the following modifiers, when replaced instead of MODIFIER, will compile cleanly?

a) public

b) protected

c) private

d) abstract

e) final

f) static

8. **Consider the following class definition:**

```
class Point {
        private int x = 0, y;
        public Point(int x, int y) {
                this.x = x;
                this.y = y;
        }
        // DEFAULT_CTOR
}
```

Which one of the following definitions of the Point constructor can be replaced without compiler errors in place of the comment DEFAULT_CTOR?

a) ```
   public Point() {
           this(0, 0);
           super();
   }
   ```

b) ```
   public Point() {
           super();
           this(0, 0);
   }
   ```

c) ```
   private Point() {
           this(0, 0);
   }
   ```

d) ```
   public Point() {
           this();
   }
   ```

e) ```
   public Point() {
           this(x, 0);
   }
   ```
   ```

9. **Consider the following program:**

```
class Base {
    public Base() {
            System.out.print("Base ");
    }
    public Base(String s) {
            System.out.print("Base: " + s);
    }
}

class Derived extends Base {
    public Derived(String s) {
            super();        // Stmt-1
            super(s);       // Stmt-2
            System.out.print("Derived ");
    }
}

class Test {
    public static void main(String []args) {
            Base a = new Derived("Hello ");
    }
}
```

Select three correct options from the following list:

a) Removing Stmt-1 will make the program compilable and it will print the following: Base Derived.

b) Removing Stmt-1 will make the program compilable and it will print the following: Base: Hello Derived.

c) Removing Stmt-2 will make the program compilable and it will print the following: Base Derived.

d) Removing both Stmt-1 and Stmt-2 will make the program compilable and it will print the following: Base Derived.

e) Removing both Stmt-1 and Stmt-2 will make the program compilable and it will print the following: Base: Hello Derived.

10. **You want to use the static member MYCONST belonging to class A in abc.org.project package. Which one of the following statements shows the correct use of static import feature?**

a) `static import abc.org.project.A;`

b) `static import abc.org.project.A.MYCONST;`

c) `import static abc.org.project.A;`

d) `import static abc.org.project.A.MYCONST;`

11. **Which one of the following programs compiles without any errors and prints "hello world" in console?**

a)
```java
import static java.lang.System.out.println;
class StaticImport {
    public static void main(String []args) {
            println("hello world");
    }
}
```

b)
```java
import static java.lang.System.out;
class StaticImport {
    public static void main(String []args) {
            out.println("hello world");
    }
}
```

c)
```java
import static java.lang.System.out.*;
class StaticImport {
    public static void main(String []args) {
            out.println("hello world");
    }
}
```

d)
```java
import static java.lang.System.out.*;

class StaticImport {
    public static void main(String []args) {
            println("hello world");
    }
}
```

12. **Consider the following program and choose the right option from the given list:**

```java
class Base {
    public void test() {
            protected int a = 10;         // #1
    }
}

class Test extends Base {                 // #2
    public static void main(String[] args) {
            System.out.printf(null);      // #3
    }
}
```

a) The compiler will report an error at statement #1.

b) The compiler will report an error at statement #2.

c) The compiler will report errors at statement #3.

d) The program will compile without any error.

13. **Consider the following program and choose the correct option from the list of options:**

```
class Base {
    public void test() {}
}

class Base1 extends Base {
    public void test() {
            System.out.println("Base1");
    }
}

class Base2 extends Base {
    public void test() {
            System.out.println("Base2");
    }
}

class Test {
    public  static void main(String[] args) {
            Base obj = new Base1();
            ((Base2)obj).test();    // CAST
    }
}
```

a) The program will print the following: Base1.

b) The program will print the following: Base2.

c) The compiler will report an error in the line marked with comment CAST.

d) The program will result in an exception (ClassCastException).

14. **Consider the following program:**

```
class Outer {
    class Inner {
            public void print() {
                    System.out.println("Inner: print");
            }
    }
}

class Test {
    public static void main(String []args) {
            // Stmt#1
            inner.print();
    }
}
```

Which one of the following statements will you replace in place of // Stmt#1 to make the program compile and run successfully to print "Inner: print" in console?

a) `Outer.Inner inner = new Outer.Inner();`

b) `Inner inner = new Outer.Inner();`

c) `Outer.Inner inner = new Outer().Inner();`

d) `Outer.Inner inner = new Outer().new Inner();`

15. **Consider the following program:**

```java
public class Outer {
        private int mem = 10;
        class Inner {
                private int imem = new Outer().mem;    // ACCESS1
        }

        public static void main(String []s) {
                System.out.println(new Outer().new Inner().imem); // ACCESS2
        }
}
```

Which one of the following options is correct?

a) When compiled, this program will result in a compiler error in line marked with comment ACCESS1.

b) When compiled, this program will result in a compiler error in line marked with comment ACCESS2.

c) When executed, this program prints 10.

d) When executed, this program prints 0.

16. **Consider the following program:**

```java
interface EnumBase { }

enum AnEnum implements EnumBase {        // IMPLEMENTS_INTERFACE
        ONLY_MEM;
}

class EnumCheck {
        public static void main(String []args) {
                if(AnEnum.ONLY_MEM instanceof AnEnum) {
                        System.out.println("yes, instance of AnEnum");
                }
                if(AnEnum.ONLY_MEM instanceof EnumBase) {
                        System.out.println("yes, instance of EnumBase");
                }
                if(AnEnum.ONLY_MEM instanceof Enum) {    // THIRD_CHECK
                        System.out.println("yes, instance of Enum");
                }
        }
}
```

Which one of the following options is correct?

a) This program results in a compiler in the line marked with comment IMPLEMENTS_INTERFACE.

b) This program results in a compiler in the line marked with comment THIRD_CHECK.

c) When executed, this program prints the following:
yes, instance of AnEnum

d) When executed, this program prints the following:
yes, instance of AnEnum
yes, instance of EnumBase

e) When executed, this program prints the following:
yes, instance of AnEnum
yes, instance of EnumBase
yes, instance of Enum

17. **Which of the following statements are true with respect to enums? (Select all that apply.)**

a) An enum can have `private` constructor.

b) An enum can have `public` constructor.

c) An enum can have `public` methods and fields.

d) An enum can implement an interface.

e) An enum can extend a class.

18. **Consider the following program and predict the behavior:**

```
class base1 {
    protected int var;
}

interface base2 {
    int var = 0; // #1
}

class Test extends base1 implements base2 { // #2
    public static void main(String args[]) {
        System.out.println("var:" + var); // #3
    }
}
```

a) The program will report a compilation error at statement #1.

b) The program will report a compilation error at statement #2.

c) The program will report a compilation error at statement #3.

d) The program will compile without any errors.

19. **Consider the following program:**

```
class WildCard {
        interface BI {}
        interface DI extends BI {}
        interface DDI extends DI {}

        static class C<T> {}
        static void foo(C<? super DI> arg) {}

        public static void main(String []args) {
                foo(new C<BI>());        // ONE
                foo(new C<DI>());        // TWO
                foo(new C<DDI>());       // THREE
                foo(new C());            // FOUR
        }
}
```

Which of the following options are correct?

a) Line marked with comment ONE will result in a compiler error.

b) Line marked with comment TWO will result in a compiler error.

c) Line marked with comment THREE will result in a compiler error.

d) Line marked with comment FOUR will result in a compiler error.

20. **Consider the following definitions:**

```
interface BI {}
interface DI extends BI {}
```

The following options provide definitions of a template class X. Which one of the options specifies class X with a type parameter whose upper bound declares DI to be the super type from which all type arguments must be derived?

a) class X <T super DI> { }

b) class X <T implements DI> { }

c) class X <T extends DI> { }

d) class X <T extends ? & DI> { }

21. **Consider the following program:**

```
class base1{}

class base2{}

interface base3{}

interface base4{}
```

```
// Stmt
public static void main(String args[]){
    }
}
```

Which one of the following statements will compile without errors if replaced in place of the line marked with comment Stmt?

a) `class Test extends base1, base2 implements base3, base4 {`

b) `class Test extends base1 implements base3, base4 {`

c) `class Test extends base1 implements base3 implements base4 {`

d) `class Test extends base1, extends base2 implements base3, base4 {`

22. **In the context of Singleton pattern, which one of the following statements is true?**

a) A Singleton class must not have any static members.

b) A Singleton class has a public constructor.

c) A Factory class may use Singleton pattern.

d) All methods of the Singleton class must be private.

23. **In the context of DAO pattern, which one of the following classes could be playing a role of TransferObject:**

a) `ImageManager`

b) `ImageFactory`

c) `Image`

d) `ImageProcessor`

24. **Which one of the following object-oriented concepts describes has-a relationship?**

a) Inheritance

b) Composite pattern

c) Inner classes

d) Composition

25. **Consider the following program:**

```
class ClassA {}

interface InterfaceB {}

class ClassC {}

class Test extends ClassA implements InterfaceB {
    String msg;
    ClassC classC;
}
```

Which one of the following statements is true?

a) Class Test is related with ClassA with a has-a relationship.

b) Class Test is related to ClassC with a composition relationship.

c) Class Test is related with String with an is-a relationship.

d) Class ClassA is related with InterfaceB with an is-a relationship.

26. **Consider the following UML diagram of a class program and choose a right option:**

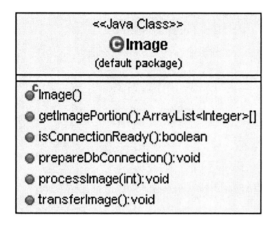

a) The class exhibits low cohesion.

b) The class implements Singleton pattern.

c) The class implements DAO pattern.

d) The class exhibits low coupling.

27. **Consider the following program:**

```
import java.util.Comparator;
import java.util.Arrays;

class CountryComparator implements Comparator<String> {
        public int compare(String country1, String country2) {
                return country2.compareTo(country2); // COMPARE_TO
        }
}

public class Sort {
        public static void main(String[] args) {
                String[] brics = {"Brazil", "Russia", "India", "China"};
                Arrays.sort(brics, null);
                for(String country : brics) {
                        System.out.print(country + " ");
                }
        }
}
```

Which one of the following options correctly describes the behavior of this program?

a) The program results in a compiler error in the line marked with the comment COMPARE_TO.

b) The program prints the following: Brazil Russia India China.

c) The program prints the following: Brazil China India Russia.

d) The program prints the following: Russia India China Brazil.

e) The program throws the exception `InvalidComparatorException`.

f) The program throws the exception `InvalidCompareException`.

g) The program throws the exception `NullPointerException`.

28. **Which one of the following class definitions will compile without any errors?**

a)
```
class P<T> {
    static T s_mem;
}
```

b)
```
class Q<T> {
    T mem;
    public Q(T arg) {
        mem = arg;
    }
}
```

c)
```
class R<T> {
    T mem;
    public R() {
        mem = new T();
    }
}
```

d)
```
class S<T> {
    T []arr;
    public S() {
        arr = new T[10];
    }
}
```

29. **Which one of the following class/interface supports "retrieval if elements based on the closest match to a given value or values?"**

a) `EnumSet`

b) `HashSet`

c) `AbstractSet`

d) `NavigableSet`

30. In a class that extends `ListResourceBundle,` which one of the following method definitions correctly overrides the `getObject()` method of the base class?

a) ```java
public String[][] getContents() {
    return new Object[][] { { "1", "Uno" }, { "2", "Duo" }, { "3", "Trie" }};
}
```

b) ```java
public Object[][] getContents() {
    return new Object[][] { { "1", "Uno" }, { "2", "Duo" }, { "3", "Trie" }};
}
```

c) ```java
private List<String> getContents() {
    return new ArrayList (Arrays.AsList({ { "1", "Uno" }, { "2", "Duo" },
    { "3", "Trie" }}));
}
```

d) ```java
protected Object[] getContents(){
    return new String[] { "Uno", "Duo", "Trie" };
}
```

31. Which one of the following interfaces declares a single method named `iterator()`? (Note: Implementing this interface allows an object to be the target of the for-each statement.)

a) `Iterable<T>`

b) `Iterator<T>`

c) `Enumeration<E>`

d) `ForEach<T>`

32. Which one of the following options is best suited for generating random numbers in a multi-threaded application?

a) Using `java.lang.Math.random()`

b) Using `java.util.concurrent.ThreadLocalRandom`

c) Using `java.util.RandomAccess`

d) Using `java.lang.ThreadLocal<T>`

33. Consider the following program:

```java
import java.util.*;

class ListFromVarargs {
    public static <T> List<T> asList1(T... elements) {
        ArrayList<T> temp = new ArrayList<>();
        for(T element : elements) {
                temp.add(element);
        }
        return temp;
    }
```

```
    public static <T> List<?> asList2(T... elements) {
        ArrayList<?> temp = new ArrayList<>();
        for(T element : elements) {
                temp.add(element);
        }
        return temp;
    }

    public static <T> List<?> asList3(T... elements) {
        ArrayList<T> temp = new ArrayList<>();
        for(T element : elements) {
                temp.add(element);
        }
        return temp;
    }

    public static <T> List<?> asList4(T... elements) {
        List<T> temp = new ArrayList<T>();
        for(T element : elements) {
                temp.add(element);
        }
        return temp;
    }
}
```

Which of the asList definitions in this program will result in a compiler error?

a) The definition of asList1 will result in a compiler error.

b) The definition of asList2 will result in a compiler error.

c) The definition of asList3 will result in a compiler error.

d) The definition of asList4 will result in a compiler error.

e) None of the definitions (asList1, asList2, asList3, asList4) will result in a compiler error.

34. **Consider the following program:**

```
import java.util.*;

class TemplateType {
        public static void main(String []args) {
                List<Map<List<Integer>, List<String>>> list =
                        new ArrayList<>();        // ADD_MAP
                Map<List<Integer>, List<String>> map = new HashMap<>();
                list.add(null);          // ADD_NULL
                list.add(map);
                list.add(new HashMap<List<Integer>,
                        List<String>>()); // ADD_HASHMAP
```

```
                    for(Map element : list) {        // ITERATE
                            System.out.print(element + " ");
                    }
            }
    }
}
```

Which one of the following options is correct?

a) This program will result in a compiler error in line marked with comment ADD_MAP.

b) This program will result in a compiler error in line marked with comment ADD_HASHMAP.

c) This program will result in a compiler error in line marked with comment ITERATE.

d) When run, this program will crash, throwing a NullPointerException in line marked with comment ADD_NULL.

e) When run, this program will print the following: null {} {}

35. **Consider the following program:**

```
class Base<T> { }

class Derived<T> { }

class Test {
    public static void main(String []args) {
            // Stmt #1
    }
}
```

Which statements can be placed in the place of //Stmt#1 and the program remains compilable (choose two):

a) Base<Number> b = new Base<Number>();

b) Base<Number> b = new Derived<Number>();

c) Base<Number> b = new Derived<Integer>();

d) Derived<Number> b = new Derived<Integer>();

e) Base<Integer> b = new Derived<Integer>();

f) Derived<Integer> b = new Derived<Integer>();

36. **Consider the following program:**

```
class Base<T> { }

class Derived<T> { }

class Test {
    public static void main(String []args) {
            //Stmt#1
    }
}
```

Which statements can be placed in the place of //Stmt#1 and the program remains compilable (select all that apply)?

a) `Base<? extends Number> b = new Base<Number>();`

b) `Base<? extends Number> b = new Derived<Number>();`

c) `Base<? extends Number> b = new Derived<Integer>();`

d) `Derived<? extends Number> b = new Derived<Integer>();`

e) `Base<?> b = new Derived<Integer>();`

f) `Derived<?> b = new Derived<Integer>();`

37. **Which of the following statements are true about `java.sql.Savepoint`? (select all that apply)**

a) Savepoint is a point within the current transaction that can be referenced from the Connection.rollback() method

b) When a transaction is rolled back to a savepoint all changes made after that savepoint are undone.

c) Savepoints must be named. It is not possible to have "unnamed savepoints".

d) java.sql.Savepoint is an abstract class; it is implemented by the classes such as JDBCSavepoint, ODBCSavepoint, and TransactionSavepoint in the java.sql package.

38. **Consider the following program and choose the appropriate option:**

```
import java.util.*;

class Test {
    public static void main(String []args) {
        Set<Integer> set = new LinkedHashSet<Integer>(); //#1
        LinkedHashSet<Integer> set2 = new HashSet<Integer>(); //#2
        SortedSet<Integer> set3 = new TreeSet<Integer>(); //#3
        SortedSet<Integer> set4 = new NavigableSet<Integer>(); //#4
    }
}
```

a) Statements #1 and #2 will compile successfully.

b) Statements #1 and #3 will compile successfully.

c) Statements #1, #2, and #3 will compile successfully.

d) Statements #2 and #4 will compile successfully.

39. **Consider the following program:**

```
import java.util.*;

class Test {
    public static void main(String []args) {
        Set<Integer> set = new TreeSet<Integer>();
```

```
                set.add(5);
                set.add(10);
                set.add(3);
                set.add(5);
                System.out.println(set);
        }
}
```

What will be the output of this program?

a) [5, 10, 3, 5]

b) [5, 10, 3]

c) [3, 5, 10]

d) [10, 5, 3]

40. **Which of the following statements are true about classes relating to formatting date and time for local cultures? (select all that apply)**

a) java.text.Format is the abstract base class that supports formatting of locale sensitive information such as date, time, and currency

b) java.text.CustomTimeFormat allows you to define custom patterns for processing time for specific locales.

c) java.text.NumberFormat derives from the java.text.Format class; it is the base class for processing numbers, currency, etc. in a locale sensitive way.

d) java.text.DateFormat derives from the java.text.Format class; it is the base class for processing date and time information based on locale.

41. **Consider the following program and choose the appropriate option:**

```
import java.util.*;

class Test {
    public static void main(String []args) {
            Map<String, int> map =
                    new HashMap<int, String>();            //#1
            Map<String, String> map2 =
                    new HashMap<String, String>();         //#2
            Map<String, String> map3 = new HashMap<>();    //#3
            Map<> map4 = new HashMap<String, String>();    //#4
        }
}
```

a) Statement #1 and #2 will compile successfully.

b) Statement #2 and #3 will compile successfully.

c) Statement #3 and #4 will compile successfully.

d) Statement #4 and #1 will compile successfully.

42. **Consider the following program and predict the output:**

```java
import java.util.*;

class Test {
    public static void main(String []args) {
        Map<Integer, String> map = new TreeMap<Integer, String>();
        map.put(5, "5");
        map.put(10, "10");
        map.put(3, "3");
        map.put(5,"25");
        System.out.println(map);
    }
}
```

a) {5=5, 10=10, 3=3, 5=25}

b) {10=10, 3=3, 5=25}

c) {3=3, 5=5, 5=25, 10=10}

d) {3=3, 5=25, 10=10}

e) {3=3, 5=5, 10=10}

43. **Consider the following program and predict the output:**

```java
import java.util.*;

class Test {
    public static void main(String []args) {
        Deque<Integer> deque = new LinkedList<>();
        deque.add(10);
        deque.add(20);
        deque.peek();
        deque.peek();
        deque.peek(); //#1
        System.out.println(deque);
    }
}
```

a) [10, 20]

b) [20, 10]

c) []

d) NoSuchElementException thrown when executing the line #1.

44. **Which of the following classes in the java.util.concurrent.atomic package inherit from java.lang.Number? (Select all that apply).**

a) AtomicBoolean

b) AtomicInteger

c) AtomicLong

d) AtomicFloat

e) AtomicDouble

45. **Consider the following program and predict the output:**

```
import java.util.HashSet;

class Student{
    public Student(int r) {
            rollNo = r;
    }
    int rollNo;
}

class Test {
    public  static void main(String[] args){
            HashSet<Student> students = new HashSet<>();
            students.add(new Student(5));
            students.add(new Student(10));
            System.out.println(students.contains(new Student(10)));
    }
}
```

a) This program prints the following: true.

b) This program prints the following: false.

c) This program results in a compiler error.

d) This program throws NoSuchElementException.

46. **Which of the following statements are true regarding resource bundles in the context of localization? (select all that apply)**

a) java.util.ResourceBundle is the base class and is an abstraction of resource bundles that contain locale-specific objects.

b) java.util.PropertyResourceBundle is a concrete subclass of java.util. ResourceBundle that manages resources for a locale using strings provided in the form of a property file.

c) Classes extending java.util.PropertyResourceBundle must override the getContents() method which has the return type Object [][].

d) java.util.ListResourceBundle defines the getKeys() method that returns enumeration of keys contained in the resource bundle.

47. **Consider the following program and predict the output:**

```
import java.util.HashSet;

class Student{
    public Student(int r) {
            rollNo = r;
    }
```

```
        int rollNo;
        public int hashCode(){
                return rollNo;
        }
}

class Test {
        public  static void main(String[] args){
                HashSet<Student> students = new HashSet<>();
                students.add(new Student(5));
                Student s10 = new Student(10);
                students.add(s10);
                System.out.println(students.contains(new Student(10)));
                System.out.println(students.contains(s10));
        }
}
```

a)   false
     true

b)   false
     false

c)   true
     false

d)   true
     true

48. **Which of the following statements are true regarding the classes or interfaces defined in the java.util.concurrent package?**

a)   The Executor interface declares a single method execute(Runnable command) that executes the given command at sometime in the future.

b)   The Callable interface declares a single method call() that computes a result.

c)   The Exchanger class provides a "synchronization point at which threads can pair and swap elements within pairs".

d)   The TimeUnit enumeration represents time duration and is useful for specifying timing parameters in concurrent programs.

49. **Consider the following program and predict the output:**

```
import java.util.*;

class Test {
    public static void main(String []args) {
        List<Integer> intList = new ArrayList<>();
        intList.add(10);
        intList.add(20);
        List list = intList;
        list.add("hello");    // ADD_STR
```

```
            for(Object o : list) {
                System.out.print(o + " ");
            }
        }
    }
```

a) This program will not print any output and will throw ClassCastException.

b) This program will first print 10 and 20 and then throw ClassCastException.

c) This program will result in a compiler error in line marked with comment ADD_STR.

d) This program will print 10, 20, and hello.

50. **Which TWO of the following options provide assignments that will compile without errors?**

a) `Map<String, String> map1 = new NavigableMap<>();`

b) `Map<String, String> map2 = new IdentityHashMap<>();`

c) `Map<String, String> map3 = new Hashtable<>();`

d) `Map<String, String> map4 = new ConcurrentMap<>();`

51. **Consider the following program:**

```
import java.util.*;

class AsList {
        public static void main(String []args) {
                String hello = "hello";
                String world = "world";
                StringBuffer helloWorld = new StringBuffer(hello + world);
                List<String> list =
                        Arrays.asList(hello, world, helloWorld.toString());
                helloWorld.append("!");
                list.remove(0);          // REMOVE
                System.out.println(list);
        }
}
```

Which one of the following options is correct?

a) When compiled, this program will result in a compiler error in linked marked with comment REMOVE.

b) When run, this program will crash with throwing the exception UnsupportedOperationException when executing the line marked with comment REMOVE.

c) When run, this program will print the following output: [hello, world, helloworld]

d) When run, this program will print the following output: [world, helloworld!]

e) When run, this program will print the following output: [world, helloworld]

52. **Consider the following program and predict the output:**

```
class Test {
    public static void main(String []args) {
            String s = new String("5");
            System.out.println(1+10+s+1+10);
    }
}
```

a) 11511

b) 1105110

c) 115110

d) 27

53. **Consider the following program and predict the output:**

```
class Test {
    public static void main(String []args) {
            String s = new String("5");
            System.out.println(1.0+10.5+s+(1.0+10.5));
    }
}
```

a) 11.5511.5

b) 11.551.010.5

c) 1.010.551.010.5

d) 11.55(1.010.5)

e) 11.55(11.5)

54. **Consider the following program:**

```
class Printf {
        public static void main(String []args) {
                System.out.printf("%3.4s %n", "hello world");
                System.out.printf("%05d", 123);
        }
}
```

Which one of the following options correctly provides the output of this program?

a) lo
    05123

b) hell
    0123

c) hello
    123

d) hell
00123

e) hello world
123

55. **Consider the following program:**

```
class PrintlnTest {
        public static void main(String[] args) {
                String two = "2";
                System.out.println("1 + 2 + 3 + 4 = "
                        + 1 + Integer.parseInt(two) + 3 + 4); // PARSE
        }
}
```

Which one of the following options correctly describes the behavior of this program?

a) When compiled, this program will give a compiler error in line marked with comment PARSE for missing catch handler for `NumberFormatException`.

b) When executed, the program prints the following: `1 + 2 + 3 + 4 = 1234`.

c) When executed, the program prints the following: `1 + 2 + 3 + 4 = 10`.

d) When executed, the program prints the following: `1 + 2 + 3 + 4 = 127`.

e) When executed, the program prints the following: `1 + 2 + 3 + 4 = 19`.

f) When executed, the program throws a `NumberFormatException` in the line marked with comment PARSE.

56. **Consider the following program and predict the output:**

```
class Test {
    public static void main(String []args) {
            int a = 7, b = 10;
            System.out.printf("no:%2$s and %1$s", a, b);
            System.out.printf("\nno:2$s and 1$s", a, b);
    }
}
```

a) no:10 and 7
no:2$s and 1$s

b) no:7 and 10
no:2$s and 1$s

c) no:10 and 7
no:10 and 7

d) no:7 and 10
no:7 and 10

e) This program will result in compiler error(s).

57. Consider the following program and predict the output (ignore any empty lines in the output):

```java
class Test {
    public static void main(String[] s) {
        String quote = "aba*abaa**aabaa***";
        String [] words = quote.split("a\\**", 10);
        for (String word : words) {
            System.out.println(word);
        }
    }
}
```

a) ab
   aba
   *aaba
   **

b) b
   b
   b

c) aba*aba
   aaba

d) This program throws a runtime exception.

58. Consider the following program and predict the output:

```java
import java.util.regex.*;

class Test {
    public static void main(String[] args) {
        String str1 = "xxzz";
        String str2 = "xyz";
        String str3 = "yzz";
        Pattern pattern = Pattern.compile("(xx)*y?z{1,}");
        Matcher matcher = pattern.matcher(str1);
        System.out.println(matcher.matches());
        System.out.println(pattern.matcher(str2).matches());
        System.out.println(
                Pattern.compile("(xx)*y?z{1,}").
                matcher(str3).matches());
    }
}
```

a) true
   false
   true

b) true
   false
   false

c) false
   false
   false

d) false
   false
   true

e) true
   true
   true

59. **Consider the following program and predict the output:**

```java
import java.util.regex.*;

class Test {
    public static void main(String[] args) {
        String str = "OCPJP 2013 OCPJP7";

        Pattern pattern = Pattern.compile("\\b\\w+\\D\\b");
        Matcher matcher = pattern.matcher(str);
        while(matcher.find()) {
            System.out.println(matcher.group());
        }
    }
}
```

a) OCPJP
   2013
   OCPJP7

b) OCPJP
   2013

c) OCPJP
   OCPJP7

d) This program does not result in any output.

60. **Consider the following program and predict the output:**

```java
import java.util.regex.*;

class Test {
    public static void main(String[] args) {
        String str =
            "Suneetha N.=9876543210, Pratish Patil=9898989898";
        Pattern pattern =
            Pattern.compile("(\\w+)(\\s\\w+)(=)(\\d{10})");
        Matcher matcher = pattern.matcher(str);
        String newStr = matcher.replaceAll("$4:$2,$1");
        System.out.println(newStr);
    }
}
```

a) 9876543210: N.,Suneetha, 9898989898: Patil,Pratish

b) Suneetha N.=9876543210, Pratish Patil=9898989898

c) Suneetha N.=9876543210, 9898989898: Patil,Pratish

d) This program throws a runtime exception.

61. **Which of the following TWO statements are true about the pre-defined streams System.in, System.out, and System.err?**

a) System.in is of type InputStream.

b) System.in is of type FileReader.

c) System.out is of type OutputStream.

d) System.err is of type ErrorStream.

e) Both System.out and System.err are of type PrintStream.

f) Both System.out and System.err are of type FileWriter.

62. **Consider the following program:**

```java
import java.io.*;

class CloseableImpl implements Closeable {
        public void close() throws IOException {
                System.out.println("In CloseableImpl.close()");
        }
}

class AutoCloseableImpl implements AutoCloseable {
        public void close() throws Exception {
                System.out.println("In AutoCloseableImpl.close()");
        }
}

class AutoCloseCheck {
        public static void main(String []args) {
                try (Closeable closeableImpl = new CloseableImpl();
                        AutoCloseable autoCloseableImpl
                                = new AutoCloseableImpl()) {
                } catch (Exception ignore) {
                        // do nothing
                }
                finally {
                        // do nothing
                }
        }
}
```

Which one of the following options correctly shows the output of this program when the program is executed?

a) This program does not print any output in console.

b) This program prints the following output:
   In AutoCloseableImpl.close()

c) This program prints the following output:
   In AutoCloseableImpl.close()
   In CloseableImpl.close()

d) This program prints the following output:
   In CloseableImpl.close()
   In AutoCloseableImpl.close()

63. **Consider the following code snippet and choose the best option:**

```java
public static void main(String []files) {
        try (FileReader inputFile =
                new FileReader(new File(files[0]))) { // #1
        }
        catch (FileNotFoundException | IOException e) { // #2
                e.printStackTrace();
        }
}
```

a) The code snippet will compile without any errors.

b) The compiler will report an error at statement #1.

c) The compiler will report an error at statement #2.

d) The compiler will report errors at statements #1 and #2.

64. **Consider the following code segment:**

```java
while( (ch = inputFile.read()) != VAL) {
        outputFile.write( (char)ch );
}
```

Assume that `inputFile` is of type `FileReader`, and `outputFile` is of type `FileWriter`, and `ch` is of type char. The method `read()` returns the character if successful, or VAL if the end of the stream has been reached. What is the correct value of this VAL checked in the while loop for end-of-stream?

a) -1

b) 0

c) 255

d) Integer.MAX_VALUE

e) Integer.MIN_VALUE

65. **Consider the following program and predict the output:**

```java
import java.io.*;

class USPresident implements Serializable{
    private static final long serialVersionUID = 1L;
    @Override
    public String toString() {
            return "US President [name=" + name +
            ", period=" + period + ", term=" + term + "]";
    }
    public USPresident(String name, String period, String term) {
            this.name = name;
            this.period = period;
            this.term = term;
    }
    private String name;
    private String period;
    private static transient String term;
}

class TransientSerialization {
    public static void main(String []args) {
            USPresident usPresident = new USPresident
                    ("Barack Obama", "2009 to --", "56th term");
            System.out.println(usPresident);
            try (ObjectOutputStream oos = new ObjectOutputStream
                    (new FileOutputStream("USPresident.data"))){
                    oos.writeObject(usPresident);
            } catch(IOException ioe) {
                    // ignore
            }
            try(ObjectInputStream ois = new ObjectInputStream
                    (new FileInputStream("USPresident.data"))){
                    Object obj = ois.readObject();
                    if(obj != null && obj instanceof USPresident){
                            USPresident presidentOfUS = (USPresident)obj;
                            System.out.println(presidentOfUS);
                    }
            }catch(IOException ioe) {
                    // ignore
            } catch (ClassNotFoundException e) {
                    // ignore
            }
    }
}
```

a) US President [name=Barack Obama, period=2009 to --, term=56th term]
    US President [name=Barack Obama, period=2009 to --, term=56th term]

b) US President [name=Barack Obama, period=2009 to --, term=56th term]
    US President [name=Barack Obama, period=2009 to --, term=null]

c) This program will result in a compiler error.

d) This program will result in a runtime exception.

66. **Which one of the following statements true?**

a) If you do not specify serialVersionUID while in serialization, your class will not compile

b) If you do not specify serialVersionUID while in serialization, JVM will work across all platforms and JVM implementations.

c) If you are implementing an Externalizable interface, you need not specify serialVerionUID.

d) If a class is serialized and you try to serialize it again, the JVM will not serialize it due to the same serialVersionUID.

67. **Consider the following program:**

```java
import java.io.*;

class CopyFile {
    public static void main(String []files) {
        if(files.length != 2) {
            System.err.println
            ("Incorrect syntax. Usage: Copy SrcFile DstFile");
            System.exit(-1);
        }
        String srcFile = files[0];
        String dstFile = files[1];

        try (BufferedReader inputFile
                = new BufferedReader(new FileReader(srcFile));
            BufferedWriter outputFile
                = new BufferedWriter(new FileWriter(dstFile))) {
            int ch = 0;
            inputFile.skip(6);
            while( (ch = inputFile.read()) != -1) {
                outputFile.write( (char)ch );
            }
            outputFile.flush();
        } catch (IOException exception) {
            System.err.println("Error "
                + exception.getMessage());
        }
    }
}
```

Assume that you have a file named HelloWorld.txt with the following contents:

```
Hello World!
```

This program is invoked from the command-line as:

```
java CopyFile HelloWorld.txt World.txt
```

Which one of the following options correctly describes the behavior of this program (assuming that both srcFile and dstFile are opened successfully)?

a)   The program will throw an IOException because skip() is called before calling read().

b)   The program will result in creating the file World.txt with the contents "World!" in it.

c)   This program will result in throwing CannotSkipException.

d)   This program will result in throwing IllegalArgumentException.

68.   **Consider the following program:**

```
import java.nio.file.*;

class SubPath {
        public static void main(String []args) {
                Path aPath = Paths.get("C:\\WINDOWS\\system32\\config\\systemprofile\\
                Start Menu\\Programs\\Accessories\\Entertainment\\Windows Media Player");
                System.out.println(aPath.subpath(3, 4));
        }
}
```

Which one of the following options is correct?

a)   This program prints the following: config\systemprofile.

b)   This program prints the following: config.

c)   This program prints the following: systemprofile.

d)   This program prints the following: system32\config.

e)   This program throws an IllegalArgumentException.

69.   **Consider the following code segment:**

```
Path testFilePath = Paths.get("C:\\WINDOWS\\system32\\config\\.\\systemprofile\\Start
Menu\\Programs\\Accessories\\Entertainment\\..\\..");
System.out.println("It's normalized absolute path is: " +
testFilePath.normalize().toAbsolutePath());
```

Which one of the following options correctly provides the output of this code segment?

a)   C:\\WINDOWS\\system32\\config\\systemprofile\\Start
     Menu\\Programs\\Accessories\\Entertainment\\

b)   C:\WINDOWS\system32\config\systemprofile\Start
     Menu\Programs\Accessories\Entertainment\

c)   C:\WINDOWS\system32\config\systemprofile\Start Menu\Programs

d)   C:\WINDOWS\system32\systemprofile\Start
     Menu\Programs\Accessories\Entertainment\

70. **Consider the following program and predict the output:**

```
class Base {
    protected void finalize() {
            System.out.println("in Base.finalize");
    }
}

class Derived extends Base {
    protected void finalize() {
            System.out.println("in Derived.finalize");
    }
}

class Test {
    public static void main(String []args) {
            Derived d = new Derived();
            d = null;
            Runtime.runFinalizersOnExit(true);
    }
}
```

a) This program prints the following: in Base.finalize.

b) This program prints the following: in Derived.finalize.

c) This program throws a CannotRunFinalizersOnExitException.

d) This program throws a NullPointerException.

71. **Consider the following program and predict the output:**

```
class Test {
    private static int mem = 0;
    public static void foo() {
            try {
                    mem = mem + 1;
            }
            catch(Exception e) {
                    e.printStackTrace();
            }
            finally {
                    mem = mem + 1;
            }
    }
    public static void main(String []args) {
            foo();
            System.out.println(mem);
    }
}
```

a) 0

b) 1

c) 2

d) 3

72. **Consider the following program:**

```java
class Base {
        public void foo() {
                assert true;    // ASSERT_BASE
        }
}

class Derived extends Base {
        public void foo() {
                assert false; // ASSERT_DERIVED
        }
}

class AssertionCheck {
        public static void main(String []args) {
                try {
                        Base base = new Base();
                        base.foo();
                }
                catch(Exception e) {
                        base = new Derived();
                        base.foo();
                }
        }
}
```

From the command line, this program is invoked as follows:

```
java -ea -da:Derived AssertionCheck
```

Which one of the following options correctly describes the behavior of this program when it is run?

a) This program crashes throwing an `AssertionError` in line marked with comment ASSERT_BASE.

b) This program crashes throwing an `AssertionError` in line marked with comment ASSERT_DERIVED.

c) This program first prints "Caught exception" and then crashes throwing an `AssertionError` in line marked with comment ASSERT_DERIVED.

d) This program completes execution normally without producing any output or throwing any exceptions.

73. **Consider the following code segment:**

```java
try (BufferedReader inputFile
    = new BufferedReader(new FileReader(srcFile));
    BufferedWriter outputFile
    = new BufferedWriter(new FileWriter(dstFile))) {  // TRY-BLOCK
    int ch = 0;
    while( (ch = inputFile.read()) != -1) {
        outputFile.write( (char)ch );
    }
} catch (FileNotFoundException
    | IOException exception) {        // MULTI-CATCH-BLOCK
    System.err.println("Error in opening or processing file "
        + exception.getMessage());
}
```

Assume that `srcFile` and `dstFile` are Strings. Which one of the following options correctly describes the behavior of this program?

a) This program will get into an infinite loop because the condition check for end-of-stream (checking != -1) is incorrect.

b) This program will get into an infinite loop because the variable ch is declared as int instead of char.

c) This program will result in a compiler error in line marked with comment TRY-BLOCK because you need to use , (comma) instead of ; (semi-colon) as separator for opening multiple resources.

d) This program will result in a compiler error in line marked with comment MULTI-CATCH-BLOCK because IOException is the base class for FileNotFoundException.

74. **Consider the following program and replace the statement #1 and #2 with appropriate declarations:**

```java
import java.io.Console;

class Login {
    public static void main(String []args) {
        Console console = System.console();
        if(console != null) {
            //#1
            //#2
            userName = console.readLine("Enter your username: ");
            password = console.readPassword("Enter password: ");
            System.out.println(userName + " ," + password);
        }
    }
}
```

a) String userName = null;
    char[] password = null;

b) String userName = null;
    String password = null;

c) char[] userName = null;
    String password = null;

d) char[] userName = null;
    char[] password = null;

75. **Assuming that** file **is a String variable, which one of the following statements is NOT a valid statement?**

a) BufferedReader inputFile = new BufferedReader(new FileReader(file));

b) FileReader inputFile = new FileReader(file);

c) FilterReader fr = new FilterReader(file);

d) FilterReader fr = new PushbackReader(new FileReader(file));

76. **Consider the following snippet:**

```
try (FileReader inputFile = new FileReader(file)) {
        //#1
        System.out.print( (char)ch );
    }
}
```

Which one of the following statements can be replaced in the place of statement #1?

a) while((ch = inputFile.read()) != null) {

b) while((ch = inputFile.read()) != -1) {

c) while((ch = inputFile.read()) != 0) {

d) while((ch = inputFile.read()) != EOF) {

77. **Among the given options, which two options will compile successfully:**

a) BufferedReader br =
        new BufferedReader(new FileReader(srcFile));
    br.getChannel();

b) RandomAccessFile raf =
        new RandomAccessFile(srcFile, "rw+");
    raf.getChannel();

c) FileInputStream ifr =
        new FileInputStream(srcFile);
    ifr.getChannel();

d) DataInputStream dis =
        new DataInputStream(new FileInputStream("temp.data"));
    dis.getChannel();

547

78. **Consider the following program and predict the output (the following files exist in the given path File09.java, File0.java, FileVisitor1.java, FileVisitor1.class):**

```java
class MyFileFindVisitor extends SimpleFileVisitor<Path> {
    private PathMatcher matcher;
    public MyFileFindVisitor(String pattern) {
        matcher =
                FileSystems.getDefault().getPathMatcher(pattern);
    }
    public FileVisitResult visitFile
            (Path path, BasicFileAttributes fileAttributes){
            find(path);
            return FileVisitResult.CONTINUE;
    }
    private void find(Path path) {
            Path name = path.getFileName();
            if(matcher.matches(name))
                    System.out.println
                            ("Matching file:" + path.getFileName());
    }
    public FileVisitResult preVisitDirectory
            (Path path, BasicFileAttributes fileAttributes){
            find(path);
            return FileVisitResult.CONTINUE;
    }
}

class FileTreeWalkFind {
    public static void main(String[] args) {
            Path startPath = Paths.get("d:\\workspace\\test\\src");
            String pattern = "glob:File[0-9]+.java";
            try {
                    Files.walkFileTree
                    (startPath, new MyFileFindVisitor(pattern));
                    System.out.println("File search completed!");
            } catch (IOException e) {
                    e.printStackTrace();
            }
    }
}
```

a) File09.java
File0.java
FileVisitor1.java
File search completed!

b) File09.java
File0.java
File search completed!

    c)   File0.java
        File search completed!

    d)   File search completed!

79.   Which one of the following statements is NOT correct in the context of NIO.2?

    a)   While finding files/directories, the default pattern format is glob; hence, you need not start the search-pattern from `"glob:"`.

    b)   You can specify the search pattern either in glob format or in regex format.

    c)   Glob format is a subset of the regex pattern format.

    d)   There will be no error or runtime exception if you specify a wrong glob search pattern.

80.   Which one of the following statements will compile without errors?

    a)   `Locale locale1 = new Locale.US;`

    b)   `Locale locale2 = Locale.US;`

    c)   `Locale locale3 = new US.Locale();`

    d)   `Locale locale4 = Locale("US");`

    e)   `Locale locale5 = new Locale(Locale.US);`

81.   Consider the following program:

```
import java.util.*;

class Format {
        public static void main(String []args) {
                Formatter formatter = new Formatter();
                Calendar calendar = Calendar.getInstance(Locale.US);
                calendar.set(/* year =*/ 2012,
                        /* month = */ Calendar.FEBRUARY, /* date = */ 1);
                formatter.format("%tY/%tm/%td",
                        calendar, calendar, calendar);
                System.out.println(formatter);
        }
}
```

Which one of the following options is correct?

    a)   The program throws a `MissingFormatArgumentException`.

    b)   The program throws an `UnknownFormatConversionException`.

    c)   The program prints the following: 2012/02/01.

    d)   The program prints the following: 12/Feb/01.

82. **Which one of the following statements is correct with respect to Closeable and AutoCloseable interfaces?**

   a) Interface Closeable extends AutoCloseable and defines one method, close().

   b) Interface Autocloseable extends Closeable and defines one method, close().

   c) Interface Closeable extends AutoCloseable and does not define any method.

   d) Interface AutoCloseable extends Closeable and does not define any method.

   e) Closeable and AutoCloseable interfaces do not share any inheritance relationship.

83. **Which one of the following code snippets shows the correct usage of try-with-resources statement?**

   a)
```
public static void main(String []files) {
        try (FileReader inputFile
            = new FileReader(new File(files[0]))) {
                //...
        }
        catch(IOException ioe) {}
}
```

   b)
```
public static void main(String []files) {
        try (FileReader inputFile
            = new FileReader(new File(files[0]))) {
                //...
        }
        finally {/*...*/}
        catch(IOException ioe) {}
}
```

   c)
```
public static void main(String []files) {
        try (FileReader inputFile
            = new FileReader(new File(files[0]))) {
                //...
        }
        catch(IOException ioe) {}
        finally {/*...*/}
}
```

   d)
```
public static void main(String []files) {
        try (FileReader inputFile
            = new FileReader(new File(files[0]))) {
                //...
        }
}
```

84. **Consider the following program and predict the output:**

```
class MyThread extends Thread {
    public MyThread(String name) {
            this.setName(name);
            start();
            System.out.println("in ctor " + getName());
    }
     public void start() {
            System.out.println("in start " + getName());
    }
    public void run() {
            System.out.println("in run " + getName());
    }
}

class Test {
    public static void main(String []args) {
            new MyThread("oops");
    }
}
```

a) in start oops
   in ctor oops

b) in start oops
   in run oops
   in ctor oops

c) in start oops
   in ctor oops
   in run oops

d) in ctor oops
   in start oops
   in run oops

85. **Which one of the following methods returns a Future object?**

a) The overloaded submit() method declared in the ExecutorService interface.

b) The execute() method declared in the Executor interface.

c) The call() method declared in the Callable interface.

d) The run() method declared in the Runnable interface.

86. **Consider the following program:**

```java
import java.util.concurrent.locks.*;

class LockUnlock {
        public static void main(String []args) {
                Lock lock = new ReentrantLock();
                try {
                        System.out.print("Lock 1 ");
                        lock.lock();
                        System.out.print("Critical section 1 ");
                        System.out.print("Lock 2 ");
                        lock.lock();    // LOCK_2
                        System.out.print("Critical section 2 ");
                } finally {
                        lock.unlock();
                        System.out.print("Unlock 2 ");
                        lock.unlock();        // UNLOCK_1
                        System.out.print("Unlock 1 ");
                }
        }
}
```

Which one of the following options is correct?

a) This program will throw an IllegalMonitorStateException in the line marked with comment LOCK_2.

b) This program will throw an IllegalMonitorStateException in the line marked with comment UNLOCK_1.

c) This program will throw an UnsupportedOperationException in the line marked with comment UNLOCK_1.

d) This program prints the following: Lock 1 Critical section 1 Lock 2 Critical section 2 Unlock 2 Unlock 1.

87. **Consider the following program:**

```java
import java.util.concurrent.locks.*;

class LockUnlock {
        public static void main(String []args) {
                Lock lock1 = new ReentrantLock();
                Lock lock2 = new ReentrantLock();
                try {
                        System.out.println("Going to lock...");
                        lock1.lock();
                        System.out.println("In critical section");
                } finally {
                        lock2.unlock();
                        System.out.println("Unlocking ...");
                }
        }
}
```

Which one of the following options is correct?

a) This program will print the following:
   "Going to lock..."
   "In critical section"
   Unlocking ...

b) This program will print the following:
   "Going to lock..."
   "In critical section"
   and then terminate normally.

c) This program will print the following:
   "Going to lock..."
   "In critical section"
   and then enter into a deadlock because lock2.unlock() waits for lock2 to get locked first.

d) This program will throw an IllegalMonitorStateException.

88. **Consider the following program:**

```java
import java.util.concurrent.Semaphore;

class ATMRoom {
        public static void main(String []args) {
                Semaphore machines = new Semaphore(2);  //#1
                new Person(machines, "Mickey");
                new Person(machines, "Donald");
                new Person(machines, "Tom");
                new Person(machines, "Jerry");
                new Person(machines, "Casper");
        }
}

class Person extends Thread {
        private Semaphore machines;
        public Person(Semaphore machines, String name) {
                this.machines = machines;
                this.setName(name);
                this.start();
        }
        public void run() {
                try {
                        System.out.println(getName()
                                + " waiting to access an ATM machine");
                        machines.acquire();
                        System.out.println(getName()
                                + " is accessing an ATM machine");
                        Thread.sleep(1000);
```

```
                          System.out.println(getName()
                                  + " is done using the ATM machine");
                          machines.release();
                  } catch(InterruptedException ie) {
                          System.err.println(ie);
                  }
          }
  }
```

Which one of the options is true if you replace the statement #1 with the following statement?

```
Semaphore machines = new Semaphore(2, true);
```

a)   The exact order in which waiting persons will get the ATM machine cannot be predicted.

b)   The ATM machine will be accessed in the order of waiting persons (because of the second parameter in semaphore constructor).

c)   It will not compile since second parameter in semaphore instantiation is not allowed.

d)   It will result in throwing an IllegalMonitorStateException.

89.   **A couple of friends are waiting for some more friends to come so that they can go to a restaurant for dinner. Which synchronization construct could be used here to programmatically simulate this situation?**

a)   Exchanger

b)   Lock

c)   CyclicBarrier

d)   RecursiveAction

90.   **An application establishes connection with a database, which returns a resultset containing two identical column names. You are using ResultSet to retrieve the associated values. In this context, which statement is true?**

a)   You can retrieve both the column values using column names.

b)   You can retrieve both the column values using column names; however, you need to specify the column names using the column index (i.e. column-name:column-index).

c)   You cannot use column names to retrieve both the values; you need to use column index to do it.

d)   Both options b and c will work.

Answer Sheet

Question No	Answer	Question No	Answer	Question No	Answer
1		31		61	
2		32		62	
3		33		63	
4		34		64	
5		35		65	
6		36		66	
7		37		67	
8		38		68	
9		39		69	
10		40		70	
11		41		71	
12		42		72	
13		43		73	
14		44		74	
15		45		75	
16		46		76	
17		47		77	
18		48		78	
19		49		79	
20		50		80	
21		51		81	
22		52		82	
23		53		83	
24		54		84	
25		55		85	
26		56		86	
27		57		87	
28		58		88	
29		59		89	
30		60		90	

Answers and Explanations

1. a) `int i = 012;`

   Putting 0 before a number makes that number an octal number. A decimal equivalent of 012 (in octal) is 10. If you attempt an implicit conversion from float, long, or double types (as given in options b, c, and d respectively) to an integer, you will a get compiler error.

2. a) Compiler error in line marked with comment NUM because Number cannot be instantiated

   Number is an abstract class, hence you cannot instantiate it using new operator. Many classes including Integer, Float, and BigDecimal derive from the Number class.

3. a) This code segment: This, that, etcetera.!

   The method `StringBuffer replace(int start, int end, String str)` has the following behavior according to the Javadoc that explains the behavior of this code segment: "Replaces the characters in a substring of this sequence with characters in the specified String. The substring begins at the specified start and extends to the character at index end - 1 or to the end of the sequence if no such character exists. First, the characters in the substring are removed and then the specified String is inserted at the start. (This sequence will be lengthened to accommodate the specified String if necessary.)"

4. b) This program prints the following: hello world! null.

   The call new `StringBuffer(10);` creates a `StringBuffer` object with initial capacity to store 10 characters; this capacity would grow as you keep calling methods like append(). After the calls to append "hello" and "world ," the call to append null results in adding the string "null" to the string buffer (it doesn't result in a `NullPointerException` or `InvalidArgumentException`). With the append of "null," the capacity of the string buffer has grown to 17 characters. So, the call `strBuffer.insert(11, '!');` successfully inserts the character '!' in the 11th position instead of resulting in an `ArrayIndexOutOfBoundsException`.

5. b) This code will result in a throwing a `NullPointerException`.

   Note that unboxing can take place in expressions when you use a wrapper type object in place of a primitive type value. In this case, in the condition check for the conditional operator (?: operator), a primitive boolean value is required, but a wrapper type object is provided. Hence auto-unboxing occurs, with the reference pointing to null. As a result, this code segment results in throwing a `NullPointerException`.

6. a) Base
   Derived
   DeriDerived

   Whenever a class gets instantiated, the constructor of its base classes (the constructor of the root of the hierarchy gets executed first) gets invoked before the constructor of the instantiated class.

7. a) `public`

    d) `abstract`

    e) `final`

    Only `public`, `abstract`, and `final` modifiers are permitted for an outer class; using `private`, `protected`, or `static` will result in a compiler error.

8. c) ```
    private Point() {
            this(0, 0);
    }
    ```

    Options a) and b): Calls to `super()` or `this()` should be the first statement in a constructor, hence both the calls cannot be there in a constructor.

    Option d): Recursive constructor invocation for `Point()` that the compiler would detect.

    Option e): You cannot refer to an instance field x while explicitly invoking a constructor using this keyword.

9.  b)  Removing `Stmt-1` will make the program compilable and it will print the following: Base: Hello Derived.

    c)  Removing `Stmt-2` will make the program compilable and it will print the following: Base Derived.

    d)  Removing both `Stmt-1` and `Stmt-2` will make the program compilable and it will print the following: Base Derived.

    If you remove Stmt-1, a call to super(s) will result in printing Base: Hello, and then constructor of the Derived class invocation will print Derived. Similarly, removal of `Stmt-2` will also produce the correct program. In fact, if you remove both these statements, you will also get a compilable program.

10. d)  `import static abc.org.project.A.MYCONST;`

11. b)  ```
    import static java.lang.System.out;
        class StaticImport {
                public static void main(String []args) {
                        out.println("hello world");
                }
        }
    ```

    The member `out` is a static member in the `System` class; you can statically import it and call `println` method on it. Note that `println` is a non-static member. Also, the statement `import static java.lang.System.out.*;` will result in a compiler error since `out` is not a class (but a static member of type `PrintStream`).

12. a) The compiler will report an error at statement #1.

    Statement #1 will result in a compiler error since the keyword `protected` is not allowed inside a method body.

13. d) The program will result in an exception (`ClassCastException`).

    The dynamic type of variable `obj` is `Base1` that you were trying to cast into `Base2`. This is not supported and so results in an exception.

14. d) `Outer.Inner inner = new Outer().new Inner();`

15. c) This program runs and prints 10.

An inner class can access even the private members of the outer class. Similarly, the private variable belonging to the inner class can be accessed in the outer class.

16. e) When executed, this program prints the following:
yes, instance of AnEnum
yes, instance of EnumBase
yes, instance of Enum

An enumeration can implement an interface (but cannot extend a class, or cannot be a base class).
Each enumeration constant is an object of its enumeration type. An enumeration automatically extends the abstract class java.util.Enum. Hence, all the three instanceof checks succeed.

17. a) Enum can have private constructor.

c) Enum can have public methods and fields.

d) Enum can implement an interface.

18. c) The program will report a compilation error at statement #3.

Statement #1 and #2 will not raise any alarm; only access to the variable var will generate an error since the access is ambiguous (since the variable is declared in both base1 and base2).

19. c) The line marked with comment THREE will result in a compiler error.

Options a) and b): For the substitution to succeed, the type substituted for the wildcard ? should be DI or one of its super types.

Option c): The type DDI is not a super type of DI, so it results in a compiler error.

Option d): The type argument is not provided, meaning that C is a raw type in the expression new C(). Hence, this will elicit a compiler warning, but not an error.

20. c) class X <T extends DI> { }

The keyword extends is used to specify the upper bound for type T; with this, only the classes or interfaces implementing the interface DI can be used as a replacement for T. Note that the extends keyword is used for any base type—irrespective of if the base type is a class or an interface.

21. b) class Test extends base1 implements base3, base4 {

You can extend from only one base class (since Java does not support multiple class inheritance). However, you can implement multiple interfaces; in that case, the list of implemented interfaces is separated by commas.

22. c) A Factory class may use Singleton pattern

A Factory class generates the desired type of objects on demand. Hence, it might be required that only one Factory object exists; in this case, Singleton can be employed in a Factory class.

23. c) Image

The DAO pattern separates the persistence logic from the rest of the business logic. In this pattern, TransferObject is a role played by an object that needs to be stored on a persistent medium. Here, only the Image class fits the description of a TransferObject.

24. d) Composition

Composition is also known as a has-a relationship, and inheritance is known as an is-a relationship. The Composite pattern is a design pattern and is not an alternative name for a has-a relationship.

25. b) Class Test is related with ClassC with a composition relationship.

When a class inherits from another class, they share an is-a relationship. On the other hand, if a class uses another class (by declaring an instance of another class), then the first class has a has-a relationship with the used class.

26. a) The class exhibits low cohesion.

The methods of the class show that the class carries out various types of operations that make this class in-cohesive.

27. b) The program prints the following: Brazil China India Russia.

For the sort() method, null value is passed as the second argument, which indicates that the elements' "natural ordering" should be used. In this case, natural ordering for Strings results in the strings sorted in ascending order. Note that passing null to the sort() method does not result in a NullPointerException.

28. b)
```
class Q<T> {
        T mem;
        public Q(T arg) {
                mem = arg;
        }
}
```

Option a): You cannot make a static reference of type T.

Option c) and d): You cannot instantiate the type T or T[] using new operator.

29. d) NavigableSet

EnumSet is a specialized Set implementation class for use with enum types. HashSet is a Set implementation that makes use of a hashing mechanism for quick retrieval of elements. AbstractSet is the abstract base class of all Set classes. NavigableSet provides "navigation methods" that can search for closest matches for a given value or values.

30. b)
```
public Object[][] getContents() {
        return new Object[][] { { "1", "Uno" }, { "2", "Duo" }, { "3", "Trie" }};
}
```

The getContents() method is declared in ListResourceBundle as follows:

```
protected abstract Object[][] getContents()
```

The other three definitions are incorrect overrides and will result in compiler error(s).

31. a) `Iterable<T>`

The interface `Iterable<T>` declares this single method:

`Iterator<T> iterator();`

This `iterator()` method returns an object of type `Iterator<T>`. A class must implement `Iterable<T>` for using its object in a `for-each` loop.

32. b) Using java.util.concurrent.ThreadLocalRandom

`java.lang.Math.random()` is not efficient for concurrent programs. Using `ThreadLocalRandom` results in less overhead and contention when compared to using `Random` objects in concurrent programs (and hence using this class type is the best option in this case).

`java.util.RandomAccess` is unrelated to random number generation. This interface is the base interface for random access data structures and is implemented by classes such as `Vector` and `ArrayList`. `java.lang.ThreadLocal<T>` class provides support for creating thread-local variables.

33. b) The definition of `asList2` will result in a compiler error.

In the `asList2` method definition, `temp` is declared as `ArrayList<?>`. Since the template type is a wild-card, you cannot put any element (or modify the container). Hence, the method call `temp.add(element);` will result in a compiler error.

34. e) When run, this program will print the following: `null {} {}`

The lines marked with comments `ADD_MAP` and `ADD_HASHMAP` are valid uses of the diamond operator to infer type arguments. In the line marked with comment `ITERATE`, the `Map` type is not parameterized, so it will result in a warning (not a compiler error). Calling the `add()` method passing `null` does not result in a `NullPointerException`. The program, when run, will successfully print the output null, {}, {} (null output indicates a null value was added to the list, and the {} output indicates that `Map` is empty).

35. a) `Base<Number> b = new Base<Number>();`

  f) `Derived<Integer> b = new Derived<Integer>();`

Note that `Base` and `Derived` are not related by an inheritance relationship. Further, for generic type parameters, subtyping doesn't work: you cannot assign a derived generic type parameter to a base type parameter.

36. a) `Base<? extends Number> b = new Base<Number>();`

  d) `Derived<? extends Number> b = new Derived<Integer>();`

  f) `Derived<?> b = new Derived<Integer>();`

When `<? extends Number>` is specified as a type, then you can use any type derived from `Number` (including `Number`); hence, options a) and d) are correct. Option f) is correct since class names are the same in both the sides, and ? in `<?>` is replaced by `Integer`, which is allowed.

37. a) Savepoint is a point within the current transaction that can be referenced from the Connection.rollback() method.

  b) When a transaction is rolled back to a savepoint, all changes made after that savepoint are undone.

Savepoints can be named or unnamed. We can identify an "unnamed savepoint" by referring to the ID generated by the underlying data source.

java.sql.Savepoint is an interface (it is not an abstract class). Classes JDBCSavepoint, ODBCSavepoint, and TransactionSavepoint do not exist in the java.sql package. Hence, options a) and b) are correct.

38.   b)   Statements #1 and #3 will compile successfully.

LinkedHashSet inherits from Set so statement #1 will compile. TreeSet inherits from SortedSet so statement #3 will also compile successfully.

LinkedHashSet is inherited from HashSet so statement #2 will not compile. Statement #4 tries to create an object of type NavigableSet which is an interface, so it will also not compile.

39.   c)   [3, 5, 10]

TreeSet is a sorted set; hence, all the inserted items are sorted in ascending order. Also, since TreeSet is a Set, it will remove any duplicate item inserted.

40.   a)   java.text.Format is the abstract base class that supports formatting of locale sensitive information such as date, time, and currency

      c)   java.text.NumberFormat derives from java.text.Format class; it is the base class for processing numbers, currency, etc. in a locale sensitive way.

      d)   java.text.DateFormat derives from java.text.Format class; it is the base class for processing date and time information based on locale.

Class java.text.SimpleDateFormat allows you to define custom patterns for processing date and time for specific locales.

41.   b)   Statement #2 and #3 will compile successfully.

Due to the diamond syntax, it is optional to specify template types in the right hand side of an object creation statement. Hence, statement #3 is right. Statement #2 is correct since HashMap is a Map. Therefore, option b) is correct.

In statement #1, the order of arguments of the declared type is different from the order of arguments in the initialized type. In statement #4, the diamond syntax is used in the declaration of the type and so is incorrect (the correct way is to use the diamond operator in the initialization type).

42.   d)   {3=3, 5=25, 10=10}

TreeMap is a Map;—a value is stored against a key, and the elements are sorted based on the key. Option c) is not possible since two values cannot exist for a key. In a Map, keys are sequential, so options a) and b) are not possible. Option e) is also not correct since you have overwritten the value 25 against key 5, which is not captured by option e).

43.   a)   [10, 20]

The method peek() retrieves an element from the head of the Deque and returns, but does not remove the element. Hence, there will be no impact on the Deque.

44. b)   AtomicInteger

c)   AtomicLong

Classes AtomicInteger and AtomicLong extend Number class.

AtomicBoolean does not extend java.lang.Number. Classes named as AtomicFloat or AtomicDouble do not exist in the java.util.concurrent.atomic package.

45. b)   This program prints the following: false.

Since methods equals() and hashcode() are not overridden for the Student class, the contains() method will not work as intended and prints false.

46. a)   ResourceBundle is the base class and is an abstraction of resource bundles that contain locale-specific objects.

d)   java.util.ListResourceBundle defines the getKeys() method that returns enumeration of keys contained in the resource bundle.

java.util.ListResourceBundle is a concrete subclass of java.util.The ResourceBundle that manages resources for a locale using strings provided in the form of a property file. Classes extending java.util.ListResourceBundle must override the getContents() method which has the return type Object [][].

47. a)   false
true

Since, the newly created object is not part of the students set, the call to contains will result in false (note that the equals() method is not overridden in this class). Object s10 is part of the students set. So option a) is the correct answer.

48. a)   The Executor interface declares a single method execute(Runnable command) that executes the given command at some time in the future.

b)   The Callable interface declares a single method call() that computes a result.

c)   The Exchanger class provides a "synchronization point at which threads can pair and swap elements within pairs".

d)   The TimeUnit enumeration represents time duration and is useful for specifying timing parameters in concurrent programs.

Options a), b), c), and d) – all four options are correct statements.

49. d)   It will print 10, 20, and hello.

The raw type List gets initialized from List<Integer> (which generates a compiler *warning* not an error), and then you add a string element to the raw List, which is allowed. Then the whole list gets iterated to print each element; each element gets cast to the Object type, so it prints 10, 20, and hello.

50. b)   Map<String, String> map2 = new IdentityHashMap<>();

c)   Map<String, String> map3 = new Hashtable<>();

The classes IdentityHashMap and Hashtable derive from the Map interface, so the assignments in the b) and c) options will compile without errors. NavigableMap and ConcurrentMap are *interfaces* that derive from the Map interface, and interfaces cannot be instantiated; hence the assignments in options a) and d) will result in compiler errors.

51. b) When run, this program will crash with throwing the exception UnsupportedOperationException when executing the line marked with the comment REMOVE.

The Arrays.asList method returns a List object that is backed by a fixed-length array. You cannot modify the List object returned by this array, so calling methods such as add() or remove() will result in throwing an UnsupportedOperationException.

52. c) 115110

The string concatenation operator works as follows: if both the operands are numbers, it performs the addition; otherwise it concats the arguments by calling the toString() method if needed. It evaluates from left to right. Hence, the expression in the program results in the string 115110.

53. a) 11.5511.5

The rule specified in the earlier explanation applies here also. However, here, the order of computation is changed using brackets. Hence, the + operator adds the numbers in the brackets first, and you get 11.5511.5.

54. d) hell
00123

In first printf() method, %3.4s indicates that you want to print the first four characters of a string. In the second printf() method call, %05d indicates that you wanted to print a minimum five digits of an integer. If the number does not have enough digits, then the number will be preceded by leading zeroes.

55. b) When executed, the program prints the following: 1 + 2 + 3 + 4 = 1234.

The string concatenation operator works as follows: if both operands are numbers, it performs the addition; otherwise, it performs string concatenation. The operator checks from left operand to right. Here, the first operand is string; therefore all operands are concatenated.

Note that parseInt need not catch NumberFormatException since it is a RuntimeException; so the lack of the catch handler will not result in a compiler error. Since the parseInt method succeeds, the program does not throw NumberFormatException.

56. a) no:10 and 7
no:2$s and 1$s

The format specifier string %$s indicates that you want to re-order the input values. A number (integer) sandwiched between a % and a $ symbol is used to re-order the input values; the number indicates which input variable you want to put here. In %2$s it indicates that you want to put the second argument. Similarly, %1$s indicates that you want to put the first argument.

57. b) b
b
b

The specified regex (i.e. "a**") will match to a string starting from an "a" followed by one or more "*" (since "**" means zero or more occurrences of "*"). Hence, when the split is called on the input string, it results in three "b"s.

The second argument indicates a limit to split, which controls the number of times the pattern is applied. Here the limit is 10, but the pattern is applied only three times, so it does not make any difference in this program.

58. a)   true
          false
          true

The specified regex expects zero or more instances of "xx", followed by a zero or one instance of "y" and further followed by one or more instances of "z."

The first string matches the regex (one instance of "xx," zero instances of "y," and more than one instances of "z"), and thus matches() returns true. The second string does not match with the regex because of one "x" (and not "xx"), thus matches() returns false. The third string matches with the specified regex (since there are zero instances of "xx," one instance of "y," and more than one instance of "z"), thus matches() prints true.

59. b)   OCPJP
          2013

The expression "\b" matches the word boundaries. The first "\b" matches the string start, "\w+" matches to OCPJP, "" matches white space, and "\b" matches the starting of the second word. Thus, it prints OCPJP in the first line. Similarly, "\b" matches the starting of the second word, "\w+" matches to 2013, "\D" matches to white space, and "\b" matches to the start of the third word. Therefore, the program prints 2013 in the second line. However, for the last word, "\b" matches to the start of the third word, "\w+" matches to the OCPJP7, but "\D" did not match with anything; hence, the third word is not printed.

60. c)   Suneetha N.=9876543210, 9898989898: Patil,Pratish

The first contact does not match with the specified regex (since "" is not covered by "\w+"); hence, the first part of the string is unchanged. The second part of string matches with the specified regex, so the replace rearranges the substring.

61. a)   System.in is of type InputStream.
     e)   Both System.out and System.err are of type PrintStream.

System.in is of type InputStream, and both System.out and System.err are of type PrintStream. These are byte streams, though they are usually used for reading and writing characters from or to the console.

62. c)   This program prints the following output:
          In AutoCloseableImpl.close()
          In CloseableImpl.close()

The types implementing AutoCloseable can be used with a try-with-resources statement. The Closeable interface extends AutoCloseable, so classes implementing Closeable can also be used with a try-with-resources statement.

The close() methods are called in the opposite order when compared to the order of resources acquired in the try-with-resources statement. So, this program calls the close() method of AutoCloseableImpl first, and after that calls the close() method on the CloseableImpl object.

63. c)   The compiler will report an error at statement #2.

Both of the specified exceptions belong to same hierarchy (FileNotFoundException derives from an IOException), so you cannot specify both exceptions together in the multi-catch handler block.

64. a) –1

The read() method returns the value –1 if end-of-stream (EOS) is reached, which is checked in this while loop.

65. a) US President [name=Barack Obama, period=2009 to --, term=56th term]
US President [name=Barack Obama, period=2009 to --, term=56th term]
Static transient variables are retained during serialization.

66. d) If a class is serialized and you try to serialize it again, the JVM will not serialize it due to the same serialVersionUID.

67. b) The program will result in creating the file World.txt with the contents "World!" in it.

The method call skip(n) skips n bytes (i.e., moves the buffer pointer by n bytes). In this case, 6 bytes need to be skipped, so the string "Hello" is not copied in the while loop while reading and writing the file contents.

Explanation for the wrong options:

Option a): The skip() method can be called before the read() method.

Option c): No exception named CannotSkipException exists.

Option d): The skip() method will throw an IllegalArgumentException only if a negative value is passed.

68. c) This program prints the following: systemprofile.

Here is the description of the subpath method: The subpath(int beginIndex, int endIndex) method returns a Path object. The returned Path object has names that begin at beginIndex till the element at index endIndex - 1. In other words, beginIndex is inclusive of the name in that index and exclusive of the name in endIndex. This method may throw an IllegalArgumentException if beginIndex is >= number of elements, or endIndex <= beginIndex, or endIndex is > number of elements.

In this program, the index starts with WINDOWS, at index 0. The given beginIndex is 3, so it is the subpath systemprofile, and it is exclusive of the endIndex with value4. Hence the output.

69. c) C:\WINDOWS\system32\config\systemprofile\Start Menu\Programs

The method normalize() removes redundant elements in the path such as . (dot symbol that indicates current directory) and .. (the double dot symbol that indicates the parent directory). Hence, the resulting path is C:\WINDOWS\system32\config\systemprofile\Start Menu\Programs.

70. b) It prints the following: in Derived.finalize.

The statement Runtime.runFinalizersOnExit(true); makes sure that the finalize method is invoked when the application exits (although the method runFinalizersOnExit() is now deprecated). Here, the dynamic type of the object is "Derived," so the finalize() method of the Derived class is invoked before the application exits.

71. c) 2

The variable mem is 0 initially. It is incremented by one in the try block and is incremented further in the finally block to 2. Note that finally will always execute irrespective of whether an exception is thrown in the try block or not. Hence, the program will print 2.

72. d) This program completes execution normally without producing any output or throwing any exceptions.

The statement `assert true;` when executed will always succeed. The statement `assert true;` when executed will always fail.

Remember that assertions are disabled by default, and –ea enables the assertion for the whole program. However, `-da` disables assertions, and `-da:Derived` instructs the JVM to disable assertions in the `Derived` class. Hence, the program completes execution normally without producing any output or throwing any exceptions.

73. d) This program will result in a compiler error in the line marked with the comment `MULTI-CATCH-BLOCK` because `IOException` is the base class for `FileNotFoundException`.

74. a) `String userName = null;`
`char[] password = null;`

The `readLine()` method returns a `String` object while the `readPassword()` method returns an array of `char`.

75. c) `FilterReader fr = new FilterReader(file);`

`FilterReader` is an abstract class and hence it cannot be instantiated.

76. b) `while( (ch = inputFile.read()) != -1) {`

The `read()` method returns -1 when the file reaches the end.

77. b) `RandomAccessFile raf = new RandomAccessFile(srcFile, "rw+");`
`raf.getChannel();`

c) `FileInputStream ifr = new FileInputStream(srcFile);`
`ifr.getChannel();`

The `getChannel()` method is supported by only the `RandomAccessFile` and `FileInputStream` classes.

78. d) File search completed!

Well, `glob` does not support "+"; hence, the specified `glob` expression does not find any file matching with the expression.

79. a) While finding files/directories, the default pattern format is `glob`; hence, you need not start the search-pattern from "glob:".

The other three statements are true.

80. b) `Locale locale2 = Locale.US;`

The `static public final Locale US` member in the `Locale` class is accessed using the expression `Locale.US`, as in option b).

81. c) The program prints the following: 2012/02/01.

The format specifier %t allows for formatting date and time information. It takes as suffix the format and part of the date or time information. The format Y is for the year displayed in four digits. The format m is for month as decimal (with months in the range 01 to 12). The format d is for the day of month as decimal (with the days in the range 01 – 31).

82. a) The interface `Closeable` extends `AutoCloseable` and defines one method, `close()`.

83. a)
```
public static void main(String []files) {
        try (FileReader inputFile
                    = new FileReader(new File(files[0]))) {
                //...
        }
        catch(IOException ioe) {}
}
```

Options b) and c) uses the `finally` block, which is not applicable with try-with-resource statements. In option d), the `catch` block is missing, which makes it wrong.

84. a) `in start oops`
    `in ctor oops`

You have overridden the `start()` method, so the `run()` method is never called!

85. a) The overloaded `submit()` method is declared in the `ExecutorService` interface.

The `executor` interface has overloaded the `submit()` method that takes "a value-returning the task for execution and returns a `Future` representing the pending results of the task."

86. d) This program prints the following: Lock 1 Critical section 1 Lock 2 Critical section 2 Unlock 2 Unlock 1.

In a re-entrant lock, you can acquire the same lock again. However, you need to release that lock the same number of times.

87. d) This program will throw an `IllegalMonitorStateException`.

Note that in this program you call the `lock()` method on the `lock1` variable and call the `unlock()` method on the `lock2` variable. Hence, in `lock2.unlock()`, you are attempting to call `unlock()` before calling `lock()` on a `Lock` object and this results in throwing an `IllegalMonitorStateException`.

88. a) The exact order in which waiting persons will get the ATM machine cannot be predicted.

The second parameter states the fairness policy of the `semaphore` object. However, there are two permits for the `semaphore` object; so you cannot predict the order in which waiting people will get the permission to access the ATM.

89. c) `CyclicBarrier`

`CyclicBarrier` is used when threads may need to wait at a predefined execution point until all other threads reach that point. This construct matches the given requirements.

90. c) You cannot use column names to retrieve both the values; you need to use column index to do it.

■ ■ ■

Mock Test – 2

The questions in this mock test are designed per the requirements of the OCPJP7 exam pattern and its standard. Take the test as if it were your real OCPJP 7 exam. Best of luck.

Time: 2 hours 30 minutes   *No. of questions:* 90

1.   **Consider the following program and predict the behavior of this program:**

```java
class Base {
        public void print() {
                System.out.println("Base:print");
        }
}

abstract class Test extends Base { //#1
        public static void main(String[] args) {
                Base obj = new Base();
                obj.print(); //#2
        }
}
```

   a)   Compiler error "an abstract class cannot extend from a concrete class" at statement #1.

   b)   Compiler error "cannot resolve call to print method" at statement #2.

   c)   The program prints the following: Base:print.

   d)   The program will throw a runtime exception of AbstractClassInstantiationException.

2.   **Consider the following program and predict the output:**

```java
class  Test {
        final Integer a;  // #1
        public void print(){
                System.out.println("a = " + a);
        }
        public static void main(String[] args) {
                Test obj = new Test();
                obj.print();
        }
}
```

a) The program will report a compiler error at statement #1.

b) The program will result in throwing a NullPointerException.

c) The program will print the following: a = 0.

d) The program will print the following: a = null.

3. **Consider the following program and predict the output:**

```java
class  Test {
        int a = 0;
        public static void print(int a) {
                this.a = a;
                System.out.println("a = " + this.a);
        }
        public static void main(String[] args) {
                Test obj = new Test();
                obj.print(10);
        }
}
```

a) The program will report a compiler error.

b) The program will generate a runtime exception.

c) The program will print the following: a = 0.

d) The program will print the following: a = 10.

4. **Consider the following program:**

```java
import java.util.*;

class Format {
        public static void main(String []args) {
                Formatter formatter = new Formatter();
                Calendar calendar = Calendar.getInstance(Locale.US);
                calendar.set(/* year =*/ 2012, /* month = */ Calendar.FEBRUARY,
                /* date = */ 1);
                formatter.format("%tY/%<tB/%<td", calendar);
                System.out.println(formatter);
        }
}
```

Which one of the following options correctly describes the behavior of this program?

a) The program throws a MissingFormatArgumentException.

b) The program throws an UnknownFormatConversionException.

c) The program throws an IllegalFormatConversionException.

d) The program prints the following: 12/February/01.

5. **Consider the following program:**

```java
import java.util.*;

public class ResourceBundle_it_IT extends ListResourceBundle {
        public Object[][] getContents() {
                return contents;
        }
        static final Object[][] contents = {
                { "1", "Uno" },
                { "2", "Duo" },
                { "3", "Trie" },
        };
        public static void main(String args[]) {
                ResourceBundle resBundle =
                        ResourceBundle.getBundle("ResourceBundle", new Locale("it", "IT", ""));
                System.out.println(resBundle.getObject(new Integer(1).toString()));
        }
}
```

Which one of the following options correctly describes the behavior of this program?

a) This program prints the following: Uno.

b) This program prints the following: 1.

c) This program will throw a MissingResourceException.

d) This program will throw a ClassCastException.

6. **Consider the following program:**

```java
import java.util.*;

class SortedOrder {
        public static void main(String []args) {
                Set<String> set = new TreeSet<String>();
                set.add("S");
                set.add("R");
                Iterator<String> iter = set.iterator();
                set.add("P");
                set.add("Q");
                while(iter.hasNext()) {
                        System.out.print(iter.next() + " ");
                }
        }
}
```

Which one of the following options correctly describes the behavior of this program?

a) The program prints the following: S R P Q.

b) The program prints the following: P Q R S.

c) The program prints the following: S R.

d) The program prints the following: R S.

e) The program throws a `ConcurrentModificationException`.

7. **Consider the following program:**

```java
import java.util.*;
import java.util.concurrent.*;

class SortedOrder {
        public static void main(String []args) {
                Set<String> set = new CopyOnWriteArraySet<String>(); // #1
                set.add("2");
                set.add("1");
                Iterator<String> iter = set.iterator();
                set.add("3");
                set.add("-1");
                while(iter.hasNext()) {
                        System.out.print(iter.next() + " ");
                }
        }
}
```

Which one of the following options correctly describes the behavior of this program?

a) The program prints the following: 2 1.

b) The program prints the following: 1 2.

c) The program prints the following: -1 1 2 3.

d) The program prints the following: 2 1 3 -1.

e) The program throws a `ConcurrentModificationException`

f) This program results in a compiler error in statement #1

8. **Which one of the following statements is FALSE?**

a) The interface Iterator<T> declares these methods: `boolean hasNext()`, `T next()`, and `void remove()`.

b) The interface Enumeration<E> declares two methods: `boolean hasMoreElements()` and `E nextElement()`.

c) The interface Iterable<T> declares three methods: `boolean hasNext()`, `T next()`, and `void remove()`.

d) Implementing Iterable<T> interface allows an object to be the target of the foreach statement.

9. **Consider the following program:**

```java
import java.io.IOException;
import java.nio.file.*;
class javals {
        public static void main(String []args) {
                Path currPath = Paths.get(".");
```

```
        try (DirectoryStream<Path> javaFiles = Files.newDirectoryStream
        (currPath, "*.{java}")) {
                for(Path javaFile : javaFiles) {
                        System.out.println(javaFile);
                }
        } catch (IOException ioe) {
                System.err.println("IO Error occurred");
                System.exit(-1);
        }
    }
}
```

Which one of the following options correctly describes the behavior of this program?

a) This program throws a PatternSyntaxException.

b) This program throws an UnsupportedOperationException.

c) This program throws an InvalidArgumentException.

d) This program lists the files ending with suffix .java in the current directory.

10. **Consider the following program:**

```
class Assert {
        public static void main(String []args) {
                try {
                        assert false;
                }
                catch (RuntimeException re) {
                        System.out.println("In the handler of RuntimeException");
                }
                catch (Exception e) {
                        System.out.println("In the handler of Exception");
                }
                catch (Error ae) {
                        System.out.println("In the handler of Error");
                }
                catch (Throwable t) {
                        System.out.println("In the handler of Throwable");
                }
        }
}
```

This program is invoked in the command line as follows:

```
java Assert
```

Which one of the following options correctly describes the behavior of this program?

a) This program prints the following: In the handler of RuntimeException.

b) This program prints the following: In the handler of Exception.

c) This program prints the following: In the handler of Error.

d) This program prints the following: In the handler of Throwable.

e) This program crashes with an uncaught exception AssertionError.

f) This program does not generate any output and terminates normally.

11. **Consider the following program:**

```
class GenericCast {
        static <E> E cast(Object item) {                    // ERROR1
                return (E) item;
        }
        public static void main(String []args) {
                Object o1 = 10;
                int i = 10;
                Integer anInteger = 10;

                Integer i1 = cast(o1);                      // ERROR2
                Integer i2 = cast(i);                       // ERROR3
                Integer i3 = cast(10);                      // ERROR4
                Integer i4 = cast(anInteger);               // ERROR5

                System.out.printf("i1 = %d, i2 = %d, i3 = %d, i4 = %d", i1, i2, i3, i4);
        }
}
```

Which one of the following options correctly describes the behavior of this program?

a) This program will result in a compiler error in the line marked with the comment ERROR1.

b) This program will result in a compiler error in the line marked with the comment ERROR2.

c) This program will result in a compiler error in the line marked with the comment ERROR3.

d) This program will result in a compiler error in the line marked with the comment ERROR4.

e) This program will result in a compiler error in the line marked with the comment ERROR5.

f) When executed, this program will print the following: i1 = 10, i2 = 10, i3 = 10, i4 = 10.

12. **Consider the following program:**

```
import java.nio.file.*;
import java.util.Iterator;

class PathInfo {
        public static void main(String[] args) {
                Path aFilePath = Paths.get("D:\\dir\\file.txt");
                Iterator<Path> paths = aFilePath.iterator();
                while(paths.hasNext()) {
                        System.out.print(paths.next() + " ");
                }
        }
}
```

Assume that the file D:\dir\file.txt does not exist in the underlying file system. Which of the following options best describes the behavior of this program when it is executed?

a) The program throws a FileNotFoundException.

b) The program throws an InvalidPathException.

c) The program throws an UnsupportedOperationException.

d) The program gets into an infinite loop printing "path element: dir" forever.

e) The program prints the following: dir file.txt.

13. **Consider the following program:**

```java
import java.io.*;

class Point2D implements Externalizable {
        private int x, y;
        public Point2D(int x, int y) {
                x = x;
        }
        public String toString() {
                return "[" + x + ", " + y + "]";
        }
        public void writeExternal(ObjectOutput out) throws IOException {
                System.out.println("Point " + x + ":" + y);
        }
        public void readExternal(ObjectInput in) throws IOException,
        ClassNotFoundException {
                /* empty */
        }
        public static void main(String []args) {
                Point2D point = new Point2D(10, 20);
                System.out.println(point);
        }
}
```

When executed, this program prints the following:

a) Point

b) [10, 0]

c) [10, 20]

d) [0, 0]

e) Point 10:20

14. **Consider the following program:**

```java
import java.util.PriorityQueue;

class PQueueTest {
        public static void main(String []args) {
                PriorityQueue<Integer> someValues = new PriorityQueue<Integer>();
```

```
                someValues.add(new Integer(10));
                someValues.add(new Integer(15));
                someValues.add(new Integer(5));
                Integer value;
                while ((value = someValues.poll()) != null) {
                        System.out.print(value + " ");
                }
        }
}
```

When executed, this program prints the following:

a) 10 10 10

b) 10 15 5

c) 5 10 15

d) 15 10 5

e) 5 5 5

15. Consider the following program:

```
class Base {}
class DeriOne extends Base {}
class DeriTwo extends Base {}

class ArrayStore {
        public static void main(String []args) {
                Base [] baseArr = new DeriOne[3];
                baseArr[0] = new DeriOne();
                baseArr[2] = new DeriTwo();
                System.out.println(baseArr.length);
        }
}
```

Which one of the following options correctly describes the behavior of this program?

a) This program prints the following: 3.

b) This program prints the following: 2.

c) This program throws an ArrayStoreException.

d) This program throws an ArrayIndexOutOfBoundsException.

16. Consider the following program:

```
import java.util.*;

class Task implements Comparable<Task> {
        int priority;
        public Task(int val) {
                priority = val;
        }
```

```
            public int compareTo(Task that) {
                    if(this.priority == that.priority)
                            return 0;
                    else if (this.priority > that.priority)
                            return -1;
                    else
                            return 1;
            }
            public String toString() {
                    return new Integer(priority).toString();
            }
    }

    class Test {
            public static void main(String []args) {
                    PriorityQueue<Task> tasks = new PriorityQueue<Task>();
                    tasks.add(new Task(10));
                    tasks.add(new Task(15));
                    tasks.add(new Task(5));
                    Task task;
                    while ( (task = tasks.poll()) != null) {
                            System.out.print(task + " ");
                    }
            }
    }
```

When executed, this program prints the following:

a)   10 10 10

b)   10 15 5

c)   5 10 15

d)   15 10 5

e)   5 5 5

17.   **Consider the following program:**

```
    import java.util.ArrayList;

    class RemoveTest {
            public static void main(String []args) {
                    ArrayList<Integer> list = new ArrayList<Integer>();
                    list.add(new Integer(2));
                    list.add(1);
                    list.add(5);
                    list.remove(2);          // REMOVE
                    System.out.println(list);
            }
    }
```

Which one of the following options correctly describes the behavior of this program?

a) When executed, this program prints the following: [2, , 5].

b) When executed, this program prints the following: [2, 1].

c) When executed, this program prints the following: [1, 5].

d) This program results in a compiler error in the line marked with the comment REMOVE.

e) This program results in a NoSuchElementException in the line marked with the comment REMOVE.

18. **Consider the following program:**

```
class Replace {
        public static void main(String []args) {
                String talk = "Pick a little, talk a little, pick a little, talk a
                little, cheep cheep cheep, talk a lot, pick a little more";
                String eat = talk.replaceAll("talk","eat").replace("cheep", "burp");
                System.out.println(eat);
        }
}
```

When executed, this program prints the following:

a) Pick a little, talk a little, pick a little, talk a little, cheep cheep cheep, talk a lot, pick a little more.

b) Pick a little, eat a little, pick a little, eat a little, cheep cheep cheep, eat a lot, pick a little more.

c) Pick a little, eat a little, pick a little, eat a little, burp cheep cheep, eat a lot, pick a little more.

d) Pick a little, eat a little, pick a little, eat a little, burp burp burp, eat a lot, pick a little more.

19. **Consider the following program:**

```
import java.util.*;
import java.util.concurrent.*;

class SetTest {
        public static void main(String []args) {
                List list = Arrays.asList(10, 5, 10, 20);
                System.out.println(list);
                System.out.println(new HashSet(list));
                System.out.println(new TreeSet(list));
                System.out.println(new ConcurrentSkipListSet(list));
        }
}
```

This program prints the following:

a) [10, 5, 10, 20]
   [20, 5, 10]
   [5, 10, 20]
   [5, 10, 20]

b) [10, 5, 10, 20]
   [5, 10, 20]
   [5, 10, 20]
   [20, 5, 10]

c) [5, 10, 20]
   [5, 10, 20]
   [5, 10, 20]
   [5, 10, 20]

d) [10, 5, 10, 20]
   [20, 5, 10]
   [5, 10, 20]
   [20, 5, 10]

20. **Consider the following program:**

```java
import java.util.regex.Pattern;

class Split {
        public static void main(String []args) {
                String date = "10-01-2012"; // 10th January 2012 in dd-mm-yyyy format
                String [] dateParts = date.split("-");
                System.out.print("Using String.split method: ");
                for(String part : dateParts) {
                        System.out.print(part + " ");
                }
                System.out.print("\nUsing regex pattern: ");
                Pattern datePattern = Pattern.compile("-");
                dateParts = datePattern.split(date);
                for(String part : dateParts) {
                        System.out.print(part + " ");
                }
        }
}
```

This program prints the following:

a) Using String.split method: 10-01-2012
   Using regex pattern: 10 01 2012

b) Using String.split method: 10 01 2012
   Using regex pattern: 10 01 2012

c) Using String.split method: 10-01-2012
   Using regex pattern: 10-01-2012

d) Using String.split method:
   Using regex pattern: 10 01 2012

e) Using String.split method: 10 01 2012
   Using regex pattern:

f) Using String.split method:
   Using regex pattern:

21. **Consider the following program:**

```
import java.util.ArrayList;

class TypeCheck {
        public static void main(String []args) {
                Class c1 = new ArrayList<String>().getClass();          // LINE A
                Class c2 = ArrayList.class;                             // LINE B
                System.out.println(c1 == c2);
        }
}
```

Which one of the following options correctly describes the behavior of this program?

a) The program will result in a compiler error in the line marked with the comment LINE A.

b) The program will result in a compiler error in the line marked with the comment LINE B.

c) When executed, the program prints the following: true.

d) When executed, the program prints the following: false.

22. **Consider the following program:**

```
class Waiter extends Thread {
        public static void main(String[] args) {
                new Waiter().start();
        }
        public void run() {
                try {
                        System.out.println("Starting to wait");
                        wait(1000);
                        System.out.println("Done waiting, returning back");
                }
                catch(InterruptedException e) {
                        System.out.println("Caught InterruptedException ");
                }
                catch(Exception e) {
                        System.out.println("Caught Exception ");
                }
        }
}
```

When executed, this program prints the following:

a) Starting to wait
   Done waiting, returning back

b) Starting to wait
   Caught InterruptedException

c) Starting to wait
   Caught Exception

d) After printing "Starting to wait," the program gets into an infinite wait and deadlocks.

23. **Consider the following program:**

```java
import java.util.ArrayList;

class ArrayListUse {
        static ArrayList<Integer> doSomething(ArrayList<Integer> values) {
                values.add(new Integer(10));
                ArrayList<Integer> tempList = new ArrayList<Integer>(values);
                tempList.add(new Integer(15));
                return tempList;
        }
        public static void main(String []args) {
                ArrayList<Integer> allValues = doSomething(new ArrayList<Integer>());
                System.out.println(allValues);
        }
}
```

This program prints the following:

a) []

b) [10]

c) [15]

d) [10, 15]

24. **Consider the following program:**

```java
class Overload {
        private Overload(Object o) {
                System.out.println("Object");
        }
        private Overload(double [] arr) {
                System.out.println("double []");
        }
        private Overload() {
                System.out.println("void");
        }
        public static void main(String[]args) {
                new Overload(null);      // MARKER
        }
}
```

Which one of the following options correctly describes the behavior of this program?

a) It throws a compiler error in the line marked with the comment `MARKER` for ambiguous overload.

b) When executed, the program prints the following: Object.

c) When executed, the program prints the following: double [].

d) When executed, the program prints the following: void.

25. **Consider the following program:**

```
class SuperClass {
        SuperClass() {
                foo();
        }
        public void foo(){
                System.out.println("In SuperClass.foo()");
        }
}
class SubClass extends SuperClass {
        public SubClass() {
                member = "HI";
        }
        public void foo() {
                System.out.println("In Derived.foo(): " + member.toLowerCase());
        }
        private String member;
        public static void main(String[] args) {
                SuperClass reference = new SubClass();
                reference.foo();
        }
}
```

This program prints the following:

a) In SuperClass.foo()

b) In Derived.foo(): hi

c) In SuperClass.foo()
   In Derived.foo(): hi

d) This program throws a NullPointerException.

26. **Consider the following program:**

```
class BaseClass {
        private void foo() {
                System.out.println("In BaseClass.foo()");
        }
        void bar() {
                System.out.println("In BaseClass.bar()");
        }
```

```
        public static void main(String[] args) {
                BaseClass po = new DerivedClass();
                po.foo();    // BASE_FOO_CALL
                po.bar();
        }
}
class DerivedClass extends BaseClass {
        void foo() {
                System.out.println("In Derived.foo()");
        }
        void bar() {
                System.out.println("In Derived.bar()");
        }
}
```

Which one of the following options correctly describes the behavior of this program?

a) This program results in a compiler error in the line marked with the comment
    BASE_FOO_CALL.

b) This program prints the following:
    In BaseClass.foo()
    In BaseClass.bar()

c) This program prints the following:
    In BaseClass.foo()
    In Derived.bar()

d) This program prints the following:
    In Derived.foo()
    In Derived.bar()

27. **Which one of the following options correctly reads a line of string from the console?**

a) BufferedReader br = new BufferedReader(System.in);
    String str = br.readLine();

b) BufferedReader br = new BufferedReader(new InputStreamReader(System.in));
    String str = br.readLine();

c) InputStreamReader isr = new InputStreamReader (new BufferedReader(System.in));
    String str = isr.readLine();

d) String str = System.in.readLine();

e) String str;
    System.in.scanf(str);

28. **Consider the following program:**

```
import java.util.Scanner;

class AutoCloseableTest {
        public static void main(String []args) {
                try (Scanner consoleScanner = new Scanner(System.in)) {
                        consoleScanner.close(); // CLOSE
                        consoleScanner.close();
                }
        }
}
```

Which one of the following statements is correct?

a) This program terminates normally without throwing any exceptions.

b) This program throws an `IllegalStateException`.

c) This program throws an `IOException`.

d) This program throws an `AlreadyClosedException`.

e) This program results in a compiler error in the line marked with the comment CLOSE.

29. **Consider the following program:**

```
import java.io.*;
class ExceptionTest {
        public static void thrower() throws Exception {
                try {
                        throw new IOException();
                } finally {
                        throw new FileNotFoundException();
                }
        }
        public static void main(String []args) {
                try {
                        thrower();
                } catch(Throwable throwable) {
                        System.out.println(throwable);
                }
        }
}
```

When executed, this program prints the following:

a) java.io.IOException

b) java.io.FileNotFoundException

c) java.lang.Exception

d) java.lang.Throwable

30. **Consider the following program:**

```
// class PQR in mock package
package mock;

public class PQR {
        public static void  foo() {
                System.out.println("foo");
        }
}

// class XYZ in mock package
package mock;
import static mock.*;

public class XYZ {
        public static PQR pqr;
}

// class StatImport
import static mock.XYZ.*;

class StatImport {
        public static void main(String []args) {
                // STMT
        }
}
```

Which one of the following statements will compile without errors when replaced with the line marked with the comment STMT?

a) foo();

b) pqr.foo();

c) PQR.foo();

d) XYZ.pqr.foo();

31. **Which of the following is NOT a problem associated with thread synchronization using mutexes?**

a) Deadlock

b) Lock starvation

c) Type erasure

d) Livelock

32. **Assume that a thread acquires a lock on an object obj; the same thread again attempts to acquire the lock on the same object obj. What will happen?**

   a) If a thread attempts to acquire a lock again, it will result in throwing an IllegalMonitorStateException.

   b) If a thread attempts to acquire a lock again, it will result in throwing an AlreadyLockAcquiredException.

   c) It is okay for a thread to acquire lock on obj again, and such an attempt will succeed.

   d) If a thread attempts to acquire a lock again, it will result in a deadlock.

33. **Consider the following program:**

```
class NullAccess {
        public static void main(String []args) {
                String str = null;
                System.out.println(str.valueOf(10));
        }
}
```

   Which of the following statements correctly describes the behavior of this program?

   a) This program will result in a compiler error.

   b) This program will throw a NullPointerException.

   c) This program will print 10 in console.

   d) This program will print null in console.

34. **There are two kinds of streams in the java.io package: character streams (i.e., those deriving from Reader and Writer interfaces) and byte streams (i.e., those deriving from InputStream and OutputStream). Which of the following statements is true regarding the differences between these two kinds of streams?**

   a) In character streams, data is handled in terms of bytes; in byte streams, data is handled in terms of Unicode characters.

   b) Character streams are suitable for reading or writing to files such as executable files, image files, and files in low-level file formats such as .zip, .class, .obj, and .exe.

   c) Byte streams are suitable for reading or writing to text-based I/O such as documents and text, XML, and HTML files.

   d) Byte streams are meant for handling binary data that is not human-readable; character streams are meant for human-readable characters.

35. **Which one of the following interfaces is empty (i.e., a marker interface that does not declare any methods)?**

   a) java.lang.AutoCloseable interface

   b) java.util.concurrent.Callable<T> interface

   c) java.lang.Cloneable interface

   d) java.lang.Comparator<T> interface

36. **Which of the following modifiers cannot be combined together for a class? (Select two options from the given options.)**

    a) final

    b) public

    c) strictfp

    d) abstract

37. **Consider the following code segment:**

```
String str = "A.B.C!";
System.out.println(str.replaceAll(".", ",").replace("!", "?"));
```

    When executed, this code segment will print the following:

    a) A,B,C!

    b) A,B,C?

    c) ,,,,,,

    d) A.B.C?

38. **Consider the following program and choose the correct option that describes its output:**

```
import java.util.concurrent.atomic.AtomicInteger;

class Increment {
        public static void main(String []args) {
                AtomicInteger i = new AtomicInteger(0);
                increment(i);
                System.out.println(i);
        }
        static void increment(AtomicInteger atomicInt){
                atomicInt.incrementAndGet();
        }
}
```

    a) 0

    b) 1

    c) This program throws an UnsafeIncrementException.

    d) This program throws a NonThreadContextException.

39. **Consider the following program and choose the correct option that describes its output:**

```
import java.util.concurrent.atomic.AtomicInteger;

class NullInstanceof {
        public static void main(String []args) {
                if(null instanceof Object)
                        System.out.println("null is instance of Object");
                if(null instanceof AtomicInteger)
                        System.out.println("null is instance of AtomicInteger");
        }
}
```

a) This program prints the following:
   null is instance of Object

b) This program prints the following:
   null is instance of Object
   null is instance of AtomicInteger

c) This program executes and terminates normally without printing any output in the console.

d) This program throws a NullPointerException.

e) This program will result in compiler error(s).

40. **What is the range of thread priority values and what is the default priority value of a thread?**

a) The range of thread priorities is 1 to 5; the default thread priority is 3.

b) The range of thread priorities is 1 to 10; the default thread priority is 6.

c) The range of thread priorities is 1 to 10; the default thread priority is 5.

d) All threads have equal priority of 1; hence, the default thread priority is also 1.

e) Threads are implemented using co-operative multi-threading approach, and not pre-emptive multithreading; as a result, they do not have any priority in Java.

41. **Which one of the following interfaces does NOT inherit from `java.util.Collection<E>` interface?**

a) Set<E>

b) Queue<E>

c) List<E>

d) Map<K, V>

42. **Which of the modifier(s) can be applied to a data member in a class?**
    (Select all that apply.)

    a) synchronized

    b) native

    c) abstract

    d) transient

    e) strictfp

43. **Which of the following method(s) from Object can be overridden?**
    (Select all that apply.)

    a) `finalize()` method

    b) `clone()` method

    c) `getClass()` method

    d) `notify()` method

    e) `wait()` method

44. **Consider the following program and predict the output:**

```
class MyThread extends Thread {
        public void run() {
                System.out.println("In run method; thread name is: "
                        + Thread.currentThread().getName());
        }
        public static void main(String args[])  {
                Thread myThread = new MyThread();
                myThread.run(); //#1
                System.out.println("In main method; thread name is: "
                        +Thread.currentThread().getName());
        }
}
```

    a) The program results in a compiler error at statement #1.

    b) The program results in a runtime exception.

    c) The program prints the following:
       In run method; thread name is: main
       In main method; thread name is: main

    d) The program prints:
       In the run method; the thread name is: thread-0
       In the main method; the thread name is: main

45.   **Consider the following program and predict the output:**

```
class MyThread extends Thread {
      public void run() {
              System.out.println("In run method; thread name is: " + Thread.
              currentThread().getName());
      }
      public static void main(String args[])  {
              Thread myThread = new MyThread();
              myThread.start();
              myThread.start();   //#1
      }
}
```

a)   The program results in a compiler error at statement #1.

b)   The program results in throwing an IllegalThreadStateException.

c)   The program prints the following:
     In the run method; thread name is: thread-0
     In the main method; thread name is: thread-0

d)   The program prints the following:
     In the run method; thread name is: thread-0

46.   **Consider the following program and predict the output:**

```
class MyThread extends Thread {
      public void run() {
              try {
                      this.join();
              } catch (InterruptedException e) {
                      e.printStackTrace();
              }
              System.out.println("In run method; thread name is: " + Thread.
              currentThread().getName());
      }
      public static void main(String args[])  {
              Thread myThread = new MyThread();
              myThread.start();
      }
}
```

a)   The program results in compiler error(s).

b)   The program results in throwing an IllegalThreadStateException.

c)   The program prints the following:
     In the run method; thread name is: thread-0

d)   The program will never terminate.

47. **Which of these statements are true with respect to Thread and Runnable? (Select all that apply.)**

a) Thread is an abstract class.

b) Thread provides a default implementation for the run() method.

c) Thread is an abstract class that extends the abstract base class Runnable.

d) Runnable is an abstract class.

48. **Which of the following state(s) is/are NOT legitimate thread state(s)? (Select all that apply.)**

a) NEW

b) EXECUTING

c) WAITING

d) TERMINATED

e) RUNNABLE

49. **Which one of the following constructor is NOT a valid constructor of Thread class?**

a) Thread()

b) Thread(String name)

c) Thread(Runnable target, Object obj)

d) Thread(Runnable target, String name)

e) Thread(ThreadGroup group, String name)

50. **Consider the following program and choose the best option:**

```
class MyThread extends Thread {
        public void run() {
                System.out.print("Burp! ");
        }
        public static void main(String args[]) throws InterruptedException  {
                Thread myThread = new MyThread();
                myThread.start();
                System.out.print ("Eat! ");
                myThread.join();
                System.out.print ("Run! ");
        }
}
```

a) When executed, it prints always the following: Eat! Burp! Run!

b) When executed, it prints one of the following: Eat! Burp! Run! or Burp! Eat! Run!

c) When executed, it prints one of the following: Eat! Burp! Run!; Burp! Eat! Run!; or Run! Eat! Burp!

d) When executed, it prints one of the following: Burp! Eat! Run! or Burp! Run! Eat!

51. **Consider the following program and choose the correct answer:**

```java
class MyThread extends Thread {
        public MyThread(String name) {
                this.setName(name);
        }
        public void run(){
                try {
                        sleep(100);
                } catch (InterruptedException e) {
                        e.printStackTrace();
                }
                play();
        }
        private void play() {
                System.out.print(getName());
                System.out.print(getName());
        }
        public static void main(String args[]) throws InterruptedException  {
                Thread tableThread = new MyThread("Table");
                Thread tennisThread = new MyThread("Tennis");
                tableThread.start();
                tennisThread.start();
        }
}
```

a)   This program will throw an IllegalMonitorStateException.

b)   This program will always print the following: Tennis Tennis Table Table.

c)   This program will always print the following: Table Table Tennis Tennis.

d)   The output of this program cannot be predicted; it depends on thread scheduling.

52. **Consider the following program and choose a right option:**

```java
class MyThread extends Thread {
        public void run(){
                System.out.println("Running");
        }
        public static void main(String args[]) throws InterruptedException  {
                Runnable r = new MyThread();        //#1
                Thread myThread = new Thread(r);   //#2
                myThread.start();
        }
}
```

a)   The program will result in a compilation error at statement #1.

b)   The program will result in a compilation error at statement #2.

c)   The program will compile with no errors and will print "Running" in the console.

d)   The program will compile with no errors but does not print any output in the console.

53. **What is the output of the following program?**

```
class EnumTest {
        enum Directions { North, East, West, South };
        enum Cards { Spade, Hearts, Club, Diamond };
        public static void main(String []args) {
                System.out.println("equals: " + Directions.East.equals(Cards.Hearts));
                System.out.println("Ordinals: " +
                        (Directions.East.ordinal() == Cards.Hearts.ordinal()));
        }
}
```

a) equals: false
    Ordinals: false

b) equals: true
    Ordinals: false

c) equals: false
    Ordinals: true

d) equals: true
    Ordinals: true

54. **Consider the following code and choose the best option:**

```
import java.util.concurrent.atomic.AtomicInteger;

class AtomicVariableTest {
        private static AtomicInteger counter = new AtomicInteger(0);
        static class Decrementer extends Thread {
                public void run() {
                        counter.decrementAndGet(); // #1
                }
        }
        static class Incrementer extends Thread {
                public void run() {
                        counter.incrementAndGet(); // #2
                }
        }
        public static void main(String []args) {
                for(int i = 0; i < 5; i++) {
                        new Incrementer().start();
                        new Decrementer().start();
                }
                System.out.println(counter);
        }
}
```

a) This program will always print 0.

b) This program will print any value between –5 to 5.

c) If you make the run() methods in the Incrementer and Decrementer classes synchronized, this program will always print 0.

d) The program will report compilation errors at statements #1 and #2.

55. **Which one of the following options is NOT correct?**

a) A Condition object can be acquired from a Lock object.

b) Executor is an interface that declares only one method, namely void execute(Runnable).

c) Using a semaphore with one resource is similar to using a lock.

d) CountDownLatch allows each thread to complete its assigned task step by step.

56. **Which one of the following options is NOT correct?**

a) A Runnable object does not return a result; a Callable object returns a result.

b) A Runnable object cannot throw a checked exception; a Callable object can throw an exception.

c) The Runnable interface has been around since Java 1.0; Callable was only introduced in Java 1.5.

d) The instances of the classes that implement Runnable or Callable are potentially executed by another thread.

e) A Callable can be executed by an ExecutorService, but a Runnable cannot be executed by an ExecutorService.

57. **Which one of the following methods will you define when you implement the ThreadFactory interface?**

a) Thread newThread(Runnable r)

b) Thread createThread(Runnable r)

c) Thread newThreadInstance(Runnable r)

d) Thread getThread(Runnable r)

58. **Which one of the following statements is NOT correct?**

a) You can use the ExecutorService to calculate moderate size mathematical equations.

b) You can use the ExecutorService to implement web crawlers.

c) You can use the Fork/Join framework to solve Tower of Hanoi problem.

d) You can use the Fork/Join framework to implement the Euclidean algorithm to find the GCD.

e) The Fork/Join framework is suitable for tasks that involve extensive user interaction and I/O operations.

59. **For the following enumeration definition, which one of the following prints the value 2 in the console?**

```
enum Pets { Cat, Dog, Parrot, Chameleon };
```

a) System.out.print(Pets.Parrot.ordinal());

b) System.out.print(Pets.Parrot);

c) System.out.print(Pets.indexAt("Parrot"));

d) System.out.print(Pets.Parrot.value());

e) System.out.print(Pets.Parrot.getInteger());

60. **Consider the following program and choose the right option:**

```
import java.util.Locale;

class Test {
        public static void main(String []args) {
                Locale locale1 = new Locale("en");   //#1
                Locale locale2 = new Locale("en", "in");   //#2
                Locale locale3 = new Locale("th", "TH", "TH"); //#3
                Locale locale4 = new Locale(locale3); //#4
                System.out.println(locale1 + " " + locale2 + " " + locale3 + "
                " + locale4);
        }
}
```

a) This program will print the following: en en_IN th_TH_TH_#u-nu-thai th_TH_TH_#u-nu-thai.

b) This program will print the following: en en_IN th_TH_TH_#u-nu-thai (followed by a runtime exception).

c) This program results in a compiler error at statement #1.

d) This program results in a compiler error at statement #2.

e) This program results in a compiler error at statement #3.

f) This program results in a compiler error at statement #4.

61. **Consider the following program and predict the output:**

```
import java.util.Locale;

class LocaleTest {
        public static void main(String []args) {
                Locale locale = new Locale("navi", "pandora");  //#1
                System.out.println(locale);
        }
}
```

a) The program results in a compiler error at statement #1.

b) The program results in a runtime exception of NoSuchLocaleException.

c) The program results in a runtime exception of MissingResourceException.

d) The program results in a runtime exception of IllegalArgumentException.

e) The program prints the following: navi_PANDORA.

62. **Which one of the following classes does NOT provide factory method(s) to instantiate the class?**

a) AtomicInteger

b) DateFormat

c) NumberFormat

d) Calendar

63. **Which of the given options are true with respect to parse() and format() methods in the NumberFormat class (choose two):**

a) The parse() method is meant for reading numbers provided as String and tries converting them to Number.

b) The format() method is used for printing the values according to the values set in the NumberFormat object.

c) The parse() method is meant for printing the values according to the values set in the NumberFormat object.

d) The format() method is used for reading numbers provided as String and tries converting them to Number.

64. **Consider the following program:**

```
String dateFormat = "d '('E')' MMM, YYYY";
// assume today's date is October 28th 2012
System.out.printf("%s", new SimpleDateFormat(dateFormat).format(new Date()));
```

This code segment prints the following:

a) 28 (44) Oct, 2012

b) 28 (Sun) Oct, 2012

c) 28 '(Sunday)' Oct, 2012

d) 28 (7) Oct, 2012

65. **Which one of the given options is NOT correct with respect to driver manager belonging to JDBC architecture?**

a) A driver manager maintains a list of available data sources and their drivers.

b) A driver manager chooses an appropriate driver to communicate to the respective DBMS.

c) A driver manager ensures the atomicity properties of a transaction.

d) A driver manager manages multiple concurrent drivers connected to their respective data sources.

66. **Which one of the following statement is NOT correct?**

    a) You need to use a Statement when you need to send a SQL statement to the database without any parameter.

    b) PreparedStatement represents a precompiled SQL statement.

    c) PreparedStatement can handle IN and OUT parameters.

    d) CallableStatement is used to execute stored procedures.

67. **You need to specify URL to establish connection to the MySQL database. Which one of the following is the correct one to use?**

    a) `String url = "jdbc:mysql://localhost:3306/";`

    b) `String url = "jdbc:mysql:localhost:3306";`

    c) `String url = "jdbc//mysql//localhost//3306/";`

    d) `String url = "jdbc/mysql/localhost/3306/";`

68. **Which one of the following statements is a correct way to instantiate a Statement object:**

    a) `Statement statement = connection.getStatement();`

    b) `Statement statement = connection.createStatement();`

    c) `Statement statement = connection.newStatement();`

    d) `Statement statement = connection.getStatementInstance();`

69. **Consider the following code snippet:**

```
try(ResultSet resultSet = statement.executeQuery("SELECT * FROM contact")){
        //Stmt #1
        resultSet.updateString("firstName", "John");
        resultSet.updateString("lastName", "K.");
        resultSet.updateString("email", "john@abc.com");
        resultSet.updateString("phoneNo", "+19753186420");
        //Stmt #2
...
}
```

    Assume that resultSet and Statement are legitimate instances. Which one of the following statements is correct with respect to Stmt #1 and Stmt #2 for successfully inserting a new row?

    a) Replacing Stmt #1 with resultSet.moveToInsertRow() alone will make the program work.

    b) Replacing Stmt #1 with resultSet.insertRow() alone will make the program work.

    c) Replacing Stmt #1 with resultSet.moveToInsertRow() and Stmt #2 with resultSet.insertRow() will make the program work.

    d) Replacing Stmt #1 with resultSet.insertRow() and Stmt #2 with resultSet.moveToInsertRow() will make the program work.

70. **Which one of the following statements is correct with respect to `ResultSet`?**

    a) Calling absolute(1) on a ResultSet instance is equivalent to calling first(), and calling absolute(-1) is equivalent to call last().

    b) Calling absolute(0) on a ResultSet instance is equivalent to calling first(), and calling absolute(-1) is equivalent to call last().

    c) Calling absolute(-1) on a ResultSet instance is equivalent to calling first(), and calling absolute(0) is equivalent to call last().

    d) Calling absolute(1) on a ResultSet instance is equivalent to calling first(), and calling absolute(0) is equivalent to call last().

71. **Which one of the following statements is NOT correct with respect to nested classes?**

    a) An outer class can access the private members of the nested class without declaring an object of the nested class.

    b) Static nested classes can access the static members of the outer class.

    c) Static nested classes can be declared abstract or final.

    d) Static nested classes can extend another class or they can be used as a base class.

72. **Which of the following classes belonging to JDK does not implement the `Singleton` pattern?**

    a) Runtime in the java.lang package.

    b) Toolkit in the java.awt package.

    c) Desktop in the java.awt package.

    d) Locale in the java.util package.

73. **In a DAO pattern implementation with multiple DAO objects and multiple persistence mechanisms (i.e. data sources), which of the following options is correct in this context?**

    a) You cannot implement multiple DAO objects and multiple data sources together using a DAO pattern.

    b) You need to implement the Observer pattern to manage the complexity of the context.

    c) You need to use the abstract factory pattern to manage the complexity of the context.

    d) You need to implement multiple instances of DAO pattern to handle the complexity of the context.

74. **Consider the following program and predict the output:**

```java
import java.nio.file.*;

class PathInfo {
        public static void main(String[] args) {
                // assume that the current directory is "D:\workspace\ch14-test"
                Path testFilePath = Paths.get(".\\Test");
                System.out.println("file name:" + testFilePath.getFileName());
```

```
            System.out.println("absolute path:" + testFilePath.toAbsolutePath());
            System.out.println("Normalized path:" + testFilePath.normalize());
    }
}
```

a) file name:Test
    absolute path:D:\workspace\ch14-test\.\Test
    Normalized path:Test

b) file name:Test
    absolute path:D:\workspace\ch14-test\Test
    Normalized path:Test

c) file name:Test
    absolute path:D:\workspace\ch14-test\.\Test
    Normalized path:D:\workspace\ch14-test\.\Test

d) file name:Test
    absolute path:D:\workspace\ch14-test\.\Test
    Normalized path:D:\workspace\ch14-test\Test

75. **Consider the following program:**

```
import java.io.*;

class Read {
        public static void main(String []args) throws IOException {
                BufferedReader br = new BufferedReader(new FileReader("names.txt"));
                System.out.println(br.readLine());
                br.mark(100);    // MARK
                System.out.println(br.readLine());
                br.reset();      // RESET
                System.out.println(br.readLine());
        }
}
```

Assume that names.txt exists in the current directory, and opening the file succeeds, and br points to a valid object. The content of the names.txt is the following:

olivea
emma
margaret
emily

Which of the following options correctly describe the behavior of this program?

a) This program prints the following:
    olivea
    emma
    margaret

b) This program prints the following:
    olivea
    emma
    olivea

c) This program prints the following:

olivea

emma

emma

d) This program throws an `IllegalArgumentException` in the line `MARK`.

e) This program throws a `CannotResetToMarkPositionException` in the line `RESET`.

76. **Consider the following program and predict the output:**

```java
import java.text.DateFormat;
import java.util.*;

class Test {
        public static void main(String[] args) {
                DateFormat df = DateFormat.getDateInstance(DateFormat.LONG, Locale.US);
                Calendar c = Calendar.getInstance();
                c.set(Calendar.YEAR, 2012);
                c.set(Calendar.MONTH, 12);
                c.set(Calendar.DAY_OF_MONTH, 1);
                System.out.println(df.format(c.getTime()));
        }
}
```

a) The program will produce a runtime exception.

b) The program will produce a compiler error.

c) It will print the following: December 1, 2012.

d) It will print the following: January 1, 2013.

77. **Consider the following program and predict the output:**

```java
class Test implements Runnable {
        public void run() {
                System.out.println(Thread.currentThread().getName());
        }
        public static void main(String arg[]) {
                Thread thread = new Thread(new Test());
                thread.run();
                thread.run();
                thread.start();
        }
}
```

a) main

main

Thread-0

b) Thread-0

main

Thread-1

c) main
Thread-0
Thread-1

d) Thread-0
Thread-1
Thread-2

78. **Consider the following program and predict the output:**

```
class Test {
        Integer I;
        int i;
        public Test(int i) {
                this.i = I + i;
                System.out.println(this.i);
        }
        public static void main(String args[]) {
                Integer I = new Integer(1);
                Test test = new Test(I);
        }
}
```

a) The program will print the following: 2.

b) The program will print the following: 1.

c) The program will report a compiler error.

d) The program will report a runtime exception.

79. **Consider the following program and predict the output:**

```
class Base {
        public void print() {
                System.out.println("Base");
        }
}

class Derived extends Base {
        public void print() {
                System.out.println("Derived");
        }
}

class Test {
        public static void main(String args[]) {
                Base obj1 = new Derived();
                Base obj2 = (Base)obj1;
                obj1.print();
                obj2.print();
        }
}
```

a)   Derived
Derived

b)   Base
Derived

c)   Derived
Base

d)   Base
Base

80.   **Consider the following program and predict the output:**

```
class Test {
        public static void main(String args[]) {
                String test = "I am preparing for OCPJP";
                String[] tokens = test.split("\\S");
                System.out.println(tokens.length);
        }
}
```

a)   0

b)   5

c)   12

d)   16

81.   **Consider the following program and predict the output:**

```
class Test {
        public void print(Integer i){
                System.out.println("Integer");
        }
        public void print(int i){
                System.out.println("int");
        }
        public void print(long i){
                System.out.println("long");
        }
        public static void main(String args[]) {
                Test test = new Test();
                test.print(10);
        }
}
```

a)   The program results in a compiler error ("ambiguous overload").

b)   long

c)   Integer

d)   int

82. **Consider the following program and choose a correct option to replace Stmt #1, which will compile without error:**

```
class Phone {
        public enum State {ONCALL, IDLE, WAITING}
}

class Test {
        public static void main(String args[]) throws InterruptedException {
                //Stmt #1
        }
}
```

a) Phone.State state = Phone.State.ONCALL;

b) State state = Phone.ONCALL;

c) State state = State.ONCALL;

d) State state = ONCALL;

83. **Consider the following declaration and choose a correct option:**

```
abstract class abstClass{
        public void print1();
        final void print2(){};
        public abstract final void print3();
        public abstract static void print4();
}
```

a) Methods print1(), print2(), and print3() will not compile.

b) Methods print1(), print3(), and print4() will not compile.

c) Methods print3() and print4() will not compile.

d) Methods print1() and print3() will not compile.

84. **Consider the following class definition:**

```
abstract class Base {
        public abstract Number getValue();
}
```

Which of the following two options are correct concrete classes extending Base class?

a) ```
    class Deri extends Base {
            protected Number getValue() {
                    return new Integer(10);
            }
    }
    ```
    ```

b)
```java
class Deri extends Base {
        public Integer getValue() {
                return new Integer(10);
        }
}
```

c)
```java
class Deri extends Base {
        public Float getValue(float flt) {
                return new Float(flt);
        }
}
```

d)
```java
class Deri extends Base {
        public java.util.concurrent.atomic.AtomicInteger getValue() {
                return new java.util.concurrent.atomic.AtomicInteger(10);
        }
}
```

85.   **Which one of the following options is correct?**

a)   An abstract class must declare all of its methods as abstract.

b)   An abstract class must contain at least one abstract method.

c)   If a method is declared abstract, its class must be declared abstract.

d)   In an abstract class, all non-abstract methods are final.

86.   **Consider the following program:**

```java
import java.util.*;

class DequeTest {
        public static void main(String []args) {
                Deque<String> deque = new ArrayDeque<String>(2);
                deque.addFirst("one ");
                deque.addFirst("two ");
                deque.addFirst("three ");
                System.out.print(deque.pollLast());
                System.out.print(deque.pollLast());
                System.out.print(deque.pollLast());
        }
}
```

What does this program print when executed?

a)   one two three

b)   three two one

c)   one one one

d)   three three three

87. **Which one of the following statements is NOT correct?**

    a) A switch can be used with enumerations (enums).

    b) A switch can be used with string type.

    c) A switch can be used with floating point type.

    d) A switch can be used with byte, char, short, or int types.

    e) A switch can be used with Byte, Character, Short, or Integer wrapper types.

88. **Consider the following program and predict its output:**

```
class Test {
        public static void main(String []args) {
                String str = null;

                switch(str) {   // #1
                        case "null":
                                System.out.println("null string"); // #2
                                break;
                }
        }
}
```

    a) This program results in a compiler error in statement #1.

    b) This program results in a compiler error in statement #2.

    c) This program results in throwing a NullPointerException.

    d) This program prints the following: null string.

89. **Which of the following interfaces does NOT extend the RowSet interface?**

    a) JdbcRowSet

    b) CachedRowSet

    c) WebRowSet

    d) TraversalRowSet

    e) JoinRowSet

90. **Which TWO of the following classes are defined in the java.util.concurrent.atomic package?**

    a) AtomicBoolean

    b) AtomicDouble

    c) AtomicReference<V>

    d) AtomicString

    e) AtomicObject<V>

Answer Sheet

Question No	Answer	Question No	Answer	Question No	Answer
1		31		61	
2		32		62	
3		33		63	
4		34		64	
5		35		65	
6		36		66	
7		37		67	
8		38		68	
9		39		69	
10		40		70	
11		41		71	
12		42		72	
13		43		73	
14		44		74	
15		45		75	
16		46		76	
17		47		77	
18		48		78	
19		49		79	
20		50		80	
21		51		81	
22		52		82	
23		53		83	
24		54		84	
25		55		85	
26		56		86	
27		57		87	
28		58		88	
29		59		89	
30		60		90	

Answers and Explanations

1. c) The program prints the following: Base:print.

   It is possible for an abstract class to extend a concrete class (though such inheritance often doesn't make much sense). Also, an abstract class can have static methods. Since you don't need to create an object of a class to invoke a static method in that class, you can invoke the main() method defined in an abstract class.

2. a) The program will report a compiler error at statement #1.

   Every final variable must be initialized. If a final variable is not initialized at the time of variable declaration (known as blank final), then it must be initialized in all the constructors of the class. Since the final variable is not initialized in this class, the code results in a compiler error.

3. a) The program will report a compiler error.

   The keyword this cannot be used in a static method, so the program will not compile.

4. d) The program prints the following: 12/February/01.

   The < symbol in a format string supports relative index with which you can reuse the argument matched by the previous format specifier. The equivalent example of passing arguments explicitly is the following:

   ```
   formatter.format("%tY/%tB/%td", calendar, calendar, calendar);
   ```

   The program used a short form by reusing the argument passed to the previous format specifier:

   ```
   formatter.format("%tY/%<tB/%<td", calendar);
   ```

5. a) This program prints the following: Uno.

   This program correctly extends ListResourceBundle and defines a resource bundle for the locale it_IT.

   The getObject() method takes String as an argument; this method returns the value of the matching key. The expression new Integer(1).toString() is equivalent of providing the key "1", so the program prints Uno in output.

6. e) The program throws a ConcurrentModificationException.

   From the documentation of TreeSet: "The iterators returned by this class's iterator method are *fail-fast*: if the set is modified at any time after the iterator is created, in any way except through the iterator's own remove method, the iterator will throw a ConcurrentModificationException."

   This program modifies the underlying TreeSet container object using the add() method using the earlier iterator. So, this program throws a ConcurrentModificationException.

7. a) The program prints the following: 2 1.

   Since the iterator was created using the snap-shot instance when the elements "2" and "1" were added, the program prints 2 and 1. Note that the CopyOnWriteArraySet does not store the elements in a sorted order. Further, modifying non-thread-safe containers such as TreeSet using methods such as add() and using the older iterator will throw a ConcurrentModificationException. However, CopyOnWriteArraySet is thread-safe and is meant to be used concurrently by multiple threads, and thus does not throw this exception.

8. c)   The interface Iterable<T> declares three methods: boolean hasNext(), T next(),
    and void remove().

    The interface Iterable<T> declares only one method, Iterator<T> iterator(), so the
    statement in option c) is false. The other statements are true.

9. d)   This program lists the files ending with suffix .java in the current directory

    The path "." specifies the current directory. The glob pattern "*.{java}" matches file
    names with suffix .java.

10. f)   This program does not generate any output and terminates normally.

    Since asserts are disabled by default, the program does not raise an AssertionError,
    so the program does not generate any output and terminates normally. If the program
    were invoked by passing -ea in the command line, it would have printed "In the handler of
    Error" (since the program would have thrown an AssertionError).

11. f)   When executed, this program will print the following: i1 = 10, i2 = 10, i3 = 10, i4 = 10.

    This is a correct implementation of generic method cast for casting between the types.
    Note that you'll get an "unchecked cast" warning (not an error) in the definition of the cast
    method since an unsafe explicit conversion is performed from Object to type E.

12. e)   The program prints the following: dir file.txt.

    The name elements in a path object are identified based on the separators. Note: To iterate
    name elements of the Path object does not actually require that the corresponding
    files/directories must exist, so it will not result in throwing any exceptions.

13. d)   [0, 0]

    In the constructor of Point2D, the statement x = x; reassigns the passed parameter
    and does not assign the member x in Point2D. Field y is not assigned, so the value is 0.
    Note that you implement the Externalizable interface to support serialization; this
    program uses the toString() method, which has nothing to do with object
    serialization/persistence.

14. c)   5 10 15

    The PriorityQueue prioritizes the elements in the queue according to its "natural
    ordering." For integers, natural ordering is in ascending order, thus the output. Note that
    the poll() method retrieves and removes the head of the queue if an element is available,
    or it returns null if the queue is empty.

15. c)   This program throws an ArrayStoreException.

    The variable baseArr is of type Base[], and it points to an array of type DeriOne. However,
    in the statement baseArr[2] = new DeriTwo(), an object of type DeriTwo is assigned
    to the type DeriOne, which does not share a parent-child inheritance relationship
    (they only have a common parent, which is Base). Hence, this assignment results in an
    ArrayStoreException.

16. d) 15 10 5

The Task class implements Comparable<Task>, which specifies how to compare its elements. The PriorityQueue method prioritizes the elements in the queue by calling the compareTo() method. The compareTo() method returns -1 if the priority of the current Task object is greater than the priority of the compared Task object. Hence the elements of the PriorityQueue are retrieved in the descending order.

17. b) When executed, this program prints the following: [2, 1].

The remove method in ArrayList removes the element at the *specified position* in the list, and shifts any subsequent elements in the list to the left.

18. d) Pick a little, eat a little, pick a little, eat a little, burp burp burp, eat a lot, pick a little more.

Both replaceAll() and replace() methods replace all occurrences of the substring from the given string. The difference between them is that replaceAll() takes regex as the first argument and replacement string as the second argument. The replace() method takes CharSequence as both the arguments (note that String implements CharSequence interface).

19. a) [10, 5, 10, 20]
        [20, 5, 10]
        [5, 10, 20]
        [5, 10, 20]

Lists are unsorted. HashSets are unsorted and retain unique elements. TreeSets are sorted and retain unique elements. ConcurrentSkipListSets are sorted and retain unique elements.

20. b) Using String.split method: 10 01 2012
        Using regex pattern: 10 01 2012

Using str.split(regex) gives the same result as Pattern.compile(regex).split(str).

21. c) When executed, the program prints the following: true.

With type erasure, details of the generic type are lost when the program is compiled. Hence, at runtime, types of the instance ArrayList<String> and the raw type ArrayList are the same.

22. c) Starting to wait
        Caught Exception

The method wait() is called without acquiring a lock, so the program will result in an IllegalMonitorStateException. This exception would be caught in the catch block for Exception, hence the output.

23. d) [10, 15]

In this program, the reference allValues is passed to the doSomething() method. In this container, the element with value 10 is added. Following that, a new container is created by copying the elements of the *current* reference, so the value 10 is copied to the new container as well. Since element 15 is added in addition to the existing element 10, and the reference to the container is returned; the program prints [10, 15].

24. c)   When executed, the program prints the following: double [].

The overload resolution matches to the most specific overload. When the argument null is passed, there are two candidates, Overload(Object) and Overload(double[]), and of these two, Overload(double[]) is the most specific overload, so the compiler resolves to calling that method.

25. d)   This program throws a `NullPointerException`.

In this program, the `SuperClass` constructor calls the method `foo()` that is overridden in the derived class. Thus, in this program, since the `SubClass` object is created, the call to the `SuperClass` constructor will result in calling the method `SubClass.foo()`.

When the derived class object is created, first the base class constructor is called, *followed by* the call to the derived class constructor. Note that the member variable is initialized only in the derived class constructor. Thus, when the base class constructor executes, the derived class constructor has not initialized the member variable to "HI" yet. So this program results in a `NullReferenceException`.

26. c)   This program prints the following:
In BaseClass.foo()
In Derived.bar()

Since a private method is not visible to any other classes, including its derived classes, it cannot be overridden.

27. b)   `BufferedReader br = new BufferedReader(new InputStreamReader(System.in));`
`String str = br.readLine();`

This is the right way to read a line of a string from the console where you pass a `System.in` reference to `InputStreamReader` and pass the returning reference to `BufferedReader`. From the `BufferedReader` reference, you can call the `readLine()` method to read the string from the console.

28. a)   This program terminates normally without throwing any exceptions.

The try-with-resources statement internally expands to call the `close()` method in the `finally` block. If the resource is explicitly closed in the `try` block, then calling `close()` again does not have any effect. From the description of the `close()` method in the `AutoCloseable` interface: "Closes this stream and releases any system resources associated with it. If the stream is already closed, then invoking this method has no effect."

29. b)   `java.io.FileNotFoundException`

If both the `try` block and `finally` block throw exceptions, the exception thrown from the try block will be ignored. Hence, the method `thrower()` throws a `FileNotFoundException`. The dynamic type of the variable `throwable` is `FileNotFoundException`, so the program prints that type name.

30. b)   `pqr.foo();`

In this program, the member pqr is imported statically. So, the `foo()` method can be accessed by qualifying it as `pqr.foo()`. Note that `foo()` itself is not imported statically, so it cannot be invoked directly in this program.

31. c)   Type erasure.

Deadlocks, lock starvation, and livelocks are problems that arise when using mutexes for thread synchronization. Type erasure is a concept related to generics where the generic type information is lost once the generic type is compiled.

32. c)   It is okay for a thread to acquire lock on `obj` again, and such an attempt will succeed.

Java locks are reentrant: a Java thread, if it has already acquired a lock, can acquire it again, and such an attempt will succeed. No exception is thrown and no deadlock occurs for this case.

33. c)   This program will print 10 in the console.

The valueOf(int) method is a static method in `String` that returns the `String` representation of the integer value that is passed as its argument. Since calling a static method does not require dereferencing the reference variable on which it is called, this program does not throw a `NullPointerException`.

34. d)   Byte streams are meant for handling binary data that is not human-readable; character streams are for human-readable characters.

In character streams, data is handled in terms of Unicode characters, whereas in byte streams, data is handled in terms of bytes. Byte streams are suitable for reading or writing to files such as executable files, image files, and files in low-level file formats such as `.zip`, `.class`, `.obj`, and `.exe`. Character streams are suitable for reading or writing to text-based I/O such as documents and text, XML, and HTML files.

35. c)   `java.lang.Cloneable` interface

The `AutoCloseable` interface declares the `close()` method. `Callable` declares `call()` method. The `Comparator<T>` interface declares `compare()` and `equals()` methods.

From the documentation of `clone()` method: "By *convention*, classes that implement this interface should override the Object.clone method. Note that this interface does *not* contain the `clone` method."

36. a)   final and d) abstract

A class cannot be final (which means it cannot be extended by any other class) and abstract (which can be extended by other classes) at the same time.

37. c)   ,,,,,,

The replaceAll() method in `String` takes a *regular expression* as the first argument. Since the character "." matches for *any* character, all the characters in the string str are replaced with commas, which is the replacement string. In the replaced string, there is no matching "!" character, so the replace() method has no effect in this code segment.

38. b)   1

Though the return value in the call `atomicInt.incrementAndGet();` is ignored, the method mutates the integer value passed through the reference variable `atomicInt`, so the changed value is printed in the `main()` method. Note that `AtomicInteger` can be used in thread or non-thread context (though it is not of any practical use when used in single-threaded programs).

39. c)   This program executes and terminates normally without printing any output in console.

It is not a compiler error to check null with the `instanceof` operator. However, if null is passed for the `instanceof` operator, it returns `false`. Since both the condition checks fail, the program does not print any output in the console.

40. c)   The range of thread priorities is 1 to 10; the default thread priority is 5.

The range of thread priorities is 1 to 10, with 10 being the highest priority. By default, the priority of a thread is 5. You can use `getPriority()` and `setPriority()` methods in the Thread class to get or set priority of threads.

41. d)   `Map<K, V>`

Other than the `Map` interface (which maps keys to values), the other three interfaces represent group of elements and derive from the `Collection` interface.

42. d)   `transient`

Other modifiers can be applied only to methods and not fields. The transient modifier is used in the context of serialization: when an object is serialized, the data member that is qualified as transient will not be part of the serialized object.

43. a)   `finalize()` method and b) `clone()` method.

The methods `finalize()` and `clone()` can be overridden. The methods `getClass()`, `notify()`, and `wait()` are final methods and so cannot be overridden.

44. c)   The program prints the following:
    In run method; thread name is: main
    In main method; thread name is: main

The correct way to invoke a thread is to call the `start()` method on a Thread object. If you directly call the `run()` method, the method will run just like any other method (in other words, it will execute sequentially in the same thread without running as a separate thread).

45. b)   The program results in throwing an `IllegalThreadStateException`

If you invoke the `start()` method on a thread object twice, it will result in a `IllegalThreadStateException`.

46. d)   The program will never terminate.

Calling `this.join()` will result in indefinite waiting since the thread is waiting for the thread itself to terminate.

47. b)   Thread provides a default implementation for the `run()` method.

Thread is a concrete class that implements the Runnable interface. The Thread class also provides a default implementation for the `run()` method.

48. b)   EXECUTING

A thread can be in one of the following states (as defined in the `java.lang.Thread.State` enumeration): NEW, RUNNABLE, BLOCKED, WAITING, TIMED_WAITING, and TERMINATED.

49. c)   `Thread(Runnable target, Object obj)`

The other constructors are valid Thread constructors.

50. b)   When executed, it prints one of the following: Eat! Burp! Run! or Burp! Eat! Run!

If the thread myThread is scheduled to run first immediately after start() is called, it will print "Burp! Eat! Run!"; otherwise it will print "Eat! Burp! Run!" The output "Run!" will always be executed last because of the join() method call in the main() method.

51. d)   The output of this program cannot be predicted; it depends on thread scheduling.

Since the threads are not synchronized in this program, the output of this program cannot be determined. Depending on how the threads are scheduled, it may even generate output such as Table Tennis Tennis Table.

52. c)   The program will compile with no errors and will print "Running" in console.

The class Thread implements the Runnable interface, so the assignment in statement #1 is valid. Also, you can create a new thread object by passing a Runnable reference to a Thread constructor, so statement #2 is also valid. Hence, the program will compile without errors and print "Running" in the console.

53. c)   equals: false
         Ordinals: true

The equals() method returns true only if the enumeration constants are the same. In this case, the enumeration constants belong to different enumerations, so the equals() method returns false. However, the ordinal values of the enumeration constants are equal since both are second elements in their respective enumerations.

54. a)   The final value of the counter will always be 0.

You have employed AtomicInteger, which provides a set of atomic methods such as incrementAndGet() and decrementAndGet(). Hence, you will always get 0 as the final value of counter. However, depending on thread scheduling, the intermediate counter values may be anywhere between -5 to +5, but the final value of the counter will always be 0. So no synchronization is needed between the threads, although they access/modify a common variable.

55. d)   CountDownLatch allows each thread to complete its assigned task step by step.

CountDownLatch allows threads to wait for a countdown to complete. It is Phaser, which allows each thread to complete its assigned task step by step. The other three statements are true.

56. e)   A callable can be executed by an ExecutorService, but a Runnable cannot be executed by an ExecutorService.

A Runnable object can also be executed by an ExecutorService. The other statements are true.

57. a)   Thread newThread(Runnable r)

The ThreadFactory interface defines only one method, Thread newThread(Runnable r). You must define this method when implementing a new thread factory with this interface.

58. e)   A Fork/Join framework is suitable for tasks that involve extensive user interaction and I/O operations.

You can use a Fork/Join framework for computationally intensive tasks that naturally can be broken down into smaller subtasks and perform computations for the subtasks. The Fork/Join framework is unsuitable when the tasks involve extensive user interaction or I/O operations since it does not fit into the framework.

59. a) `System.out.print(Pets.Parrot.ordinal());`

Option a) The ordinal method prints the position of the enumeration constant within an enumeration.

Option b) The call print(Pets.Parrot); prints the string "Parrot" to console.

Options c), d) and e) There are no methods named indexAt(), value(), or getInteger() in Enum

60. f) This program results in a compiler error at #4.

The `Locale` class supports three constructors that are used in statements #1, #2, and #3; however, there is no constructor in the `Locale` class that takes another `Locale` object as argument, so the compiler gives an error for statement #4.

61. e) The program prints the following: navi_PANDORA.

To create a `Locale` object using the constructor `Locale` (String language, String country), any `String` values can be passed; just attempting to create a `Locale` object will not result in throwing exceptions (other than a `NullPointerException`, which could be raised for passing null `String`s).

The `toString()` method of `Locale` class returns a string representation of the `Locale` object consisting of language, country, variant, etc.

62. a) `AtomicInteger`

The class `DateFormat` provides methods such as `getDateInstance()` and `getTimeInstance()`, `NumberFormat` provides methods such as `getInstance()` and `getNumberInstance()`, and `Calendar` provides the method getInstance(), which are factory methods. The `AtomicInteger` class does not support any `factory` methods. (In fact, it does not have any static methods!)

63. a) The parse() method is meant for reading numbers provided as `String` and try converting them to `Number`.

b) The format() method is used for printing the values according to the values set in the NumberFormat object.

The parse() method is meant for creating a `Number` object from a `String` object that has numeric value, and format() method is meant for converting a numeric value into a `String` object.

64. b) `28 (Sun) Oct, 2012`

Relevant letters and their meaning:

```
d    Day in month
E    Day name in week
M    Month in year
Y    Year
```

Calling new `Date()`; object creates a `Date` object for the current date. Within the date format string "d '('E')' MMM, YYYY", the opening and closing parenthesis are given within single quotes (i.e., '('E')' to ensure that it is not treated as a format specifier character), so the single quotes are not part of the output itself.

65. c) A driver manager ensures the atomicity properties of a transaction.

66. c) `PreparedStatement` can handle IN and OUT parameters.

`PreparedStatement` can handle only IN parameters; `CallableStatement` can handle IN, OUT, and INOUT parameters.

67. a) `String url = "jdbc:mysql://localhost:3306/";`

68. b) `Statement statement = connection.createStatement();`

69. c) Replacing `Stmt #1` with `resultSet.moveToInsertRow();` and `Stmt #2` with `resultSet.insertRow();` will make the program work.

You need to call the `moveToInsertRow()` method in order to insert a new row (this method prepares the result set for creating a new row). Once the row is updated, you need to call `insertRow()` to insert the row into result set and the database.

70. a) Calling `absolute(1)` on a `ResultSet` instance is equivalent to calling `first()`, and calling `absolute(-1)` is equivalent to calling `last()`.

71. a) An outer class can access the private members of the nested class without declaring an object of the nested class.

An outer class can access the private members of the nested class only by declaring an object of the nested class.

72. d) `Locale` is in the `Java.util` package

The `Locale` class has three public constructors, so it does not implement the `Singleton` pattern. The other three classes implement the `Singleton` pattern.

73. c) You need to use the abstract factory pattern to manage the complexity of the context.

Using the abstract factory pattern, you can create appropriate data source instances with applicable DAO objects.

74. a) `file name:Test`
`absolute path:D:\workspace\ch14-test\.\Test`
`Normalized path:Test`

The absolute path adds the path from the root directory; however, it does not normalize the path. Hence, ".\" will be retained in the resultant path. On the other hand, the `normalize()` method normalizes the path but does not make it absolute.

75. c) This program prints the following:
`olivea`
`emma`
`emma`

The method `void mark(int limit)` in `BufferedReader` marks the current position for resetting the stream to the marked position. The argument limit specifies the number of characters that may be read while still preserving the mark. This program marks the position after "olivea" is read, so after reading "emma," when the marker is reset and the line is read again, it reads "emma" once again.

76. d) It will print the following: January 1, 2013.

The month index starts from 0; thus, if you give the month an index of 12, it will increase the year by one and start counting from January.

77. a) `main`
      `main`
      `Thread-0`

Calling `run()` directly will not create a new thread. The correct way is to call the `start()` method, which in turn will call the `run()` method in a new thread.

78. d) The program will report a runtime exception.

The member variable `I` is not initialized and accessed in the constructor, which results in a `NullPointerException`. The `main()` method declares a local variable named `I` whose scope is limited to the `main()` method.

79. a) `Derived`
      `Derived`

The dynamic type of the instance variable `obj2` remains the same (i.e., `Derived`). Thus, when `print()` is called on `obj2`, it calls the derived class version of the method.

80. d) 16

The specified regex is "\\S" and not "\\s"; the first regex specifies non-whitespace characters and the other one specifies whitespace characters.

81. d) int

If `Integer` and `long` types are specified, a literal will match to `int`. So, the program prints `int`.

82. a) Phone.State state = Phone.State.ONCALL;

83. b) Methods `print1()`, `print3()`, and `print4()` will not compile

The method `print2()` is correct since it defines a method and declares it final, which is acceptable.

The method `print1()` is incorrect since either a method has a body or it needs to be declared as `abstract` in an abstract class. Method `print3()` is not correct since a method cannot be `abstract` and `final` at the same time. Similarly, `print4()` is also not correct since a method cannot be static and `abstract` at the same time.

84. b) ```
class Deri extends Base {
    public Integer getValue() {
        return new Integer(10);
    }
}
```

d)  ```
class Deri extends Base {
    public java.util.concurrent.atomic.AtomicInteger getValue() {
        return new java.util.concurrent.atomic.AtomicInteger(10);
    }
}
```

Option a) attempts to assign weaker access privilege by declaring the method protected when the base method is public, and thus is incorrect.

Option b) makes use of a co-variant return type (note that `Integer` extends `Number`), and defines the overriding method correctly.

616

In option c) the method Float getValue(float flt) does not override the getValue() method in Base since the signature does not match, so it is incorrect.

Option d) makes use of co-variant return type (note that AtomicInteger extends Number), and defines the overriding method correctly.

85. c) If a method is declared abstract, its class must be declared abstract.

86. a) Prints the following: one two three.

The addFirst() inserts an element in the front of the Deque object and pollLast() method retrieves and removes the element from the other end of the object. Since the elements "one," "two," and "three" are inserted in one end and retrieved in another end, the elements are retrieved in the same order as they were inserted.

87. c) A switch can be used with a floating point type.

A switch statement can be used with enums, strings, and primitive types byte, char, short, and int and their wrapper types; it cannot be used with a floating-point type.

88. c) This program results in throwing a NullPointerException.

If a null value is passed to a switch statement, it results in a NullPointerException.

89. d) TraversalRowSet

The interfaces deriving from JdbcRowSet are CachedRowSet, WebRowSet, JoinRowSet, and FilteredRowSet.

90. a) AtomicBoolean and c) AtomicReference<V>

The class AtomicBoolean supports atomically updatable Boolean values. The class AtomicReference<V> supports atomically updatable references of type V. Classes AtomicDouble, AtomicString, and AtomicObject are not part of the java.util.concurrent.atomic package.

Index

F

P, Q

W, X, Y

Z

CPSIA information can be obtained at www.ICGtesting.com
Printed in the USA
LVOW090456020313

322388LV00004B/243/P